Frommer's®
Paris

Our Paris

by Darwin Porter & Danforth Prince

THE CITY OF LIGHT HAS BEEN CELEBRATED IN SUCH A TORRENT OF SONGS, poems, stories, books, paintings, and movies that for millions of people she is an abstraction rather than a city. To provincial Frenchmen, Paris is the center of the universe, the place where laws and careers are made and broken. To many American visitors, she is still "Gay Paree," the fairytale town inviting you for a fling, the hub of everything "continental," and the epitome of that nebulous attribute known as chic.

Some of these images are so old they date from the time called "between the wars." Yet they live on, post-millennium, and through the old clichés runs a thread of an eternal reality, an aura of enchantment Paris casts that neither François Mitterrand's *grands projets*, nor the commercialization of French culture (baguettes now sold in supermarkets) have been able to dispel.

Whether you see Paris for the 1st or 50th time, the effect always strikes a curiously personal note. Paris beckons to *me*. As novelist Romain Gary so evocatively put it: "The kid will come from Nebraska or Heidelberg, from Poland or Senegal, and Paris will be born again—new, brand-new and unexpected, and the Arch of Triumph will rise again, and the Seine will flow for the first time, and there will be new areas, unknown and unexplored, called Montmartre and Montparnasse . . . and it will all be for the first time, a completely new city, built suddenly for you and you alone."

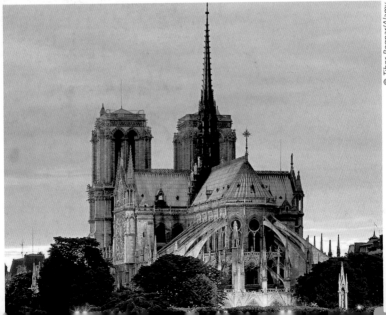

© Tibor Bognar/Alamy

Baseball great Joe DiMaggio once said, "There are two great rear views in the world—my wife's backside [he was married to Marilyn Monroe at the time] and the back of **NOTRE-DAME (left)** in Paris." Jumpin' Joe got it right: Jean Ravy's spectacular flying buttresses at the east end of the cathedral seem to take flight, jutting out for 15m (50 ft.) like a giant insect with pincers. Illuminated at night, this architectural fantasy is actually firmly grounded—or, as E. E. Cummings noted, "does not budge an inch for all the idiocies of this world."

With the French flag waving in the breeze in the foreground, the majestic **ARC DE TRIOMPHE (above)** is lit at night, while all around it manic Parisian drivers turn the dozen radiating avenues converging here into a racetrack. After the Battle of Austerlitz in 1805, Napoléon promised his soldiers, "You shall go home beneath triumphal arches." Not completed until 1836, the arch is home to the Tomb of the Unknown Soldier from World War I. An eternal flame burns here to commemorate the thousands of Frenchmen who died in the 20th century's two world wars.

PARIS FASHION (left) is often outrageous, as lean, trim, and mean models, who survive on grapefruit and Perrier, parade down the catwalks of the leading couture houses—in this case with an overly groomed French poodle named Fifi.

A Chinese-American architect, I.M. Pei, in 1989 launched his "glass pyramid" in the Cour Napoléon at the **LOUVRE** (below), the Western world's largest museum, and faced a barrage of protests from outraged Parisians. Former French president Giscard d'Estaing bluntly stated that it had turned the palace "into a cultural drugstore that looks like an airport." As time has gone by, the rage has died down, as both visitors and Parisians alike have come to appreciate the fact that the pyramid has increased gallery space by 80%.

Immortalized by Utrillo's painting of the cabaret, the original Cabaret des Assassins was in 1880 rechristened **AU LAPIN AGILE** (above) or "The Nimble Rabbit," based on a drawing by humorist André Gill who pictured a rabbit in a bow tie escaping from a stew pot. The fave of Montmartre bohemians, including Picasso, the Rabbit still attracts nostalgia seekers who join in the sing-alongs of folk songs, love ballads, army marching tunes, sea chanteys, and music hall ditties.

The most macabre sight in Paris, the **CATACOMBS** (right), has an ominous sign posted over the entrance door. "Stop! This is the Empire of Death!" The creation of this ghoulish attraction began in 1786 when the city ordered the removal of million of graves from unsanitary burial ground at Les Halles. Rotting corpses and skeletons were hauled in large carts through the streets of Paris at night to their new home in the miles of quarries that make up the Catacombs where workers neatly arranged the remains.

In the **JARDIN DES HALLES (above)**, site of the long-gone market stalls of the "underbelly of Paris," stands the bulky church of St-Eustache, with its bastardized Gothic and Renaissance architecture. This landmark church was the burial place of Molière and the site of the infant baptisms of Madame de Pompadour and Cardinal Richelieu. Today it attracts children who scamper across its courtyard art, a sculptured head with gigantic hand—called *l'Ecoute*—a creation of Henri de Miller.

The Cathedral of Notre-Dame in Paris has long been celebrated for its *GALERIE DES CHIMERES* (right) that lines a large upper gallery between the building's twin towers. These fabulous monsters stand guard over one of the most panoramic vistas of Paris. Architect Viollet-le-Duc's stone bestiary of gremlins, demons, and gargoyles were believed to keep evil spirits away from the cathedral.

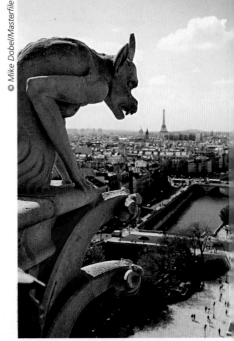

An Art Nouveau glass roof crowns the **WINTER GARDEN OF THE HOTEL MEURICE** (right), a pocket of posh since 1835 when it fancifully billed itself as "the Home of Kings." Kings and eccentrics have paraded through this Winter Garden, none more notable than longtime resident Salvador Dalí.

Gilded and partially undraped golden statuettes at the honey-colored 1930s Palais de Chaillot open onto a picture-postcard panoramic sweep of the once-controversial **EIFFEL TOWER** (below). The shady Jardins du Trocadero slope down to the River Seine leading to this monument that was the tallest building in the world, towering 300m (984 ft.) when it was constructed in 1889 for the Paris Exposition.

PLACE DES VOSGES (left), the heart of the once seedy but now gentrified Marais, is our favorite square in all of Paris and one of the most beautiful in the world. Still intact after 4 centuries, it was the former stamping ground of royal mistresses, cavaliers, government ministers, French noblemen, courtiers, and marquises. Victor Hugo, the French poet, dramatist, and novelist lived here from 1833 to 1848, completing most of *Les Misérables*. Oblivious to the history, French schoolgirls in the foreground enjoy a sunny day in front of a fountain where sculpted lions' heads spew cooling waters.

The oldest bridge in Paris, **PONT NEUF (NEW BRIDGE) (above)**, dates from 1607 when it became the city's first bridge to be constructed without houses on top of it. It spans the Seine with a dozen broad arches at the river's widest point, and has turrets for jugglers, acrobats, and street peddlers. It became such a major thoroughfare that, according to legend, "You can't cross Pont Neuf without meeting a monk, a whore, and a white stallion."

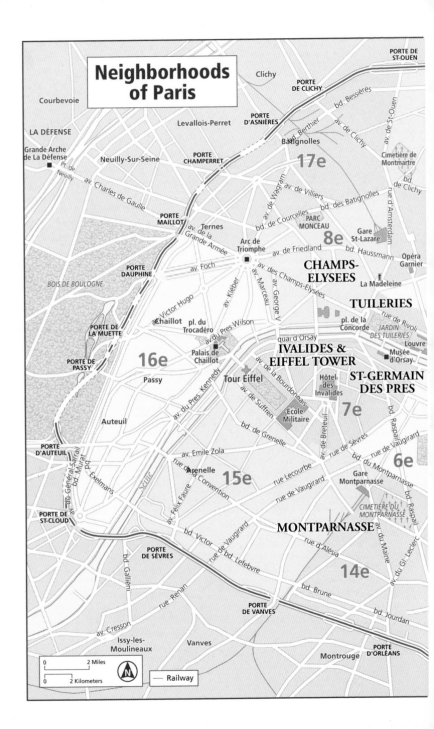

Neighborhoods
of Paris

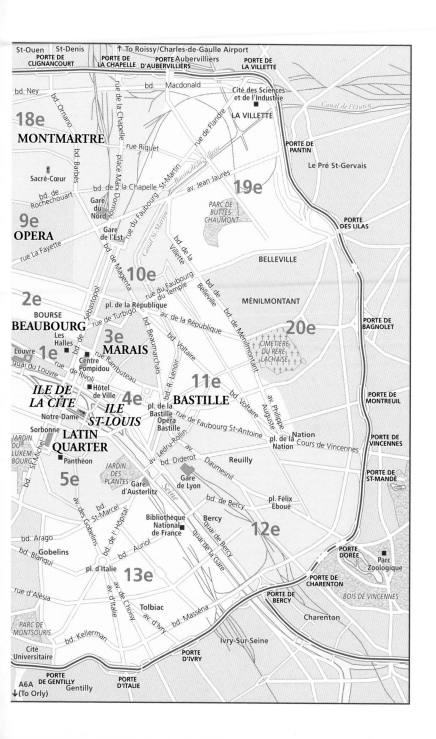

Paris' Best Museums & Galleries

Centre Pompidou **5**
Musée de Cluny **8**
Musée de la Carnavalet **7**
Musée d'Orsay **9**
Musée des Arts Decoratifs **3**
Musée du Louvre **4**
Musée Guimet **1**
Musée Picasso **6**
Musée Rodin **10**
Petit Palais **2**

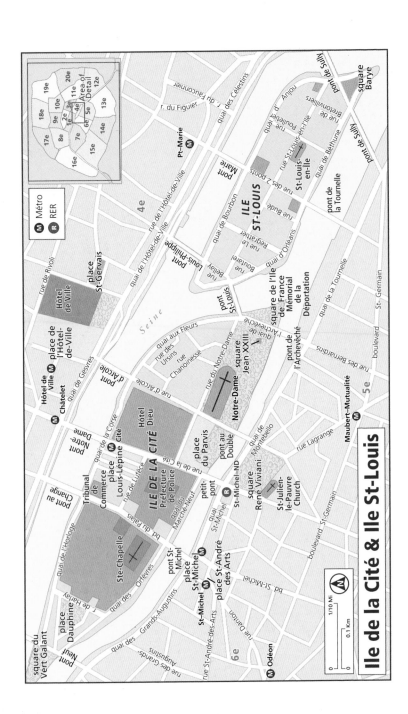

Ile de la Cité & Ile St-Louis

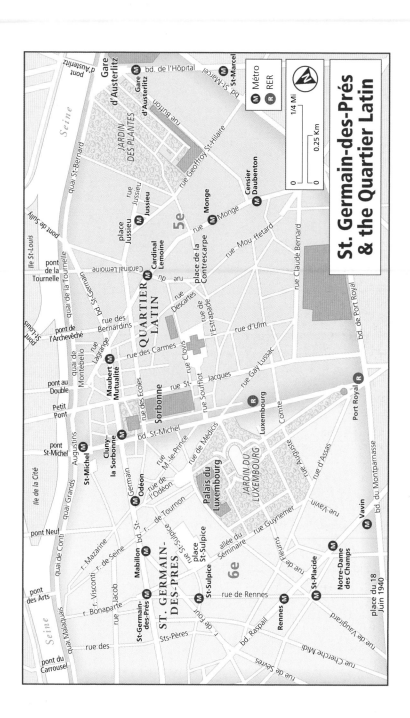

St. Germain-des-Prés
& the Quartier Latin

M Métro
R RER

0   0.25 Km
0   1/4 Mi

Seine

pont d'Austerlitz

Gare
d'Austerlitz

M Gare
d'Austerlitz

bd. de l'Hôpital

M St-Marcel

bd. St-Marcel

rue Buffon

quai St-Bernard

JARDIN
DES PLANTES

rue Geoffroy St-Hilaire

Censier
Daubenton

M

5e

rue Jussieu

place
Jussieu

M Jussieu

rue Monge

M Monge

rue Mouffetard

Ile St-Louis

pont
de la
Tournelle

quai de la Tournelle

bd. St-Germain

Cardinal
Lemoine

M Cardinal Lemoine

rue du

place de la
Contrescarpe

rue Claude Bernard

pont de
l'Archevéché

rue des
Bernardins

QUARTIER
LATIN

rue
Descartes

rue de
l'Estrapade

rue d'Ulm

bd. de Port Royal

pont St-Louis

quai de
Montebello

rue
Lagrange

rue des Carmes

rue des Écoles

M Maubert
Mutualité

Sorbonne

rue St-
Jacques

rue Clovis

rue Soufflot

rue Gay Lussac

pont au
Double

Petit
Pont

Luxembourg
R

Comte

Port Royal R

pont
St-Michel

St-Michel M

Augustins

quai des Grands

Cluny-
la Sorbonne M

bd. St-Michel

M Odéon

Germain

rue de
M.-le-Prince

rue de Médicis

JARDIN DU
LUXEMBOURG

rue d'Assas

Ile de la Cité

pont Neuf

quai de Conti

rue de
l'Odéon

Palais du
Luxembourg

rue Guynemer

rue Auguste

bd. du Montparnasse

r. Mazarine

r. de Seine

bd. St-

r. de Tournon

place
St-Sulpice

allée du
Séminaire

rue de Fleurus

M Vavin

Vavin

pont
des Arts

r. Visconti

r. Jacob

St-Germain-
des-Prés M

Mabillon M

rue St-Sulpice

St-Sulpice M

ST. GERMAIN-
DES-PRÉS

6e

rue de Rennes

Rennes M

St-Placide M

place du 18
Juin 1940

Seine

quai Malaquais

r. Bonaparte

rue des

Sts-Pères

r. de Four

bd. Raspail

rue de Sèvres

rue Cherche Midi

rue de Vaugirard

Notre-Dame
des Champs M

pont du
Carrousel

A Seine River View

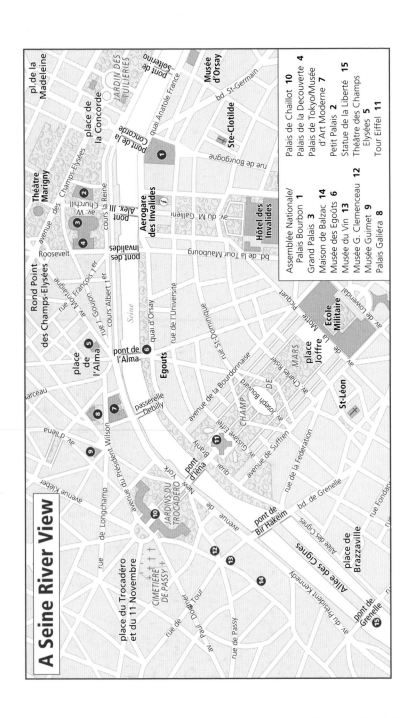

place du Trocadéro et du 11 Novembre

CIMETIÈRE DE PASSY

JARDINS DU TROCADÉRO

place de la Madeleine

pl. de la Madeleine

JARDIN DES TUILERIES

pont de Solférino

place de la Concorde

pont de la Concorde

Musée d'Orsay

bd. St-Germain

Ste-Clotilde

quai Anatole France

Théâtre Marigny

avenue des Champs-Elysées

av. W. Churchill

cours la Reine

pont Alex. III

Aerogare des Invalides

rue de Bourgogne

Rond Point des Champs-Elysées

Roosevelt

av. Montaigne

rue François 1er

rue J.-Goujon

cours Albert 1er

pont des Invalides

Hôtel des Invalides

av. du M. Gallieni

bd. de la Tour Maubourg

marceau

place de l'Alma

pont de l'Alma

quai d'Orsay

Egouts

rue de l'Université

Seine

av. d'Iéna

passerelle Debilly

avenue de la Bourdonnaise

rue St-Dominique

av. de La Motte Picquet

Ecole Militaire

place Joffre

CHAMP DE MARS

av. Charles Risler

av. Joseph Bouvard

av. de Suffren

av. de Lowendal

avenue Kléber

avenue du Président-Wilson

New York

pont d'Iéna

quai Branly

av. Gustave Eiffel

rue de la Federation

St-Léon

rue de Longchamp

avenue de

pont de Bir Hakeim

bd. de Grenelle

rue Fondand

rue de Tour

rue Paul Doumer

rue de Passy

CIMETIÈRE DE PASSY

Allée des Cygnes

place de Brazzaville

av. du Président Kennedy

pont de Grenelle

Legend

Assemblée Nationale/ Palais Bourbon **1**
Grand Palais **3**
Maison de Balzac **14**
Musée des Egoûts **6**
Musée du Vin **13**
Musée G. Clemenceau **12**
Musée Guimet **9**
Palais Galiéra **8**

Palais de Chaillot **10**
Palais de la Decouverte **4**
Palais de Tokyo/Musée d'Art Moderne **7**
Petit Palais **2**
Statue de la Liberté **15**
Théâtre des Champs Elysées **5**
Tour Eiffel **11**

Frommer's®

Paris

2008

by Darwin Porter & Danforth Prince

Here's what the critics say about Frommer's:

"Amazingly easy to use. Very portable, very complete."

—*Booklist*

"Detailed, accurate, and easy-to-read information for all price ranges."
—*Glamour Magazine*

"Hotel information is close to encyclopedic."

—*Des Moines Sunday Register*

"Frommer's Guides have a way of giving you a real feel for a place."
—*Knight Ridder Newspapers*

Wiley Publishing, Inc.

About the Authors

As a team of veteran travel writers, **Darwin Porter** and **Danforth Prince** have produced numerous titles for Frommer's, including best-selling guides to Italy, France, the Caribbean, England, and Germany. Porter, a former bureau chief of the *Miami Herald,* is also a Hollywood biographer. His recent releases include *The Secret Life of Humphrey Bogart* and *Katherine the Great,* the latter a close-up of the private life of the late Katherine Hepburn. Prince was formerly employed by the Paris bureau of the *New York Times* and is today the president of Blood Moon Productions and other media-related firms.

Published by:

Wiley Publishing, Inc.

111 River St.
Hoboken, NJ 07030-5774

ISBN: 978-0-470-13822-9

Editor: Marc Nadeau
Production Editor: Michael Brumitt
Cartographer: Tim Lohnes
Photo Editor: Richard Fox
Anniversary Logo Design: Richard Pacifico
Production by Wiley Indianapolis Composition Services

For information on our other products and services or to obtain technical support, please contact our Customer Care Department within the U.S. at 800/762-2974, outside the U.S. at 317/572-3993 or fax 317/572-4002.

Wiley also publishes its books in a variety of electronic formats. Some content that appears in print may not be available in electronic formats.

Manufactured in the United States of America

5 4 3 2 1

Contents

List of Maps

An Invitation to the Reader

In researching this book, we discovered many wonderful places—hotels, restaurants, shops, and more. We're sure you'll find others. Please tell us about them, so we can share the information with your fellow travelers in upcoming editions. If you were disappointed with a recommendation, we'd love to know that, too. Please write to:

Frommer's Paris 2008
Wiley Publishing, Inc. • 111 River St. • Hoboken, NJ 07030-5774

An Additional Note

Please be advised that travel information is subject to change at any time—and this is especially true of prices. We therefore suggest that you write or call ahead for confirmation when making your travel plans. The authors, editors, and publisher cannot be held responsible for the experiences of readers while traveling. Your safety is important to us, however, so we encourage you to stay alert and be aware of your surroundings. Keep a close eye on cameras, purses, and wallets, all favorite targets of thieves and pickpockets.

Other Great Guides for Your Trip:

Frommer's France 2008

Frommer's Provence & the Riviera

Frommer's Europe

Frommer's French PhraseFinder & Dictionary

Suzy Gershman's Born to Shop Paris

France For Dummies

Frommer's Star Ratings, Icons & Abbreviations

Every hotel, restaurant, and attraction listing in this guide has been ranked for quality, value, service, amenities, and special features using a **star-rating system.** In country, state, and regional guides, we also rate towns and regions to help you narrow down your choices and budget your time accordingly. Hotels and restaurants are rated on a scale of zero (recommended) to three stars (exceptional). Attractions, shopping, nightlife, towns, and regions are rated according to the following scale: zero stars (recommended), one star (highly recommended), two stars (very highly recommended), and three stars (must-see).

In addition to the star-rating system, we also use **seven feature icons** that point you to the great deals, in-the-know advice, and unique experiences that separate travelers from tourists. Throughout the book, look for:

Finds	Special finds—those places only insiders know about
Fun Fact	Fun facts—details that make travelers more informed and their trips more fun
Kids	Best bets for kids and advice for the whole family
Moments	Special moments—those experiences that memories are made of
Overrated	Places or experiences not worth your time or money
Tips	Insider tips—great ways to save time and money
Value	Great values—where to get the best deals

The following **abbreviations** are used for credit cards:

AE American Express	DISC Discover	V Visa
DC Diners Club	MC MasterCard	

Frommers.com

Now that you have this guidebook to help you plan a great trip, visit our website at **www.frommers.com** for additional travel information on more than 3,500 destinations. We update features regularly to give you instant access to the most current trip-planning information available. At Frommers.com, you'll find scoops on the best airfares, lodging rates, and car rental bargains. You can even book your travel online through our reliable travel booking partners. Other popular features include:

- Online updates of our most popular guidebooks
- Vacation sweepstakes and contest giveaways
- Newsletters highlighting the hottest travel trends
- Online travel message boards with featured travel discussions

What's New in Paris

In a jittery world and with an uncertain economy, Paris remains one of the most visited places on the planet. Travelers, of course, come to revisit Paris's glorious past, as reflected in its art and architecture, but they are also intrigued by the City of Light's cutting-edge style, cuisine, and fashion. Here are some of the latest developments in an ever-changing world metropolis:

ACCOMMODATIONS The hotel getting all the press is the provocatively named **Hotel Amour,** 8 rue de Navarin, 9e (© **01-48-78-31-80**), where doubles begin at $117. It is centrally located just off the rue des Martyrs, currently the hippest street in Paris. You join the starlets and bright young things checking in here. Walk up the steps to the bedrooms (there's no elevator). The beds are so incredibly comfortable we asked about them, only to learn they come from the same company that supplies the Ritz. Expect to encounter an oddball charm and comfort food served on site, including *steak frites.*

The film, *Amélie,* first made the Goutte d'Or neighborhood of Montmartre world famous. Thousands continue to flock to this up-and-coming sector because that movie was shot in the area. It was inevitable that some entrepreneur would open a hotel there. But what a hotel. **Kube Rooms & Bars,** 1–5 Passage Ruelle, 18e (© **01-42-05-20-00**), is unique in Paris. Design-savvy clients check into this cube, "the most modern of shapes," according to the owners. Their reception area was inspired by the architecturally controversial glass box in front of the Louvre. Rectangular beds are lit from below and appear to levitate. Expect shag-covered sofas and faux fur throws. The Ice Kube Bar is made with—you guessed it—ice. Guests stay in here for half an hour before deep freeze sets in. Instead of room keys, guests are electronically fingerprinted.

DINING The most famous restaurateur in Paris, Claude Terrail, owner of **La Tour d'Argent,** 15–17 quai de la Tournelle (© **01-43-54-23-31**), died in the summer of 2006, at the age of 88. His restaurant, once hailed as the best in Europe, is still known for its duck specialties, its vast wine cellar, and its spectacular views of the River Seine (as well as Notre-Dame). Over the years he hosted such notables as Queen Elizabeth II, President John F. Kennedy, and Marilyn Monroe. His death is not expected to have a lasting effect on the restaurant. By 2003, he'd already handed over management to his son, André, though Terrail came in every day for lunch and dinner until his death.

Because of a bad economy, Paris in 2006 and early 2007 didn't see the rash of good restaurant openings that it usually does. However, in the 8th Arrondissement, **Citrus Etoile,** 6 rue Arsène Houssaye (© **01-42-89-15-51**), attracted serious foodies to its excellent French food served at moderate—for Paris—prices. Chef Gilles Epié earned his fame as a private chef in Hollywood before returning to Paris with his American fashion-model wife. Together, in a minimalist background, they receive a health-conscious, trendy crowd, watching their waistlines but also demanding a cuisine prepared with razor-sharp technique.

ATTRACTIONS   In the shadow of the Eiffel Tower, the museum getting all the press is Jean Nouvel's sweeping **Musée du Quai Branly,** 206–208 rue de l'Université, 7e (© **01-56-61-70-00**). With an exterior wall planted with 150 exotic plant species, it is devoted to the art of Africa, the Americas, the South Pacific, and Asia. In all, nearly 300,000 tribal artifacts are on parade in this $256-million project. During its decade-long construction there were many scandals, such as when the museum's curator discovered that the terra-cotta figurines from Nigeria were stolen. Galleries stand on sculpted pillars that evoke totems. Nouvel said he wanted to "create something unique, poetic, and disturbing."

Another major opening was the long-closed **Musée de l'Orangerie,** Jardin des Tuileries, 1er (© **01-44-77-80-07**). Claude Monet's celebrated *Nymphéas* are displayed as the artist intended them to be—that is, lit by sunlight. The spacious oval-shaped galleries evoke the shape of the garden ponds at the artist's Giverny estate. Over the years, we've come here many times to gaze upon Marie Laurencin's *Portrait of Mademoiselle Chanel* from 1923.

It's had a number of roles in its long life, but today the newly reopened **Jeu de Paume,** 1 place de la Concorde, 8e (© **01-47-03-12-50**), is devoted to photography and video, exploring a world of images. It presents ever-changing exhibitions, many of them daringly avant-garde, and is one of the finest museums of its type in the world.

SHOPPING   For those who do not get their Value Added Tax (VAT) refunded in France, a new office in North America is processing and handling this tax as well as providing information for confused shoppers. **Global Refund** closed its New York office and now operates from Box 2020 Station, Main Brampton, Ontario L6T 353 (© **800/993-4313** or 905/791-9078; www.globalrefund.com).

AFTER DARK   At last, Paris has a permanent home for its orchestras with the reopening of restored **Salle Pleyel,** 252 rue du Faubourg-St-Honoré, 8e (© **01-42-52-13-13**). Pleyel is the Carnegie Hall of Paris. Opening first in 1927, the auditorium saw the likes of Ravel, Debussy, and Stravinsky performing their masterpieces here. Its acoustics and seating are now better than ever. The Orchestre Philharmonique de Radio France and the Orchestre de Paris now call Salle Pleyel home.

The Best of Paris

Discovering the City of Light and making it your own has always been the most compelling reason to visit Paris. If you're a first-timer, everything, of course, will be new to you. If you've been away for awhile, expect changes: Taxi drivers may no longer correct your fractured French, but address you in English—tantamount to a revolution. More Parisians have a rudimentary knowledge of the language, and France, at least at first glance, seems less xenophobic than in past years. Paris, aware of its role within a united Europe, is an international city. Parisians are attracted to foreign music, videos, and films, especially those from America, even though most French people vehemently disagree with the political dictates emerging from George Bush's Washington.

Though Paris is in flux culturally and socially, it lures travelers for the same reasons as always. You'll still find such classic sights as the Tour Eiffel, Notre-Dame, the Arc de Triomphe, Sacré-Coeur, and all those atmospheric cafes, as well as daringly futuristic projects such as the Grande Arche de La Défense, the Cité des Sciences et de l'Industrie, the Cité de la Musique, and the Bibliothèque François-Mitterrand. Don't forget the parks, gardens, and squares; the Champs-Elysées and other grand boulevards; and the river Seine and its quays. Paris's beauty is still overwhelming, especially at night, when it truly is the City of Light.

1 The Most Unforgettable Travel Experiences

- **Whiling Away an Afternoon in a Parisian Cafe:** The cafes are where passionate meetings of writers, artists, philosophers, thinkers, and revolutionaries once took place—and perhaps still do. Parisians stop by their favorite cafes to meet lovers and friends, to make new ones, or to sit in solitude with a newspaper or book. For our recommendations, see section 6, "The Top Cafes," in chapter 7, "Where to Dine."

- **Taking Afternoon Tea à la Française:** Drinking tea in London has its charm, but the Parisian *salon de thé* is unique. Skip the cucumber-and-watercress sandwiches and delve into a luscious dessert like the Mont Blanc, a creamy purée of sweetened chestnuts and meringue. The grandest Parisian tea salon is **Angélina,** 226 rue de Rivoli, 1er (© **01-42-60-82-00;** Métro: Tuileries or Concorde; p. 134).

- **Strolling along the Seine:** Such painters as Sisley, Turner, and Monet have fallen under the Seine's spell. On its banks, lovers still walk hand in hand, anglers cast their lines, and *bouquinistes* (secondhand-book dealers) peddle their mix of postcards, 100-year-old pornography, and tattered histories of Indochina. For more details on the sights and moments of Paris, see chapter 8, "Exploring Paris."

- **Spending a Day at the Races:** Paris boasts eight tracks for horse racing. The most famous and the classiest is **Hippodrome de Longchamp,** in the Bois de Boulogne, the site of the Prix de l'Arc de Triomphe and Grand Prix (p. 229). These and other top races are major social events, so you'll have to dress up (buy your outfit on rue du Faubourg St-Honoré). Take the Métro to Porte d'Auteuil and then a bus from there to the track. The racing newspaper *Paris Turf* and weekly entertainment magazines have details about race times.

- **Calling on the Dead:** You don't have to be a ghoul to be thrilled by a visit to Europe's most famous cemetery, **Père-Lachaise** (p. 224). You can pay your respects to the earthly remains of Gertrude Stein and her longtime companion, Alice B. Toklas; Oscar Wilde; Yves Montand and Simone Signoret; Edith Piaf; Isadora Duncan; Abélard and Héloïse; Frédéric Chopin; Marcel Proust; Eugène Delacroix; Jim Morrison; and others. The tomb designs are intriguing and often eerie. Laid out in 1803 on a hill in Ménilmontant, the cemetery offers surprises with its bizarre monuments, unexpected views, and ornate sculpture.

- **Checking Out the Marchés:** A daily Parisian ritual is ambling through one of the open-air markets to buy fresh food—perhaps a properly creamy Camembert or a pumpkin-gold cantaloupe—to be eaten before sundown. Our favorite market is on rue Montorgueil, beginning at rue Rambuteau, 1er (Métro: Les Halles). During mornings at this grubby little cluster of food stalls, we've spotted some of France's finest chefs stocking up for the day. For more details, see "Food Markets" in chapter 10.

- **Window-Shopping in the Faubourg St-Honoré:** In the 1700s, the wealthiest Parisians resided in the Faubourg St-Honoré; today, the quarter is home to stores catering to the rich, particularly on rue du Faubourg St-Honoré and avenue Montaigne. Even if you don't buy anything, it's great to window-shop big names such as Hermès, Dior, Laroche, Courrèges, Cardin, and Saint Laurent. If you want to browse in the stores, be sure to dress the part. See chapter 10, "Shopping," for the lowdown on these boutiques.

- **Exploring Ile de la Cité's Flower Market:** A fine finish to any day (Mon–Sat) spent meandering along the Seine is a stroll through the **Marché aux Fleurs,** place Louis-Lépine (p. 267). You can buy rare flowers, the gems of the French Riviera—bouquets that have inspired artists throughout the centuries. Even the most basic hotel room will feel like a luxury suite once you fill it with bunches of carnations, lavender, roses, and tulips. On Sundays, the area is transformed into the **Marché aux Oiseaux,** where you can admire rare birds from around the world.

- **Going Gourmet at Fauchon:** An exotic world of food, **Fauchon** (p. 173) offers more than 20,000 products from around the globe. Everything you never knew you were missing is in aisle after aisle of coffees, spices, pastries, fruits, vegetables, rare Armagnacs, and much more. Take your pick: Tonganese mangoes, Scottish smoked salmon, preserved cocks' combs, Romanian rose-petal jelly, blue-red Indian pomegranates, golden Tunisian dates, larks stuffed with foie gras, dark morels from France's rich soil, Finnish reindeer's tongue, century-old eggs from China, and a Creole punch from Martinique, reputed to be the best anywhere.

- **Attending a Ballet or an Opera:** In 1989, the **Opéra Bastille** (p. 274) was inaugurated to compete with the grande dame of the music scene, the **Opéra Garnier** (p. 275), which then was used solely for dance and soon closed for renovations. The Opéra Garnier reopened a few years ago, and opera has joined dance in the rococo splendor created by Charles Garnier, beneath a controversial ceiling by Chagall. The modern Opéra Bastille, France's largest opera house, with curtains by designer Issey Miyake, has opera and symphony performances in four concert halls (its main hall seats 2,700). Whether for a performance of Bizet or Tharp, dress with pomp and circumstance.

• **Sipping Cocktails at Willi's:** Back in the early 1970s, the first-timer to Paris might have arrived with a copy of Hemingway's *A Moveable Feast* and, taking the author's endorsement to heart, headed for Harry's Bar at "Sank roo doe Noo." Harry's is still around but now draws an older, more conservative clientele. Today's chic younger expats head for **Willi's Wine Bar,** 13 rue des Petits-Champs, 1er (© 01-42-61-05-09; Métro: Bourse, Palais Royal, or Pyramides; p. 286). Here, the long-haired young bartenders are mostly English, as are the waitresses, who are dressed in Laura Ashley garb. The place is like an informal club for Brits, Australians, and Yanks, especially in the afternoon. Some 300 wines await your selection.

2 The Best Splurge Hotels

• **Hôtel Ritz** (15 place Vendôme, 1er; © 800/223-6800 or 01-43-16-30-30; www.ritzparis.com). This hotel, which gave the world the word "ritzy," meaning posh, occupies a magnificent palace overlooking the octagonal borders of one of the most perfect squares in the world. The decor is pure opulence. Marcel Proust wrote parts of *Remembrance of Things Past* here, and the world's greatest chef, Georges-Auguste Escoffier, perfected many of his recipes in the Ritz kitchens. See p. 84.

• **Four Seasons Hotel George V** (31 av. George V, 8e; © 800/332-3442 or 01-49-52-70-00; www.fourseasons.com). Humorist Art Buchwald once wrote, "Paris without the George V would be Cleveland." The swanky address has long been a favorite of celebrities in every field, including Duke Ellington, who once wrote in his memoirs that his suite was so big that he couldn't find the way out. Its public and private rooms are decorated with a vast array of antiques and Louis XIV tapestries worth millions. See p. 96.

• **Hôtel Meurice** (228 rue de Rivoli, 1er; © 01-44-58-10-10; www.meuricehotel.com) has been restored to its former glory. It reigned as the queen-bee hotel of Paris in the 19th century and has made a comeback to preside over post-millennium Paris as well. From its Winter Garden to its sumptuous bedrooms that sheltered kings, this one is a winner. See p. 81.

• **Hôtel Pershing Hall** (49 rue Pierre Charron, 8e; © 01-58-36-58-00; www.pershing-hall.com) is not as well known as the previous hotels, but it too ranks among Paris's pockets of posh. Converted from an elegant town house of the 19th century, it was drastically altered by Andrée Putnam, one of France's most celebrated modern designers, into this citadel of fine living. Built for the Comte de Paris and his mistress, it was the Paris headquarters for General John Pershing in World War I—hence, its name.

It's lavish, lush, and luxurious. See p. 98.

- **Plaza Athénée** (25 av. Montaigne, 8e; ℂ **866/732-1106** or 01-53-67-66-65; www.plaza-athenee-paris.com) is still the favorite lunchtime hangout for Parisian couturiers. It's also a lot more than that, providing luxurious accommodations for the likes of the Rockefellers and super-wealthy Brazilians. This swanky citadel is graced with potted palms, crystal chandeliers, and elegant furnishings—you name it: Louis XV, Louis XVI, Regency, whatever. Its ivy-covered courtyard is a slice of heaven. See p. 98.
- **Hôtel d'Aubusson** (33 rue Dauphine, 6e; ℂ **01-43-29-43-43**; www.hotel daubusson.com) lies in the heart of St-Germain-des-Prés and is our favorite boutique hotel in Paris. It takes its name from the original Aubusson tapestries gracing its elegant public rooms. Antiques and luxurious accessories make a stay here evocative of a visit to a classy private home, filled with tasteful, beautifully decorated bedrooms and intimate public salons with baronial furnishings evocative of the era of Louis XV. You can sleep under a ceiling with exposed beams in a canopied bed. See p. 109.
- **L'Hôtel** (13 rue des Beaux-Arts, 6e; ℂ **01-44-41-99-00**; www.l-hotel. com) is precious—just precious—the Left Bank's most charming little town house hotel. And, yes, this former fleabag was where the great Oscar Wilde died, disgraced and penniless. That was Glenn Close or Robert De Niro you saw walking through the lobby, but not Elizabeth Taylor, because the rooms were too small for her luggage. The hotel is a triumph of Directoire architecture, and the ambience is oh, so seductive. See p. 109.

3 The Best Moderately Priced Hotels

- **Hôtel Duo** (11 rue du Temple, 4e; ℂ **01-42-72-72-22**; www.duoparis. com) is a winner in the increasingly fashionable Marais district, convenient to the Picasso Museum and the Centre Pompidou. Parisian fashionistas have made this a favorite nesting place. The old architecture, including time-worn stones and exposed beams, has been respected; otherwise, the place is as up-to-date as tomorrow. A member of the staff jokingly suggested to us that this sophisticated rendezvous is "not for virgins." See p. 91.
- **Hôtel des Deux-Iles** (59 rue St-Louis-en-l'Ile, 4e; ℂ **01-43-26-13-35**; www.deuxiles-paris-hotel.com). There exists no more platinum real estate, at least in our view, than the Ile St-Louis, Paris's most beautiful isle in the Seine. For a charming, yet unpretentious, hotel on this island, we'd choose this restored 18th-century town house. We like the abundance of fresh flowers and the fireplace in the cellar bar. The rooms are a bit small, but this is one of the city's greatest locations for a hotel, and that should count for something. See p. 90.
- **Hôtel Saint-Louis** (75 rue St-Louis-en-l'Ile, 4e; ℂ **01-46-34-04-80**). Like Hôtel des Deux-Iles, this cozy nest, a restored 17th-century town house, occupies a "world apart" on a tiny island in the middle of the Seine. The rooms may be *petit,* but the charm of the place compensates, with its exposed ceiling beams, wooden Louis XIII furnishings, and modern bathrooms. Opt for a fifth-floor bedroom for a panoramic view over the rooftops of Paris. See p. 91.

- **Galileo Hôtel** (54 rue Galilee, 8e; ✆ **01-47-20-66-06;** www.galileo-paris-hotel.com). In the super-expensive 8th Arrondissement, site of the Champs-Elysées and France's most expensive street, avenue Montaigne, this is a holdout since it's actually affordable to many visitors. In the epicenter of Paris, this restored town house is imbued with Parisian elegance and charm. Though understated, the bedrooms are tastefully furnished and most comfortable, and a few choice ones have glass-covered verandas. See p. 100.

- **Hotel Trocadéro La Tour** (5 bis rue Massenet, 16e; ✆ **01-45-24-43-03;** www.paris-hotel-trocaderolatour.com). In a tony district known for its well-heeled bourgeoisie and upscale rents, this restored late-19th-century town house charges reasonable prices—for Paris, that is. Subdued elegance and refined comfort are just part of its allure, along with its view of the Eiffel Tower in the distance. From its tree-filled courtyard to its elegant, tastefully decorated bedrooms, this one is a winner and not as well known as it should be. See p. 101.

- **Hôtel de l'Abbaye Saint-Germain** (10 rue Cassette, 6e; ✆ **01-45-44-38-11;** www.hotel-abbaye.com). For those who'd like to stay in the heart of the Quartier Latin in the 5th Arrondissement, this charming boutique hotel, originally a convent in the 1700s, has been restored with a certain grace and sophisticated flair. Brightly painted rooms with traditional French furnishings are inviting and comfortable, and the maintenance is first-rate. Grace notes include a courtyard with a fountain, along with flowerbeds and climbing ivy. Try for the upper-floor room with a terrace overlooking Paris. See p. 110.

- **Résidence des Arts** (14 rue Git-le-Coeur, 6e; ✆ **01-55-42-71-11;** www.hotelresidencedesartsparis.com). If your own "studio" in Left Bank Paris has always been a dream, you can rent one here, or else a tastefully decorated suite or apartment—all at an affordable price. In the heart of the Quartier Latin, this hotel was carved from a former apartment building to which two upper floors were added in 1998. Some of the units come with kitchenettes, and a bistro and restaurant are on site. See p. 113.

4 The Most Unforgettable Dining Experiences

- **Le Grand Véfour** (17 rue de Beaujolais, 1er; ✆ **01-42-96-56-27**). Seductively and appropriately time-worn, this dining room is where Napoleon sat wooing Joséphine. Its Louis XVI–Directoire interior is a protected historic monument. With its haute cuisine, it has been the haunt of celebrities since 1760. Its cuisine, mercifully, is even better than ever, because it insists on hiring only the world's leading chefs. This monument to the past still tantalizes 21st-century palates. See p. 128.

- **Aux Lyonnais** (32 rue St-Marc, 2e; ✆ **01-42-96-65-04**). Paris's bistro of bistros has been taken over by Alain Ducasse, the six-star Michelin chef and self-proclaimed "greatest in the world." In spite of that takeover, Aux Lyonnais remains the quintessential Parisian dining choice for Lyonnais specialties. As any city dweller of Lyon will tell you, that city is the gastronomic capital of France. The market-fresh produce is as new as the 1890s bistro is old, with its backdrop of potted palms, etched glass, and globe lamps in the best of the Belle Epoque style. See p. 135.

- **Au Pied de Cochon** (6 rue Coquillière, 1er; © **01-40-13-77-00**). For years, it's been a Paris tradition to stop off at this joint in Les Halles for the famous onion soup at 3 o'clock in the morning after a night of revelry. The true Parisian also orders the restaurant's namesake—grilled pigs' feet with béarnaise sauce. You can also do as your grandpa did and wash down a dozen different varieties of oysters at the time-mellowed bar—along with champagne, but of course. See p. 132.

- **Taillevent** (15 rue Lamennais, 8e; © **01-44-95-15-01**). Forget about sending the kids to college and instead enjoy one of the most memorable meals of your life at what is consistently hailed as Paris's temple of haute cuisine. Named after a 14th-century chef to the king and the author of the first French cookbook, this restaurant comes as close to perfection as any in the world. In all of our years of dining here, the chef has never had a bad day. This is a true temple of grand cuisine with one of the world's top 10 wine lists. Although we've enjoyed much of the innovative cuisine of Alain Solivères, we are also grateful that he's kept that airy, sausage-shaped lobster soufflé on the menu. See p. 148.

- **Carré des Feuillants** (14 rue de Castiglione, 1er; © **01-42-86-82-82**): Chef Alain Dutournier presides over this temple of haute gastronomy, thrilling diners with his take on new French cuisine. As always, deluxe ingredients are prepared with one of the most finely honed techniques in all of Paris. This chef knows the value of simplicity touched with inspiration. See p. 128.

- **Lasserre** (17 av. Franklin D. Roosevelt, 8e; © **01-43-59-53-43**): Each new generation discovered this elegant bastion of chic for itself. A tradition since the late 1930s, Lasserre has seen the faces of the Golden Age (everyone from Marlene Dietrich to Audrey Hepburn) but also welcomes the stars of today, tempting them with sublime cuisine both modern and traditional. See p. 145.

- **Crémerie-Restaurant Polidor** (41 rue Monsieur-le-Prince, 6e; © **01-43-26-95-34**). A longtime favorite of students, artists, and the literati such as James Joyce and Jack Kerouac, this bistro in St-Germain-des-Prés has been around since 1845. We've been such regulars that our favorite waitress used to store our linen napkins in a wooden drawer for use on another night. One habitué we met here claimed he'd been dining at Polidor 2 or 3 nights a week for half a century. The pumpkin soup, the *boeuf bourguignon*, the *blanquette de veau*—yes, the same recipes that delighted Hemingway—are still served here. See p. 165.

- **L'Atelier de Joël Robuchon** (5–7 rue de Montalembert, 7e; © **01-42-22-56-56**). What a discovery. When Joël Robuchon retired in the mid-1990s, he was hailed as the greatest chef in France, which may as well mean the world. Bored with retirement, he made a more modest comeback with this 7th Arrondissement delight. His innovative dishes are far less elaborate than they were in days of yore, but he still makes the best mashed potatoes the world has ever known, along with other market-fresh concoctions that will win your heart. We're talking the likes of such dishes as caramelized quail glazed with a shallot-perfumed sauce. See p. 168.

• **La Petite Chaise** (36 rue de Grenelle, 7e; ℂ **01-42-22-13-35**). Even on the most rushed of visits to Paris, we always drop in here for one of the best prix-fixe menus at the more affordable restaurants in Paris. "The Little Chair" (its English name) first opened as an inn in 1680, when it was used for both food and its bedrooms upstairs, where discretion for afternoon dalliances was virtually assured. The time-honored cuisine is as French as Charles de Gaulle—and that is as it should be. See p. 170.

5 The Best Things to Do for Free (or Almost)

• **Meeting the Natives.** There is no page number to which you can turn for guidance here. You're on your own. But meeting Parisians, and experiencing their cynical metropolitanism, is one of the adventures of traveling to Paris—and it's free. Tolerance, gentleness, and patience are not their strongest points; they don't suffer fools gladly, but adore eccentrics. Visitors often find Parisians brusque to the point of rudeness and preoccupied with their own affairs. However, this hard-boiled crust often protects a soft center. Compliment a surly bistro owner on her cuisine, and—nine times out of 10—she'll melt before your eyes. Admire a Parisian's dog or praise a window display, and you'll find a loquaciously knowledgeable companion for the next 5 minutes. Ask about the correct pronunciation of a French word (before you mispronounce it), and a Parisian may become your language teacher. Try to meet a Parisian halfway with some kind of personalized contact. Only then do you learn their best qualities: their famed charm, their *savoir-faire*—and, yes, believe it or not, the delightful courtesy that marks their social life.

• **Trailing les Américains.** At 35 rue de Picpus, a few blocks from the place de la Nation, is a spot over which the Stars and Stripes have flown for more than a century and a half. It lies in a small secluded cemetery, marking the **grave of the Marquis de Lafayette**—the man who, during the American Revolution, forged the chain that has linked the two countries ever since. Col. Charles E. Stanton came here to utter the famous words, *Lafayette, nous voila!* ("Lafayette, we are here!") to announce the arrival of the World War I doughboys on French soil. At the pont de Grenelle, at Passy, you'll find the original model of the **Statue of Liberty** that France presented to the people of the United States. One of the most impressive paintings in the **Musée de l'Armée** (p. 193) shows the Battle of Yorktown, which—however you learned it in school—was a combined Franco-American victory. Throughout the city, you'll keep coming across statues, monuments, streets, squares, and plaques commemorating George Washington, Benjamin Franklin, Presidents Wilson and Roosevelt, Generals Pershing and Eisenhower, and scores of lesser Yankee names.

• **Attending a Free Concert.** Summer brings a Paris joy: free concerts in parks and churches all over the city. Pick up an entertainment weekly for details. Some of the best concerts are held at the **American Church in Paris,** 65 quai d'Orsay, 7e (ℂ **01-40-62-05-00;** Métro: Invalides or Alma-Marceau; p. 276), which sponsors free concerts from September to June on Sunday at 5pm. You can also attend free concerts at **Eglise**

St-Merry, 78 rue St-Martin, 4e (℗ **01-42-71-48-15;** Métro: Hôtel-de-Ville; p. 276). These performances are staged based on the availability of the performers, from September to July on Saturday at 9pm and again on Sunday at 4pm.

- **Hanging Out at the Place des Vosges.** Deep in the Marais, place des Vosges is more an enchanted island than a city square. This serenely lovely oasis is the oldest square in Paris and the most entrancing. Laid out in 1605 by order of Henri IV, it was the scene of innumerable cavaliers' duels. In the middle is a tiny park where you can sit and sun, listen to the splashing waters of the fountains, or else watch the kids at play. On three sides is an encircling arcaded walk, supported by arches and paved with ancient, worn flagstones. Sit sipping an espresso as the day passes you by. It's our all-time favorite spot in Paris for people-watching. See p. 64.

- **Viewing Avant-Garde Art.** Space is too tight to document the dozens of art galleries that abound in Paris, but the true devotee will find that not all great art in Paris is displayed in a museum. There is a tendency, however, for owners to open galleries around major museums, hoping to lure the art lovers in. This is especially true around the Musée Picasso and the Centre Pompidou, both in the Marais. Our favorite gallery in the Marais is **La Maison Rouge,** the red house at 10 bd. de la Bastille, 12e (℗ **01-40-01-08-81;** Métro: Quai de la Rapée). It displays an ever-changing array of the "hottest" work—and the most avant-garde—of Parisian artists. The more traditional galleries are found in St-Germain-des-Prés, with **Galerie Adrien Maeght,** 42 rue du Bac, 7e (℗ **01-45-48-45-15;** p. 253) being the market leader.

- **Seeing Paris from a Bus.** Most tours of Paris are expensive, but for only 1.30€ ($1.70) you can ride one of the city's public buses traversing some of the most scenic streets. Our favorite is no. 29, which begins at historic Gare St-Lazare (Métro: St-Lazare), subject of Monet's painting *La Gare St-Lazare* at Musée d'Orsay. Featured in Zola's novel *La Bête Humaine,* the station also has a bus line. Aboard no. 29, you pass the famous Opéra Garnier (home of the Phantom) and proceed into the Marais district, passing by Paris's most beautiful square, place des Vosges. You end up at the Bastille district, home of the new opera. What we like about this bus is that it takes you along the side streets of Paris and not the major boulevards. It's a close encounter with back-street Paris and a cheap way to see the city without commentary.

- **Strolling the World's Grandest Promenade.** Pointing from place de la Concorde like a broad, straight arrow to the Arc de Triomphe at the far end, the **Champs-Elysées** (the main street of Paris) presents its grandest spectacle at night. Guidebook writers to Paris grow tired of repeating "the most in the world," but, of course, the Champs-Elysées is the world's most famous promenade. For the first third of the stroll from place de la Concorde, the avenue is hedged by chestnut trees. Then it changes into a double row of palatial hotels and shops, movie houses, office buildings, and block after block of sidewalk cafes. The automobile showrooms and gift stores have marred the Belle Epoque elegance of this stretch, but it's still the greatest vantage point from which to watch Paris roll by.

- **Cooling Off in the Jardin des Tuileries.** Right-Bank Parisians head to the Tuileries Gardens to cool off on a hot summer day. The park stretches on the Right Bank of the Seine from the place de la Concorde to the doorstep of the Louvre. This exquisitely formal garden was laid out as a royal pleasure ground in 1564, but was thrown open to the public by the French Revolution. Filled with statues, fountains, and mathematically trimmed hedges, it's a bit too formal for English gardeners who like their green spaces a little wilder. Its nicest feature is a series of round ponds on which kids sail armadas of model boats. Stand on the elevated terrace by the Seine, enjoying panoramic views over Paris, including the Arc de Triomphe and the Cour Napoléon of the Louvre. The sculptures by Rodin aren't bad either. Food stands and cafes with refreshing drinks await you.

6 The Best Museums

- **Musée du Louvre** (34–36 quai du Louvre, 1er; ℂ **01-40-20-53-17;** www.louvre.fr). The Louvre's exterior is a triumph of French architecture, and its interior shelters an embarrassment of art, one of the greatest treasure troves known to Western civilization. Of the Louvre's more than 300,000 paintings, only a small percentage can be displayed at one time. The museum maintains its staid dignity and timelessness even though thousands of visitors traipse daily through its corridors, looking for the *Mona Lisa* or the *Venus de Milo*. I. M. Pei's controversial Great Pyramid nearly offsets the grandeur of the Cour Carrée, but it has a real functional purpose, as you will soon see. See p. 195.

- **Musée d'Orsay** (1 rue de Bellechasse, 7e; ℂ **01-40-49-48-14;** www.musee-orsay.fr). The spidery glass-and-iron canopies of an abandoned railway station frame one of Europe's greatest museums of art. Devoted mainly to paintings of the 19th century, d'Orsay contains some of the most celebrated masterpieces of the French Impressionists, along with sculptures and decorative objects whose designs forever changed the way European artists interpreted line, movement, and color. In case you didn't know, d'Orsay is also where *Whistler's Mother* sits in her rocker. See p. 194.

- **Centre Pompidou** (place Georges-Pompidou, 4e; ℂ **01-44-78-12-33;** www.centrepompidou.fr). "The most avant-garde building in the world," or so it is known, is a citadel of modern art, with exhibitions drawn from more than 40,000 works. Everything seemingly is here—from Calder's 1928 *Josephine Baker* (one of his earliest versions of the mobile) to a recreation of Brancusi's Jazz Age studio. See p. 199.

- **Musée Jacquemart-André** (158 bd. Haussmann, 8e; ℂ **01-45-62-11-59;** www.musee-jacquemart-andre.com). The 19th-century town house, with its gilt salons and elegant winding staircase, contains the best small collection of 18th-century decorative art in Paris. The building and its contents were a bequest to the Institut de France by the late Mme Nélie Jacquemart-André, herself an artist of note. To her amazing collection of rare French decorative art, she added a rich trove of painting and sculpture from the Dutch and Flemish schools, as well as paintings and objets d'art from the Italian Renaissance. See p. 203.

- **Musée National du Moyen Age/ Thermes de Cluny** (in the Hotel de

Cluny, 6 place Paul-Painlevé, 5e; ② **01-45-62-11-59**; www.musee-moyenage.fr). This is an enchantress of a museum, housing some of the most beautiful medieval art still in existence. The museum occupies one of the two Gothic private residences left from Paris in the 15th century. Dark, rough-walled, and evocative, the Cluny is devoted to the church art and castle crafts of the Middle Ages. It is more celebrated for its tapestries—among them the world-famed series of *The Lady and the Unicorn,* gracefully displayed in a circular room on the second floor. Downstairs you can visit the ruins of Roman baths, dating from around A.D. 200. See p. 204.

- **Musée Marmottan-Claude Monet** (2 rue Louis-Boilly, 16e; ② **01-44-96-50-33**; www.marmottan.com). On the edge of the Bois de Boulogne, this once rarely visited museum is now one of the most frequented in Paris. It was rescued from obscurity on February 5, 1966, when the museum fell heir to more than 130 paintings, watercolors, pastels, and drawings of Claude Monet, the "father of Impressionism." A gift of Monet's son Michel, the bequest is one of the greatest art acquisitions in France. Had an old widow in Brooklyn suddenly inherited the fortune of a J. P. Morgan, the event would not have been more startling. Exhibited here is the painting, *Impression, Sunrise,* which named the artistic movement. See p. 203.

- **Musée Picasso** (in the Hotel Salé, 5 rue de Thorigny, 3e; ② **01-42-71-25-21**; www.musee-picasso.fr). Deep in the heart of the Marais, this museum has been hailed in the press as a repository "for Picasso's Picassos." The state acquired the world's greatest collection in lieu of a $50-million inheritance tax: 203 paintings, 158 sculptures, 16 collages, 19 bas-reliefs, 88 ceramics, and more than 1,500 sketches and 1,600 engravings. The work spans 75 years of Picasso's life. See p. 205.

- **Musée Rodin** (in the Hotel Biron, 77 rue de Varenne, 7e; ② **01-44-18-61-10**; www.musee-rodin.fr). Auguste Rodin, the man credited with freeing French sculpture from classicism, once lived at, and had his studio in, this charming 18th-century mansion across from Napoleon's tomb. Today, the house and its garden are filled with his works, a soul-satisfying feast for the Rodin enthusiast. In the cobbled Court of Honor, within the walls as you enter, you'll see *The Thinker* crouched on his pedestal. The *Burghers of Calais* are grouped off to the left; and, to the far left, the writhing *Gates of Hell* can be seen, atop which another *Thinker* once more meditates. In the almost-too-packed rooms, men and angels emerge from blocks of marble, their hands twisted in supplication, and the nude torso of Balzac rises from a tree. See p. 205.

7 The Best Neighborhoods for Getting Lost

- **Montmartre.** Striding a hill atop Paris, Montmartre used to be a village of artists, glorified by masters such as Utrillo, and painted, sketched, sculpted, and photographed by 10,000 lesser lights. Today, it's overrun by tourists, building speculators, and nightclub entrepreneurs who moved in as the artists moved out. However, a few still linger and so does much of the villagelike charm. Of all the places for wandering the cobbled streets of old Paris, Montmartre, especially in its back streets and alleyways, gets our vote. The center point is the place du Tertre, where you can head out on your journey of exploration. Gleaming through the trees from here is the Basilica of Sacré-Coeur, built in an oddly Oriental neo-Byzantine style. Behind the church and clinging to the hillside below are steep and crooked little streets that seem—almost—to have survived the relentless march of progress. Rue des Saules still has Montmartre's last vineyard. The rue Lepic still looks—almost—the way Renoir, the melancholic Van Gogh, and the dwarfish genius Toulouse-Lautrec saw it. See p. 67.

- **Quartier Latin.** Over the Seine on the Left Bank, the Latin Quarter lies in the 5th Arrondissement and consists of streets winding around the Paris University, of which the Sorbonne is only a part. The logical starting point is place Saint-Michel, right on the river, with an impressive fountain. From here you can wander at leisure, getting lost as you discover the doglegged cluster of alleys adjoining the river—rue de la Huchette, rue de la Harpe, rue St-Séverin. Each generation makes discoveries of its own, and everything is new again. End up by strolling along Boulevard St-Germain, lined with sophisticated cafes and some of the most avant-garde fashion shops in Paris. See p. 64.

- **Le Marais.** Very few cities on earth boast an entire district that can be labeled a sight. Paris has several, including the vaguely defined maze of streets north of place de la Bastille, known as Le Marais, or "the marshland." During the 17th century, this was a region of aristocratic mansions,

which lost their elegance when the fashionable set moved elsewhere. The houses lost status, but they remain standing and restored today, as the once-decaying Marais has been gentrified. Today, it's one of the most fashionable districts in Paris, home to funky shops, offbeat hotels, dozens of bistros, hot bars, and "gay Paree." See p. 63.

- **Ile St-Louis.** A footbridge behind Notre-Dame leads to another enchanting island on the Seine, a world of tree-shaded quays, town houses with courtyards, and antiques shops. This smaller and more tranquil of the Seine islands has remained much as it was in the 17th century. Over the years, many illustrious French have called St-Louis home, none more famous than Voltaire. Sober patrician houses stand along the four quays, and the feverish beat of Paris seems 100 miles away. This is our favorite real estate for wandering in the whole city. See p. 63.

- **Ile de la Cité.** "The cradle of Paris," where the city was born, is actually an island shaped like a great ship in the middle of the Seine. Home to France's greatest cathedral, Notre-Dame, it invites exploration and wandering. Home to French kings until the 14th century, Cité still has a curiously medieval air, with massive gray walls rising up all around you, relieved by tiny patches of parkland. The island is home to Sainte-Chapelle and the Conciergerie. After these stellar attractions, save time for wandering about and discovering Cité's secrets, such as the square du Vert Galant. See p. 63.

2

A Traveler's Guide to Paris's Art & Architecture

Paris is one of the artistic capitals of Europe. For centuries the city has produced, and been home to, countless artists and artistic movements. This chapter will help you find the best examples of each period in the city's museums and architecture.

1 Art 101

GOTHIC (1100–1400)

Almost all artistic expression in medieval France was church-related. Paris retains almost no art from the Classical or Romanesque eras, but much remains from the medieval Gothic era, when artists created sculpture and stained glass for churches.

Because Mass was in Latin, many images were used to communicate the Bible's most important lessons to the mostly illiterate populace. **Bas reliefs** (sculpture that projects slightly from a flat surface) were used to illustrate key tales that inspired faith in God and fear of sin (last judgments were favorites). These reliefs were wrapped around column capitals, festooned onto facades, and fitted into the **tympanum** (the arched spaces above doorways; the complete door, tympanum, arch, and supporting pillars assemblage is the **portal**).

The French were also becoming masters of **stained glass.** Many painterly conventions began in this era on windowpanes, or as elaborate doodles in the margins of **illuminated manuscripts,** which developed into altarpieces of the colorful **International Gothic** style.

In both Gothic painting and sculpture, figures tend to be highly stylized, flowing, and rhythmic. The figures' features and gestures are exaggerated for symbolic or emotional emphasis.

Outstanding examples include:

- **Cathédrale de Chartres** (1194–1220). A day trip from Paris, the cathedral of Chartres boasts magnificent sculpture and some of the best stained glass in Europe.
- **Cathédrale de Notre-Dame** (1163–1250). The Gothic high points of the Notre-Dame cathedral are the sculpture on the facade, an interior choir screen lined with deep-relief carvings, and three rose windows filled with stained glass.
- **Sainte-Chapelle** (1240–50). The finest stained glass in the world adorns this tiny chapel.
- **The Lady and the Unicorn Tapestries** (1499–1514). These famed tapestries shine brightly as a final statement of medieval sensibilities while borrowing some burgeoning Renaissance conventions. Find them in the **Musée de Cluny.**

THE RENAISSANCE (1400–1600)

Renaissance means "rebirth," in this case the return of classical ideals originating in Greece and Rome. Humanist thinkers rediscovered the wisdom of the ancients, while artists strove for greater naturalism, using newly developed techniques such as linear perspective to achieve new heights of realism. Famous practitioners of the style include **Michelangelo** (1475–1564) and **Leonardo da Vinci** (1452–1519). **Mannerism,** the late-16th-century branch of the High Renaissance, took Michelangelo's bright color palette and twisting figures to extremes and exhausted the movement.

Aside from collecting Italian art, the French had little to do with the Renaissance, which started in Italy and was quickly picked up in Germany and the Low Countries. France owes many of its early Renaissance treasures to **François I,** who imported art (paintings by Raphael and Titian) and artists (Leonardo da Vinci). Henri II's Florentine wife, **Catherine de Médicis,** also collected 16th-century Italian masterpieces.

Significant artists and examples to look for in Paris include:

- **Italian Artists.** Many works by Italy's finest reside in the **Louvre,** including paintings by **Giotto, Fra Angelico,** and **Veronese;** sculptures by **Michelangelo;** and a handful of works by **Leonardo da Vinci,** who moved to a Loire Valley château for the last 3 years of his life and whose *Mona Lisa* (1503–05), perhaps the world's most famous painting, hangs here.

- **The School of Fontainebleau.** This group of artists working on the **Palais de Fontainebleau** outside Paris from 1530 to 1560 were imported Italian mannerists who combined painting, stucco, sculpture, and woodwork to decorate the château's Galerie François I. They included **Niccolò dell'Abbate, Benvenuto Cellini, Primaticcio,** and **Rosso Fiorentino.** (If you don't make it out to Fontainebleau, check out Cellini's sculpture *Diana of Fontainebleau* [1543–44] in the Louvre.)

THE BAROQUE (1600–1800)

The 17th-century **baroque style** is hard to pin down. In some ways it was a result of the Catholic Counter-Reformation, reaffirming spirituality in a simplified, monumental, and religious version of Renaissance ideals. Another version of the baroque style delved even deeper into classical modes and a kind of super-realism based on peasants as models and the exaggerated *chiaroscuro* (interplay or contrast of light and dark) of Italian painter Caravaggio.

Some view those two styles as extensions of Renaissance experiments and find the true baroque in later compositions—all explosions of dynamic fury, movement, color, and figures—that are well balanced but in such cluttered abundance as to appear untamed. **Rococo** is this later baroque art gone awry, frothy, and chaotic.

Significant practitioners of the baroque with examples in the **Louvre** include:

- **Nicolas Poussin** (1594–1665). The most classical French painter, Poussin created mythological scenes that presaged the Romantic movement. His balance and predilection to paint from nature influenced French Impressionists such as Cézanne.

- **Antoine Watteau** (1684–1721). Watteau indulged in the wild, untamed complexity of the rococo. Cruise the Louvre for his colorful, theatrical works. He began the short-lived *fête galante* style that featured china-doll figures against stylized landscapes of woodlands or ballrooms.

- **François Boucher** (1703–70). Louis XV's rococo court painter, Boucher studied Watteau and produced lots of decorative landscapes and genre works.
- **Jean-Honoré Fragonard** (1732–1806). Boucher's student and the master of rococo, Fragonard painted an overindulgence of pink-cheeked, genteel lovers frolicking against billowing treescapes. The Louvre hangs his famous painting, *The Bathers.*

NEOCLASSICAL & ROMANTIC (1770–1890)

As the baroque got excessive, the rococo got cute, and the somber Counter-Reformation got serious about the limits on religious art, several artists looked for relief to the ancients. Viewing new excavations of Greek and Roman sites (Pompeii and Paestum) and statuary became integral parts of the Grand Tour through Italy, while the Enlightenment (and growing Revolutionary) interest in Greek democracy beat an intellectual path to the distant past. This gave rise to a **neoclassical** artistic style that emphasized symmetry, austerity, clean lines, and classical themes, such as depictions of events from history or mythology.

The **romantics,** on the other hand, felt that both the ancients and the Renaissance had gotten it wrong and that the Middle Ages was the place to be. They idealized romantic tales of chivalry and held a deep respect for nature, human rights, and the nobility of peasantry. Their paintings were heroic, historic, and (melo)dramatic, and quested for beauty.

Some great artists and movements of the era, all with examples in the **Louvre,** include:

- **Jacques-Louis David** (1748–1825). David dropped the baroque after a year of study in Rome exposed him to neoclassicism, which he brought back to Paris and displayed in such paintings as *The Oath of the Horatii* (1784) and *Coronation of Napoléon and Joséphine* (1805–08).
- **Jean Ingres** (1780–1867). Trained with David, Ingres became a defender of the neoclassicists and the Royal French Academy, and opposed the romantics. His *Grand Odalisque* (1814) hangs in the Louvre.
- **Theodore Géricault** (1791–1824). One of the great early romantics, Géricault produced the large, dramatic history painting *The Raft of the Medusa* (1819), which served as a model for the movement.
- **Eugène Delacroix** (1798–1863). His *Liberty Leading the People* (1830) was painted in the romantic style, but the artist was also experimenting with color and brushstroke.
- **The Barbizon School.** This school of landscape painters, founded in the 1830s by **Théodore Rousseau** (1812–67), painted directly from nature at Barbizon near Paris. **Jean François Millet** (1814–75) preferred classical scenes and local peasants; his works are at the **Musée d'Orsay. Jean Baptiste Camille Corot** (1796–1875), the third Barbizon great, was a sort of idealistic proto-Impressionist.

IMPRESSIONISM (1870–1920)

Formal, rigid neoclassicism and idealized romanticism rankled some late-19th-century artists interested in painting directly from nature. Seeking to capture the *impression* light made as it reflected off objects, they adopted a free, open style; deceptively loose compositions; swift, visible brushwork; and often light colors. For subject matter, they turned away from the classical themes of previous styles to landscapes and scenes of modern life. Unless specified below, you'll find some of the best examples of their works in the **Musée d'Orsay.**

Impressionist greats include:

- **Edouard Manet** (1832–83). His groundbreaking *Picnic on the Grass* (1863) and *Olympia* (1863) were not examples of Impressionism proper, but they helped inspire the movement with their harsh realism, visible brushstrokes, and thick outlines.
- **Claude Monet** (1840–1926). The Impressionist movement officially began with an 1874 exhibition in which Monet exhibited his loose, Turner-inspired *Impression, Sunrise* (1874), now in the **Musée Marmottan,** which one critic picked to lambaste the entire exhibition, deriding it all as "Impressionist." Far from being insulted, the antiestablishment artists in the show adopted the word for their exhibits, held through the 1880s.
- **Pierre-Auguste Renoir** (1841–1919). Originally, Renoir was a porcelain painter, which helps explain his figures' ivory skin and chubby pink cheeks.
- **Edgar Degas** (1834–1917). Degas was an accomplished painter, sculptor, and draftsman—his pastels of dancers and bathers are particularly memorable.
- **Auguste Rodin** (1840–1917). The greatest Impressionist-era sculptor, Rodin crafted remarkably expressive bronzes, refusing to idealize the human figure as did his neoclassical predecessors. The **Musée Rodin,** his former Paris studio, contains, among other works, his *Burghers of Calais* (1886), *The Kiss* (1886–98), and *The Thinker* (1880).

POST-IMPRESSIONISM (1880–1930)

Few experimental French artists of the late 19th century were technically Impressionists, though many were friends with those in the movement. The smaller movements or styles are usually lumped together as "post-Impressionism."

Again, you'll find the best examples of their works at the **Musée d'Orsay,** though you'll find pieces by Matisse, Chagall, and the cubists, including Picasso, in the **Centre Pompidou.** Important post-Impressionists include:

- **Paul Cézanne** (1839–1906). He adopted the short brushstrokes, love of landscape, and light color palette of his Impressionist friends, but Cézanne was more formal and deliberate in his style. He sought to give his art monumentality and permanence, even if the subjects were simple still lifes, portraits, or landscapes.
- **Paul Gauguin** (1848–1903). Gauguin could never settle himself or his work, trying Brittany first, where he developed **synthetism** (black outlines around solid colors), and later hopping around the South Pacific, where he was inspired by local styles and colors.
- **Georges Seurat** (1859–91), **Paul Signac** (1863–1935), and **Camille Jacob Pissarro** (1830–1903). Together these artists developed **divisionism** and its more formal cousin, **pointillism.** Rather than mixing, say, yellow and blue paint together to make green, they applied tiny dots of yellow and blue right next to each other so that the viewer's eye mixed them together to make green.
- **Henri de Toulouse-Lautrec** (1864–1901). Most famous for his work with thinned-down oils, Toulouse-Lautrec created paintings and posters of wispy, fluid lines anticipating Art Nouveau and often depicting the bohemian life of Paris's dance halls and cafes. In Montmartre, you can still visit the **Moulin Rouge,** the cabaret he immortalized on canvas.

- **Vincent van Gogh** (1853–90) spent most of his tortured artistic career in France. He combined divisionism, synthetism, and a touch of Japanese influence, and painted with thick, short strokes. Never particularly accepted by any artistic circle, he is the most popular painter in the world today (his paintings fetch record sums at auction, and he sells more postcards and posters than any other artist), even though he sold only one painting in his short life.
- **Henri Matisse** (1869–1954). He took a hint from synthetism and added wild colors and strong patterns to create **fauvism** (a critic described those who used the style as *fauves*, meaning "wild beasts"). Matisse continued exploring these themes, even when most artists were turning to cubism. When his health failed, he began assembling brightly colored collages of paper cutouts.
- **Pablo Picasso** (1881–1973). Along with **Georges Braque** (1882–1963), this Barcelona-born artist painted objects from all points of view at once, rather than using such optical tricks as perspective to fool viewers into seeing three dimensions. The fractured result was **cubism** and was expanded upon by the likes of **Fernand Léger** (1881–1955) and **Juan Gris** (1887–1927), while Picasso moved on to other styles. You can see art from all of his periods at the **Musée Picasso** in the Marais.

2 Architecture 101

While each architectural era has its distinctive features, there are some elements, general floor plans, and terms common to many.

From the Romanesque period on, most **churches** consist either of a single wide **aisle,** or a wide central **nave** flanked by two narrow aisles. A row of **columns,** or square stacks of masonry called **piers,** connected by **arches,** separate the aisles from the nave.

This main nave/aisle assemblage is usually crossed by a perpendicular corridor called a **transept** near the far, east end of the church so that the floor plan looks like a Latin cross (shaped like a lowercase "t"). At the east end sits the holy **altar.** This is usually on a raised dais and in the entrance to—or, especially later, just in front of—the large **chapel** formed by the shorter, far end of the cross. If this large, main chapel is rounded off on the end, it is called an **apse;** it is often elongated and filled with the stalls of the **choir.** Some churches, especially after the Renaissance when mathematical proportion became important, were built on a Greek cross plan, each axis the same length, like a giant "+."

It's worth pointing out that very few buildings (especially churches) were built in one particular style. These massive, expensive structures often took centuries to complete, during which time tastes would change and plans would be altered.

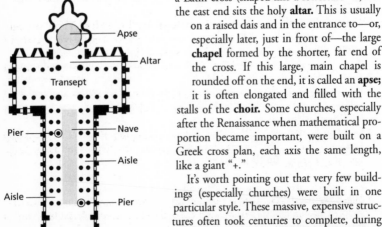

Church Floor Plan

ANCIENT ROMAN (125 B.C.–A.D. 450)

France was Rome's first transalpine conquest, and the legions of Julius Caesar quickly subdued the Celtic tribes across France, converting it into Roman Gaul and importing Roman building concepts.

IDENTIFIABLE FEATURES

- Load-bearing arches
- Use of concrete and brick

BEST EXAMPLES

- **Parvis Archaeological Excavations.** The Romanized village of Lutèce, later renamed after its native *Parisii* tribe of Celtic Gauls, is partially excavated under place du Parvis in front of Notre-Dame.
- **Musée de Cluny.** This medieval monastery was built on top of a **Roman baths complex,** remnants of which are still visible on the grounds outside and in the huge preserved *frigidarium* (the cold-water bath), which is now a room of the museum. The museum itself also contains ancient statuary.

ROMANESQUE (800–1100)

Romanesque architects concentrated on building large churches with wide aisles to accommodate the population that came to hear Mass and worship at the altars of various saints. The Romanesque style took its inspiration from ancient Rome (hence the name). Early Christians in Italy had adapted the basilica (ancient Roman law-court buildings) to become churches. Few examples of the Romanesque style remain in Paris, however, with most churches having been rebuilt in later eras.

IDENTIFIABLE FEATURES

- **Rounded arches.** These load-bearing architectural devices allowed the architects to open up wide naves and spaces, channeling all the weight of the stone walls and ceiling across the curve of the arch and down into the ground via the columns or pilasters.
- **Thick walls, infrequent and small windows, and huge piers.** These were necessary to support the weight of all that masonry, giving Romanesque churches a dark, somber, mysterious, and often oppressive feeling.
- **Apse.** This rounded space behind the altar in many Romanesque churches opens up the holiest, east end of the church.
- **Radiating chapels.** These smaller chapels began to sprout off the east end of the church, especially later in the Romanesque period, often in the form of a fan of minichapels radiating off the apse.
- **Ambulatory.** This curving corridor separates the altar and choir area from the ring of smaller, radiating chapels. This, too, was a convention of the later Romanesque period and carried into the Gothic style.

BEST EXAMPLES

- **St-Germain-des-Prés.** The overall building is Romanesque, including the fine sculpted column capitals near the entrance of the left aisle; only the far left corner is original, the others are copies. By the time builders got to creating the choir, the early Gothic style was on—note the pointed arches. Over the (early Renaissance) portal is a Romanesque carving of the *Last Judgment.*
- **St-Julien-le-Pauvre.** This small church has a general Romanesque plan overwritten by later Gothic embellishments, including the facade.

GOTHIC (1100–1500)

By the 12th century, engineering developments freed church architecture from the heavy, thick walls of Romanesque structures and allowed ceilings to soar, walls to thin, and windows to proliferate.

Instead of dark, somber, relatively unadorned Romanesque interiors that forced the eyes of the faithful toward the altar, the Gothic interiors enticed churchgoers' gazes upward to high ceilings filled with light. The priests still conducted Mass in Latin, but now peasants could "read" the stories told in pictures in the stained-glass windows.

The squat, brooding exteriors of the Romanesque fortresses of God were replaced by graceful buttresses and spires that soared above town centers.

IDENTIFIABLE FEATURES

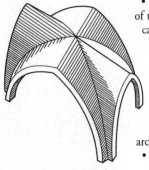

Cross Vault

• **Pointed arches.** The most significant development of the Gothic era was the discovery that pointed arches carry far more weight than rounded ones.

• **Cross vaults.** Instead of being flat, the square patch of ceiling between four columns arches up to a point in the center, creating four sail shapes, like the underside of a pyramid. The "X" separating these four sails is often reinforced with ridges, called **ribbing.** As the Gothic style progressed, four-sided cross vaults became six- or eight-sided as architects played with the angles.

• **Flying buttresses.** These freestanding exterior pillars, connected by graceful, thin arms of stone, help to channel the weight of the building and its roof out and down into the ground. To help counter the cross forces involved in this engineering sleight of hand, the piers of buttresses were often topped by heavy pinnacles, which took the form of minispires or statues.

• **Spires.** These pinnacles of masonry seem to defy gravity and reach toward heaven itself.

• **Gargoyles.** Disguised as wide-mouthed creatures, gargoyles are actually drain spouts.

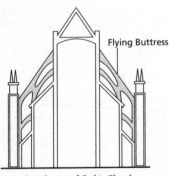

Cross Section of Gothic Church

• **Tracery.** These lacy spider webs of carved stone grace the pointed ends of windows and sometimes the spans of ceiling vaults.

• **Stained glass.** Because pointed arches can carry more weight than rounded ones, windows could be larger and more numerous. They were often filled with Bible stories and symbolism writ in the colorful patterns of stained glass.

• **Rose windows.** Huge circular windows filled with tracery and "petals" of stained glass, rose windows often appear as the centerpieces of facades and, in some larger churches, at the ends of transepts as well.

Flying Buttress

- **Ambulatory.** The Gothic style made much greater use of this corridor of space wrapping behind the apse and often around a **choir** (the boxed-off area, usually behind the altar, where the choir sat and sang).
- **Choir screen.** Serving as the inner wall of the ambulatory and the outer wall of the choir section, choir screens are often decorated with carvings or serve as tombs.

BEST EXAMPLES

- **Basilique St-Denis** (1140–44). Today you'll find the world's first Gothic cathedral in a Paris suburb.
- **Cathédrale de Chartres** (1194–1220). This Gothic masterpiece boasts good statuary, a soaring spire, and some 150 glorious stained-glass windows.
- **Cathédrale de Notre-Dame** (1163–1250). This famous cathedral possesses pinnacled flying buttresses, a trio of France's best rose windows, good portal carvings, a choir screen of deeply carved reliefs, and spiffy gargoyles (though many of those are actually 19th-century neo-Gothic).

Cathédrale de Chartres

RENAISSANCE (1500–1630)

In architecture, as in painting, the Renaissance style came from Italy and was only slowly adapted by the French. As in painting, its rules stressed proportion, order, classical inspiration, and precision to create unified, balanced structures.

IDENTIFIABLE FEATURES

- **Proportion and symmetry.** Other than a close eye to these Renaissance ideals, little specifically identifies buildings of this period.
- **Steeply pitched roofs.** Many roofs are of pale stone with dark gray tiles. This feature is a throwback to medieval sensibilities, but because almost no medieval mansions survive in Paris, the buildings that *do* sport steep roofs tend to be Renaissance.
- **Dormer windows.** These tend to be tall and made of stone, which differentiates them from the less extravagant, wooden ones of later periods.

BEST EXAMPLES

- **Hôtel Carnavalet** (1544). This Renaissance mansion is the only 16th-century hotel left in Paris. It contains the **Musée Carnavalet,** a museum devoted to the history of Paris and the French Revolution.
- **Place des Vosges.** This square is lined by Renaissance mansions rising above a lovely arcaded corridor that wraps all the way around.

CLASSICISM & ROCOCO (1630–1800)

While Italy and Germany embraced the opulent baroque, France took the fundamentals of Renaissance **classicism** even further, becoming more imitative of ancient models—this represents a change from the Renaissance preference to find inspiration in the classic era.

During the reign of Louis XIV, art and architecture were subservient to political ends. Buildings were grandiose and severely ordered on the Versailles model. Opulence was saved for interior decoration, which increasingly (especially 1715–50, after the death of Louis XIV) became an excessively detailed and self-indulgent **rococo** (*rocaille* in French). Externally, this later style is only noticeable by a greater elegance and delicacy.

Rococo tastes didn't last long, though, and soon a **neoclassical** movement was raising structures, such as Paris's **Panthéon** (1758), which were even more strictly based on ancient models than was the earlier classicism.

IDENTIFIABLE FEATURES

- **Symmetrical, rectangular structures.** French classicism concentrated on horizontal and vertical lines and simple proportions.
- **Classical throwbacks.** Classicism was favored for the very fact that it brought back such elements as classical orders (Doric, Ionic, and Corinthian) and projecting central sections topped by triangular pediments.

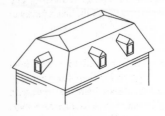
Mansard Roof

- **Mansard roofs.** A defining feature and true French trademark developed by **François Mansart** (1598–1666) in the early 15th century, a mansard roof has a double slope, the lower being longer and steeper than the upper.
- **Dormer windows.** Unlike the larger Renaissance ones flanked by showy stone scrolls, later dormers tended to be lower, less extravagant, and wooden.
- ***Oeil-de-bouef* windows.** These small, round "ox-eye" windows poke out of the roof's slope.
- **Excessive detail.** Rococo interior decoration is often asymmetrical and abstract with shell-like forms and many C- and S-curves. Naturalistic flowers and trees are sometimes playfully introduced.

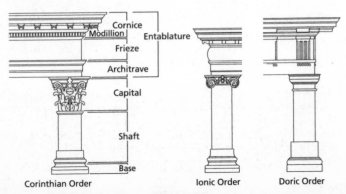

Cornice
Modillion
Frieze
Architrave
Capital
Shaft
Base

Entablature

Corinthian Order   Ionic Order   Doric Order

Classical Orders

BEST EXAMPLES

- **Palais du Louvre** (1650–70). A collaborative classical masterpiece, the Louvre was designed as a palace. **Le Vau** (1612–70) was its chief architect, along with collaborators **François Mansart** (1598–1666), the interior decorator **Charles Le Brun** (1619–90), and the unparalleled landscape gardener **André Le Nôtre** (1613–1700). The structure subsequently had several purposes (see chapter 8 for the complete history) before becoming a museum.
- **Versailles** (1669–85). Versailles is France's—indeed, Europe's—grandest palace, the Divine Monarchy writ as a statement of fussily decorative, politically charged classical architecture, though the interior was redecorated in more flamboyant styles. The chief architects of its complete overhaul under Louis XIV were the oft-used team (see Palais du Louvre, above) of **Le Vau, Mansart, Le Brun,** and **Le Nôtre.** Mansart's grand-nephew (and Louis XIV's chief architect) **Jules Hardouin-Mansart** (1646–1708) took over after Le Vau's death, changing much of the exterior look. The **Clock Room** is a good example of rococo interior decoration.
- **Panthéon** (1758). This Left Bank monument is a perfect example of the strict neoclassical style.

THE 19TH CENTURY

Architectural styles in 19th-century Paris were eclectic, beginning in a severe classical mode and ending with an identity crisis torn between Industrial Age technology and Art Nouveau organic. The "Identifiable Features" section explores the main facets of competing styles during this turbulent century.

IDENTIFIABLE FEATURES

- **First Empire.** Elegant, neoclassical furnishings—distinguished by strong lines often accented with a simple curve—became the rage during Napoleon's reign.
- **Second Empire.** Napoleon III's reign saw the eclectic Second Empire reinterpret classicism in an ornate, dramatic mode. Urban planning was the architectural rage, and Paris became a city of wide boulevards courtesy of **Baron Georges-Eugène Haussmann** (1809–91), commissioned by Napoleon III in 1852 to redesign the city. Paris owes much of its remarkably unified look to Haussmann, who drew his beloved thoroughfares directly across the city, tearing down existing structures along the way. He lined the boulevards with simple, six-story apartment blocks, such as elongated 18th-century town houses with continuous balconies wrapping around the third and sixth floors and mansard roofs with dormer windows.
- **Third Republic.** Expositions in 1878, 1889, and 1900 were the catalysts for constructing huge glass-and-steel structures that showed off modern techniques and the engineering prowess of the Industrial Revolution. This produced such Parisian monuments as the Tour Eiffel and Sacré-Coeur.

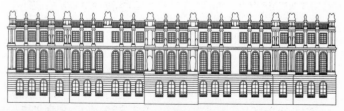

Versailles

- **Art Nouveau.** These architects and decorators rebelled against the Third Republic era of mass production by stressing the uniqueness of craft. They created asymmetrical, curvaceous designs based on organic inspiration (plants and flowers) in such mediums as wrought iron, stained glass, tile, and hand-painted wallpaper.

BEST EXAMPLES

- **Palais de Fontainebleau.** Napoleon spent his imperial decade (1804–14) refurbishing his quarters in this palace in First Empire style.
- **Arc de Triomphe** (1836). Napoleon's oversize imitation of a Roman triumphal arch is the ultimate paean to the classic era. The arch presides over **L'Etoile,** an intersection of 12 wide boulevards laid out by Baron Haussmann in the Second Empire.
- **Tour Eiffel** (1889). Under the Third Republic, the French wanted to show how far they had come in the 100 years since the Revolution. They hired **Gustave Eiffel** (1832–1923) to slap together the world's tallest structure, a temporary 320m (1,050-ft.) tower made of riveted steel girders. Everyone agreed it was tall; most thought it was ugly and completely lacking in aesthetics. Its usefulness as a radio transmitter saved Eiffel's tower from being torn down.
- **Métro station entrances.** Art Nouveau was less an architectural mode than a decorative movement. You can still find some of the original Art Nouveau Métro entrances designed by **Hector Guimard** (1867–1942). A recently renovated entrance is at the Porte Dauphine station on the No. 2 line.

THE 20TH CENTURY

France commissioned some ambitious architectural projects in the last century, most of them the *grand projets* of the late François Mitterrand. The majority were considered controversial or even offensive when completed. Only slowly have structures such as the Centre Pompidou or Louvre's glass pyramids become accepted. Over time, a lucky few may even become as beloved as the once-despised Tour Eiffel.

Tour Eiffel

IDENTIFIABLE FEATURES

Other than a concerted effort to be unique, break convention, and look stunningly modern, nothing communally identifies France's recent architecture.

BEST EXAMPLES

- **Centre Pompidou** (1977). Britisher Richard Rogers (b. 1933) and Italian Renzo Piano (b. 1937) turned architecture inside out—literally—to craft Paris's eye-popping modern-art museum. Exposed pipes, steel supports, and plastic-tube escalators wrap around the exterior.
- **Louvre's glass pyramids** (1989). Chinese-American architect I. M. Pei (b. 1917) was called in to cap the Louvre's new underground entrance with these pyramids in the center of the Palais du Louvre's 17th-century courtyard.
- **Opéra Bastille** (1989). In 1989, Paris's opera company moved into this curvaceous, dark glass mound of space designed by Canadian Carlos Ott. Unfortunately, the acoustics have been lambasted.

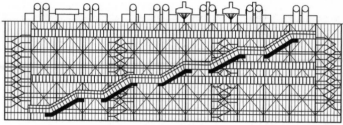

Centre Pompidou

3

Planning Your Trip to Paris

This chapter provides the nuts-and-bolts details you need before setting off for Paris—everything from information sources to money matters to the major airlines and how to save money on your flight.

1 Visitor Information

TOURIST OFFICES

Your best source of information is the **French Government Tourist Office,** which you can reach at the following addresses:

IN THE UNITED STATES 444 Madison Ave., 16th Floor, New York, NY 10022 (© **514/288-1904;** fax 212/838-7855); 875 N. Michigan Ave., Suite 3214, Chicago, IL 60611 (© **514/288-1904**); 9454 Wilshire Blvd., Suite 715, Beverly Hills, CA 90212 (© **514/288-1904**). To request additional information, call **France on Call** at © **900/990-0040;** 50¢ per min.

IN CANADA Maison de la France/French Government Tourist Office, 1800 av. McGill College, Suite 1010, Montreal, H3A 2W9 (© **514/288-1904**).

IN THE UNITED KINGDOM Maison de la France/French Government Tourist Office, 178 Piccadilly, London, W1J 9AL (© **090/6824-4123;** 60p per minute).

IN AUSTRALIA French Tourist Bureau, 25 Bligh St., Sydney, NSW 2000 (© **02/9231-5244;** fax 02/9221-8682).

WEBSITES

The French Government Tourist Office's home on the Internet is at **www.franceguide.com** or **www.francetourism.com**. The website of the Paris Convention and Visitors Bureau, at **www.paris-touristoffice.com** or **www.parisinfo.com**, provides information on hotels, restaurants, attractions, entertainment, and events.

For general information, see "Staying Connected," later in this chapter.

2 Entry Requirements

PASSPORTS

For information on how to get a passport, go to "Passports" in the "Fast Facts" section in chapter 5—the websites listed provide downloadable passport applications, as well as the current fees for processing passport applications. For an up-to-date, country-by-country listing of passport requirements around the world,

go to the "Foreign Entry Requirement" Web page of the U.S. Department of State at **http://travel.state.gov**. All non-French nationals need a **valid passport** to enter France (check its expiration date). Passport requirements for children are the same as for adults. If your passport is lost or stolen, go to your consulate as soon as possible for a replacement.

MEDICAL REQUIREMENTS

For information on medical requirements and recommendations, see "Health," later in this chapter.

CUSTOMS
WHAT YOU CAN BRING INTO PARIS

Customs restrictions differ for citizens of European Union (EU) countries and non-EU countries.

For Non-EU Nationals   You can bring in, duty-free, 200 cigarettes, or 100 cigarillos, or 50 cigars, or 250 grams of smoking tobacco. You can also bring in 2 liters of wine and either 1 liter of alcohol more than 22% or 2 liters of alcohol less than 22%. In addition, you can bring in 60cc (2 oz.) of perfume and a quarter-liter of eau de toilette. Visitors age 15 and older may bring in other goods totaling 175€ ($228); the allowance for those age 14 and younger is 90€ ($117). (Customs officials tend to be lenient about general merchandise, realizing the limits are unrealistically low.)

For EU Citizens   Visitors from European Union countries can bring into France any amount of goods as long as they're intended for personal use—not for resale.

WHAT YOU CAN TAKE HOME FROM PARIS
U.S. Citizens

Returning U.S. citizens who have been away for at least 48 hours are allowed to bring back, once every 30 days, $800 worth of merchandise duty-free. You'll be charged a flat rate of 4% duty on the next $1,000 worth of purchases. Be sure to have your receipts handy. On mailed gifts, the duty-free limit is $200. With some exceptions, you cannot bring fresh fruits and vegetables into the United States.

For more specifics on what you can bring back and the corresponding fees, download the invaluable free pamphlet *Know Before You Go* online at www.cbp. gov. (Click on "Travel," and then click on "Know Before You Go! Online Brochure.") Or contact the U.S. Customs & Border Protection (CBP), 1300 Pennsylvania Ave., NW, Washington, DC 20229 (© **877/287-8667**) and request the pamphlet.

Canadian Citizens

Canadian citizens are allowed a C$750 exemption, and you're allowed to bring back duty-free 1 carton of cigarettes, or 2.2 pounds of tobacco, 40 imperial ounces of liquor, and 50 cigars. In addition, you're allowed to mail gifts to Canada valued at less than C$60 a day, provided they're unsolicited and don't contain alcohol or tobacco (write on the package "Unsolicited gift, less than $60 value"). All valuables should be declared on the Y-38 form before departure from Canada, including serial numbers of valuables you already own, such as expensive foreign cameras. *Note:* The C$750 exemption can be used only once a year and only after an absence of 7 days.

For a clear summary of Canadian rules, write for the booklet *I Declare,* issued by the Canada Border Services Agency (© **800/461-9999** in Canada, or 204/983-3500; www.cbsa-asfc.gc.ca).

U.K. Citizens

Citizens of the U.K. who are returning from a European Union (EU) country will go through a separate Customs Exit (called the "Blue Exit") especially for EU travelers. In essence, there is no limit on what you can bring back from an EU country, as long as the items are for personal use (this includes gifts) and you have already paid the necessary duty and tax. However, customs law sets out guidance levels. If you bring in more than these levels, you may be asked to prove that the goods are for your own use. Guidance levels on goods bought in the EU for your own use are 3,200 cigarettes, 200 cigars,

400 cigarillos, 3 kilograms of smoking tobacco, 10 liters of spirits, 90 liters of wine, 20 liters of fortified wine (such as port or sherry), and 110 liters of beer.

For more information, contact HM Revenue Customs at (2) **0845/010-9000** (from outside the U.K., 02920/501-261), or consult their website at www.hmrc. gov.uk.

Australian Citizens

The duty-free allowance in Australia is A$900 or, for those younger than 18, A$450. Citizens can bring in 250 cigarettes or 250 grams of loose tobacco and 2.25 liters of alcohol. If you're returning with valuables you already own, such as foreign-made cameras, you should file form B263.

A helpful brochure, available from Australian consulates or Customs offices, is *Know Before You Go.* For more information, call the Australian Customs Service at (2) **1300/363-263,** or log on to www.customs.gov.au.

New Zealand Citizens

The duty-free allowance for New Zealand is NZ$700. Citizens older than 17 can bring in 200 cigarettes, 50 cigars, or 250 grams of tobacco (or a mixture of all three if their combined weight doesn't exceed 250g), plus 4.5 liters of wine and beer or 1.125 liters of liquor. New Zealand currency does not carry import or export restrictions. Fill out a certificate of export, listing the valuables you are taking out of the country; that way, you can bring them back without paying duty.

Most questions are answered in a free pamphlet available at New Zealand consulates and Customs offices: *New Zealand Customs Guide for Travellers, Notice no. 4.* For more information, contact New Zealand Customs Service, The Customhouse, 17–21 Whitmore St., Box 2218, Wellington ((2) **04/473-6099** or 0800/428-786; www.customs.govt.nz).

3 When to Go

In August, Parisians traditionally leave for their annual holidays, and the city serves visitors on a skeleton staff. July has also become a popular vacation month, when many restaurateurs take holidays.

Hotels, especially first class and deluxe, are easy to come by in July and August. Budget hotels, on the other hand, are likely to be full during these months of student invasion. You should also try to avoid late September and the first 2 weeks in October, when the annual auto show attracts thousands of enthusiasts.

Balmy weather in Paris has prompted more popular songs and love ballads than

weather conditions in any other city. But the weather here is actually quite fickle. Rain is more common than snow throughout the winter, prompting longtime residents to complain about the occasional bone-chilling dampness.

In recent years, Paris has had about 15 snow days a year, and there are only a few oppressively hot days (over 86°F, or 30°C) in summer. What will most likely chill a Parisian heart, however, are the winds that sweep along the city's boulevards, channeled by bordering buildings. Other than these occasional winds and rain (which add an undeniable drama to

Paris's Average Daytime Temperatures & Rainfall

	Jan	Feb	Mar	Apr	May	June	July	Aug	Sept	Oct	Nov	Dec
Temp. °F	38	39	46	51	58	64	66	66	61	53	45	40
Temp. °C	3	4	8	11	14	18	19	19	16	12	7	4
Rainfall (in.)	3.2	2.9	2.4	2.7	3.2	3.5	3.3	3.7	3.3	3.0	3.5	3.1

many of the city's panoramas), Paris has some of the most pleasant weather of any capital in Europe, with an average temperature of 53°F (12°C).

Holidays in France are known as *jours fériés*. Shops and banks are closed, as well as many (but not all) restaurants and museums. For a list of major holidays, see "Fast Facts: Paris" in chapter 5.

PARIS CALENDAR OF EVENTS

Check the Paris Tourist Office website at **www.paris-touristoffice.com** for up-to-the-minute details on these and other events.

January

International Ready-to-Wear Fashion Shows (Salon International de Prêt-à-Porter), Parc des Expositions (Hall #7), 15e. Hundreds of designers, from the giants to the unknown, unveil their visions (hallucinations?) of what you will be wearing in 6 months. The event in the Porte de Versailles convention facilities is geared to wholesalers, retailers, buyers, journalists, and industry professionals, but for the merely fashion-conscious, the rules are usually bent. Much more exclusive are the *défilés* (fashion shows) at the headquarters of houses like Lagerfeld, Lanvin, Courrèges, and Valentino. For details, call ✆ 01-44-94-70-00; www.pretparis.com. End of January.

February

Special Exhibitions, Special Concerts: During Paris's grayest month, look for a splash of expositions and concerts designed to perk up the city. Concerts and theaters spring up at such diverse sites as the **Cité de la Musique,** 221 av. Jean-Jaurès, 19e (✆ 01-44-84-45-00; www.cite-musique.fr; Métro: Porte-de-Pantin); the **Théâtre des Champs-Elysées,** 15 av. Montaigne, 8e (✆ 01-49-52-50-50; www.theatrechamps elysees.fr; Métro: Alma-Marceau); and

the **Maison de Radio-France,** 116 av. du Président-Kennedy, 16e (✆ 01-56-40-15-16; www.radiofrance.fr; Métro: Passy-Ranelagh). Also look for openings of new operas at the **Opéra Bastille,** 2 place de la Bastille, 4e (✆ 01-40-01-17-89; www.opera-de-paris.fr; Métro: Bastille); operas and dance at the **Opéra Garnier,** place de l'Opéra, 9e (✆ 01-40-01-25-14; Métro: Opéra); and concerts at the **Auditorium du Louvre,** 1er (✆ 01-40-20-50-50; www.louvre.fr; Métro: Musée du Louvre), and the **Salle Cortot,** 78 rue Cardinet, 17e (✆ 01-47-63-80-16; Métro: Malesherbes). A copy of *Pariscope* or *L'Officiel des Spectacles*, available at most newsstands, is the best info source.

March

Foire du Trône, Bois de Vincennes, 12e. A mammoth amusement park that its fans call France's largest country fair, the Foire du Trône originated in A.D. 957, when merchants met with farmers to exchange grain and wine. This high-tech continuation of that tradition, held on the lawns of the Pelouse de Reuilly, has a Ferris wheel, carousels, acrobats, fire eaters, and diversions that seem like a Gallic Coney Island. It's open daily from 2pm to midnight. Call ✆ 01-46-27-52-29; www.foiredutrone.com. End of March to end of May.

April

International Marathon of Paris. Beginning on the Champs-Elysées at 9am, runners take over Paris's boulevards in a race that draws competitors from around the world. Depending on their speed and endurance, participants arrive at the finishing point on avenue Foch, 16e, beginning about 2½ hours later. For details, call ✆ 01-41-33-14-00; www.parismarathon.com. Early April.

Les Grandes Eaux Musicales, Versailles. These musical events are intended to re-create the atmosphere of the ancient regime. The fountains around the palace are turned on, with special emphasis on the Neptune Fountain, which sits squarely in front of the best view of the château. You can promenade in the garden and listen to the music of French composers (Couperin, Charpentier, and Lully) and others (Mozart or Haydn) whose careers thrived during the years of the palace's construction. The music is recorded, but the vistas are monumental, and the music, the fountains, and the architectural vistas of the world's grandest château all operate in unison. The events occur every Saturday and Sunday from 11:15am till noon and 2:30pm till 5pm between April and early September. For details, call ☎ **01-30-83-78-88;** www.chateau versailles-spectacles.fr.

May

VE Day (in French: *Jour de l'Armistice*), citywide. The celebration commemorating the capitulation of the Nazis on May 7, 1945, lasts 4 days in Paris, with a parade along the Champs-Elysées and additional ceremonies in Reims. Pro-American sentiments are probably higher during this festival than at any other time of year. May 5 to May 8.

Grand Steeplechase de Paris, Auteuil and Longchamp racetracks, Bois de Boulogne. In this equestrian event, obstacle courses at both Auteuil and Longchamp racetracks are laid out to incorporate hurdles and crossings over streams. The result is a rougher, more rustic counterpoint to the flatbed races conducted at Chantilly (see below). For details, call ☎ **01-49-10-20-30** or see www.france-galop.com. Mid-May.

French Open Tennis Championship, Stade Roland-Garros, 16e. The Open features 10 days of Grand Slam men's and women's tennis, with European and South American players traditionally dominating on the hot, dusty red courts. For details, call ☎ **01-47-43-48-00;** www.fft.fr. Late May to early June.

June

Fête de St-Denis, St-Denis. This series presents a month of artfully contrived music in the burial place of the French kings, a grim, early Gothic monument in this industrialized northern suburb. For details, call ☎ **01-48-13-12-10;** www.festival-saint-denis.fr. Early June to July.

Prix du Jockey Club & Prix Diane-Hermès, Hippodrome de Chantilly. Thoroughbreds from as far away as Kentucky and Brunei, as well as mounts sponsored by Europe's old and new fortunes, compete in a very civil competition broadcast around France and talked about in horse circles around the world. On race days, as many as 30 trains depart from Paris's Gare du Nord for Chantilly, where they're met by free shuttle buses to the track. For details on this and all other equine events in this calendar, call ☎ **08-21-21-32-13;** www.france-galop.com. First week of June (Jockey Club) and second week of June (Prix Diane-Hermès).

Paris Air Show, Le Bourget. This is where France's military-industrial complex shows off enough high-tech hardware to make anyone think twice about invading La Patrie. Fans, competitors, and industrial spies mob the airport's exhibition halls for a taste of what Gallic technocrats have wrought. For details, call ☎ **01-53-23-33-33;** www.salon-du-bourget.fr. Mid-June.

Fête de la Musique, citywide. This celebration at the summer solstice is the only day that noise laws don't apply in Paris. Musicians and wannabes pour into the streets, where you can make music with anything, even if it means banging two garbage cans together or driving around blowing your car horn (illegal otherwise). You might hear anything from Russians playing balalaikas to Cubans playing mambo rhythms. Musical parties pop up in virtually all the open spaces, with more organized concerts at place de la Bastille and place de la République, and in La Villette and the Latin Quarter. For details, call © **01-40-03-94-70;** www.fetedela musique.culture.fr. Mid-June.

Fête Chopin, Orangerie du Parc de Bagatelle, Versailles. Hear all the Chopin you want at these piano recitals from the works of the Polish exile who lived most of his life in Paris. For details, call © **01-45-00-22-19;** www.frederic-chopin.com. Mid-June to mid-July.

Festival Musique en l'Ile. A series of concerts, most including dignified masses composed from the 17th to the late–19th centuries, is presented at the Church St-Louis-en-l'Ile and the Church St-Germain-des-Prés. For more information, call La Toison d'Art at © **01-44-62-00-55;** www.latoison dart.com. Late June to late August.

La Course des Garçons de Café, throughout the city. Although it has diminished somewhat in importance in Paris since the postwar years, when it was much more visible, there's no more amusing race in Paris. Balancing heavy trays, the *garçons* (both waiters and waitresses) line up in front of the Hôtel de Ville in the 4th Arrondissement and then race for 8km (5 miles) through the streets, ending back at the Hôtel de Ville. Some, obviously, don't

make it. A Sunday in the last week of June or first week of July.

Gay Pride Parade, place de la République to place de la Bastille. A week of expositions and parties climaxes in a parade patterned after those in New York and San Francisco. It's followed by a dance at the Palais de Bercy, a convention hall/sports arena. For more information about gay pride and any other aspect of gay, lesbian, and transgendered life in and around Paris, contact Lesbian and Gay Pride, Ile de France, 3 rue Keller, BP 255, 75524 Paris Cedex 11. For information about the parade, call or fax © **01-72-70-39-22;** www.inter-lgbt.org. Late June.

July

Tour de France. This is Europe's most visible, highly contested, and overabundantly televised bicycle race. Crews of wind tunnel–tested athletes speed along an itinerary tracing the six sides of the French "hexagon," detouring deep into the Massif Central and across the Swiss Alps. The race is decided at a finish line drawn across the Champs-Elysées. For details, call © **01-41-33-15-00;** www.letour.fr. First 3 weeks of July.

Bastille Day, citywide. This celebration of the 1789 storming of the Bastille is the birth date of modern France, and festivities reach their peak in Paris with street fairs, pageants, fireworks, and feasts. The day begins with a parade down the Champs-Elysées and ends with fireworks in Montmartre. Wherever you are, before the end of the day, you'll hear Piaf warbling "La Foule" ("The Crowd"), the song that celebrated her passion for the stranger she met and later lost in a crowd on Bastille Day, and lots of people singing "La Marseillaise." July 14.

Paris Quartier d'Eté, Latin Quarter. For 4 weeks, the Arènes de Lutèce or the Sorbonne's Cour d'Honneur host pop orchestral concerts. The dozen or so concerts are grander than the outdoor setting would imply and include performances by the Orchestre de Paris, Orchestre National de France, and Baroque Orchestra of the European Union. On the fringes, you can find plays, jazz, and parades in the Tuileries Gardens. For details, call ℂ **01-44-94-98-00;** www.quartierdete.com. Mid-July to mid-August.

September

International Ready-to-Wear Fashion Shows (Salon International de Prêt-à-Porter), Parc des Expositions, 15e. More of what took place at the fashion shows in January (see above), with an emphasis on what *le beau monde* (the rich and the beautiful) will be wearing next spring. For details, call ℂ **01-44-94-70-00;** www.pretparis.com. Early September.

La Villette Jazz Festival, La Villette. This homage to the art of jazz incorporates 50 concerts in churches, auditoriums, and concert halls in all neighborhoods of this Paris suburb. Past festivals have welcomed Herbie Hancock, Shirley Horn, Michel Portal, and other artists from around the world. For details, call ℂ **01-40-03-75-75;** www.jazzalavillett.com. Early September.

Biennale des Antiquaires, Carrousel du Louvre, 99 rue de Rivoli, 1er. Antiques dealers and lovers from all over gather at this gilded event in even-numbered years. Precious furnishings and objets d'art are displayed in the underground exhibit halls linked to the Louvre, or perhaps in the Grand Palais once it's restored. For details, call ℂ **01-44-51-74-74;** www.biennaledesantiquaires.com. Usually third week in September. Next events: 2008 and 2010.

Fête d'Automne (Autumn Festival), citywide. Paris welcomes the return of its residents from their August holidays with an ongoing and eclectic festival of modern music, ballet, theater, and art. Venues include art galleries, churches, concert halls, auditoriums, and parks citywide. There's an emphasis on experimental works, which the festival's promoters scatter judiciously among more traditional productions. Depending on the event, tickets cost from 15€ to 75€ ($20–$98). For details, contact the **Fête d'Automne,** 156 rue de Rivoli, 75001 Paris (ℂ **01-53-45-17-00;** www.festival-automne.com). Mid-September to late December.

October

Prix de l'Arc de Triomphe, Hippodrome de Longchamp, 16e. France's answer to England's Ascot is the country's most prestigious horse race, culminating the equine season in Europe. For details, call ℂ **01-44-30-75-00;** www.france-galop.com. Early October.

Paris Auto Show, Parc des Expositions, 15e. Glitzy attendees and lots of hype attend this showcase for European car design. The show takes place in even-numbered years near the Porte de Versailles. In addition, a permanent exhibit on French auto design at the Cité des Sciences et de l'Industrie is upgraded and enriched during October. For details, call ℂ **01-56-88-22-40;** www.mondial-automobile.com. Two weeks in October (dates vary).

November

Armistice Day, citywide. The signing of the controversial document that ended World War I is celebrated with a military parade from the Arc de Triomphe to the Hôtel des Invalides. November 11.

Fête d'Art Sacré (Festival of Sacred Art). A series of classical concerts is held in five of the oldest churches of

Paris. For details, call the Paris Tourist Office (© **01-49-52-53-54**). Mid-November to mid-December.

Release of the Beaujolais Nouveau, citywide. Parisians eagerly await the yearly release of the first new Beaujolais, that fruity wine from Burgundy. Signs are posted in bistros, wine bars, and cafes—these places report their heaviest patronage of the year during this celebration of the grape. Third Thursday in November.

December

Le Salon Nautique de Paris (Boat Fair), Parc des Expositions, 15e. This is Europe's most visible exposition of what's afloat and of interest to wholesalers, retailers, boat owners (or wannabes), and anyone involved in the business of waterborne holidaymaking. For details, call © **01-41-90-47-22**, or check on the Web at www.salonnautiqueparis.com. Ten days in early December.

Fête de St-Sylvestre (New Year's Eve), citywide. It's most boisterously celebrated in the Latin Quarter around the Sorbonne. At midnight, the city explodes. Strangers kiss strangers, and boulevard St-Michel and the Champs-Elysées become virtual pedestrian malls. December 31.

4 Getting There

BY PLANE

Paris has two international airports: **Orly** (© **01-49-75-15-15**), 14km (8¾ miles) south of the city, and **Charles de Gaulle (Roissy;** © **01-48-62-22-80**), 23km (14 miles) northeast. A 13€ ($17) Air France shuttle operates between the two every 30 minutes, taking 50 to 75 minutes. Orly is more convenient to central Paris, with cheaper transportation costs, but you really don't have a choice here in most cases. Transatlantic flights land at Charles de Gaulle, with Orly used for domestic and charter flights. For information on both airports, go to www.aeroportsdeparis.fr.

High season on most airlines' routes to Paris is usually June to the beginning of September. This is the most expensive and most crowded time to travel. **Shoulder season** is April to May, early September to October, and December 15 to December 24. **Low season** is November 1 to December 14 and December 25 to March 31.

THE MAJOR AIRLINES

FROM NORTH AMERICA One of the best choices for travelers in the southeastern United States and the Midwest is **Delta Airlines** (© **800/221-1212;** www.delta.com). Delta flies direct to Paris from Atlanta, which is a hub for frequent flights from cities such as New Orleans, Phoenix, Columbia (South Carolina), and Cincinnati. Delta also operates daily nonstop flights to Paris from Cincinnati and New York.

Another good option is **Continental Airlines** (© **800/231-0856;** www.continental.com), serving the Northeast and much of the Southwest through its busy hubs in Newark (New Jersey) and Houston. Continental provides nonstop flights to Paris from both cities.

The French flag carrier, **Air France** (© **800/237-2747;** www.airfrance.com), uses Paris as a hub and offers daily or several-times-a-week flights to Paris from Newark; Washington, D.C.; Miami; Chicago; New York; Houston; San Francisco; Los Angeles; Boston; Cincinnati; Atlanta; Montreal; Toronto; and Mexico City.

In 2004, Air France acquired control of KLM Royal Dutch Airlines, which is leading to the creation of **Air France-KLM,** the world's biggest airline in terms of revenue. In the lifetime of this edition, KLM and Air France will begin coordinating their schedules and fares, acting as a unit. Airline spokespersons predict that the merger in time will lead to lower costs, lower fares, and better connections between flights.

American Airlines (© 800/433-7300; www.aa.com) provides daily nonstop flights to Paris from Dallas/Fort Worth, Chicago, Miami, Boston, and New York.

US Airways (© 800/428-4322; www. usairways.com) offers daily nonstop service from Philadelphia to Paris.

If you'd like to see London before traveling on to Paris, **British Airways** (© 800/247-9293; www.britishairways. com) has dozens of flights from North American cities to London. You can fly first from, say, New York to London and then take the BA shuttle flight to Paris following a holiday in England.

Canadians usually choose **Air Canada** (© 888/247-2262 from the U.S. and Canada; www.aircanada.ca) for flights to Paris from Toronto and Montreal. Nonstop flights from Montreal and Toronto depart every evening. Two of the nonstop flights from Toronto are shared with Air France and feature Air France aircraft.

FROM THE UNITED KINGDOM From London, **Air France** (© 0845/084-5111; www.airfrance.com) and **British Airways** (© 0870/850-9850 in the U.K.; www.britishairways.com) fly frequently to Paris, offering up to 17 flights daily from Heathrow. **Aer Lingus** (© 866/IRISH-AIR; www.aerlingus.com) has frequent direct flights from Dublin to Paris throughout the day. Many commercial travelers also use regular flights from the London City Airport in the Docklands. There are also direct flights to Paris from major cities such as Manchester, Edinburgh, and Southampton. For more information, contact Air France, British Airways, or **British Midland** (© 0870/607-0555; www.flybmi.com).

FROM AUSTRALIA Getting to Paris from Australia is rather difficult, because **Air France** (© 02-92-44-21-00; www. airfrance.com) has discontinued all direct flights to and from that country, requiring transfers through, among others, Singapore, with ongoing service to and from Sydney provided by Qantas. Consequently, on virtually any route, and with any airline you take, you have to change planes at least once en route. **British Airways** (© 1300-767-177; www.british airways.com) flies daily from both Sydney and Melbourne to London in time for any of several connecting flights to Paris. **Qantas** (© 612/13-13-13-68-46; www.qantas.com.au) can route passengers from Australia into London, where plentiful connections exist for the hop across the Channel.

GETTING INTO TOWN FROM THE AIRPORT

CHARLES DE GAULLE AIRPORT (ROISSY) At Charles de Gaulle, foreign carriers use Aérogare 1, and Air France uses Aérogare 2. From Aérogare 1, take a walkway to the passport checkpoint and the Customs area. A **shuttle bus** *(navette)* links the terminals.

The free shuttle bus connecting Aérogare 1 with Aérogare 2 also transports passengers to the Roissy rail station, from which fast **RER trains** (Line B) leave every 15 minutes daily between 5:30am to 11:30pm for such Métro stations as Gare du Nord, Châtelet, Luxembourg, Port Royal, and Denfert-Rochereau. A typical RER fare from Roissy to any point in central Paris is 13€ ($17) in first class or 8€ ($10) in second.

You can also take either of two Air France shuttle buses, both of which depart from Roissy for points within central Paris. Line 2 departs at 15-minute intervals every day between 6am and 11pm, charging 10€ ($13) each way for the 40-minute transit to the place de l'Etoile,

Value Airport Shuttle

A commuter service is provided by **PariShuttle**, 103 rue Villiers de l'Isle Adam, 75020 Paris (*©* **01-53-39-18-18**; www.parishuttle.com). Before collecting your baggage at the airport, you can call its toll-free number (*©* **08-00-69-96-99**) and make your way later to the arranged meeting point. You can also call and reserve by phone before your arrival in Paris. PariShuttle will take you to your desired address in Paris, and service in the eight-seat minivans runs 7 days a week. The cost is 25€ ($33) per person or 19€ ($25) per person if two or more people are traveling together.

with a stop en route at Porte Maillot. Line 4 departs at 30-minute intervals every day between 7am and 9:30pm, charging 12€ ($16) for the 50-minute trip to the Gare Montparnasse, making an intermediate stop at the Gare de Lyon en route. From any of those points within central Paris, Métro lines can carry you on to virtually any other point within the city.

Another option, the **Roissybus** (*©* **01-48-04-18-24**), departs from a point near the corner of the rue Scribe and place de l'Opéra every 15 minutes from 5:45am to 11pm. The cost for the 50-minute ride is 8.20€ ($11).

Taxis from Roissy into the city run about 45€ ($59) on the meter. At night (8pm–7am) fares are about 40% higher. Long queues of both taxis and passengers form outside each of the airport's terminals in a surprisingly orderly fashion.

ORLY AIRPORT   Orly has two terminals: Orly Sud (south) for international flights and Orly Ouest (west) for domestic flights. A free shuttle bus links them.

Air France buses (*©* **01-41-56-89-00**) leave from Exit E of Orly Ouest and from Exit K, Platform 5, of Orly Sud every 15 to 20 minutes from 5:40am to 11pm for Gare St-Michel, Gare d'Austerlitz, or Gare Montparnasse in central Paris at a cost of 11€ ($14) one-way. Another bus goes direct to Roissy Airport (CDG).

An alternative method for reaching central Paris involves taking a **monorail** (Orly Val) to the RER station of Anthony and then the RER train into downtown Paris. The Orly Val makes stops at the north and south terminals, and continues at 8-minute intervals for the 10-minute ride to the Anthony RER station. At Anthony, you'll board an RER train (Line B) for the 30-minute ride into the city. The cost of the Orly Val monorail plus the RER (Line B) transit into Paris is 9€ ($12), a fare that may seem a bit high, but that offsets the horrendous construction costs of a monorail that sails above the congested roadways encircling the airport.

A **taxi** from Orly to the center of Paris costs about 40€ ($52), more at night and on weekends. Returning to the airport, **buses** to Orly leave from the Invalides terminal to either Orly Sud or Orly Ouest every 15 minutes, taking about 30 minutes.

Caution: Don't take a meterless taxi from Orly Sud or Orly Ouest—it's much safer (and usually cheaper) to hire a metered cab from the taxi queues, which are under the scrutiny of a police officer.

LONG-HAUL FLIGHTS: HOW TO STAY COMFORTABLE

- Your choice of airline and airplane will definitely affect your leg room. Find more details about U.S. airlines at www.seatguru.com. For international airlines, the research firm Skytrax has posted a list of average seat pitches at www.airlinequality.com.

- Emergency exit seats and bulkhead seats typically have the most legroom. Emergency exit seats are usually left unassigned until the day of a flight, (to ensure that someone able-bodied fills the seats); it's worth getting to the ticket counter early to snag one of these spots for a long flight. Many passengers find that bulkhead seating (the row facing the wall at the front of the cabin) offers more legroom, but keep in mind that bulkheads are where airlines often put baby bassinets, so you may be sitting next to an infant.
- To have two seats for yourself in a three-seat row, try for an aisle seat in a center section toward the back of coach. If you're traveling with a companion, book an aisle and a window seat. Middle seats are usually booked last, so you might end up with three seats to yourselves.
- Ask about entertainment options. Many airlines offer seatback video systems where you get to choose your movies or play video games—but only on some of their planes. (Boeing 777s are your best bet.)
- To sleep, avoid the last row of any section or the row in front of an emergency exit, as these seats are the least likely to recline. Avoid seats near highly trafficked toilet areas. Avoid seats in the back of many jets—these can be narrower than those in the rest of coach. You also may want to reserve a window seat so you can rest your head and avoid being bumped in the aisle.
- Get up, walk around, and stretch every 60 to 90 minutes to keep your blood flowing. See the box "Avoiding 'Economy-Class Syndrome,'" under "Health," later in this chapter.
- Drink water before, during, and after your flight to combat the lack of humidity in airplane cabins. Avoid alcohol, which will dehydrate you.

- If you're flying with kids, don't forget to carry on toys, books, pacifiers, and chewing gum to help them relieve ear pressure buildup during ascent and descent.

BY CAR

Driving in Paris is definitely not recommended. Parking is difficult; traffic is dense; and networks of one-way streets make navigation, even with the best of maps, a problem. If you do drive, remember that Paris is encircled by a ring road called the *périphérique.* Always obtain detailed directions to your destination, including the name of the exit on the périphérique you're looking for (exits aren't numbered). Avoid rush hours. Few hotels, except the luxury ones, have garages, but the staff will usually be able to direct you to one nearby.

The **major highways** into Paris are the A1 from the north (Great Britain and Benelux); A13 from Rouen, Normandy, and northwest France; A10 from Bordeaux, the Pyrenees, France's southwest, and Spain; A6 from Lyon, the French Alps, the Riviera, and Italy; and A4 from Metz, Nancy, and Strasbourg in eastern France.

BY TRAIN

If you're already in Europe, you might decide to travel to Paris by train, especially if you have a **Eurailpass.** Rail passes or individual rail tickets within Europe are available at most travel agencies, at any office of **Rail Europe** (✆ **888/382-7245;** www.raileurope.com), or at **Eurostar** (✆ **800/EUROSTAR** in the U.S., 0870/ 510-4105 in London, 01-70-70-99-49 in Paris; www.eurostar.com).

There are six major train stations in Paris: **Gare d'Austerlitz,** 55 quai d'Austerlitz, 13e (serving the southwest, with trains from the Loire Valley, the Bordeaux country, and the Pyrenees); **Gare de l'Est,** place du 11 Novembre 1918, 10e (serving the east, with trains from Strasbourg,

Nancy, Reims, and beyond to Zurich, Basel, Luxembourg, and Austria); **Gare de Lyon,** 20 bd. Diderot, 12e (serving the southeast with trains from the Côte d'Azur and Provence to Geneva, Lausanne, and Italy); **Gare Montparnasse,** 17 bd. Vaugirard, 15e (serving the west, with trains from Brittany); **Gare du Nord,** 18 rue de Dunkerque, 15e (serving the north, with trains from Holland, Denmark, Belgium, and Germany); and **Gare St-Lazare,** 13 rue d'Amsterdam, 8e (serving the northwest, with trains from Normandy).

For general train information and to make reservations, call **Rail Europe** at ℂ **01-70-70-60-88** daily from 7am to 8pm. Buses operate between rail stations. Each of these stations has a Métro stop, making the whole city easily accessible. Taxis are also available at designated stands at every station. Look for the sign that says TETE DE STATION. Be alert in train stations, especially at night.

BY FERRY FROM ENGLAND

Despite competition from the Channel Tunnel (Chunnel), services aboard ferries and hydrofoils operate day and night in all seasons, with the exception of last-minute cancellations during storms. Many Channel crossings are timed to coincide with the arrival/departure of major trains (especially those between London and Paris); trains let you off a short walk from the piers. Most ferries carry cars, trucks, and massive amounts of freight, but some hydrofoils take passengers only. The major routes include at least 12 trips a day between Dover or Folkestone and Calais or Boulogne. Hovercraft and hydrofoils make the trip from Dover to Calais, the shortest distance across the Channel, in 40 minutes during good weather; the slower-moving ferries can take several hours, depending on weather and tides. If you're bringing a car, it's important to make reservations, as space below decks is usually crowded.

Timetables can vary depending on the weather and many other factors.

The leading operator of ferries across the Channel is **P&O Ferries** (ℂ **0870/520-0333** in England; www.poferries.com). It operates car and passenger ferries between Portsmouth, England, and Cherbourg, France (three departures a day; 4¼ hr. each way during daylight hours, 7 hr. each way at night); between Portsmouth and Le Havre, France (three a day; 5½ hr. each way). The most popular routes are between Dover and Calais, France (25 sailings a day; 75 min. each way), which costs 19€ ($25) one-way for adults; children under 4 go free.

The shortest and most popular route is between Calais and Dover. **Hoverspeed** operates at least 12 hovercraft crossings daily; the trip takes 35 minutes. It also runs a SeaCat (a catamaran propelled by jet engines) that takes longer, just under 1 hour, between Dover and Calais. For reservations and information, call Hoverspeed (ℂ **800/677-8585** in North America or 0870/164-2114 in England; www.hoverspeed.com). Typical one-way fares are 19€ ($25) per person.

If you plan to transport a rental car between England and France, check in advance with the rental company about license and insurance requirements and additional drop-off charges. Be aware that many car-rental companies, for insurance reasons, forbid transport of one of their vehicles over the water between England and France. Transport of a car each way begins at 150€ ($195).

UNDER THE CHANNEL

One of the great engineering feats of our time, the $15-billion Channel Tunnel (Chunnel) opened in 1994, and the **Eurostar Express** now has daily service from London to both Paris and Brussels. The 50km (31-mile) journey takes 35 minutes, though actual time spent in the Chunnel is only 19 minutes. Stores selling duty-free goods, restaurants, service stations, and bilingual staffs are available to travelers on both sides of the Channel.

Eurostar tickets are available through **Rail Europe** (℗ 888/382-7245; www.raileurope.com). In Great Britain, make reservations for Eurostar at ℗ **0870/518-6186;** in the United States, call ℗ **800/EUROSTAR.** Chunnel train travel is roughly competitive with air travel, if you calculate door-to-door travel time. Trains leave from London's Waterloo Station and arrive in Paris at the Gare du Nord.

The tunnel also accommodates passenger cars, charter buses, taxis, and motorcycles, transporting them under the Channel from Folkestone, England, to Calais, France. It operates 24 hours a day, running every 15 minutes during peak travel times and at least once an hour at night. You can buy tickets at the tollbooth at the tunnel's entrance. With **Eurotunnel** (℗ 0870/535-3535; www.eurotunnel.com), gone are the days of weather-related delays, seasickness, and advance reservations.

Before they board Eurotunnel, motorists stop at a tollbooth and pass through British and French immigration at the same time. Then they drive onto a 1km-long (half-mile) train and travel through the tunnel. During the ride, motorists stay in air-conditioned carriages, remaining inside their cars or stepping outside to stretch their legs. When the trip is completed, they simply drive off. Total travel time is about an hour. Once on French soil, British drivers must remember to drive on the right-hand side of the road.

5 Money & Costs

CURRENCY

The **euro,** the single European currency, became the official currency of France and 11 other participating countries on January 1, 1999. The euro didn't go into general circulation until January 1, 2002. The old currency, the French franc, disappeared into history on March 1, 2002, replaced by the euro, which is officially abbreviated "EUR" or €. Exchange rates of participating countries are locked into a common currency fluctuating against the dollar, and the difference could affect the relative costs of your trip. For up-to-the-minute currency conversions, go to **www.xe.com/ucc.** For more details on the euro, check out **www.europa.eu.int/euro**.

Most banks in Paris are open Monday to Friday from 9am to 4:30pm, and a few are open Saturday; ask at your hotel for the location of the one nearest you. Most post offices will convert currency, and exchanges are also available at Paris airports and train stations and along most of the major boulevards. They charge a small commission. Some exchange places charge favorable rates to lure you into their stores. For example, **Paris Vision,** 214 rue de Rivoli, 1er (℗ **01-42-60-31-25;** Métro: Tuileries), maintains a minibank in the back of a travel agency, open daily from 7am to 9pm. Its rates are only a fraction less favorable than those offered for large blocks of money as listed by the Paris stock exchange.

The prices in Paris are roughly comparable to London or New York, though Paris is less expensive than London these days. It remains one of the priciest capitals to visit in Western Europe, though it's far cheaper than Oslo. Worldwide, its prices are "moderate" when stacked up against such international destinations as Tokyo.

ATMs

The easiest and best way to get cash away from home is from an ATM (automated teller machine), sometimes referred to as a "cash machine," or a "cashpoint." The **Cirrus** (℗ **800/424-7787;** www.mastercard.com) and **PLUS** (℗ **800/843-7587;**

What Things Cost in Paris

	U.S.$	UK£
Taxi from Charles de Gaulle Airport to the city center	65	34
Taxi from Orly Airport to the city center	59	30
Public transportation for a trip within the city	1.80	95p
Double room at The Ritz (very expensive)	884	460
Double room at Lord Byron (moderate)	228	119
Double room at Hotel DE Nevers (inexpensive)	116	60
Lunch for one, without wine, at Chez Georges (moderate)	60	31
Lunch for one, without wine, at Crémerie-Restaurant Polidor (inexpensive)	14	8
Dinner for one, without wine, at Le Grand Véfour (very expensive)	300	156
Dinner for one, without wine, at Ladurée (moderate)	42	22
Dinner for one, without wine at Aux Charpentiers (inexpensive)	31	16
Glass of wine	1.40–2.60	75p–1.35
Coca-Cola	3.20	1.65
Cup of coffee	2	1.05
Admission to the Louvre	10	5.20
Movie ticket	10–12	5.20–6.25
Theater ticket (at the Comédie-Française)	32	17

www.visa.com) networks span the globe; look at the back of your bank card to see which network you're on, and then call or check online for ATM locations at your destination. Be sure you know your personal identification number (PIN) and daily withdrawal limit before you depart. You may need a **four-digit** personal identification number or **PIN** (six digits may not work) to use ATMs in Paris. If you have a six-digit code, you may want to consider getting a new one for your trip.

Note: Remember that many banks impose a fee every time you use a card at another bank's ATM, and that fee can be higher for international transactions (up to $5 or more) than for domestic ones. In addition, the bank from which you withdraw cash may charge its own fee. For international withdrawal fees, ask your bank.

CREDIT CARDS

Credit cards are another safe way to carry money. They also provide a convenient record of all your expenses, and they generally offer relatively good exchange rates. You can withdraw cash advances from your credit cards at banks or ATMs, provided you know your PIN. Keep in mind that you'll pay interest from the moment of your withdrawal, even if you pay your monthly bills on time. Also, note that many banks now assess a 1% to 3% transaction fee on all charges you incur abroad (whether you're using the local currency or your native currency). The credit cards most commonly accepted in Paris are American Express, Diners Club, Master-Card, and Visa, but not the Discover card. For emergency numbers, see "Lost & Found" in "Fast Facts: Paris" in chapter 5.

TRAVELER'S CHECKS

Traveler's checks are still an option in Paris, but with 24-hour ATMs around every corner, they are fading in use. However, the frugal traveler still carries them because they are cheaper than withdrawing money from the ATM every day.

You can buy traveler's checks at most banks. They are offered in denominations of $20, $50, $100, $500, and sometimes $1,000. Generally, you'll pay a service charge ranging from 1% to 4%.

The most popular traveler's checks are offered by: American Express (© 800/807-6233 or 800/221-7282 for card-holders—this number accepts collect calls, offers service in several foreign languages, and exempts AmEx gold and platinum cardholders from the 1% fee); Visa (© 800/732-1322)—AAA members can obtain Visa checks for a $9.95 fee (for checks up to $1,500) at most AAA offices or by calling © 866/339-3378; and MasterCard (© 800/223-9920).

6 Travel Insurance

Because Paris is far from home for most of us, and a number of things can go wrong—lost luggage, trip cancellation, a medical emergency—buying insurance makes sense. Check your existing insurance policies and credit card coverage before you buy travel insurance. You may already be covered for lost luggage, cancelled tickets, or medical expenses.

The cost of travel insurance varies widely, depending on the cost and length of your trip, your age and health, and the type of trip you're taking, but expect to pay between 5% and 8% of the vacation itself. You can get estimates from various providers through **InsureMyTrip.com**. Enter your trip cost and dates, your age, and other information, for prices from more than a dozen companies.

TRIP-CANCELLATION INSURANCE

Trip-cancellation insurance will help retrieve your money if you have to back out of a trip or depart early, or if your travel supplier goes bankrupt. Permissible reasons for trip cancellation can range from sickness to natural disasters to the Department of State declaring a destination unsafe for travel.

For more information, contact one of the following recommended insurers: **Access America** (© 800/729-6021; www.accessamerica.com); **Travel Guard International** (© 800/826-4919; www.travelguard.com); **Travel Insured International** (© 800/243-3174; www.travelinsured.com); and **Travelex Insurance Services** (© 800/228-9792; www.travelex-insurance.com).

MEDICAL INSURANCE

For travel overseas, most U.S. health plans (including Medicare and Medicaid) do not provide coverage, and the ones that do often require you to pay for services upfront and reimburse you only after you return home. As a safety net, you may want to buy travel medical insurance, particularly if you're traveling to a remote or high-risk area where emergency evacuation might be necessary. If you require additional medical insurance, try **MEDEX Assistance** (© 800/732-5309;

www.medexassist.com) or **Travel Assistance International** (© 800/821-2828; www.travelassistance.com; for general information on services, call the company's Worldwide Assistance Services, Inc., at © 800/777-8710; www.worldwideassistance.com).

LOST-LUGGAGE INSURANCE

On flights within the U.S., checked baggage is covered up to $2,500 per ticketed passenger. On international flights (including U.S. portions of international trips), baggage coverage is limited to approximately $9.07 per pound, up to approximately $635 per checked bag. If you plan to check items more valuable than what's covered by the standard liability, see if your homeowner's policy covers your valuables. As an added discretion, you might also ask for baggage insurance as part of your comprehensive travel-insurance package.

If your luggage is lost, immediately file a lost-luggage claim at the airport, detailing the luggage contents. Most airlines require that you report delayed, damaged, or lost baggage within 4 hours of arrival. The airlines are required to deliver luggage, once found, directly to your house or destination free of charge.

7 Health

STAYING HEALTHY
GENERAL AVAILABILITY
OF HEALTHCARE

In general, Paris is a "safe" destination, although problems can and do occur anywhere. You don't need shots, most foodstuffs are safe, and the water in Paris is potable. If you're concerned, order bottled water. It is easy to get a prescription filled in Paris, and nearly all hospitals have English-speaking doctors with well-trained medical staffs. It's also easy to get over-the-counter medicine, if necessary, in Paris. In other words, France is part of the civilized world.

Contact the **International Association for Medical Assistance to Travelers** (IAMAT; © 716/754-4883 or, in Canada, 416/652-0137; www.iamat.org) for tips on travel and health concerns in the countries you're visiting, and for lists of local, English-speaking doctors. The **U.S. Centers for Disease Control and Prevention** (© 800/394-1945;

Avoiding "Economy-Class Syndrome"

Deep vein thrombosis, or as it's know in the world of flying, "economy-class syndrome," is a blood clot that develops in a deep vein. It's a potentially deadly condition that can be caused by sitting in cramped conditions—such as an airplane cabin—for too long. During a flight (especially a long-haul flight), get up, walk around, and stretch your legs every 60 to 90 minutes to keep your blood flowing. Other preventative measures include frequent flexing of the legs while sitting, drinking lots of water, and avoiding alcohol and sleeping pills. If you have a history of deep vein thrombosis, heart disease, or another condition that puts you at high risk, some experts recommend wearing compression stockings or taking anticoagulants when you fly; always ask your physician about the best course for you. Symptoms of deep vein thrombosis include leg pain or swelling, or even shortness of breath.

www.cdc.gov) provides up-to-date information on health hazards by region or country and offers tips on food safety. The website www.tripprep.com, sponsored by a consortium of travel medicine practitioners, may also offer helpful advice on traveling abroad. You can find listings of reliable clinics overseas at the International Society of Travel Medicine (www.istm.org).

WHAT TO DO IF YOU GET SICK AWAY FROM HOME

In most cases, your existing health plan will provide the coverage you need. But double-check; you may want to buy **travel medical insurance** instead. (See "Medical Insurance," above.) Bring your insurance ID card with you when you travel.

Some large Paris hotels have a doctor on staff. You can also try the **American Hospital,** 63 bd. Victor-Hugo, in the suburb of Neuilly-sur-Seine (© **01-46-41-25-25;** Métro: Pont-de-Levallois or Pont-de-Neuilly; bus no. 82), which operates a 24-hour emergency service. The bilingual staff accepts Blue Cross and other American insurance plans.

For emergency dental service, call **S.O.S. Dentaire,** 87 bd. Du Port-Royal, 13e (© **01-43-37-51-00;** Métro: Gobelins), Monday to Friday from 8pm to midnight and Saturday and Sunday from 9am to midnight. Staff members will arrange an appointment with a qualified dentist either on the day of your call or for early in the morning of the following day. You can also call or visit the American Hospital.

We list hospitals, clinics, and emergency numbers under "Hospitals" in "Fast Facts" in chapter 5.

If you suffer from a chronic illness, consult your doctor before your departure. Pack **prescription medications** in your carry-on luggage, and carry them in their original containers, with pharmacy labels—otherwise, they won't make it through airport security. If you have liquid or gel prescriptions in containers larger than 3 oz., remember to put them in your checked bag as they may be confiscated at security checkpoints. Carry the generic name of prescription medicines, in case a local pharmacist is unfamiliar with the brand name. For travel abroad, you may have to pay all medical costs upfront and be reimbursed later. See "Medical Insurance" under "Travel Insurance," above.

8 Safety

The most common menace in Paris is the plague of pickpockets and roving gangs of Gypsy children who surround you, distract you, and steal your purse or wallet. They prey on tourists around attractions like the Louvre, Eiffel Tower, and Notre-Dame, and they can often strike in the Métro, sometimes blocking a victim from the escalator. A band of these young thieves can clean your pockets even while you try to fend them off. Their method is to get very close to a target, ask for a handout (sometimes), and deftly help themselves to your money or passport.

Never leave valuables in a car, and never travel with your car unlocked. A U.S. Department of State travel advisory warns that every car (whether parked, stopped at a traffic light, or moving) can be a potential target for armed robbery. In these uncertain times, it is prudent to check the U.S. Department of State's travel advisories at **http://travel.state. gov/travel/warnings.html**.

The government of France maintains a national antiterrorism plan; in times of heightened security concerns, the government mobilizes police and armed forces, and installs them at airports; train and Métro stations; and high-profile locations such as schools, embassies, and government installations.

In recent years, Paris has experienced political assassinations and random bombings. One U.S. citizen was injured in these attacks, but none has been killed. All passengers on subways and trains are urged to be aware of their surroundings and to report any unattended baggage to the nearest authority.

Student demonstrations, labor protests, or other demonstrations have turned into violent confrontations between demonstrators and police. Americans are advised to avoid street demonstrations.

Gangs of thieves operate on the rail link from Charles de Gaulle Airport to downtown Paris by preying on jet-lagged, luggage-burdened tourists. Often, one thief distracts the tourist with a question about directions while an accomplice takes a momentarily unguarded backpack, briefcase, or purse. Thieves also time their thefts to coincide with train stops so that they may quickly exit the car. Travelers may wish to consider traveling from the airport to the city by bus or taxi.

Although public safety is not as much a problem in Paris at it is in some large American cities, concerns are growing. Robbery at gunpoint or knifepoint is uncommon, but not unknown. Be careful, especially late at night. There have been a number of violent armed robberies, including knife attacks, in the vicinity of the Eiffel Tower late at night.

Thieves on motorcycles have been known to reach into moving cars by opening the car door or reaching through an open window to steal purses and other bags visible inside. Those traveling by car in Paris should remember to keep windows closed and doors locked.

The No. 1 subway line, which runs by many major tourist attractions (including the Grand Arch at La Defense, Arc de Triomphe, Champs-Elysées, Concorde, Louvre, and Bastille), is the site of many thefts. Pickpockets are especially active on this Métro line during the summer months.

Gare du Nord train station, where the express trains from the airport arrive in Paris, is also a high-risk area for pickpocketing and theft.

Many thefts occur at the major department stores (Galeries Lafayette, Printemps, and La Samaritaine), where tourists often leave wallets, passports, and credit cards on cashier counters during transactions.

In hotels, thieves frequent lobbies and breakfast rooms, and take advantage of a minute of inattention to snatch jackets, purses, and backpacks. Also, while many hotels do have safety latches that allow guests to secure their rooms while they are inside, this feature is not as universal as it is in the United States. If no chain or latch is present, a chair placed up against the door is usually an effective obstacle to surreptitious entry during the night.

In restaurants, many Americans have reported that women's purses placed on the floor under the table at the feet of the diner are stolen during the meal.

DEALING WITH DISCRIMINATION

Discrimination against West and North African immigrants to France—a population estimated to number more than a million—does exist. Anyone who might be taken for an immigrant (often illegal) from Africa is subject to verbal abuse. Racism is more prevalent in the southeast of France than Paris. So far, there has been almost no harassment of African-American tourists to Paris or France itself. Many expatriate Americans, in fact, including such cultural figures as Josephine Baker and author James Baldwin, fled to Paris in decades past to escape the racism of America. **S.O.S. Racisme,** 51 av. de Flandre, 19e (© **01-40-35-36-55;** www.sos-racisme.org), offers legal advice to victims of prejudice and will even intervene to help with the police.

Regrettably, anti-Semitism has been on the rise in Europe, especially in France, which has registered a significant increase in incidents against Jews. French Jews (not visitors from abroad) have suffered assaults and attacks against synagogues, cemeteries, schools, and other Jewish property. Officials say they believe that

attacks in France are linked to the worsening of the Israeli-Palestinian conflict. Some sources—none official—recommend that travelers conceal Star of David jewelry and such items to ensure personal safety while traveling in France.

Officially, the government of France welcomes Jewish visitors and promises a vigorous defense of their safety and concerns. The French Government Tourist Office website (www.franceguide.com) has a "Jewish Traveler Guide" section with more information.

9 Specialized Travel Resources

TRAVELERS WITH DISABILITIES
Most disabilities shouldn't stop anyone from traveling. There are more options and resources out there than ever before. Facilities in Paris for travelers with disabilities are certainly better than you'll find in most cities. Nearly all modern hotels in France now have rooms designed especially for persons with disabilities. Older hotels, unless renovated, may not provide important features such as elevators, special toilet facilities, or ramps for wheelchair accessibility. Depending on your needs, it's best to contact each hotel directly and make your needs known before you arrive.

Most high-speed trains in France can deal with wheelchairs, and guide dogs ride free. Older trains have compartments for wheelchair boarding. On the Paris Métro, persons with disabilities can sit in wider seats. Some stations don't have escalators or elevators, however, and this may present problems.

The **Association des Paralysés de France,** 17 bd. Auguste-Blanqui, 75013 Paris (© **01-40-78-69-66;** www.apf.asso.fr), is an organization that provides documentation, moral support, and travel ideas for individuals who use wheelchairs.

Many travel agencies offer customized tours and itineraries for travelers with disabilities. Among them are **Flying Wheels Travel** (© **507/451-5005;** www.flyingwheelstravel.com); **Access-Able Travel Source** (© **303/232-2979;** www.access-able.com); and **Accessible Journeys** (© **800/846-4537** or 610/521-0339; www.disabilitytravel.com).

Organizations that offer assistance to travelers with disabilities include **Moss-Rehab** (© **800/CALL-MOSS;** www.mossresourcenet.org), the **American Foundation for the Blind (AFB;** © **800/232-5463;** www.afb.org), and **SATH (Society for Accessible Travel & Hospitality;** © **212/447-7284;** www.sath.org). AirAmbulanceCard.com is now partnered with SATH and allows you to preselect topnotch hospitals in case of an emergency.

Check out the quarterly magazine *Emerging Horizons* (www.emerginghorizons.com) and *Open World* magazine, published by SATH. Dated, though still useful, *Access in Paris: A Guide for Those Who Have Problems Getting Around,* by Gordon Couch and Ben Roberts (Cpg, Inc., 1994), is available in paperback online. It has reviews of wheelchair- and crutch-dependent accessible hotels, restaurants, attractions, and modes of transportation, and it was researched by travelers with and without disabilities.

GAY & LESBIAN TRAVELERS

Paris is one of the world's most tolerant cities toward gays and lesbians, and no special laws discriminate against them. "Gay Paree" has a large gay population, with dozens of gay clubs, restaurants, organizations, and services. The Marais has become a favorite area for gays to live and socialize in Paris.

Ecoute Gay, 7 place du Commerce, 15e (℃ **01-44-93-01-02**), is a hotline designed for the counseling of persons with gay-related problems and issues. The phone is staffed every Monday, Tuesday, and Friday from 6 to 10pm by volunteers, some not as helpful as others. Also helpful is **La Maison des Femmes,** 163 rue de Charenton, 12e (℃ **01-43-43-41-13;** http://maisondesfemmes.free.fr; Métro: Charonne), offering information about Paris for lesbians and bisexual women, and sometimes sponsoring informal dinners and get-togethers. Call anytime for a recorded announcement about the hours when someone will be available in that particular week.

Lesbian or bisexual women may also pick up a copy of *Lesbia,* if only to check out the ads. These and other publications are available at Paris's largest gay bookstore, **Les Mots à la Bouche,** 6 rue Ste-Croix-de-la-Bretonnerie, 4e (℃ **01-42-78-88-30;** www.motsbouche.com). Hours are Monday to Saturday from 11am to 11pm and Sunday from 2 to 8pm. Both French- and English-language publications are available.

The International Gay & Lesbian Travel Association (IGLTA; ℃ **800/448-8550** or 954/776-2626; www.iglta.org) is the trade association for the gay and lesbian travel industry, and offers an online directory of gay- and lesbian-friendly travel businesses; go to its website and click on "Members."

Many agencies offer tours and travel itineraries specifically for gay and lesbian travelers, among them **Above and Beyond Tours** (℃ **800/397-2681;** www.abovebeyondtours.com).

Gay.com Travel (℃ **415/644-8044;** www.gay.com/travel or www.outandabout.com), is an excellent online successor to the popular *Out & About* print magazine. It provides regularly updated information about gay-owned, gay-oriented, and gay-friendly lodging, dining, sightseeing, nightlife, and shopping establishments in every important destination worldwide.

The following travel guides are available at many bookstores, or you can order them from any online bookseller: *Frommer's Gay & Lesbian Europe* (www.frommers.com), an excellent travel resource to the top European cities and resorts; *Spartacus International Gay Guide* (Bruno Gmünder Verlag; www.spartacusworld.com/gayguide) and *Odysseus: The International Gay Travel Planner* (Odysseus Enterprises Ltd.); and the **Damron guides** (www.damron.com), with separate, annual books for gay men and lesbians.

SENIOR TRAVEL

Mention the fact that you're a senior citizen when you make your travel reservations. In most cities, people over the age of 60 qualify for reduced admission to theaters, museums, and other attractions, as well as discounted fares on public transportation.

At any rail station in France, seniors (60 and older, with proof of age) can get **A La Carte Senior,** available online at www.senior-sncf.com. The pass costs 53€ ($69) and is good for a 50% discount on unlimited rail travel throughout the year. The *carte* also offers reduced prices on some regional bus lines and half-price admission at state-owned museums. There are some restrictions—for example, you can't use it between 3pm

Traveling with Minors

It's always wise to have plenty of documentation when traveling in today's world with children. For changing details on entry requirements for children traveling abroad, keep up to date by going to the U.S. Department of State website: www.travel.state.gov/travel/tips/brochures/brochures_1229.html.

To prevent international child abduction, EU governments have initiated procedures at entry and exit points. These often (but not always) include requiring documentary evidence of relationship and permission for the child's travel from the parent or legal guardian not present. Having such documentation on hand, even if not required, facilitates entries and exits. All children must have their own passports. To obtain a passport, the child **must** be present—that is, in person—at the center issuing the passport. Both parents must be present as well. If not, then a notarized statement from the parents is required.

Any questions that parents or guardians might have can be answered by calling the **National Passport Information Center** at © 877/487-6868 Monday to Friday 8am to 8pm Eastern Standard Time.

Sunday and noon Monday or from noon Friday to noon Saturday. There's no discount on the Paris network of commuter trains.

Members of **AARP** (formerly known as the American Association of Retired Persons), 601 E. St. NW, Washington, DC 20049 (© **888/687-2277;** www. aarp.org), get discounts on hotels, airfares, and car rentals. AARP offers members a wide range of benefits, including *AARP: The Magazine* and a monthly newsletter. Anyone over age 50 can join.

Many reliable agencies and organizations target the 50-plus market. **Elderhostel** (© **800/454-5768;** www.elder hostel.org) arranges study programs for those ages 55 and older.

Recommended publications offering travel resources and discounts for seniors include the quarterly magazine *Travel 50 & Beyond* (www.travel50andbeyond. com); *Travel Unlimited: Uncommon Adventures for the Mature Traveler* (Avalon); *101 Tips for Mature Travelers,* available from Grand Circle Travel (© **800/959-0405;** www.gct.com); *The 50+ Traveler's Guidebook* (St. Martin's Press); and *Unbelievably Good Deals and Great Adventures That You* *Absolutely Can't Get Unless You're Over 50* (McGraw-Hill), by Joann Rattner Heilman.

WOMEN TRAVELERS

Women in Paris face some additional safety concerns, but less so than in most of the rest of the world. The usual precautions are advised—that is, to stick to secure hotels in the major tourist districts and avoid late-night walks along the Seine or through the relatively deserted back streets of Paris. Try to ride on the Métro in cars with other passengers, not in lonely compartments. As the world grows more politically correct, the old macho attitudes of cat-calling at an attractive woman are dying out, though still prevalent among many of the newly arrived immigrants from less developed countries. Carry a purse with a zipper and a thick strap that you can drape across your body, and avoid wearing a money belt or waist pack. Also avoid ghettoized or seedy districts of the city. If you travel in the neighborhoods previewed in this guide, you should avoid trouble. Of course, proper dress is always discreet. Parisians tend to frown on the wearing of "shorty short shorts" on their streets. In

Paris, donning Paris Hilton garb for a night on the town might mean you'll be mistaken for a prostitute.

STUDENT TRAVEL

If you're traveling internationally, you'd be wise to arm yourself with an **International Student Identity Card (ISIC)**, which offers substantial savings on rail passes, plane tickets, and entrance fees. It also provides you with basic health and life insurance and a 24-hour help line. The card is available from **STA Travel** (℡ **800/781-4040** in North America; www.sta.com or www.statravel.com; or www.statravel.co.uk in the U.K.), the biggest student travel agency in the world. If you're no longer a student but are still younger than 26, you can get an **International Youth Travel Card (IYTC)** from the same people, which entitles you to some discounts (but not on museum admissions). **Travel CUTS** (℡ **800/592-2887**; www.travelcuts.com) offers similar services for both Canadians and U.S. residents. Irish students may prefer to turn to **USIT** (℡ **01/602-1904**; www.usitnow.ie), an Ireland-based specialist in student, youth, and independent travel.

SINGLE TRAVELERS

On package vacations, single travelers are often hit with a "single supplement" to the base price. To avoid it, you can agree to room with other single travelers or find a compatible roommate before you go, from one of the many roommate locator agencies.

Travel Buddies Single Travel Club (℡ **800/998-9099**; www.travelbuddies worldwide.com), based in Canada, runs small, intimate, single-friendly group trips and will match you with a roommate free of charge. **Travel Chums** (℡ **212/787-2621**; www.travelchums.com) is an Internet-only travel-companion matching service with elements of an online personals–type site, hosted by the respected New York–based Shaw Guides travel service. **Singles Travel International** (℡ **877/765-6874**; www.singles travelintl.com) offers singles-only trips to such places as Paris.

10 Sustainable Tourism/Ecotourism

Each time you take a flight or drive a car CO_2 is released into the atmosphere. You can help neutralize this danger to our planet through "carbon offsetting"— paying someone to reduce your CO_2 emissions by the same amount you've added. Carbon offsets can be purchased in the U.S. from companies such as **Carbonfund.org** (www.carbonfund.org) and **TerraPass** (www.terrapass.org), and from **Climate Care** (www.climatecare.org) in the U.K.

Although one could argue that any vacation that includes an airplane flight can't be truly "green," you can go on holiday and still contribute positively to the environment. You can offset carbon emissions from your flight in other ways. Choose forward-looking companies that embrace responsible development practices, helping preserve destinations for the future by working alongside local people.

Responsible Travel (www.responsible travel.com) contains a great source of sustainable travel ideas run by a spokesperson for responsible tourism in the travel industry. **Sustainable Travel International** (www.sustainabletravelinternational.org) promotes responsible tourism practices and issues an annual *Green Gear & Gift Guide*.

You can find eco-friendly travel tips, statistics, and touring companies and associations—listed by destination under "Travel Choice"—at the TIES website, www.ecotourism.org. Also check out **Conservation International** (www. conservation.org)—which, with *National Geographic Traveler*, annually presents

World Legacy Awards (www.wlaward. org) to those travel tour operators, businesses, organizations, and places that have made a significant contribution to sustainable tourism.

In the U.K., **Tourism Concern** (www. tourismconcern.org.uk) works to reduce social and environmental problems connected to tourism and find ways of improving tourism so that local benefits are increased.

The **Association of British Travel Agents** (**ABTA;** www.abtamembers.org) acts as a focal point for the U.K. travel industry and is one of the leading groups spearheading responsible tourism.

The **Association of Independent Tour Operators** (**AITO;** www.aito.co.uk) is a group of interesting specialist operators leading the field in making holidays sustainable.

11 Staying Connected

TELEPHONES

Public phones are found in cafes, restaurants, Métro stations, post offices, airports, and train stations, and occasionally on the streets. Finding a coin-operated telephone in France is an arduous task. A simpler and more widely accepted method of payment is the *télécarte,* a prepaid calling card available at kiosks, post offices, and Métro stations and costing 11€ to 16€ ($14–$21) for 50 and 120 units, respectively. A local call costs one unit, which provides you 6 to 18 minutes of conversation, depending on the rate. Télécarte is good for local calls in Paris or anywhere else in France, but is not valid for international calls. Avoid making calls from your hotel, which may double or triple the charges.

To call **long distance within France,** dial the 10-digit number (9-digit in some cases outside Paris) of the person or place you're calling. To reach the long-distance operator for AT&T, the Direct Access Number is: ℂ **08-00-99-00-11** or 08-05-70-12-88; for Canada, dial ℂ **08-00-99-00-16** or 08-00-99-02-16.

If you have a **phone card,** you can recharge it anywhere, anytime, with **eKit** (www.ekit.com), via the Web. You can recharge over the phone using a self-service recharge menu. If you prefer to speak to someone, you can call eKit's 24-hour Customer Service: ℂ **800/706-1333** in the U.S.; ℂ **0800/032-6297** in Britain;

ℂ **800/150-812** in Australia; and ℂ **866/626-9724** in Canada. With eKit, you can save up to 70% on calls in 200 countries worldwide, including France. One of the many advantages is that family and friends can leave you messages at no cost to them.

To call Paris:
1. Dial the international access code: 011 from the U.S.; 00 from the U.K., Ireland, or New Zealand; or 0011 from Australia.
2. Dial the country code 33.
3. Dial the city code 1 and then the number.

To make international calls: To make international calls from Paris, first dial 00 and then the country code (U.S. or Canada 1, U.K. 44, Ireland 353, Australia 61, New Zealand 64). Next you dial the area code and number. For example, if you wanted to call the British Embassy in Washington, D.C., you would dial ℂ **00-1-202-588-7800.**

For directory assistance: For numbers inside and outside France, dial ℂ **118-008.**

For operator assistance: With the inauguration of increasing numbers of cellphones (each of which has a different carrier), and with the decentralization of what used to be the P. T. T., local operators within France are less and less widespread. Even if you dial "0," depending on where you are within France, it might not get you a live body. According to the director of phone services in Paris, everyone automatically expects that dialers know the codes of the countries or regions they're trying to reach.

As for reaching an operator for the **placement of calls outside of France,** the system involves bypassing French operators completely and relying on the operators based within the country you're trying to call. In any event, the prefix for accessing a foreign (i.e., non-French) operator involves dialing the access codes **0800-99-00** followed by the **country code.**

Toll-free numbers: Numbers beginning with **0800** within France are toll-free, but calling a 1-800 number in the States from France is not toll-free. In fact, it costs the same as an overseas call.

CELLPHONES

The three letters that define much of the world's wireless capabilities are **GSM** (Global System for Mobile Communications), a big, seamless network that makes for easy cross-border cellphone use throughout Europe and dozens of other countries worldwide. In the U.S., T-Mobile, AT&T Wireless, and Cingular use this quasi-universal system; in Canada, Microcell and some Rogers customers are GSM, and all Europeans and most Australians use GSM. GSM phones function with a removable plastic SIM card, encoded with your phone number and account information. If your cellphone is on a GSM system, and you have a world-capable multiband phone such as many Sony Ericsson, Motorola, or Samsung models, you can make and receive calls across civilized areas around much of the globe. Just call your wireless operator and ask for international roaming to be activated on your account. Unfortunately, per-minute charges can be high—usually $1 to $1.50 in Western Europe.

Buying a phone can be economically attractive, as France has cheap prepaid phone systems. Once you arrive, stop by a local cellphone shop and get the cheapest package; you'll probably pay less than $70 for a phone and a starter calling card. Local calls may be as low as 10¢ per minute, and in France incoming calls are free.

VOICE OVER INTERNET PROTOCOL (VOIP)

If you have Web access while traveling, you might consider a broadband-based telephone service (in technical terms, **Voice over Internet Protocol,** or **VoIP**) such as Skype (www.skype.com) or Vonage (www.vonage.com), which allows you to make free international calls if you use their services from your laptop or in a cybercafe.

INTERNET ACCESS AWAY FROM HOME
WITHOUT YOUR OWN COMPUTER

To find cybercafes in Paris, check **www. cybercaptive.com** and **www.cybercafe. com**. The latter lists 20 such cafes scattered throughout central Paris. The most popular in Paris seems to be **Luxembourg Micro,** 81 bd. Saint-Michel, 5e (© **01-46-33-27-98;** Métro: Luxembourg; www.luxembourg-micro.com). For 20 minutes, you pay 1€ ($1.30); for 30 minutes 1.50€ ($1.95), and for an hour 2.50€ ($3.25). It's open daily from 9am to 11pm.

WITH YOUR OWN COMPUTER

More and more hotels, cafes, and retailers are signing on as Wi-Fi (wireless fidelity) "hotspots." Mac owners have their own networking technology: Apple AirPort. T-Mobile Hotspot (**www.t-mobile.com/ hotspot**) serves up wireless connections in the U.S. Boingo (**www.boingo.com**) and Wayport (**www.wayport.com**) have set up networks in airports and high-class hotel lobbies. iPass providers (see below) also give you access to a few hundred wireless hotel lobby setups. To locate other hotspots that provide free wireless networks in cities around the world, go to **www.personaltelco.net**.

For dial-up access, most business-class hotels throughout the world offer dataports for laptop modems, and a few thousand hotels in the U.S. and Europe now offer free high-speed Internet access. In addition, major Internet Service Providers (ISPs) have local access numbers around the world, allowing you to go online by placing a local call. The iPass network also has dial-up numbers around the world. You'll have to sign up with an iPass provider, who will then tell you how to set up your computer for your destination(s). For a list of iPass providers, go to **www.ipass.com** and click on "Individuals Buy Now." One solid provider is i2roam (© **866/811-6209** or 920/233-5863; www.i2roam.com).

Wherever you go, bring a connection kit of the right power and phone adapters, a spare phone cord, and a spare Ethernet network cable—or find out whether your hotel supplies them to guests. See "Electricity" in "Fast Facts: Paris" in chapter 5.

12 Package Tours for the Independent Traveler

Package tours are simply a way to buy the airfare, accommodations, and other elements of your trip (such as car rentals, airport transfers, and sometimes even activities) at the same time and often at discounted prices.

One good source of package deals is the airlines themselves. Most major airlines offer air/land packages, including **American Airlines Vacations** (© **800/321-2121**; www.aavacations.com), **Delta Vacations** (© **800/654-6559**; www.deltavacations.com), **Continental Airlines Vacations** (© **800/301-3800**; www.covacations.com), and **United Vacations** (© **888/854-3899**; www.unitedvacations.com). Several big **online travel agencies**—Expedia, Travelocity, Orbitz, Site59, and Lastminute.com—also do a brisk business in packages.

The French Experience, 370 Lexington Ave., Room 511, New York, NY 10017 (© **800/283-7262** or 212/986-3800; fax 646/349-3276; www.french experience.com), offers inexpensive tickets to Paris on most major airlines and arranges tours and stays in various types and categories of country inns, hotels, private châteaux, and B&Bs. In addition, it takes reservations for about 38 small hotels in Paris and arranges short-term apartment rentals in the city or farmhouse rentals in the countryside. It also offers all-inclusive packages in Paris and prearranged package tours of various regions in France. Tours can be adapted to suit individual needs.

Travel packages are also listed in the travel section of your local Sunday newspaper. Or check ads in the national travel magazines, such as *Arthur Frommer's Budget Travel, Travel + Leisure, National Geographic Traveler,* and *Condé Nast Traveler.*

13 Escorted General Interest Tours

Escorted tours are structured group tours, with a group leader. The price usually includes everything from airfare to hotels, meals, tours, admission costs, and local transportation. The two largest tour operators conducting escorted tours of France and Europe are **Globus/Cosmos** (© **866/755-8581**; www.globusandcosmos.com) and **Trafalgar** (© **800/854-0103**; www.trafalgartours.com). Both companies have first-class tours that run about $100 a day and budget tours for even less. The differences are mainly in hotel location and the number of activities. There's little difference in the companies' services, so choose your tour based on the itinerary and preferred date of departure. Brochures are available at travel agencies, and all tours must be booked through travel agents.

Despite the fact that escorted tours require big deposits and predetermine hotels, restaurants, and itineraries, many people derive security and peace of mind from the structure they offer. Escorted tours—whether they're navigated by bus, motor coach, train, or boat—let travelers sit back and enjoy the trip without having to drive or worry about details. They take you to the maximum number of sights in the minimum amount of time with the least amount of hassle. They're particularly convenient for people with limited mobility and they can be a great way to make new friends.

On the downside, you'll have little opportunity for serendipitous interactions with locals. The tours can be jam-packed with activities, leaving little room for individual sightseeing, whim, or adventure—plus they often focus on the heavily touristed sites, so you miss out on many a lesser-known gem.

FINDING A SPECIALTY PACKAGE

What about special-interest tours? For a city as diverse and popular as Paris, there are only a few specialty tours.

One outfit that coordinates hotel stays with major musical events, usually within at least one (and often both) of the city's opera houses, is **Dailey-Thorp Travel,** P.O. Box 670, Big Horn, WY 82833 (© **800/998-4677** or 307/673-1555; fax 307/674-7474; www.daileythorp.com). Stays in Paris last between 3 and 7 days and, in many cases, are tied in with opera performances in other cities (usually London, Berlin, or Milan) as well. Expect accommodations in deluxe hotels such as the Grand, the Louvre, or the Scribe, and a staff that has made arrangements for all the nuts and bolts of your arrival in, and artistic exposure to, Paris.

Die-hard tennis fans set their calendars by the events that transpire each year in Paris's Roland-Garros stadium at the French Open. If you're unsure about how to match the dates of your visit with tennis tournaments that will be watched around the world, consider the California-based company that specializes in this issue: **Advantage Tennis Tours,** 33 White Sail Drive, Suite 100, Laguna Niguel, CA 92677 (© **800/341-8687;** www.advantagetennistours.com).

Packages usually include either 5 or 6 nights of hotel accommodations in Paris, 2 or 3 days on Center Court, the organizational skills of a bilingual hostess, and a chance to meet and mingle with tennis fans of many different nationalities during at least one catered lunch. There will even be an opportunity to grab a racquet and play some tennis on your own, in between bouts of sightseeing. Rates, per person, without airfare, begin at $2,775, double occupancy, depending on your choice of hotel and the duration of your visit.

4

Suggested Paris Itineraries

For visitors on the run, who are forced by their schedules to see Paris in anywhere from 1 to 3 days, we've devised a trio of self-guided tours, written as three 1-day itineraries. With these ready-made itineraries, you can have a complete, unforgettable trip, even though time is short.

"It's not possible!" a Parisian may warn you. Actually, seeing Paris in 1 to 3 days is possible, but it calls for some discipline and fast moving on your part.

Of course, even as we present these itineraries for "conquering" Paris in a nutshell, we must warn you that a month is really needed to develop an acquaintance with Paris. Save that for another visit when you'll have more time. Start your voyage of discovery right outside your hotel door.

1 The Best of Paris in 1 Day

Since time is wasting, arise early and begin your day with some live "theater" by walking the streets around your hotel—Right Bank or Left Bank, it doesn't matter at this point. This walk can acclimate you to the sights, sounds, and smells of the City of Light faster than anything, and it gets you centered before catching a taxi or hopping aboard the Métro for a ride underground to your first attraction.

We suggest you duck into a cafe for breakfast, and it doesn't matter where. On virtually every street in Paris, there is usually more than one cafe.

Any neighborhood will provide a slice of Parisian life, so order breakfast as thousands of locals do. Sit back, enjoy, and breathe deeply before beginning your descent on Paris. **Start:** *Métro to Palais Royal-Musée du Louvre.*

❶ **Musée du Louvre** ✿✿✿
You know you must see the Louvre, perhaps the greatest museum of art in the world. You wouldn't dare go home without storming that citadel. Since it opens at 9am, be among the first in line.

We've been going to this repository of art for years and, on every visit, discover something we've overlooked before. This palatial treasure trove is richly endowed, and some of its art is the most acclaimed on earth. With your clock ticking, at least call on the "great ladies of the Louvre": the *Mona Lisa* with her enigmatic smile, the sexy *Venus de Milo,* and *Winged Victory*

(alas, without a head). Try to allot at least 2 hours of viewing time for some world-class masterpieces. See p. 195.

Around 11am, go for a walk along:
❷ **The Quays of the Seine** ✿✿✿
After leaving the Louvre, walk south toward the river and head east for a stroll along the Seine. You'll encounter the most splendid panoramic vistas that Paris has to offer. Trees shade the banks of the river, and 14 bridges span the Seine. So much of the city's fortune has depended on this river, and you'll be in the nerve center of Paris life as you stroll along.

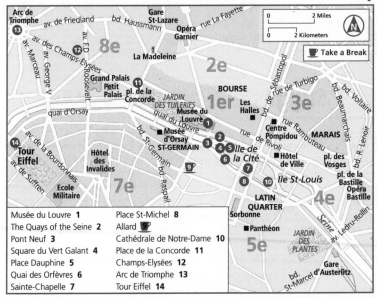

Arc de Triomphe · av. de Friedland · Gare St-Lazare · bd. Haussmann · Opéra Garnier · rue La Fayette

0 — 2 Miles
0 — 2 Kilometers

🍴 Take a Break

av. des Champs-Elysées · av. F.D. Roosevelt · av. George V · av. Marceau · 8e

La Madeleine · 2e · rue de Sébastopol · bd. de rue de Turbigo · bd. Voltaire

Grand Palais · Petit Palais · pl. de la Concorde · JARDIN DES TUILERIES · BOURSE · Les Halles · 1er · Centre Pompidou · rue de Rivoli · rue Rambuteau · MARAIS · bd. Beaumarchais · bd. R. Lenoir · 3e

quai d'Orsay · Musée du Louvre **1** · Musée d'Orsay · ST-GERMAIN · Ile de la Cité · Hôtel de Ville · pl. des Vosges · pl. de la Bastille

Tour Eiffel **14** · av. de la Bourdonnais · av. de Suffren · Hôtel des Invalides · bd. St-Germain · bd. Raspail · Ile St-Louis · Opéra Bastille · 4e

Ecole Militaire · 7e · LATIN QUARTER · Sorbonne · ■ Panthéon · JARDIN DES PLANTES · 5e · Seine · av. Ledru-Rollin

Gare d'Austerlitz · bd. St-Marcel

Musée du Louvre **1**	Place St-Michel **8**
The Quays of the Seine **2**	Allard 🍴
Pont Neuf **3**	Cathédrale de Notre-Dame **10**
Square du Vert Galant **4**	Place de la Concorde **11**
Place Dauphine **5**	Champs-Elysées **12**
Quai des Orfèvres **6**	Arc de Triomphe **13**
Sainte-Chapelle **7**	Tour Eiffel **14**

You'll see Paris's greatest island on the Seine, the Cité, emerging before you.

Cross over the:

❸ Pont Neuf ⚛

The oldest and most evocative of the bridges of Paris, Pont Neuf (p. 227) dates from 1578 and still looks the same. From the bridge, the view down (or up) the river is perhaps the most memorable in Paris.

Walk down the steps emerging on your right along Pont Neuf to:

❹ Square du Vert Galant

The steps take you behind the statue dedicated to Henri IV to the square du Vert Galant (p. 227) at the western tip of Ile de la Cité. The square takes its designation from the nickname given Henri IV, meaning "gay old spark." The square is the best vantage point for viewing Pont Neuf and the Louvre. As you stand on this square, you'll be at the "prow" of Cité if you liken the island to a giant ship.

After taking in that view, continue east, pausing at:

❺ Place Dauphine

This square—perfect for a picnic—was named in honor of the Dauphin, the future Louis XIII. It faces the towering mass of La Conciergerie (p. 215), whose gloomy precincts and memories of the French Revolution you can save for another visit to Paris.

With time moving on, head east along:

❻ Quai des Orfèvres

This Seine-bordering quay leads east to Notre-Dame. It was the former market of the jewelers of 17th- and 18th-century Paris. Marie Antoinette's celebrated necklace, subject of countless legends, was fashioned here.

The quay leads you to:

❼ Sainte-Chapelle ⚛⚛⚛

This Gothic chapel (p. 197) is sublime, and entering its upper chapel is like climbing into Tiffany's most deluxe jewel box. As the colored light from the 13th-century windows shines through, you'll bathe in perhaps the most brilliantly colored "walls of glass" in the world. Taking in the deep glow of these astonishing windows is one of the great joys of a visit to the City of Light. The windows, the oldest in Paris, are known not only for their brilliant colors, but also for the vitality of their characters, including everybody from Adam and Eve to St. John the Baptist and the Virgin.

After a visit, it's time for lunch. Because first-day visitors have little time to absorb Left Bank life, here's your chance.

Continue east along quai des Orfèvres until you come to the Pont St-Michel. Cross the bridge to the Left Bank of Paris, arriving at the Latin Quarter centering on:

❽ Place St-Michel

One of the inner chambers of Left Bank life, this square was named in memory of the ancient chapel of St-Michel that stood here once upon a time. The square, a bustling hub of Sorbonne life, centers on a fountain from 1860 designed by Gabriel Davioud, rising 23m (75 ft.) high and stretching out to 5m (15 ft.), a "monster" spouting water. A bronze statue depicts Saint Michael fighting the dragon.

Why not do lunch in one of the most evocative of all Left Bank bistros?

☕ **ALLARD** ✸

Arm yourself with a good map to reach Allard, which lies only a 5-minute walk southwest of place St-Michel. You can easily get lost in the narrow maze of Left Bank streets. Little has changed at this classic bistro with its mellow decor and traditional menu. Against a nostalgic ambience of Paris of the 1930s, you can join cosmopolitan patrons enjoying the sole meunière or canard d'olives, finishing off with that most divine pastry known to all Parisians as *tarte tatin*. And, yes, if you've never tried them before, you'll find frogs' legs on the menu. See p. 164.

41 rue St-André-des-Arts, 6e. ✆ 01-43-26-48-23.

After lunch, walk back to place St-Michel.

Still on the Left Bank, continue east along quai St-Michel until it becomes quai de Montebello. At the "green lung" or park, square Rene Viviani, pause to take in the most dramatic view of Notre-Dame across the Seine. Then cross the bridge, Pont au Double, to visit the cathedral itself.

❿ Cathédrale de Notre-Dame ✸✸✸

In so many ways, the exterior is more exciting than the vast and hollow interior that, since its denuding during the French Revolution, is almost tomblike. One of the supreme masterpieces of Gothic art, Notre-Dame cathedral still evokes Victor Hugo's novel *The Hunchback of Notre-Dame.* You stand in awe, taking in the majestic and perfectly balanced portals. After a walk through the somber interior, climb the towers (around to the left facing the building) for a close encounter with tons of bells and an eerie inspection of what are history's most bizarre gargoyles, some so terribly impish that they seem to be mocking you. See p. 191.

After Notre-Dame, take the Métro to the:

⓫ Place de la Concorde ✸✸✸

This octagonal traffic hub, built in 1757, is dominated by an Egyptian obelisk from Luxor, the oldest manmade object in Paris, from 1200 B.C. In the Reign of Terror at the time of the French Revolution, the dreaded guillotine was erected on this spot to claim thousands of heads. For a spectacular view, look down the Champs-Elysées.

The grandest walk in Paris begins here, leading all the way to the Arc de Triomphe (see below). It's a distance of 3.2km (2 miles) and is the most popular walk in Paris.

However, since your afternoon is short, you may want to skip most of it, taking the Métro to F. D. Roosevelt and continuing west from there. At

least you'll see the busiest and most commercial part of the:

🔟 Champs-Elysées 🟊🟊🟊

Called "the highway of French grandeur," this boulevard was designed for promenading. It's witnessed some of the greatest moments in French history and some of its worst defeats, such as when Hitler's armies paraded down the street in 1940. Louis XIV ordered the construction of the 1.8km (1-mile) avenue in 1667. Without worrying about any particular monument, stroll along its avenue of sidewalk cafes, automobile showrooms, airline offices, cinemas, lingerie stores, and even hamburger joints. The Champs has obviously lost its *fin-de-siècle* elegance as evoked by Marcel Proust in *Remembrance of Things Past.* But then, what hasn't?

At the end of the broad boulevard, you approach:

🔟 Arc de Triomphe 🟊🟊🟊

The greatest triumphal arch in the world, the 49m (161-ft.) arch can be climbed for one of the most panoramic views of Paris. The arch marks the intersections of the 8th, 16th, and 17th arrondissements. Sculptures, including François Rude's famous *La Marseillaise,* depicting the uprising of 1792 (p. 180), are embedded in the arch.

With the afternoon fading, take the Métro to the Champ de Mars-Tour Eiffel for an ascent up the:

🔟 Tour Eiffel 🟊🟊🟊

It's open until 11pm or midnight, so don't worry about missing it. A close encounter with this tower, a 10,000-ton dark metal structure, is more inspiring up close than when seen from afar. A source of wonder since the 1889 World Exposition, this 317m (1,040-ft.) tower was the world's tallest building until the Chrysler Building went up in New York in 1930. If the afternoon is clear, you can see for 65km (40 miles). See p. 198.

2 The Best of Paris in 2 Days

If you've already made your way through "The Best of Paris in 1 Day," you'll find that your second full-day tour takes in other fascinating sections of Paris, including Ile St-Louis (the most beautiful island in the Seine) and Montmartre, (the hill crowning Paris), along with major attractions such as the greatest works of the Impressionists in the Musée d'Orsay, Napoleon's Tomb, and other amusements. ***Start:*** *the Pont-Marie Métro stop.*

❶ Ile St-Louis 🟊🟊

The neighboring island to La Cité is Ile St-Louis (p. 227), lying to the immediate east of the larger island. Beautiful antique town houses with charming courtyards, tree-shaded quays opening onto the Seine, mansions that once housed such famous literati as Voltaire and his mistress, antiques shops, and little restaurants and cafes fill the narrow streets on this island of platinum real estate. A great way to break in your second day in Paris is by wandering the streets and quays in

the early morning before the museums and attractions open. After arriving at Pont-Marie on the Right Bank, head south across the bridge, Pont-Marie, to Ile St-Louis. Cut immediately to your right and walk along quai de Bourbon. We suggest that you circle the entire Seine-bordering quays, including those south of the island, quai d'Orléans and quai de Béthune. When you reach square Barye in the far southeastern corner, take in the scenic view down river before crossing by Pont de Sully. At this point you can cut inland and walk the entire length of rue St-Louis-en-l'Ile, which will take you along the "main street" and the most historic part of the island.

After your stroll, take the Métro to Solférino.

❷ Musée d'Orsay 𝕬𝕬𝕬

This splendid museum will take up the rest of your morning, at least 2 hours. It shelters the world's greatest collection of the Impressionists, including all the old masters, such as Manet, Monet, and Van Gogh. You'll even get to see the fabled painting of *Whistler's Mother*—and it's by an American. This former railway station also presents a vast array of sculpture and decorative arts, with other departments devoted to architecture, photography, and cinema. Most of the works span the period from 1848 to 1914 and the beginning of World War I. To speed you on your way, English-language information is available at the entrance. Audio guides offer analyses of more than 50 masterpieces on display. See p. 194.

Because it's time for lunch, we suggest you eat on-site.

🍽 **RESTAURANT DU MUSÉE D'ORSAY**

Serving first-class cuisine, this elegant restaurant should be visited if only for its setting, although the food is excellent. Gabriel Ferrier designed this Belle Epoque room with its panoramic vista of the Seine and its splendid chandeliers. Main dishes are reasonably priced at 10€ to 18€ ($13–$23). Lunch is also served Tuesday to Sunday 11:30am to 2:30pm, afternoon tea from Friday to Wednesday 3:30 to 5:30pm, and dinner daily from Thursday 7 to 9:30pm. If you want something cheaper, you can patronize **Café des Hauteurs**, on the fifth floor behind one of the former train station's huge iron clocks. It's open Tuesday to Wednesday and Friday to Sunday 10am to 5pm, Thursday 10am to 9pm. For food on the run, patronize a self-service food stand directly above the cafe; it's open Tuesday to Sunday 11am to 5pm. 1 rue de Bellechasse, 7e. 🕿 **01-40-49-48-14.**

After lunch, take the Métro to:

❹ Hotel des Invalides/Napoleon's Tomb 𝕬𝕬𝕬

Still beloved by many French people, the little megalomaniac who tried to conquer Europe lies locked away (or at least his remains are) with some of his family members in six coffins of red Finnish porphyry. After seeing the tomb in Eglise du Dome, you can leave at once or else take a quick look at the **Musée de l'Armée** located here. This is a gaudy celebration of French military history, but most first-timers to Paris skip it. See p. 193.

From Invalides take the Métro over to the Right Bank, getting off at the Alma-Marceau stop. Here, you can embark on one of the:

❺ Bateaux-Mouche Cruises of the Seine

We know of no better way to enjoy Paris than on one of these scenic boat tours from the riverbank point of view. They allow for one of the most dramatic vistas of Notre-Dame. Tours depart every 20 to 30 minutes during the day and are in English, lasting about 75 minutes. First, you sail east all the way to Ile St-Louis, and then you return west past the Eiffel Tower.

As the afternoon fades, head for "the top of Paris," the legendary Montmartre district, reached by Métro going north to the Abbesses stop.

❻ Basilique du Sacré-Coeur 𝕬𝕬

Before heading for Sacré-Coeur, you can wander around the legendary square, **place du Tertre** (p. 181 of our walking tour of Montmartre). Dozens of young artists wait for you to give them the nod to paint your portrait. This may sound corny to sophisticated travelers, but thousands of visitors consider these portraits their most memorable souvenirs of Paris. Perhaps your portrait will be painted by tomorrow's Toulouse-Lautrec. The basilica of Sacré-Coeur, or the Church of the

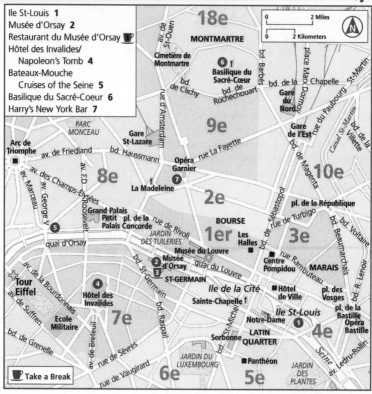

Ile St-Louis **1**
Musée d'Orsay **2**
Restaurant du Musée d'Orsay **3**
Hôtel des Invalides/
  Napoleon's Tomb **4**
Bateaux-Mouche
  Cruises of the Seine **5**
Basilique du Sacré-Coeur **6**
Harry's New York Bar **7**

Sacred Heart, with its many cupolas, is a brilliant white and as much a part of the Paris skyline as the Eiffel Tower. Ascend to the dome at 80m (262 ft.) for one of the greatest panoramas in all of Europe, extending for 65km (40 miles) on a clear afternoon. After coming down from the dome, we always like to sit with dozens of other visitors on the steps of Sacré-Coeur, watching the afternoon fade and the lights go on all over Paris.

After dinner, perhaps in one of the little bistros that surround place du Tertre, head for a Paris landmark for your final toast to the City of Light. Take the Métro to Opéra or Pyramides.

❼ Harry's New York Bar

This is the official headquarters of the International Bar Flies (p. 291). Such cocktails as the Bloody Mary, the Sidecar, and the White Lady were created here. The bar looks much as it did at the time of the Liberation, when Hemingway was one of its patrons. The main bar attracts sports fans, especially rugby rooters, but the downstairs piano bar is more attuned to a romantic conversation over a cocktail.

A final stroll through the streets of Paris before turning in will be your *adieu* to the favorite city of everybody (well, almost).

3 The Best of Paris in 3 Days

Having survived 2 days in the capital of France, you are by now a veteran Parisian. Now it's time to "Hit the Road, Jack" (or Jill) and head for the single most glorious monument to pomp and pomposity that France ever erected to royal pretensions and kingly vanity. *Start: RER line C to Versailles Rive Gauche station.*

---

❶ Château de Versailles ✫✫✫

There is nothing in all of Paris to equal this regal wonder, former stomping ground of everyone from Madame de Pompadour, the royal mistress, to Marie Antoinette, the Austrian princess doomed to marry a French king who lost his head. The palace opens at 9am, so try to arrive at that time because it will take a minimum of 3 hours to see just some of the highlights.

A first-time visitor will want to concentrate on the **Grands Appartements** ✫✫✫, the glittering **Hall of Mirrors** ✫✫✫, and the **Petits Appartements** ✫✫ where Louis XV died in 1774 of smallpox. Other "don't miss" attractions include the **Opéra** that Gabriel designed for Louis XV in 1748 and the **Royal Chapel** ✫✫✫ that Hardouin-Mansart didn't live to complete. There's more. For your final hour, wander through Le Nôtre's "Garden of Eden"—in other words, the **Gardens of Versailles** ✫✫✫, paying a visit to the **Grand Trianon** ✫✫ where Nixon once slept in the room in which Madame de Pompadour died, and the **Petit Trianon** ✫✫ that Louis XV used for trysts with his mistress, Madame du Barry. See p. 294.

⓶ LE POTAGER DU ROY ✫

This is one of the best of the middle-bracket restaurants of Versailles. Philippe Letourneur makes it easy for you by offering one of the best, most generous, and well-prepared *prix-fixe* menus in Versailles, although it's rather pricey. The choice of ingredients is skillful and the preparation inventive. The menu is adjusted to take advantage of the best produce of any season.
1 rue du Maréchal-Joffre. ✆ **01-39-50-35-34.** See p. 299.

Note: Should your time be too precious for a sit-down meal, you can have a fast lunch on the run and save those dwindling hours to see more of Paris itself. You can visit a deli in the morning before leaving Paris and secure the makings of a *piquenique,* which you can enjoy by the canal in the Gardens of Versailles after touring the palace. Within various corners of the gardens, you'll also encounter snack bars discreetly tucked away. There's even a McDonald's on the walk back from the palace to the train station, which you'll need to visit anyway to take the RER back to Paris.

Once in Paris, take the Métro to Rambuteau, Hôtel-de-Ville, or Châtelet-Les Halles to visit:

❸ Centre Pompidou ✫✫✫

The exterior is controversial, called daringly innovative and avant-garde or else "the eyesore of Paris." But inside, virtually everyone agrees that this museum dominating Beaubourg is a repository of one of the world's greatest collections of modern art. Amazingly, more art lovers visit Pompidou per day than they do the Louvre or the Eiffel Tower. Beginning with Rousseau's *Snake Charmer* and ending with the latest acquisition from the 21st century, you can view the greatest modern artists of the 20th century: the inevitable Picassos, but also Chagall, Francis Bacon, Calder, Magritte, Matisse, Mondrian, Pollock, Kandinsky—and the beat goes on. Allow at least 2 hours. See p. 199.

Take the Métro to:

❹ Place des Vosges ✫✫✫

Having tasted the glories of such districts as Montmartre and Ile St-Louis, it's time

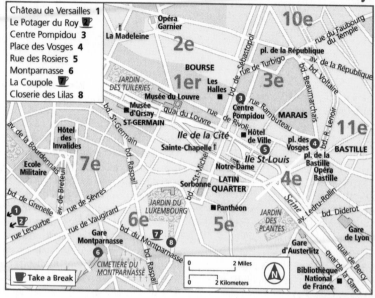

Château de Versailles **1**
Le Potager du Roy **2**
Centre Pompidou **3**
Place des Vosges **4**
Rue des Rosiers **5**
Montparnasse **6**
La Coupole **7**
Closerie des Lilas **8**

Take a Break

to discover the charms of one of Paris's most enchanting neighborhoods, the Marais. Place des Vosges, one of the world's most perfectly designed and harmonious squares, is found at the very center of the Marais. For those with extra time, we've designed a complete walking tour of the Marais (p. 243). But most 3-day visitors, especially if they visit Versailles, will not have time to see the entire district.

The oldest square in Paris is flanked by 36 matching pavilions with red-and-gold brick-and-stone facades. Architecturally, this square represents the first time in Paris that an arcade was used to link houses. Balconies were also designed for the first time—not just for decorative reasons, but to be used. The most famous resident of this square (no. 6) was the French writer Victor Hugo, who lived here from 1833 to 1848 until Napoleon III came to power and Hugo fled into voluntary exile in the Channel Islands. His home is now a museum (p. 219), which at this point may have to be saved until your next trip to Paris.

Arm yourself with a good map and spend at least an hour wandering the narrow Marais streets to the west of place des Vosges. You can make discoveries on every block as you explore trendy cafes and funky shops. At the northern tier of the place des Vosges, head west along rue des Francs Bourgeois, one of the most historic streets.

At some point, dip south to visit the parallel street:

⑤ Rue des Rosiers

"The Street of Rose Bushes" (its English name) remains from the heyday of the old Jewish ghetto that once flourished here. The street, deep in the heart of the Marais, is still packed with kosher butchers, bakeries, and falafel shops. In the 1960s, the waves of North African Sephardim radically changed the street. In World War II, despite Nazi attempts to exterminate the Jews, their families survived and are still living in the Marais. A synagogue is at 25 rue des Rosiers.

One more famous neighborhood awaits discovery.

⑥ Montparnasse ✦✦✦

Take the Métro to Montparnasse-Bienvenüe. Montparnasse was once the retreat of bohemian artists and the working class. Today, it's been as successfully gentrified with urban renewal projects as the Marais. The district teems with cafes (many of literary fame), cinemas, and nightclubs, along with artisan shops and bars. For a description of some of the highlights of the area, see coverage beginning on p. 229. For the best overview, take an elevator to the 56th floor of **Tour Montparnasse** (© 01-45-38-52-56), which, when it was built, was accused of bringing Manhattan to Paris. The tower, completed in 1973, rises 206m (676 ft.) above the Parisian skyline.

After taking in the view, descend on the most famous cafe of Montparnasse.

⑦ LA COUPOLE ✦

One doesn't see as many writers and publishers as before, but this is still the best viewing platform for Montparnasse life. In this citadel to the bohemian life of Paris in the 1920s and 1930s, Hemingway, Picasso, and Louis Armstrong once scribbled, sketched, or composed. Chanteuse Josephine Baker would show up accompanied by her lion cub, and Jean-Paul Sartre would dine here. Eugène Ionesco always ordered the *café liegeois*. Henry Miller came for his morning porridge, and the famous "Kiki of Montparnasse" picked up tricks here to service back in her hotel room. James Joyce patronized the joint, as did F. Scott Fitzgerald when he didn't have much money; when the royalty check came in, he fled to the Ritz Bar. Join the local fauna for the memories if for no other reason.

102 bd. du Montparnasse, 14e. © 01-43-20-14-20. See p. 175.

You can order drinks here and sit back to enjoy the cafe scene in Montparnasse, perhaps not as colorful as in days gone by, but still a lively, bustling place to be at night.

For dinner on your final night, head for a restaurant that is a virtual sightseeing attraction as well as a place for food:

⑧ Closerie des Lilas ✦

After taking the Métro Port Royal or Vavin, descend on this legend that has been wining and dining some of the most famous figures of the past 2 centuries since it opened back in 1847. It is "The Pleasure Garden of the Lilacs" (its English name), a virtual French monument. Follow the sounds of a jazz pianist and enter its hallowed precincts, heading for the *bateau* (boat) section for a champagne julep (the bartender's special). You can dine expensively in the main restaurant with formal service or else enjoy the more democratically priced brasserie. Should you be on the strictest of budgets, you can order a coffee or beer at the bar and soak up the atmosphere, the way Hemingway did between royalty checks when he was broke and had to kill a pigeon in the park for his dinner. Today, the lilacs of its namesake no longer bloom, Trotsky has long been assassinated, and Henry James is a mere skeleton of himself (if that). But young Parisians, including rising film stars, models, the pretty, and the chic, still patronize the place, giving you a close encounter with Paris after dark. And, yes, it's still going in August when the rest of the town shuts down. Have a nightcap at the bar and promise a return to Paris.

171 bd. du Montparnasse, 6e. © 01-40-51-34-50. See p 163.

5

Getting to Know the City of Light

Ernest Hemingway called the many splendors of Paris a "moveable feast" and wrote, "There is never any ending to Paris, and the memory of each person who has lived in it differs from that of any other." It's this aura of personal discovery that has always been the most compelling reason to come to Paris. Perhaps that's why France has been called *le deuxième pays de tout le monde* (everybody's second country).

The Seine not only divides Paris into the Right Bank and the Left Bank, but also seems to split the city into two vastly different sections and ways of life. Depending on your time, interest, and budget, you may quickly decide which section of Paris suits you best.

The old clichés about the Left Bank being for poor, struggling artists and the Right Bank being for the well-heeled were broken down long ago. The very heart of the Left Bank, including the areas around Odéon and St-Germain-des-Prés, are as chic as anything on the Right Bank—and just as expensive.

The history of Paris repeats itself. In the old days, Montmartre was the artists' quarter until prices and tourism drove these "bohemians" to less expensive *quartiers* such as Montparnasse. But Montparnasse long ago became gold-plated real estate.

So where does the struggling artist go today? Not to the central core of the Right or Left Bank, but farther afield. First, it was the Marais, until that district, too, saw rents spiral and the average visitor carried an American Express gold card. Now it's farther east, into the 11th Arrondissement, a blue-collar neighborhood between the Marais, Ménilmontant, and République. The heartbeat of this area is rue Oberkampf.

1 Essentials

VISITOR INFORMATION

The **Paris Convention and Visitors Bureau** (© **08-92-68-30-00;** 0.35€/45¢ per minute; www.paris-info.com) has offices throughout the city, with the main headquarters at 25–27 rue des Pyramides, 1er (Métro: Pyramides). It's open Monday to Saturday 10am to 7pm, Sunday and holidays from 11am to 7pm. Less comprehensive branch offices include **Opéra-Grands Magasins,** 11 rue Scribe, 9e (Métro: Opera), open Monday to Saturday 9am to 6:30pm; **Espace Tourisme Ile-de-France,** in the Carrousel du Louvre, 99 rue de Rivoli, 1er (Métro: Palais–Royal–Louvre), open daily 10am to 7pm; in the **Gare de Lyon,** 20 bd. Diderot, Paris 12e (Métro: Gare de Lyon), open Monday to Saturday 8am to 6pm; in the **Gare du Nord,** 18 rue de Dunkerque, 10e (Métro: Gare du Nord), open daily 8am to 6pm; and in **Montmartre,** 21 place du Tertre, 18e (Métro: Abbesses or Lamarck–Caulaincourt), open daily 10am to 7pm. You can walk in at any branch to make a hotel reservation; the service charge is free

> **Tips Country & City Telephone Codes**
>
> The country code for France is **33**. The city code for Paris (as well as for all cities in the Ile de France region) is **1**; use this code if you're calling from outside France. If you're calling Paris from within Paris or from anywhere else in France, use **01**, which is now built into all phone numbers in the Ile de France, making them 10 digits long.

for hostels and between 2€ to 6€ ($2.60–$7.80) for hotels, depending on their category and price range. The offices are extremely busy year-round, especially in midsummer, so be prepared to wait in line.

CITY LAYOUT

Paris is surprisingly compact. Occupying 105 sq. km (41 sq. miles), it's home to more than 2.15 million people. The city is divided into 20 municipal wards called **arrondissements,** each with its own mayor, city hall, police station, and central post office. Some even have remnants of market squares.

The river Seine divides Paris into the *Rive Droite* **(Right Bank)** to the north and the *Rive Gauche* **(Left Bank)** to the south. These designations make sense when you stand on a bridge and face downstream; watching the water flow out toward the sea, to your right is the north bank, to your left, the south. Thirty-two bridges link the banks of the Seine, some providing access to the two small islands at the heart of the city, **Ile de la Cité,** the city's birthplace and site of Notre-Dame, and **Ile St-Louis,** a moat-guarded oasis of sober 17th-century mansions. These islands can cause some confusion to walkers who think they've just crossed a bridge from one bank to the other, only to find themselves caught up in an almost medieval maze of narrow streets and old buildings.

The "main street" on the Right Bank is the **Champs-Elysées,** beginning at the Arc de Triomphe and running to place de la Concorde. Haussmann also created avenue de l'Opéra (as well as the Opéra) and the 12 avenues that radiate starlike from the Arc de Triomphe, giving it its original name, place de l'Etoile (the star); it was renamed place Charles de Gaulle following the general's death and is often referred to as **place Charles de Gaulle–Etoile.**

FINDING AN ADDRESS

The key to finding any address in Paris is looking for the arrondissement number, rendered either as a number followed by "e" (2e, 3e, and so on) or more formally as part of the postal code (the last two digits indicate the arrondissement—75007 indicates the 7th Arrondissement, 75017 the 17th). Numbers on buildings running parallel to the Seine usually follow the course of the river—east to west. On north–south streets, numbering begins at the river.

If you're staying more than 2 or 3 days, buy one of the inexpensive little books that include the *plan de Paris* by arrondissement, available at all major newsstands and bookshops. If you can find it, the forest-green "Paris Classique l'Indispensable" is a thorough, well-indexed, and accurate guide to the city and its suburbs. Most map guides provide you with a Métro map, a foldout map of the city, and indexed maps of each arrondissement, with all streets listed and keyed. We've given you a head start by including a **full-color foldout map** at the back of this guide.

ARRONDISSEMENTS IN BRIEF

Each of Paris's 20 arrondissements possesses a unique style and flavor. You'll want to decide which district appeals most to you and then try to find accommodations there. Later on, try to visit as many areas as you can so you get the full taste of Paris.

For a map of Paris's arrondissements, please refer to the color map titled "Neighborhoods of Paris" at the beginning of this book.

1ST ARRONDISSEMENT (MUSEE DU LOUVRE/LES HALLES) "I never knew what a palace was until I had a glimpse of the Louvre," wrote Nathaniel Hawthorne. Perhaps the world's greatest art museum, the **Louvre,** a former royal residence, still lures visitors to the 1st Arrondissement. Walk through the **Jardin des Tuileries,** Paris's most formal garden (laid out by Le Nôtre, gardener to Louis XIV). Pause to take in the classic beauty of **place Vendôme,** the opulent home of the Hôtel Ritz. Zola's "belly of Paris" (Les Halles) is no longer the food-and-meat market of Paris (traders moved to the new, more accessible suburb of Rungis); today the **Forum des Halles** is a center of shopping, entertainment, and culture.

2ND ARRONDISSEMENT (LA BOURSE) Home to the **Bourse** (stock exchange), this Right Bank district lies between the Grands Boulevards and rue Etienne-Marcel. From Monday to Friday, brokers play the market until it's time to break for lunch, when the movers and shakers of French capitalism channel their hysteria into the area restaurants. Much of the eastern end of the arrondissement (**Le Sentier**) is devoted to wholesale outlets of the Paris garment district, where thousands of garments are sold (usually in bulk) to buyers from clothing stores throughout Europe. "Everything that exists elsewhere exists in Paris," wrote Victor Hugo in Les Misérables, and this district provides ample evidence of that.

3RD ARRONDISSEMENT (LE MARAIS) This district embraces much of Le Marais (the swamp), one of the best-loved Right Bank neighborhoods. (It extends into the 4th as well.) After decades of decay, Le Marais recently made a comeback, though it may never again enjoy the prosperity of its 17th-century aristocratic heyday; today it contains Paris's **gay neighborhood,** with lots of gay/lesbian restaurants, bars, and stores, as well as the remains of the old Jewish quarter, centered on **rue des Rosiers.** Two of the chief attractions are the **Musée Picasso,** a kind of pirate's ransom of painting and sculpture, which the Picasso estate had to turn over to the French government in lieu of the artist's astronomical death duties, and the **Musée Carnavalet,** which brings to life the history of Paris from prehistoric times to the present.

4TH ARRONDISSEMENT (ILE DE LA CITE/ILE ST-LOUIS & BEAUBOURG) It seems as if the 4th has it all: Notre-Dame on Ile de la Cité, and Ile St-Louis and its aristocratic town houses, courtyards, and antiques shops. **Ile St-Louis,** a former cow pasture and dueling ground, is home to dozens of 17th-century mansions and 6,000 lucky Louisiens, its permanent residents. Seek out **Ile de la Cité**'s two Gothic churches, **Sainte-Chapelle** and **Notre-Dame,** a majestic structure that, according to poet E. E. Cummings, "doesn't budge an inch for all the idiocies of this world." You'll find France's finest bird and flower markets along with the nation's law courts, which Balzac described as a "cathedral of chicanery." It was here that Marie Antoinette was sentenced

to death in 1793. The 4th is also home to the freshly renovated **Centre Pompidou,** one of the top three attractions in France. After all this pomp and glory, you can retreat to **place des Vosges,** a square of perfect harmony and beauty where Victor Hugo lived from 1832 to 1848 and penned many of his famous masterpieces. (His house is now a museum—see p. 219.)

5TH ARRONDISSEMENT (QUARTIER LATIN)

The Latin Quarter is the intellectual heart and soul of Paris. Bookstores, schools, churches, clubs, student dives, Roman ruins, publishing houses, and expensive boutiques characterize the district. Discussions of Artaud or Molière over cups of coffee may be rarer than in the past, but they aren't out of place. Beginning with the founding of the **Sorbonne** in 1253, the quarter was called Latin because students and professors spoke the language. You'll follow in the footsteps of Descartes, Verlaine, Camus, Sartre, James Thurber, Elliot Paul, and Hemingway as you explore. Changing times have brought Greek, Moroccan, and Vietnamese immigrants, among others, offering everything from couscous to fiery-hot spring rolls and souvlaki. The 5th borders the Seine, and you'll want to stroll along quai de Montebello, inspecting the inventories of the *bouquinistes* (secondhand-book dealers), who sell everything from antique Daumier prints to yellowing copies of Balzac's *Père Goriot* in the shadow of Notre-Dame. The 5th also has the **Panthéon,** built by Louis XV after he recovered from gout and wanted to do something nice for St. Geneviève, Paris's patron saint. It's the resting place of Rousseau, Gambetta, Zola, Braille, Hugo, Voltaire, and Jean Moulin, the World War II Resistance leader whom the Gestapo tortured to death.

6TH ARRONDISSEMENT (ST-GERMAIN/LUXEMBOURG)

This is the heartland of Paris publishing and, for some, the most colorful Left Bank quarter, where waves of young artists still emerge from the Ecole des Beaux-Arts. The secret of the district lies in discovering its narrow streets, hidden squares, and magnificent gardens. To be really authentic, stroll with an unwrapped loaf of sourdough bread from the wood-fired ovens of **Poilâne** at 8 rue du Cherche-Midi. Everywhere you turn, you'll encounter historic and literary associations, nowhere more so than on **rue Jacob.** At no. 7, Racine lived with his uncle as a teenager; Richard Wagner resided at no. 14 from 1841 to 1842; Ingres lived at no. 27 (now it's the office of the French publishing house Editions du Seuil); and Hemingway once occupied a tiny upstairs room at no. 44. The 6th takes in the **Jardin du Luxembourg,** a 24-hectare (59-acre) playground where Isadora Duncan went dancing in the predawn hours and a destitute Ernest Hemingway went looking for pigeons for lunch, carrying them in a baby carriage back to his humble flat for cooking.

7TH ARRONDISSEMENT (EIFFEL TOWER/MUSEE D'ORSAY)

Paris's most famous symbol, **la Tour Eiffel,** dominates Paris and especially the 7th, a Left Bank district of residences and offices. The tower is one of the most recognizable landmarks in the world, despite the fact that many Parisians (especially its nearest neighbors) hated it when it was unveiled in 1889. Many of Paris's most imposing monuments are in the 7th, like the **Hôtel des Invalides,** which contains Napoleon's Tomb and the Musée de l'Armée, and the **Musée d'Orsay,** the world's premier showcase of 19th-century French art and culture, housed in the old Gare d'Orsay. But there's much hidden charm here as well. **Rue du Bac** was home to the swashbuckling heroes of Dumas's *The Three Musketeers* and to James McNeill Whistler, who moved to no. 110 after selling *Mother.* Auguste Rodin lived at what's now the **Musée Rodin,** 77 rue de Varenne, until his death in 1917.

8TH ARRONDISSEMENT (CHAMPS-ELYSEES/MADELEINE) The showcase of the 8th is the **Champs-Elysées,** stretching from the **Arc de Triomphe** to the Egyptian obelisk on **place de la Concorde.** By the 1980s, the Champs-Elysées had become a garish strip, with too much traffic, too many fast-food joints, and panhandlers. In the 1990s, Jacques Chirac, then the Gaullist mayor, launched a cleanup, broadening the sidewalks and planting new trees. Now you'll find fashion houses, elegant hotels, restaurants, and shops. Everything in the 8th is the city's best, grandest, and most impressive. It has the best restaurant **(Taillevent),** the sexiest strip joint **(Crazy Horse Saloon),** the most splendid square **(place de la Concorde),** the best rooftop cafe **(La Samaritaine),** the grandest hotel (the **Crillon**), the most impressive arch **(Arc de Triomphe),** the most expensive residential street **(avenue Montaigne),** the world's oldest subway station **(Franklin-D.-Roosevelt),** and the most ancient monument (the 3,300-year-old **Obelisk of Luxor**).

9TH ARRONDISSEMENT (OPERA GARNIER/PIGALLE) From the Quartier de l'Opéra to the strip joints of Pigalle (the infamous "Pig Alley" of World War II GIs), the 9th endures, even if fashion prefers other addresses. Over the decades, the 9th has been celebrated in literature and song for the music halls that brought gaiety to the city. The building at 17 bd. de la Madeleine was where Marie Duplessis, who gained fame as the heroine Marguerite Gautier in Alexandre Dumas the younger's *La Dame aux Camellias,* died. (Greta Garbo played her in the film *Camille.*) **Place Pigalle** has nightclubs, but is no longer home to cafe La Nouvelle Athènes, where Degas, Pissarro, and Manet used to meet. Other attractions include the **Folies-Bergère,** where cancan dancers have been high-kicking since 1868. It is the rococo **Opéra Garnier** (home of the Phantom) that made the 9th the last hurrah of Second Empire opulence. Renoir hated it, but generations later, Chagall painted its ceilings. Pavlova danced *Swan Lake* here, and Nijinsky took the night off to go cruising.

10TH ARRONDISSEMENT (GARE DU NORD/GARE DE L'EST) The **Gare du Nord** and **Gare de l'Est,** along with porno houses and dreary commercial zones, make the 10th one of the least desirable arrondissements for living, dining, or sightseeing. We try to avoid it except for one of our longtime favorite restaurants: **Brasserie Flo** (© **01-47-70-13-59**), 7 cour des Petites-Ecuries, best known for its formidable *choucroute,* a heap of sauerkraut garnished with everything.

11TH ARRONDISSEMENT (OPERA BASTILLE) For many years, this quarter seemed to sink lower and lower into decay, overcrowded by working-class immigrants from the far reaches of the former Empire. The opening of the **Opéra Bastille,** however, has given the 11th new hope and new life. The facility, called the "people's opera house," stands on the landmark place de la Bastille, where on July 14, 1789, 633 Parisians stormed the fortress and seized the ammunition depot, as the French Revolution swept across the city. Over the years, the prison held such luminaries as Voltaire and the

Marquis de Sade. The area between the Marais, Ménilmontant, and République is now being called "blue-collar chic," as the *artistes* of Paris who've been driven from the costlier sections of the Marais can now be found walking the gritty sidewalks of rue Oberkampf. Hip Parisians in search of a more cutting-edge experience are now living and working among the decaying 19th-century apartments and the 1960s public housing with graffiti-splattered walls.

12TH ARRONDISSEMENT (BOIS DE VINCENNES/GARE DE LYON) Very few out-of-towners came here until a French chef opened a restaurant called **Au Trou Gascon** (p. 144). The 12th's major attraction remains the **Bois de Vincennes,** sprawling on the eastern periphery of Paris. This park is a longtime favorite of French families who enjoy its zoos and museums, its royal châteaux and boating lakes, and its **Parc Floral de Paris,** a celebrated flower garden boasting springtime rhododendrons and autumn dahlias. Venture into the dreary **Gare de Lyon** for **Le Train Bleu,** 20 bd. Diderot (✆ **01-43-43-09-06**), in the Gare de Lyon, 12e, a restaurant whose ceiling frescoes and Art Nouveau decor are national artistic treasures; the food is good, too. The 12th, once a depressing urban wasteland, has been singled out for budgetary resuscitation and is beginning to sport new housing, shops, gardens, and restaurants. Many will occupy the site of the former Reuilly rail tracks.

13TH ARRONDISSEMENT (GARE D'AUSTERLITZ) Centered on the grimy **Gare d'Austerlitz,** the 13th might have its devotees, but we've yet to meet one. British snobs who flitted in and out of the train station were among the first of the district's foreign

visitors and wrote the 13th off as a dreary working-class counterpart of London's East End. The 13th is also home to Paris's **Chinatown,** stretching for 13 square blocks around the Tolbiac Métro stop. It emerged out of the refugee crisis at the end of the Vietnam War, taking over a neighborhood that held mostly Arab-speaking peoples. Today, recognizing overcrowding in the district, the Paris civic authorities are imposing new, not particularly welcome, restrictions on population densities.

14TH ARRONDISSEMENT (MONTPARNASSE) The northern end of this large arrondissement is devoted to **Montparnasse,** home of the "Lost Generation" and stomping ground of Stein, Toklas, Hemingway, and other American expatriates of the 1920s. After World War II, it ceased to be the center of intellectual life, but the memory lingers in its cafes. One of the monuments that sets the tone of the neighborhood is **Rodin's statue of Balzac** at the junction of boulevards Montparnasse and Raspail. At this corner are some of the world's most famous **literary cafes,** including La Rotonde, Le Select, La Dôme, and La Coupole. Though Gertrude Stein avoided them (she loathed cafes), other American expats, including Hemingway and Fitzgerald, had no qualms about enjoying a drink here (or quite a few of them, for that matter). Stein stayed at home (27 rue de Fleurus) with Alice B. Toklas, collecting paintings, including those of Picasso, and entertaining the likes of Max Jacob, Apollinaire, T. S. Eliot, and Matisse.

15TH ARRONDISSEMENT (GARE MONTPARNASSE/INSTITUT PASTEUR) This is a mostly residential district beginning at **Gare Montparnasse** and stretching to the Seine.

In size and population, it's the largest quarter of Paris, but it draws few tourists and has few attractions except for the **Parc des Expositions,** the **Cimetière du Montparnasse,** and the **Institut Pasteur.** In the early 20th century, many artists—like Chagall, Léger, and Modigliani—lived here in a shared atelier known as "The Beehive."

16TH ARRONDISSEMENT (TROCADERO/BOIS DE BOULOGNE)

Originally the village of Passy, where Benjamin Franklin lived during most of his time in Paris, this district is still reminiscent of Proust's world. Highlights include the **Bois de Boulogne;** the **Jardin du Trocadéro;** the **Maison de Balzac;** the **Musée Guimet** (famous for its Asian collections); and the **Cimetière de Passy,** resting place of Manet, Talleyrand, Giraudoux, and Debussy. One of the largest arrondissements, it's known today for its well-heeled bourgeoisie, its upscale rents, and some rather posh (and, according to its critics, rather smug) residential boulevards. The arrondissement also has the best vantage point to view the Eiffel Tower: **place du Trocadéro.**

17TH ARRONDISSEMENT (PARC MONCEAU/PLACE CLICHY)

Flanking the northern periphery of Paris, the 17th incorporates neighborhoods of bourgeois respectability (in its west end) and less affluent neighborhoods in its east end. It boasts two of the great restaurants of Paris, **Guy Savoy** and **Michel Rostang** (see chapter 7, "Where to Dine").

18TH ARRONDISSEMENT (MONTMARTRE)

The 18th is the most famous outer quarter of Paris, containing **Montmartre,** the **Moulin Rouge, Sacré-Coeur,** and ultratouristy **place du Tertre.** Utrillo was its native son, Renoir lived here, and Toulouse-Lautrec adopted the area as his own. The most famous enclave of artists in Paris's history, the **Bateau-Lavoir** of Picasso fame, gathered here. Max Jacob, Matisse, and Braque were all frequent visitors. Today, place Blanche is known for its prostitutes, and Montmartre is filled with honky-tonks, souvenir shops, and terrible restaurants. You can still find pockets of quiet beauty, though. The city's most famous flea market, the **Marché aux Puces de Clignancourt,** is another landmark.

19TH ARRONDISSEMENT (LA VILLETTE)

Today, visitors come to what was once the village of La Villette to see the angular **Cité des Sciences et de l'Industrie,** a spectacular science museum and park built on a site that for years was devoted to the city's slaughterhouses. Mostly residential and not at all upscale, the district is one of the most ethnically diverse in Paris, the home of people from all parts of the former Empire. A highlight is **Les Buttes Chaumont,** a park where kids can enjoy puppet shows and donkey rides.

20TH ARRONDISSEMENT (PERE-LACHAISE CEMETERY)

The 20th's greatest landmark is **Père-Lachaise Cemetery,** the resting place of Edith Piaf, Marcel Proust, Oscar Wilde, Isadora Duncan, Sarah Bernhardt, Gertrude Stein and Alice B. Toklas, Colette, Jim Morrison, and many others. Otherwise, the 20th arrondissement is a dreary and sometimes volatile melting pot comprising residents from France's former colonies. Though nostalgia buffs sometimes head here to visit Piaf's former neighborhood, **Ménilmontant-Belleville,** it has been almost totally bulldozed and rebuilt since the bad old days when she grew up here.

Around Paris

for strollers who enjoy rambling through unexpected alleyways and
plazas. Only when you're dead tired and can't walk another step, or have to go all the
way across town in a hurry, should you consider using the Métro, a swift but dull
means of urban transport.

BY METRO (SUBWAY) The Métro (© 08-92-68-77-14; www.ratp.fr) is the most
efficient and fastest way to get around Paris. All lines are numbered, and the final destination of each line is clearly marked on subway maps, in the system's underground
passageways, and on the train cars. The Métro runs daily from 5:30am to 1:15am. It's
reasonably safe at any hour, but beware of pickpockets.

To familiarize yourself with the Métro, check out the color map on the inside back
cover of this book. Most stations display a map of the Métro at the entrance. To locate
your correct train on a map, find your destination, follow the line to the end of its
route, and note the name of the final stop, which is that line's direction. In the station, follow the signs for your direction in the passageways until you see the label on
a train. Many larger stations have maps with push-button indicators that light up your
route when you press the button for your destination.

Transfer stations are *correspondances*—some require long walks; Châtelet is the most
difficult—but most trips require only one transfer. When transferring, follow the
orange CORRESPONDANCE signs to the proper platform. Don't follow a SORTIE (exit)
sign, or you'll have to pay again to get back on the train.

On the urban lines, one ticket for 1.40€ ($1.80) lets you travel to any point. On
the Sceaux, Boissy-St-Léger, and St-Germain-en-Laye lines to the suburbs, fares are
based on distance. A *carnet* is the best buy—10 tickets for about 11€ ($14).

At the turnstile entrances to the station, insert your ticket and pass through. At
some exits, tickets are also checked, so hold onto yours. There are occasional ticket
checks on trains and platforms and in passageways, too.

Value Discount Transit Passes

The **Paris-Visite** (© 08-92-68-77-14) is valid for 1, 2, 3, or 5 days on public
transport, including the Métro, buses, the funicular ride to Montmartre,
and RER trains. For access to zones 1 to 3, which includes central Paris and
its nearby suburbs, its cost ranges from 8.50€ ($11) for 1 day to 27€ ($35)
for 5 days. Get it at RATP (Régie Autonome des Transports Parisiens) offices,
the tourist office, and Métro stations.

Another discount pass is **Carte Mobilis,** which allows unlimited travel on
bus, subway, and RER lines during a 1-day period for 5.50€ to 19€ ($7.15–
$25), depending on the zone. Ask for it at any Métro station.

Most economical, for anyone who arrives in Paris early in the week, is a
Carte Orange. Sold at large Métro stations, it allows 1 week of unlimited
Métro or bus transit within central Paris and its immediate outskirts for 16€
to 44€ ($21–$57). The pass is valid from any Monday to the following Sunday, and it's sold only on Monday, Tuesday, and Wednesday. You'll have to
submit a passport-size photo.

RER TRAINS   A suburban train system, RER (Réseau Express Regional) passes through the heart of Paris, traveling faster than the Métro and running daily from 5:30am to 12:30am. This system works like the Métro and requires the same tickets. The major stops within central Paris, linking the RER to the Métro, are Nation, Gare de Lyon, Charles de Gaulle-Etoile, and Gare-Etoile, and Gare du Nord as well as Châtelet-Les-Halles. All of these stops are on the Right Bank. On the Left Bank, RER stops include Denfert-Rochereau and St-Michel. The five RER lines are marked A through E. Different branches are labeled by a number, the C5 Line serving Versailles-Rive Gauche, for example. Electric signboards next to each track outline all the possible stops along the way. Make sure that the little square next to your intended stop is lit.

BY BUS   Buses are much slower than the Métro. The majority run from 6:30am to 9:30pm (a few operate until 12:30am, and 10 operate during early morning hours). Service is limited on Sundays and holidays. Bus and Métro fares are the same; you can use the same tickets on both. Most bus rides require one ticket, but some destinations require two (never more than two within the city limits).

At certain stops, signs list destinations and bus numbers serving that point. Destinations are usually listed north to south and east to west. Most stops are also posted on the sides of the buses. During rush hours, you may have to take a ticket from a dispensing machine, indicating your position in the line at the stop.

If you intend to use the buses a lot, pick up an RATP bus map at the office on place de la Madeleine, 8e, or at the tourist offices at RATP headquarters, 54 Quai de La Rapée, 12e. For detailed recorded information (in English) on bus and Métro routes, call © **01-58-76-16-16.** Open Monday to Friday 7am to 9pm.

The RATP also operates the **Balabus,** big-windowed orange-and-white motor coaches that run only during limited hours: Sunday and national holidays from noon to 8:30pm, from April 15 to the end of September. Itineraries run in both directions between Gare de Lyon and the Grande Arche de La Défense, encompassing some of the city's most beautiful vistas. It's a great deal—three Métro tickets, for 1.40€ ($1.80) each, will carry you the entire route. You'll recognize the bus and the route it follows by the Bb symbol emblazoned on each bus's side and on signs posted beside the route it follows.

BY TAXI   It's virtually impossible to get a taxi at rush hour, so don't even try. Taxi drivers are organized into a lobby that limits their number to 15,000.

Watch out for common rip-offs: Always check the meter to make sure you're not paying the previous passenger's fare; beware of cabs without meters, which often wait outside nightclubs for tipsy patrons; or settle the tab in advance.

You can hail regular cabs on the street when their signs read LIBRE. Taxis are easier to find at the many stands near Métro stations. The flag drops at 5.50€ ($7.15), and from 10am to 5pm you pay .77€ ($1) per kilometer. From 5pm to 10am, you pay 1.09€ ($1.40) per kilometer. On airport trips, you're not required to pay for the driver's empty return ride.

You're allowed several pieces of luggage free if they're transported inside and are less than 5kg (11 lb.). Heavier suitcases carried in the trunk cost 1€ to 1.50€ ($1.30–$1.95) apiece. Tip 12% to 15%—the latter usually elicits a *merci*. For radio cabs, call **Les Taxis Bleus** (© **08-25-16-10-10**) or **Taxi G7** (© **01-47-39-47-39**)—but note that you'll be charged from the point where the taxi begins the drive to pick you up.

BY BOAT The **Batobus** (© 08-25-05-01-01; www.batobus.com) is a 150-passenger ferry with big windows. Every day between April and December, the boats operate along the Seine, stopping at such points of interest as the **Eiffel Tower, Musée d'Orsay,** the **Louvre, Notre-Dame,** and the **Hôtel de Ville.** Unlike the Bateaux-Mouche (see chapter 8), the Batobus does not provide recorded commentary. The only fare option available is a day pass valid for either 1, 2, or 5 days, each allowing as many entrances and exits as you want. A 1-day pass costs 11€ ($14) for adults, 5€ ($6.50) for students and children under 16; a 2-day pass costs 13€ ($17) for adults, 6€ ($7.80) for students and children under 16; a 5-day pass costs 16€ ($21) for adults, 7€ ($9.10) for students and children under 16. Boats operate daily (closed most of Jan) every 25 to 30 minutes, starting between 10 and 10:30am and ending between 4:30 and 10:30pm, depending on the season of the year.

BY BICYCLE

Bicycling through the streets and parks of Paris, perhaps with a baguette tucked under your arm, might have become your fantasy after seeing your first Maurice Chevalier film. In recent years, the city has added many miles of right-hand lanes designated for cyclists, as well as hundreds of bike racks. (When these aren't available, many Parisians simply chain their bikes to fences or lampposts.) Cycling is especially popular in the larger parks and gardens.

Fat Tire Bike Tours, 24 rue Edgar Faure, 15e (© **01-56-58-10-54;** www.fattire biketours.com; Métro: Grenelle), rents bicycles hourly, by the day, week, or month, charging 2€ ($2.60) per hour; 15€ ($20) per day/24 hours; 25€ ($33) 2 consecutive days/48 hours; 50€ ($65) weekly; and 65€ ($85) monthly. You must leave a 250€ ($325) deposit. This company (formerly Mike's Bike Tours) also provides bike tours. A day tour costs 24€ ($31), with a night tour going for 28€ ($36).

BY CAR

Don't even think about driving in Paris. The streets are narrow, with confusing one-way designations, and parking is next to impossible. Besides, most visitors don't have the ruthlessness required to survive in Parisian traffic. Think about renting a car only if you plan to explore the Ile de France and beyond.

To rent a car, you'll need to present a passport, a driver's license, and a credit card. You also have to meet the company's minimum-age requirement. (For the least expensive cars, this is 21 at Hertz, 23 at Avis, and 25 at Budget. More expensive cars may require that you be at least 25.) It usually isn't obligatory within France, but certain companies have asked for the presentation of an International Driver's License, even though this is becoming increasingly superfluous in western Europe.

Note: The best deal is usually a weekly rental with unlimited mileage. All car-rental bills in France are subject to a 19.6% government tax. Though the rental company won't usually mind if you drive your car into, say, Germany, Switzerland, Italy, or Spain, it's often forbidden to transport your car by ferry, including across the Channel to England.

In France, a **collision damage waiver (CDW)** is usually factored into the overall rate quoted, but you should always verify this, of course, before taking a car on the road. At most companies, the CDW waiver provision won't protect you against theft, so if this is the case, ask about purchasing extra theft protection.

Automatic transmission is a luxury in Europe, so if you want it, you'll pay dearly.

Budget (© **800/472-3325** in the U.S., or 800/268-8900 in Canada; www.budget. com) has about 30 locations in Paris and at Orly (© **01-49-75-56-05**) and Charles de Gaulle (© **01-48-62-70-22**). For rentals of more than 7 days, you can usually pick up a car in one French city and drop it off in another, but there are extra charges. Drop-offs in cities within an easy drive of the French border (including Geneva and Frankfurt) incur no extra charge; you can arrange drop-offs in other non-French cities for a reasonable surcharge.

Hertz (© **800/654-3131** in the U.S. and Canada; www.hertz.com) maintains about 15 locations in Paris, including offices at the city's airports. The main office is at 27 place St-Ferdinand, 17e (© **01-45-74-97-39**; Métro: Argentine). Be sure to ask about promotional discounts.

Avis (© **800/331-1212** in the U.S. and Canada; www.avis.com) has offices at both Paris airports and an inner-city headquarters at 5 rue Bixio, 7e (© **01-44-18-10-50**; Métro: Ecole Militaire), near the Eiffel Tower.

National (© **800/CAR-RENT** in the U.S. and Canada; www.nationalcar.com) is represented in Paris by Europcar; one office is at 48 rue de Berri, 8e (© **01-53-93-73-40**; Métro: St. Philippe du Roule). It has offices at both Paris airports and at about a dozen other locations. For the lowest rates, reserve in advance from North America.

Two U.S.-based agencies that don't have Paris offices, but act as booking agents for Paris-based agencies, are **Kemwel Holiday Auto** (© **800/678-0678**; www.kemwel. com) and **Auto Europe** (© **800/223-5555**; www.autoeurope.com). They can make bookings in the United States only, so call before your trip.

FAST FACTS: Paris

American Express The office at 11 rue Scribe, 9e (© **01-47-77-79-28**) is open as a travel agency, a tour operator, and a mail pickup service every Monday to Friday from 9:30am to 6:30pm, Saturday 9am to 5:30pm. Its banking section can fill most needs and, for issues involving American Express credit cards, transfers of funds, and credit-related issues, it's open Monday to Saturday from 9am to 6:30pm.

Area Codes The area code for Paris is **01**. In some special cases, such as for certain transportation information, it might be 08.

ATM Networks See "Money," p. 38.

Babysitters The best deal comes from **Babychou** Services, 31 rue Moulin de la Pointe, 13e (© **01-43-13-33-23**; fax 01-43-13-33-20). You pay 16€ ($21) for the booking, plus 8€ ($10) per hour for one kid, 9€ ($12) per hour for two kids, and 10€ ($13) for three.

Business Hours Opening hours in France are erratic, as befits a nation of individualists. Most museums close 1 day a week (often Tues) and national holidays; hours tend to be from 9:30am to 5pm. Some museums, particularly the smaller ones, close for lunch from noon to 2pm. Most museums are open Saturday, but many close Sunday morning and reopen in the afternoon (see chapter 8 for specific times). Generally, **offices** are open Monday to Friday from 9am to 5pm, but don't count on it—always call first. **Large stores** are open from 9 or 9:30am (often 10am) to 6 or 7pm without a break for lunch. Some **shops,** particularly those operated by non-native French owners, open at 8am and close at 8 or 9pm. In some **small stores,** the lunch break can last 3 hours, beginning at 1pm.

Car Rentals See "Getting Around Paris," p. 71.

Cashpoints See "Money," p. 38.

Currency See "Money," p. 38.

Driving Rules See "Getting Around Paris," p. 70.

Drugstores After regular hours, have your concierge contact the Commissariat de Police for the nearest 24-hour pharmacy. French law requires one pharmacy in any given neighborhood to stay open 24 hours. You'll find the address posted on the doors or windows of all other drugstores. One of the most central all-nighters is **Pharmacy Les Champs "Derhy,"** 84 av. des Champs-Elysées, 8e (℗ **01-45-62-02-41;** Métro: George V).

Electricity In general, expect 200 volts AC (60 cycles), though you'll encounter 110 and 115 volts in some older establishments. Adapters are needed to fit sockets. Many hotels have two-pin (in some cases, three-pin) sockets for electric razors. It's best to ask at your hotel before plugging in any electrical appliance.

Embassies & Consulates If you have a passport, immigration, legal, or other problem, contact your consulate. Call before you go—they often keep odd hours and observe both French and home-country holidays. The Embassy of the **United States,** 2 av. Gabriel, 8e (℗ **01-43-12-22-22;** Métro: Concorde), is open Monday to Friday 9am to 6pm. The Embassy of **Canada** is at 35 av. Montaigne, 8e (℗ **01-44-43-29-00;** Métro: Franklin-D.-Roosevelt or Alma-Marceau), open Monday to Friday 9am to noon and 2 to 5pm. The Embassy of the **United Kingdom** is at 35 rue du Faubourg St-Honoré, 8e (℗ **01-44-51-31-00;** Métro: Concorde or Madeleine), open Monday to Friday 9:30am to 1pm and 2:30 to 5pm. The Embassy of **Ireland** is at 4 rue Rude, 16e (℗ **01-44-17-67-00;** Métro: Etoile), open Monday to Friday 9:30am to 1pm and 2:30 to 5:30pm. The Embassy of **Australia** is at 4 rue Jean-Rey, 15e (℗ **01-40-59-33-00;** Métro: Bir Hakeim), open Monday to Friday 9:15am to noon and 2:30 to 4:30pm. The embassy of **New Zealand** is at 7 ter rue Léonard-de-Vinci, 16e (℗ **01-45-01-43-43;** Métro: Victor Hugo), open Monday to Friday 9am to 1pm and 2:30 to 6pm. The embassy of **South Africa,** 59 quai d'Orsay, 7e (℗ **01-53-59-23-89;** Métro: Invalides), is open Monday to Friday 9am to noon.

Emergencies For the police, call ℗ **17;** to report a fire, call ℗ **18.** For an ambulance, call ℗ **15** or 01-45-67-50-50.

Etiquette & Customs The French are known for a certain classic stylishness and conservatism in dress. What looks good on a holiday in Jamaica might instantly mark you out as a foreigner on the Right Bank of Paris. Parisians like pleasantries: Say *Bonjour Madame/Monsieur* when entering an establishment and *Au Revoir* when you depart. Always say *Pardon* when you accidentally bump into someone. Bread is served with each meal, and it's polite to wipe your plate with it. Waiters will not bring the check until asked. French etiquette requires you to keep your hands above the table and not below, in your lap. For more information, refer to *The Global Etiquette Guide to Europe:*

Everything You Need to Know for Business and Travel Success by Dean Foster (Wiley Publishing).

Holidays Major holidays are January 1 (New Year's Day), Easter, Ascension Day (40 days after Easter), Pentecost (seventh Sunday after Easter), May 1 (May Day), May 8 (VE Day), July 14 (Bastille Day), August 15 (Assumption of the Virgin Mary), November 1 (All Saints Day), November 11 (Armistice Day), and December 25 (Christmas). For more information on holidays, see "Paris Calendar of Events," p. 29.

Hospitals Open Monday to Saturday from 8am to 7pm, **Central Médical Europe,** 44 rue d'Amsterdam, 9e (℘ **01-42-81-93-33;** Métro: Liège or St-Lazare), maintains contacts with medical and dental practitioners in all fields. Appointments are recommended. Another choice is the **American Hospital of Paris,** 63 bd. Victor-Hugo, Neuilly, 17e (℘ **01-46-41-25-25;** Métro: Pont de Levallois or Pont de Neuilly; bus: 82), which operates 24-hour medical and dental services. An additional clinic is the **Centre Figuier,** 2 rue du Figuier, 4e (℘ **01-49-96-62-70;** Métro: St-Paul). Call before visiting.

Hotlines S.O.S. Help can be reached at ℘ **01-46-21-46-46.** The 24-hr. Pharmacy Hotline is ℘ **01-45-62-02-41.** S.O.S. Dentaire can be reached at ℘ **01-43-37-51-00.**

Internet Access See "Internet Access Away from Home," p. 49.

Language English is widely understood. It is said that everyone who lives in the 6th Arrondissement speaks English. It is more understood by young people than their elders. English is common in all the tourist areas—museums, hotels, restaurants, cafes, and nightclubs. For useful French words and phrases, as well as food and menu terms, refer to the glossary in Appendix B of this book. A good phrasebook is *Frommer's French PhraseFinder & Dictionary.* For those who would also like an audio component, *Berlitz French CD Pack with Book* is a good choice.

Legal Aid In an emergency, especially if you get into trouble with the law, your country's embassy or consulate will provide legal advice. For serious emergencies, the staff might even advance you some money. See "Embassies & Consulates" above.

Liquor Laws Supermarkets, grocery stores, and cafes sell alcoholic beverages. The legal drinking age is 16, but persons under that age can be served alcohol in a bar or restaurant if accompanied by a parent or legal guardian. Wine and liquor are sold every day of the week, year-round. Hours of cafes vary. Some open at 6am, serving drinks to 3am; others are open 24 hours. Bars and nightclubs may stay open as late as they wish. The Breathalyzer test is used in France, and a motorist is considered "legally intoxicated" with .5 grams of alcohol per liter of blood (the more liberal U.S. law varies among states, with many states in the range of .6 to .8g per liter). If convicted, a motorist faces a stiff fine and a possible prison term of 2 months to 2 years. If bodily injury results, sentences can range from 2 years to life.

Lost & Found To speed the process of replacing your personal documents if they're lost or stolen, make a photocopy of the first few pages of your passport and write down your credit card numbers (and the serial numbers of your traveler's checks, if you're using them). Leave this information with someone at home—to be faxed to you in an emergency—and swap it with your traveling companion. Be sure to tell all of your credit card companies the minute you discover your wallet has been lost or stolen, and file a report at the nearest police precinct. Your credit card company or insurer may require a police report number or record of the loss.

Use the following numbers in France to report your lost or stolen credit card: **American Express** (call collect) © 336/393-1111; **MasterCard** © 08-00-90-13-87, www.mastercard.com; **Visa** © 08-00-90-11-79, www.visaeurope.com. Your credit card company may be able to wire you a cash advance immediately or deliver an emergency card in a day or two.

If you need emergency cash over the weekend when all banks and American Express offices are closed, you can have money wired to you via **Western Union** (© 800/325-6000; www.westernunion.com). **Travelers Express/MoneyGram** is the largest company in the U.S. for money orders. You can transfer funds either online or by phone in about 10 minutes (© 800/MONEYGRAM; www.money gram.com).

Identity theft and fraud are potential complications of losing your wallet, especially if you lose your driver's license with your cash and credit cards. Notify the major credit-reporting bureaus immediately; placing a fraud alert on your records may protect you against liability for criminal activity. The three major U.S. credit-reporting agencies are **Equifax** (© 800/766-0008; www.equifax. com), **Experian** (© 888/397-3742; www.experian.com), and **TransUnion** (© 800/ 680-7289; www.transunion.com).

If you've lost all forms of photo ID, call your airline and explain the situation; your carrier may let you board the plane if you have a copy of your passport or birth certificate and a copy of the police report you've filed.

Mail Most post offices in Paris are open Monday to Friday from 8am to 7pm and every Saturday from 8am to noon. One of the biggest and most central of them is the main post office for the 1st Arrondissement, at 52 rue du Louvre (© 01-40-28-76-00; Métro: Musée du Louvre). It maintains the hours noted above for services including the sale of postal money orders, mail collection and distribution, and the expedition of faxes. For the purposes of selling stamps and accepting packages, it's open on a limited basis 24 hours a day. If you find it inconvenient to go to the post office to buy stamps, they're sold at the reception desks of many hotels and at cafes designated with red TABAC signs.

Measurements See the chart on the inside front cover of this book for details on converting metric measurements to nonmetric equivalents.

Newspapers & Magazines English-language newspapers are available at nearly every kiosk. Published Monday to Saturday, the *International Herald-Tribune* is the most popular paper with visiting Americans and Canadians; the *Guardian* provides a British point of view. For those who read in French, the leading domestic newspapers are *Le Monde, Le Figaro,* and *Libération;* the top magazines are *L'Express, Le Point,* and *Le Nouvel Observateur.* Kiosks are generally open daily from 8am to 9pm.

Passports Allow plenty of time before your trip to apply for a passport; processing normally takes 3 weeks but can take longer during busy periods (especially spring). And keep in mind that if you need a passport in a hurry, you'll pay a higher processing fee.

For Residents of the United States: Whether you're applying in person or by mail, you can download passport applications from the U.S. Department of State website at http://travel.state.gov. To find your regional passport office, either check the U.S. Department of State website or call the toll-free number of the **National Passport Information Center** (© 877/487-2778) for automated information.

For Residents of Canada: Passport applications are available at travel agencies throughout Canada or from the central **Passport Office,** Department of Foreign Affairs and International Trade, Ottawa, ON K1A 0G3 (© 800/567-6868; www.ppt.gc.ca).

For Residents of Ireland: You can apply for a 10-year passport at the **Passport Office,** Setanta Centre, Molesworth Street, Dublin 2 (© 01/671-1633; www.irlgov.ie/iveagh). Those younger than age 18 and older than 65 must apply for a 12€ 3-year passport. You can also apply at 1A South Mall, Cork (© 021/494-4700) or at most main post offices.

For Residents of Australia: You can pick up an application from your local post office or any branch of Passports Australia, but you must schedule an interview at the passport office to present your application materials. Call the **Australian Passport Information Service** at © 131-232 or visit the government website at www.smarttraveler.gov.au.

For Residents of New Zealand: You can pick up a passport application at any New Zealand Passports Office or download it from their website. Contact the **Passports Office** at © 0800/225-050 in New Zealand or 04/474-8100, or log on to www.passports.govt.nz.

Police In an emergency, call © 17. For non-emergency situations, the principal préfecture is at 9 bd. du Palais, 4e (© 01-53-73-53-73; Métro: Cité).

Restrooms If you're in dire need, duck into a cafe or brasserie to use the toilet. It's customary to make some small purchase if you do so. In the street, the domed self-cleaning lavatories are a decent option if you have small change; Métro stations and underground garages usually have public lavatories, but the degree of cleanliness varies.

Safety See "Safety," p. 42.

Smoking Smoking is acceptable at most restaurants and cafes, but not in museums and other public areas.

Taxes As a member of the European Union, France routinely imposes a value-added tax (VAT in English; TVA in French) on many goods and services. The standard VAT is 19.6% on merchandise, including clothing, appliances, liquor, leather goods, shoes, furs, jewelry, perfumes, cameras, and even caviar. Refunds are made for the tax on certain goods and merchandise, but not on services. The minimum purchase is 175€ ($228) at one time for nationals or residents of countries outside the EU. Hotel taxes in Paris range from around .70€ (90¢) to around 1.50€ ($1.95; Ritz rate) per person per day.

Telephones Public phones are found in cafes, restaurants, Métro stations, post offices, airports, and train stations, and occasionally on the streets. Finding a coin-operated telephone in France is an arduous task. A simpler and more widely accepted method of payment is the *télécarte,* a prepaid calling card available at kiosks, post offices, and Métro stations and costing 11€ to 16€ ($14–$21) for 50 and 120 units, respectively. A local call costs one unit, which provides you 6 to 18 minutes of conversation, depending on the rate. Télécarte is good for local calls in Paris or anywhere else in France, but is not valid for international calls. Avoid making calls from your hotel, which may double or triple the charges.

To call **long distance within France,** dial the 10-digit number (9-digit in some cases outside Paris) of the person or place you're calling. To reach the long-distance operator for AT&T, the Direct Access Number is: ☎ **0800-99-0011** or 0805-701-288; for Canada, dial ☎ **0800-99-00-16** or 0800-99-02-16.

If you have a **phone card,** you can recharge it anywhere, anytime, with **eKit,** via the Web. You can recharge over the phone using a self-service recharge menu. If you prefer to speak to someone, you can call eKit's 24-hour Customer Service: ☎ **888/310-4168** in the U.S.; ☎ **0800/028-2402** in Britain; ☎ **800/094-747** in Australia; and ☎ **866/626-9724** in Canada. With eKit, you can save up to 70% on calls in 200 countries worldwide, including France. One of the many advantages is that family and friends can leave you messages at no cost to them.

To call Paris:
1. Dial the international access code: 011 from the U.S.; 00 from the U.K., Ireland, or New Zealand; or 0011 from Australia.
2. Dial the country code 33.
3. Dial the city code 1 and then the number.

To make international calls: To make international calls from Paris, first dial 00 and then the country code (U.S. or Canada 1, U.K. 44, Ireland 353, Australia 61, New Zealand 64). Next you dial the area code and number. For example, if you wanted to call the British Embassy in Washington, D.C., you would dial ☎ **00-1-202-588-7800.**

For directory assistance: For numbers inside and outside France, dial ☎ 118-008.

For operator assistance: With the inauguration of increasing numbers of cellphones (each of which has a different carrier), and with the decentralization of what used to be the P. T. T., local operators within France are less and less widespread. Even if you dial "0," depending on where you are within France, it might not get you a live body. Everyone automatically expects that, according to the director of phone services in Paris, dialers know the codes of the countries or regions they're trying to reach.

As for reaching an operator for the **placement of calls outside of France,** the system involves bypassing French operators completely, and relying on the operators based within the country you're trying to call. In any event, the prefix for accessing a foreign (i.e., non-French) operator involves dialing the access codes **0800-99-00** followed by the **country code.**

Toll-free numbers: Numbers beginning with **0800** within France are toll-free, but calling a 1-800 number in the States from France is not toll-free. In fact, it costs the same as an overseas call.

Time France is usually 6 hours ahead of Eastern Standard Time and 9 hours ahead of Pacific Standard Time in the United States. French daylight saving time lasts from around April to September, when clocks are set 1 hour ahead of the standard time.

Tipping By law, all bills show *service compris,* which means the tip is included; additional gratuities are customarily given as follows: For **hotel staff,** tip the porter 1.05€ to 1.50€ ($1.35–$1.95) per item of baggage and 1.50€ ($1.95) per day for the chambermaid. You're not obligated to tip the concierge, doorman, or anyone else unless you use his or her services. In **cafes** and **restaurants,** waiter service is usually included, though you can leave some small change, if you like. Tip **taxi drivers** 12% to 15% of the amount on the meter. In **theaters** and **restaurants,** give cloakroom attendants at least .75€ ($1) per item. Give **restroom attendants** in nightclubs and such places about .30€ (40¢). Tip the **hairdresser** about 15%, and don't forget to tip the person who gives you a shampoo or a manicure 1.50€ ($1.95). For **guides** for group visits to museums and monuments, .75€ to 1.50€ ($1–$1.95) is a reasonable tip.

Useful Phone Numbers U.S. Department of State Travel Advisory ✆ **202/647-5225** (manned 24 hrs.); U.S. Passport Agency ✆ **202/647-0518**; U.S. Centers for Disease Control International Traveler's Hotline ✆ **404/332-4559**; Postal info ✆ **01-40-28-20-40**; Federal Express ✆ **01-40-06-90-16** or 08-20-12-38-00.

Water Drinking water is generally safe, though some who were unused to it have gotten diarrhea. If you ask for water in a restaurant, it will be bottled water (for which you'll pay) unless you specifically request *une carafe d'eau* (tap water).

6

Where to Stay

Paris boasts some 2,000 hotels—with about 80,000 rooms—spread across its 20 arrondissements. They range from the Ritz and the Crillon to dives so repellent that even George Orwell, author of *Down and Out in Paris and London,* wouldn't have considered checking in. (Of course, you won't find those in this guide!) We've included deluxe places for those who can afford to live like the Sultan of Brunei, as well as a wide range of moderate and inexpensive choices for the rest of us.

Most visitors, at least those from North America, come to Paris in July and August. Many French people are on vacation, and trade fairs and conventions come to a halt, so there are usually plenty of rooms, even though these months are traditionally the peak season for European travel. In most hotels, February is as busy as April or September, due to the volume of business travelers and tourists taking advantage of off-season discounts.

Because hot weather rarely lasts long in Paris, few hotels, except the deluxe ones, provide air-conditioning. If you're trapped in a garret on a hot summer night, you'll have to sweat it out. You can open your window to get cooler air, but you also may get noise from outside. To avoid this, request a room in back when reserving.

READING THE GOVERNMENT RATINGS

The French government grades hotels with a star system, ranging from one star for a simple inn to four stars for a deluxe hotel. Moderately priced hotels usually get two or three stars. This system is based on a complex formula of room sizes, facilities, plumbing, elevators, dining options, renovations, and so on. In one-star hotels, the bathrooms are often shared, the facilities are extremely limited (such as no elevator), the rooms may not have phones or TVs, and breakfast is often the only meal served. Two- or three-star hotels usually have elevators, and rooms will likely have baths, phones, and TVs. In four-star hotels, you'll get all the amenities plus facilities and services such as room service, 24-hour concierges, elevators, and perhaps even health clubs.

However, the system is a bit misleading. For tax reasons, a four-star hotel might elect to have a three-star rating, which, with the hotel's permission, is granted by the government. The government won't add a star where it's not merited, but will remove one at the hotel's request.

WHICH BANK IS FOR YOU?

The river dividing Paris geographically and culturally demands that you make a choice. Are you more Left Bank, wanting a room in the heart of Saint-Germain, where Jean-Paul Sartre and Simone de Beauvoir once spent their nights? Or are you more Right Bank, preferring sumptuous quarters such as those at the Crillon, where Tom Cruise once slept? Would you rather look for that special old curio in a dusty shop on the Left Bank's rue Jacob, or inspect the latest Lagerfeld or Dior couture on the

Right Bank's avenue Montaigne? Each of Paris's neighborhoods has its own flavor, and your experiences and memories of the city will likely be formed by where you choose to stay.

If you desire chic surroundings, choose a Right Bank hotel. That puts you near the most elegant shops and within walking distance of major sights such as the Arc de Triomphe, place de la Concorde, the Jardin des Tuileries, the Opéra Garnier, and the Louvre. The best Right Bank hotels are near the Arc de Triomphe in the 8th Arrondissement, though many first-class lodgings cluster near the Trocadéro and Bois de Boulogne in the 16th or near the Palais des Congrès in the 17th. If you'd like to be near place Vendôme, try for a hotel in the 1st. Also popular are the increasingly fashionable Marais and Bastille in the 3rd, 4th, and 11th arrondissements, and Les Halles/Beaubourg, home of the Centre Pompidou and Les Halles shopping mall, in the 1st.

If you want less formality and tiny bohemian streets, head for the Left Bank, where prices are traditionally lower. Hotels that cater to students are found in the 5th and 6th arrondissements, the 5th being known as the Latin Quarter. These areas, with their literary overtones, boast the Sorbonne, the Panthéon, the Jardin du Luxembourg, cafe life, bookstores, and publishing houses. The 6th Arrondissement provides a touch of avant-garde St-Germain.

North American and Canadian chain hotels include Marriott, Hilton, Radisson, Holiday Inn, and Four Seasons, plus Starwood (encompassing Westin and Sheraton). The French also have chain hotels or hotel associations that feature Sofitel, Mercure, Ibis, Novotel, and, in some cases, Logis de France and Relais de Silence. The latter two are mostly in the countryside.

For apartment or cottage stays of 2 weeks or more, **Idyll Untours** (② **888/868-6871;** www.untours.com) provides exceptional lodgings for a reasonable price—which includes air/ground transportation, cooking facilities, and on-call support from a local resident. Best of all: Untours—named the "Most Generous Company in America" by Newman's Own—donates most profits to provide low-interest loans to underprivileged entrepreneurs around the world (see website for details).

1 Best Hotel Bets

For full details on the following hotels, see the listings later in this chapter.

- **Best for Families:** An affordable Left Bank choice is the **Hôtel de Fleurie,** 32–34 rue Grégoire-de-Tours, 6e (② **01-53-73-70-00**), in the heart of St-Germain-des-Prés. The accommodations are thoughtfully appointed, and many connecting rooms with two large beds are perfect for families. Children younger than 12 stay free with a parent. See p. 110.
- **Best Value:** Not far from the Champs-Elysées, the **Résidence Lord Byron,** 5 rue Chateaubriand, 8e (② **01-43-59-89-98**), is a classy little getaway that's far from opulent, but is clean and comfortable and worth every euro. See p. 101.
- **Best Location:** Only a 2-minute walk from Paris's most historic and beautiful square, **Hôtel de la Place des Vosges,** 12 rue de Birague, 4e (② **01-42-72-60-46**), is a little charmer. In a building 350 years old, it is small and inviting, with some decorative touches that evoke the era of Louis XIII. See p. 91.
- **Best View:** Of the 33 rooms at the **Hôtel du Quai Voltaire,** 19 quai Voltaire, 7e (② **01-42-61-50-91**), 28 open onto views of the Seine. If you stay here, you'll be

following in the footsteps of Wilde, Baudelaire, and Wagner. This 17th-century abbey was transformed into a hotel back in 1856 and has been welcoming guests who appreciate its tattered charms ever since. See p. 119.

- **Best for Nostalgia:** If you yearn for a Left Bank "literary" address, make it the **Odéon Hôtel,** 3 rue de l'Odéon (© **01-43-25-90-67**), in the heart of the 6th Arrondissement, filled with the ghosts of Gide, Hemingway, Fitzgerald, Joyce, and Stein and Toklas. Evoking a Norman country inn, this charming hotel lures guests with its high crooked ceilings, exposed beams, and memories of yesterday. See p. 111.

- **Best-Kept Secret:** Built in 1913 and long in a seedy state, the fully restored **Terrass Hôtel,** 12 rue Joseph-de-Maistre, 18e (© **01-44-92-34-14**), is now the only four-star choice in Montmartre, an area not known for luxury accommodations. Its rooms take in far-ranging views of the Tour Eiffel, Arc de Triomphe, and Opéra Garnier. See p. 95.

- **Best Historic Hotel:** Inaugurated by Napoleon III in 1855, the **Hôtel du Louvre,** place André-Malraux, 1er (© **800/888-4747** in the U.S. and Canada or 01-44-58 38-38 in France), was once described by a French journalist as "a palace of the people, rising adjacent to the palace of kings." Today, the hotel offers luxurious accommodations and panoramic views down avenue de l'Opéra. See p. 81.

- **Most Trendy Hotel:** It's all the rage. Right off the Champs-Elysées, **Hotel Le A,** 4 rue d'Artois, 8e (© **01-42-56-99-99**), forsakes the traditional for a style so contemporary that it could be called avant-garde. It's as if the Paris hotel scene is reinventing itself with modern technology. See p. 99.

A Room in Paris

If you want to stay somewhere more intimate (and in some cases, more restrictive) than a hotel, consider booking a room within a private home. An agency promoting upmarket B&B accommodations in Paris is **Alcôve & Agapes,** 8 bis rue Coysevox, 75018 Paris (© **01-44-85-06-05**; fax 01-44-85-06-14; www.bed-and-breakfast-in-paris.com). Reservations are made through the Internet only.

This outfit is a bridge between travelers who seek rooms in private homes and Parisians who wish to welcome visitors. Most hosts speak at least some English, range in age from 30 to 75, and have at least some points of view about entertainment and dining options within the neighborhood. Available options include individual bedrooms, usually within large, old-fashioned private apartments, as well as "unhosted" accommodations where the apartment is otherwise empty and without the benefit (or restrictions) of a live-in host.

Rates for occupancy by either one or two persons, with breakfast included, range from 65€ to 195€ ($85–$254) per unit, depending on the apartment, the neighborhood, the setup, and the plumbing. In cases where a client occupies an unhosted apartment, the refrigerators will be stocked with sufficient breakfast supplies for the number of days you are staying (3-night minimum stay).

2 On the Right Bank

We'll begin with the most centrally located arrondissements on the Right Bank and then work our way through the more outlying neighborhoods and to the area around the Arc de Triomphe.

1ST ARRONDISSEMENT (LOUVRE/LES HALLES)
VERY EXPENSIVE

Hôtel de Vendôme 𝕲𝕲   This jewel box was the embassy of Texas when that state was a nation. The hotel opened in 1998 at one of the world's most prestigious addresses. It is comparable to the Hôtel Costes but with a less flashy clientele. Though the guest rooms are moderate in size, they're opulent and designed in classic Second Empire style, with luxurious beds; well-upholstered, handcarved furnishings; and first-rate marble bathrooms with tub/shower combinations. Suites have generous space and such extras as blackout draperies and quadruple-glazed windows. The security is fantastic, with TV intercoms. This new version of the hotel replaced a lackluster one that stood here for a century, and its facade and roof are classified as historic monuments by the French government.

1 place Vendôme, 75001 Paris. ℂ 01-55-04-55-00. Fax 01-49-27-97-89. www.hoteldevendome.com. 29 units. High season 604€–674€ ($785–$876) double; 914€ ($1,188) junior suite, from 1,154€ ($1,500) suite; winter 514€–720€ ($668–$936) double, 794€ ($1,032) junior suite, from 974€ ($1,266) suite. AE, DC, MC, V. Parking 25€ ($33). Métro: Concorde or Opéra. **Amenities:** Restaurant; piano bar; room service; massage; babysitting; laundry service; dry cleaning; rooms for those w/limited mobility. *In room:* A/C, TV, minibar, hair dryer, safe.

Hôtel du Louvre 𝕲 *Kids*   When Napoleon III inaugurated the hotel in 1855, it was described as "a palace of the people, rising adjacent to the palace of kings." In 1897, Camille Pissarro moved into a room with a view that inspired many of his landscapes. Its decor features marble, bronze, and gilt. The guest rooms are filled with souvenirs of the Belle Epoque, along with elegant fabrics, carpeting, double-glazed windows, comfortable beds, and wood furniture. Suites provide greater dimensions and better exposures, as well as such upgrades as antiques, trouser presses, and robes. All rooms have well-maintained bathrooms with a choice of tub or shower.

Place André-Malraux, 75001 Paris. ℂ 800/888-4747 in the U.S. and Canada, or 01-44-58-38-38. Fax 01-44-58-38-01. www.hoteldulouvre.com. 177 units. 255€–500€ ($332–$650) double; 700€–1,800€ ($910–$2,340) suite. AE, DC, MC, V. Parking 24€ ($31). Métro: Palais-Royal–Louvre or Louvre–Rivoli. **Amenities:** Restaurant; bar; pool; fitness center; business center; room service; in-room massage; babysitting; laundry service; dry cleaning; nonsmoking rooms; rooms for those w/limited mobility. *In room:* A/C, TV, minibar, hair dryer, safe.

Hôtel Meurice 𝕲𝕲𝕲   After a massive renovation, this landmark is better than ever. It lies between the place de la Concorde and the Grand Louvre, facing the Tuileries Gardens. The hotel is more media-hip, style-conscious, and better located than the George V. Since the 1800s, it has welcomed the royal, the rich, and even the radical. The mad genius Salvador Dalí made the Meurice his headquarters. The mosaic floors, plaster ceilings, handcarved moldings, and Art Nouveau glass roof atop the Winter Garden look new. Each room is individually decorated with period pieces, fine carpets, Italian and French fabrics, marble bathrooms, and modern features such as fax and Internet access. Our favorites and the least expensive are the sixth-floor rooms. Some have painted ceilings of puffy clouds and blue skies, along with canopy beds. Suites are among the most lavish in France. Beds are sumptuous, furnished in luxurious fabrics; bathrooms are well maintained, with tub/shower combinations.

Where to Stay on the Right Bank (1–4, 9–12 & 18e)

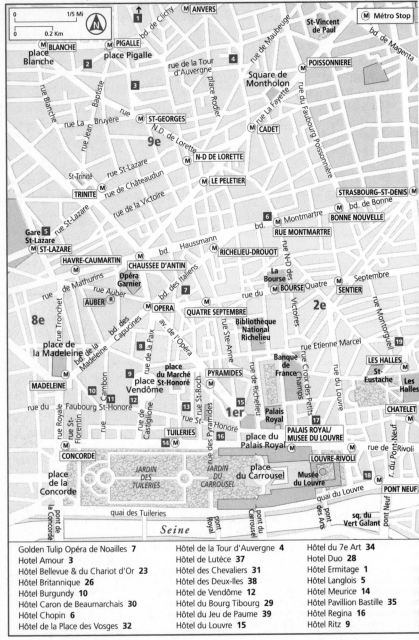

Golden Tulip Opéra de Noailles **7**
Hotel Amour **3**
Hôtel Bellevue & du Chariot d'Or **23**
Hôtel Britannique **26**
Hôtel Burgundy **10**
Hôtel Caron de Beaumarchais **30**
Hôtel de la Place des Vosges **32**

Hôtel de la Tour d'Auvergne **4**
Hôtel de Lutéce **37**
Hôtel des Chevaliers **31**
Hôtel des Deux-Iles **38**
Hôtel de Vendôme **12**
Hôtel du Bourg Tibourg **29**
Hôtel du Jeu de Paume **39**
Hôtel du Louvre **15**

Hôtel du 7e Art **34**
Hotel Duo **28**
Hôtel Ermitage **1**
Hôtel Langlois **5**
Hôtel Meurice **14**
Hôtel Pavillion Bastille **35**
Hôtel Regina **16**
Hôtel Ritz **9**

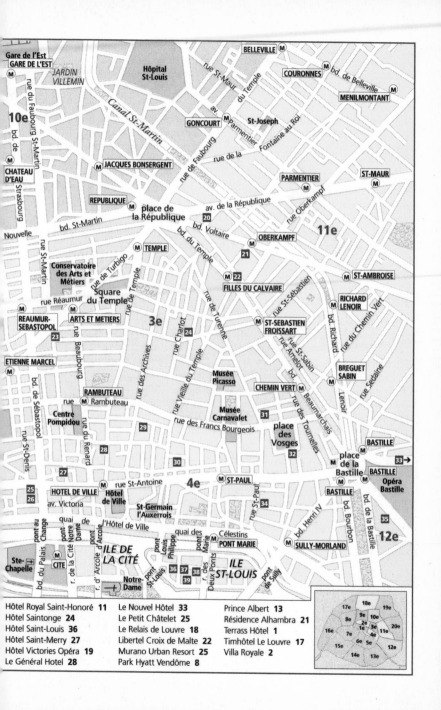

Hôtel Royal Saint-Honoré 11
Hôtel Saintonge 24
Hôtel Saint-Louis 36
Hôtel Saint-Merry 27
Hôtel Victories Opéra 19
Le Général Hotel 28

Le Nouvel Hôtel 33
Le Petit Châtelet 25
Le Relais de Louvre 18
Libertel Croix de Malte 22
Murano Urban Resort 25
Park Hyatt Vendôme 8

Prince Albert 13
Résidence Alhambra 21
Terrass Hôtel 1
Timhôtel Le Louvre 17
Villa Royale 2

228 rue de Rivoli, 75001 Paris. ℂ **01-44-58-10-10.** Fax 01-44-58-10-15. www.meuricehotel.com. 160 units. 720€–800€ ($936–$1,040) double; 1,250€–6,300€ ($1,625–$8,190) suite. AE, DC, MC, V. Parking 24€ ($31). Métro: Tuileries or Concorde. **Amenities:** 2 restaurants; bar; gym; full-service spa; room service; massage; babysitting; laundry service; dry cleaning; nonsmoking rooms; rooms for those w/limited mobility. *In room:* A/C, TV, fax, minibar, hair dryer, safe.

Hôtel Regina ⨁   Restored to its old-fashioned grandeur, Hôtel Regina is adjacent to rue de Rivoli's equestrian statue of Joan of Arc opposite the Louvre. Since 1999, the management has poured millions into a full-fledged renovation, retaining the patina of the Art Nouveau interior and making historically appropriate improvements. The guest rooms are richly decorated and spacious; those overlooking the Tuileries enjoy panoramic views as far away as the Eiffel Tower. The bathrooms, each with tub and shower, are midsize to large, many with stained-glass windows. The public areas contain every period of Louis furniture imaginable, Oriental carpets, 18th-century paintings, and bowls of flowers. Fountains play in a flagstone-covered courtyard. This hotel has more grace notes than its closest competitor, Hôtel du Louvre.

2 place des Pyramides, 75001 Paris. ℂ **01-42-60-31-10.** Fax 01-40-15-95-16. www.regina-hotel.com. 120 units. 420€–480€ ($546–$624) double; 580€–645€ ($754–$839) junior suite; from 790€ ($1,027) suite. AE, DC, DISC, MC, V. Parking 20€ ($26). Métro: Pyramides or Tuileries. **Amenities:** Restaurant; bar; room service; babysitting; laundry service; dry cleaning; nonsmoking room; rooms for those w/limited mobility. *In room:* A/C, TV, Wi-Fi, minibar, safe.

Hôtel Ritz ⨁⨁⨁   The Ritz is Europe's greatest hotel, an enduring symbol of elegance on one of Paris's most beautiful and historic squares. César Ritz, the "little shepherd boy from Niederwald," converted the Hôtel de Lazun into a luxury hotel in 1898. With the help of the culinary master Escoffier, he made the Ritz a miracle of luxury. In 1979, the Ritz family sold the hotel to Mohammed al Fayed, who refurbished it and added a cooking school. The hotel annexed two town houses, joined by an arcade lined with display cases representing 125 of Paris's leading boutiques. The public salons are furnished with museum-caliber antiques. Each guest room is uniquely decorated, most with Louis XIV or XV reproductions; all have fine rugs, marble fireplaces, tapestries, brass beds, and more. The spacious bathrooms are the city's most luxurious, with deluxe toiletries, sumptuous tubs, scales, private phones, cords to summon maids and valets, robes, full-length and make-up mirrors, and dual basins. Ever since Edward VII got stuck in a too-narrow bathtub with his lover, the tubs at the Ritz have been deep and big.

15 place Vendôme, 75001 Paris. ℂ **800/223-6800** in the U.S. and Canada, or 01-43-16-30-30. Fax 01-43-16-45-38. www.ritzparis.com. 168 units. 680€–770€ ($884–$1,001) double; from 900€ ($1,170) suite. AE, DC, MC, V. Parking 44€ ($57). Métro: Opéra, Concorde, or Madeleine. **Amenities:** Restaurant; 4 bars; nightclub; indoor pool; health club; sauna; room service; in-room massage; babysitting; laundry service; dry cleaning; nonsmoking rooms; rooms for those w/limited mobility. *In room:* A/C, TV, minibar, hair dryer, iron/ironing board, safe.

EXPENSIVE

Hôtel Burgundy ⨁   The Burgundy is one of the less expensive hotels in a mortgage-the-house sea of super-priced accommodations. The frequently renovated building was constructed in the 1830s as two adjacent town houses—one a pension where Baudelaire wrote poetry in the 1860s, the other a bordello. British-born managers who insisted on using the English name linked the houses. The hotel hosts many North and South Americans and has conservatively decorated rooms, each with a bathroom with full tub and shower.

8 rue Duphot, 75001 Paris. ℂ **01-42-60-34-12.** Fax 01-47-03-95-20. www.burgundyhotel.com. 89 units. 173€–238€ ($225–$309) double; 318€–353€ ($413–$459) suite. AE, DC, MC, V. Métro: Madeleine or Concorde. **Amenities:** Restaurant; bar; room service; babysitting; laundry service; dry cleaning. *In room:* TV, minibar, hair dryer.

Hôtel Royal Saint-Honoré ⭐⭐   This renovated, government-rated four-star hotel enjoys one of the most fashionable locations in Paris, lying between place Vendôme and the Tuileries. Although its facade dates from 1830, it has been practically rebuilt inside and turned into an oasis of charm. The fashionistas and the glitterati check into the tony Hôtel Costes nearby, while the Royal Saint-Honoré attracts a more conservative (read, less rich) clientele. At the doorstep are famous shops such as Chanel, Hermès, Lanvin, Guerlin, and Cartier. After its latest overhaul, the hotel is imbued with luxurious contemporary styling with impressive redwood English furnishings, Louis XVI–styled paneling in the breakfast room, and an on-site cafe that is also a chic bar. Bedrooms are midsize to spacious, with Louis XVI–style or Directoire wood pieces, botanical prints on the walls, and color-coordinated upholsteries and fabrics. The tubs are a bit narrow, but the appointments are first-rate.

221 rue St-Honoré, 75001 Paris. ℂ **01-42-60-32-79.** Fax 01-42-60-47-44. www.hotel-royal-st-honore.com. 72 units. 300€–420€ ($390–$546) double; 450€–580€ ($585–$754) suite. AE, DC, MC, V. Métro: Tuileries. **Amenities:** Restaurant; bar; room service; babysitting; laundry service; dry cleaning; nonsmoking rooms; rooms for those w/limited mobility. *In room:* A/C, TV, Wi-Fi, minibar, hair dryer, safe.

MODERATE

Hôtel Britannique *Value*   Conservatively modern and plush, this is a much-renovated 19th-century hotel near Les Halles and Notre-Dame. The place is not only British in name, but also seems to cultivate English graciousness. The guest rooms are small, but immaculate and soundproof, with comfortable beds and well-maintained bathrooms with tub/shower combinations. A satellite receiver gets U.S. and U.K. television shows. The reading room is a cozy retreat.

20 av. Victoria, 75001 Paris. ℂ **01-42-33-74-59.** Fax 01-42-33-82-65. www.hotel-britannique.fr. 39 units. 168€–193€ ($218–$251) double; 247€–288€ ($321–$374) suite. AE, DC, MC, V. Métro: Châtelet. **Amenities:** Bar; room service; laundry service; dry cleaning. *In room:* A/C, TV, minibar, hair dryer, safe.

Le Relais du Louvre   One of the neighborhood's most up-to-date hotels, Relais du Louvre overlooks the neoclassical colonnade at the eastern end of the Louvre. Between 1800 and 1941, its upper floors contained the printing presses that recorded the goings-on in Paris's House of Representatives. Its street level held the Café Momus, favored by Voltaire, Hugo, and intellectuals of the day, and is where Puccini set one of the pivotal scenes of *La Bohème*. Bedrooms are outfitted in monochromatic schemes of blue, yellow, or soft reds, usually with copies of Directoire-style (French 1830s) furniture. All units have tub/shower combinations except for four of the simplest and smallest singles, which have only a shower. Many rooms are a bit small, but others contain roomy sitting areas.

19 rue des Prêtres-St-Germain-l'Auxerrois, 75001 Paris. ℂ **01-40-41-96-42.** Fax 01-40-41-96-44. www.relaisdulouvre.com. 21 units. 160€–198€ ($208–$257) double; 232€–265€ ($302–$345) suite. AE, DC, MC, V. Parking 22€ ($29). Métro: Louvre or Pont Neuf. **Amenities:** Room service; babysitting; laundry service; dry cleaning; nonsmoking rooms. *In room:* A/C, TV, Wi-Fi, minibar, hair dryer, safe.

INEXPENSIVE

Le Petit Châtelet ⭐ *Value*   Small, unpretentious, and inexpensive, this hotel has a difficult-to-detect front entrance (it's tucked within a cluster of more highly visible restaurants); a clientele that includes lots of musicians playing at the nearby jazz clubs; and a warm-toned decorative scheme loosely inspired by India, Southeast Asia, and Africa. Bedrooms are small, a bit battered, and artfully accessorized with musical instruments and framed paintings—in some cases originals. Bathrooms are compact,

---

Tips   Splish, Splash—Taking a Bath

Throughout the hotels in this chapter, expect the bathrooms in very expensive and expensive hotels to be a bit larger than normal, with fine toiletries, plush towels, and perhaps bathrobes. The bathrooms in moderate and inexpensive hotels tend to be cramped but still acceptable, with towels that are less plush than those at expensive places.

Be aware that some hotels offer tub/shower combinations, some offer shower stalls, and some offer a mix. If something particular is important to you, request your preference when reserving. Almost all hotels, except the inexpensive ones, include hair dryers in the bathrooms.

---

with showers but not bathtubs and tile work. There's no elevator, so be prepared to climb as many as six flights of stairs. The largest room, and the only one with its own private terrace, is on the top floor. All of the rooms in this hotel that don't have private bathrooms are designated as singles. Accommodations facing the street can be noisy, but double-glazed windows keep out most of the noise, except during the heat of midsummer, when you might have to leave the windows open.

9 rue St-Denis, 75001 Paris. ℂ **01-42-33-32-31.** www.fapeco.com. 11 units. 75€–160€ ($98–$208) (apartment) double. AE, MC, V. Métro: Châtelet. **Amenities:** Restaurant; bar; nonsmoking rooms. *In room:* A/C, TV.

Prince Albert *(Value)*   A government-rated two-star hotel, this undiscovered lodging enjoys a great location near the place Vendôme and the Louvre area. It is a century-and-a-half old but has been brought completely up-to-date and has a certain charm—all at an affordable price. Built in the 1820s, the rooms are still evocative of 19th-century Paris, with their high ceilings. The furnishings, however, are modern and comfortable. About two-thirds of the bathrooms contain showers; the rest, bathtubs. Accommodations reveal that a decorator has come by, one fond of the color schemes of pink or green—sometimes with flowery fabrics.

5 rue Saint-Hyacinthe, 75001 Paris. ℂ **01-42-61-58-36.** Fax 01-42-60-04-06. www.hotelprincealbert.com. 30 units. 109€–120€ ($142–$156) double. AE, DC, MC, V. Métro: Tuileries. *In room:* A/C (in some), TV, Wi-Fi, minibar, hair dryer, safe.

Timhôtel Le Louvre *(Kids)*   This hotel and its sibling in the 2nd Arrondissement, the Timhôtel Palais-Royal, are part of a new breed of government-rated, two-star, family-friendly hotels cropping up in France. These Timhôtels share the same manager and temperament. Though the rooms at the Palais-Royal branch are a bit larger than the ones here, this branch is so close to the Louvre that it's almost irresistible. The ambience is modern, with monochromatic rooms and wall-to-wall carpeting. Each unit's bathroom comes with a tub and shower.

4 rue Croix des Petits-Champs, 75001 Paris. ℂ **01-42-60-34-86.** Fax 01-42-60-10-39. www.timhotel.fr. 56 units. 99€–150€ ($129–$195) double. AE, DC, MC, V. Métro: Palais-Royal. The 46-room **Timhôtel Palais-Royal** is at 3 rue de la Banque, 75002 Paris (ℂ **01-42-61-53-90;** fax 01-42-60-05-39; Métro: Bourse). **Amenities (at both branches):** Restaurant (breakfast only); nonsmoking rooms; rooms for those w/limited mobility rooms. *In room:* A/C, TV.

2ND ARRONDISSEMENT (LA BOURSE)
VERY EXPENSIVE
Park Hyatt Vendôme *(★★★)*   American interior designer Ed Tuttle took five separate Haussmann-era buildings and wove them into a seamless whole to create this

citadel of 21st-century luxury living. High ceilings, colonnades, and interior court-yards speak of the buildings' former lives, but other than the facades, all is completely modern inside—not just contemporary, but luxe modern. The third Hyatt in Paris, this palace enjoys the greatest and most prestigious location in "Ritz Hotel country." Graced with modern art, this place is filled with elegant fabrics, huge mirrors, walk-in closets, mahogany doors, and Jim Thompson silk. Bedrooms and bathrooms are spacious and state-of-the-art, with elegant furnishings and glamorous bathrooms with "rain showers," plus separate tubs.

5 rue de la Paix, 75002 Paris. ✆ **01-58-71-12-34.** Fax 01-58-71-12-35. www.paris.vendome.hyatt.com. 166 units. 650€–760€ ($845–$988) double; from 860€ ($1,118) suite. AE, DC, DISC, MC, V. Métro: Tuileries or Opéra. **Amenities:** 2 restaurants; bar; lounge with fireplace; health club; spa; room service; babysitting; laundry service; dry cleaning. *In room:* A/C, TV, minibar, hair dryer, safe.

EXPENSIVE
Hôtel Victoires Opéra ✪   Head to this little charmer in the fashion district if you want a reasonably priced place convenient to Les Halles and the Pompidou as well as to the Marais, with its shops and mix of gay and straight restaurants. It's a classically decorated hotel, evoking the era of Louis Philippe. Renovations in 2001 included the addition of a private bathroom to every room. The rooms are comfortable but rather small in most cases, except for the junior suites. Most of the rooms come with tubs; the rest, with showers. Skip the hotel breakfast (which costs extra) and cross the street to Stohrer at no. 51, one of Paris's most historic patisseries, founded in 1730 by the *pâtissier* to Louis XV.

56 rue de Montorgueil, 75002 Paris. ✆ **01-42-36-41-08.** Fax 01-45-08-08-79. www.hotelvictoiresopera.com. 24 units. 214€–275€ ($278–$358) double; 335€ ($436) junior suite. AE, DC, MC, V. Métro: Les Halles. **Amenities:** Room service; laundry service; dry cleaning; rooms for those w/limited mobility. *In room:* A/C, TV, Wi-Fi, minibar, hair dryer, safe.

MODERATE
Golden Tulip Opéra de Noailles   If you're looking for a postmodern hotel in the style of Putman and Starck, book here. Proprietor Martine Falck has turned this old-fashioned place in a great location into a refined Art Deco choice with bold colors and cutting-edge style, yet the prices remain reasonable. The guest rooms come in various shapes and sizes, but all are comfortable and have a tub/shower combo. A favorite is no. 601, which has its own Japanese indoor garden.

9 rue de la Michodière, 75002 Paris. ✆ **800/344-1212** in the U.S., or 01-47-42-92-90. Fax 01-49-24-92-71. www.paris-hotel-noailles.com. 59 units. 210€–330€ ($273–$429) double; 310€–480€ ($403–$624) suite. AE, DC, MC, V. Métro: 4 Septembre or Opéra. RER: Opéra. **Amenities:** Bar; health club; sauna; room service; massage; babysitting; laundry service; dry cleaning. *In room:* A/C, TV, minibar, hair dryer, safe.

3RD ARRONDISSEMENT (LE MARAIS)
EXPENSIVE
Murano Urban Resort ✪ *Finds*   This hotel oddity, not everyone's cup of tea but charming for some, was created late in 2004, when two abandoned buildings—one a run-down five-story apartment house; the other a three-story parking garage—were interconnected and upgraded into a new and coherent whole. The result is a trendset-ting, aggressively minimalist hotel with an angular sense of design that will either impress you with its purity or not. The decorative theme, as conceived by Lyon-based designer Raymond Morel, revolves around the transparency of Murano glass. You'll find a Murano glass chandelier in the green-toned lobby, another in a key spot on the ground floor, and very large glass-framed mirrors in some of the upper hallways. The

mirrors and chandeliers are metaphors for the games that residents can play with light in their respective, and otherwise sparsely furnished, units: Up to three sets of curtains in any room filter sunlight in patterns that range from gauzy and bright to complete blackouts. Additionally, individual settings switch on and off a spectrum of lights in up to six colors. Collectively, they create the semblance of noonday sun; individually and separately, they create moods that range from cheerful to pensive, depending (in theory) on an occupant's mood. Two of the suites have small (about 14-sq.-m/151-sq.-ft.) swimming pools on their private terraces.

13 bd. du Temple, 75003 Paris. ℂ 01-42-71-20-00. Fax 01-42-71-21-01. www.muranoresort.com. 52 units. 400€–650€ ($520–$845) double; from 750€ ($975) suite. AE, DC, MC, V. Métro: Filles du Calvaire. **Amenities:** Restaurant; bar; fitness center; spa; Jacuzzi; car-rental facilities; room service; nonsmoking rooms; rooms for those w/limited mobility; photo service. *In room:* A/C, TV, hair dryer, safe.

INEXPENSIVE

Hôtel Bellevue & du Chariot d'Or   Originally built in 1860 as part of the majestic redevelopment of central Paris by Baron Haussmann, this hotel has a grand facade and inexpensive, relatively comfortable and cozy, simple bedrooms that are priced as a distinct bargain within the neighborhood. The hotel has become more desirable because of its location in the once-neglected Arts et Métiers district north of the Pompidou Center. The second part of its name—"Chariot d'Or" (Golden Carriage)—derives from the medieval custom of placing brides-to-be (along with their dowries) in a flower-draped ceremonial carriage. It carried them across a former courtyard near the entrance to the Church of St-Martin des Champs, which still stands within a 2-minute walk from the hotel. During the occupation of Paris during World War II, the site was commandeered as a garrison for rank-and-file Nazi troops. Expect a polite and well-spoken reception staff, a rather grand entrance hallway, and comfortable bedrooms to which touches of warmth have been added.

39 rue de Turbigo, 75003 Paris. ℂ 01-48-87-45-60. Fax 01-48-87-95-04. www.hotelbellevue75.com. 59 units. 68€ ($88) double. AE, DC, MC, V. Métro: Châtelet–Les Halles or Réaumur-Sebastopol. **Amenities:** Bar; babysitting; rooms for those w/limited mobility. *In room:* TV, safe.

Hôtel des Chevaliers   Half a block from the place des Vosges, this hotel occupies a corner building whose 17th-century vestiges have been elevated to high art. These include the remnants of a well in the cellar, a stone barrel vault covering the breakfast area, and Louis XIII accessories that will remind you of the hotel's origins. Each guest room is comfortable and well maintained, and all bathrooms come with both tub and shower. Units on the top floor have exposed ceiling beams. Some are larger than others, with an extra bed making them suitable for those traveling with a child or for three people on the road together.

30 rue de Turenne, 75003 Paris. ℂ 01-42-72-73-47. Fax 01-42-72-54-10. www.chevaliers-paris-hotel.com. 24 units. 150€ ($195) double; 165€ ($215) triple. AE, MC, V. Métro: Chemin Vert or St-Paul. **Amenities:** Bar; laundry service; dry cleaning. *In room:* A/C, TV, minibar, hair dryer, safe.

Hôtel Saintonge ★ *Finds*   Its rooms are small, but there's a coziness about this hotel that you might appreciate, especially if you're attracted to beamed ceilings, patches of exposed and very old masonry, and charmingly claustrophobic upstairs hallways. It rises seven stories above a quiet neighborhood in the Marais, one of the many structures that functioned as private houses in the 17th century and have been converted to hotels or private apartments. Breakfast is served beneath the vaulted ceiling of what used to be a cellar-level storage area; the lobby boasts hand-hewn beams and a tile floor; and bedrooms have tall windows or, if they're on the building's uppermost floor, angled ceilings that evoke the feeling of an artist's studio in a garret. The hotel has few amenities other than the breakfast room, but considering the wealth of museums and architecture in the surrounding neighborhood, no one seems to care. Bathrooms are sheathed in tile, most only with a shower.

16 rue Saintonge, 75003 Paris. ✆ 01-42-77-91-13. Fax 01-48-87-76-41. www.saintongemarais.com. 23 units. 115€ ($150) double; 170€ ($221) suite. AE, DC, MC, V. Métro: Filles du Calvaire or République. **Amenities:** Room service; babysitting; laundry service; dry cleaning; nonsmoking rooms; rooms for those w/limited mobility. *In room:* TV, minibar, hair dryer, safe.

4TH ARRONDISSEMENT (ILE DE LA CITÉ/ ILE ST-LOUIS & BEAUBOURG)
EXPENSIVE

Hôtel du Bourg Tibourg ✿ *Finds*   Don't come here expecting large rooms with lots of elbow room: What you get is a sophisticated and supercharged color palette, a sense of high-profile design, and a deliberately cluttered venue that looks like an Edwardian town house decorated by an obsessive-compulsive individual on psychedelic drugs. It is set behind an uncomplicated, cream-colored facade in the Marais and marked only with a discreet brass plaque and a pair of carriage lamps. Its rooms have been radically overhauled by superstar decorator Jacques Garcia. Bedrooms are genuinely tiny, but rich with neo-romantic, neo-Gothic, and in some cases neo-Venetian swirls and curlicues. Each is quirky, idiosyncratic, richly upholstered, and supercharged with tassels, faux leopard skin, contrasting stripes, fringes, and lavish window treatments. Our advice: Either come alone or bring only a very intimate friend to share these cramped, overcharged premises, and leave most of your luggage behind. The place is precious, not for cowboys or claustrophobes, and, if you like the micro-approach to intensive decorating, absolutely charming. Rooms facing the front get more sunlight; rooms facing the courtyard tend to be quieter. Breakfast is served in your bedroom or beneath the vaulted ceiling of the building's cellar.

19 rue du Bourg-Tibourg, 75004 Paris. ✆ 01-42-78-47-39. Fax 01-40-29-07-00. www.hotelbourgtibourg.com. 30 units. 220€–250€ ($286–$325) double; 350€ ($455) suite. Parking 26€ ($34). AE, DC, MC, V. Métro: Hôtel de Ville. **Amenities:** Room service; laundry service. *In room:* A/C, TV, minibar, hair dryer, safe.

Hôtel du Jeu de Paume ✿   This small-scale hotel encompasses a pair of 17th-century town houses accessible through a timbered passageway from the street outside. The rooms are a bit larger than those of some nearby competitors. Originally, the hotel was a clubhouse used by members of the court of Louis XIII, who amused themselves with *les jeux de paume* (an early form of tennis) nearby. Public areas are outfitted in a simple version of Art Deco. Guest rooms are freshly decorated in sleek contemporary style, with elegant materials such as oaken floors and fine craftsmanship. Some have wooden beamed ceilings. All contain well-maintained bathrooms with tub/shower combinations. The most luxurious units are the five duplexes and two junior suites, each individually decorated and opening onto an indoor courtyard.

54 rue St-Louis en l'Ile, 75004 Paris. ✆ 01-43-26-14-18. Fax 01-40-46-02-76. www.jeudepaumehotel.com. 30 units. 230€–335€ ($299–$436) double; 395€–545€ ($514–$709) suite. AE, DC, MC, V. Métro: Pont Marie. **Amenities:** Bar; gym; sauna; room service; babysitting; laundry service; dry cleaning. *In room:* TV, minibar, hair dryer, safe.

MODERATE
Hôtel Caron de Beaumarchais *Value*   Built in the 18th century, this good-value choice features floors of artfully worn gray stone, antique reproductions, and elaborate

fabrics based on antique patterns. Hotelier Alain Bigeard intends his primrose-colored guest rooms to evoke the taste of the French gentry in the 18th century, when the Marais was the scene of high-society dances or even duels. Most rooms retain their original ceiling beams. The smallest units overlook the courtyard, and the top-floor rooms are tiny, but have panoramic balcony views across the Right Bank. All but two bedrooms have a tub/shower combination.

12 rue Vieille-du-Temple, 75004 Paris. © 01-42-72-34-12. Fax 01-42-72-34-63. www.carondebeaumarchais.com. 19 units. 125€–162€ ($163–$211) double. AE, MC, V. Métro: St-Paul or Hôtel-de-Ville. **Amenities:** Breakfast room; babysitting. *In room:* A/C, TV, minibar, hair dryer.

Hôtel de Lutèce This hotel feels like a country house in Brittany. The lounge, with its old fireplace, is furnished with antiques and contemporary paintings. Each of the guest rooms boasts antiques, adding to a refined atmosphere that attracts celebrities such as the duke and duchess of Bedford. Each unit comes with either tub or shower. The suites, though larger than the doubles, are often like doubles with extended sitting areas. Each is tastefully furnished, with an antique or two. The hotel is comparable in style and amenities to the Deux-Iles (see below), under the same ownership.

65 rue St-Louis-en-l'Ile, 75004 Paris. © 01-43-26-23-52. Fax 01-43-29-60-25. www.paris-hotel-lutece.com. 23 units. 185€ ($241) double; 205€ ($267) triple. AE, MC, V. Métro: Pont Marie or Cité. **Amenities:** Laundry service; dry cleaning. *In room:* A/C, TV, hair dryer, safe.

Hôtel des Deux-Iles This is an unpretentious but charming choice in a great location. In a restored 18th-century town house, the hotel has elaborate decor, with bamboo and reed furniture and French provincial touches. The guest rooms are on the small side, but the beds are very comfortable and the bathrooms well maintained, with tubs or shower units. A garden off the lobby leads to a basement breakfast room that has a fireplace.

59 rue St-Louis-en-l'Ile, 75004 Paris. © 01-43-26-13-35. Fax 01-43-29-60-25. www.deuxiles-paris-hotel.com. 17 units. 170€ ($221) double. AE, MC, V. Métro: Pont Marie. **Amenities:** Room service; laundry service; dry cleaning; nonsmoking rooms. *In room:* A/C, TV, hair dryer, safe.

(Kids) Family-Friendly Hotels

Hôtel de Fleurie (p. 110) In the heart of St-Germain-des-Prés, this has long been a Left Bank family favorite. The hotel is known for its *chambres familiales*—two connecting rooms with a pair of large beds in each room. Children younger than 12 stay free with a parent.

Hôtel du Ministère (p. 100) For the family on a budget that doesn't mind cramped quarters, the Ministère is one of the best bets in this expensive area near the Champs-Elysées.

Résidence Lord Byron (p. 101) The Byron is not only a good value and an unusually family-oriented place for the swanky 8th Arrondissement, but also is only a short walk from many major monuments.

Timhôtel Le Louvre (p. 86) This is an especially convenient choice because it offers some rooms with four beds for the price of a double. The location near the Louvre is irresistible.

Hôtel Duo ⟨F⟩ *(Finds)*   Fashionistas flock to this restored hotel in the Marais, which is one of the cutting-edge places to stay in Paris. The location is convenient to the Centre Pompidou, Notre-Dame, the Louvre, and the Picasso Museum. The building has been in the family of Veronique Turmel since 1918. In 2002, she decided to completely convert the interior while retaining the facade. She hired Jean-Philippe Nuel, who kept many of the original architectural features, including exposed beams, old stones, and hardwood floors. He created a medieval look graced with Wengé-wood furnishings, white walls, and bronzed sconces—old-world charm in a tasteful and refined setting. The midsize bedrooms are completely up-to-date, with beautiful and comfortable furnishings, along with impressive bathrooms with tub and shower. The so-called breakfast "cave" is a charming room with slipcovered chairs and sea-grass matting.

11 rue du Temple, 75004 Paris. ℭ **01-42-72-72-22.** Fax 01-42-72-03-53. www.duoparis.com. 58 units. 170€–300€ ($221–$390) double, 350€–480€ ($455–$624) suite. AE, DC, MC, V. Métro: Hôtel-de-Ville. **Amenities:** Lounge for drinks; fitness center; room service; laundry service; dry cleaning. *In room:* A/C, TV, minibar, hair dryer, safe.

Hôtel Saint-Louis ⟨F⟩ *(Value)*   Proprietors Guy and Andrée Record maintain a charming family atmosphere at this antiques-filled hotel in a 17th-century town house. The hotel represents an incredible value, considering its prime location on Ile St-Louis. Expect cozy, slightly cramped rooms, each with a small bathroom containing a tub/shower combination. With mansard roofs and old-fashioned moldings, the top-floor units sport tiny balconies that afford sweeping views. The breakfast room is in the cellar, which has 17th-century stone vaulting.

75 rue St-Louis-en-l'Ile, 75004 Paris. ℭ **01-46-34-04-80.** Fax 01-46-34-02-13. 19 units. 140€–220€ ($182–$286) double. MC, V. Métro: Pont Marie or St-Michel-Notre-Dame. **Amenities:** Babysitting. *In room:* TV, hair dryer, safe.

Hôtel Saint-Merry ⟨F⟩ *(Finds)*   The rebirth of this once-notorious brothel as a charming, upscale hotel is an example of how the area has been gentrified. It contains only a dozen rooms, each relatively small but accented with neo-Gothic detail: exposed stone, 18th-century ceiling beams, and lots of quirky architecture. Suites, much larger than doubles, have upgraded furnishings. All units contain tiled bathrooms with showers or tubs; some have a TV and a minibar. According to the staff, the clientele here is about 50% gay males; the other half is straight and tends to be involved in the arts scene in the surrounding neighborhood. Before it became a bordello, it was conceived as the presbytery of the nearby Church of Saint-Merry.

78 rue de la Verrerie, 75004 Paris. ℭ **01-42-78-14-15.** Fax 01-40-29-06-82. www.hotel-saintmerry.com. 12 units. 160€–230€ ($208–$299) double; 335€–400€ ($436–$520) suite. AE, MC, V. Métro: Hôtel de Ville or Châtelet. **Amenities:** Room service; babysitting; laundry service; dry cleaning. *In room:* TV (in some), minibar (in some), hair dryer, safe.

INEXPENSIVE

Hôtel de la Place des Vosges ⟨F⟩ *(Value)*   Built about 350 years ago, during the same era as the majestic square for which it's named (a 2-min. walk away), this is a well-managed, small-scale property with reasonable prices and lots of charm. The structure was once used as a stable for the mules of Henri IV. Many of the small guest rooms have beamed ceilings; tiled bathrooms (with tub or shower); small TVs hanging from the ceiling; and a sense of cozy, well-ordered efficiency. The most desirable and expensive room is top-floor no. 60, overlooking the rooftops of Paris, with a luxurious private bathroom. Patches of chiseled stone in various parts of the hotel add a decorative touch.

> ⌠*Value* **Good, Clean Rooms for around $55 a Night**
>
> Largely unnoticed by U.S. visitors—as yet—a French Revolution is quietly taking place. Some two dozen modern, amenity-packed hotels have sprouted up in Paris under the **Ibis Hotel** banner. These cookie-cutter properties have become the McDonald's of French budget lodgings. Operated by Accor Hotels (© **800/ 221-4542**), they have attractive but tiny rooms and simple but comfortable decor, and they are cost-efficient, albeit without any particular antique or glamorous trappings. If you stay at Motel 6 and Red Roof Inns in the United States, it's a comparable experience. You can book a room at an Ibis for the price of two martinis at the George V.

12 rue de Birague, 75004 Paris. © **01-42-72-60-46.** Fax 01-42-72-02-64. www.hotelplacedesvosges.com. 16 units. 120€–140€ ($156–$182) double. AE, DC, MC, V. Métro: Bastille. **Amenities:** Room service; nonsmoking rooms. *In room:* TV, hair dryer, safe.

Hôtel du 7e Art The hotel occupies one of many 17th-century buildings classified as historic monuments in this neighborhood. Don't expect grand luxury: rooms are cramped and outfitted with the simplest furniture, relieved by 1950s-era movie posters. Each has white walls, and some of them—including those under the sloping mansard-style roof—have exposed ceiling beams. All have small bathrooms with either a tub or shower. The five-story building has a lobby bar and a breakfast room but no elevator. The "7th Art" is a reference to filmmaking.

20 rue St-Paul, 75004 Paris. © **01-44-54-85-00.** Fax 01-42-77-69-10. 23 units. 85€–145€ ($111–$189) double. AE, DC, MC, V. Métro: St-Paul. **Amenities:** Bar; coin-operated laundry. *In room:* A/C, TV, hair dryer, safe.

RIGHT BANK: 9TH ARRONDISSEMENT (OPERA GARNIER/PIGALLE)
EXPENSIVE
Hotel Amour The dramatic transformation of what had previously been a somewhat nondescript hotel brought it into sync with the increasingly hip neighborhood, just off the rue des Martyrs, which contains it. It's the kind of hotel that services the needs of suburbanites looking for lodgings in the town center on a weekend, or young business travelers looking for a buzz in the lobby even before replicating a buzz in their bedroom upstairs. And in this case, there's a lot to be entertained and amused by within a venue that the "nouveau chic" has deemed worth hanging out in. One critic even claimed that thanks to the hotel bar being frequented by young European fashionistas, each flaunting their respective allure and neurosis, "waiting in a queue for the toilets has never been so entertaining." Each bedroom is outfitted in ways radically different from its neighbors: Each has a very comfortable mattress—they come from the same company that supplies the (much more expensive) Hotel Ritz—and no TV and no telephone. (The assumption being that anyone hip enough to check in here already has a working cellphone of his or her own.) Each of the decors varies widely, including some with a minimalist white-on-white decor with touches of faux baroque; others with works by graffiti artists applied directly to the walls. Overall, the place has an oddball charm that's generating a lot of press in Paris these days.

8 rue Navarin, 75009 Paris. © **01-48-78-31-80.** www.hotelamour.com. 20 units. 90€–190€ ($117–$247) double. AE, MC, V. Métro: St-Georges. **Amenities:** Restaurant; bar; room service. *In room:* A/C, Wi-Fi, minibar, no phone.

Villa Royale *(Finds)*   Paris can be many things to many people, and if your vision of the city involves the scarlet-toned settings once associated with the Moulin Rouge, and the paintings of Toulouse-Lautrec, this designer hotel might be for you. It does a flourishing business renting small but carefully decorated rooms, each of which evokes Paris's sometimes kitschy world of glitzy and risqué nightlife entertainment. Expect rooms outfitted Liberace-style, with rococo gewgaws, velvet and velour upholsteries, jewel-toned walls, and TV screens that are sometimes encased in gilded frames. Each is named after someone from the world of French entertainment, including namesakes inspired by La Bardot, La Deneuve—even Claude Debussy. Bathrooms are small but efficient, each sheathed in white ceramic tiles, containing showers and clothes steamers.

2 rue Duperré, 75009 Paris. © **01-55-31-78-78.** Fax 01-55-31-78-70. www.leshotelsdeparis.com. 31 units. 210€–350€ ($273–$455) double. AE, DC, MC, V. Métro: Pigalle. Bus: 30 or 54. **Amenities:** Laundry service; dry cleaning; room service. *In room:* A/C, TV, Wi-Fi (in some), hair dryer, safe.

MODERATE

Hôtel de la Tour d'Auvergne   Here's a good bet for those who want to be near the Opéra or the Gare du Nord. This building was erected before Baron Haussmann reconfigured Paris's avenues around 1870. Later, Modigliani rented a room for 6 months, and Victor Hugo and Auguste Rodin lived on this street. The interior has been modernized into a glossy internationalism. The guest rooms are meticulously coordinated, yet the small decorative canopies over the headboards make them feel cluttered. Though the views over the back courtyard are uninspired, some guests prefer the quiet of the rear rooms. Every year, five rooms are renovated, and each unit comes with a tub/shower combination.

10 rue de la Tour d'Auvergne, 75009 Paris. © **01-48-78-61-60.** Fax 01-49-95-99-00. www.hotel-tour-auvergne-opera-paris.federal-hotel.com. 24 units. 130€–190€ ($169–$247) double. AE, DC, MC, V. Métro: Cadet. **Amenities:** Bar; room service; nonsmoking rooms. *In room:* A/C, TV, minibar, hair dryer.

Hôtel Langlois   This hotel used to be known as Hôtel des Croises, but when it was used as a setting for the Jonathan Demme film *The Truth About Charlie,* the hotel owners changed the name to match the one used in the film. It's a well-proportioned, restored town house with a main stairwell and spacious landing. An antique wrought-iron elevator running up the center of the building adds an old-fashioned Parisian touch. The rooms are well proportioned but not overly large; those in the front get the most light. Units in the rear are darker but quieter. Rooms, with their aura of *Ecole de Nancy* (a florid Art Nouveau style), have well-chosen antiques, tasteful rugs and fabrics, even an occasional fireplace. Bathrooms are modernized, with tub and shower. We suggest avoiding the upper floors in summer; there's no air-conditioning, and the heat is often stifling.

63 rue St-Lazare, 75009 Paris. © **01-48-74-78-24.** Fax 01-49-95-04-43. www.hotel-langlois.com. 27 units. 114€–130€ ($148–$169) double; 170€ ($221) suite. AE, DC, MC, V. Métro: Trinité. **Amenities:** Breakfast room; room service. *In room:* A/C, TV, minibar, hair dryer.

INEXPENSIVE

Hôtel Chopin *(Value)*   Enter this intimate, offbeat hotel through a passageway that includes a toy store, a bookstore, the exit from the Musée Grevin, and the architectural trappings of its original construction in 1846. Just off the Grands Boulevards, this old-fashioned hotel evokes the charm of yesteryear. In honor of its namesake, the Chopin has a piano in its reception area. The inviting lobby welcomes you behind its 1850s facade of elegant woodwork and Victorian-era glass. In the style of Paris of long ago, the comfortably furnished bedrooms open onto a glass-topped arcade instead of the hysterically busy street, so they are rather tranquil. We prefer the bedrooms on the top floor, as they are larger and quieter, with views over the rooftops of Paris. The least expensive bedrooms lie behind the elevator bank and get less light.

10 bd. Montmartre or 46 passage Jouffroy, 75009 Paris. ℂ **01-47-70-58-10.** www.hotel-chopin.com. Fax 01-42-47-00-70. 36 units. 81€–92€ ($105–$120) double. AE, MC, V. Métro: Grands-Boulevards. *In room:* TV, hair dryer, safe.

11TH ARRONDISSEMENT (OPERA BASTILLE)
EXPENSIVE
Le Général Hotel As the neighborhood around place de la République and rue Oberkampf becomes increasingly tuned to Paris's sense of counterculture chic, it's inevitable that new hotels will crop up as the neighborhood becomes more gentrified. This is a good example of that neighborhood's improving fortunes. Opened within the premises of a run-down hotel that was radically renovated and decorated by noted designer Jean-Philippe Nuel, the hotel's interior revolves around prominent rectilinear lines, spartan-looking decors, and an intelligent distribution of spaces. The result is a seven-story hotel with floors linked by two separate elevator banks and pale, monochromatic beige-and-off-white color schemes, and with furniture that is either dark (i.e., rosewood-toned) or pale (i.e., birch- or maple-toned). Midsize bathrooms are outfitted in white ceramic tiles, with tubs and showers.

5–7 rue Rampon, 75011 Paris. ℂ **01-47-00-41-57.** Fax 01-47-00-21-56. www.legeneralhotel.com. 47 units. 168€– 228€ ($218–$296) double; 238€–268€ ($309–$348) suite. AE, MC, V. Métro: République. **Amenities:** Bar; fitness center; sauna; business center; laundry service; dry cleaning. *In room:* A/C, TV, hair dryer, safe.

INEXPENSIVE
Libertel Croix de Malte A member of a nationwide chain of government-rated two-star hotels, this is a well-maintained lodging choice. The hotel consists of two buildings of two and three floors, one of which is accessible through a shared breakfast room. There's a landscaped courtyard in back with access to a lobby bar. The cozy guest rooms contain brightly painted modern furniture accented with vivid green, blue, and pink patterns that flash back to the 1960s. About half of the units contain tubs; the rest are equipped with showers.

5 rue de Malte, 75011 Paris. ℂ **01-48-05-09-36.** Fax 01-43-57-02-54. www.hotelcroixdemalte-paris.com. 29 units. From 80€–105€ ($104–$137) double. AE, DC, MC, V. Métro: Oberkampf. **Amenities:** Bar; room service (breakfast); babysitting. *In room:* TV, Wi-Fi, hair dryer.

Résidence Alhambra Named for the famous cabaret/vaudeville theater that once stood nearby, the Alhambra dates from the 1800s. A radical renovation in 2002 gave the hotel its fine contemporary format. In the rear garden, where breakfast is served, its two-story chalet offers eight additional guest rooms. The small accommodations are bland but comfortable, each in a dull pastel scheme that includes white and ocher. Ten private bathrooms contain tub/shower combos; the rest, showers.

13 rue de Malte, 75011 Paris. ℂ **01-47-00-35-52.** Fax 01-43-57-98-75. www.hotelalhambra.fr. 58 units. 68€–84€ ($88–$109) double; 92€–110€ ($120–$143) triple. AE, DC, MC, V. Métro: Oberkampf. **Amenities:** Garden. *In room:* TV, Wi-Fi.

12TH ARRONDISSEMENT (BOIS DE VINCENNES/GARE DE LYON)
MODERATE
Hôtel Pavillon Bastille This is a bold, innovative hotel in a town house across from the Opéra Bastille, a block south of place de la Bastille. It was completely renovated

in 2007. A 17th-century fountain graces the courtyard. The guest rooms have twin or double beds, partially mirrored walls, and contemporary built-in furniture. Each unit comes with a tub/shower combo.

65 rue de Lyon, 75012 Paris. ⓒ **01-43-43-65-65.** Fax 01-43-43-96-52. www.paris-hotel-pavillonbastille.com. 25 units. 170€ ($221) double; 213€ ($277) suite. AE, DC, MC, V. Métro: Bastille. **Amenities:** Bar; room service; babysitting; laundry service; dry cleaning. *In room:* A/C, TV, Wi-Fi, minibar, hair dryer, safe.

INEXPENSIVE
Le Nouvel Hôtel This hotel evokes the French provinces more than urban Paris. Surrounded by greenery in a neighborhood rarely visited by tourists, the Nouvel conjures a day when parts of Paris still seemed like small country towns. The most attractive spot is the inside courtyard, site of warm-weather breakfasts. Winding halls lead to small guest rooms overlooking the courtyard or, less appealingly, the street. Each contains flowered fabrics and old-fashioned furniture, but only three have baths; the rest are equipped with showers.

24 av. du Bel-Air, 75012 Paris. ⓒ **01-43-43-01-81.** Fax 01-43-44-64-13. www.nouvel-hotel-paris.com. 28 units. 78€–109€ ($101–$142) double. MC, V. Métro: Nation. **Amenities:** Garden; nonsmoking rooms. *In room:* TV.

18TH ARRONDISSEMENT (MONTMARTRE)
EXPENSIVE
Kube Rooms & Bars ⓕ *(Finds)* It's relatively new, it's comfortable, it's being talked about within trendy circles of Paris, and it manages to combine its lodgings with a sense of being within a youth-obsessed dance club where the party goes on and on. Design-savvy clients usually appreciate the way the architect (in-the-news Raymond Morel) made repeated use of the cube, a form that the owners refer to as "the most modern of shapes." It occupies the six-story premises of what was built in the late 1800s as the administrative headquarters of a now-defunct brewery *(Les bières de la Meuse),* which these writers remember from beerfests of yesteryear. There's a restaurant and a dance lounge on the street level, where a DJ spins tunes most evenings from a mezzanine that looks down on the dance floor, and a sense of hard-partying 20-somethings that can be either invigorating or tiresome, depending on your point of view.

Bedrooms (and everything else about the place) seem to revel in the concept of the rectangular cube as a newly re-conceived decorative device. Rectangular beds are lit from below and appear to float. Expect shag-covered sofas, fuzzy faux-fur slippers in tones of high-voltage yellow, and a sense of compact efficiency that, despite the minimalist angularity and self-conscious sense of "design," is hard to ignore. Instead of room keys, guests are electronically fingerprinted. On the premises is the Ice Kube Bar, a deep-cooled conversational oddity whose bartop is fashioned from—you guessed it—ice. For a per person price of 38€ ($49), clients reserve a 30-minute block of time within the deep freeze, receive a lecture on the odder natures of the place from a bundled-up staff, are assigned thermally insulated parkas, and are offered as much vodka, served within goblets fashioned from ice, as they can drink within the pre-assigned 30-minute block.

3–5 Passage Ruelle, 75018 Paris. ⓒ **01-42-05-20-00.** Fax 01-42-05-21-01. www.kubehotel.com. 41 units. 300€–350€ ($390–$455) double; 400€–750€ ($520–$975) suite. Parking 30€ ($39). Métro: La Chapelle. **Amenities:** Restaurant; bar/lounge with a DJ several nights a week; fitness center; laundry service; dry cleaning. *In room:* A/C, TV, Wi-Fi, safe, hair dryer.

Terrass Hôtel ⓕⓕ *(Finds)* Built in 1913, this is the only government-rated four-star hotel on the Butte Montmartre. In an area filled with some of Paris's seediest hotels, this place is easily in a class of its own. Its main advantage is its location amid Montmartre's bohemian atmosphere (or what's left of it). Staffed by English-speaking employees, it has a large marble-floored lobby ringed with blond-oak paneling and accented with 18th-century antiques and valuable paintings. The guest rooms are high-ceilinged and well upholstered, often with views. All the bathrooms are well maintained, each with a shower and about half with both a shower and tub.

12 rue Joseph-de-Maistre, 75018 Paris. © 01-44-92-34-14. Fax 01-44-92-34-30. www.terrass-hotel.com. 98 units. 260€–355€ ($338–$462) double; 355€ ($462) suite. AE, DC, MC, V. Métro: Place de Clichy or Blanche. **Amenities:** 2 restaurants; bar; room service; babysitting; laundry service; dry cleaning; nonsmoking rooms; rooms for those w/limited mobility; Internet in lobby. *In room:* A/C, TV, minibar, coffeemaker, hair dryer, safe.

INEXPENSIVE
Hôtel Ermitage   Built in 1870 of chiseled limestone in the Napoleon III style, this hotel's facade evokes a perfectly proportioned small villa. It's set in a calm area, a brief uphill stroll from Sacré-Coeur. Views extend over Paris, and there's a garden in the back courtyard. The small guest rooms are like those in a countryside *auberge* (inn), with exposed ceiling beams, flowered wallpaper, and casement windows opening onto the garden or a street seemingly airlifted from the provinces. All the bedrooms come with small tub/shower combinations.

24 rue Lamarck, 75018 Paris. © 01-42-64-79-22. Fax 01-42-64-10-33. www.ermitagesacrecoeur.fr. 12 units. 90€ ($117) double. Rates include breakfast. No credit cards. Métro: Lamarck-Caulaincourt. **Amenities:** Room service; babysitting; garden.

8TH ARRONDISSEMENT (CHAMPS-ELYSEES/MADELEINE)
VERY EXPENSIVE
Concorde St-Lazare ✦   Across from the St-Lazare rail station, this hotel—the area's best—first greeted visitors flocking to the Universal Exposition of 1889. Many rooms (medium-size to quite large) have high ceilings, especially those on the lower floors, which also have double-glazed windows to cut down on the noise. The beds are plush and comfortable, and bathrooms come with tub/shower combinations.

108 rue St-Lazare, 75008 Paris. © 800/888-4747 in the U.S. outside New York state, 0800/02-89-880 in London, or 01-40-08-44-44. Fax 01-42-93-01-20. www.concordestlazare-paris.com. 266 units. 390€–450€ ($507–$585) double; from 690€ ($897) suite. AE, DC, MC, V. Parking 26€ ($34). Métro: St-Lazare. **Amenities:** Restaurant; bar; cafe; room service; babysitting; laundry service; dry cleaning; nonsmoking rooms. *In room:* A/C, TV, Wi-Fi, minibar, hair dryer, safe.

Four Seasons Hotel George V ✦✦✦   In its latest reincarnation, with all its glitz and glamour, this hotel is one of the best in the world. The George V's history is as gilt-edged as they come. It opened in 1928 in honor of George V of England, grandfather of Queen Elizabeth. During the liberation of Paris, it housed Dwight D. Eisenhower. After its acquisition by Saudi Prince Al Waleed and a 2-year renovation, it was reopened under the banner of Toronto-based Four Seasons. The guest rooms are about as close as you'll come to residency in a well-upholstered private home where teams of decorators have lavished vast amounts of attention and money. The beds rival those at the Ritz and Meurice in comfort. It's deluxe all the way. The renovation reduced the number of units from 300 to 245, which now come in three sizes. The largest are magnificent; the smallest are, in the words of a spokesperson, *"très agreeable."* Each unit comes with a large bathroom with a separate tub and shower. Security is tight—a fact appreciated by sometimes-notorious guests.

31 av. George V, 75008 Paris. © 800/332-3442 in the U.S. and Canada, or 01-49-52-70-00. Fax 01-49-52-70-10. www.fourseasons.com. 245 units. 710€–910€ ($923–$1,183) double; 1,350€ ($1,755) suite. Parking 40€ ($52).

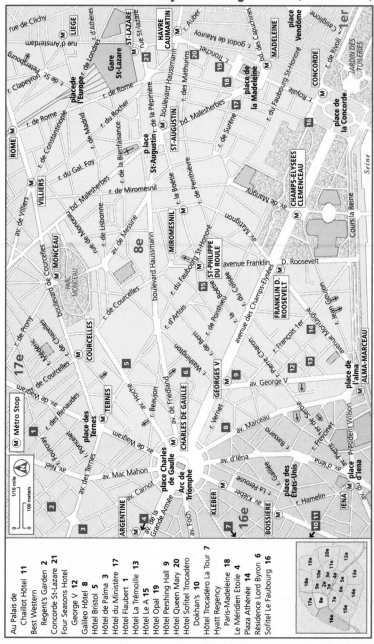

Au Palais de
  Chaillot Hôtel **11**
Best Western
  Regent's Garden **2**
Concorde St-Lazare **21**
Four Seasons Hotel
  George V **12**
Galileo Hôtel **8**
Hôtel Bristol **5**
Hôtel de Palma **3**
Hôtel du Ministère **17**
Hôtel Flaubert **1**
Hôtel La Trémoille **13**
Hôtel Le A **15**
Hôtel Opal **19**
Hôtel Pershing Hall **9**
Hôtel Queen Mary **20**
Hôtel Sofitel Trocadéro
  Dokhan's **10**
Hôtel Trocadéro La Tour **7**
Hyatt Regency
  Paris-Madeleine **18**
Le Méridien Etoile **4**
Plaza Athénée **14**
Résidence Lord Byron **6**
Sofitel Le Faubourg **16**

AE, DC, MC, V. Métro: George V. **Amenities:** 2 restaurants; 2 lounges; indoor pool; fitness center; spa; sauna; room service; massage; babysitting; laundry service; dry cleaning; nonsmoking rooms; rooms for those w/limited mobility. *In room:* A/C, TV, minibar, hair dryer, safe.

Hôtel Bristol ★★★   This palace is near the Palais d'Elysée (home of the French president), on the shopping street parallel to the Champs-Elysées. In terms of style and glamour, here's how the lineup reads in Paris: (1) Ritz, (2) Plaza Athénée, (3) Bristol, and (4) George V. The 18th-century Parisian facade has a glass-and-wrought-iron entryway, where uniformed English-speaking attendants greet you. Hippolyte Jammet founded the Bristol in 1924, installing many antiques and Louis XV and XVI furnishings. The guest rooms are opulent, with antiques or well-made reproductions, inlaid wood, bronze, crystal, Oriental carpets, and original oil paintings. Each room is freshened every 3 years, and each comes with a luxurious bathroom with tub/shower combos. Personalized old-world service is rigidly maintained here—some guests find it forbidding; others absolutely adore it. In 2007 the Bristol was building an extension of the existing hotel, which will add to the room count, of course.

112 rue du Faubourg St-Honoré, 75008 Paris. ℂ 01-53-43-43-00. Fax 01-53-43-43-01. www.lebristolparis.com. 162 units. 710€–810€ ($923–$1,053) double; 900€–1,100€ ($1,170–$1,430) junior suite; from 930€ ($1,209) suite. AE, DC, MC, V. Free parking. Métro: Miromesnil or Champs-Elysées. **Amenities:** Restaurant; bar; indoor pool; fitness room; spa; sauna; hammam (steam bath); salon; room service; babysitting; laundry service; dry cleaning. *In room:* A/C, TV, minibar, hair dryer, safe.

Hôtel Pershing Hall ★★★   Set on a hyperstylish street that parallels the avenue Montaigne, this hotel was created when a late-19th-century town house was radically altered by one of France's most celebrated modern designers, Andrée Putnam. Admittedly, she had fascinating raw materials. The five-story town house was built in 1890 by the Comte de Paris—who at the time was heir apparent to the French monarchy, had it been fully restored—as a home for his mistress. During World War I, it was transformed into the Paris headquarters of American Gen. John Pershing. Today, the walls of the soaring courtyard are draped in lush tropical plants from Southeast Asia, which thrive in the microclimate of the courtyard. Inside, don't expect an homage to the imperial days of the French monarchy, as all appointments have been replaced in favor of the warm, but artfully spartan and rectilinear style favored by the woman who designed the original decor of Air France's Concorde. Visitors find a lavish use of quarried stone, tile, mosaics, and hardwoods; a subtle color scheme of warm beiges and grays; bead curtains; bathtubs with claw-and-ball feet; and comfortable, subtly contemporary furniture.

49 rue Pierre Charron, 75008 Paris. ℂ 01-58-36-58-00. Fax 01-58-36-58-01. www.pershing-hall.com. 26 units. 420€–500€ ($546–$650) double; 720€–1,000€ ($936–$1,300) suite. AE, DC, MC, V. Métro: George V. **Amenities:** Restaurant; bar; gym; spa; sauna; babysitting; laundry service; dry cleaning; nonsmoking rooms; rooms for those w/limited mobility. *In room:* A/C, TV, minibar, hair dryer, safe.

Plaza Athénée ★★★   The Plaza Athénée, an 1889 Art Nouveau marvel, is a landmark of discretion and style. In the 8th Arrondissement, only the Bristol can compare. About half the celebrities visiting Paris have been pampered here; in the old days, Mata Hari used to frequent the place. Superbly decorated subdivisions within the hotel include the **Bar Montaigne,** whose audaciously designed countertops are crafted from crystal that's lit from beneath. It's been described as an enormous iceberg that self-illuminates when you touch it. The **Salon Gobelins** (with tapestries against rich paneling) and the **Salon Marie Antoinette,** a richly paneled and grand room, are two public rooms that add to the ambience of this lavish hotel. There's also a calm, quiet interior courtyard draped with vines and dotted with geraniums. The quietest guest rooms overlook a courtyard with awnings and parasol-shaded tables; they have ample closet space, and their large tiled bathrooms contain double basins and separate tubs and showers. Some rooms overlooking avenue Montaigne have views of the Eiffel Tower. The hotel is also home to **Restaurant Plaza Athénée,** where Alain Ducasse presents an award-winning menu focusing on "rare and precious ingredients." See p. 148 for complete review.

25 av. Montaigne, 75008 Paris. ② **866/732-1106** in the U.S. and Canada, or 01-53-67-66-65. Fax 01-53-67-66-66. www.plaza-athenee-paris.com. 188 units. 635€–740€ ($857–$962) double; from 940€ ($1,222) junior suite. AE, DC, MC, V. Parking 25€ ($35). Métro: Franklin-D.-Roosevelt or Alma-Marceau. **Amenities:** 3 restaurants; bar; tea room; fitness center; sauna; hammam (steam bath); room service; massage; babysitting; laundry service; dry cleaning; nonsmoking rooms; rooms for those w/limited mobility. *In room:* A/C, TV, minibar, hair dryer, iron, safe.

EXPENSIVE

Hotel La Trémoille ✦   In the heart of Paris and a 2-minute walk from the Champs-Elysées, this is a preferred Right Bank address for fashionistas, as it lies in the heart of the haute couture district. Built in the 19th century, the hotel opened again following a $23-million renovation that returned the swank address to much of its original elegance and charm. It blends modern and traditional styles. Originally a private residence, the hotel is outfitted in a Louis XV style, all in woodwork and tapestries. In the old days, you might have encountered General de Gaulle or even Orson Welles. Today, Johnny Depp is a regular visitor. Rooms are cozy and comfortable, each decorated in harmonies of tawny, ocher, gray, and white, with much use of silks, synthetic furs, and mohair. Bathrooms, done in elegant gray-and-black marble, contain tubs and showers.

14 rue de la Trémoille, 75008 Paris. ② **01-56-52-14-00.** Fax 01-40-70-01-08. www.hotel-tremoille.com. 93 units. 420€–575€ ($546–$748) double; from 625€ ($813) suite. AE, DC, MC, V. Métro: Alma-Marceau. **Amenities:** Restaurant; bar; fitness center; sauna; room service; laundry service; dry cleaning. *In room:* A/C, TV, minibar, hair dryer, safe.

Hotel Le A ✦   Lying only 2 blocks from the Champs-Elysées, this town house has been converted to an elegant enclave. It's true the rooms are a bit small—the staff refers to them as cozy—but the overall comfort may still entice your soul. A well-known designer, Frédéric Mechiche, was responsible for the ultramodern contemporary design. A spacious lounge with a library is filled with books on art and design. Walls are painted with bold abstractions. The hotel bar under a 19th-century glass roof, with a tasteful black and white decor, has become a favorite rendezvous with the fashionistas of the era. Rooms represent supreme comfort with adjustable lights, electronic blinds, and other modern amenities, including state-of-the-art bathrooms with tubs, showers, or both. The elevator ceiling that changes color every few seconds is a bit much, however.

4 rue d'Artois, 75008 Paris. ② **01-42-56-99-99.** Fax 01-42-56-99-90. www.paris-selection.com. 26 units. 345€– 450€ ($449–$585) double, 472€ ($614) junior suite. Rates include continental breakfast. AE, DC, MC, V. Parking: 24€ ($31). **Amenities:** Lounge; bar; laundry service; nonsmoking rooms; library. *In room:* A/C, TV, Wi-Fi, minibar, hair dryer, safe.

Hyatt Regency Paris-Madeleine ✦✦   In the heart of the financial district, this is Paris's latest luxury hotel and represents Hyatt's first venture into the heart of the French capital. This is our top recommendation for those visiting Paris on business, as rooms are designed not only for rest, but also for work—large writing desks, three phones, modem sockets, voice mail, individual fax machines, you name it. As you enter, the hotel evokes a noble, romantic private home with a lavish use of quality materials such as sycamore wood. Bedrooms are spacious with large beds and luxurious, tiled bathrooms with tubs and showers. Some of the units boast exceptional views over the rooftops of Paris.

24 bd. Malesherbes, 75008 Paris. © 01-55-27-12-34. Fax 01-55-27-12-35. www.paris.madeleine.hyatt.com. 86 units. 360€–520€ ($468–$676) double; from 895€ ($1,164) suite. AE, DC, MC, V. Free parking. Métro: Madeleine. **Amenities:** 2 restaurants; bar; fitness center; spa; sauna; hammam (steam bath); business center; salon; room service; massage; babysitting; laundry service; dry cleaning; nonsmoking rooms; rooms for those w/limited mobility. *In room:* A/C, TV, Wi-Fi, minibar, hair dryer, iron, safe.

Sofitel Le Faubourg   Cozy, well upholstered, and businesslike, this hotel in the heart of Paris was created by linking two buildings dating from the 18th and 19th centuries. Celebrity guests such as David Bowie seem to appreciate its low-key but high-quality accommodations and the personalized service. It's decorated throughout with a mixture of modern and traditional French styles, with feng shui touches. Rooms come in various sizes but are comfortable, quiet, and of a decent size—even the short-stay one-person rooms which, though small, are not claustrophobic. If there's a specific feature you want—a balcony, a view, high ceilings—inquire about these when booking.

15 rue Boissy d'Anglais, 75008 Paris. © 800/SOFITEL or 01-44-94-14-14. Fax 01-44-94-14-28. www.sofitel.com. 174 units. 465€–558€ ($605–$725) double; from 995€ ($1,294) suite. AE, DC, MC, V. Parking 29€ ($38). Métro: Concorde. **Amenities:** Restaurant; bar; fitness center; hammam (steam bath); business center; room service; laundry service; dry cleaning; nonsmoking rooms; rooms for those w/limited mobility. *In room:* A/C, TV, minibar, hair dryer, safe.

MODERATE

Galileo Hotel 🗝 *(Finds)*   This is one of the 8th's most charming hotels. Proprietors Roland and Elisabeth Buffat have won friends from all over with their Hôtel des Deux-Iles and Hôtel de Lutèce on St-Louis-en-l'Ile (see earlier in this chapter). A short walk from the Champs-Elysées, this town house is the epitome of French elegance and charm. The medium-size rooms are a study in understated taste. Beautifully kept bathrooms hold a tub or shower. Within this hotel, rooms with numbers ending in 3 (i.e., 103, 203, 303, 403, and 503) are more spacious than the others. Rooms 501 and 502 have private glassed-in verandas that you can use even in winter. For this neighborhood, the prices are moderate.

54 rue Galilée, 75008 Paris. © 01-47-20-66-06. Fax 01-47-20-67-17. www.galileo-paris-hotel.com. 27 units. 174€ ($226) double. AE, DC, MC, V. Parking 23€ ($30). Métro: Charles-de-Gaulle–Etoile or George V. **Amenities:** Laundry service; dry cleaning; 1 room for those w/limited mobility. *In room:* A/C, TV, minibar, hair dryer, safe.

Hôtel du Ministère 🗝   The Ministère is a winning choice near the Champs-Elysées, though it's far from Paris's cheapest budget hotel. The guest rooms are on the small side, but they are comfortable and well maintained; many have oak beams and fine furnishings. Avoid rooms on the top floor, which are cramped. Each unit's bathroom holds a tub/shower combination. Junior suites are only slightly larger than regular doubles, but the extra space may be worth the money.

31 rue de Surène, 75008 Paris. © 01-42-66-21-43. Fax 01-42-66-96-04. www.ministerehotel.com. 28 units. 179€–209€ ($233–$272) double. AE, MC, V. Métro: Madeleine. **Amenities:** Bar; room service; laundry service; dry cleaning; nonsmoking rooms. *In room:* A/C, TV, minibar, hair dryer, safe.

Hôtel Opal *(Finds)*   Built around 1900, this hotel is a real find behind La Madeleine church and near the Opéra Garnier. Throughout most of 2007 this hotel was undergoing a major renovation, so look for changes after its opening. Rooms are somewhat tight, but very well furnished and comfortable, and many of them are air-conditioned. Those on the top floor are reached by a narrow staircase; some have skylights. Most rooms have twin beds, and all of them come with a tub/shower combo. Reception will make arrangements for parking at a nearby garage.

19 rue Tronchet, 75008 Paris. ☎ 01-42-65-77-97. Fax 01-49-24-06-58. www.hotelopal.com. 34 units. 175€–230€ ($228–$299) double. Extra bed 15€ ($20). AE, DC, V. Métro: Madeleine. **Amenities:** Breakfast room; room service; laundry service; dry cleaning. *In room:* A/C (in some), TV, Wi-Fi, minibar, hair dryer, safe.

Hôtel Queen Mary *Kids*   Meticulously renovated inside and out, this early 1900s hotel has an iron-and-glass canopy, wrought iron, and the kind of detailing normally reserved for more expensive hotels. The public rooms have touches of greenery and reproductions of antiques; guest rooms contain upholstered headboards, comfortable beds, and mahogany furnishings, plus a carafe of sherry. All units are renovated, and most come with a tub/shower combination (six have showers only). Suites and triples are slightly more spacious than regular doubles and are beautifully furnished.

9 rue Greffulhe, 75008 Paris. ☎ 01-42-66-40-50. Fax 01-42-66-94-92. www.hotelqueenmary.com. 36 units. 189€–219€ ($246–$285) double; 299€ ($389) triple. AE, DC, MC, V. Métro: Madeleine or Havre-Caumartin. **Amenities:** Bar; room service; rooms for those w/limited mobility. *In room:* A/C, TV, minibar, hair dryer, safe.

Résidence Lord Byron *Kids*   Off the Champs-Elysées on a curving street of handsome buildings, the Lord Byron may not be as grand as other hotels in the neighborhood, but it's more affordable. Unassuming and a bit staid, it offers exactly what repeat guests want: a sense of luxury, solitude, and understatement. Beds are old-fashioned, and bathrooms are well kept; most have shower units. It's a fine choice for families, who often book suites for the larger living space. You can eat breakfast in the dining room or in the shaded inner garden.

5 rue Chateaubriand, 75008 Paris. ☎ 01-43-59-89-98. Fax 01-42-89-46-04. www.escapade-paris.com. 31 units. 175€–195€ ($228–$254) double; 265€ ($345) suite. AE, DC, MC, V. Parking 20€ ($26). Métro: George V. RER: Etoile. **Amenities:** Room service; babysitting; laundry service; dry cleaning. *In room:* A/C, TV, minibar, hair dryer, safe.

16TH ARRONDISSEMENT (TROCADERO/BOIS DE BOULOGNE)
VERY EXPENSIVE
Hôtel Sofitel Trocadéro Dokhan's *Kids Kids*   If not for the porters walking through its public areas carrying luggage, you might suspect that this well-accessorized hotel was a private home. It's in a stately, 19th-century Haussmann-styled building vaguely inspired by Palladio and contains accessories such as antique paneling, Regency-era armchairs, and chandeliers. Each guest room has a different decorative style, with antiques or good reproductions, lots of personalized touches, triple-glazed windows, and beautifully maintained bathrooms with tubs. Beds are often antique reproductions with maximum comfort. Suites have larger living space and spacious bathrooms with such extras as make-up mirrors and luxe toiletries.

117 rue Lauriston, 75116 Paris. ☎ 01-53-65-66-99. Fax 01-53-65-66-88. www.sofitel.com. 45 units. 220€–450€ ($286–$585) double; from 850€ ($1,105) suite. AE, DC, MC, V. Parking 30€ ($39). Métro: Trocadéro. **Amenities:** Champagne bar; room service; massage; babysitting; laundry service; dry cleaning; nonsmoking rooms. *In room:* A/C, TV, fax, minibar, hair dryer, safe.

MODERATE
Hotel Trocadéro La Tour *Kids Finds*   Originally built in the late 19th century, this eight-story building is a well-maintained, well-managed hotel with comfortable, well-accessorized bedrooms and a location that's near the best viewing platform for the Eiffel Tower (place de Trocadéro) in Paris. The hotel is one of subdued elegance and refined comfort, filled with grace notes such as a lobby that evokes a library, a bar wainscoted in mahogany for teatime, and a tree-filled courtyard. The rather spacious

bedrooms are each outfitted with a slightly different floor plan and color scheme, usually a coordinated palette of pale pastels. Each of the bathrooms has marble or tile trim and a tub/shower combination. The staff is kindly, albeit overworked and a bit harassed.

5 bis rue Massenet, 75116 Paris. (℗ **01-45-24-43-03**. Fax 01-45-24-41-39. www.paris-hotel-trocaderolatour.com. 41 units. 159€–195€ ($207–$254) double; 169€–260€ ($220–$338) suite. AE, DC, MC, V. Métro: La Muette or Passy. **Amenities:** Bar; babysitting; laundry service; dry cleaning; nonsmoking rooms. *In room:* A/C, TV, Wi-Fi, minibar, hair dryer, safe.

INEXPENSIVE

Au Palais de Chaillot Hôtel When American-trained brothers Thierry and Cyrille Pien opened this hotel, budget travelers flocked here. Located between the Champs-Elysées and Trocadéro, the town house was restored from top to bottom, and the result is a contemporary yet informal variation on Parisian chic. The guest rooms come in various shapes and sizes, and are furnished with a light touch, with bright colors and wicker. Rooms 61, 62, and 63 afford partial views of the Eiffel Tower. Each comes with a neatly tiled, shower-only bathroom (tubs in junior suites).

35 av. Raymond-Poincaré, 75016 Paris. (℗ **01-53-70-09-09**. Fax 01-53-70-09-08. www.chaillotel.com. 28 units. 125€–145€ ($163–$189) double; 170€ ($221) junior suite; 20€ ($26) extra bed. AE, DC, MC, V. Métro: Victor Hugo or Trocadéro. **Amenities:** Room service; laundry service. *In room:* AC, TV, hair dryer, safe.

17TH ARRONDISSEMENT (PARC MONCEAU/PLACE CLICHY)
EXPENSIVE

Le Méridien Etoile This hotel made records as the largest in Paris when it was built in 1972. Rising nine stories above a rather dull residential and commercial neighborhood at the northwestern fringe of Paris, near the exposition halls at Porte Maillot, it's the flagship of the Méridien chain. Rooms are contemporary looking, not overly large, and standardized, reflecting a bland but completely acceptable international style. Rooms on the hotel's uppermost two floors are a bit plusher than rooms on the lower floors and have a more personalized approach, including a separate breakfast and bar/lounge, separate check-in facilities, and a separate concierge. Expect a lot of corporate bustle at this megahotel, a hard-working staff, and occasional touches of charm that help overcome the hotel's sense of anonymity. *Hint:* The enormous size of this hotel, and the ongoing efforts of the sales and marketing staff to keep its occupancy levels high, lead to promotional rates that can be much as 50% less than the official rates quoted below. Thanks to a business-oriented clientele, the demand is lower on weekends, so be sure to ask for discounts if you're staying then.

81 bd. Gouvion Saint-Cyr, 75017 Paris. (℗ **01-40-68-34-34**. Fax 01-40-68-31-31. www.lemeridien-etoile.com. 1,025 units. 185€–450€ ($241–$585) double; from 625€ ($813) suite. AE, DC, MC, V. Parking 23€ ($30). Métro: Porte Maillot. **Amenities:** 2 restaurants; bar; jazz club/nightclub; car rental; business center; gift shop; room service; babysitting; laundry service; dry cleaning; nonsmoking rooms; rooms for those w/limited mobility; currency exchange. *In room:* A/C, TV, minibar, hair dryer, safe.

MODERATE

Best Western Regent's Garden ⊛ Near the convention center (Palais des Congrès) and the Arc de Triomphe, the Regent's Garden boasts a proud heritage: Napoleon III built this château for his physician. The interior resembles a classically decorated country house. Guest rooms have flower prints on the walls, traditional French furniture, and tall soundproof windows, plus neatly organized private bathrooms with both a tub and shower. A garden with ivy-covered walls and umbrella-shaded tables makes for a perfect place to meet other guests.

6 rue Pierre-Demours, 75017 Paris. © **800/528-1234** in the U.S., or 01-45-74-07-30. Fax 01-40-55-01-42. www.
hotel-paris-garden.com. 39 units. 189€–319€ ($246–$415) double. AE, DC, MC, V. Parking 12€ ($16). Métro: Ternes
or Charles de Gaulle–Etoile. **Amenities:** Babysitting; garden; nonsmoking rooms. *In room:* A/C, TV, Wi-Fi, minibar, hair
dryer, safe.

INEXPENSIVE
Hôtel de Palma ★ *Finds*   Although this hotel is off the beaten track for most visitors, some patrons like the quiet residential neighborhood that surrounds it, as well as its quick access by Métro to other parts of Paris. The location is only a 15-minute walk to the Air France/Roissy bus stops. Built at the beginning of the 20th century expressly as a hotel, this seven-story structure totters on the borderline between a government-rated two-star hotel and a three-star hotel, with very reasonable prices for a hostelry in that category. The lobby, with its rattan chairs and prints of animals from the savannah, has a vaguely African colonial aura. The bedrooms, with their warm, sunny colors, evoke Provence. About two-thirds of the rooms contain showers, and the other one-third tubs; there are no tub/shower combinations. Only the bedrooms on the sixth floor are air-conditioned. In honor of the hotel's namesake, the breakfast room is adorned with potted palms.

46 rue Brunel, 75017 Paris. © **01-45-74-74-51.** Fax 01-45-74-40-90. www.hotelpalma-paris.com. 37 units.
135€–145€ ($176–$189) double. AE, DC, MC, V. Métro: Argentine. RER: Neuilly–Porte Maillot. **Amenities:** Bar; room
service. *In room:* A/C (in some), TV, hair dryer.

Hôtel Flaubert   For an inexpensive retreat in the 17th, this is as good as it gets. The staff long ago became accustomed to handling the problems their international guests might have. Terra-cotta tiles and bentwood furniture in the public areas make for an efficient, if not lushly comfortable, setting for breakfast. Though the climbing plants in the courtyard overshadow the guest rooms, the accommodations are appealing and, particularly those beneath the mansard's eaves, cozy. In 2000, management added about a dozen new rooms, thanks to the acquisition and refurbishment of a building next door. Throughout, rooms are modern, relatively small scale, and comfortable. About half of the private bathrooms contain tubs, the others showers.

19 rue Rennequin, 75017 Paris. © **01-46-22-44-35.** Fax 01-43-80-32-34. www.hotelflaubert.com. 41 units. 112€
($146) double. AE, DC, MC, V. Métro: Ternes. **Amenities:** Room service; garden. *In room:* TV.

3 On the Left Bank
We'll begin with the most centrally located arrondissements on the Left Bank and then work our way through the more outlying neighborhoods and to the area near the Eiffel Tower.

5TH ARRONDISSEMENT (QUARTIER LATIN)
MODERATE
Grand Hôtel Saint-Michel   Built in the 19th century, this hotel is larger and more businesslike than many town house–style inns nearby. It basks in the reflected glow of Brazilian dissident Georges Amado, whose memoirs recorded his 2-year sojourn in one of the rooms. In 1997, the hotel completed a renovation and moved from two- to three-star status, and it has been continuously renovated since. The public areas are tasteful, with portraits and rich upholsteries. All but four rooms have tub/shower combinations. The improvements enlarged some rooms, lowering their ceilings and adding amenities, but retained old-fashioned touches such as wrought-iron balconies (on the fifth floor). Triple rooms have an extra bed and are suitable for families who

Where to Stay on the Left Bank (5–6 & 13–14e)

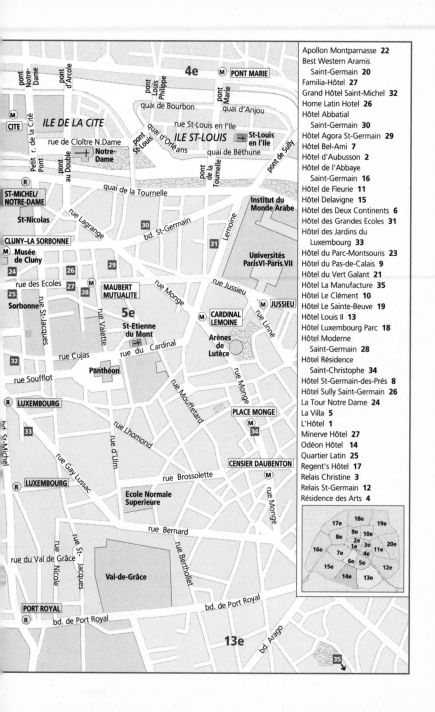

4e Ⓜ PONT MARIE

pont Notre-Dame
pont d'Arcole
pont Louis Philippe
pont Marie

quai de Bourbon
quai d'Anjou

Ⓜ CITE

ILE DE LA CITE

rue de la Cité
Petit r. de la Cité
Petit Pont
pont au Double

rue de Cloître N.Dame
rue St-Louis en l'Ile
pont St-Louis
quai d'Orléans

ILE ST-LOUIS
St-Louis en l'Ile

Notre-Dame
quai de Béthune
pont de Sully

quai de la Tournelle
pont de la Tournelle

Ⓡ ST-MICHEL/ NOTRE-DAME

St-Nicolas

rue Lagrange

Institut du Monde Arabe

CLUNY–LA SORBONNE

Ⓜ Musée de Cluny

bd. St-Germain

24   26   29

rue des Ecoles   27   Ⓜ 28
25

MAUBERT MUTUALITE

Sorbonne

rue St-Jacques

rue Monge   rue Jussieu

30

31

Lemoine

Universités Paris VI-Paris VII

Ⓜ JUSSIEU

rue Linné

5e

St-Etienne du Mont

rue Valette

Ⓜ CARDINAL LEMOINE

Arènes de Lutèce

rue Cujas   rue du Cardinal

Panthéon

rue Soufflot

rue Mouffetard

rue Monge

Ⓡ LUXEMBOURG

33

bd. St-Michel

rue L'homond

rue d'Ulm

PLACE MONGE
Ⓜ
34

rue Gay Lussac

rue Brossolette

CENSIER DAUBENTON
Ⓜ

Ⓡ LUXEMBOURG

Ecole Normale Superieure

rue Bernard

rue Monge

rue St-Jacques
rue Nicole

rue du Val de Grâce

Val-de-Grâce

rue Berthollet

Ⓡ PORT ROYAL

PORT ROYAL

bd. de Port Royal

bd. de Port Royal

13e

bd. Arago

35

17e 18e 19e
9e 10e
8e 2e 3e 20e
1e 11e
16e 7e 4e
6e 5e 12e
15e 14e 13e

share a private bathroom with tub and shower. Others have only shower, toilet, and sink. Sixth-floor rooms have views over the rooftops.

19 rue Cujas, 75005 Paris. ☎ 01-46-33-33-02. Fax 01-40-46-96-33. 45 units. 170€ ($221) double; 220€ ($286) triple. AE, DC, MC, V. Métro: Cluny–La Sorbonne. RER: Luxembourg or St-Michel. **Amenities:** Bar; room service; babysitting; laundry service; dry cleaning; rooms for those w/limited mobility. *In room:* A/C, TV, minibar, hair dryer, safe.

Hôtel Abbatial Saint-Germain

The origins of this hotel run deep: Interior renovations have revealed such 17th-century touches as dovecotes and oak beams. A restoration made the public areas appealing and brought the small guest rooms, furnished in faux Louis XVI, up to modern standards. Rooms were again restored in 2005. All the beds are fitted with immaculate linens. All windows are double-glazed, and the fifth- and sixth-floor units enjoy views over Notre-Dame. The neatly kept bathrooms are equipped with showers.

46 bd. St-Germain, 75005 Paris. ☎ 01-46-34-02-12. Fax 01-43-25-47-73. www.abbatial.com. 43 units. 145€– 189€ ($189–$246) double. AE, MC, V. Parking 19€ ($25). Métro: Cluny–La Sorbonne. **Amenities:** Room service; babysitting; nonsmoking rooms. *In room:* A/C, TV, minibar, hair dryer, safe.

Hôtel Agora St-Germain

One of the neighborhood's best moderately priced choices, this hotel occupies a building constructed in the early 1600s, probably to house a group of guardsmen protecting the brother of the king at his lodgings nearby. It's in the heart of artistic/historic Paris and offers compact, soundproof guest rooms that were each renovated in 2005. All but seven of the bedrooms have tub/shower combinations; the rest have only showers.

42 rue des Bernardins, 75005 Paris. ☎ 01-46-34-13-00. Fax 01-46-34-75-05. www.agorasaintgermain.com. 39 units. 169€–189€ ($220–$246) double. AE, DC, MC, V. Parking 22€ ($29). Métro: Maubert-Mutualité. **Amenities:** Room service; laundry service; dry cleaning. *In room:* A/C, TV, Wi-Fi, minibar, hair dryer, safe.

Hôtel des Jardins du Luxembourg

Built during Baron Haussmann's 19th-century overhaul of Paris, this hotel boasts an imposing facade of honey-colored stone accented with ornate iron balconies. Sigmund Freud stayed here in 1885. The interior is outfitted in strong, clean lines, often with groupings of Art Deco furnishings. The high-ceilinged guest rooms, some with Provençal tiles and ornate moldings, are well maintained, the sizes ranging from small to medium. Best of all, they overlook a quiet dead-end alley, ensuring relatively peaceful nights. Some have balconies overlooking the rooftops. Ongoing renovations have kept the bedrooms looking spiffy. Each unit comes with a neat, tidily arranged bathroom with a tub/shower combo.

5 Impasse Royer-Collard, 75005 Paris. ☎ 01-40-46-08-88. Fax 01-40-46-02-28. www.les-jardins-du-luxembourg. com. 26 units. 140€–150€ ($182–$195) double. AE, DC, MC, V. Parking 16€ ($20). Métro: Cluny–La Sorbonne. RER: Luxembourg. **Amenities:** Bar; sauna; room service; babysitting; laundry service; dry cleaning; nonsmoking rooms; rooms for those w/limited mobility. *In room:* A/C, TV, Wi-Fi, minibar, hair dryer, safe.

Hôtel Sully Saint-Germain ⭐

With its medieval-style decoration and its numerous and beautiful antiques, this hotel is a winning choice with a bit of charm. A government-rated three-star hotel, it captures much of the spirit of the Quartier Latin in the St-Germain-des-Prés area in the heart of the Left Bank. At your doorstep are some of Paris's major attractions, including Notre-Dame, Cluny Abbey, the banks of the Seine, and even the Louvre and Orsay museums. The public rooms are not overly adorned but are furnished with taste and comfort in mind. The midsize bedrooms, with brass beds set against stone walls, are handsomely furnished and comfortable. They're not grand, but are imbued with Parisian charm.

31 rue des Ecoles, 75005 Paris. ✆ **01-43-26-56-02.** Fax 01-43-29-74-42. www.hotel-paris-sully.com. 61 units. 110€–160€ ($143–$208) double; 220€ ($286) junior suite. AE, DC, MC, V. Métro: Maubert-Mutualité. **Amenities:** Bar; fitness room; Jacuzzi; sauna; hammam (steam bath); room service; laundry service; dry cleaning; nonsmoking rooms. *In room:* A/C, TV, Wi-Fi, minibar, hair dryer, safe.

La Tour Notre Dame ⚘   In the heart of the Sorbonne district, this restored Latin Quarter hotel rises seven floors over a 17th-century vaulted cellar where breakfast is served. A hotel of Rive Gauche character, it is ideally situated for Left Bank living, lying between St-Germain-des-Prés and the cathedral of Notre-Dame, opposite the Sorbonne and the Cluny Museum. Bedrooms, many with exposed beams, have been given a decorator's touch, and they are adorned with certain romantic accents. Liberty prints and Empire-era furniture decorate many of the bedrooms, which are beautifully maintained. Sixty percent of the bathrooms contain a shower; the rest, bathtubs.

20 rue du Sommerard, 75005 Paris. ✆ **01-43-54-47-60.** Fax 01-43-26-42-34. www.la-tour-notre-dame.com. 48 units. 172€–232€ ($224–$302) double. AE, DC, MC, V. Métro: Cluny–Sorbonne. RER: Saint-Michel or Notre-Dame. **Amenities:** Bar; business center; laundry service. *In room:* TV, Wi-Fi, minibar, hair dryer, safe.

Quartier Latin   Between the Sorbonne and the Musée de Cluny, this hotel captures the flavor of the Paris literati better than any other in Paris. Its decor was conceived by Didier Gomez in 1997, who referred to it as "contemporary with cultural references." That means walls stenciled with passages from Victor Hugo or photographs of Colette and André Gide. Even the breakfast room is stocked with bookshelves and its ceiling inscribed with quotes from Baudelaire. Bibliomania continues in the lobby, which is filled with floor-to-ceiling bookcases. Bedrooms are decorated comfortably and tastefully in blue and white, with such delicacies as linen curtains, along with fine wood furnishings, plus white-tiled bathrooms that are large and equipped with tub or shower. In all, this is a "novel" hotel and ideal for bookworms.

9 rue des Ecoles, 75005 Paris. ✆ **01-44-27-06-45.** Fax 01-43-25-36-70. www.hotelquartierlatin.com. 29 units. 177€–220€ ($230–$286) double. AE, MC, V. Métro: Cardinal Lemoine. **Amenities:** Room service; babysitting; laundry service; dry cleaning; nonsmoking rooms; rooms for those w/limited mobility. *In room:* A/C, TV, Wi-Fi, minibar, hair dryer, safe.

INEXPENSIVE

Familia-Hôtel   As the name implies, this hotel has been family-run for decades. Many personal touches make the place unique. Finely executed sepia-colored frescoes of Parisian scenes grace the walls of 14 rooms. Eight units have restored stone walls, and seven boast balconies with delightful views over the Latin Quarter. Half of the bathrooms come with tubs as well as showers. The dynamic owners renovate the rooms as often as needed to maintain the highest level of comfort.

11 rue des Ecoles, 75005 Paris. ✆ **01-43-54-55-27.** Fax 01-43-29-61-77. www.hotel-paris-familia.com. 30 units. 97€–127€ ($126–$165) double, 154€ ($200) triple; 176€ ($229) quad. Parking 20€ ($26). AE, DC, MC, V. Métro: Jussieu or Maubert-Mutualité. **Amenities:** Car rental; nonsmoking rooms. *In room:* TV, minibar, hair dryer.

Home Latin Hotel *Value*   This is one of Paris's most famous budget hotels, known since the 1970s for its simple lodgings. The functional rooms are renovated; some have small balconies overlooking the street. Those facing the courtyard are quieter than those on the street. The elevator goes only to the fifth floor, but to make up for the stair climb, the sixth floor's *chambres mansardées* offer a romantic location under the eaves and panoramic views. Thirty-nine units come with a shower only; the rest have a tub/shower combination.

15–17 rue du Sommerard, 75005 Paris. ℂ **01-43-26-25-21.** Fax 01-43-29-87-04. www.homelatinhotel.com. 54 units. 106€ ($138) double; 127€ ($165) triple. AE, DC, MC, V. Métro: St-Michel or Maubert-Mutualité. *In room:* TV, hair dryer.

Hôtel des Grandes Ecoles *(Value* Few hotels in the neighborhood offer so much low-key charm at such reasonable prices. It's composed of a trio of high-ceilinged buildings, interconnected via a sheltered courtyard, where in warm weather, singing birds provide a worthy substitute for the TVs deliberately missing from the rooms. Accommodations, as reflected by the price, range from snug, cozy doubles to more spacious chambers. All units were renovated in 2001, with lesser repairs continuing regularly since then, and the small bathrooms with showers were also spruced up. Each room is comfortable, but with a lot of luggage, the very smallest would be cramped. The decor is old-fashioned, with feminine touches such as flowered upholsteries and ruffles. Many have views of a garden whose trellises and flower beds evoke the countryside.

75 rue de Cardinal-Lemoine, 75005 Paris. ℂ **01-43-26-79-23.** Fax 01-43-25-28-15. www.hotel-grandes-ecoles.com. 51 units. 110€–135€ ($143–$176) double. Extra bed 20€ ($26). MC, V. Parking 30€ ($39). Métro: Cardinal Lemoine, Jussieu, or Monge. RER: Port-Royal, Luxembourg. **Amenities:** Room service; babysitting; garden; nonsmoking rooms; rooms for those w/limited mobility. *In room:* Wi-Fi, hair dryer.

Hôtel Moderne Saint-Germain ℱ In the heart of the Latin Quarter, between the Pantheon and Saint-Michel, the Hôtel Moderne is better than ever since it ended the 20th century with a complete overhaul. Though the rooms are small, this is still one of the neighborhood's better three-star hotels. Its charming owner, Mme Gibon, welcomes guests to her spotless accommodations. In the units fronting rue des Ecoles, double-glazed windows hush the traffic. About half of the bathrooms have a tub as well as a shower. Guests can use the sauna and Jacuzzi at the Hôtel Sully next door.

33 rue des Ecoles, 75005 Paris. ℂ **01-43-54-37-78.** Fax 01-43-29-91-31. www.hotel-paris-stgermain.com. 45 units. 150€ ($195) double; 180€ ($234) triple. AE, DC, MC, V. Parking 26€ ($34). Métro: Maubert-Mutualité. **Amenities:** Fitness center; room service; laundry service; dry cleaning; nonsmoking rooms. *In room:* A/C, TV, hair dryer.

Hôtel-Résidence Saint-Christophe This hotel, in one of the Latin Quarter's undiscovered areas, offers a gracious English-speaking staff. It was created in 1987, when an older hotel was connected to a butcher shop. All the small to medium-size rooms have Louis XV–style furniture and carpeting. Half of the bathrooms have tubs in addition to showers.

17 rue Lacépède, 75005 Paris. ℂ **01-43-31-81-54.** Fax 01-43-31-12-54. www.charm-hotel-paris.com. 31 units. 110€–150€ ($143–$195) double. AE, DC, MC, V. Métro: Place Monge. **Amenities:** Nonsmoking rooms. *In room:* TV, minibar, hair dryer.

Minerve Hôtel This is a well-managed, government-rated two-star hotel in the heart of the Latin Quarter, with good-size, comfortable rooms and a staff with a sense of humor. Bedrooms have contemporary-looking mahogany furniture and walls covered in fabric. Try for one of 10 rooms with balconies where you can look out over the street life of Paris and, in some cases, enjoy a view of Notre-Dame. Depending on your room assignment, bathrooms range in dimension from cramped to midsize, each with a tub/shower combination. If there's no space at the Minerve, a staff member will arrange an equivalent (and equivalently priced) lodging in its sibling, the Familia, next door (see description above).

13 rue des Ecoles, 75005 Paris. ℂ **01-43-26-26-04.** Fax 01-44-07-01-96. www.hotel-paris-minerve.com. 54 units. 98€–132€ ($127–$172) double. AE, DC, MC, V. Métro: Cardinal Lemoine. **Amenities:** Room service; Wi-Fi (in lobby); 1 room for those w/limited mobility. *In room:* A/C, TV, hair dryer.

6TH ARRONDISSEMENT (ST-GERMAIN/LUXEMBOURG)
VERY EXPENSIVE

Hotel Bel-Ami ⭐ *(Finds)*   Until 2002, this was a simple government-rated three-star hotel that was known by a different name (L'Alliance St-Germain). Beginning at that time, the hotel was restored, floor by floor, to this four-star hotel, designed to appeal to fashion-conscious patrons, in the heart of the Left Bank cafe district. Its name translates as "handsome (male) friend." You'll get the feeling that this is an arts-conscious hotel whose minimalist public areas were built only after months of careful design by a team of trend-following architects. Expect color schemes of lilac walls, acid-green sofas, copper-colored tiles, bleached ash, and industrial-style lighting fixtures. Bedrooms contain a palette of earth tones, such as pistachio ice cream or pumpkin pie, and an almost aggressively minimalist, even cubist, design. Bathrooms are artfully spartan, usually with tub/shower combinations and white marble trim. The hip and well-meaning staff sometimes gets overwhelmed by the ego-driven needs of demanding clients.

7–11 rue St. Benoît, 75006 Paris. ⓒ **01-42-61-53-53.** Fax 01-49-27-09-33. www.hotel-bel-ami.com. 115 units. 270€–440€ ($351–$572) double; 490€–540€ ($637–$702) suite. AE, DC, MC, V. Métro: St-Germain-des-Prés. **Amenities:** Bar; espresso bar; fitness center; room service; laundry service; dry cleaning; computer workstations with Internet access (in the lobby). *In room:* TV, minibar, safe.

Hôtel d'Aubusson ⭐⭐⭐   This mansion in the heart of St-Germain-des-Prés was the site of the city's first literary salon. Fully restored, it is today one of the best of the luxe boutique hotels of Paris. It's graced with original Aubusson tapestries. Lying 2 blocks south of pont Neuf and the Seine, the hotel has taken over a former private residence from the 1600s, to which is attached a 1950s building. It opens onto a beautiful courtyard. You enter a grand hall under a beamed ceiling with a baronial fireplace and furnishings in the style of Louis XV. There are also a number of smaller, more intimate lounges. The bedrooms are midsize to large, each attractively and comfortably furnished, often in a Directoire style and sometimes with exposed ceiling beams. Antiques are often placed in front of the original stone walls. For the most traditional flair, ask for one of the rooms on the top two floors. The best units are labeled deluxe, and these are quite large and graced with canopied beds.

33 rue Dauphine, Paris 75006. ⓒ **01-43-29-43-43.** Fax 01-43-29-12-62. www.hoteldaubusson.com. 49 units. 295€–450€ ($384–$585) double. AE, DC, MC, V. Parking: 25€ ($33). Métro: Odéon. **Amenities:** Bar; cafe; room service; babysitting; laundry service; dry cleaning; nonsmoking rooms; rooms for those w/limited mobility. *In room:* A/C, TV, Wi-Fi, minibar, hair dryer, safe.

L'Hôtel   Ranking just a notch below the Relais Christine, this is one of the Left Bank's most charming boutique hotels. It was once a 19th-century fleabag whose major distinction was that Oscar Wilde died in one of its bedrooms, but today's guests aren't anywhere near destitution. In 2000, superstar aesthete Jacques Garcia redecorated the hotel, retaining its Victorian-baroque sense. Other than for maintenance purposes, the decor has remained virtually intact ever since. Guest rooms vary in size, style, and price; all have decorative fireplaces and fabric-covered walls. All the sumptuous beds have tasteful fabrics and crisp linens. About half the bathrooms are small, tubless nooks. Room themes reflect China, Russia, Japan, India, or high-camp Victorian. The Cardinal room is all scarlet, the Viollet-le-Duc room is neo-Gothic, and the room where Wilde died is Victorian. One spacious room contains the furnishings (including multiple mirrors) and memorabilia of stage star Mistinguett. The cellar holds a small swimming pool and hammam (steam bath).

13 rue des Beaux-Arts, 75006 Paris. ℂ 01-44-41-99-00. Fax 01-43-25-64-81. www.l-hotel.com. 20 units. 255€–740€ ($332–$962) double; 640€–740€ ($832–$962) suite. AE, DC, MC, V. Métro: St-Germain-des-Prés. **Amenities:** Restaurant; bar (see chapter 11); indoor pool; steam room; room service; babysitting; laundry service; dry cleaning. *In room:* A/C, TV, minibar, hair dryer, safe.

Relais Christine   This hotel welcomes you into a former 16th-century Augustinian cloister. From a cobblestone street, you enter a symmetrical courtyard and find an elegant reception area with sculpture and Renaissance antiques. Each room is uniquely decorated with wooden beams and Louis XIII–style furnishings; the rooms come in a range of styles and shapes. Some are among the Left Bank's largest, with extras such as mirrored closets, plush carpets, thermostats, and some balconies facing the courtyard. The least attractive rooms are in the interior. Bed configurations vary, but all mattresses are on the soft side, offering comfort with quality linens. Each unit comes with a tub and shower. Since 2003, at least four, if not five, of the rooms have been renovated annually.

3 rue Christine, 75006 Paris. ℂ 01-40-51-60-80. Fax 01-40-51-60-81. www.relais-christine.com. 51 units. 335€–450€ ($436–$585) double; 530€–750€ ($689–$975) duplex or suite. AE, DC, MC, V. Free parking. Métro: Odéon or St-Michel. **Amenities:** Honor bar; gym; room service; massage; babysitting; laundry service; dry cleaning; nonsmoking rooms. *In room:* A/C, TV, minibar, hair dryer, safe.

Relais St-Germain   It's difficult to exaggerate the charm of this deeply personalized and intimate hotel created from side-by-side 17th-century town houses. You'll navigate your way through a labyrinth of narrow and winding hallways to soundproofed bedrooms that are spacious, and artfully and individually decorated in a style that evokes late-19th-century Paris at its most sensual. Two of the rooms have outdoor terraces. Come here for a discreet escape from the anonymity of larger, less personalized hotels, and for an injection of boutique-style Parisian charm. Even *Vogue* magazine referred to this place as "an oasis of Left-Bank charm." We heartily agree.

9 carrefour de l'Odéon, 75006 Paris. ℂ 01-43-29-12-05. Fax 01-46-33-45-30. www.hotelrsg.com. 22 units. 275€–360€ ($358–$468) double; 420€ ($546) suite. Rates include breakfast. AE, DC, MC, V. **Amenities:** Restaurant; room service; Internet access; laundry service; dry cleaning. *In room:* A/C, TV, dataport, minibar, hair dryer, safe.

EXPENSIVE

Hôtel de Fleurie 🌟 *Kids*   Off the boulevard St-Germain on a colorful little street, the Fleurie is one of the best of the city's "new" old hotels; its statuary-studded facade recaptures 17th-century elegance, and the stone walls in the salon have been exposed. Many of the guest rooms have elaborate draperies and antique reproductions. All of the bedrooms were renovated early in the millennium. Some rooms have tub/shower combinations; others, a full bathroom with a shower stall. Because some rooms are larger than others and contain an extra bed for one or two children, the hotel has long been a family favorite.

32–34 rue Grégoire-de-Tours, 75006 Paris. ℂ 01-53-73-70-00. Fax 01-53-73-70-20. www.fleurie-hotel-paris.com. 29 units. 170€–280€ ($221–$364) double; 305€–350€ ($397–$455) family room. Children younger than 13 stay free in parent's room. AE, DC, MC, V. Métro: Odéon or Mabillon. **Amenities:** Bar; car rental; room service; babysitting; laundry service; dry cleaning; rooms for those w/limited mobility. *In room:* A/C, TV, minibar, hair dryer, safe.

Hôtel de l'Abbaye Saint-Germain 🌟   This is one of the district's most charming boutique hotels, built as a convent in the early 18th century. Its brightly colored rooms have traditional furniture, plus touches of sophisticated flair. In front is a small garden and in back is a verdant courtyard with a fountain, raised flower beds, and masses of ivy and climbing vines. If you don't mind the expense, one of the most charming rooms has a terrace overlooking the upper floors of neighboring buildings. Guest rooms are midsize to large, with tiled, full bathrooms, and are continually maintained. Suites are generous in size and full of Left Bank charm, often with antique reproductions.

10 rue Cassette, 75006 Paris. © **01-45-44-38-11.** Fax 01-45-48-07-86. www.hotel-abbaye.com. 44 units. 221€–330€ ($287–$429) double; 410€–462€ ($533–$601) suite. Rates include breakfast. AE, MC, V. Métro: St-Sulpice. **Amenities:** Bar; room service; laundry service; dry cleaning. *In room:* A/C, TV, hair dryer, safe.

Hôtel Le Sainte-Beuve ✦ *Finds*   Lying off the tree-lined boulevard Raspail, this Montparnasse choice is close to the "Lost Generation" cafes made famous in the pages of Ernest Hemingway's *The Sun Also Rises.* The famous English decorator, David Hicks, had a hand in the stylish decor. If you stay here, you're just 3 minutes from the Luxembourg Gardens. You enter a small reception area opening into a Georgian parlor with plush sofas, armchairs, columns, and even a marble fireplace for those nippy Paris nights. Bedrooms are often furnished in part with antiques, but have all the modern comforts. Some come with small sitting rooms; all have marble bathrooms equipped with everything from deluxe toiletries to make-up mirrors. The cheaper rooms are small. If you can afford it, ask for one of the deluxe units that also have love seats and safes.

9 rue Ste-Beuve, 75006 Paris. © **01-45-48-20-07.** Fax 01-45-48-67-52. www.hotel-sainte-beuve.fr. 22 units. 138€–192€ ($179–$250) double; 246€ ($320) deluxe double; 288€ ($374) junior suite. AE, DC, MC, V. Métro: Notre-Dame-des-Champs or Vavin. **Amenities:** Bar; room service; babysitting; laundry service; dry cleaning. *In room:* A/C, TV, Wi-Fi, minibar, hair dryer, safe.

Hôtel Luxembourg Parc ✦✦   Near the Luxembourg Gardens for those lovely strolls, this elegant bastion of fine living has been called a small-scale version of the swank Hôtel de Crillon. In one of the Left Bank's most charming and historic districts, a 17th-century palace has been beautifully restored and decorated. The bedrooms are decorated in the styles of Louis XV, Louis XVI, and Napoleon III. The bar is an elegant rendezvous point and the library is relaxing. Bathrooms are generous in size, and units contain such thoughtful touches as bathrobes and plenty of hangers. The around-the-clock room service is actually takeout from nearby restaurants. The breakfast room on the ground floor overlooks the Luxembourg Gardens.

42 rue de Vaugirard, 75006 Paris. © **01-53-10-36-50.** Fax 01-53-10-36-59. www.luxembourg-paris-hotel.com. 23 units. 290€–550€ ($377–$715) double. AE, DC, MC, V. Métro: Luxembourg. **Amenities:** Bar; room service; fitness center; laundry service; rooms for those w/limited mobility. *In room:* A/C, TV, Wi-Fi, minibar, hair dryer, safe.

La Villa ✦   This hotel's facade resembles those of many of the other buildings in the neighborhood. Inside, however, the decor is a minimalist ultramodern creation rejecting traditional French aesthetics. The public areas and guest rooms contain Bauhaus-like furniture; the lobby's angular lines are softened with bouquets of leaves and flowers. Most unusual are the tubs, whose stainless steel and pink, black, or beige marble are decidedly postmodern. Everything was renovated in 2000 and all but four units contain a complete tub and shower.

29 rue Jacob, 75006 Paris. © **01-43-26-60-00.** Fax 01-46-34-63-63. www.villa-saintgermain.com. 31 units. 265€–335€ ($345–$436) double; 445€ ($579) suite. AE, DC, MC, V. Métro: St-Germain-des-Prés. **Amenities:** Bar; room service; babysitting; rooms for those w/limited mobility. *In room:* A/C, TV, Wi-Fi, minibar, hair dryer, safe.

Odéon Hôtel ✦   Reminiscent of a modernized Norman country inn, the Odéon has such rustic touches as exposed beams, stone walls, high ceilings, and tapestries mixed with contemporary fabrics, mirrored ceilings, and black leather furnishings.

Near the Théâtre de l'Odéon and boulevard St-Germain, the Odéon stands on the first street in Paris to have pavements (ca. 1779). By the 20th century, this area began attracting such writers as Gertrude Stein and her coterie. The guest rooms are small to medium in size but charming; each comes with a tub/shower combination. The beds are excellent, with reading lamps and bedside controls.

3 rue de l'Odéon, 75006 Paris. ℂ 01-43-25-90-67. Fax 01-43-25-55-98. www.odeonhotel.fr. 33 units. 170€–270€ ($221–$351) double. AE, DC, MC, V. Métro: Odéon. **Amenities:** Bar; room service; babysitting; laundry service; dry cleaning; nonsmoking rooms. *In room:* A/C, TV, hair dryer, safe.

MODERATE

Best Western Aramis Saint-Germain   Between St-Germain-des-Prés and Montparnasse, this is a recently renovated hotel that is attractively modernized and gracefully comfortable. Individually decorated bedrooms are midsize and furnished in a sleek, modern fashion, each with a private tiled bathroom with tub and shower. Nine of the bedrooms also contain a private Jacuzzi, and rooms are also soundproofed. The English-speaking staff is helpful.

124 rue de Rennes, 75006 Paris. ℂ 800/528-1234 in the U.S., or 01-45-48-03-75. Fax 01-45-44-99-29. www.hotel-aramis.com. 42 units. 160€–210€ ($208–$273) double; 200€–250€ ($260–$325) triple. Rooms with Jacuzzi 30€ ($39) extra. AE, DC, MC, V. Métro: Rennes or Sainte Placide. **Amenities:** Private bar; babysitting; laundry service; dry cleaning; nonsmoking rooms. *In room:* A/C, TV, Wi-Fi, minibar, coffeemaker, hair dryer, safe.

Hôtel des Deux Continents   Built from three interconnected historic buildings, each between three and six stories high, this hotel is a reliable choice with a sense of Latin Quarter style. The carefully coordinated guest rooms range from small to medium size and include reproductions of antique furnishings and soundproof upholstered walls. Rooms are equipped with neatly tiled shower bathrooms, a third of which also have tubs.

25 rue Jacob, 75006 Paris. ℂ 01-43-26-72-46. Fax 01-43-25-67-80. www.2continents-hotel.com. 41 units. 152€–170€ ($198–$221) double; 200€ ($260) triple. MC, V. Métro: St-Germain-des-Prés. *In room:* A/C, TV, Wi-Fi, hair dryer.

Hôtel du Pas-de-Calais   The Pas-de-Calais goes back to the 17th century. It retains its elegant facade, with wooden doors. Novelist Chateaubriand lived here from 1811 to 1814, but its most famous guest was Jean-Paul Sartre, who struggled with the play *Les Mains Sales (Dirty Hands)* in room no. 41. The hotel is a bit weak on style, but as one longtime guest confided, "We still stay here for the memories." Rooms are small; inner units surround a courtyard with two garden tables and several trellises. Each bathroom has a tub and shower.

59 rue des Sts-Pères, 75006 Paris. ℂ 01-45-48-78-74. Fax 01-45-44-94-57. www.hotelpasdecalais.com. 38 units. 160€–230€ ($208–$299) double; 300€ ($390) suite. AE, DC, MC, V. Parking 25€ ($33). Métro: St-Germain-des-Prés or Sèvres-Babylone. **Amenities:** Bar; room service; babysitting; laundry service; dry cleaning; nonsmoking rooms; rooms for those w/limited mobility. *In room:* A/C, TV, hair dryer, safe.

Hôtel Louis II   In an 18th-century building, this hotel offers guest rooms decorated in rustic French tones. Afternoon drinks and morning coffee are served in the reception salon, where gilt-framed mirrors, fresh flowers, and antiques radiate a provincial aura, like something out of Proust. The generally small, soundproof rooms with exposed beams and lace bedding complete the impression. Many visitors ask for the romantic attic rooms.

2 rue St-Sulpice, 75006 Paris. ℂ 01-46-33-13-80. Fax 01-46-33-17-29. www.hotel-louis2.com. 22 units. 190€–220€ ($247–$286) double; 290€ ($377) junior suite. AE, DC, MC, V. Métro: Odéon. **Amenities:** Room service; laundry service; dry cleaning. *In room:* A/C (in some), TV, Wi-Fi, minibar, hair dryer, safe.

Hôtel St-Germain-des-Prés   Most of this hotel's attraction comes from its location in the Latin Quarter, behind a well-known Left Bank street. Janet Flanner, the legendary 1920s *New Yorker* correspondent, lived here for awhile. The guest rooms are small but charming, with antique ceiling beams and safes; air-conditioning is available in most. The public areas are severely elegant. Most of the bathrooms contain tubs and all come with showers.

36 rue Bonaparte, 75006 Paris. ℂ 01-43-26-00-19. Fax 01-40-46-83-63. 30 units. 170€–265€ ($221–$345) double; 325€ ($423) suite. Rates include breakfast. AE, MC, V. Métro: St-Germain-des-Prés. **Amenities:** Room service; babysitting; laundry service; dry cleaning; nonsmoking rooms. *In room:* A/C, TV, Wi-Fi, minibar, hair dryer, safe.

Résidence des Arts ⍟   A converted 1550 residence, this winner is filled with handsomely decorated suites, studios, and apartments in the heart of the Latin Quarter. The structure was an apartment building until the mid-1990s, and two additional floors were added when it opened for business in 1998. Regular doubles are rented with shower-only bathrooms. Each suite and apartment has a large sitting room with a hide-a-bed and a separate bedroom with a king-size bed. Suites and apartments have full bathrooms with tubs and showers, and each apartment comes with a kitchenette. The furnishings are tasteful and comfortable, and the service is first-rate. A bistro and restaurant are connected to the hotel.

14 rue Git-le-Coeur, 75006 Paris. ℂ 01-55-42-71-11. Fax 01-55-42-71-00. www.hotelresidencedesartsparis.com. 11 units. 190€–225€ ($247–$293) double; 280€–350€ ($364–$455) junior suite. AE, DC, MC, V. Métro: St-Michel. **Amenities:** Restaurant; bar; room service; babysitting; laundry service; dry cleaning; nonsmoking rooms. *In room:* A/C, TV, Wi-Fi, kitchenette, minibar, hair dryer, safe (in some).

INEXPENSIVE

Hôtel Delavigne   Despite modernization, you still get a sense of the 18th-century origins of the building, which is next to the Luxembourg Gardens. The public areas reveal a rustic use of chiseled stone, some of it original. The high-ceilinged guest rooms are tasteful, sometimes with wooden furniture, often with upholstered headboards, and sometimes with Spanish-style wrought iron. All but four of the bathrooms have both a tub and a shower.

1 rue Casimir-Delavigne, 75006 Paris. ℂ 01-43-29-31-50. Fax 01-43-29-78-56. www.hoteldelavigne.com. 34 units. 140€–155€ ($182–$202) double; 170€ ($221) triple. AE (accepted for Internet reservations only), MC, V. Métro: Odéon. **Amenities:** Room service; massage; babysitting; laundry service; dry cleaning. *In room:* TV, hair dryer, safe.

Hôtel Le Clément   This hotel sits on a narrow street within sight of the towers of St-Sulpice church. The building dates to the 1700s, but was renovated several years ago. Rooms are comfortably furnished but often small, although in 2000 some walls in the smaller rooms were knocked down, creating larger units. Most of the bathrooms contain tubs; two units have shower-only bathrooms.

6 rue Clément, 75006 Paris. ℂ 01-43-26-53-60. Fax 01-44-07-06-83. www.hotel-clement.com. 28 units. 117€–150€ ($152–$195) double; 145€–150€ ($189–$195) suite. AE, DC, MC, V. Métro: Mabillon. **Amenities:** Bar; room service. *In room:* A/C, TV, hair dryer, safe.

Regent's Hôtel *Value*   In the heart of St-Germain-des-Prés, this is a smart Left Bank address. This hotel is in a neighborhood of tony boutiques and fashionable hair salons, just a short walk from the Jardin du Luxembourg, where Hemingway strolled as a poor struggling artist looking for pigeons to kill for his dinner. This is a high-quality choice at reasonable prices, considering its location. Inside, carved-wood headboards, fluffy bedspreads, and flower boxes in the windows evoke sunny Provence. We prefer the rooms on the top floor, with their slender balconies overlooking Paris rooftops.

All the furnishings are comfortable, and the bathrooms, with tub and shower, are completely restored. Some rooms open onto a secluded courtyard where breakfast is served if the weather behaves. A few rooms are big enough to accommodate a family of four.

44 rue Madame, 75006 Paris. ✆ **01-45-48-02-81.** Fax 01-45-44-85-73. www.france-hotel-guide.com. 34 units. 80€–110€ ($104–$143) double; 95€–125€ ($124–$163) triple. AE, MC, V. Métro: Rennes or St-Sulpice. RER: Luxembourg. **Amenities:** Car rental; room service; babysitting; rooms for those w/limited mobility. *In room:* TV, hair dryer, safe.

13TH ARRONDISSEMENT (GARE D'AUSTERLITZ)
MODERATE
Hôtel La Manufacture ⚘ *Finds*   If you don't mind its offbeat 13th Arrondissement location, this undiscovered hotel, with good rooms and decent prices, lying on a small street near place d'Italie, is a real find. It is only 10 minutes by Métro from the stations at Montparnasse and Gare de Lyon. Small to midsize bedrooms are decorated in printed fabrics and soothing pastels, and the large bathrooms are spotlessly maintained, each with a shower. The most desirable room is no. 74 because of its distant views of the Eiffel Tower. This restored 19th-century building has a wrought-iron door and is graced with iron lamps, wicker chairs, oak floors, and bright paintings. It contains a number of old-fashioned armoires called *chapeau de gendarme* (police hat). The staff is one of the most helpful we've discovered in our tours of Paris's small hotels. Each day the staff serves a different set of pastries.

8 rue Philippe de Champagne (av. des Gobelins), 75013 Paris. ✆ **01-45-35-45-25.** Fax 01-45-35-45-40. www.hotel-la-manufacture.com. 56 units. 133€–225€ ($173–$293) double; 199€–240€ ($259–$312) triple. AE, DC, MC, V. Métro: Place d'Italie. **Amenities:** Bar; breakfast room; room service; laundry service; dry cleaning; nonsmoking rooms. *In room:* A/C, TV, hair dryer, iron.

INEXPENSIVE
Hôtel du Vert Galant   Verdant climbing plants and shrubs make this hotel feel like an *auberge* (inn) deep in the French countryside. The smallish guest rooms have tiled or carpeted floors, unfussy furniture, and (in most cases) views of the garden or the public park across the street. All bathrooms have showers, and nearly three-fourths of them also contain tubs. One of the hotel's best aspects is the Basque restaurant next door, the Auberge Etchegorry, sharing the same management; hotel guests receive a discount.

41 rue Croulebarbe, 75013 Paris. ✆ **01-44-08-83-50.** Fax 01-44-08-83-69. www.vertgalant.com. 15 units. 90€–120€ ($117–$156) double. AE, MC, V. Parking 15€ ($20). Métro: Corvisart or Gobelins. RER: Gare d'Austerlitz. **Amenities:** Restaurant; room service; laundry service; dry cleaning. *In room:* TV, Wi-Fi, minibar, hair dryer, safe.

14TH ARRONDISSEMENT (MONTPARNASSE)
INEXPENSIVE
Apollon Montparnasse   This privately owned hotel lies in Montparnasse, former home of such Left Bank residents as Gertrude Stein and Alice B. Toklas. Since opening, the hotel has established a reputation for its good rates and very comfortable bedrooms, which are midsize and furnished with flower spreads and draperies. Each bedroom has a well-maintained bathroom with tub or shower.

91 rue de l'Ouest, 75014 Paris. ✆ **01-43-95-62-00.** Fax 01-43-95-62-10. www.apollon-montparnasse.com. 33 units. 89€–94€ ($116–$122) double. AE, DC, MC, V. Métro: Pernety. **Amenities:** Breakfast lounge; room service. *In room:* AC, TV, Wi-Fi, minibar, hair dryer, safe.

Hôtel du Parc-Montsouris   The residential neighborhood is far removed from central Paris's bustle, the staff is a bit absent-minded, and the decor doesn't pretend to be stylish, but the prices are reasonable enough that this government-rated two-star hotel attracts loyal repeat guests. They might be parents of students studying at the nearby Cité Universitaire or provincial clothiers attending fashion shows at the nearby Porte de Versailles. The guest rooms are low-key and quiet, each renovated in the late 1990s. Singles and doubles are small, but the triples are spacious, the apartments even more so. Bathrooms contain tubs and showers, except for the seven with showers only.

4 rue du Parc de Montsouris, 75014 Paris. ℂ **01-45-89-09-72.** Fax 01-45-80-92-72. www.hotel-parc-montsouris. com. 35 units. 72€ ($94) double; 81€ ($105) triple; 100€ ($130) apt. AE, DC, MC, V. Métro: Porte d'Orléans. RER: Cité-Universitaire. **Amenities:** Room service; laundry service; dry cleaning. *In room:* TV, Wi-Fi, hair dryer.

7TH ARRONDISSEMENT (EIFFEL TOWER/MUSEE D'ORSAY)
VERY EXPENSIVE
Hôtel Montalembert   Unusually elegant for the Left Bank, the Montalembert dates from 1926, when it was built in the Beaux Arts style. Its beige, cream, and gold decor borrows elements of Bauhaus and postmodern design. The guest rooms are spacious except for some standard doubles that are small unless you're a very thin model. Frette linens decorate roomy beds topped with cabana-stripe duvets that crown deluxe French mattresses. The bathrooms are luxurious with deep tubs, Cascais marble, and tall pivoting mirrors.

3 rue de Montalembert, 75007 Paris. ℂ **800/786-6397** in the U.S. and Canada, or 01-45-49-68-68. Fax 01-45-49-69-49. www.montalembert.com. 56 units. 350€–450€ ($455–$585) double; 580€–800€ ($754–$1,040) suite. AE, DC, MC, V. Parking 39€ ($51). Métro: Rue du Bac. **Amenities:** Restaurant; bar; access to nearby health club; room service; laundry service; dry cleaning. *In room:* A/C, TV, minibar, hair dryer, safe.

EXPENSIVE
Bourgogne & Montana   Across from the Palais Bourbon and just 2 blocks from the Seine, this boutique hotel resides in the same tony neighborhood as such famous Parisian residents as Karl Lagerfeld. It is only a short walk to the landmark place du Palais-Bourbon and the boulevard St-Germain. A six-floor hotel, the building itself dates from 1791. Two of the bedrooms open onto the Grand Palais or the Assemblée Nationale, and from some windows you can see all the way down to the place de la Concorde. A 1924 cage elevator takes visitors to the accommodations, which are mid-size for the most part, although some are small and have no view whatsoever. Each room is individually decorated, often in Empire style or with Empire reproductions. All contain tiled bathrooms that, though small, are equipped with tubs and showers. The lounge is also small, but has a marble-topped bar. Rollet Pradier, one of the city's best *patisseries,* lies just across the street.

3 rue de Bourgogne, 75007 Paris. ℂ **01-45-51-20-22.** Fax 01-45-56-11-98. www.bourgogne-montana.com. 32 units. 170€–250€ ($221–$325) double; 305€ ($397) suite. Rates include breakfast. AE, DC, MC, V. Métro: Invalides. **Amenities:** Bar; room service; babysitting; laundry service; dry cleaning. *In room:* A/C, TV, Wi-Fi, minibar, hair dryer.

Hôtel de l'Académie 👁👁   The exterior walls and old ceiling beams are all that remain of this 18th-century residence of the duc de Rohan's private guards. Other than its Renaissance origins and associations with the duc de Rohan, this place is locally famous for having housed poet and novelist Antonio Marchado, "the Victor Hugo of Spain," between 1909 and 1914. In 1999, the hotel was completely renovated to include an elegant reception area. The up-to-date guest rooms, each renovated in 2003 and 2004, have a lush Ile-de-France decor and views over the neighborhood's 18th- and 19th-century buildings. By American standards, the rooms are small, but they're average for Paris. All but eight bathrooms have full tub/shower combos.

32 rue des Sts-Pères, 75007 Paris. ☎ **800/246-0041** in the U.S. and Canada, or 01-45-49-80-00. Fax 01-45-44-75-24. www.academiehotel.com. 33 units. 199€–229€ ($259–$298) double; 299€ ($389) suite. AE, DC, MC, V. Parking 23€ ($30). Métro: St-Germain-des-Prés. **Amenities:** Room service; babysitting; laundry service; dry cleaning; nonsmoking rooms. *In room:* A/C, TV, Wi-Fi, minibar, hair dryer, safe.

Hôtel de l'Université ⭐ Long favored by well-heeled parents of North American students studying in Paris, this 300-year-old, antiques-filled town house enjoys a location in a discreetly upscale neighborhood. Room no. 54 is a favorite, containing a rattan bed, period pieces, and a terrace. Another charmer is room no. 35, which has a nonworking fireplace and opens onto a courtyard with a fountain. Many of the bathrooms were renovated throughout the hotel. Each unit comes with a well-maintained bathroom equipped with a tub/shower combination. Beds have plush comfort and discreet French styling. You'll sleep well here.

22 rue de l'Université, 75007 Paris. ☎ **01-42-61-09-39.** Fax 01-42-60-40-84. www.hoteluniversite.com. 27 units. 165€–180€ ($215–$234) double. AE, DC, MC, V. Métro: St-Germain-des-Prés. **Amenities:** Room service. *In room:* A/C, TV, minibar, hair dryer, safe.

Hôtel Le Tourville ⭐ This is a well-managed, personalized town house between the Eiffel Tower and Les Invalides. It originated in the 1930s as a hotel and was revitalized much later into the charmer of today. Bedrooms offer original art, antique furnishings or reproductions, and wooden furniture covered in modern, sometimes bold, upholsteries. Four of the rooms, including the suite, have private terraces. Beds are queens or twins, each of which was recently replaced. About half of the well-maintained bathrooms have tub/shower combinations, and most were renovated in 2004. The staff is well trained, with the kinds of personalities that make you want to linger at the reception desk. Breakfast is the only meal served, but you can get a drink in the lobby.

16 av. de Tourville, 75007 Paris. ☎ **01-47-05-62-62.** Fax 01-47-05-43-90. www.hoteltourville.com. 30 units. 170€–250€ ($221–$325) double; 330€ ($429) suite. AE, MC, V. Métro: Ecole Militaire. **Amenities:** Bar; room service; laundry service; dry cleaning; nonsmoking rooms; rooms for those w/limited mobility. *In room:* A/C, TV, hair dryer.

Hôtel Verneuil ⭐ *(Finds)* Small-scale and personal, this hotel, in the words of a recent critic, "combines modernist sympathies with nostalgia for *la vieille France* [old-fashioned France]." Built in the 1600s as a town house, it is a creative and intimate jumble of charm and coziness inside. Expect a mixture of antique and contemporary furniture; lots of books; and, in the bedrooms, *trompe l'oeil* ceilings, antique beams, quilts, and walls covered in fabric that comes in a rainbow of colors. The well-kept bathrooms come with tub/shower combinations.

8 rue de Verneuil, 75007 Paris. ☎ **01-42-60-82-14.** Fax 01-42-61-40-38. www.hotelverneuil.com. 26 units. 155€–210€ ($202–$273) double. AE, DC, MC, V. Métro: St-Germain-des-Prés. **Amenities:** Bar; room service; babysitting; laundry service; dry cleaning. *In room:* A/C (in some), TV, minibar, hair dryer, safe.

MODERATE

Best Western Derby Eiffel This hotel faces the Ecole Militaire and contains airy public areas. Our favorite is a glass-roofed conservatory in back, filled year-round with plants and used as a breakfast area. The soundproof and modern guest rooms employ thick fabrics and soothing neutral colors. Most front-facing rooms have views of the Eiffel Tower. In 1998, enormous sums were spent upgrading the rooms and bathrooms and improving the hotel's interior aesthetics, and renovations have been going on ever since. All bathrooms have showers and half-tubs.

Where to Stay on the Left Bank (7e)

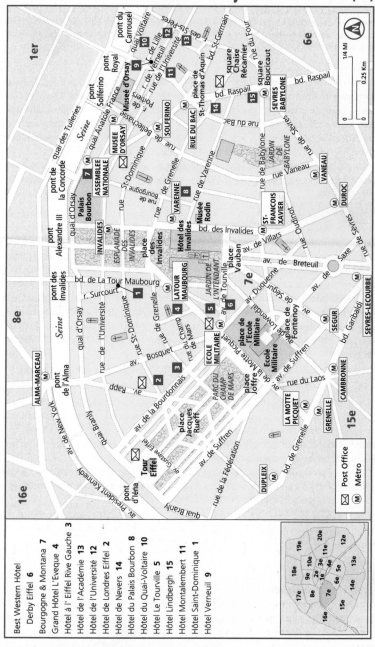

Best Western Hôtel
    Derby Eiffel **6**
Bourgogne & Montana **7**
Grand Hôtel L'Eveque **4**
Hôtel à l' Eiffel Rive Gauche **3**
Hôtel de l'Académie **13**
Hôtel de l'Université **12**
Hôtel de Londres Eiffel **2**
Hôtel de Nevers **14**
Hôtel du Palais Bourbon **8**
Hôtel du Quai-Voltaire **10**
Hôtel Le Tourville **5**
Hôtel Lindbergh **15**
Hôtel Montalembert **11**
Hôtel Saint-Dominique **1**
Hôtel Verneuil **9**

⊠ Post Office
Ⓜ Métro

5 av. Duquesne, 75007 Paris. ℂ **800/528-1234** in the U.S. and Canada, or 01-47-05-12-05. www.bestwestern.com. Fax 01-47-05-43-43. 43 units. 135€–180€ ($176–$234) double; 165€ ($215) triple. AE, DC, MC, V. Métro: Ecole Militaire. **Amenities:** Room service; babysitting; laundry service; dry cleaning; nonsmoking rooms. *In room:* A/C, TV, minibar, hair dryer, safe.

INEXPENSIVE

Grand Hôtel L'Eveque   Built in the 1930s, this hotel draws lots of English-speaking guests, many of whom appreciate its proximity to the Eiffel Tower. The pastel-colored guest rooms retain an Art Deco inspiration, just enough space to be comfortable, and double-insulated windows overlooking a courtyard in back or the street in front. Suites are only slightly larger than double rooms. The small bathrooms contain shower units.

29 rue Cler, 75007 Paris. ℂ **01-47-05-49-15.** Fax 01-45-50-49-36. www.hotel-leveque.com. 50 units. 90€–115€ ($117–$150) double; 130€ ($169) triple. AE, MC, V. Métro: Ecole Militaire. **Amenities:** Breakfast room. *In room:* A/C, TV, hair dryer, safe.

Hôtel à l'Eiffel Rive Gauche   The charm of this family-owned and -run, intimate hotel derives from a very small on-site team and the sense that you've entered a distinctive universe that's very closely linked to the surrounding upscale residential neighborhood. Built around 1900, the hotel retains such original touches as the black-and-white, checkerboard-patterned floor tiles from the 1930s. Bedrooms are outfitted in tones of off-white and dark Bordeaux, with vaguely French Empire themes scattered with some angular furniture from the 1960s and 1970s. The hotel lies on a tranquil street in the heart of the so-called "Triangle" (Eiffel, Invalides, and Champs-Elysées).

6 rue du Gros Caillou, 75007 Paris. ℂ **01-45-51-24-56.** Fax 01-45-51-11-77. www.hotel-eiffel.com. 29 units. 75€–125€ ($98–$163) double; 95€–145€ ($124–$189) triple; 105€–175€ ($137–$228) quad. MC, V. Métro: Ecole Militaire. *In room:* TV, fridge, hair dryer, safe.

Hôtel de Londres Eiffel   Small and charming, this independently run hotel is just a 2-minute walk from the Eiffel Tower. Completely renovated, it is "dressed" in colors of yellow and raspberry, which is far more harmonious and elegant than the combination sounds. In a residential district (one of the best in Paris), the bedrooms are midsize and tastefully decorated, each with an individual decoration. The top floors open onto views of the illuminated Eiffel Tower at night. Bathrooms are small but well equipped, with either a tub or shower.

1 rue Augereau, 75007 Paris. ℂ **01-45-51-63-02.** Fax 01-47-05-28-96. www.londres-eiffel.com. 30 units. 150€–165€ ($195–$215) double. AE, DC, MC. Parking 34€ ($44). Métro: Ecole Militaire. **Amenities:** Rooms for those w/ limited mobility. *In room:* A/C, TV, minibar, hair dryer.

Hôtel de Nevers   This is one of the neighborhood's most historic choices—it was a convent from 1627 to 1790. In 2000, many aspects were upgraded and renovated. The building is *classé,* meaning any restoration must respect the original architecture. That precludes an elevator, so you'll have to use the beautiful wrought-iron staircase. The cozy, pleasant guest rooms contain a mix of antique and reproduction furniture. Room nos. 10 and 11 are especially sought after for their terraces overlooking a corner of rue du Bac or a rear courtyard. About half of the units have tub/shower combinations.

83 rue du Bac, 75007 Paris. ℂ **01-45-44-61-30.** Fax 01-42-22-29-47. 11 units. 89€–99€ ($116–$129) double. MC, V. Métro: Rue du Bac. **Amenities:** Room service. *In room:* TV, minibar, hair dryer.

Hôtel du Palais Bourbon   The solid stone walls of this 18th-century building aren't as grand as those of the embassies and stately homes nearby. But don't be put off by the tight entranceway and rather dark halls: Though the guest rooms on the upper floors are larger, all the rooms are pleasantly decorated, with carefully crafted built-in furniture. Each bathroom contains both a tub and a shower.

49 rue de Bourgogne, 75007 Paris. ✆ **01-44-11-30-70.** Fax 01-45-55-20-21. www.hotel-palais-bourbon.com. 32 units. 110€–125€ ($143–$163) double; 145€ ($189) triple; 162€ ($211) quad. Rates include breakfast. MC, V. Métro: Varenne. **Amenities:** Room service (breakfast only); laundry service; dry cleaning; nonsmoking rooms. *In room:* A/C, TV, minibar, hair dryer, safe.

Hôtel du Quai Voltaire   Built in the 1600s as an abbey and transformed into a hotel in 1856, the Quai Voltaire is best known for such illustrious guests as Wilde, Richard Wagner, and Baudelaire, who occupied room nos. 47, 55, and 56, respectively. Camille Pissarro painted *Le Pont Royal* from the window of his fourth-floor room. Many guest rooms in this modest inn have been renovated; most overlook the bookstalls and boats of the Seine. Each unit comes with a tub-and-shower bathroom, except for five that have a shower only.

19 quai Voltaire, 75007 Paris. ✆ **01-42-61-50-91.** Fax 01-42-61-62-26. www.quaivoltaire.fr. 33 units. 124€–132€ ($161–$172) double; 159€ ($207) triple. AE, DC, MC, V. Parking 24€ ($31). Métro: Musée d'Orsay or Rue du Bac. **Amenities:** Bar; room service; laundry service. *In room:* Hair dryer.

Hôtel Lindbergh   A 5-minute walk from St-Germain-des-Prés, this hotel provides streamlined, simple guest rooms. About two-thirds of the bathrooms contain tubs as well as showers. Breakfast is the only meal served, but the staff will point out good restaurants nearby—an inexpensive bistro, Le Cigale, is quite close.

5 rue Chomel, 75007 Paris. ✆ **01-45-48-35-53.** Fax 01-45-49-31-48. www.hotellindbergh.com. 26 units. 136€–160€ ($177–$208) double; 174€–180€ ($226–$234) triple; 184€–190€ ($239–$247) quad. AE, DC, MC, V. Parking 27€ ($35). Métro: Sèvres-Babylone or St-Sulpice. **Amenities:** Limited room service (breakfast only); laundry service; dry cleaning; 1 room for those w/limited mobility. *In room:* TV, Wi-Fi (in some), hair dryer.

Hôtel Saint-Dominique   Part of this place's charm derives from its division into three buildings connected through an open-air courtyard. The most visible of these was an 18th-century convent—you can still see its ceiling beams and structural timbers in the reception area. The guest rooms aren't large, but each is warm and simply decorated. About a third of the bathrooms have full tub/shower combinations; the remaining have only showers. About half of the rooms have been renovated since 2004.

62 rue St-Dominique, 75007 Paris. ✆ **01-47-05-51-44.** Fax 01-47-05-81-28. www.hotelstdominique.com. 34 units. 93€–121€ ($121–$157) double. AE, MC, V. Métro: Latour-Maubourg or Invalides. **Amenities:** Room service. *In room:* TV, minibar, hair dryer, safe.

4 Near the Airports

ORLY

MODERATE

Hilton Paris Orly Airport ✦   Boxy and bland, the Hilton at Orly is a well-maintained, especially convenient business hotel. Noise from incoming planes can't penetrate the guest rooms' sound barriers, giving you a decent shot at a night's sleep. (Unlike the 24-hr. Charles de Gaulle Airport, Orly is closed to arriving flights from midnight to 6am.) The rooms are standard for a chain hotel; each was renovated in the late 1990s, with tub/shower combinations.

Aéroport Orly, 267 Orly Sud, 94544 Orly Aérogare Cedex. ✆ **800/445-8667** in the U.S. and Canada, or 01-45-12-45-12. Fax 01-45-12-45-00. www.hilton.com. 351 units. 130€–210€ ($169–$273) double; 205€–285€ ($267–$371) suite. AE, DC, MC, V. Parking 14€ ($18). Free shuttle bus between hotel and both Orly terminals. **Amenities:** Restaurant; bar; fitness center; sauna; room service; babysitting; laundry service; dry cleaning; nonsmoking rooms; rooms for those w/limited mobility. *In room:* A/C, TV, hair dryer.

INEXPENSIVE

Kyriad Air Plus   Also boxy and contemporary-looking, and connected with Orly by frequent 10-minute complimentary shuttle-bus rides, this 1990s hotel offers standard bedrooms. Rooms are comfortable, insulated against airport noise, and a bit larger than you might expect. Each unit comes with a neatly tiled bathroom with tub and shower.

58 voie Nouvelle (near the Parc Georges Méliès), 94544 Orly. ☎ 01-41-80-75-75. Fax 01-41-80-12-12. airplus@club-internet.fr. 72 units. 65€–73€ ($85–$95) double. AE, DC, MC, V. Parking 9.50€ ($12). Transit to and from airport by complimentary shuttle bus. **Amenities:** Restaurant; room service; nonsmoking rooms; rooms for those w/limited mobility. *In room:* A/C, TV, Wi-Fi, coffeemaker, hair dryer.

CHARLES DE GAULLE

EXPENSIVE

Hôtel Sofitel Paris Aéroport CDG ✹   Many travelers pass happily through this bustling, somewhat anonymous member of the French chain. It employs a multilingual staff accustomed to accommodating international business travelers. The conservatively furnished guest rooms are soundproof havens against the all-night roar of jets. Suites are larger and more comfortable, although they are not especially elegant and are consistent with the chain format. Each unit comes with a tiled bathroom with tub and shower.

Aéroport Charles de Gaulle, Zone Central, B.P. 20248, 95713 Roissy. ☎ 800/221-4542 in the U.S. and Canada, or 01-49-19-29-29. Fax 01-49-19-29-00. www.sofitel.com. 350 units. 275€–465€ ($358–$605) double; from 950€ ($1,235) suite. AE, DC, MC, V. Parking 12€ ($16). Free shuttle to and from airport. **Amenities:** Restaurant; bar; fitness center; indoor pool; business center; room service; laundry service; dry cleaning; nonsmoking rooms; rooms for those w/limited mobility. *In room:* A/C, TV, minibar, hair dryer, safe.

Hyatt Regency Paris–Charles de Gaulle ✹   This property is adjacent to the Charles de Gaulle Airport. Lying only a 25-minute drive from Disneyland Paris and a half-hour from the attractions of central Paris, the Roissy property was designed by the renowned architect Helmut Jahn. He created a stunning five-story structure of sleek design and tech-smart features. Inaugurated in 1994, this is the first hotel of its size to be built in Paris since 1975, and as airport hotels go, the cutting-edge architecture puts it in a class by itself. The builder allowed natural glass to flow into the hotel, with a spectacular glass atrium overlooking the lobby. Jet-lagged passengers find ultimate comfort in the elegantly furnished and soundproof guest rooms, which meld American convenience with European style. The state-of-the-art bathrooms contain separate showers and tubs.

351 av. du Bois de la Pie, 95912 Roissy. ☎ 01-48-17-12-34. Fax 01-48-17-17-17. http://paris.charlesdegaulle.hyatt. com. 388 units. 130€–330€ ($169–$429) double; 230€–370€ ($299–$481) suite. AE, DC, MC, V. RER1 train to airport, and then Hyatt shuttle. **Amenities:** Restaurant; bar; indoor pool; 2 tennis courts; fitness center; sauna; nearby jogging track; room service; babysitting; laundry service; dry cleaning. *In room:* A/C, TV, Wi-Fi, minibar, hair dryer, safe.

INEXPENSIVE

Hôtel Campanile de Roissy   This hotel is less expensive than most other lodgings near the airport. Its cement-and-glass design is barely masked by a thin overlay of cheerful-looking and rustic artifacts. Generally, this is an efficiently decorated, but not particularly stylish, place to stay, with a well-meaning but overworked staff. Each unit comes with a small, shower-only bathroom.

Parc de Roissy, 95700 Val-d'Oise. ☎ 01-34-29-80-40. Fax 01-34-29-80-39. www.campanile.fr. 260 units. 65€–135€ ($85–$176) double. AE, DC, MC, V. Free shuttle to and from Roissy. **Amenities:** Restaurant; bar; laundry service; dry cleaning; nonsmoking rooms; rooms for those w/limited mobility. *In room:* TV, hair dryer.

I don't speak sign language.

A hotel can close for all kinds of reasons.
Our Guarantee ensures that if your hotel's undergoing construction, we'll
let you know in advance. In fact, we cover your entire travel experience.
See www.travelocity.com/guarantee for details.

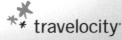

travelocity
You'll never roam alone.

©2007 Travelocity.com LP. LS1 # 20b8372-501

Where to Dine

Welcome to the city that prides itself on being the world's culinary capital. Only in Paris can you turn onto the nearest little crooked side street; enter the first nondescript bistro you see; sit down at a bare, wobbly table; order from an illegibly hand-scrawled menu; and get a wonderfully memorable meal.

See below for a list of our favorites: the best chef, the best view, the best old-fashioned bistro, and more.

1 Best Dining Bets

- **Best Chef:** Proud owner of six Michelin stars, **Alain Ducasse,** at the Restaurant Plaza Athénée, 25 av. Montaigne, 8e (© **01-53-67-66-65;** www.alain-ducasse. com), has taken Paris by storm, dividing his time between his restaurant here and the one in Monte Carlo. He combines produce from every French region in a cuisine that's contemporary but not quite new, embracing the Mediterranean without abandoning France. See p. 148.
- **Best Modern French Cuisine:** A temple of gastronomy is found at **Carré des Feuillants,** 14 rue de Castiglione, 1er (© **01-42-86-82-82;** www.carredesfeuillants.fr), near place Vendôme and the Tuileries. Alain Dutournier is one of the leading chefs of France, and he restored this 17th-century convent, turning it into a citadel of refined cuisine and mouthwatering specialties. See p. 128.
- **Best Provençal Cuisine:** With two of Michelin's coveted stars, **Les Elysées du Vernet,** 25 rue Vernet, 8e (© **01-44-31-98-98;** www.hotelvernet.com), hosts *tout Paris* (all of Paris) and the media. Montpellier-born chef Alain Solivérès has emerged as one of the greatest in Paris, challenging some big-name chefs. His Provençal cookery is the freshest and among the best in the entire country. See p. 146.
- **Best Old-Fashioned Bistro:** Established in 1931 and bouncing back from a period of decline, **Allard,** 41 rue St-André-des-Arts, 6e (© **01-43-26-48-23**), is better than ever, from its zinc bar to its repertoire of French classics—escargots, frogs' legs, foie gras, *boeuf à la mode* (marinated beef), and cassoulet. This is a good bet for real Left Bank bistro ambience. See p. 164.
- **Best Provincial Restaurant:** The cuisine of the Auvergne in central France is showcased at **Bath's,** 9 rue de la Trémoille, 8e (© **01-40-70-01-09**). In a cozy, elegant setting, you can dine on the best dishes of this province, including ravioli stuffed with Cantal cheese and filet of beef with lentils. See p. 148.
- **Best for Romance:** There is no more romantic atmosphere among restaurants than the long-established **Le Grand Véfour,** 17 rue de Beaujolais, 1er (© **01-42-96-56-27**). When Aristotle Onassis was wooing Jackie Kennedy, he took her here, preferring to dine with his mistress, Maria Callas, at the "more vulgar" Maxim's.

Sublime dishes are served against a restaurant decor that was established during the reign of Louis XV. See p. 128.

- **Best Brasserie:** Head for the Left Bank and the **Brasserie Balzar,** 49 rue des Ecoles, 5e (© **01-43-54-13-67;** www.brasseriebalzar.com), which opened in 1898. If you dine on the familiar French food here, you'll be following in the footsteps of Sartre and Camus and others. You can even have a complete dinner in the middle of the afternoon. See p. 160.
- **Best Seafood:** The fattest lobsters and prawns in the Rungis market emerge on platters at **Goumard,** 9 rue Duphot, 1er (© **01-42-60-36-07;** www.goumard. com), so chic that even the toilets are historic monuments. Nothing interferes with the taste of the sea: You'd have to fly to the Riviera to find a better bouillabaisse. See p. 129.
- **Best Kosher Food:** If corned beef, pastrami, herring, and dill pickles thrill you, head to **rue des Rosiers** in the 4th Arrondissement (Métro: St-Paul). John Russell wrote that rue des Rosiers is the "last sanctuary of certain ways of life; what you see there in miniature is Warsaw before the ghetto was razed." North African overtones reflect the long-ago arrival of Jews from Morocco, Tunisia, and Algeria. The best time to go is Sunday morning: You can wander the streets, eating as you go—apple strudel; Jewish rye bread; pickled lemons; smoked salmon; and *merguez,* a spicy smoked sausage from Algeria.
- **Best Vegetarian Cuisine:** One of the best-known veggie restaurants in the Marais is **Le Marais,** 54 rue Ste-Croix-de-la-Bretonnerie, 4e (© **01-48-87-48-71**). Choose from the array of soups and salads, or have a mushroom tart or a *galette* (a flat pastry) of wheat with raw vegetables. In this rustic 17th-century setting, you can expect flavorful, wholesome, and generous meals. See p. 139.
- **Best Wine Cellar:** At the elegant **Lasserre,** 17 av. Franklin D. Roosevelt, 8e (© **01-43-59-53-43;** www.restaurant-lasserre.com), you'll find not only wonderful food, but also one of the great wine cellars of France, with some 160,000 bottles. See p. 145.

2 Food for Thought

WHAT'S COOKING IN FRANCE   Once you arrive in Paris, you'll find that the word "French," although used frequently, isn't very helpful in describing cuisine. "French" covers such a broad scope that it doesn't prepare you for the offerings of the specialty chefs. Even the Parisians themselves might ask, "What *type* of French cooking?"

Sometimes a chef will include regional specialties, classic dishes, and even modern cuisine all on one menu. In that case, such a restaurant is truly "French." Other chefs prefer a more narrow focus and feature the cooking of one region or one style—classic or modern. Still others prefer to strike a middle ground between classic and modern; they're called "creative."

Regional cuisine showcases the diversity of the provinces of France, from Alsace on the German border to the Basque country at the frontier of Spain. The climate has a lot to do with this diversified offering—olive oil, garlic, and tomatoes from Provence in the south to oysters and saltwater fish from Brittany. Every region is known for special dishes—Burgundy for its escargots plucked off the grapevines; Périgord for its truffles and foie gras; Normandy for its soft, rich cheeses, Calvados, and cream sauces; and Alsace for its sauerkraut and wines. Today, one or more restaurants in Paris represent almost every region of France. You can go on a complete culinary tour of the country without leaving the city.

Few chefs today use the expression **"nouvelle cuisine,"** now called "modern." This cooking style, which burst upon us in the early 1970s, is now old hat (or should we say old *toque?*). It was a rebellion against the fats, butter, and sauces of haute cuisine, and used reductions of foodstuff to create flavor, along with vegetable purées and lighter ingredients. Portions were reduced. Diners were shocked to see a piece of *boeuf* (beef) the size of an egg on their plate under a slice of fresh

> **Tips Mystifying Menu?**
>
> If you need help distinguishing a *boeuf à la mode* from a *crème brûlée,* turn to the glossary in appendix B.

kiwi. Created in the name of innovation, many of these dishes were successful, while others, such as asparagus ice cream, were dismal failures.

From nouvelle cuisine grew *cuisine improvisée,* which is creative cookery based on the freshest ingredients available. Chefs make their selections at the morning market and then rush back to their kitchens to create spontaneously, often while dictating the menu of the day to an assistant who rushes it into print.

But fans of the great chef Escoffier can rest assured that modern hasn't replaced **classic cuisine**—France is still awash in béchamel and ablaze with cognac. *Haute gastronomie* is alive and thriving at restaurants not only in Paris, but also throughout France. This richly extravagant fare is often lethal in price as it makes use of expensive ingredients, including fatted ducks, lobster, truffles, and plenty of butter and cream, plus sauces that consume endless time in their preparation. Breaking from Escoffier, many chefs today have forged ahead with a **"new classic cuisine,"** in which they have taken classic dishes and branded them with their own distinctive style and flavor, often reducing the calories.

PARIS'S RANGE OF RESTAURANTS   Paris boasts a surplus of restaurants and cafes. Ultra-expensive **temples of gastronomy** include Alain Ducasse, L'Astor, Taillevent, Pierre Gagnaire, Lasserre, Jacques Cagna, Le Grand Véfour, and La Tour d'Argent. Savvy diners confine their trips to luxe places for special occasions. An array of other choices awaits, including simpler restaurants dispensing cuisine from every province of France and former colonies such as Morocco and Algeria.

Paris has hundreds of restaurants serving exotic **international fare,** reflecting the changing complexion of Paris itself and the city's increasing appreciation for food from other cultures. Your most memorable meal in Paris may turn out to be Vietnamese or West African.

You'll also find hundreds of bistros, brasseries, and cafes. In modern times, their designations and roles have become almost meaningless. Traditionally, a **bistro** was a small restaurant, often with Mom at the cash register and Pop in the kitchen. Menus are most often handwritten or mimeographed, and the selection of dishes tends to be small. They can be chic and elegant, sometimes heavily Mediterranean, and often dispensing gutsy fare, including the *pot-au-feu* (beef simmered with vegetables) that the chef's grandmother prepared for him as a kid.

French for "brewery," most **brasseries** have an Alsatian connection, and that means lots of beer, although Alsatian wines are also featured. Brasseries are almost always brightly lit and open 24 hours. Both snacks and full meals are available. The Alsatian establishments serve sauerkraut with an array of pork products.

Tips Dining Savoir-Faire

- Most restaurants serve lunch between noon and 2:30pm and dinner from 7 to 10pm. In a cafe, if you stand at the bar for a drink, coffee, or sandwich, prices are reduced from what they would be if you were seated at a table. French cookery reaches perfection when accompanied by wine. The general label on bottles of national wine is known as *Appellation d'Origine Contrôllée* (abbreviated AOC). Wine labels are narrowed down to a particular vine-growing region. Of course, labels are only part of the story: It's the vintage that counts.

- Some of the most satisfying wines come from unlabeled house bottles or carafes, called *vin de la maison.* They're also the cheapest wines served. Some restaurants include a beverage in their fixed-price menu *(boisson compris).* French beers are cheaper than imported beers. One of the best French beers has a German sounding name. It's Kronenbourg, and it's bottled in Alsace.

- Three-star dining remains quite expensive, with appetizers sometimes priced at 58€ ($75) and dinners easily costing 185€ to 250€ ($241–$325) per person in the top dining rooms of celebrated chefs. But you can get around that high price tag in many places by **dining at lunch** (when prices are always cheaper) or ordering a prix-fixe meal at lunch or dinner.

- The **prix-fixe (fixed-price) menu** or *le menu* is a set meal that the chef prepares that day. It is most often fresh and promptly served, and represents a greater bargain than dining a la carte. Of course, it's limited, so you'll have to like the choices provided. Sometimes there are one to three menus, beginning with the less expensive and going up for a more elaborate meal. A lot depends on your pocketbook and appetite.

- In France, **lunch** (as well as dinner) tends to be a full-course meal with meat, vegetables, salad, bread, cheese, dessert, wine, and coffee. It may be difficult to find a restaurant that serves the type of light lunch North Americans usually eat. Cafes, however, offer sandwiches, soup, and salads in a relaxed setting.

- **Coffee** in France is served after the meal and carries an extra charge. The French consider it barbaric to drink coffee during the meal and, unless you order it with milk *(au lait),* it'll be served black. In more conscientious places, it's prepared as the traditional *café filtre,* a slow but rewarding java draw.

- In years gone by, no man would consider dining out, even at the neighborhood bistro, without a suit and tie, and no woman would be seen without a smart dress or suit. That **dress code** is more relaxed now, except in first-class and luxe establishments. Relaxed doesn't mean sloppy jeans and jogging attire, however. Parisians still value style, even when dressing informally.

- Sometimes service is added to your tab—usually 12% to 15%. If not, look for the words *service non compris* on your bill. That means that the cost of service was not added, and you'll be expected to leave a **tip.**

The **cafe** is a French institution and not just a place for an aperitif, a café au lait, or a croissant. Many cafes serve rib-sticking fare as well, certainly *entrecôte* (rib steak) with french fries, but often classics such as *blanquette de veau* (veal in white sauce). For more cafe lore, see section 6, "The Top Cafes," later in this chapter.

More attention in the late 1990s focused on the **wine bar**, a host of which we recommend in chapter 11, "Paris After Dark." Originally, wine bars concentrated on their lists of wines, featuring many esoteric choices and ignoring the food except for some *charcuterie* (cold cuts) and cheeses. Today, you're likely to be offered various daily specials, from homemade foie gras to *boeuf à la mode* (marinated beef braised with red wine and served with vegetables).

Paris prices may seem extravagant to visitors from other parts of the world, particularly those who don't live in big cities, but there has been an emergence of moderately priced **informal restaurants** here, and we recommend several.

Although not as fashionable as before, **baby bistros** are still around. At these reasonably priced spinoffs from deluxe restaurants, you can get a taste of the cuisine of famous chefs without breaking the bank. We cover the best of them.

3 Restaurants by Cuisine

ALGERIAN
Wally Le Saharien (9e, $$, p. 140)

ALSATIAN
Bofinger ✧ (4e, $$, p. 138)
Brasserie Flo (10e, $$, p. 141)
Jenny (3e, $, p. 137)

AMERICAN
Breakfast in America (5e, $, p. 161)
Joe Allen ✧ (1er, $$, p. 133)

ASIAN
Cabaret (1er, $$, p. 132)
Kambodjia (16e, $, p. 155)
Le Pré Verre ✧ (5e, $$, p. 161)

AUVERGNAT
Bath's (8e, $$$, p. 148)
Chez Savy ✧ (8e, $, p. 153)
L'Ambassade d'Auvergne ✧ (3e, $, p. 137)

BASQUE
Au Bascou ✧ (3e, $, p. 136)
Auberge Etchegorry (13e, $$, p. 166)
Chez l'Ami Jean (7e, $, p. 171)

BRETON
Chez Michel (10e, $$, p. 141)

BURGUNDIAN
Chez Pauline ✧ (1er, $$$, p. 129)

CAFES
Brasserie Lipp (6e, $$$, p. 174)
Café Beaubourg (4e, $$, p. 174)
Café de Flore ✧✧ (6e, $$$, p. 174)
Café de la Musique (19e, $$, p. 175)
Café de l'Industrie (11e, $, p. 177)
Cafe des Deux Moulins (18e, $, p. 177)
Fouquet's ✧ (8e, $$$, p. 174)
La Belle Hortense (4e, $$, p. 175)
La Coupole ✧ (14e, $$, p. 175)
La Palette ✧✧ (6e, $$, p. 176)
La Rotonde (6e, $$, p. 176)
Le Procope ✧✧ (6e, $$, p. 176)
Le Rouquet ✧ (7e, $, p. 177)
Les Deux Magots ✧✧ (6e, $$, p. 176)

CAMBODIAN
Kambodgia (16e, $, p. 155)

CANTONESE
Chez Vong ✧ (1er, $$$, p. 129)
China Club ✧ (12e, $$, p. 144)

Key to Abbreviations: $$$$ = Very Expensive $$$ = Expensive $$ = Moderate $ = Inexpensive

CHINESE

China Club ✴ (12e, $$, p. 144)
Le Canton (6e, $, p. 166)

CORSICAN

Chez La Vieille ✴ (1er, $$, p. 132)

FRENCH (MODERN)

Alcazar Restaurant ✴ (6e, $$, p. 163)
Bofinger (4e, $$, p. 138)
Cabaret (1er, $$, p. 132)
Café Panique ✴ (10e, $, p. 142)
Carré des Feuillants ✴✴✴ (1er, $$$$, p. 128)
Citrus Etoile, 151
Cristal Room ✴✴ (16e, $$$, p. 154)
Jacques Cagna ✴✴✴ (6e, $$$$, p. 162)
L'Absinthe (1er, $$, p. 133)
L'Arpège ✴✴✴ (7e, $$$$, p. 168)
Lasserre ✴✴✴ (8e, $$$$, p. 145)
L'Astrance ✴✴✴ (16e, $$$, p. 155)
L'Atelier de Joël Robuchon ✴✴ (7e, $$$, p. 168)
Le Chamarré ✴✴✴ (7e, $$$, p. 170)
Le Violon d'Ingres ✴✴✴ (7e, $$$, p. 170)
Marty ✴ (5e, $$, p. 161)
Michel Rostang ✴✴✴ (17e, $$$$, p. 156)
Pierre Gagnaire ✴✴✴ (8e, $$$$, p. 146)
Publicis Drugstore (8e, $$, p. 152)
Restaurant de l'Astor ✴ (8e, $$$, p. 149)
Restaurant Plaza Athénée (Alain Ducasse) ✴✴✴ (8e, $$$$, p. 148)
1728 ✴ (8e, $$$, p. 150)
Taillevent ✴✴✴ (8e, $$$$, p. 148)
Ze Kitchen Galerie ✴ (6e, $$, p. 165)

FRENCH (TRADITIONAL)

Allard ✴ (6e, $$, p. 164)
Angélina ✴✴ (1er, $, p. 134)
Au Petit Monsieur (11e, $$, p. 142)
Au Petit Riche ✴ (9e, $$, p. 140)
Au Pied de Cochon ✴✴ (1er, $$, p. 132)
Au Pied de Fouet (7e, $, p. 170)
Aux Charpentiers (6e, $, p. 165)

Aux Lyonnais ✴ (2e, $$, p. 135)
Bar des Théâtres ✴ (8e, $, p. 152)
Bath's (8e, $$$, p. 148)
Benoit ✴ (4e, $$$, p. 137)
Bistrot Paul Bert ✴ (11e, $$, p. 143)
Bofinger ✴ (4e, $$, p. 138)
Brasserie Balzar ✴ (5e, $$, p. 160)
Café Constant ✴ (7e, $, p. 171)
Chartier (9e, $, p. 141)
Chez André (8e, $$, p. 151)
Chez Georges (2e, $$, p. 135)
Chez Georges (17e, $$, p. 156)
Chez Gramond ✴ (6e, $$, p. 164)
Chez Jean ✴ (9e, $$, p. 140)
Chez La Vieille ✴ (1er, $$, p. 132)
Chez Pauline ✴ (1er, $$$, p. 129)
Chez Ramulaud ✴ (11e, $$, p. 143)
Closerie des Lilas ✴ (6e, $$$, p. 163)
Crémerie-Restaurant Polidor ✴ (6e, $, p. 165)
Guy Savoy ✴✴✴ (17e, $$$$, p. 155)
Hiramatsu ✴ (16e, $$$$, p. 153)
Jacques Cagna ✴✴✴ (6e, $$$$, p. 162)
Jamin ✴✴✴ (16e, $$$$, p. 153)
La Butte Chaillot ✴ (16e, $$, p. 155)
La Cagouille ✴ (14e, $$, p. 167)
Ladurée ✴ (8e, $$, p. 151)
La Grille (10e, $$, p. 141)
La Maison Blanche ✴✴ (8e, $$$, p. 149)
L'Ambassade d'Auvergne ✴ (3e, $, p. 137)
L'Ambroisie ✴(4e, $$$$, p. 137)
L'Ami Louis ✴ (3e, $$$, p. 136)
L'Angle du Faubourg ✴✴ (8e, $$$, p. 149)
La Petite Chaise (7e, $$, p. 170)
La Petite Hostellerie ✴ (5e, $, p. 162)
La Poule au Pot (1er, $$, p. 133)
La Régalade (14e, $$, p. 167)
La Rôtisserie d'en Face ✴ (6e, $$, p. 164)
Lasserre ✴✴✴ (8e, $$$$, p. 145)
La Tour d'Argent (5e, $$$$, p. 157)
L'Ebauchoir ✴ (12e, $, p. 145)
Le Caveau François Villon (1er, $, p. 134)
Le Cinq ✴✴✴ (8e, $$$$, p. 146)

Le Grand Véfour ★★★ (1er, $$$$, p. 128)
Le Pamphlet ★ (3e, $$, p. 136)
Le Petit Marguery (13e, $$, p. 166)
Le Petit Pontoise ★ (5e, $$, p. 160)
Le Pré Verre ★ (5e, $$, p. 161)
Les Gourmets des Ternes (8e, $$, p. 151)
Le Vaudeville (2e, $$, p. 135)
Le Vieux Bistro ★ (4e, $$, p. 139)
Michel Rostang ★★★ (17e, $$$$, p. 156)
Perraudin ★★ (5e, $$, p. 161)
Restaurant Caïus ★ (17e, $$, p. 157)
Restaurant Plaza Athénée (Alain Ducasse) ★★★ (8e, $$$$, p. 148)
Taillevent ★★★ (8e, $$$$, p. 148)

FUSION
Market ★ (8e, $$, p. 152)

GASCONY
Au Trou Gascon ★★★ (12e, $$$, p. 144)

INDIAN
Yugaraj (6e, $$, p. 164)

INTERNATIONAL
Georges ★ (4e, $$, p. 138)
Le Fumoir ★ (1er, $$, p. 133)
Senso ★★ (8e, $$$, p. 150)
Spoon, Food & Wine ★ (8e, $$$, p. 150)
Ze Kitchen Galerie ★ (6e, $$, p. 165)

ITALIAN
Il Cortile ★★ (1er, $$, p. 132)
Swann & Vincent (12e, $$, p. 144)

JAPANESE
1728 ★ (8e, $$$, p. 150)

LATE NIGHT
Au Pied de Cochon ★★ (1er, $$, p. 132)
La Poule au Pot (1er, $$, p. 133)
Le Vaudeville (2e, $$, p. 135)

LEBANESE
Al Dar (5e, $$, p. 160)

LOIRE VALLEY (ANJOU)
Au Petit Riche ★ (9e, $$, p. 140)

LYONNAIS
Aux Lyonnais ★ (2e, $$, p. 135)
Chez Henri (6e, $, p. 165)

MAURITIEN
Le Chamarré ★★★ (7e, $$$, p. 170)

MEDITERRANEAN
Il Cortile ★★ (1er, $$, p. 132)

MOROCCAN
Mansouria (11e, $$, p. 143)

ORGANIC
Le Grain de Folie (18e, $, p. 145)

POITEVINE
Le Petit Marguery (13e, $$, p. 166)

PROVENÇAL
Chez Janou (3e, $, p. 136)
La Bastide Odéon ★ (6e, $, p. 166)
La Maison Blanche ★★ (8e, $$$, p. 149)
Les Elysées du Vernet ★★★ (8e, $$$$, p. 146)

SEAFOOD
Goumard ★★★ (1er, $$$, p. 129)
La Cagouille ★ (14e, $$, p. 167)
La Grille (10e, $$, p. 141)
Le Marais (4e, $, p. 139)

SENEGALESE
Le Manguier (11e, $, p. 143)

SEYCHELLE ISLANDS
Coco de Mer ★ (5e, $, p. 162)

SOUTHWESTERN FRENCH
Chez l'Ami Jean (7e, $, p. 171)
La Braisière ★★ (17e, $$, p. 156)
La Fermette du Sud-Ouest ★ (1er, $, p. 134)
L'Assiette (14e, $$, p. 168)
Le Pamphlet ★ (3e, $$, p. 136)
Pinxo ★ (1er, $$, p. 134)
Restaurant d'Hélène/Salon d'Hélène ★★★ (6e, $$$$, p. 163)

> **Tips　Leave Home without Them**
>
> No matter how long you stay in Paris, we suggest you indulge in at least one break-the-bank French meal at a fabulous restaurant. It will be a memory you'll treasure long after you've recovered from paying the tab. However, to get a table at one of these places, **you must reserve far in advance**—at least a day or two ahead, sometimes even a few weeks or months ahead! We suggest you look over these listings and call for reservations before you leave home or at least as soon as you get into town.

TEA

Angélina ★★ (1er, $, p. 134)

THAI

Blue Elephant ★ (11e, $$$, p. 142)

VEGETARIAN

Le Grain de Folie (18e, $, p. 145)
Le Marais (4e, $, p. 139)

VIETNAMESE

Kim Anh (15e, $$, p. 171)
Le Canton (6e, $, p. 166)

4 On the Right Bank

We'll begin with the most centrally located arrondissements on the Right Bank and then work our way through the more outlying neighborhoods and to the area around the Arc de Triomphe.

1ST ARRONDISSEMENT
VERY EXPENSIVE

Carré des Feuillants ★★★ MODERN FRENCH　This is a bastion of perfection, an enclave of haute gastronomy. When chef Alain Dutournier turned this 17th-century convent between the place Vendôme and the Tuileries into a restaurant, it was an overnight success. The interior is artfully simple and even, in the eyes of some diners, spartan-looking. It has a vaguely Asian feel, shared by a series of small, monochromatic dining rooms that are mostly outfitted in tones of off-white, black, and beige, and that overlook a flowering courtyard and a glass-enclosed kitchen. You'll find a sophisticated reinterpretation of cuisine from France's southwest, using seasonal ingredients and lots of know-how. Examples include a cappuccino of chestnuts with white truffles; a "cake" of Jerusalem artichokes studded with foie gras and black truffles; grilled monkfish with crispy potatoes and French caviar (from the Gironde region of France), served with a cabbage lasagna and horseradish sauce; and grilled wood pigeon with chutney and polenta.

14 rue de Castiglione (near place Vendôme and the Tuileries), 1er. ✆ **01-42-86-82-82.** Fax 01-42-86-07-71. www.carredesfeuillants.fr. Reservations required far in advance. Main courses 55€–70€ ($72–$91); fixed-price lunch 65€–165€ ($85–$215); fixed-price dinner 165€ ($215). AE, DC, MC, V. Mon–Fri noon–2:30pm and 7:30–10pm. Closed Aug. Métro: Tuileries, Concorde, Opéra, or Madeleine.

Le Grand Véfour ★★★ TRADITIONAL FRENCH　This is the all-time winner: a great chef, the most beautiful restaurant decor in Paris, and a history-infused citadel of classic French cuisine. This restaurant has been around since the reign of Louis XV. Napoleon, Danton, Hugo, Colette, and Cocteau dined here—as the brass plaques on the tables testify—and it's still a gastronomic experience. Guy Martin, chef for the past decade, bases many items on recipes from the French Alps. He prepares such heavenly dishes as filet of lamb cooked with sweet Muscat wine, carved into rib sections and served with the smoked essence of its own juice. Other specialties are noisettes of lamb with star anise, Breton lobster, and cabbage sorbet in dark-chocolate sauce. The desserts are often grand, such as the *gourmandises au chocolat* (medley of chocolate), served with chocolate sorbet.

17 rue de Beaujolais, 1er. ⓒ 01-42-96-56-27. Fax 01-42-86-80-71. Reservations required far in advance. Main courses 75€–100€ ($98–$130); fixed-price menu 78€ ($101) lunch, 265€ ($345) dinner. AE, DC, MC, V. Mon–Fri 12:30–1:45pm; Mon–Thurs 8–9:30pm. Closed Aug. Métro: Louvre–Palais-Royal or Pyramides.

EXPENSIVE

Chez Pauline ⓡ *(Finds* BURGUNDIAN/TRADITIONAL FRENCH   Fans say this *bistro de luxe* is a less expensive, less majestic version of Le Grand Véfour. The early-1900s setting is grand enough to impress a business client and lighthearted enough to attract a roster of VIPs. Tables sit on two levels, among polished mirrors, red leather banquettes, and memorabilia of long-ago Paris. The emphasis is on the cuisine of central France—especially Burgundy—shown by the liberal use of wine in such favorites as cassoulet of Burgundian snails with bacon and tomatoes, *boeuf bourguignon* (braised beef in red-wine sauce) with tagliatelle, terrine of parsleyed ham, and roast venison in red wine. Also wonderful is the roasted Bresse chicken with dauphinois potatoes.

5 rue Villedo, 1er. ⓒ 01-42-96-20-70. Reservations recommended. Main courses 25€–35€ ($33–$46); fixed-price lunch 27€–45€ ($35–$59); fixed-price dinner 40€–55€ ($52–$72). AE, DC, V. Mon–Fri 12:15–2:30pm; Mon–Sat 7:15–10:30pm. Closed Sat May–Aug. Métro: Pyramides.

Chez Vong ⓡ CANTONESE   This is the kind of Les Halles restaurant you head for when you've had your fill of grand cuisine and pretensions. The decor is a soothing mix of greens and browns, steeped in a Chinese-colonial ambience that evokes early-1900s Shanghai. Menu items feature shrimp and scallops served as spicy as you like, including a super-hot version with garlic and red peppers, "joyous beef" with pepper sauce, chicken in puff pastry with ginger, and an array of fish dishes. The whims of fashion have deemed this one of the restaurants of the moment, so it's full of folks from the worlds of entertainment and the arts.

10 rue de la Grande-Truanderie, 1er. ⓒ 01-40-26-09-36. www.chez-vong.com. Reservations recommended. Main courses 25€–30€ ($33–$39); fixed-price lunch Mon–Fri 23€ ($30). AE, DC, MC, V. Mon–Sat noon–2:30pm and 7pm–midnight. Métro: Etienne-Marcel or Les Halles.

Goumard ⓡⓡⓡ SEAFOOD   Opened in 1872, this landmark is one of Paris's leading seafood restaurants. It's so devoted to the fine art of preparing fish that other food is banned from the menu (the staff will verbally present a limited roster of meat dishes). The decor consists of a collection of Lalique crystal fish in artificial aquariums. Even more unusual are the restrooms, classified as historic monuments; the Art Nouveau master cabinetmaker Majorelle designed the commodes in the early 1900s. Much of the seafood is flown in from Brittany daily. Examples are *craquant* (crisp-cooked) crayfish in herb salad, flash-fried scallops with black truffles, lobster soup with coconut, and grilled turbot salad on a bed of artichokes with tarragon. Nothing (no excess butter, spices, or salt) is allowed to interfere with the natural flavor of the sea.

9 rue Duphot, 1er. ⓒ 01-42-60-36-07. Fax 01-42-60-04-54. www.goumard.com. Reservations required far in advance. Main courses 39€–75€ ($51–$98); fixed-price menu 46€ ($60). AE, DC, MC, V. Daily noon–2:30pm and 7:30–10:30pm. Métro: Madeleine or Concorde.

Where to Dine on the Right Bank (1–4, 9–12 & 18–19e)

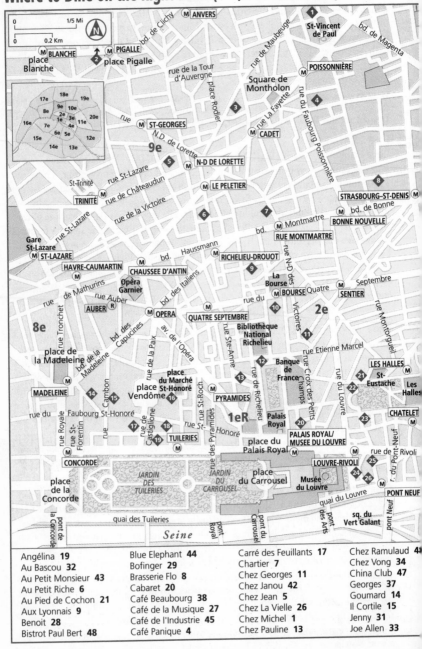

Angélina **19**	Blue Elephant **44**	Carré des Feuillants **17**	Chez Ramulaud **4**
Au Bascou **32**	Bofinger **29**	Chartier **7**	Chez Vong **34**
Au Petit Monsieur **43**	Brasserie Flo **8**	Chez Georges **11**	China Club **47**
Au Petit Riche **6**	Cabaret **20**	Chez Janou **42**	Georges **37**
Au Pied de Cochon **21**	Café Beaubourg **38**	Chez Jean **5**	Goumard **14**
Aux Lyonnais **9**	Café de la Musique **27**	Chez La Vielle **26**	Il Cortile **15**
Benoit **28**	Café de l'Industrie **45**	Chez Michel **1**	Jenny **31**
Bistrot Paul Bert **48**	Café Panique **4**	Chez Pauline **13**	Joe Allen **33**

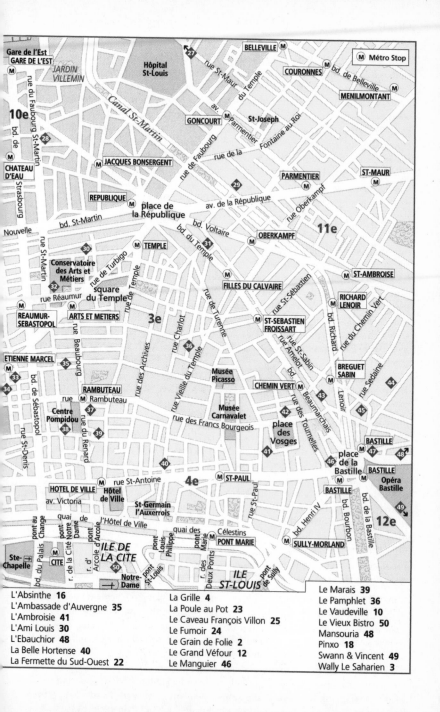

Gare de l'Est
GARE DE L'EST
JARDIN VILLEMIN
Hôpital St-Louis
BELLEVILLE Ⓜ
COURONNES
bd. de Belleville
Ⓜ Métro Stop
MENILMONTANT
Canal St-Martin
rue St-Maur
du Temple
10e
av. Parmentier
GONCOURT Ⓜ St-Joseph
bd. de
CHATEAU D'EAU
Strasbourg
Ⓜ JACQUES BONSERGENT
rue de Faubourg
rue de la
Fontaine au Roi
PARMENTIER Ⓜ
ST-MAUR Ⓜ
REPUBLIQUE Ⓜ
place de la République
av. de la République
rue Oberkampf
11e
bd. St-Martin
bd. Voltaire
OBERKAMPF Ⓜ
rue St-Martin
Nouvelle
Conservatoire des Arts et Métiers
Ⓜ TEMPLE
bd. du Temple
rue de Turbigo
square du Temple
FILLES DU CALVAIRE
ST-AMBROISE Ⓜ
rue Réaumur
RICHARD LENOIR Ⓜ
REAUMUR-SEBASTOPOL Ⓜ
ARTS ET METIERS Ⓜ
3e
rue de Temple
rue Charlot
rue de Turenne
rue St-Sébastien
ST-SEBASTIEN FROISSART Ⓜ
rue du Chemin Vert
ETIENNE MARCEL Ⓜ
rue Beaubourg
rue des Archives
rue Vieille du Temple
Musée Picasso
rue St-Sabin
rue Amelot
bd. Richard
BREGUET SABIN Ⓜ
rue Sedaine
bd. de Sébastopol
RAMBUTEAU
rue Ⓜ Rambuteau
Musée Carnavalet
rue des Francs Bourgeois
CHEMIN VERT Ⓜ
bd. Beaumarchais
Lenoir
Centre Pompidou
rue du Renard
rue St-Denis
place des Vosges
rue des Tournelles
BASTILLE Ⓜ
rue St-Antoine
4e
ST-PAUL Ⓜ
place de la Bastille
BASTILLE Ⓜ
HOTEL DE VILLE Ⓜ
av. Victoria
Hôtel de Ville
St-Germain l'Auxerrois
rue St-Paul
BASTILLE Ⓜ
Opéra Bastille
pont au Change
pont Notre Dame
quai de l'Hôtel de Ville
quai des Célestins
PONT MARIE Ⓜ
bd. Henri IV
bd. Bourbon
bd. de la Bastille
12e
Ste-Chapelle
bd. du Palais
CITE Ⓜ
r. de la Cité
r. d'Arcole
pont d'Arcole
ILE DE LA CITE
pont Louis Philippe
pont Marie
r. des Deux Ponts
PONT MARIE
ILE ST-LOUIS
pont de Sully
SULLY-MORLAND Ⓜ
Notre-Dame
pont St-Louis

L'Absinthe 16
L'Ambassade d'Auvergne 35
L'Ambroisie 41
L'Ami Louis 30
L'Ebauchior 48
La Belle Hortense 40
La Fermette du Sud-Ouest 22

La Grille 4
La Poule au Pot 23
Le Caveau François Villon 25
Le Fumoir 24
Le Grain de Folie 2
Le Grand Véfour 12
Le Manguier 46

Le Marais 39
Le Pamphlet 36
Le Vaudeville 10
Le Vieux Bistro 50
Mansouria 48
Pinxo 18
Swann & Vincent 49
Wally Le Saharien 3

MODERATE

Au Pied de Cochon ★★ LATE NIGHT/TRADITIONAL FRENCH   Their famous onion soup and namesake specialty (grilled pigs' feet with béarnaise sauce) still lure visitors, and where else in Paris can you get such a good meal at 3am? Other specialties include a platter named after the medieval patron saint of sausage makers, *la temptation de St-Antoine*, which includes grilled pig's tail, pig's snout, and half a pig's foot, all served with béarnaise and *pommes frites;* and *andouillettes* (chitterling sausages) with béarnaise. Two flavorful but less unusual dishes: a *jarret* (shin) of pork, caramelized in honey and served on a bed of sauerkraut, and grilled pork ribs with sage sauce. On the street outside, you can buy some of the freshest oysters in town.

6 rue Coquillière, 1er. ☎ 01-40-13-77-00. www.pieddecochon.com. Reservations recommended for lunch and dinner hours. Main courses 16€–35€ ($21–$46). AE, DC, MC, V. Daily 24 hr. Métro: Les Halles or Louvre.

Cabaret ASIAN/MODERN FRENCH   You'll either admire this restaurant for its sense of cutting-edge glamour or become irritated with its inflated sense of grandeur, its artfully vague lack of organization, and, in some cases, its genuinely silly sense of chichi. Depending on when you arrive, your meal will be served either on the street level or in the cellar, where a well-publicized team of hot designers (including Jacques Garcia and Ora-Ito) have installed a postmodern decor that's coy, minimalist, and thought-provoking. A bar crafted from mirrors, exotic hardwoods, and replicas of beds is spread across the lounge–disco area. Recommended dishes include crab claws with a sweet-and-sour sauce, fried slices of foie gras with green asparagus tips, pasta shells with Parmesan cream sauce, and T-bone of veal with a ginger-flavored lime sauce.

2 place du Palais-Royal, 1er. ☎ 01-58-62-56-25. www.cabaret.fr. Reservations recommended. Main courses 20€–30€ ($26–$39). AE, MC, V. Restaurant Tues–Sat 8–10:45pm. Club Tues–Sat 11:30pm–5 or 6am. Métro: Palais-Royal.

Chez La Vieille ★ (Finds) CORSICAN/TRADITIONAL FRENCH   Except on Thursday night, when a clientele of mostly local residents is likely to drop in for dinner, Chez La Vieille serves only lunch. Amid a crush of local office workers and visitors to the nearby Louvre, you'll be served the first course and your dessert from a trolley, and wait for the staff to bring your main course directly from the kitchen. This method evokes a large communal meal in a private home or perhaps a boardinghouse. Starters change with the season and the mood of the staff, and include homemade terrines (there's one made from wild boar), stuffed cabbages and tomatoes, and more. Main courses might include *pot-au-feu* (beef stew with carrots) or perhaps braised calf's liver.

1 rue Bailleul, 1er. ☎ 01-42-60-15-78. Reservations recommended. Main courses 18€–29€ ($23–$38); fixed-price lunch 27€ ($35). AE, MC, V. Mon–Fri noon–2:30pm; Thurs 7:30–9pm. Closed Aug. Métro: Louvre-Rivoli.

Il Cortile ★★ ITALIAN/MEDITERRANEAN   Flanking the verdant courtyard of a small hotel, this much-talked-about restaurant serves the best Italian food in Paris. The cuisine is fresh, inventive, and seasonal. Dishes are from throughout Italy, with emphasis on the North. Look for such items as farfalle pasta with squid ink and fresh shellfish, and award-winning guinea fowl (spit-roasted and served with artfully shaped slices of the bird's gizzard, heart, and liver) with polenta. The service is flawless: The French and Italian-speaking staff is diplomatic and good humored. If you want to see what's cooking, ask for a seat in the dining room with a view of the rotisserie, where hens and guinea fowl slowly spin. In warm weather, tables fill an enclosed patio.

In the Hôtel Castille, 37 rue Cambon, 1er. ℂ 01-44-58-45-67. www.castille.com. Reservations recommended. Main courses 20€–40€ ($26–$52); fixed-price menu 95€ ($124). AE, DC, DISC, MC, V. Mon–Fri 12:30–2:30pm and 7:30–10:30pm. Métro: Concorde or Madeleine.

Joe Allen ★ (Kids) AMERICAN

The first American restaurant in Les Halles is aging well. Joe Allen long ago invaded the place with his hamburger. Though the New York restaurateur admits "it's a silly idea," it works, and this place serves Paris's best burger. While listening to the jukebox, you can order black-bean soup, chili, sirloin steak, ribs, or apple pie. Joe Allen is getting more sophisticated, catering to modern tastes with dishes such as grilled salmon with coconut rice and sun-dried tomatoes. His saloon is the only place in Paris serving New York cheesecake and real pecan pie. A very popular brunch is served Saturday and Sunday from noon to 4pm, costing 18€ ($23). Without a dinner reservation, expect a 30-minute wait at the New York Bar.

30 rue Pierre-Lescot, 1er. ℂ 01-42-36-70-13. www.joeallenrestaurant.com. Reservations recommended for dinner. Main courses 16€ ($21); fixed-price menu 23€ ($30); brunch 22€ ($29). AE, MC, V. Daily noon–1am; Sat–Sun brunch noon–4pm. Métro: Etienne-Marcel.

L'Absinthe MODERN FRENCH

Charming and airy, its pair (upstairs/downstairs) of dining rooms are gracefully paneled, and an enormous antique clock dominates a panorama over the chattering and animated dining room. Best of all for foodies who follow this sort of thing, this upscale bistro is associated with one of the mightiest names of mega-celebrity French gastronomy: It's owned and its dining room is supervised by Caroline, daughter of Michel Rostang. In summer, tables spill outside onto an all-pedestrian, see-and-be-seen stretch of street with dauntingly upscale boutiques. Come here for well-prepared, but not particularly innovative bistro-style food. The best examples are crayfish ravioli, scallops sautéed with bacon and sherry, poached codfish with a garlicky aioli sauce, and a served-pink version of standing rack of veal. Service is quirky, a wee bit judgmental, and at its worst a bit cranky.

24 place du Marché St-Honoré, 1er. ℂ 01-49-26-90-04. www.michelrostang.com. Reservations recommended. Fixed-price menu 29€–36€ ($38–$47). AE, DC, MC, V. Mon–Fri noon–2pm; Mon–Sat 7:15–10:30pm. Métro: Tuileries.

La Poule au Pot LATE NIGHT/TRADITIONAL FRENCH

Established in 1935, this bistro welcomes late-night carousers and showbiz personalities looking for a meal after a performance. (Past aficionados have included the Rolling Stones, Prince, and Dustin Hoffman.) The decor is authentically Art Deco; the ambience, nurturing. Time-tested and savory menu items include a salad of warm goat cheese on toast; onion soup; pan-fried stingray with capers; Burgundy-style snails; country pâté on a bed of onion marmalade; and a succulent version of the restaurant's namesake—chicken in a pot, with slices of pâté and fresh vegetables.

9 rue Vauvilliers, 1er. ℂ 01-42-36-32-96. www.lapouleaupot.fr. Reservations recommended. Main courses 23€–35€ ($30–$45); fixed-price menu 33€ ($43). MC, V. Tues–Sun 7pm–5am. Métro: Louvre or Les Halles.

Le Fumoir ★ INTERNATIONAL

This upscale brasserie is in an antique building a few steps from the Louvre. It's one of the most fashionable places in Paris for a bite or drink. You can order salads, pastries, and drinks at off-hours, and platters of more substantial food at mealtimes. Examples are codfish with onions and herbs, rack of veal simmered in its own juices with tarragon, calves' liver with onions, and herring in mustard-flavored cream sauce.

6 rue de l'Amiral-Coligny, 1er. ℂ 01-42-92-00-24. www.lefumoir.com. Reservations recommended. Main courses 18€–28€ ($23–$36). AE, MC, V. Salads, pastries, and snacks daily 11am–2pm; full menu Mon–Fri 7:30–11:30pm, Sat–Sun 7:30pm–midnight. Métro: Louvre-Rivoli.

Pinxo ✶ *(Finds)* SOUTHWESTERN FRENCH   This is the cost-conscious brasserie that's associated with megachef Alain Dutournier's terribly stylish, and much more expensive, Carré des Feuillants, which is on a nearby street. Within Pinxo, a good-looking waitstaff encourages clients to share their starters and platters with their table-mates. This becomes relatively easy because anytime something appears on a plate, it's replicated, sometimes with variations, three times. The setting manages to elevate kitchen drudgery to a high, and high-tech, art form. Expect a wooden floor, white walls, and views that extend directly into an all-black open kitchen-cum-theater. Most foods here are grilled or at least prepared with heart-healthy cooking oils. Examples include a mixture of Aquitaine beef on the same plate as a steak, a tartare, and a blood sausage, all of them accompanied by a slice of foie gras. Filet of goose comes with water-cress, cannelloni, sliced star fruit, and mushrooms. Some platters are piled high with, among other items, tuna ceviche, herring, and crabmeat spring rolls. Dessert might include a platter topped with three glasses: one with a chestnut and rum sabayon, one with a portion of coffee-flavored honey cake, and one with litchi-flavored custard.

In the Plaza-Paris-Vendôme Hôtel, 9 rue d'Alger, 1er. ℂ 01-40-20-72-00. www.carredesfeuillants.fr. Reservations recommended. Main courses 16€–26€ ($21–$34). AE, MC, V. Daily 12:15–2:30pm and 7:15–11:30pm. Métro: Tuileries.

INEXPENSIVE

Angélina ✶✶ TEA/TRADITIONAL FRENCH   In the high-rent area near the InterContinental, this *salon de thé* (tea salon) combines fashion-industry glitter and bourgeois respectability. The carpets are plush, the ceilings high, and the accessories have the right amount of patina. This place has no equal when it comes to viewing the lionesses of haute couture over tea and sandwiches. The waitresses bear silver trays with pastries, drinks, and tea or coffee to marble-topped tables. Lunch usually offers a salad and a *plat du jour* (dish of the day) such as *salade gourmande* (gourmet salad) with foie gras and smoked breast of duck on a bed of fresh salad greens. An enduring specialty here is hot chocolate, priced at 6€ ($7.80) for a pot suitable for one person. Another specialty, designed to go well with tea, is the Mont Blanc, a combination of chestnut cream and meringue.

226 rue de Rivoli, 1er. ℂ 01-42-60-82-00. Reservations not accepted for tea. Pot of tea for 1 6€ ($7.80); sand-wiches and salads 6€–14€ ($7.80–$18); main courses 14€–18€ ($18–$23). AE, MC, V. Mon–Sat 8am–6:45pm; Sun 9am–6:45pm. Métro: Tuileries or Concorde.

La Fermette du Sud-Ouest ✶ SOUTHWESTERN FRENCH   This restaurant, which occupies the site of a 1500s convent, is in the heart of one of Paris's oldest neighborhoods. After the Revolution, the convent was converted into a coaching inn, preserving the original stonework and massive beams. La Fermette prepares rich, savory stews and confits celebrating agrarian France, and serves them on the ground floor and on a mezzanine resembling a choir loft. Menu items include ever-popular *magret* (breast) of duckling with flap mushrooms, *andouillettes* (chitterling sausages), and a sometimes startling array of *cochonailles* (pork products and byproducts) that you probably have to be French to appreciate.

31 rue Coquillière, 1er. ℂ 01-42-36-73-55. Reservations recommended. Main courses 12€–21€ ($16–$27); fixed-price lunch 15€ ($20); fixed-price dinner 23€ ($30). MC, V. Mon–Sat noon–2pm and 7:30–10pm. Métro: Les Halles.

Le Caveau François Villon TRADITIONAL FRENCH   The food here is compe-tently prepared but not noteworthy, and the 40 or so tables crowded into the cellar-level dining room are claustrophobically close together. But there's something fun and spontaneous about the place, and readers have written to us proclaiming the good times they've had and the insights they've garnered into French humor and conviviality. The masonry in the basement dates from the late 1400s, around the time when François Villon, the restaurant's namesake, was composing his French-language poetry. Get a table in the cellar, since that's where the guitarist who entertains here spends most of his time, on every working night from 8:30pm till closing. Menu items change with the seasons, but usually include the house version of foie gras, a spinach salad with caramelized bacon; an assortment of terrines and pâtés made from chicken or pork; and a grilled confit of duckling with a galette of potatoes. The entertainment is convivial and, at times, even a bit bawdy.

64 rue de l'Arbre Sec, 1er. © 01-42-36-10-92. www.caveauvillon.com. Reservations recommended. Fixed-price lunches 20€–26€ ($26–$34); fixed-price dinners 26€ ($34). AE, DC, MC, V. Tues–Fri noon–2:15pm; Mon–Sat 7pm–midnight. Métro: Louvre.

2ND ARRONDISSEMENT
MODERATE

Aux Lyonnais ✦ LYONNAIS/TRADITIONAL FRENCH   After a meal here, you'll know why Lyon is called the gastronomic capital of France. There is no better Lyonnais bistro in Paris than this time-mellowed place vaguely associated with Alain Ducasse. The day's menu is based on the freshest produce in the market that morning. It's offered against an 1890s bistro backdrop of potted palms, etched glass, and globe lamps. Inventiveness and solid technique characterize such dishes as parsleyed calves' liver, pike dumplings (the best in Paris), skate meunière, and peppery *coq au vin* (chicken stewed in red wine) with *crème fraîche* (fresh cream) macaroni. Foie gras is a starter, or you can opt for a *charcuterie* (deli meat) platter. The best for last: a heaven-sent Cointreau soufflé.

32 rue St-Marc, 2e. © 01-42-96-65-04. www.alain-ducasse.com. Reservations required. Main courses 22€–25€ ($29–$33); 3-course fixed-price menu 28€–32€ ($36–$42). AE, DC, MC, V. Tues–Fri noon–1:30pm and Tues–Sat 7:30–10pm. Métro: Grands-Boulevards.

Chez Georges TRADITIONAL FRENCH   Three generations of the same family run this bistro, which opened in 1964 near La Bourse (the stock exchange). At lunch it's packed with stock-exchange members. It serves *la cuisine bourgeoise* (comfort food). Waiters bring around bowls of appetizers, such as celery rémoulade, to get you started. You can follow with sweetbreads with morels, duck breast with cèpe mushrooms, cassoulet, or *pot-au-feu* (beef simmered with vegetables). The sole filet with a sauce made from Pouilly wine and *crème fraîche* (fresh cream) is a delight.

1 rue du Mail, 2e. © 01-42-60-07-11. Reservations required. Main courses 25€–33€ ($33–$43). AE, MC, V. Mon–Fri noon–2pm and 7–10pm. Closed Aug. Métro: Bourse.

Le Vaudeville LATE NIGHT/TRADITIONAL FRENCH   Adjacent to La Bourse (stock exchange), this bistro retains its marble walls and Art Deco carvings from 1918. In summer, tables dot a terrace among banks of geraniums. The place is boisterous and informal, often welcoming groups of six or eight diners at a time. The roster of platters includes snails in garlic butter, shellfish, smoked salmon, sauerkraut, and grilled meats. Three dishes reign as enduring favorites: fresh grilled codfish with mashed potatoes and truffle juice, fresh escalope of warm foie gras with grapes or raspberries, and fresh pasta with morels. The prix-fixe menu is a good deal.

29 rue Vivienne, 2e. ℂ 01-40-20-04-62. www.vaudevilleparis.com. Reservations recommended in the evenings. Main courses 15€–30€ ($20–$39); fixed-price menu 20€ ($26) for 2 courses, 30€ ($39) for 3 courses. AE, DC, MC, V. Daily noon–3pm and 7pm–1am. Métro: Bourse.

3RD ARRONDISSEMENT
EXPENSIVE

L'Ami Louis ✿ TRADITIONAL FRENCH   L'Ami Louis is in one of central Paris's least fashionable neighborhoods, far removed from the part of the Marais that has become chic, and its facade has seen better days. It was one of Paris's most famous brasseries in the 1930s, thanks to its excellent food served in copious portions and its old-fashioned decor. Its traditions, even the hostile waiters, are fervently maintained today. Amid a "brown gravy" decor (the walls retain a smoky patina), dishes such as grilled veal kidneys, roasted suckling lamb, confit of duckling, and slices of foie gras are served on marble-topped tables. Though some say the ingredients aren't as good as in the restaurant's heyday, the sauces are as thick as they were between the wars.

32 rue du Vertbois, 3e. ℂ 01-48-87-77-48. Reservations required far in advance. Main courses 36€–60€ ($47–$78). AE, DC, MC, V. Wed–Sun noon–1:30pm and 8–11:30pm. Closed July 19–Aug 25. Métro: Temple.

MODERATE

Le Pamphlet ✿ *Value* SOUTHWESTERN FRENCH/TRADITIONAL FRENCH   This is the kind of rustic, country-comfortable inn where Parisians book a table at least 48 hours in advance and then schedule the event in their appointment books as a midweek break from urban life. Part of the charm here involves discussing the political theories of strong-willed and gruffly charming owner and chef Alain Carrère. The menu changes several times a week. Your meal might begin with *rillettes* (a rough-textured terrine) of rabbit with crayfish, a thick cream of crabmeat soup garnished with baby peas, or a thin potato tart with marinated wild salmon and fine herbs. Recommended main courses include a rack of Pyrénéan lamb served with *croustillant* (a crisp pastry) enriched with Rocamadour goat cheese, or braised sea bass with carrots, leeks, and a shrimp-flavored cream sauce. We think this place is a lot of fun, and if you can handle its eccentricities, you may agree.

38 rue Debelleyme, 3e. ℂ 01-42-72-39-24. Reservations required, usually 48 hr. in advance for dinner. Fixed-price menu 35€–55€ ($46–$72). MC, V. Tues–Fri noon–2:30pm and Mon–Sat 7:30–11pm. Closed 1st 2 weeks of Jan and 2 weeks in mid-Aug. Métro: Filles du Calvaire.

INEXPENSIVE

Au Bascou ✿ *Finds* BASQUE   The succulent cuisine of France's "deep southwest" is the specialty here, where art objects, paintings, and tones of ocher celebrate the beauty of the region, and hanging clusters of pimentos add spice to the air. For a ray of sunshine, try *pipérade basquaise* (a spicy omelet loaded with peppers and onions); pimentos stuffed with purée of codfish; and *axoa* of veal (shoulder of calf served with pimento-and-pepper-based green sauce). Also noteworthy is thick-sliced filet of cod served with essence of tomatoes.

38 rue Réaumur, 3e. ℂ 01-42-72-69-25. Reservations recommended. Main courses 16€ ($21), fixed-price menu 16€–18€ ($21–$23). AE, DC, MC, V. Mon–Fri noon–2pm and 8–10:30pm. Closed Aug and week of Christmas. Métro: Arts-et-Métiers.

Chez Janou PROVENÇAL   On one of the 17th-century streets behind place des Vosges, a pair of cramped but cozy dining rooms filled with memorabilia from Provence make up this loud and somewhat raucous bistro. The service is brusque and

sometimes hectic. But the food will remind you of a visit to your Fr
mother's kitchen—dishes such as shrimp with pastis sauce, *brouillade de*
(baked eggs with oyster mushrooms), spinach salad with goat cheese, fondu
touille, gratin of mussels, and simple but savory *magret* (breast) of duck with ro

2 rue Roger-Verlomme, 3e. ✆ **01-42-72-28-41.** Reservations recommended. Main courses 13€–18€ ($1
fixed-price lunch 14€ ($18). AE, MC, V. Daily noon–3pm and 7:30pm–midnight. Métro: Chemin Vert.

Jenny *(Value* ALSATIAN One of the city's most famous Alsatian restaurants was estab
lished in 1930 by members of the Jenny family. Little has changed since its inauguration except that the clientele is a lot more contemporary-looking than in the old days.
Up to 220 diners can fit into this nostalgia-laden setting, where Alsatian *Gemütlichkeit*
prevails. An ongoing specialty is the *choucroute* (sauerkraut) *de chez Jenny,* piled high
with sausages, tender pork knuckles, and slices of ham. Also available are oysters,
onion soup, grilled meats, and grilled fish. Any of these tastes wonderful accompanied
by one of the Alsatian wines that fill the wine list.

39 bd. du Temple, 3e. ✆ **01-44-54-39-00.** Reservations recommended. Main courses 17€–30€ ($22–$39); fixed-
price menu 19€–29€ ($25–$38). AE, DC, MC, V. Sun–Thurs noon–midnight; Fri–Sat noon–1am. Métro: République.

L'Ambassade d'Auvergne ✸ AUVERGNAT/TRADITIONAL FRENCH You
enter this rustic tavern through a bar with heavy oak beams, hanging hams, and
ceramic plates. It showcases the culinary bounty of France's most isolated region, the
Auvergne, whose pork products are widely celebrated. Try chicory salad with apples
and pieces of country ham; pork braised with cabbage, turnips, and white beans; or
grilled tripe sausages with mashed potatoes and Cantal cheese with garlic. Nonpork
specialties are pan-fried duck liver with gingerbread, perch steamed in verbena tea,
and roasted rack of lamb with wild mushrooms.

22 rue de Grenier St-Lazare, 3e. ✆ **01-42-72-31-22.** www.ambassade-auvergne.com. Reservations recommended.
Main courses 14€–22€ ($18–$29); fixed-price menu 28€ ($36). AE, MC, V. Daily noon–2pm and 7:30–10:30pm.
Métro: Rambuteau.

4TH ARRONDISSEMENT
VERY EXPENSIVE
L'Ambroisie ✸ *(Overrated* FRENCH One of Paris's most talented chefs, Bernard
Pacaud, drew attention with his vivid flavors and gastronomical skill, but culinary standards here are declining. At this 17th-century town house, the decor resembles an Italian palazzo. Pacaud's tables are nearly always filled with diners drawn here by all that
praise in Michelin. The dishes change seasonally and may include fricassee of Breton
lobster with chestnuts, served with purée of pumpkin; turbot braised with endive,
served with julienne of black truffles; or *poulard de Bresse demi-deuil homage à la Mère
Brazier* (chicken roasted with black truffles and truffled vegetables). There is a rather
snobby attitude here: It's a bit shocking when one calls for a reservation to be asked to
state one's nationality.

9 place des Vosges, 4e. ✆ **01-42-78-51-45.** Reservations required far in advance. Main courses 80€–140€
($104–$182). AE, MC, V. Tues–Sat noon–1:30pm and 8–9:30pm. Métro: St-Paul or Chemin Vert.

EXPENSIVE
Benoit ✸ TRADITIONAL FRENCH There's something weighty about this historical monument; every mayor of Paris has dined here since the restaurant was
founded in 1912 by the grandfather of the present owner. He's one of the last
bistrotiers who occasionally purchases Beaujolais in casks and then bottles it in his own

Ice-Cream Break at Berthillon

...er more than 3 dozen years in business, the *salon*
...ue St-Louis-en-l'Ile, 4e (€ **01-43-54-31-61**; Métro:
...world's best selection of ice cream. Try gingerbread,
...sse, rhubarb, melon, kumquat, black currant, or any fresh
...there are more than 70 flavors and nothing artificial (but only
...able at any given moment). Parisians flock here in such numbers
...ndarmes have been called out to direct the traffic of ice-cream aficiona-
...It's open Wednesday to Sunday 10am to 8pm.

cellars. The setting is theatrical, and the service can be attentive or arrogant, depending on a delicate chemistry that only longtime fans of this place understand. Prices are
higher than you'd expect for bistro fare, but it all seems part of the self-satisfied norm
here, and clients keep coming back for more. The satisfying cuisine is full of flavor,
based on time-tested classics. Traditional crowd-pleasers include salmon that's both
marinated and smoked; snails served in their shells with garlic butter; slow-cooked pot
roast with carrots; and cassoulet, a white-bean-and-pork dish.

20 rue St-Martin, 4e. (€ **01-42-72-25-76**. www.alain-ducasse.com. Reservations required. Main courses 25€–40€
($33–$52); fixed-price lunch 38€ ($49). AE. Daily noon–2pm and 7:30–10pm. Métro: Hôtel de Ville.

MODERATE

Bofinger *Overrated* ALSATIAN/MODERN & TRADITIONAL FRENCH
Opened in the 1860s, Bofinger is the oldest Alsatian brasserie in town, but it's grown
tired and stale over the years. Nonetheless, it's packed every night with visitors because
of its world fame. If the food isn't what it used to be, the atmosphere for some will be
worth trekking over here. It's a Belle Epoque dining palace, resplendent with brass and
stained glass. Affiliated with La Coupole, Julien, and Brasserie Flo, the restaurant has
updated its menu, retaining the most popular traditional dishes, such as sauerkraut
and *sole meunière* (sole in lemon butter sauce). Recent additions include roasted leg of
lamb with fondant of artichoke hearts and parsley purée, grilled turbot with a fennel
sauce, and stingray with chives and burnt-butter sauce. Shellfish, including fresh oysters and lobster, is almost always available in season. Weather permitting, you can dine
on an outdoor terrace. In light of the restaurant's rich history, a staff member conducts
brief complimentary tours.

5–7 rue de la Bastille, 4e. (€ **01-42-72-87-82**. www.bofingerparis.com. Reservations recommended. Main courses
15€–35€ ($20–$46); fixed-price menu 30€ ($39). AE, DC, MC, V. Mon–Fri noon–3pm and 6:30pm–1am; Sat–Sun
noon–1am. Métro: Bastille.

Georges ☆ INTERNATIONAL   The Centre Pompidou is again in the spotlight;
all of artsy Paris is talking about this place. Georges is in a large space on the top floor
of Paris's most comprehensive arts complex, with views through bay windows over
most of the city. The decor is minimalist and postmodern, with lots of brushed aluminum and stainless steel. Tables are made from sandblasted glass, lit from below, and
accessorized with hypermodern cutlery. Menu items are mostly Continental, with
hints of Asia. Some combinations surprise—macaroni with lobster, for example. Others seem exotic, including roasted ostrich steak. Aside from these dishes, some of the
best items on the menu are roasted scallops with lemon butter and tuna steak spiced

with coriander. To get here, head for the ex‗
Pompidou's main entrance. Tell the guard ‗
might not be allowed up.

Centre Pompidou, 6th Floor, 19 rue Beaubourg, 4e. ② 01‗
mended for lunch. Main courses 15€–43€ ($20–$56). AE, ‗

Le Vieux Bistro ℛ (Finds) TRADITIONA‗
fashioned bistros in the heart of Paris. Fev‗
forbidding view of the massive walls of P‗
curtains from the windows of the front ‗
souvenir stands and then settle into one ‗
which is a bit heavy, evokes the French staples y‗
in the heart of France. The specialty is *boeuf bourguignon* (be‗
sauce), and in winter, the menu features lots of game dishes. You can order ‗
garlic butter; filet mignon with Roquefort sauce; and a classic dessert, *tarte tatin* (pie
studded with apples and sugar, drenched with Calvados, and capped with fresh cream).

14 rue du Cloître-Notre-Dame, 4e. ② 01-43-54-18-95. Main courses 18€–28€ ($23–$36). AE, MC, V. Daily
noon–2pm and 7–10pm. Métro: Cité.

INEXPENSIVE

Le Marais SEAFOOD/VEGETARIAN   Housed in a 17th-century building with
stonework that forms part of the earth-toned decor, this is one of the best-known vegetarian restaurants in Le Marais. The owners serve a limited array of organic wine, and
smoking is forbidden. Flavorful, healthful meals come in generous portions. Choose
from a variety of soups and salads; galette of wheat served with crudités and mushroom
tarts; or a country plate composed of fried mushrooms and potatoes, garlic, and goat
cheese, served with a salad. There's also a wide choice of fish dishes.

(*Moments*   **A Parisian *Piquenique***

One of the best ways to save money while still enjoying Parisian cuisine is
to picnic. Go to a *fromagerie* for cheese; to a *boulangerie* for a baguette;
to a *charcuterie* for pâté, sausage, or salad; and to a *patisserie* for luscious
pastries. Add a bottle of Côtes du Rhone—it goes well with picnics—and
you'll have the makings of a delightful, typically French meal you can take
to the nearest park or along the banks of the Seine. Pretend you're in
Manet's *Déjeuner sur l'herbe,* and enjoy! (Don't forget the corkscrew!)

The best spot for a picnic is a cozy nook along the **Seine.** Another great
place for picnics (also boating, walks, and jogging) is the **Bois de Boulogne**
(Métro: Porte Maillot), covering some 809 hectares (2,000 acres) at the western edge of Paris. At night it becomes a twilight zone of sex and drugs, but
it's lovely during the day. Even though they're in a state of restoration, the
splendid gardens of **Versailles** are another fine picnic spot. You can also
enjoy your meal on the grass on a day trip to the cathedral city of **Chartres.**
Go to bucolic **Parc André Gagon,** a 5-minute walk northwest of the fabled
cathedral.

54 rue Ste-Croix-de-la-Bretonnerie
19€ ($25). MC, V. Mon-Sat no‗

Like its counter‗
Montmartre, ‗
Drouot), off‗
rock. The‗
tas, an‗
Thu‗

, 4e. ℂ **01-48-87-48-71.** Main courses 8.50€–14€ ($11–$18); fixed-price menu
n–midnight. Métro: Hôtel de Ville. RER: Châtelet–Les Halles.

SEMENT

arts from Hong Kong to Reykjavík, the **Hard Rock Cafe,** 14 bd.
9e (ℂ **01-53-24-60-00;** Métro: Grands Boulevards or Richelieu-
ers musical memorabilia as well as musical selections from 35 years of
crowd appreciates the juicy steaks, hamburgers, veggie burgers, salads, pas-
heaping platters of informal French-inspired food. It's open Monday to
sday from 9am to 1am and Friday to Sunday from 9am to 2am.

MODERATE

Au Petit Riche ✛ LOIRE VALLEY (ANJOU)/TRADITIONAL FRENCH No,
that's not Flaubert or Balzac walking through the door, but should they miraculously
return, the decor of old Paris, with the original gas lamps and time-mellowed paneling,
will make them feel at home. This place opened in 1865 as the restaurant associated with
the very large and then-solvent Café Riche next door. After Café burned down, the
restaurant continued to attract lawyers, set designers, and machinists from the nearby
Opéra Garnier, eventually becoming a well-known restaurant. Charles Aznavour is an
occasional patron, along with politicians and anyone interested in the nostalgia of *La
Vieille France.* Expect an impressive roster of Loire Valley wines and food that combines
Loire Valley classics with traditional French fare. Examples include roasted rack of veal
prepared *à l'ancienne,* a long-standing house special of *tartare* of beef, roasted whitefish
in meat drippings, and seasonal game dishes such as civet of rabbit.

25 rue Le Peletier, 9e. ℂ **01-47-70-68-68.** www.aupetitriche.com. Reservations recommended. Main courses
15€–30€ ($20–$39); fixed-price lunch 27€ ($34); fixed-price dinner 30€ ($38). AE, DC, MC, V. Mon–Sat
noon–2:15pm and 7pm–midnight. Métro: Le Peletier or Richelieu-Drouot.

Chez Jean ✛ TRADITIONAL FRENCH The crowd is young, the food is sophisticated, and the vintage 1950s aura makes you think that American expatriate novelist James Baldwin will arrive any minute. Surrounded by well-oiled pine panels and
polished copper, you can choose from some of grandmother's favorites as well as more
modern dishes. Owner Jean-Frederic Guidoni worked for more than 20 years at one
of the world's most expensive restaurants, Taillevent, but within his own milieu, he
demonstrates his own innovative touch at prices that are much more reasonable. For
starters, consider a succulent version of Brazilian-style shrimp resting on toast that's
been smeared with pulverized olives, capers, and pork sausage; a savory version of a
cheesy alpine staple, *raclette,* made with mustard sauce and *Curé Nantais* cheese; and
slow-braised pork cooked for 7 hours and served on a bed of carrots, apricots, and
confit of lemon. Our most recent dessert was a brownie with a clementine-flavored
sorbet and "perfumed juices."

8 rue St-Lazare, 9e. ℂ **01-48-78-62-73.** Reservations recommended far in advance. Main courses 25€–34€
($33–$44); fixed-price menu 34€ ($44). AE, DC, MC, V. Mon–Fri noon–2:30pm and 7:30–10:30pm. Métro: Notre-
Dame de Lorette, Opéra, or Cadet.

Wally Le Saharien ALGERIAN Head to this dining room—lined with desert
photos and tribal artifacts crafted from ceramics, wood, and weavings—for an insight
into the spicy, slow-cooked cuisine that fueled the colonial expansion of France into
North Africa. The prix-fixe dinner menu begins with a trio of starters: spicy soup,
stuffed and grilled sardines, and a savory *pastilla* of pigeon in puff pastry. Next comes

any of several kinds of couscous or a *méchouia* (slow-cooked tart) of lamb dusted with an optional coating of sugar. *Merguez*, the cumin-laden spicy sausage of the North African world, factors importantly into any meal, as do homemade pastries.

36 rue Rodier, 9e. ℂ 01-42-85-51-90. Reservations recommended. A la carte main courses (lunch only) 19€–23€ ($25–$30); fixed-price dinner 44€ ($57). MC, V. Tues–Sat noon–2pm and 7–10pm. Métro: Anvers.

INEXPENSIVE

Chartier TRADITIONAL FRENCH   Opened in 1896, this unpretentious *fin-de-siècle* restaurant is now an official historic monument featuring a whimsical mural with trees, a flowering staircase, and an early depiction of an airplane (it was painted in 1929 by an artist who traded his work for food). The menu follows brasserie-style traditions, including items you might not dare to eat—boiled veal's head, tripe, tongue, sweetbreads, lamb's brains, chitterling sausages—as well as some old-time tempters. The waiter will steer you through such dishes as *boeuf bourguignon* (braised beef in red-wine sauce), *pot-au-feu* (combining beef, turnips, cabbage, and carrots), *pavé* (a thick slice) of rump steak, and at least five kinds of fish.

7 rue du Faubourg Montmartre, 9e. ℂ 01-47-70-86-29. Main courses 9€–11€ ($12–$14). Fixed-price menus 16€–21€ ($21–$27). AE, DC, MC, V. Daily 11:30am–3pm and 6–10pm. Métro: Grands Boulevards.

10TH ARRONDISSEMENT
MODERATE

Brasserie Flo ⭐ ALSATIAN   This remote restaurant is hard to find, but once you arrive (after walking through passageway after passageway), you'll see that *fin-de-siècle* Paris lives on. The restaurant opened in 1860 and has changed its decor very little. The specialty is *la formidable choucroute* (a mound of sauerkraut with boiled ham, bacon, and sausage) for two. Onion soup and *sole meunière* (sole in lemon butter sauce) are always good, as are warm foie gras and guinea hen with lentils. Look for the *plats du jour,* ranging from roast pigeon to veal fricassee with sorrel.

7 cour des Petites-Ecuries, 10e. ℂ 01-47-70-13-59. www.flobrasserie.com. Reservations recommended. Main courses 15€–30€ ($20–$39); fixed-price menus 21€–31€ ($27–$40). AE, DC, MC, V. Daily noon–3pm and 7pm–1am. Métro: Château d'Eau or Strasbourg-St-Denis.

Chez Michel BRETON   Adapting to the tastes and income of its loyal crowd, this restaurant near the Gare du Nord serves generous portions of well-prepared Breton dishes. In a pair of dining rooms accented with exposed wood, you'll enjoy the fruits of the fields and seacoast, densely flavored and traditional; they include veal chops fried in butter and served with gratin of potatoes enriched with calf's foot gelatin, and codfish filets served on a bed of tomatoes and onions with a tapenade of black olives. Other regional choices include a Celtic stew (*kig ha farz,* in Breton dialect) made from stewed veal and pork, and served with grilled lard, herbs, and baby vegetables; and *les craquelins de Saint Mâlo* (small Breton-style tarts) stuffed with aromatic goat cheese.

10 rue de Belzunce, 10e. ℂ 01-44-53-06-20. Reservations recommended. Fixed-price menu 30€ ($39). MC, V. Tues–Fri noon–2pm; Mon–Fri 7pm–midnight. Métro: Gare du Nord.

La Grille Ⓥalue SEAFOOD/TRADITIONAL FRENCH   Few other moderate restaurants are as hotly pursued by Parisians as this nine-table holdover from another age. For at least a century after the French Revolution, fishermen from Dieppe used this place as a springboard for carousing and cabaret-watching after delivering their fish to Les Halles market. Since the late 1960s, the charming, outspoken M. and Mme Cullérre, who in 2005 received an award from the French tourist office for their contribution to tourism in Paris, have run this restaurant. They have become distinctive, albeit slightly eccentric, neighborhood fixtures. The Holy Grail at La Grille is an entire turbot prepared tableside with an emulsified white-butter sauce. Other recommended dishes are seafood terrine, *boeuf bourguignon* (braised beef in red-wine sauce), and marinated sardine filets. The high-calorie, high-satisfaction desserts include chocolate mousse and vanilla custard. (The restaurant name derives from the 200-year-old wrought-iron grills in front, classified as national treasures.)

80 rue du Faubourg-Poissonnière, 10e. (℃ 01-47-70-89-73. Reservations required. Main courses 25€–32€ ($33–$42). AE, MC, V. Mon–Fri noon–2:30pm and 7–10pm. Métro: Poissonnière.

INEXPENSIVE
Café Panique ⚑ *Finds* MODERN FRENCH   Welcome to the New France and one of Paris's best-kept secrets. Although this cafe opened its doors in the '90s, it was only really discovered post-millennium when word seeped out about its easygoing atmosphere and affordable prices. Come here for the mellow ambience and the scrumptious food. The Café has improved its kitchen since its debut, and today's chefs offer such delights as *magret de canard* (breast of duckling) or scallops with a fresh orange flavoring. A marvelous monkfish flavored with fresh basil is also featured, as is a veal "cake" with onions and a flavoring of white wine.

12 rue des Messagerie, 10e. (℃ 01-47-70-06-84. Reservations recommended. Main courses 19€ ($25). Fixed-price lunch 19€ ($25), fixed-price dinner 23€–35€ ($30–$46). MC, V. Mon–Fri noon–2pm and 7:30–10pm. Closed Sat–Sun and in Aug. Métro: Poissonnière.

11TH ARRONDISSEMENT
EXPENSIVE
Blue Elephant ⚑ THAI   At this branch of a chain of Thai restaurants, the decor evokes the jungles of Southeast Asia, interspersed with sculptures and paintings. The menu items are succulent, infused with lemon grass, curries, and the aromas that make Thai cuisine distinctive. Examples are a salad made with pomelo (a citrus fruit larger and tarter than a grapefruit), studded with shrimp and herbs; salmon soufflé served in banana leaves; and grilled fish with passion fruit. If you have trouble deciding which delicacy is for you, consider a *plateau royal,* a main course that contains five different specialties of the Thai repertoire (shrimp, chicken, fish, and vegetable dishes), all of them artfully arranged.

43 rue de la Roquette, 11e. (℃ 01-47-00-42-00. www.blueelephant.com. Reservations recommended. Main courses 22€–27€ ($29–$35); fixed-price lunch 16€–48€ ($21–$62); fixed-price dinner 44€–48€ ($57–$62). AE, DC, MC, V. Mon–Fri noon–2:30pm; Sun 2 brunches noon–2pm and 2:30–4:30pm; Mon–Wed 7–11pm; Thurs–Sat 7pm–midnight. Métro: Bastille.

MODERATE
Au Petit Monsieur ⚑ *Finds* TRADITIONAL FRENCH   A meal at this restaurant, tucked away in the 11th Arrondissement, is like dining in the French countryside. Under wooden beams and held up by old stone walls, the three dining rooms are decorated with country crockery. Patrons dine at bare wooden tables, using kitchen towels as napkins. Both modernists and upholders of French culinary tradition find a happy home here. Everything is served by a capable staff sensitive to your needs and orders. The fixed-price lunch and dinner menus are changed every day. Appetizers often begin with a tureen of soup from which you help yourself. Count yourself lucky if it's the well-flavored pumpkin with tasty homemade croutons and Parmesan. Delicate red mullet often comes with eggplant "caviar" and an arugula salad, the fish

enhanced by a sprinkle of basil juice. Since dining here, we've become addicted to fennel ice cream.

50 rue Amelot, 11e. ☎ 01-43-55-54-04. Reservations required. Fixed-price lunch 16€–26€ ($21–$34); fixed-price dinner 35€ ($46). AE, V. Tues–Fri noon–2pm and Tues–Sat 7–10pm. Métro: Chemin Vert.

Bistrot Paul Bert ⊛ TRADITIONAL FRENCH   Some critics define this as the best and most appealing middle-bracket restaurant in the 11th Arrondissement, and judging by the crowds that pack in here on a Saturday night, we're inclined to agree. Expect a crowded, noisy, usually convivial ambience where diners' necks strain to read the blackboard specials and where overworked, independent-minded waiters don't lightly suffer fools of any nationality. Menu items evoke the classic traditions that have flourished here at least since the 1950s. Classics include chicken braised in yellow wine from the Jura, veal kidneys in mustard sauce, monkfish served with an herb-flavored cream sauce, and braised filet of sea bass with risotto.

18 rue Paul-Bert, 11e. ☎ 01-43-72-24-01. Reservations recommended. Main courses 10€–20€ ($13–$26); fixed-price lunch 16€–32€ ($21–$42); fixed-price dinner 32€ ($42). MC, V. Tues–Sat noon–2:30pm and 7:30–11pm. Closed Aug. Métro: Faidherbe-Chaligny.

Chez Ramulaud ⊛ TRADITIONAL FRENCH   This establishment may seem like the average Parisian restaurant from the outside, but on any given Sunday, you will encounter the friendlier side of Paris in this almost completely gentrified neighborhood. A trio of musicians *chante* French golden oldies, and a few empty wine bottles later, the foodies are singing along. The wine prices are reasonable, and you tip for the musicians. So, almost overnight, Chez Ramulaud has become the place to be in Paris on a Sunday. Actually it's a good choice for lunch or dinner at any time. Tried-and-true specialties lure a list of habitués. Rump steak is perfectly prepared with a nutty sauce, or else you can order a cakelike pasta made with spicy sausage and crab. For dessert, the chef is justifiably proud of his white chocolate mousse made with pistachios.

269 rue du Faubourg-Saint-Antoine, 11e. ☎ 01-43-72-23-29. Reservations recommended. Main courses 18€–23€ ($23–$30). Fixed-price menu 29€ ($38); fixed-price lunch 15€ ($20). MC, V. Sun–Fri noon–2:30pm, Mon–Thurs 8–11pm, Fri–Sat 8pm–midnight. Métro: Faidherbe-Chaligny.

Mansouria MOROCCAN   One of Paris's most charming Moroccan restaurants occupies a much-restored building midway between place de la Bastille and place de la Nation. The minimalist decor combines futuristic architecture with bare sand-colored walls, accented only with sets of antique doors and portals from the sub-Sahara. Look for seven kinds of couscous, including versions with chicken; beef brochettes; or lamb, onions, and almonds. *Tagines* are succulent dishes of chicken or fish prepared with aromatic herbs and slow-cooked in clay pots that are carried to your table.

11 rue Faidherbe, 11e. ☎ 01-43-71-00-16. Reservations recommended. Main courses 16€–24€ ($21–$31); fixed-price dinner 30€–46€ ($39–$60); fixed-price lunch 29€–39€ ($38–$51). MC, V. Wed–Sat noon–2pm; Tues–Sat 7:30–11pm. Métro: Faidherbe-Chaligny.

INEXPENSIVE

Le Manguier SENEGALESE   Many of the patrons who dine here don't know much about Senegalese cuisine, but thanks to a charming welcome and live music presenting African jazz at its most compelling, they tend to come back. The decor evokes a West African fishing village. You can order zesty fare such as roast chicken marinated with lime and served with onions; smoked shark meat; and the national dish, *tieboudiene* (a blend of fish, rice, and fresh vegetables). The medley is perked up with a selection of fiery sauces you apply yourself. The drinks of choice are beer, a rum-based cocktail called *Le Dakar,* and wine.

67 av. Parmentier, 11e. ✆ **01-48-07-03-27.** Reservations recommended. Main courses 12€–15€ ($16–$20). AE, DC, MC, V. Tues–Sat noon–3pm and 7pm–2am. Métro: Parmentier.

12TH ARRONDISSEMENT
EXPENSIVE

Au Trou Gascon ✸✸✸ GASCONY   One of Paris's most acclaimed chefs, Alain Dutournier, lures fashionable palates to an unchic area. He launched his career in southwest France's Gascony region. His parents mortgaged their inn to allow Dutournier to open an early-1900s bistro in a little-known part of the 12th Arrondissement. Word spread of a savant in the kitchen who practiced authentic *cuisine moderne.* His wife, Nicole, is the welcoming hostess, and the wine steward has distinguished himself for his exciting cave containing several little-known wines along with a fabulous collection of Armagnacs. You can start with duck foie gras cooked in a terrine or Gascony-cured ham. The best main courses include fresh tuna with braised cabbage; a superb cassoulet; and chicken from the Chalosse region of Landes, which Dutournier roasts and serves in its own drippings.

40 rue Taine, 12e. ✆ **01-43-44-34-26.** Reservations recommended a day in advance. Main courses 28€–30€ ($36–$39); fixed-price lunch 36€ ($47); fixed-price dinner 50€ ($65). AE, DC, MC, V. Mon–Fri noon–2pm and 8–10pm. Closed Aug. Métro: Daumesnil.

MODERATE

China Club ✸ CANTONESE/CHINESE   Evoking 1930s Hong Kong, this favorite is still going strong, laughing at upstart new Asian restaurants, and serving some of the best Asian cuisine in Paris. The food is mainly Cantonese, prepared with flair. The menu is vast, with plenty of choices. Nearly everything is good, especially sautéed shrimp and calamari, Shanghai chicken, and red rice sautéed with vegetables. Before dinner, you might want to enjoy a drink in the upstairs smoking lounge. Downstairs, the Sing Song club has live music, including something called Sino-French jazz on Thursday, Friday, and Saturday.

50 rue de Charenton, 12e. ✆ **01-43-43-82-02.** www.chinaclub.cc. Main courses 13€–29€ ($17–$38); fixed-price dinner 28€ ($36). AE, DC, MC, V. Sun–Thurs 7pm–2am; Fri–Sat 7pm–3am. Closed July 20–Aug 20. Métro: Bastille.

Swann & Vincent ITALIAN   This is the kind of Italian trattoria that readers write to us about, praising both the quality of the food and the cheerful amiability that brightens up an evening in a neighborhood not generally frequented by foreign visitors. The setting evokes an old-time Parisian brasserie from the turn of the 20th century, thanks to paneled walls, Bordeaux-colored banquettes, big mirrors, a decor that hasn't changed much since the late 1940s, and a prominent bar top crafted from ocher-colored marble. You can begin your meal with a fried combination of calamari and shrimp or perhaps a visit to the antipasti buffet for a medley of mostly fish and vegetarian starters. After that, you'll be tempted with a wide array of pastas, any of which can be configured either as a full or half portion. Main courses include roasted racks of lamb or pork, veal cutlets prepared *alla milanese* (fried in butter with breadcrumbs) or *alla parmigiana* (with a layer of cheese), or simply braised and served with lemon-butter or mushroom sauce. Desserts might include *pannacotta* (similar to a flan) or tiramisu.

7 rue St-Nicolas, 12e. ✆ **01-43-43-49-40.** Reservations recommended. Fixed-price lunch (Mon–Fri only) 15€ ($20); main courses 12€–16€ ($16–$21). MC, V. Daily noon–2:45pm and 7:30–11:45pm. Métro: Ledru-Rolin.

INEXPENSIVE

L'Ebauchoir ★ *Finds* TRADITIONAL FRENCH Tucked into a neighborhood rarely visited by foreigners and featuring a 1950s decor that is so out it's in, this bistro attracts carpenters, plumbers, and electricians, as well as an occasional journalist and screenwriter. With buffed aluminum trim and plaster-and-stucco walls tinted dark orange-yellow and Bordeaux, the place might remind you of a factory canteen. You can order surprisingly generous and well-prepared stuffed sardines, snapper filet with olive oil and garlic, crabmeat soup, tuna steak with orange-flavored butter, fried calf's liver with coriander and honey, and rack of lamb combined with saddle of lamb.

43 rue de Citeaux, 12e. © 01-43-42-49-31. Reservations recommended for dinner. Main courses 15€–25€ ($20–$33); fixed-price lunch 14€ ($18); fixed-price dinner 23€ ($30). AE, MC, V. Tues–Sat noon–2:30pm; Mon–Sat 8–11pm. Métro: Faidherbe-Chaligny.

18TH ARRONDISSEMENT
INEXPENSIVE

Le Grain de Folie ORGANIC/VEGETARIAN Simple and wholesome, this cuisine is inspired by France, Greece, California, Turkey, and India. The menu includes an array of theme salads, cereals, tarts, terrines, and casseroles. Dessert selections might include an old-fashioned tart or a fruit salad. The decor includes potted plants and exposed stone. You can choose one of an array of wines or a frothy glass of vegetable juice to accompany your meal. This place may be a bit difficult to find, but it's worth the search. Marie-Cécite is the charming owner.

24 rue de Lavieuville, 18e. © 01-42-58-15-57. Reservations recommended. Main courses 10€–12€ ($13–$16); fixed-price menus 12€–16€ ($16–$21). No credit cards. Tues–Sat 12:30–2:30pm and 7:30–11pm; Sun 11:30am–10pm. Métro: Abbesses.

8TH ARRONDISSEMENT
VERY EXPENSIVE

Lasserre ★★★ MODERN & TRADITIONAL FRENCH It's so old, it's new again. This elegant restaurant was a bistro before World War II and has since become a legend. The main salon stretches two stories high, with a mezzanine on each side. Tall, silk-draped, arched windows frame the tables set with fine porcelain, gold-edged crystal glasses, and silver candelabras. The ceiling is painted with white clouds and a cerulean sky, but in good weather, the staff slides back the roof to reveal the real sky. The faces of Audrey Hepburn, Maria Callas, and Marlene Dietrich have given way to young British royals and statuesque models from Brazil. A spectacular chef, Jean-Louis Nomicos, is a master of taste and texture, and he's brought renewed life to this swank citadel. The appetizers are among Paris's finest, including truffle salad, grilled foie gras of duckling served with a confit of green apples, Chablis-flavored Belon oysters, and a hyper-upscale version of macaroni with foie gras and truffles. The signature main course is poached sole filets *Club de la Casserole,* in puff pastry with asparagus tips and asparagus-flavored cream sauce; also wonderful are the veal kidneys flambé and pigeon André Malraux. For dessert, and evocative of the new menu, the chef serves roasted baby pineapples in passion-fruit juice with coconut sorbet. The wine cellar, with some 160,000 bottles, is one of Paris's most remarkable.

17 av. Franklin D. Roosevelt, 8e. © 01-43-59-53-43. Fax 01-45-63-72-23. www.restaurant-lasserre.com. Reservations required far in advance. Main courses 55€–75€ ($72–$98); fixed-price dinner 75€–185€ ($98–$241). AE, MC, V. Thurs–Fri 12:15–2pm; Mon–Sat 7:30–10pm. Closed Aug. Métro: Franklin-D-Roosevelt.

Le Cinq ★★★ TRADITIONAL FRENCH   Since it was established in 1928 in honor of the king of England, there has always been a world-class dining venue associated with the Hotel George V. The configuration today dates from its acquisition by Toronto's Four Seasons group, which poured time, money, talent, and taste into a high-ceilinged room whose majestic decor evokes the Grand Trianon at Versailles. Within a gray and very pale pink dining room that shimmers with gold inlays, your dining needs will be supervised by a sophisticated staff that intuitively understands the needs and priorities of the hotel's widely divergent international clientele. Within 3 years of this restaurant's birth, it had been awarded three coveted stars by the Guide Michelin—an honor that's accorded only very rarely. The menu changes frequently, but enduring favorites include a tart of artichokes and black Périgord truffles; a fricassee of Breton crayfish with coriander and lime sauce; North Atlantic lobster with chestnuts; and a classic that has been on the menu since the days of Mistinguett and Piaf—Bresse chicken "in the style of the George V," stuffed with crayfish and herbs. Desserts are artful and ornate: The best examples include hazelnut meringue with hazelnut mousse and mandarin oranges; and a high-caloric collection, compiled onto a single hyperindulgent platter, of all-chocolate desserts, *exclusivement tout chocolat*.

In the Four Seasons Hotel George V, 31 av. George V, 8e. (✆ **01-49-52-71-54**. Fax 01-49-52-71-81. www.fourseasons. com. Reservations recommended 4 weeks in advance for dinner, 1 week in advance for lunch. Main courses 53€–120€ ($69–$156); fixed-price lunches 75€–120€ ($98–$156), fixed-price dinners 120€–210€ ($156–$273). AE, DC, MC, V. Daily noon–2:30pm and 6:30–10:30pm. Métro: George V.

Les Elysées du Vernet ★★★ PROVENÇAL   This restaurant is a gastronomic wonder. It has a panoramic glass ceiling, a gray-and-green translucent dome designed by Gustav Eiffel, the architect who conceived the famous tower. Chef Eric Brifford keeps the crowds lined up. Menu items focus on Provençal models and change every 2 months, based on whatever is fresh. Begin your meal with a truffle-studded tart or perhaps a salad of scallops served with caviar and mango-flavored vinaigrette. Move on to a casserole of wild boar *(cochon noir)* from the Pyrenees with wild mushrooms or perhaps a whole red snapper, simply grilled and succulent, and served with butter or hollandaise sauce, according to your wishes. Dessert might be a soft lemon-flavored pastry, prepared like a soufflé and served with mascarpone sauce. Candles illuminate the place; during dinner, live piano music reverberates off the dome.

In the Hôtel Vernet, 25 rue Vernet, 8e. (✆ **01-44-31-98-98**. www.hotelvernet.com. Reservations required. Main courses 45€–88€ ($59–$114); *menu gastronomique* 130€ ($169). AE, DC, MC, V. Tues–Fri 12:30–2pm; Mon–Fri 7:30–10pm. Métro: George V.

Pierre Gagnaire ★★★ MODERN FRENCH   If you're able to get a reservation, it's worth the effort. The menus are seasonal to take advantage of France's rich bounty; owner Pierre Gagnaire demands perfection, and the chef has a dazzling way with flavors and textures. Stellar examples are crayfish cooked tempura-style with thin-sliced, flash-seared vegetables and sweet-and-sour sauce; and turbot cooked in a bag and served with fennel and Provençal lemons. Chicken with truffles comes in two stages— first the breast in wine-based aspic and then the thighs, chopped into roughly textured pieces. For dessert, try chocolate soufflé with a frozen parfait and pistachios.

6 rue Balzac, 8e. (✆ **01-58-36-12-50**. Fax 01-58-36-12-51. www.pierre-gagnaire.com. Reservations required. Main courses 65€–120€ ($85–$156); fixed-price menu 90€ ($117) lunch, 260€ ($338) dinner. AE, DC, MC, V. Mon–Fri noon–1:30pm; Sun–Fri 7:30–10pm. Métro: George V.

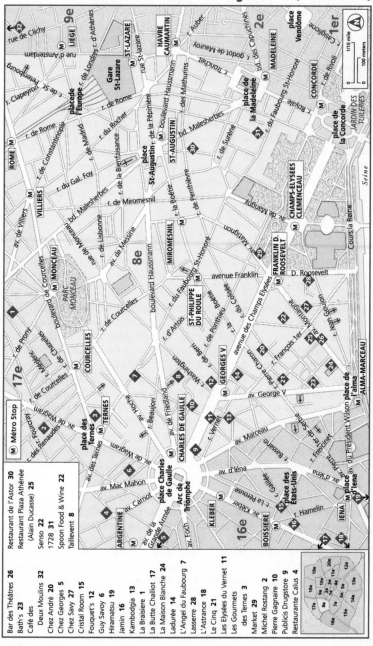

Where to Dine on the Right Bank (8 & 16–17e)

Bar des Théâtres **26**
Bath's **23**
Café des Deux Moulins **32**
Chez André **20**
Chez Georges **5**
Chez Savy **27**
Cristal Room **15**
Fouquet's **12**
Guy Savoy **6**
Hiramatsu **19**
Jamin **16**
Kambodgia **13**
La Braisière **1**
La Butte Chaillot **17**
La Maison Blanche **24**
Ladurée **14**
L'Angel du Faubourg **7**
Lasserre **28**
L'Astrance **18**
Le Cinq **21**
Les Elysées du Vernet **11**
Les Gourmets des Ternes **3**
Market **29**
Michel Rostang **2**
Pierre Gagnaire **10**
Publicis Drugstore **9**
Restaurante Caïus **4**

Restaurant de l'Astor **30**
Restaurant Plaza Athénée (Alain Ducasse) **25**
Senso **22**
1728 **31**
Spoon Food & Wine **22**
Taillevent **8**

147

Restaurant Plaza Athénée (Alain Ducasse) ✩✩✩ MODERN & TRADITIONAL FRENCH   Few other chefs have been catapulted to international fame as quickly as Alain Ducasse. There's a lot of marketing and glitter involved, but what you'll find in this world-renowned hotel is a lobby-level hideaway that top-notch decorator Patrick Jouin originally decorated around the turn of the millennium and then artfully redecorated, much to the fascination of *haute* Paris. The six-star chef, Alain Ducasse, who supervises the kitchens here, divides his time among Paris, Monaco, New York, and Tokyo. In this, his Parisian stronghold, he places a special emphasis on "rare and precious ingredients," whipping up flavorful and very expensive combinations of caviar, lobster, crayfish, truffles (both black and white), and shellfish. Cuisine is vaguely Mediterranean and decidedly contemporary, yet based on traditional models. Examples include chilled crayfish served with Osetra caviar; succulent versions of Bresse chicken with truffles; and thick, oozing slabs of pork crisp-grilled to perfection. The wine list is superb, with some selections deriving from the best vintages of France, Germany, Switzerland, Spain, California, and Italy.

In the Hôtel Plaza Athénée, 25 av. Montaigne, 8e. ℂ **01-53-67-65-00.** Fax 01-53-67-65-12. www.alain-ducasse. com. Reservations required 4–6 weeks in advance. Main courses 80€–150€ ($104–$195); fixed-price menus 220€–320€ ($286–$416). AE, DC, MC, V. Thurs–Fri 12:45–2:15pm; Mon–Fri 7:45–10:15pm. Closed mid-July to Aug 22 and 10 days in late Dec. Métro: Alma-Marceau.

Taillevent ✩✩✩ MODERN & TRADITIONAL FRENCH   This is the Parisian *ne plus ultra* of gastronomy. Taillevent opened in 1946 and has climbed steadily in excellence; today it ranks as Paris's outstanding all-around restaurant, challenged only by Lucas-Carton and Pierre Gagnaire. It's in a grand 19th-century town house off the Champs-Elysées, with paneled rooms and crystal chandeliers. The place is small, which permits the owner to give personal attention to every facet of the operation and maintain a discreet atmosphere. You might begin with *boudin* (sausage) of Breton lobster à la Nage, cream of watercress soup with Sevruga caviar, or duck liver with spice bread and ginger. Main courses include red snapper with black olives, Scottish salmon with a sauce of olive oil and lemons, and cassoulet of crayfish. Dessert might be *nougatine glacé* with pears. The wine list is among the best in Paris.

15 rue Lamennais, 8e. ℂ **01-44-95-15-01.** Fax 01-42-25-95-18. www.taillevent.com. Reservations required 4–6 weeks in advance. Main courses 34€–90€ ($44–$117); *dégustation* 140€–190€ ($182–$247). AE, DC, MC, V. Mon–Fri noon–2:30pm and 7–10pm. Closed Aug. Métro: George V.

EXPENSIVE

Bath's AUVERGNAT/TRADITIONAL FRENCH   The rocky and agrarian region of central France known as L'Auvergne has never been considered particularly chic. This restaurant, however, more than any other Auvergnat restaurant in Paris, manages to transform the region's provincial image into something that's cozy but elegant. The setting is a well-upholstered, ocher-colored dining room where menu items are divided between the pork-based culinary specialties of the Auvergne and lighter dishes from the rest of France. The finest examples include ravioli stuffed with a pungent cantal cheese from the Auvergne; cream of lentil soup studded with foie gras "bonbons"; filet of beef from Salers (a part of the Auvergne) served with lentils; and something not native to the Auvergne, a cassoulet (stew pot) of lobster. Jean-Yves Bath, the owner and chef, earned a Michelin star just a few months after the place opened in 1999.

9 rue de la Trémoille, 8e. ℂ **01-40-70-01-09.** Reservations required. Main courses 20€–44€ ($26–$57); fixed-price lunch 30€ ($39); fixed-price dinner 70€ ($91). AE, DC, MC, V. Mon–Fri noon–2:30pm and 7:30–10:30pm. Closed Aug. Métro: Alma-Marceau.

> ### *Finds* The Best Food Shopping in Paris
>
> Master chef Alain Ducasse continues to expand his empire with the opening of **BE**, 73 bd. de Courcelles, 8e ((C) **01-46-22-20-20**; Métro: Courcelles). Short for *Boulangerie Epicerie*, BE is part bakery and part upmarket deli. As a baker, Eric Kayser is famous in Paris, and he sells some 400 products from all over the globe, including 15 varieties of French bread baked fresh at least eight times a day. You can stop off here for the makings of a picnic, costing about 20€ to 30€ ($26–$39) per person, depending on your selection. There are only 22 seats. If a table is free, grab it. You can eat an array of freshly made salads for 5.50€ to 8.50€ ($7.15–$11); delicious homemade soups at 4€ ($5.20); and some of the best and most delectable sandwiches in Paris, costing from 4.20€ to 8€ ($5.45–$10). Of course, if you want some walnut oil from the Dordogne or some lavender honey from Moustiers-Ste-Marie, they are standing on the shelves as well. Open Monday to Saturday 7am to 8pm.

La Maison Blanche 🐱🐱 PROVENÇAL/TRADITIONAL FRENCH   Jacques and his twin brother, Lauren Pourcel, were two of the most famous chefs in the southerly province of Languedoc before heading north to Paris. The setting would be the envy of any restaurant in the world: Positioned on the uppermost (seventh) floor of the Art Deco–style Theatre des Champs-Elysées, it has contemporary, all-white-and-purple decor, sweeping views across the Seine, and two dining rooms. Clientele tends to be rich, non-French, and a bit pretentious, but in light of the brilliant food and the sublime setting, who cares? The menu changes with the inspiration of the chefs and the seasons, but stellar examples include filet of grilled sole with citrus sauce; rack of roasted lamb with sesame seeds; and filet of partridge cooked on the bone with caramelized turnips and Szechuan-style spicy peppers, dribbled with a syrup of licorice-flavored blackberries.

15 av. Montaigne, 8e. (C) 01-47-23-55-99. Reservations required. Main courses 38€–73€ ($49–$95); fixed-price lunch with wine 65€ ($85). AE, DC, MC, V. Mon–Fri noon–1:45pm; daily 8–10:45pm. Métro: Alma-Marceau.

L'Angle du Faubourg 🐱🐱 TRADITIONAL FRENCH   Throughout the 1980s and early 1990s, a reservation at the ultra-upscale Taillevent was sought after by diplomats, billionaires, and *demi-mondains* from around Europe. In 2001, the Taillevent's owner, M. Vrinat, opened a cost-conscious bistro that capitalizes on Taillevent's reputation, but at much lower prices. Lunches here tend to be efficient, relatively quick, and businesslike; dinners are more leisurely, even romantic. The restaurant has an ultramodern dining room, additional seating in the cellar, and a menu that simplifies Taillevent's lofty culinary ideas. The best examples include cream of endive soup with mustard grains; risotto with ingredients that change weekly (during our visit, it was studded with braised radicchio); and a grilled, low-fat version of *daurade* (bream), served with artichokes and a reduction of mushrooms, appreciated by the many diet-conscious *photo-modèles* who stop in.

195 rue du Faubourg St-Honoré, 8e. (C) 01-40-74-20-20. www.taillevent.com. Reservations required. Main courses 19€–35€ ($25–$46); fixed-price menu 35€–70€ ($46–$91). AE, DC, MC, V. Mon–Fri noon–2:30pm and 7–10:30pm. Métro: Terme or Etoile.

Restaurant de l'Astor 🐱 MODERN FRENCH   The vaguely Art Deco decor by superstar Frederick Mechiche includes tones of black and champagne. The restaurant attracts some of the leading politicians of France, many of whom walk the short distance from the dining room to the Elysée Palace and government ministries. The cuisine, as conceived and concocted by Laurent Delarbre is utterly sublime. Menu items change with the seasons, but include, among other items, cream of coconut soup with a *tartare* of pig's foot and fried slices of foie gras; roasted scallops with a confit of fennel and licorice; and rosettes of lamb basted with champagne and served with bacon-studded lard. Everything here is artfully presented, with a sort of reverential hush.

In the Hôtel Saint-Honoré, 11 rue d'Astorg, 8e. ℭ 01-53-05-05-05. Reservations recommended. Main courses 31€–34€ ($40–$44); fixed-price lunches 47€ ($60), fixed-price dinners 50€–70€ ($65–$91). AE, DC, MC, V. Mon–Fri noon–2pm and 7:30–10pm. Métro: Madeleine.

Senso ℱ INTERNATIONAL   The new power lunch venue of the hour is **Senso,** in the revamped La Trémoille. On exquisitely beautiful dishes, some of the most delectable food in Paris is served, including such exotic treats as squid stuffed with chorizo and sole with fresh ginger and spinach. The contemporary French cuisine also features stuffed tomatoes with beef and fresh herbs and, an unusual combination, chateaubriand served with Provençal monkfish soup. Designed by the famous Sir Terrence Conran, the restaurant is ultramodern in its appointments. The fashionably cool bar area is decorated with ivory leather sofas and subtle lighting, which changes from blue to red throughout the day.

In the Hotel La Trémoille, 14 rue de la Trémoille, 8e. ℭ 01-56-52-14-14. www.hotel-tremoille.com. Reservations required. Main courses 25€–40€ ($33–$52). Fixed-price menus 50€–65€ ($65–$85). Daily noon–3pm and 7pm–2am. Métro: Alma-Marceau.

1728 ℱ *Finds* JAPANESE/MODERN FRENCH   An 18th-century town house, just off Faubourg-St-Honoré where the Marquis de Lafayette lived, has been turned into this chic rendezvous. The decor is sumptuous, just like it was in the 1700s, with paintings on the wall—each for sale—and low marble dining tables and chairs. Call the place what you like—upmarket tea salon or cafe. Start with the tuna tartare or even a well-stuffed club sandwich at lunch. The tiger shrimp is savory and is scented with malt whisky. For a main course, one of the most delightful offerings is steamed sea bass, flavored with ginger and served with snow peas and zucchini. Other fine selections include filet of sole with a saffron-laced sauce and filet of beef in a sauce made of Chinese truffles. The pastries are supplied from the famous Pierre Hermé bakeries.

8 rue d'Anjou, 8e. ℭ 01-40-17-04-77. www.restaurant-1728.com. Reservations recommended for main meals. Main courses 25€–40€ ($33–$52). AE, MC, V. Mon–Fri noon–midnight, Mon–Sat 8pm–midnight. Closed 3 weeks in Aug. Métro: Concorde.

Spoon, Food & Wine ℱ INTERNATIONAL   This hypermodern venture by star chef Alain Ducasse is both hailed as a "restaurant for the millennium" and condemned as surreal and a bit absurd. Despite that, there can be a 2-week wait for a dinner reservation. This upscale but affordable restaurant may be the least pretentious and most hip of Ducasse's ventures. The somewhat claustrophobic dining room blends Parisian and Californian references, and the menu (which changes every 2 months) roams the world. Examples include deliberately undercooked grilled squid (part of it evokes sushi) with curry sauce; grilled Waguy beef (an Australia-derived version of Kobe beef); and spareribs with a devil's marmalade. Vegetarians appreciate stir-fried dishes in which you can mix and match up to 15 ingredients.

In the Hôtel Marignan-Elysée, 14 rue Marignan, 8e. ℭ 01-40-76-34-44. www.spoon.tm.fr. Reservations recommended 1–2 weeks in advance. Main courses 10€–40€ ($13–$52). AE, DC, MC, V. Mon–Fri noon–2pm and 7–10:30pm. Métro: Franklin-D-Roosevelt.

MODERATE

Chez André TRADITIONAL FRENCH   Chez André is one of the neighborhood's favorite bistros with an ambience that evokes France of the 1950s and a clientele that includes everyday folk, as well as some of the most prosperous residents of this extremely upscale neighborhood. Outside, a discreet red awning stretches over an array of shellfish on ice; inside, an Art Nouveau decor includes etched glass and masses of flowers. This has been a landmark on rue Marbeuf since 1937. It remains as it was when it was founded (thanks to an agreement made with the original owners). The old-style cuisine on the menu includes pâté of thrush; Roquefort in puff pastry; grilled veal kidneys; roast rack of lamb; a *potage du jour* (soup of the day); fresh shellfish; and, on Fridays, bouillabaisse. Several reasonably priced wines are offered as well.

12 rue Marbeuf (at rue Clément-Marot), 8e. ☎ 01-47-20-59-57. Reservations recommended. Main courses 18€–35€ ($23–$46); fixed-price menu 34€ ($44). AE, DC, MC, V. Daily noon–1am. Métro: Franklin-D-Roosevelt.

Citrus Etoile ⋆ FRENCH   It's a good example of a hip, well-connected, and stylish restaurant-of-the-minute, where part of the fun involves seeing and being seen by the politically connected and trend-conscious crowd. The decor is minimalist, black, white, and orange, a bemused blend of the best of California (former home of the owners and inspiration for some of the cuisine) and France. If you opt for a meal here, you'll be in good hands: Chef Gilles Epié used to be a caterer and private chef in Hollywood before returning to Paris with his fashion-model wife Elizabeth (an American, who supervises the dining room) to open this in-vogue dining venue near the Arch of Triumph. Menu items are health-conscious, artfully simple, "uncluttered," and flavorful. Begin with asparagus with salmon caviar, lime juice, and crumbled egg yolks; braised scallops with parmesan cheese and olive oil; or perhaps some slices of foie gras with truffles and port wine sauce. Delightful main courses include John Dory, served with its skin on a bed of laurel leaves with grated parmesan cheese; breast of pigeon with foie gras and green cabbage; and lobster cooked in a bouillon of green asparagus and tarragon.

6 rue Arsène Houssaye, 8e. ☎ 01-42-89-15-51. www.citrusetoile.fr. Reservations recommended. Main courses 16€–31€ ($21–$40); set menus 29€–38€ ($38–$49). AE, MC, V. Mon–Fri 12:30–2:30pm and 7:30–10:30pm. Métro: Etoile.

Ladurée ⋆ TRADITIONAL FRENCH   Ladurée, acclaimed since 1862 as one of Paris's grand cafes, adds a touch of class to the neighborhood. This offshoot of the original near La Madeleine caters to an international set. The stylish, somewhat chaotic venue changes from tearoom to full-fledged restaurant at least twice each day. The Belle Epoque setting is ideal for sampling Ladurée's macaroons—not the coconut version familiar to Americans, but two almond meringue cookies, flavored with vanilla, coffee, strawberry, pistachio, or another flavor, held together with butter cream. The talented chefs constantly adjust to take advantage of the freshest ingredients. The menu may include crisp, tender pork filet with potato-and-parsley purée; sea bass with leeks; and marinated red mullet on a salad of cold ratatouille. One downside: Service isn't always efficient.

75 av. des Champs-Elysées, 8e. ☎ 01-40-75-08-75. www.laduree.fr. Reservations required for restaurant. Main courses 29€–44€ ($38–$57); fixed-price lunch 27€–32€ ($35–$42); fixed-price dinner 32€ ($42); fixed-price breakfast 16€–24€ ($21–$31); pastries from 6€ ($7.80). AE, DC, MC, V. Daily 7:30am–1am. Métro: George V.

Les Gourmets des Ternes *Value* TRADITIONAL FRENCH   This restaurant caters to hordes who appreciate its affordable prices and lack of pretension. Despite the brusque service, diners have included the mayor of Atlanta (who wrote the bistro a thank-you letter), Sean Penn, and Oliver Stone, as well as hundreds of folks from this neighborhood. Thriving in this spot since 1892, the place retains an early-1900s paneled decor, with some additions from the 1950s, including Bordeaux-colored banquettes, mirrors, wooden panels, touches of brass, and paper tablecloths. The finely grilled signature dishes include rib steak with marrow sauce and fries; country pâtés and sausages; sole, turbot, and monkfish; and desserts such as peach Melba and *baba au rhum* (rum cake with raisins).

87 bd. de Courcelles, 8e. ☎ 01-42-27-43-04. Main courses 16€–35€ ($21–$46). AE, MC, V. Mon–Fri noon–2:30pm and 7–10pm. Métro: Ternes.

Market 👶 FUSION   The creative force here is Alsatian Jean-Georges Vongerichten, whose restaurants in New York, Hong Kong, London, and Las Vegas are classified by local critics as both megahip and top tier. The Paris gemstone in the Vongerichten empire holds 130 diners in a richly paneled postmodern decor, designed by decorating mogul Christian Liaigre, dotted with carved masks from Oceania (Polynesia) and Borneo and with art objects on loan from the Paris branch of Christie's auction house. Menu items include a pizza with black truffles and Fontina cheese; foie gras with a purée of quince, corn pancakes, and wild cranberries; or crabmeat salad with mango. Main courses might feature *daurade* (bream or porgy) baked in a salt crust; a faux-filet with exotic mushrooms; or a "black plate" for two diners, loaded high with shellfish and their garnishes. There's a wine list that most oenophiles consider extremely interesting.

15 av. Matignon, 8e. ☎ 01-56-43-40-90. Reservations required. Fixed-price lunch 34€ ($44); pizzas 19€–29€ ($25–$38); main courses 22€–40€ ($29–$52). AE, MC, V. Daily noon–3pm and 7:30–11:30pm; Sat–Sun brunch noon–6pm. Métro: Champs-Elysées–Clemenceau.

Publicis Drugstore MODERN FRENCH   In 1958 the founder of this company, Marcel Bleustein-Blanchet, following a visit to the United States, created a new concept for Paris that became a legend. Years later, a fire in one drugstore and a bombing in a Left Bank branch ended its glory. But Le Drugstore has made a spectacular comeback. Truman Capote once defined a city as a place where you can purchase a canary at 3 o'clock in the morning. In Paris, the Drugstore is a place where you can purchase a 200€ ($260) teddy bear or order a deluxe hamburger with foie gras in the wee hours. The Drugstore stands on the site of the old Astoria Hotel, the home of General Eisenhower when he was supreme commander of the Allied Forces in Europe. Today it houses a brasserie and a restaurant, a bookshop, a wine shop, two cinemas, a newsstand, and a luxury grocery store. The famed chef, Alain Ducasse, planned the menu offered in both dining places. Every food item from grilled scallops to ham with truffles Ducasse-style is served here. Naturally, the Brasserie has the cheaper prices; a more refined service and better cuisine is at Le Marcel.

133 av. des Champs-Elysées, 8e. ☎ 01-44-43-77-64. Reservations required for Le Marcel. Brasserie: main courses 16€–29€ ($21–$38); fixed-price menus 41€ ($53). Le Marcel: main courses 30€–40€ ($39–$52); fixed-price menu 50€ ($65). AE, DC, MC, V. Brasserie: Mon–Fri 8am–2am. Le Marcel: Mon–Fri noon–3pm and 7–10pm. Métro: Charles de Gaulle (Etoile) or Georges V.

INEXPENSIVE

Bar des Théâtres TRADITIONAL FRENCH   Its local patrons in the 8th arrondissement have long called this bar/restaurant "The Temple of the God Steak Tartare." For those daring souls who still eat this blood-rare red meat specialty, this long-established restaurant is said to make the best dish. Even though it's situated in the most lethally priced district of Paris, over the years it has kept its prices reasonable.

Across the street is the Théâtre des Champs-Elysées, and many of its performers, especially actors and musicians, make the bar their "local" while appearing here. The chef also specializes in a delectable *magret de canard* (breast of duckling), and you can even order caviar and foie gras, but those items would put this into a very expensive category.

6 av. Montaigne, 8e. ☎ 01-47-23-34-63. Reservations recommended. Main courses 15€–25€ ($20–$33). AE, DC, MC, V. Mon–Fri 6am–2am; Sat–Sun 10am–2am. Métro: Alma Marceau.

Chez Savy ✿ *Value* AUVERGNAT   Set within one of Paris's most stratospherically expensive neighborhoods, this old-time brasserie has prices that, compared to nearby competitors, seem modest. Founded in 1923 and with an old-fashioned bistro decor (mirrors, brass hardware, polished paneling, banquettes) that hasn't changed much since the Jazz Age, it has a pair of long and narrow dining rooms, the first of which is known as *le wagon* (the dining car). Come here for the kind of hearty, flavorful food that your great-grandmother (had she been from the Auvergne) would have prepared for a holiday meal around 1910. Sauces here are likely to have been enriched with bone marrow; pork chitterlings are laboriously processed into earthy versions of *andouillettes;* and accompaniments to a main course might include a *petit farçou,* a thick crepe enriched with such green leafy vegetables as chard, spinach, and leeks. Lamb here is superb, especially the slow-cooked haunches, cooked with rosemary until the meat is literally falling off the bone. Wines are strong and heady; cheeses (cantal, Roquefort, and others) are fresh from farms in central France and satisfying.

23 rue Bayard, 8e. ☎ 01-47-23-46-98. Reservations recommended. Main courses 22€–28€ ($29–$36); fixed-price lunch 20€–24€ ($26–$31); fixed-price dinner 29€ ($38). AE, DC, MC, V. Mon–Fri noon–2:30pm and 7:30–11pm. Closed Aug. Métro: Franklin-D-Roosevelt.

16TH ARRONDISSEMENT
VERY EXPENSIVE

Hiramatsu ✿ *Finds* TRADITIONAL FRENCH   Other than the fact that chef Hiroyuki Hiramatsu and most of his staff are Japanese, the only Asian touch at this restaurant is a hot, wet towel that arrives before the meal, in the Japanese style. Everything else is unabashedly French: the contemporary dining room, seating just 40, that's outfitted in mostly monochromatic tones of black and white; the rows of windows, each of which is set with shimmering panes of red-and-blue cut glass; the mini-salon where smokers can run in for a quick puff and/or a pre- or post-dinner drink (the dining room is nonsmoking); and a polite staff wearing gray-and-white uniforms. Menu items change frequently, but are always artfully presented. Examples include lightly smoked and marinated salmon served with *fines herbes,* deliberately undercooked crayfish served with a mousseline of mushrooms and a watercress-and-truffle salad, fried scallops served with a "brick" of rhubarb and a splash of champagne sauce, and saddle of roasted venison in puff pastry with vanilla and walnut gnocchi and a puree of celeriac and green apples.

52 rue de Longchamps, 16e. ☎ 01-56-81-08-80. www.hiramatsu.co.jp. Reservations required. Main courses 38€–60€ ($49–$78); fixed-price lunch 48€ ($62); fixed-price dinner 95€–130€ ($124–$169). AE, DC, MC, V. Mon–Fri 12:30–2pm and 7:30–9:30pm. Métro: Trocadéro.

Jamin ✿✿✿ TRADITIONAL FRENCH   This is where Paris's great chef of the 1980s, Joël Robuchon, made his mark. Now Robuchon's 17-year second-in-command, Benoit Guichard, is completely in charge, inspired by his master but an imaginative chef in his own right. He prepares a brief but well-chosen menu. Lunch can be simple, though each dish, such as a beautifully seasoned salmon tartare, is done to perfection. Menu items change with the seasons but might, at the time of your arrival, include a ravioli of crayfish with tarragon-flavored red wine sauce; a "blood sausage" of chicken garnished with truffles and served with an herb-flavored salad; line-caught sea bass sautéed in butter with capers and lemon (in the "style of Grenoble"), resting on a bed of butter-cooked carrots; and Bresse chicken served with a sauce made from its drippings and a generous dose of cream.

32 rue de Longchamp, 16e. ℂ 01-45-53-00-07. Fax 01-45-53-00-15. Reservations required 1 week in advance. Main courses 48€–80€ ($62–$104); fixed-price lunch 50€–130€ ($65–$169); fixed-price dinner 95€–130€ ($124–$169). AE, DC, MC, V. Mon–Fri 12:30–2pm and 7:45–9:45pm. Métro: Trocadéro.

EXPENSIVE

Cristal Room 🎨🎨 MODERN FRENCH The Taittinger family of champagne fame has opened this Baccarat crystal–laden room in a former town house of the art patroness, Marie-Laure de Noailles. She was known as the benefactor of such artists as Man Ray and Salvador Dalí. For the new restaurant setting, Philippe Starck was called in to create the minimalist decor, with a bow to the Surrealists. The chef is the brilliant Thierry Burlot, a total original, creating his own take on such classics as oyster ravioli or even a caramel soufflé, each dish having a distinctive flavor. Start, perhaps, with a delectable foie gras from Landes and follow with such delights as marinated shrimp in a red curry or lobster carpaccio.

Kids Family-Friendly Restaurants

Meals at Paris's grand restaurants are rarely suitable for young children. Nevertheless, many parents drag their kids along, often to the annoyance of other diners. You may have to make some compromises, such as dining earlier than most Parisians. **Hotel dining rooms** can be another good choice for family dining. They usually have children's menus or at least one or two *plats du jour* cooked for children, such as spaghetti with meat sauce.

If you take your child to a **moderate** or an **inexpensive restaurant,** ask if they will serve a child's plate. If not, order a *plat du jour* or *plat garni* (a garnished main-course platter), which will be suitable for most children, particularly if a dessert is to follow. Most **cafes** welcome children during the day and early evening. At a cafe, children seem to like the sandwiches (try a *croque monsieur,* or toasted ham and cheese), the omelets, and the *pommes frites* (french fries).

Crémerie-Restaurant Polidor (p. 165)   One of the most popular restaurants on the Left Bank, this reasonably priced dining room is so family friendly, it calls its food *cuisine familiale.* This might be the best place to introduce your child to bistro food.

Hard Rock Cafe (p. 140)   At the Paris branch of this chain, good old American burgers and more are served against a background of rock memorabilia and music.

Joe Allen (p. 133)   This American restaurant in Les Halles delivers everything from chili to chocolate-mousse pie to the best burgers in Paris.

11 place des Etats-Unis, 16e. ✆ **01-40-22-11-10.** Reservations required. Main courses 30€–49€ ($39–$64). AE, MC, V. Mon–Sat noon–2:30pm; Mon–Sat 8–9:30pm. Closed last week in Dec. Métro: Boissière.

L'Astrance ✫✫✫ MODERN FRENCH   It's small, it's charming, and its creative flair derives from the partnership of two former employees (some say "disciples") of megachef Alain Passard, scion of L'Arpège, an ultraglam restaurant in the 7th Arrondissement. The perfectly mannered Christophe Rohat, supervising the dining room, is the more visible of the two, but Pascal Barbot, the chef creating the food that emerges from the kitchens, has become a true culinary force. Expect a crisply contemporary dining room. The menu, from which flavors practically jump off the plates, might include an unusual form of "ravioli," wherein thin slices of avocado encase a filling of seasoned crabmeat, all of it accompanied by salted almonds and a splash of almond oil. A mussel salad is enriched with cumin, chervil, and carrots, and buckwheat blinis come layered with a confit of shallots and a cupful of oyster-based "cappuccino."

4 rue Beethoven, 16e. ✆ **01-40-50-84-40.** Reservations required 3 or 4 weeks in advance. Main courses 24€–38€ ($31–$50). Fixed-price lunch 45€–130€ ($59–$169); fixed-price dinner 50€–150€ ($65–$195). AE, DC, MC, V. Tues–Fri 12:30–1:30pm and Tues–Sat 8:30–11:45pm. Closed in Aug. Métro: Trocadéro.

MODERATE

La Butte Chaillot ✫ *Value* TRADITIONAL FRENCH   This baby bistro showcases culinary high priest Guy Savoy and draws a crowd from the affluent neighborhood's corporate offices. Diners congregate in posh but congested areas. Menu items change weekly (sometimes daily) and betray a strange sense of mass production not unlike that found in a luxury cruise ship's dining room. Examples are a sophisticated medley of terrines; a "low-fat" version of chunky mushroom soup; a salad of snails and herbed potatoes; succulent rack of lamb; and roasted rabbit with sage and a compote of onions, bacon, and mushrooms.

110 bis av. Kléber, 16e. ✆ **01-47-27-88-88.** www.buttechaillot.com. Reservations recommended. Main courses 16€–27€ ($21–$35); fixed-price menus 33€ ($43). AE, DC, MC, V. Sun–Fri noon–2:30pm; daily 7–11pm. Métro: Trocadéro.

INEXPENSIVE

Kambodgia ASIAN/CAMBODIAN   The waiters, all dressed in black cotton tunics, will welcome you to this excellent eatery that serves some of the best and most flavorful Asian dishes in Paris. The basement atmosphere has been called "Zen-like," but the service is welcoming, and it's a good choice for a romantic dinner not far from the Champs-Elysées. Two of our favorite dishes: a superb seafood *pot-au-feu* (stew) and chicken roasted with honey and lemon. One Cambodian dish that's a delight is ginger fish wrapped in a banana leaf.

15 rue de Bassano, 16e. ✆ **01-47-23-31-80.** www.kambodgia.com. Reservations required. Main courses 15€–22€ ($20–$29); fixed-price lunch 19€–24€ ($25–$31). AE, MC, V. Mon–Fri noon–2:30pm; Mon–Sat 7:30–10:30pm. Closed Aug. Métro: George V.

17TH ARRONDISSEMENT
VERY EXPENSIVE

Guy Savoy ✫✫✫ TRADITIONAL FRENCH   One of the hottest chefs in Europe, Guy Savoy serves the kind of food he likes to eat, prepared with consummate skill. We think he has a slight edge over his rival Michel Rostang (see below), though Ducasse, at least in media coverage, surpasses them both. The decor is a sober, monochromatic, and deliberately understated foil for the superb and fussed-over food: "a contemporary-looking study in browns and off-whites." Although the superb meals comprise as many as nine courses, the portions are small; you won't necessarily be satiated at the end. The menu changes with the seasons and may include cream of artichoke soup with Parmesan and black truffles, roasted rack of veal served with truffle-studded mashed potatoes, duckling foie gras with aspic and gray salt, or sea bass grilled in a salt shell and served with a sauce of sweet herbs. If you come in the right season, you may have a chance to order game, such as mallard and venison. Savoy is fascinated with mushrooms and has been known to serve a dozen types, especially in autumn.

18 rue Troyon, 17e. ℂ **01-43-80-40-61**. Fax 01-46-22-43-09. www.guysavoy.com. Reservations for dinner required 1 month in advance; 2–3 days in advance for lunch. Main courses 72€–160€ ($94–$208); *menu dégustation* 230€–285€ ($299–$371). AE, DC, MC, V. Tues–Fri noon–2pm; Tues–Sat 7–10:30pm. Métro: Charles-de-Gaulle–Etoile or Ternes.

Michel Rostang ✦✦✦ MODERN & TRADITIONAL FRENCH   Michel Rostang is one of Paris's most creative chefs, the fifth generation of a distinguished French "cooking family." His restaurant contains four dining rooms paneled in mahogany, cherrywood, or pearwood; some have frosted Lalique crystal panels. Changing every 2 months, the menu offers modern improvements on *cuisine bourgeoise.* Truffles are the dish of choice in midwinter, and you'll find racks of suckling lamb from the salt marshes of France's western coast in spring; in game season, look for pheasant and venison. Year-round staples are quail eggs with sea urchins; fricassee of sole; quenelles of whitefish with a lobster sauce; *canard au sang* (duck prepared in a duck press with a sauce of red wine, foie gras, and its own blood); and Bresse chicken with mushroom purée and a salad composed of the chicken's thighs.

20 rue Rennequin, 17e. ℂ **01-47-63-40-77**. Fax 01-47-63-82-75. www.michelrostang.com. Reservations required 1 week in advance. Main courses 60€–98€ ($78–$127); fixed-price menu 70€–230€ ($91–$299) lunch; 175€–230€ ($228–$299) dinner. AE, DC, MC, V. Tues–Fri 12:30–2:30pm; Mon–Sat 7:30–10:30pm. Closed 3 weeks in Aug. Métro: Ternes.

MODERATE

Chez Georges TRADITIONAL FRENCH   Not to be confused with a bistro of the same name in the 2nd Arrondissement, this is a worthy choice. It has flourished since 1926 despite an obscure location. The setting has changed little—cheerfully harassed waiters barge through a dining room sheathed with old-fashioned paneling and etched glass, and savory odors emerge from the busy kitchen. Two enduring specialties are leg of lamb with white kidney beans and standing rib roast with herbs (especially thyme) in its own juices and *au gratin* of potatoes. Preceding these might be Baltic herring in cream sauce; a savory *pot-au-feu;* or a selection of sausages and pork products eaten with bread, butter, and sour pickles.

273 bd. Pereire, 17e. ℂ **01-45-74-31-00**. Reservations recommended. Main courses 19€–30€ ($25–$39). MC, V. Daily noon–2:30pm and 7pm–midnight. Métro: Porte Maillot.

La Braisière ✦✦ *(Finds* SOUTHWESTERN FRENCH   In this very residential arrondissement, Jacques Faussat is all the rage, winning his first Michelin star in 2004. Born in the Pyrenees, he brings the savory cuisine of the southwest to this 40-seat restaurant, whose entrance is dominated by an enormous vase of flowers in a Medici-inspired Renaissance vase. The decor is cozy, warm, and intimate, the restaurant evoking upscale chic in one of the French provinces. From the first bite, we fell in love with Faussat's savory, ambitious cuisine, with its contrast in texture and flavor. Nothing is finer for a starter than his signature appetizer of blue lobster with mangos. You can also delight in the foie gras before going on to one of the beautifully prepared and

---

Tips **Can You Dine Badly in Paris?**

The answer is an emphatic yes. Our mailbox fills with complaints from readers who've encountered haughty service and paid outrageous prices for swill. Often, these complaints are about restaurants catering to tourists. Avoid them by following our suggestions or looking in nontouristy areas for new discoveries. If you ask Parisians for recommendations, specify that you're looking for restaurants where *they* would dine, not where they think you, as a tourist, would dine.

---

seasoned fish dishes, such as "lacquered" red tuna served with onions, braised endive, and Szechuan peppers. The lamb from the Pyrenees is among the best we've ever had. The dessert specialty, familiar to residents of Gascony, is *tortière,* made with a light phyllo pastry over stewed prunes flavored with Armagnac and cinnamon, and garnished with the world's best fig ice cream.

54 rue Cardinet, 17e. ℭ **01-47-63-40-37.** Reservations required. Main courses 27€–29€ ($35–$38). Fixed-price lunch 33€ ($43). AE, DC, MC, V. Mon–Fri noon–2:30pm and Mon–Sat 7:30–10:30pm. Closed Aug. Métro: Malesherbes.

Restaurant Caïus ⭐ *(Value)* TRADITIONAL FRENCH   This chic place, popular for business lunches and dinners, also draws residents and shoppers. It's ringed with wood paneling, banquettes, and teakwood chairs. The new owner, Jean-Marc Notelet, has brought renewed vigor to the kitchen. His cuisine, however, remains traditionally French and is based on spices and a judicious use of pepper. The dining room is a showcase for the chef's enticing cuisine, which is based on authentically flavor-filled local foodstuffs. We were intrigued by his rooster from the Somme Valley. This was served with *topinébours,* a rare type of potato whose origins are in medieval France—very esoteric. Among other masterful offerings were dorado braised with Belgian endives and root vegetables, and a confit of beef with fava beans and aged vinegar along with celery whipped into almond milk.

6 rue d'Armaillé, 17e. ℭ **01-42-27-19-20.** Reservations recommended. Main courses 19€–21€ ($25–$27); fixed-price lunch 23€ ($30); fixed-price dinner 38€ ($49). AE, DC, MC, V. Mon–Fri noon–2:30pm; Mon–Sat 7:30–10pm. Métro: Charles-de-Gaulle–Etoile.

5 On the Left Bank

We'll begin with the most centrally located arrondissements on the Left Bank and then work our way through the more outlying neighborhoods and to the area near the Eiffel Tower.

5TH ARRONDISSEMENT
VERY EXPENSIVE

La Tour d'Argent *(Overrated)* TRADITIONAL FRENCH   This penthouse restaurant, a national institution, enjoys a panoramic view over the Seine and Notre-Dame. Although its reputation as the best in Paris has long been eclipsed, dining here remains an unsurpassed event, not because of the diminishing culinary reputation of this place, but because of the view of those flying buttresses of Notre-Dame. A restaurant of some sort has stood on this site since 1582: Mme de Sévigné refers to a cafe here in her letters, and Dumas used it in one of his novels. The fame of La Tour d'Argent spread

Where to Dine on the Left Bank (5–6 & 13–14e)

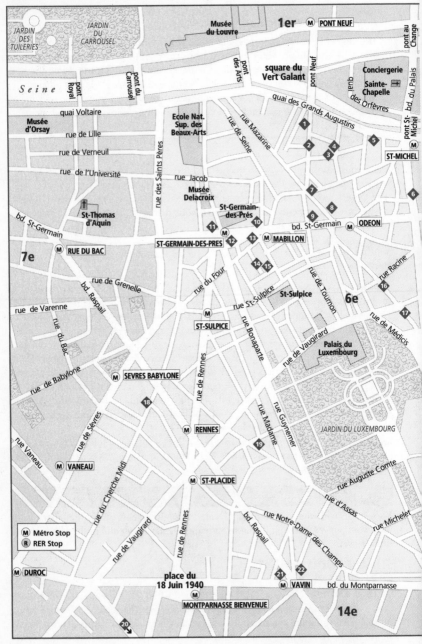

JARDIN DES TUILERIES

JARDIN DU CARROUSEL

Musée du Louvre

1er

PONT NEUF

pont au Change

pont des Arts

pont du Carrousel

pont Royal

square du Vert Galant

pont Neuf

Conciergerie

Sainte-Chapelle

quai de l'Horloge

bd. du Palais

Seine

quai Voltaire

quai des Grands Augustins

quai des Orfèvres

Musée d'Orsay

rue de Lille

Ecole Nat. Sup. des Beaux-Arts

rue Mazarine

rue de Seine

pont St-Michel

rue de Verneuil

1

rue de l'Université

rue des Saints Pères

2

5

ST-MICHEL

3

rue Jacob

7

6

Musée Delacroix

8

St-Germain-des-Prés

9

bd. St-Germain

ODEON

St-Thomas d'Aquin

10

11

bd. St-Germain

ST-GERMAIN-DES-PRES

12

13

MABILLON

bd. St-Germain

RUE DU BAC

7e

rue du Four

14 **15**

St-Sulpice

rue de Tournon

rue Racine

16

rue de Grenelle

rue St-Sulpice

6e

17

rue de Médicis

bd. Raspail

ST-SULPICE

rue Bonaparte

rue de Vaugirard

Palais du Luxembourg

rue de Varenne

rue du Bac

rue de Rennes

rue de Babylone

SEVRES BABYLONE

rue de Sèvres

18

rue Madame

rue Guynemer

JARDIN DU LUXEMBOURG

rue Vaneau

RENNES

19

VANEAU

ST-PLACIDE

rue Auguste Comte

rue d'Assas

rue du Cherche Midi

rue de Vaugirard

rue de Rennes

bd. Raspail

rue Notre-Dame des Champs

rue Michelet

Ⓜ Métro Stop
Ⓡ RER Stop

DUROC

place du 18 Juin 1940

21 **22**

VAVIN

bd. du Montparnasse

14e

MONTPARNASSE BIENVENUE

20

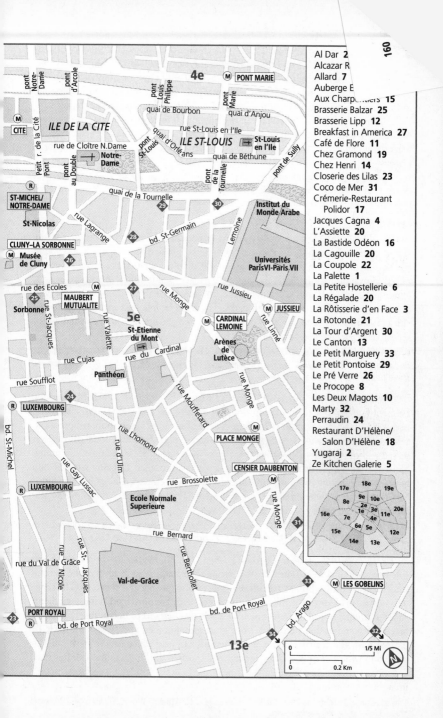

4e

Ⓜ PONT MARIE

pont Notre-Dame
pont d'Arcole
pont Louis Philippe
pont Marie

quai de Bourbon
quai d'Anjou

Ⓜ CITE

ILE DE LA CITÉ

rue de Cloître N.Dame
Petit Pont
pont au Double
rue du Double

rue St-Louis en l'Ile
ILE ST-LOUIS
quai d'Orléans
quai St-Louis

🚉 **St-Louis en l'Ile**

quai de Béthune

Notre-Dame

quai de Bethune
pont de la Tournelle
pont de Sully

ST-MICHEL/ NOTRE-DAME
Ⓡ

quai de la Tournelle

St-Nicolas

rue Lagrange

Institut du Monde Arabe

CLUNY–LA SORBONNE

bd. St-Germain

Ⓜ Musée de Cluny

rue des Ecoles

MAUBERT MUTUALITE
Ⓜ

rue Monge

rue Jussieu

Universités ParisVI–Päris VII

Ⓜ JUSSIEU

Sorbonne

rue St-Jacques
rue Valette

5e
St-Etienne du Mont

rue du Cardinal

Ⓜ CARDINAL LEMOINE

Arènes de Lutèce

rue Linné

rue Cujas

rue Soufflot

Panthéon

rue Mouffetard

rue Monge

Ⓡ LUXEMBOURG

bd. St-Michel

rue Gay Lussac

rue Lhomond

rue d'Ulm

PLACE MONGE
Ⓜ

CENSIER DAUBENTON
Ⓜ

Ⓡ LUXEMBOURG

Ecole Normale Superieure

rue Brossolette

rue Monge

rue Bernard

Ⓡ

rue du Val de Grâce
rue St-Jacques
rue Nicole

Val-de-Grâce

rue Berthollet

Ⓜ LES GOBELINS

PORT ROYAL
Ⓡ
23

bd. de Port Royal

bd. de Port Royal

bd. Arago

13e

0   1/5 Mi
0   0.2 Km

N

17e 18e 19e
8e 9e 10e
2e 3e 20e
16e 1e 11e
7e 4e
6e 5e 12e
15e
14e 13e

during its ownership by Frédéric Delair, who in the 1890s started the practice of issuing certificates to diners who ordered *caneton* (pressed duckling). The birds are numbered: The first was served to Edward VII in 1890, and now the number is over 1.2 million! For decades, the restaurant was owned by Claude Terrail, who became the most famous restaurateur in Europe. He died in 2006, and today management is handled by his son, André. A good part of the menu is devoted to duck, but the kitchen, of course, knows how to prepare other dishes. There are plenty of other places nearby where you can order food even better than that served here—and at only half the price.

15–17 quai de la Tournelle, 5e. ℂ 01-43-54-23-31. Fax 01-44-07-12-04. www.latourdargent.com. Reservations required far in advance. Main courses 60€–85€ ($78–$111); fixed-price lunch 70€ ($91). AE, DC, MC, V. Wed–Sun noon–1:15pm; Tues–Sun 7:30–9pm. Métro: St-Michel or Pont Marie.

MODERATE

Al Dar LEBANESE   This well-respected restaurant works hard to popularize the savory cuisine of Lebanon. Within a modern decor whose colors might remind you of the arid scrublands of the Middle East, you'll dine on such dishes as tabbouleh, a refreshing combination of finely chopped parsley, mint, milk, tomatoes, onions, lemon juice, olive oil, and salt; baba ghanoush, pulverized and seasoned eggplant; and hummus, pulverized chickpeas with herbs. These can be followed with savory roasted chicken; tender minced lamb with mint, cumin, and Mediterranean herbs; and any of several delectable tagines and couscous.

8 rue Frédéric-Sauton, 5e. ℂ 01-43-25-17-15. Reservations recommended. Main courses 14€–18€ ($18–$23); fixed-price lunch 17€–27€ ($22–$35); fixed-price dinner 38€–53€ ($49–$69). AE, DC, MC, V. Daily noon–3pm and 7pm–12:30am. Métro: Maubert-Mutualité.

Brasserie Balzar ⊛ TRADITIONAL FRENCH   Opened in 1898, Brasserie Balzar is battered but cheerful, with some of Paris's most colorful waiters. The menu makes almost no concessions to modern cuisine; it includes onion soup, pepper steak, sole meunière, sauerkraut with ham and sausage, pigs' feet, and fried calves' liver served without garnish. Be warned that if you want just coffee or a drink, you probably won't get a table at mealtimes. But the staff, accustomed to many patrons' odd hours, will be happy to serve you dinner in the midafternoon. Guests have included Sartre and Camus (who often got into arguments), James Thurber, and countless professors from the nearby Sorbonne.

49 rue des Ecoles, 5e. ℂ 01-43-54-13-67. www.brasseriebalzar.com. Reservations strongly recommended. Main courses 18€–31€ ($23–$40). AE, DC, MC, V. Daily noon–11:45pm. Métro: Odéon or Cluny–La Sorbonne.

Le Petit Pontoise ⊛ *Finds* TRADITIONAL FRENCH   Lying on a little-visited side street, off quai de la Tournelle, this restaurant is frequented by both professors and students from the Sorbonne. It's tiny, but the portions are big and generous. The clientele—often made up of regulars—is pampered with comfort food. Fine ingredients and a technique honed to perfection have made this a citadel of fine dining. You could take your grandmother here, even your great-grandmother, and she would likely be pleased with the seared scallops in the garlicky tomato sauce or the fresh chicken cooked in wine and mushrooms. Tender, well-flavored duckling comes with foie gras, and you can also take delight in the stew of pigs' cheeks and fresh vegetables, served in an iron casserole.

9 rue de Pontoise, 5e. ℂ 01-43-29-25-20. Main courses 14€–24€ ($18–$31). AE, MC, V. Daily noon–2:30pm and 7:30–10:30pm. Métro: Maubert-Mutualité.

Le Pré Verre ⚐ *Value* ASIAN/TRADITIONAL FRENCH Around the corner from the Sorbonne in the heart of the Latin Quarter comes a refreshing restaurant where you can get seriously good food—all for an affordable price. Even if this is not an earth-shattering gastronomic experience, it is solid and reliable, with good cooking and market-fresh ingredients. The Delacourcelle brothers are firmly based in the French tradition, but they have added innovative modern twists by giving extra spicing to the food, many of the flavorings inspired by Asia. In a welcoming, relaxed, and convivial atmosphere, tables are placed so close together that you're literally dining and rubbing elbows with the same people. For something bourgeois, dig into the well-flavored terrines for starters. One of these—and the most delectable—is made with layers of foie gras and mashed potatoes. Your meal might begin with oysters marinated with ginger and poppy seeds or scallops with cinnamon. Main courses might include suckling pig with aromatic spices and crisp-cooked cabbage, or roasted codfish.

8 rue Thenard, 5e. © 01-43-54-59-47. www.lepreverre.com. Reservations required. Fixed-price menu at lunch 13€–27€ ($17–$35), at dinner 27€ ($35). MC, V. Tues–Sat noon–2pm and 7:30–10pm. Closed Aug. Métro: Maubert-Mutualité.

Marty ⚐ *Finds* MODERN FRENCH Charming, with a stone-trimmed decor that's authentic to the era (1913) when it was established, this restaurant has been "discovered" by new generations of restaurant-goers. Named after its founders, Etienne and Marthe Marty, its fame now extends beyond the 5th Arrondissement. Service is attentive, and lots of Jazz Age murals grace the walls. Food is savory, satisfying, and unfussy. Views from the hideaway tables on the mezzanine sweep over the entire human comedy, which is loud, large, and animated, unfolding above and below you. Begin a meal with tartare of sea bream flavored with anise and lime, lobster ravioli with sherry vinegar, or fresh oysters. Continue with suprême of guinea fowl with vegetable moussaka; a platter that combines grilled squid with grilled strips of red mullet or perhaps fried scallops with garlic sauce.

20 av. des Gobelins, 5e. © 01-43-31-39-51. Main courses 19€–27€ ($25–$35); fixed-price menu 33€ ($43). AE, DC, MC, V. Daily noon–3pm and 7–11pm. Métro: Gobelins.

Perraudin ⚐⚐ TRADITIONAL FRENCH Everything about this place—decor, cuisine, prices, and service—attempts to duplicate an early-1900s bistro. This one was built in 1870 as an outlet for coal and wine. It evolved into the wood-paneled bistro you see today, where little has changed since Zola was buried in the Panthéon nearby. The marble-topped tables, mirrors, and vaudeville posters have been here forever. Reservations aren't made in advance: Diners usually drink a glass of kir at the zinc-topped bar as they wait. Onion tart, pumpkin soup, and terrine are all good appetizers. The menu includes roast leg of lamb with dauphinois potatoes, *boeuf bourguignon* (beef in red-wine sauce), and grilled salmon with sage sauce. The charming, lovely owner and chef, Mme Rameau, has fed many of the grandest scholars and professors in Europe. She accepts reservations only for early-bird diners, between 7 and 8pm.

157 rue St-Jacques, 5e. © 01-46-33-15-75. Main courses 16€–29€ ($21–$38); fixed-price lunch 18€ ($23); fixed-price dinner 28€ ($36). MC, V. Mon–Sat noon–2:15pm and 7–10pm. Closed 3 weeks in Aug. Métro: Cluny–La Sorbonne. RER: Luxembourg.

INEXPENSIVE

Breakfast in America AMERICAN Connecticut-born Hollywood screenwriter Craig Carlson opened this replica of a down-home U.S.-based diner in 2003, building it with funds from members of the California film community who donated

...ia from their films. Its self-proclaimed mission involves dispensing proper, ...g American breakfasts and diner food to a generation of Parisians who ...rior to their visits here, that coffee comes only as espresso, and that quantities, per meal, are rigidly limited. To their delight, coffee cups here are "bottomless," and food items, especially breakfast items, evoke the good old days of America's bountiful agrarian past. The venue replicates a 1950s-era railway car, replete with scarlet-and-black Naugahyde banquettes, faux windows with mirrored insets, and an unabashedly Americanized staff. Breakfast (heaping portions of the egg-and-waffle-and-bacon combinations, as well as omelets) is served throughout the day and evening. Also available are half a dozen variations of burgers, as well as tacos, club sandwiches, and BLTs.

17 rue des Ecoles, 5e. ☎ 01-43-54-50-28. Reservations not accepted. Breakfast platters 5.95€–9.50€ ($7.75–$12); fixed-price Sunday brunch 15€ ($20); lunch and dinner platters and "blue-plate specials" 6.50€–10€ ($8.45–$13). MC, V. Daily 8:30am–10:30pm. Métro: Cardinal Lemoine or Jussieu.

Coco de Mer ★ *Finds* SEYCHELLE ISLANDS   The theme of this restaurant tugs at the emotions of Parisians who have spent their holidays on the beaches of the Seychelles, in the Indian Ocean. It contains several dining rooms, one of which is outfitted like a beach, with a sand-covered floor, replicas of palm trees, and a scattering of conch shells. Menu items feature such exotic dishes as tartare of tuna flavored with ginger, olive oil, salt, and pepper; and smoked swordfish, served as carpaccio or in thin slices with mango mousse and spicy sauce. Main courses focus on fish, including a species of red snapper *(boirzoes)* imported from the Seychelles. Dessert might be a *crème de banana gratinée*.

34 bd. St-Marcel, 5e. ☎ 01-47-07-06-64. Reservations recommended. Main courses 14€–20€ ($18–$26); fixed-price menus 30€–40€ ($39–$52). AE, DC, MC, V. Tues–Sat noon–3pm; Mon–Sat 7:30pm–midnight. Métro: Les Gobelins or St-Marcel.

La Petite Hostellerie ★ *Value* TRADITIONAL FRENCH   This 1902 restaurant has a ground-floor dining room that's usually crowded and a larger upstairs one with 18th-century woodwork. People come for the cozy ambience and decor, French country cooking, polite service, and excellent prices. The fixed-price dinner might feature favorites such as *boeuf bourguignon* (braised beef in red-wine sauce), roasted rabbit with mustard sauce, or duckling *à l'orange*. Start with onion soup or stuffed mussels, and finish with cheese or peach Melba.

35 rue de la Harpe (a side street north of bd. St-Germain, just east of bd. St-Michel), 5e. ☎ 01-43-54-47-12. All main courses 10€–12€ ($13–$16); fixed-price menu 10€–20€ ($13–$26). DC, MC, V. Wed–Sun noon–2pm and Tues–Sun 6:30–11pm. Métro: St-Michel or Cluny–La Sorbonne.

6TH ARRONDISSEMENT
VERY EXPENSIVE

Jacques Cagna ★★★ MODERN & TRADITIONAL FRENCH   St-Germain knows no finer dining than at Jacques Cagna, a sophisticated restaurant in a 17th-century town house with massive timbers, burnished paneling, and 17th-century Dutch paintings. Jacques Cagna is one of the best classically trained chefs in Paris, though he has become a half-apostle to *cuisine moderne*. This is evident in his delectable carpaccio of pearly sea bream with caviar-lavished *céleric rémoulade* (celery root in mayonnaise with capers, parsley, gherkins, spring onions, chervil, chopped tarragon, and anchovy essence). Also sublime are the carpaccio of dorado; roasted crayfish with fresh herbs; fried foie gras of duckling served with caramelized fruits of the season (in winter, that usually means pears and quince); sweetbreads cooked in a salt crust and served with mushrooms and rosemary sauce; and standing roast of veal with a lime-and-ginger sauce.

14 rue des Grands-Augustins, 6e. (℃) **01-43-26-49-39**. Fax 01-43-54-54-48. www.jacquescagna.com. Reservations required in advance. Main courses 42€–85€ ($55–$111); fixed-price lunch 45€–100€ ($59–$130); fixed-price dinner 100€ ($130). AE, DC, MC, V. Tues–Fri noon–2pm; Mon–Sat 7:30–10:15pm. Closed 3 weeks in Aug. Métro: St-Michel or Odéon.

Restaurant d'Hélène/Salon d'Hélène ✦✦✦ SOUTHWESTERN FRENCH
Hélène Darroze is the most famous female chef in Paris, a Basque-born *wunderkind* whose southwestern French cuisine is a superb modern take on a classic. Be very clear about what you want before entering: The upstairs dining room (Le Restaurant d'Hélène, with elaborately set round tables) is more formal, horrendously expensive, and more sedate than the bistro (Le Salon d'Hélène). In both areas, expect bright, pop-influenced decor and relatively slow service. Upstairs, menus are artfully composed and presented as part of fixed-price meals that contain, among other things, confit of foie gras with chutney, salad of white beans and clams, and roast wild duck stuffed with foie gras and truffles. On street level, food focuses on an array of *plats du jour* (skate Grenobloise with lemon and capers) and tapas, two or three of which can be combined to create a meal. Tapas might include raw marinated tuna with Basque-derived red pepper sauce or cannelloni gratinéed with Basque sheep's milk cheese and smoked Basque ham.

4 rue d'Assas, 6e. (℃) **01-42-22-00-11**. Reservations required. Restaurant fixed-price dinner 175€–250€ ($228–$325); fixed-price lunch 72€–250€ ($94–$325); tapas 9€–36€ ($12–$47). In-salon fixed-price lunch 35€–45€ ($46–$59); fixed-price dinner 88€–150€ ($114–$195). AE, MC, V. Tues–Sat 12:30–2:15pm and 7:30–10pm. Métro: Sèvres-Babylone.

EXPENSIVE
Closerie des Lilas ✦ *Overrated* TRADITIONAL FRENCH
Opened in 1847, the Closerie was a social and culinary magnet for the avant-garde. The famous people who have sat in the "Pleasure Garden of the Lilacs" include Gertrude Stein and Alice B. Toklas, Ingres, Henry James, Chateaubriand, Picasso, Hemingway, Apollinaire, Lenin and Trotsky (at the chessboard), and Whistler. Today, the crowd consists of tourists or members of the Paris publishing world. The place resounds with the sometimes-loud sounds of a jazz pianist every night after 7pm, making the interior seem more claustrophobic than it is. If you're asked to wait for a table, you can make the wait more enjoyable by ordering the world's best champagne julep at the bar. The food is often disappointing. Try veal kidneys with mustard, veal ribs in cider sauce, steak tartare, pikeperch quenelles, or filet of beef with green peppercorn sauce. You'll be more comfortable here if you realize in advance that there are two distinctly different seating areas inside this place: the crowded and relatively inexpensive brasserie (also known as *le bateau,* the boat), and the more expensive and nominally more sedate *restaurant,* where service is a bit more formal and attentive.

171 bd. du Montparnasse, 6e. (℃) **01-40-51-34-50**. Reservations recommended 2–3 days in advance (for restaurant only). Restaurant main courses 35€–45€ ($46–$59); brasserie main courses 19€–24€ ($25–$31). AE, DC, MC, V. Restaurant daily noon–2pm and 7–11pm. Brasserie daily 11:30am–1am. Métro: Port Royal or Vavin.

MODERATE
Alcazar Restaurant ✦ MODERN FRENCH
Paris's highest-profile *brasserie de luxe* is this high-tech place funded by British restaurateur Sir Terence Conran. It features a red-and-white futuristic decor in a street-level dining room and a busy

upstairs bar (La Mezzanine de l'Alcazar). The menu includes rack of veal sautéed with wild mushrooms, roasted rack of lamb with thyme, Charolais duckling with honey and spices, monkfish with saffron in puff pastry, and shellfish and oysters from the waters of Brittany. The wines are as stylish and diverse as you'd expect.

62 rue Mazarine, 6e. ℂ 01-53-10-19-99. Reservations recommended. Main courses 18€–32€ ($23–$42); fixed-price lunch 20€–30€ ($26–$39); fixed-price dinner 40€ ($52). AE, DC, MC, V. Daily noon–3pm and 7pm–midnight. Métro: Odéon.

Allard ✪ TRADITIONAL FRENCH   This old-time bistro, opened in 1931, is still going strong. It was once the city's leading bistro, although today the competition is too great for it to reclaim that reputation. Over the years, the front room's zinc bar has been a haven for many celebrities, including Mme Pompidou; actor Alain Delon; and, since then, a gaggle of French celebrities. Allard serves all the old specialties, with quality ingredients deftly handled by the kitchen. Try snails, foie gras, veal stew, or frogs' legs or turbot in a *beurre blanc* sauce. We head here on Monday for the cassoulet Toulousian (casserole of white beans and goose and other meats) and on Saturday for *coq au vin*.

41 rue St-André-des-Arts, 6e. ℂ 01-43-26-48-23. Reservations required. Main courses 19€–39€ ($25–$51); fixed-price lunch 24€–32€ ($31–$42); fixed-price dinner 32€ ($42). AE, DC, MC, V. Mon–Sat noon–3pm and 7:30–11pm. Métro: St-Michel or Odéon.

Chez Gramond ✪ *Finds* TRADITIONAL FRENCH   Aficionados of the way France used to be seek out this place, and if you're looking for the kind of cuisine that used to satisfy the *grands intellectuels* of the Latin Quarter in the 1960s, you might find it appealing. It seats only 20 people, each of whom is treated to the savoir-faire of Auvergne-born Jean-Claude Gramond and his charming wife, Jeannine. Listed in purple ink that's duplicated on an old-time mimeograph machine, the menu items may include a marinade of mushrooms with coriander; a *navarin* (rich stew) of lamb with scotch beans; roasted grouse with figs; scallops cooked with white wine, leeks, and shallots; partridge (this is increasingly rare and expensive) served with an *émincé* (shredded mixture) of cabbage; sautéed pheasant with a Calvados-flavored cream sauce; two different preparations of rabbit, one of which is a traditional *civet* (a wild hare); or duckling with orange sauce. Try the soufflé Grand Marnier for dessert.

5 rue de Fleurus, 6e. ℂ 01-42-22-28-89. Reservations recommended. Main courses 23€–35€ ($30–$46). MC, V. Mon–Sat noon–2:30pm and 7–10:30pm. Closed in Aug. Métro: Notre-Dame des Champs.

La Rôtisserie d'en Face ✪ *Value* TRADITIONAL FRENCH   This is Paris's most popular baby bistro, operated by Jacques Cagna, whose expensive namesake restaurant is across the street. The informal place features a postmodern decor with high-tech lighting, yellow walls, and red banquettes. The simply prepared food is very good and employs high-quality ingredients. It includes several types of ravioli, pâté of duckling *en croûte* with foie gras, fish, scallops, *friture d'éperlans* (tiny fried freshwater fish), and smoked Scottish salmon with spinach. The Barbary duckling in red-wine sauce is incomparable.

2 rue Christine, 6e. ℂ 01-43-26-40-98. Reservations recommended. Main courses 22€ ($29); fixed-price menu 25€–29€ ($33–$38). AE, DC, MC, V. Mon–Fri noon–2:30pm; Mon–Sat 7–11pm. Métro: Odéon or St-Michel.

Yugaraj INDIAN   On two floors of an old Latin Quarter building, Yugaraj serves flavorful food based on the recipes of northern and (to a lesser degree) southern India. In recently renovated rooms done in vivid shades of ocher, with a formally dressed staff and lots of intricately carved Kashmiri panels and statues, you can sample the spicy, aromatic tandoori dishes that are all the rage in France. Seafood specialties are usually made with warm-water fish imported from the Seychelles, including *thiof, capitaine,* and *bourgeois,* prepared as they would be in Calcutta, with tomatoes, onions, cumin, coriander, ginger, and garlic.

14 rue Dauphine, 6e. ℂ 01-43-26-44-91. Reservations recommended. Main courses 20€–32€ ($26–$42); fixed-price lunch 19€–29€ ($25–$38); fixed-price dinner 32€–34€ ($42–$44). AE, DC, MC, V. Tues–Wed and Fri–Sun noon–2pm; Tues–Sun 7–10:30pm. Métro: Pont-Neuf or Odéon.

Ze Kitchen Galerie ⭐ *Finds* INTERNATIONAL/MODERN FRENCH   The owner and head chef of this restaurant trained in haute Parisian gastronomy under culinary czar Guy Savoy. The setting is a colorful loft space in an antique building, with an open-to-view showcase kitchen. Most of the paintings on display are for sale (the place doubles as an art gallery). Menu items, like the paintings, change about every 5 weeks; appetizers are subdivided into pastas, soups, and fish; and main courses are divided into meats and fish that are usually *à la plancha* (grilled). The best examples include platters of oysters, mussels, and sea urchins served with herb sauce and *crostini* (breadsticks), and grilled shoulder of wild boar with tamarind sauce. Desserts are modern and unusual; an imaginative example is a pumpkin beignet with corn-flavored ice cream, roasted fruit, apples, ginger, and vanilla sauce. A meal might also be followed with the restaurant's "cappuccino of the month," a frothy dessert concoction whose ingredients change with the seasons.

4 rue des Grands-Augustins, 6e. ℂ 01-44-32-00-32. Reservations recommended. Main courses 22€–30€ ($29–$39); fixed-price lunch with wine 23€–34€ ($30–$44). AE, DC, MC, V. Mon–Fri noon–2:30pm; Mon–Sat 7–11pm. Métro: St-Michel.

INEXPENSIVE

Aux Charpentiers TRADITIONAL FRENCH   This old bistro, which opened more than 130 years ago, attracts those seeking the Left Bank of yesteryear. It was once the rendezvous spot of the master carpenters, whose guild was next door. Nowadays, it's where young men take dates. Though the food isn't imaginative, it's well prepared in the best tradition of *cuisine bourgeoise*—hearty but not effete. Appetizers include pâté of duck and rabbit terrine. Recommended as a main course is roast duck with olives. The *plats du jour* recall French home cooking: salt pork with lentils, *pot-au-feu,* and stuffed cabbage. The wine list has a selection of Bordeaux, including Château Gaussens.

10 rue Mabillon, 6e. ℂ 01-43-26-30-05. Reservations required. Main courses 19€–25€ ($25–$33); fixed-price lunch 20€ ($26); fixed-price dinner 26€ ($34). AE, DC, MC, V. Daily noon–3pm and 7–11:30pm. Métro: St-Germain-des-Prés or Mabillon.

Chez Henri LYONNAIS   This is that cozy bistro, all wood and velvet, that you hope to find in Paris. Chez Henri is classic and it also specializes in the dishes of the Lyon region, still hailed as the gastronomic center of France. The elegantly decorated place is warm and welcoming and feeds you well, all at a reasonable price. Its slow-cooked lamb with prunes and potatoes gratin is worth crossing town to devour, as is their *magret de canard* (breast of duckling) with honey. Their delicate fish dishes such as red mullet in a cream sauce are always excellent. We like to finish off with crème brûlée based on a coveted family recipe.

16 rue Princesse, 6e. ℂ 01-43-33-51-12. Reservations recommended. Main courses 12€–18€ ($16–$23). MC, V. Daily noon–2:30pm and 7–11:30pm. Métro: Mabillon.

Crémerie-Restaurant Polidor ⭐ *Kids* TRADITIONAL FRENCH   Crémerie Polidor is the most traditional bistro in the Odéon area, serving *cuisine familiale.* Its name dates from the early 1900s, when it specialized in frosted cream desserts, but the restaurant can trace its history to 1845. The Crémerie was André Gide's favorite, and Joyce, Hemingway, Valéry, Artaud, and Kerouac also dined here. Peer beyond the lace curtains and brass hat racks to see drawers where in olden days, regular customers used to lock up their cloth napkins. Try pumpkin soup followed by *boeuf bourguignon, confit de canard,* or *blanquette de veau.* For dessert, order a chocolate, raspberry, or lemon tart—the best in all Paris.

41 rue Monsieur-le-Prince, 6e. *©* **01-43-26-95-34.** Main courses 11€–16€ ($14–$21); fixed-price lunch (Mon–Fri) 12€–30€ ($16–$39), dinner 20€–30€ ($26–$39). No credit cards. Daily noon–2:30pm; Mon–Sat 7pm–12:30am; Sun 7–11pm. Métro: Odéon.

La Bastide Odéon 🍷 *Finds* PROVENÇAL   The sunny climes of Provence come through in the pale yellow walls, oak tables, and bouquets of wheat and dried roses. Chef Gilles Ajuelos prepares a market-based cuisine. His simplest first courses are the most satisfying, such as pumpkin soup with oysters and mussels, and eggplant-stuffed roasted rabbit with olive toast and balsamic vinegar. Main courses include a warm napoleon of grilled eggplants served "in the style of the Riviera," and roasted chicken with a confit of Provençal garlic and fried potatoes. A winning dessert is almond pie with prune and Armagnac ice cream.

7 rue Corneille, 6e. *©* **01-43-26-03-65.** Reservations recommended. Main courses 19€ ($25); fixed-price lunch 26€ ($34). AE, MC, V. Tues–Sat 12:30–2pm and 7:30–10:30pm. Métro: Odéon. RER: Luxembourg.

Le Canton *Finds* CHINESE/VIETNAMESE   The cuisine is exotic, especially the Vietnamese dishes, and the setting is relaxing and evocative of Asia. Best of all, the food is affordable and better than that served at the nearby fast-food joints. Begin with any of the versions of *nem* (Vietnamese ravioli) stuffed with shrimp and vegetables. Main courses include salt-and-pepper shrimp; Szechuan-style chicken; and the best-selling shrimp quick-fried with black soybeans, garlic, peppers, and onions. The soups are wonderful.

5 rue Gozlin, 6e. *©* **01-43-26-51-86.** Reservations recommended. Main courses 9€–13€ ($12–$17); fixed-price lunch 14€ ($18); fixed-price dinner 17€ ($22). MC, V. Mon–Sat noon–2:30pm and 7–10:30pm. Métro: St-Germain-des-Prés.

13TH ARRONDISSEMENT
MODERATE

Auberge Etchegorry BASQUE   Its windows overlook a verdant patch of lawn that's so green, you might for a moment imagine you've entered a rustic countryside inn. Dark paneling, deep colors, hanging hams and pigtails of garlic, and lacy curtains emulate the Basque country, the corner of southwestern France adjacent to Spain. Victor Hugo and Chateaubriand ate here in centuries past. The cramped tables are a drawback, but not much of one in this rich atmosphere. The menu includes a roster of such specialties as cassoulet, *magret* (breast) of duckling, beef filet with peppercorns, a peppery omelet known as *pipérades,* cocottes of mussels, and terrines or pan-fried slices of foie gras.

41 rue Croulebarbe, 13e. *©* **01-44-08-83-51.** www.etchegorry.com. Reservations recommended. All courses 15€ ($20); fixed-price lunch 20€ ($26); fixed-price dinner 28€–38€ ($36–$49). AE, MC, V. Tues–Sat noon–2:30pm and Tues–Fri 7:30–10:30pm. Métro: Gobelins or Corvisart.

Le Petit Marguery POITEVINE/TRADITIONAL FRENCH   This place feels like a turn-of-the-20th-century bistro, with antique floor tiles, banquettes, vested waiters, and a color scheme of dark rose. Menu items are based in old-fashioned traditions, especially those from the Poitou region of west-central France, with emphasis on game dishes in autumn and fresh produce in summer. The finest examples include slices of wild duck breast dusted with white pepper and strewn over mounds of shredded cabbage; a *petit salé* (family-style stew) of duckling that's served with braised cabbage and garlic-flavored cream sauce; roasted suckling lamb; homemade ravioli stuffed with sea scallops on a bed of shellfish sauce; and a variety of homemade terrines (including an excellent version from blood sausage). There are also two very fine dishes, classics from *la cuisine bourgeoise* (comfort food) of the late 19th century: *lièvre à la royale* and *coq à la Pictavienne,* whereby a hare *(lièvre)* or rooster *(coq)* is deboned, marinated, roasted, and served in a sauce that combines red wine, some of the animal's blood, and foie gras. The restaurant's specialty dessert is a soufflé with Grand Marnier.

9 bd. du Port-Royal, 13e. ① 01-43-31-58-59. Reservations recommended. 3-course lunch 23€–35€ ($30–$46); 3-course dinner 34€ ($44). AE, DC, MC, V. Tues–Sat noon–2pm and 7:30–10pm. Closed Aug. Métro: Gobelins.

14TH ARRONDISSEMENT
MODERATE

La Cagouille ⋆ (Finds) TRADITIONAL FRENCH/SEAFOOD   Don't expect to find meat at this temple of seafood—owner Gérard Allamandou refuses to feature it. Everything about La Cagouille is a testimonial to a modern version of the culinary arts of La Charente, the flat sandy district on the Atlantic south of Bordeaux. In a trio of oak-sheathed dining rooms, you'll sample seafood prepared as naturally as possible, with no fancy sauces or elaborate techniques. Allamandou's preferred fish is red mullet, which might be sautéed in oil or baked in rock salt. The name derives from the regional symbol of La Charente, the sea snail, whose preparation its namesake elevates to a fine culinary art. Look for a vast assemblage of wines and cognacs.

10–12 place Constantin-Brancusi, 14e. ① 01-43-22-09-01. www.la-cagouille.fr. Reservations recommended. Main courses 20€–35€ ($26–$46); fixed-price menu 26€–42€ ($34–$55). MC, V. Daily noon–2:30pm and 7:30–10:30pm. Métro: Gaîté.

La Régalade FRENCH TRADITIONAL   The setting is a bistro with banquettes the color of aged Bordeaux wine, congenial service, and unexpectedly good food. The prix-fixe menu presents a choice of at least 10 starters, 10 main courses, and about a dozen fresh desserts or selections from a cheese tray. The menu changes weekly (sometimes daily) according to the availability of the ingredients, but examples that particularly impressed us include cream of walnut soup poured over a flan of foie gras, roasted Pyrénéan lamb served with thyme and a confit of roasted garlic, filet of wild

---

Chinatown Paris Style

More and more visitors are discovering that Paris, like New York, has a Chinatown. Take the Métro to Porte d'Ivry or Place d'Italie in the 13th Arrondissement. **Quartier Chinois,** a 5-minute walk from Place d'Italie, centers on avenue d'Ivry. Here you will find 250,000 Asians (the population grows all the time) living in a center of food stores, Asian restaurants and markets, and rows of teas and spices straight from China. The center of the sector is **Tang Frères,** the largest Asian-food market in Europe. Spend a morning exploring here and stick around for lunch. We'd recommend **Le Mer de Chine** at 159 des Rentiers, 13e (① **01-45-84-22-49;** Métro: Place d'Italie), serving the best Cantonese cuisine in Paris.

boar with a red-wine sauce, and an always-popular platter of fried goose liver served on toasted slices of spice bread.

49 av. Jean-Moulin, 14e. ✆ 01-45-45-68-58. Reservations recommended. Fixed-price menu 30€ ($39). MC, V. Tues–Fri noon–2pm; Mon–Fri 7–11pm. Métro: Alésia.

L'Assiette SOUTHWESTERN FRENCH   Everything here appeals to a nostalgic crowd seeking down-to-earth prices and flavorful food. The place was a *charcuterie* (pork butcher's shop) in the 1930s and maintains some of its old accessories. Mitterrand used to drop in for oysters, crayfish, sea urchins, and clams. The food is inspired by Paris's long tradition of bistro cuisine, with a few twists. Examples are chanterelle mushroom salad; *rillettes* (roughly textured pâté) of mackerel; very fresh fish; and homemade desserts, including a crumbly version of apple cake with fresh North African figs. Particularly delicious is *petit salé* (stew with vegetables) of duckling with wine from the Poitou region.

181 rue du Château, 14e. ✆ 01-43-22-64-86. Reservations recommended. Fixed-price menus 50€ ($65). AE, MC, V. Sat–Sun noon–2:30pm and Tues–Sun 8–10:30pm. Closed Aug. Métro: Gaité.

7TH ARRONDISSEMENT
VERY EXPENSIVE
L'Arpège ★★★ MODERN FRENCH   L'Arpège is best known for Alain Passard's specialties—no restaurant in the 7th serves better food. Surrounded by etched glass, burnished steel, monochromatic oil paintings, and pearwood paneling, you can enjoy such specialties as couscous of vegetables and shellfish, lobster braised in the yellow wine of the Jura, braised monkfish in a mustard sauce, pigeon roasted with almonds and honey-flavored mead, and carpaccio of crayfish with caviar-flavored cream sauce. Although Passard is loath to include red meat on his menus, Kobe beef and venison sometimes appear. He focuses on fish, shellfish, poultry, and—his passion—vegetables. These he elevates to levels unequaled by any other chef in Paris. The signature dessert is a candied tomato stuffed with 12 kinds of dried and fresh fruit, served with anise-flavored ice cream.

84 rue de Varenne, 7e. ✆ 01-47-05-09-06. Fax 01-44-18-98-39. www.alain-passard.com. Reservations required 2 weeks in advance. Main courses 48€–180€ ($62–$234). AE, DC, MC, V. Mon–Fri 12:30–2:30pm and 8–10:30pm. Métro: Varenne.

EXPENSIVE
L'Atelier de Joël Robuchon ★★ MODERN FRENCH   Upon his retirement in the mid-1990s, Joël Robuchon was hailed around the world as the greatest chef in France. Well, he's back, but in a style and format that's either swank and stylish or a bit unnerving, depending on your point of view. All of the restaurant's 41 seats are pulled up to a bar-style countertop that surrounds an open-to-view kitchen. Reservations are accepted only for the earliest service, beginning every night at 6:30. You might start with pumpkin and cauliflower soup with smoky bacon or divine chicken liver terrine. Among the sublime main courses are caramelized quail glazed with shallot-perfumed sauce; buttery, tender langoustines in pastry; ravioli of crayfish with foie gras sauce; and a succulent version of sole meunière. Duckling comes roasted, braised, and flavored with spices such as ginger, nutmeg, and cinnamon. The fish and shellfish are shipped fresh from Brittany.

5–7 rue de Montalembert, 7e. ✆ 01-42-22-56-56. www.robuchon.com. Reservations required. Main courses 30€–70€ ($39–$91); fixed-price menu 110€ ($143). MC, V. Daily 11:30am–3:30pm and 6:30pm–midnight. Métro: Rue du Bac.

Where to Dine on the Left Bank (7 & 15e)

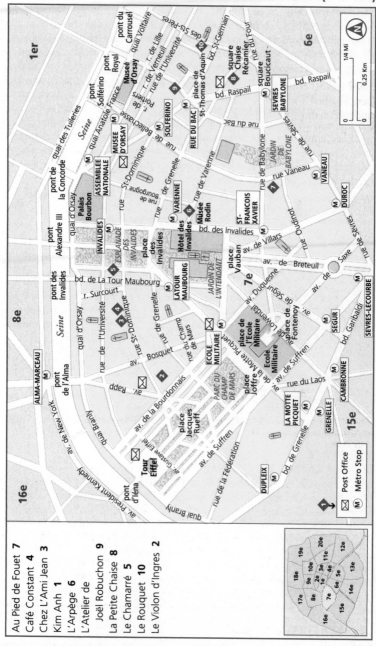

Au Pied de Fouet **7**
Café Constant **4**
Chez L'Ami Jean **3**
Kim Anh **1**
L'Arpège **6**
L'Atelier de
  Joël Robuchon **9**
La Petite Chaise **8**
Le Chamarré **5**
Le Rouquet **10**
Le Violon d'Ingres **2**

Le Chamarré ★★★ *(Finds)* MAURITIEN/MODERN FRENCH   Come here for food that appeals to your brain as much as it does to your palate. Founded in 2002, it immediately shot into the Parisian consciousness, thanks to the inspired cuisine of a pair of French and Mauritien chefs. The restaurant's name translates as "nuances of color," and its French cuisine is subtly influenced by the heat, aromas, and flavors of Mauritius. Try chicken with curry Indian rice and herbs, line-caught sea bass served with an emulsion of limes and comfit of leeks with banana leaves, Auvergnat flap mushrooms prepared with eggplant caviar and linden-leaf tea, grilled octopus with garlic, Breton lobster braised in bouillabaisse, suckling pig infused with four different spices and served with a sweet-and-sour mousseline sauce, and French-derived grilled slices of suckling veal with fried mushroom and walnut oil. Desserts are unusual, with ingredients you might not associate with sweets, such as sliced and fried eggplant with vanilla sauce and laurel-flavored ice cream.

13 bd. de la Tour-Maubourg, 7e. ✆ **01-47-05-50-18**. www.lechamarre.com. Reservations required. Main courses 25€–35€ ($33–$46); fixed-price lunch 40€ ($52); fixed-price dinner 65€–130€ ($85–$169). AE, DC, MC, V. Mon–Fri noon–2:30pm and 7:30–10:30pm; Sat 7:30–10:30pm. Closed Aug. Métro: Invalides.

Le Violon d'Ingres ★★★ MODERN FRENCH   This restaurant is Paris's pièce de résistance. Chef-owner Christian Constant is "the new Robuchon." Those fortunate enough to dine in Violon's warm atmosphere rave about the artistic dishes. They range from pan-fried foie gras with gingerbread and spinach salad to more elegant main courses such as lobster ravioli with crushed vine-ripened tomatoes; beefsteak *à la plancha*, served with a shallot and parsley sauce; roasted veal in light, creamy milk sauce, served with tender spring vegetables; and a selection from the rotisserie, including spit-roasted leg of lamb rubbed with fresh garlic and thyme. The service is charming and discreet; the wine selection, well chosen. The Constant family has tied up the dining rituals along this street, with less expensive, less formal restaurants flanking Le Violon d'Ingres.

135 rue St-Dominique, 7e. ✆ **01-45-55-15-05**. Fax 01-45-55-48-42. Reservations required at least 2 days in advance. Main courses 40€–46€ ($52–$60); *menu dégustation* 110€ ($143); fixed-price lunch 50€–110€ ($65–$143); fixed-price dinner 80€–110€ ($104–$143). AE, DC, MC, V. Tues–Sat noon–2:30pm and 7–10:30pm. Métro: Invalides or Ecole-Militaire.

MODERATE
La Petite Chaise TRADITIONAL FRENCH   This is Paris's oldest restaurant, opened as an inn in 1680 by the baron de la Chaise at the edge of a hunting preserve. (According to lore, the baron used the upstairs bedrooms for afternoon dalliances, between fox and pheasant hunts.) Very Parisian, the "Little Chair" invites you into a world of cramped but attractive tables, old wood paneling, and ornate wall sconces. A vigorous chef has brought renewed taste and flavor to this longtime favorite, and the four-course set menu offers a large choice of dishes in each category. Examples are *magret* (breast) of duck with sweet-and-sour sauce, *pot-au-feu* whose ingredients change with the seasons, and grilled sea bass on a bed of fennel with a light butter sauce.

36 rue de Grenelle, 7e. ✆ **01-42-22-13-35**. Reservations recommended. Main courses all 19€ ($25). Fixed-price menu 19€–31€ ($25–$40). MC, V. Daily noon–2pm and 7–11pm. Métro: Sèvres-Babylone or Rue du Bac.

INEXPENSIVE
Au Pied de Fouet TRADITIONAL FRENCH   This is one of the neighborhood's oldest and most reasonably priced restaurants. In the 1700s, it was a stopover for carriages en route to Paris, offering wine, food, and stables. Don't expect a leisurely or

attentive meal: Food and drink will disappear quickly from your table, under the gaze of others waiting their turn. The dishes are solid and unpretentious and include *blanquette de veau* (veal stew), chicken in vinegar sauce (a house specialty), *petit salé* (a savory family-style stew made from pork and vegetables and served with lentils), and filet of sea wolf or filet of codfish. If you demand a polite staff, go elsewhere. The waiters are among the rudest in Paris. Some visitors claim that's part of the charm of this place. You decide.

45 rue de Babylone, 7e. © 01-47-05-12-27. Main courses 9€–12€ ($12–$16). MC, V. Mon–Sat noon–2:30pm; Mon–Fri 7–9:30pm. Closed Aug. Métro: Vaneau.

Café Constant ✪ *Value* TRADITIONAL FRENCH   This is the least expensive of the trio of nearly adjacent restaurants established along the rue St-Dominique by megachef Christian Constant, whose mainstream, ultraluxe restaurant (Le Violin d'Ingres) is also recommended. Café Constant prides itself on fast service, fast turnover, and well-prepared but not particularly complicated cuisine that's a good value within this posh and expensive neighborhood. Within two separate dining rooms, one on the ground floor and a smaller one upstairs, you can order starters, each priced at 8€ ($10); main courses, each priced at 12€ ($16); and desserts, each priced at 7€ ($9.10). Examples include a *terrine de kako,* made with pork and foie gras and served with lentils and vinaigrette sauce; a tartare of oysters and salmon, flavored with ginger; veal scallops "Cordon Bleu," which are layered with ham and cheese, breaded, and fried; and quenelles of whitefish. Since reservations aren't accepted except for large groups, most potential diners are asked to wait at the wood-topped bar for a table to become available. Waits are usually not long.

139 rue St-Dominique, 7e. © 01-47-53-73-34. Reservations accepted only for groups of 5 or more. Main courses 12€ ($16). MC, V. Tues–Sat noon–2:30pm and 7–10:30pm. Métro: Invalides.

Chez l'Ami Jean BASQUE/SOUTHWESTERN FRENCH   This restaurant was opened by a Basque nationalist in 1931, and fans claim its Basque cuisine and setting are the most authentic on the Left Bank. Decorative details include wood panels; memorabilia from *pelote* (a Basque game similar to jai alai), rugby, and soccer. Dishes include Bayonne ham; herb-laden Béarn-influenced vegetable soups; confit of duck with small sautéed potatoes; and fine slices of veal with fresh herbs, onions, red peppers, and a light tomato sauce. In springtime, look for a specialty rarely found elsewhere: *saumon de l'Adour* (Adour salmon) with béarnaise sauce.

27 rue Malar, 7e. © 01-47-05-86-89. Reservations recommended. Main courses 18€–25€ ($23–$33); 3-course Basque dinner 29€ ($38); fixed-price lunch 15€ ($20). MC, V. Tues–Sat noon–2pm and 7pm–midnight. Closed Aug. Métro: Invalides.

15TH ARRONDISSEMENT
MODERATE

Kim Anh VIETNAMESE   This is one of the best addresses in Paris for the savory, spicy cuisine of its former colony. It's a bit lost down in the 15th, but many Parisian foodies journey here anyway. The cuisine includes the sharp, spicy, sour, and succulent flavors of Vietnam, as prepared in pork, chicken, fish, and beef dishes, many of them excellent. Waiters are very patient in explaining various dishes to newcomers. We are especially fond of the caramelized langoustines and most definitely the stuffed crabs and steamed pork ravioli.

51 av. Emile Zola, 15e. © 01-45-79-40-96. Reservations recommended. Main courses 20€–40€ ($26–$52); fixed-price menu 34€ ($44). AE, MC, V. Tues–Sun 7–11pm. Métro: Charles-Michels.

In Pursuit of the Perfect Parisian Pastry

Could it be true, as rumor has it, that more eggs, sugar, cream, and butter per capita are consumed in Paris than in any other city? From a modern-day Proust sampling a madeleine to a child munching a *pain au chocolat* (chocolate-filled croissant), everyone in Paris seems to be looking for two things: the perfect lover and the perfect pastry, not necessarily in that order. As a Parisian food critic once said, "A day without a pastry is a day in hell!"

Who'd think of beginning a morning in Paris without a **croissant** or two—freshly baked, flaky, light, and made with real butter, preferably from Norman cows. The Greeks may have invented pastry making, but the French perfected it. Some French pastries have made a greater impact than others. The croissant and the *brioche*, a yeasty sweet breakfast bread, are baked around the world today, as is the fabled *éclair au chocolat* (chocolate éclair), a pastry filled with whipped cream or pastry cream and topped with chocolate. Another pastry you should sample on its home turf is the **Napolitain**—layers of cake flour and almonds alternating with fruit purée. (Don't confuse this term with *Neapolitan*, meaning sweets and cakes made with layers of two or more colors, each layer flavored differently.) Very much in vogue is the *mille-feuille* ("thousand leaves"), made by arranging thin layers of flaky pastry on top of one another, along with layers of cream or fruit purée or jam; the American version is the napoleon.

Here are some of our favorite patisseries: **Stohrer,** 51 rue Montorgueil, 2e (𝄪 01-42-33-38-20; Métro: Sentier or Les Halles), has been going strong ever since it was opened by Louis XV's pastry chef in 1730. A pastry always associated with this place is *puits d'amour* (well of love), which consists of caramelized puff pastry filled with vanilla ice cream. Available at any time is one of the most luscious desserts in Paris, *baba au rhum,* or its even richer cousin, *un Ali Baba,* which also incorporates cream-based rum-and-raisin filling. Stohrer boasts an interior decor classified as a national historic treasure, with frescoes of damsels in 18th-century costume bearing flowers and (what else?) pastries.

Opened in 1862, a few steps from La Madeleine, **Ladurée Royale,** 16 rue Royale, 8e (𝄪 01-42-60-21-79; Métro: Concorde or Madeleine), is Paris's dowager tearoom. Its pastry chefs are known for the macaron, a pastry for

6 The Top Cafes

As surely everyone knows, the cafe is a Parisian institution. Parisians use cafes as combination club/tavern/snack bars, almost as extensions of their living rooms. They're spots where you can sit alone reading your newspaper, doing your homework, or writing your memoirs; meet a friend or lover; nibble on a hard-boiled egg; or drink yourself into oblivion. At cafes, you meet your dates, and then go on to a show or stay and talk. Above all, cafes are for people-watching.

Coffee, of course, is the chief drink. It comes black, in a small cup, unless you specifically order it *au lait* (with milk). *Thé* (tea, pronounced *tay*) is also fairly popular but which this place is celebrated. Karl Lagerfeld comes here and raves about them, as did the late ambassador Pamela Harriman. This isn't the sticky coconut-version macaroon known to many, but two almond meringue cookies, flavored with chocolate, vanilla, pistachio, coffee, or other flavor, stuck together with butter cream. You may also want to try **Le Faubourg,** a lusciously dense chocolate cake with layers of caramel and apricots.

In business since Napoleon was in power, **Dalloyau,** 101 rue du Faubourg St-Honoré, 8e (© **01-42-99-90-00;** Métro: St-Philippe du Roule), has a name instantly recognizable throughout Paris; it supplies pastries to the Elysée Palace (the French White House) and many Rothschild mansions nearby. Its specialties are **Le Dalloyau,** praline cake filled with almond meringue that's marvelously light-textured; and **un Opéra,** composed of an almond-flavored biscuit layered with butter cream, chocolate, coffee, and cashews. Unlike Stohrer, Dalloyau has a tearoom (open daily 8:30am–7:30pm) one floor above street level, where ladies who lunch can drop in for a slice of pastry that Dalloyau warns is "too fragile to transport, or to mail, over long distances."

As readers of French literature know, the taste of the *madeleine* (a scalloped tea cake) triggered the memory of the narrator in Marcel Proust's *Remembrance of Things Past.* Known since the 18th century, the madeleine also inspired chef Christophe Adam at **Fauchon's,** 26 place de la Madeleine, 8e (© **01-70-39-38-00;** Métro: Madeleine) to tinker with the classic cookie recipe. Today he prepares madeleines in such flavors as orange, coffee-sesame, and pistachio.

We always head for **Pierre Hermé,** 72 rue Bonaparte, 6e (© **01-43-54-47-77;** Métro: Saint-Sulpice), for truffles with chocolate and pistachios or truffles praline. The macaroons, probably of Venetian origin, are worth crossing town to sample, especially if the cream filling is flavored with fresh raspberries or litchis.

Parisians started eating éclairs, that cream-filled chocolate-covered shell of choux pastry, in the 1800s. Surprisingly it is a Japanese chef, **Sadaharu Aoki,** 56 bd. Port Royale, 13e (© **01-45-35-36-80;** Métro: Les Gobelins), who makes the best éclairs in today's Paris. He even does a mâcha green tea version, with green tea powder imported from Kyoto.

generally not of a high quality. If you prefer beer, we advise you to pay a bit more for the imported German, Dutch, or Danish brands, which are much better than the local brew. If you insist on a French beer, at least order it *à pression* (draft), which is superior. There's also a vast variety of fruit drinks, as well as Coca-Cola, which can be rather expensive. French chocolate drinks—either hot or iced—are absolutely superb and on par with the finest Dutch brands. They're made from ground chocolate, not a chemical compound.

Now, just a few words on cafe etiquette: You don't pay when you get your order—only when you intend to leave. Payment indicates you've had all you want. *Service compris* means the tip is included in your bill, so it isn't necessary to tip extra; still, most people leave an extra euro or so. You'll hear the locals call for the *"garçon,"* but as a foreigner, it would be more polite to say *"monsieur."* All waitresses, on the other hand, are addressed as *"mademoiselle,"* regardless of age or marital status. In the smaller cafes, you may have to share your table. In that case, even if you haven't exchanged a word with your table companion, when you leave it's customary to bid him or her *au revoir.*

For the locations of these cafes, see the corresponding arrondissement maps earlier in this chapter.

EXPENSIVE

Brasserie Lipp This is a Left Bank institution. On the day of Paris's liberation in 1944, late owner Roger Cazes welcomed Hemingway as the first man to drop in for a drink. Since its acquisition a few years ago by members of the Bertrand Group (the force behind Paris's St. James Club), the mechanics whereby you can obtain a table in this cultural monument are a lot easier, and a lot less arbitrary, than when Cazes granted or denied a table in his joint based, basically, on whether he considered you worthy. Reservations are accepted today and usually respected for dining tables, but not cafe tables. The specialty is *choucroute garni.* You get not only sauerkraut, but also a thick layer of ham and braised pork, which you can wash down with the house Riesling (an Alsatian white wine) or beer.

151 bd. St-Germain, 6e. ☏ 01-45-48-53-91. www.brasserie-lipp.fr. Main courses 18€–26€ ($23–$34); full meals with a modest wine average 50€ ($65); café au lait 4€ ($5.20). AE, DC, MC, V. Daily 11am–2am; restaurant service 12:15pm–12:45am. Métro: St-Germain-des-Prés.

Café de Flore ★★ It's the most famous cafe in the world, still fighting to maintain a Left Bank aura despite hordes of visitors from around the world. Sartre—the granddaddy of existentialism, a key figure in the Resistance, and a renowned cafe-sitter—often came here during World War II. Wearing a leather jacket and beret, he sat and wrote his trilogy *Les Chemins de la Liberté (The Roads to Freedom).* Camus, Picasso, and Apollinaire also frequented the Flore. The cafe is still going strong, though the famous patrons have moved on and tourists have taken up all the tables. According to the spokeswoman: "We will never change the decor." The menu offers omelets, salads, club sandwiches, and more.

172 bd. St-Germain, 6e. ☏ 01-45-48-55-26. www.cafe-de-flore.com. Café espresso 4.60€ ($6); glass of beer 9€ ($12); snacks from 16€ ($21). AE, DC, MC, V. Daily 7:30am–1:30am. Métro: St-Germain-des-Prés.

Fouquet's For people-watching, this is definitely on the see-and-be-seen circuit. Fouquet's has been collecting anecdotes and a patina since it was founded in 1901. A celebrity favorite, it has attracted Chaplin, Chevalier, Dietrich, Churchill, Roosevelt, and Jackie Onassis. The premier cafe on the Champs-Elysées sits behind a barricade of potted flowers at the edge of the sidewalk. Today, it's owned by the well-managed hotel and dining conglomerate Lucien Barrière. You can choose a table in the sunshine or retreat to the glassed-in elegance of the leather banquettes and rattan furniture of the grillroom. This is a full-fledged restaurant, with a beautiful formal dining room on the second floor.

99 av. des Champs-Elysées, 8e. ☏ 01-47-23-50-00. Glass of wine from 9€ ($12); sandwiches 10€–21€ ($13–$27); main courses 30€–55€ ($39–$72); fixed-price lunch or dinner 80€ ($104). AE, DC, MC, V. Daily 8am–2am. Restaurant daily noon–3pm and 7pm–12:30am; bar and brasserie 9am–2am. Métro: George V.

MODERATE

Café Beaubourg Next to the all-pedestrian plaza of the Centre Pompidou, this is a trendy cafe with soaring concrete columns and a minimalist decor. Many of the regulars work in the neighborhood's eclectic shops and galleries. You can order salads, omelets, grilled steak, chicken *cordon bleu,* pastries, and daily platters. In warm weather, tables are set up on the sprawling outdoor terrace, providing an appropriate niche for watching the young and the restless go by.

100 rue St-Martin, 4e. ✆ **01-48-87-63-96.** Glass of wine 5€–9€ ($6.50–$12); beer 6€–7.50€ ($7.80–$9.75); American breakfast 15€–24€ ($20–$31); sandwiches and platters 6€–25€ ($7.80–$33). AE, DC, MC, V. Mon–Fri 8am–1am, Sat–Sun 8am–2am. Métro: Rambuteau or Hôtel-de-Ville.

Café de la Musique   This cafe's location, in one of the grandest of Mitterrand's *grands travaux,* guarantees a crowd passionately devoted to music; the recorded sounds that play in the background are likely to be more diverse and more eclectic than those in any other cafe in Paris. The red-and-green velour setting might remind you of a modern opera house. Although it originated in the late 1990s as a cafe serving light platters, sandwiches, and drinks, its cuisine became dramatically more sophisticated in 2002, the year it was taken over by culinary legend and nightlife impresario Alain Poudou. The menu was inspired by the cuisine served

Did You Know?

You'll pay substantially less in a cafe if you stand at the counter rather than sit at a table, partly because there's no service charge, and partly because clients tend to linger at tables.

in one of Paris's trendiest hotels, the Costes, and is likely to include lobster-studded risotto, roasted rack of lamb with thyme, fresh salads of the type you'd find in Italy, brochettes of shrimp with spinach, and baked salmon in a white-wine cream sauce. As the evening progresses, this place takes on more of the ambience of a hip nightclub as DJs spin various kinds of music.

In the Cité de la Musique, place Fontaine aux Lions, 213 av. Jean-Jaurès, 19e. ✆ **01-48-03-15-91.** www.cite-musique.fr. Main courses 16€–28€ ($21–$36). AE, DC, MC, V. Daily 8am–2am; restaurant daily 8am–1am. Métro: Porte de Pantin.

La Belle Hortense   This is the most literary cafe in a neighborhood (the Marais) that's loaded with literary antecedents and references. It contains an erudite and accessible staff; an inventory of French literary classics as well as modern tomes about art, psychoanalysis, history, and culture; and two high-ceilinged, 19th-century rooms little changed since the days of Baudelaire and Balzac. Near the entrance is a zinc-covered bar that sells glasses of wine. If you're fluent in French, you might be interested in attending a reading, a book signing, or a lecture. Some kind of public gathering, conducted only in rapid, colloquial French, is scheduled every Tuesday, Wednesday, and Thursday, usually at 8pm. One particularly intriguing and ongoing series involves three trained actors, each reading sequential passages from a book.

31 rue Vieille du Temple, 4e. ✆ **01-48-04-71-60.** Glass of wine 4€–9€ ($5.20–$12); coffee 1.30€ ($1.70); snacks from 12€ ($16). MC, V. Daily 5pm–2am. Métro: Hôtel de Ville or St-Paul.

La Coupole ✪   Born in 1927 and once a leading center of artistic life, La Coupole is now the epitome of the grand Paris brasserie in Montparnasse. Former patrons included Josephine Baker, Henry Miller, Dalí, Calder, Hemingway, Fitzgerald, and Picasso. At one of its sidewalk tables, you can sit and watch the passing scene and order a coffee or a cognac VSOP. The food is quite good, despite the fact that the dining room resembles an enormous rail-station waiting room. Try main dishes such as sole meunière, a very good rump steak, fresh oysters, shellfish, grilled lobster with flambéed whisky sauce, and curried lamb. The waiters are as rude and inattentive as ever, and the patrons would have it no other way.

102 bd. du Montparnasse, 14e. ℂ 01-43-20-14-20. www.flobrasserie.com. Breakfast buffet 15€–19€ ($20–$25); main courses 18€–40€ ($23–$52); fixed-price lunch 16€–32€ ($21–$42), dinner 35€ ($46). AE, DC, MC, V. Daily 8:30am–1am (breakfast buffet Mon–Fri 8:30–10:30am). Métro: Vavin.

La Palette 👁👁 The staff here defiantly maintains old-fashioned Parisian traditions that haven't changed much since the days of Picasso and Braque—the same drinks (Ricard and Pernod, among others) are still popular. A bustle of comings and goings makes La Palette an insider's version of a battered, artistically evocative Latin Quarter cafe. The interior, inhabited by amiably crotchety waiters, consists of tiled murals, installed around 1935, advertising the virtues of a brand of liqueur that's no longer manufactured. If you happen to drop in during mealtime, you'll have a limited selection of salads and *croque monsieur* (toasted ham and cheese), plus one *plat du jour* per day, always priced at 12€ ($16), which may include roast beef, lamb stew, fish, and gigot of lamb. The food is well prepared, and the dish of the day is usually announced as a kind of surprise to the joint's devoted fans.

43 rue de Seine, 6e. ℂ 01-43-26-68-15. Sandwiches, omelets, and *plats du jour* 6€–13€ ($7.80–$17). MC, V. Cafe and bar Mon–Sat 9am–2am; restaurant Mon–Sat 11:30am–3pm. Métro: Mabillon or St-Germain-des-Prés.

La Rotonde Once patronized by Hemingway, the original Rotonde faded into history but is immortalized in the pages of *The Sun Also Rises,* in which Papa wrote, "No matter what cafe in Montparnasse you ask a taxi driver to bring you to from the right bank of the river, they always take you to the Rotonde." Lavishly upgraded, its reincarnation has a paneled Art Deco elegance and shares the site with a cinema. The menu includes such hearty fare as pepper steak with *pommes frites* (french fries), shellfish in season, a superb and genuinely succulent version of sole meunière, and sea-bass filets with herb-flavored lemon sauce.

105 bd. du Montparnasse, 6e. ℂ 01-43-26-48-26. Glass of wine from 3.90€–8.50€ ($5.05–$11); main courses 20€–38€ ($26–$49); fixed-price lunch 15€–35€ ($20–$46); fixed-price dinner 35€ ($46). AE, MC, V. Cafe daily 7:15am–2am; food service daily noon–1am. Métro: Vavin.

Le Procope 👁👁 To fans of French history, this is the holy grail of Parisian cafes. Opened in 1686, it occupies a three-story town house categorized as a historic monument. Inside, nine salons and dining rooms, each of whose 300-year-old walls have been carefully preserved and painted a deep red, are available for languorous afternoon coffee breaks or well-presented meals. Menu items include platters of shellfish, onion soup au gratin, *coq au vin* (chicken stewed in wine), duck breast in honey sauce, and grilled versions of various meats and fish. Every day between 3 and 7pm, the place makes itself available to sightseers who come to look but not necessarily eat and drink at the site that welcomed such movers and shakers as Diderot, Voltaire, George Sand, Victor Hugo, and Oscar Wilde. Of special charm is the ground-floor room outfitted like an antique library.

13 rue de l'Ancienne-Comédie, 6e. ℂ 01-40-46-79-00. www.procope.com. Reservations recommended. Coffee 2.95€ ($3.85); glass of beer 4.80€–6.50€ ($6.25–$8.45); main courses 17€–45€ ($22–$59). AE, DC, MC, V. Daily noon–midnight. Métro: Odéon.

Les Deux Magots 👁👁 This legendary hangout for the sophisticated residents of St-Germain-des-Prés becomes a tourist favorite in summer. Visitors monopolize the few sidewalk tables as the waiters rush about, seemingly oblivious to anyone's needs.

Regulars from around the neighborhood reclaim it in the off season. [...] was once a gathering place of the intellectual elite, such as Sartre, de [...] Giraudoux. Inside are the two large statues of *magots* (Confucian wise m[...] the cafe its name. The crystal chandeliers are too brightly lit, but the regula[...] to the glare. After all, some of them even read their daily papers here. You c[...] salads, pastries, ice cream, or one of the daily specials; the fresh fish is usually g[...]

6 place St-Germain-des-Prés, 6e. ℃ 01-45-48-55-25. www.lesdeuxmagots.fr. Café au lait 5€ ($6.50); whisky s[...] 12€–16€ ($16–$21); main courses 18€–26€ ($23–$34). AE, DC, V. Daily 7:30am–1:30am. Métro: St-Germai[...] des-Prés.

INEXPENSIVE

Café de l'Industrie   Founded in the years before World War II, at no. 16 rue St-Sabin, it received a vital new lease on life after the opening of the nearby Opéra de la Bastille. In 2003, it expanded into a second venue (no. 17 rue St-Sabin) just across the street from its original premises and did everything it could to replicate the spirit and decor of the original. To perk up business at the newer venue, management schedules live jazz every Monday, Tuesday, and Wednesday from 9pm to midnight. Both venues maintain the same hours and serve the same food at the same prices. Each is known for decanting obscure vintages from the Touraine and the region around Beaujolais and Bordeaux. If you're hungry, consider any of the generous *plats du jour* such as leeks steeped in vinaigrette or minced chicken with tarragon.

16–17 rue St-Sabin, 11e. ℃ 01-47-00-13-53. Main courses 9€–19€ ($12–$25). MC, V. Daily 10am–2am. Métro: Bastille or Breguier-Sabin.

Café des Deux Moulins   *Amélie* was a quirky low-budget film that was nominated for five Oscars and was seen by more than 25 million people around the world following its release in 2001. The film was set in Montmartre, and the cafe featured in the film has developed into a mandatory stopping-off place for the constantly arriving "cult of *Amélie*." In the film, Amélie worked as a waitress at the Café des Deux Moulins. The musty atmosphere, with its 1950s decor, mustard-colored ceiling, and lace curtains, has been preserved—even the wall lamps and unisex toilet. The menu remains much the same as it always was—escalopes of veal in a cream sauce, beef filets, calf's liver, green frisée salad with bacon bits and warm goat cheese, and pigs' brains with lentils. The kitchen serves hamburgers, but with an egg on top. Of course, the classic dish is a demi-Camembert with a glass of Côtes du Rhône.

15 rue Lepic, 18e. ℃ 01-42-54-90-50. Main courses 9€–16€ ($12–$21). MC, V. Daily 7:30am–2am. Métro: Blanche.

Le Rouquet ⭐ *(Finds)*   Despite its conventional food, Le Rouquet enjoys an enviable cachet and sense of chic, partly because it competes on a less flamboyant scale with the nearby Café de Flore and Les Deux Magots and partly because the decor hasn't changed since a 1954 remodeling. Less than 60 yards from St-Germain church, you can sit for as long as you want, watching a crowd of stylish Italians and Americans performing rituals of shopping and people-watching, which have barely altered since Le Rouquet's founding in 1922.

188 bd. St-Germain, 7e. ℃ 01-45-48-06-93. Café au lait 2.40€ ($3.10) at counter, 4.20€ ($5.45) at table; plats du jour 12€ ($16). MC, V. Mon–Sat 7am–9pm. Métro: St-Germain-des-Prés.

TOP CAFES 177

...es Deux Magots
... Beauvoir, and
...en) that give
...s are used
...n order
...od.
...da

...ring Paris

...is a city where taking in the street life—shopping, strolling, and hanging out—should claim as much of your time as sightseeing in churches or museums. Having a picnic in the Bois de Boulogne, taking a sunrise stroll along the Seine,

spending an afternoon at a flea market—Paris bewitches you with these kinds of experiences. For all of the Louvre's beauty, you'll probably remember the Latin Quarter's crooked alleyways better than the 370th oil painting of your visit.

1 Attractions by Arrondissement

For the locations of these sights, see the **"Top Paris Attractions"** map on p. 182 and the individual **arrondissement maps** that follow.

Musée de l'Armée (p. 193)
Musée des Plans-Reliefs (p. 193)
Musée d'Orsay ✦✦✦ (p. 194)
Musée Rodin ✦✦ (p. 205)
Palais Bourbon/Assemblée
 Nationale ✦ (p. 217)
Tour Eiffel ✦✦✦ (p. 198)

13TH ARRONDISSEMENT
Bibliothèque Nationale de France
 (p. 215)
Manufacture Nationale des
 Gobelins ✦ (p. 208)

14TH ARRONDISSEMENT
Cimetière du Montparnasse ✦
 (p. 222)
Les Catacombes ✦ (p. 225)
Tour Montparnasse (p. 230)

15TH ARRONDISSEMENT
Musée Bourdelle ✦ (p. 206)
Musée National de Céramique de
 Sèvres ✦✦ (p. 209)

2 The Top Attractions: From the Arc de Triomphe to the Tour Eiffel

Arc de Triomphe ✦✦✦   At the western end of the Champs-Elysées, the Arc de Triomphe suggests an ancient Roman arch, only it's larger. Actually, it's the biggest triumphal arch in the world, about 49m (161 ft.) high and 44m (144 ft.) wide. To reach it, *don't try to cross the square,* Paris's busiest traffic hub. With a dozen streets radiating from the "Star," the roundabout has been called by one writer "vehicular roulette with more balls than numbers" (death is certain!). Take the underground passage, and live a little longer.

Commissioned by Napoleon in 1806 to commemorate the victories of his Grand Armée, the arch wasn't ready for the entrance of his empress, Marie-Louise, in 1810 (he had divorced Joséphine because she couldn't provide him an heir). It wasn't completed until 1836, under the reign of Louis-Philippe. Four years later, Napoleon's remains, brought from St. Helena, passed under the arch on their journey to his tomb at the Hôtel des Invalides. Since that time, it has become the focal point for state funerals. It's also the site of the tomb of the Unknown Soldier, in whose honor an eternal flame burns.

The greatest state funeral was Victor Hugo's in 1885; his coffin was placed under the arch, and much of Paris came to pay tribute. Another notable funeral was in 1929 for Ferdinand Foch, commander of the Allied forces in World War I. The arch has been the centerpiece of some of France's proudest moments and some of its most humiliating defeats, notably in 1871 and 1940. The memory of German troops marching under the arch is still painful to the French. Who can forget the 1940 newsreel of the Frenchman standing on the Champs-Elysées weeping as the Nazi storm troopers goose-stepped through Paris? The arch's happiest moment occurred in 1944, when the liberation-of-Paris parade passed beneath it. That same year, Eisenhower paid a visit to the tomb of the Unknown Soldier, a new tradition among leaders of state and important figures. After Charles de Gaulle's death, the French government (despite protests from anti-Gaullists) voted to change the name of this site from place de l'Etoile to place Charles de Gaulle. Nowadays it's often known as place Charles de Gaulle–Etoile.

Tips **Best City View**

From the observation deck of the Arc de Triomphe, you can see up the Champs-Elysées and such landmarks as the Louvre, the Eiffel Tower, Sacré-Coeur, and La Défense. Although we don't want to get into any arguments about this, we think the view of Paris from this perspective is the grandest in the entire city.

Of the sculptures on the monument, the best known is Rude's *Marseillaise*, or *The Departure of the Volunteers*. J. P. Cortot's *Triumph of Napoléon in 1810* and Etex's *Resistance of 1814* and *Peace of 1815* also adorn the facade. The monument is engraved with the names of hundreds of generals (those underlined died in battle) who commanded French troops in Napoleonic victories.

You can take an elevator or climb the stairway to the top, where there's an exhibition hall with lithographs and photos depicting the arch throughout its history, as well as an observation deck with a fantastic view.

Place Charles-de-Gaulle–Etoile, 8e. ✆ 01-55-37-73-77. www.monum.fr. Admission 10€ ($13) adults, 8€ ($10) under 25, free for children 18 and under. Apr–Sept daily 10am–11pm; Oct–Mar daily 10am–10:30pm. Métro: Charles-de-Gaulle–Etoile. Bus: 22, 30, 31, 52, 73, or 92.

Basilique du Sacré-Coeur Sacré-Coeur is one of Paris's most characteristic landmarks and has been the subject of much controversy. One Parisian called it "a lunatic's confectionery dream." An offended Zola declared it "the basilica of the ridiculous." Sacré-Coeur has had warm supporters as well, including poet Max Jacob and artist Maurice Utrillo. Utrillo never tired of drawing and painting it, and he and Jacob came here regularly to pray. Atop the *butte* (hill) in Montmartre, its multiple gleaming white domes and *campanile* (bell tower) loom over Paris like a 12th-century Byzantine church. But it's not that old. After France's 1870 defeat by the Prussians, the basilica was planned as a votive offering to cure France's misfortunes. Rich and poor alike contributed money to build it. Construction began in 1876, and though the church wasn't consecrated until 1919, perpetual prayers of adoration have been made here day and night since 1885. The interior is brilliantly decorated with mosaics: Look for the striking Christ on the ceiling and the mural of his Passion at the back of the altar. The stained-glass windows were shattered during the struggle for Paris in 1944 but have been well replaced. The crypt contains what some of the devout believe is Christ's sacred heart—hence, the name of the church.

Insider's tip: Although the view from the Arc de Triomphe is the greatest panorama of Paris, we also want to endorse the view from the gallery around the inner dome of Sacré-Coeur. On a clear day, your eyes take in a sweep of Paris extending for 48km (30 miles) into the Ile de France. You can also walk around the inner dome, an attraction even better than the interior of Sacré-Coeur itself.

Place St-Pierre, 18e. ✆ 01-53-41-89-09. www.sacre-coeur-montmartre.com. Free admission to basilica; joint ticket to dome and crypt 5€ ($6.50) adults. Basilica daily 6am–11pm; dome and crypt daily 9am–6pm. Métro: Abbesses; take elevator to surface and follow signs to funicular.

Top Paris Attractions

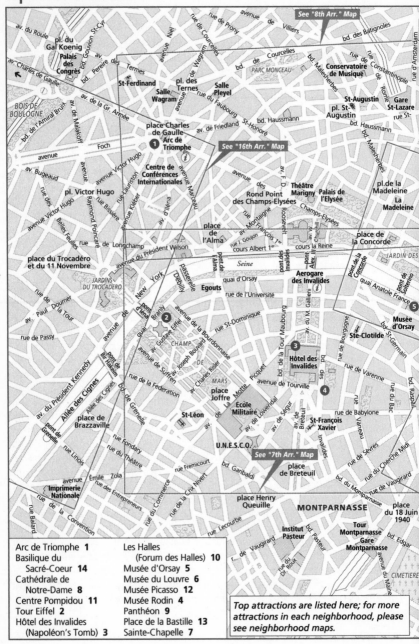

See "8th Arr." Map

See "16th Arr." Map

See "7th Arr." Map

av. du Roule
pl. du
Gal Koenig
**Palais
des
Congrès**
av. Charles de Gaulle
bd. Pereire des

avenue de Villiers
rue de Prony
rue de Courcelles
rue Niel
av. de Wagram
bd. des Batignolles
rue de Constantinople
rue d'Amsterdam

BOIS DE
BOULOGNE
bd. de l'Amiral Bruix
av. de la Gr. Armée
Foch
av. de Malakoff

St-Ferdinand
Termes
**Salle
Wagram**
pl. des
Ternes
rue du Faubourg St-Honoré
**Salle
Pleyel**

de Courcelles
PARC MONCEAU
bd. Malesherbes
bd. Haussmann

**Conservatoire
de Musique**

St-Augustin
pl. St-
Augustin
bd. Haussmann
bd. Malesherbes

**Gare
St-Lazare**
rue St-

place Charles
de Gaulle
❶ **Arc de
Triomphe**
av. de Friedland
St-Honoré

**Centre de
Conférences
Internationales**
avenue Victor Hugo
av. Bugeaud
avenue Victor Hugo
av. Kléber
av. Marceau
av. d'Iéna

pl. Victor Hugo
rue Lauriston
rue Bassière
rue Raymond Poincaré
Belles Feuilles
rue de Longchamp

avenue des Champs-Elysées
**Rond Point
des Champs-Elysées**
**Théâtre
Marigny**
**Palais de
l'Elysée**
av. F. D. Roosevelt
av. de Montaigne
av. W. Churchill

**pl.de la
Madeleine**
**La
Madeleine**

place
de
l'Alma
rue J. Goujon
cours Albert 1er
rue François 1er
cours la Reine

**place de
la Concorde**
pont de la Concorde
JARDIN DES

**place du Trocadéro
et du 11 Novembre**
avenue du Président Wilson
JARDINS
DU TROCADÉRO
rue de Passy
av. Paul Doumer
rue de Doumer

Seine
pont de l'Alma
quai d'Orsay
rue de l'Université
rue St-Dominique
Passerelle Debilly
avenue de New York

Egouts
**Aerogare
des Invalides**
av. du M. Gallieni
pont des Invalides
pont Alex. III
quai Anatole France
pont de Solferino

**Musée
d'Orsay** ❺
Ste-Clotilde
bd. St-Germain

av. du Président Kennedy
pont de Bir-Hakeim
Allée des Cygnes
Allée des Cygnes
pont d'Iéna
quai Branly
avenue de la Bourdonnais
av. de Suffren
av. Joseph Bourdon
**CHAMP
DE
MARS**
av. Charles Ridet
av. de la Motte Picquet

❷ **Tour
Eiffel**
Gustave Eiffel

**Hôtel des
Invalides** ❸
bd. de la Tour Maubourg
rue de Grenelle
rue de Bourgogne
rue de Varenne
rue du Bac
bd. Raspail

❹ **Musée
Rodin**

**place de
Brazzaville**
pont de Grenelle
rue Linois
bd. de Grenelle
rue de la Fédération
St-Léon
rue Fondary
rue du Théâtre
avenue Émile Zola
rue des Entrepreneurs

**place
Joffre**
**Ecole
Militaire**
av. de Lowendal
av. de Ségur
av. de Breteuil
rue de Sèvres
rue de Babylone
rue Vaneau
rue du Cherche Midi

**St-François
Xavier**

U.N.E.S.C.O.
bd. Garibaldi
rue Fremicourt
rue du Commerce
rue de la Croix Nivert
rue Lecourbe

**place
de Breteuil**

**Imprimerie
Nationale**
rue de la Convention
rue Balard

**place Henry
Queuille**
Institut
Pasteur
bd. Pasteur
de Vaugirard
rue du Dr Roux

MONTPARNASSE
**Tour
Montparnasse**
**Gare
Montparnasse**
bd. Edgar
**place
du 18 Juin
1940**
avenue du Maine
CIMETIÈRE

*Top attractions are listed here; for more
attractions in each neighborhood, please
see neighborhood maps.*

Arc de Triomphe **1**
Basilique du
    Sacré-Coeur **14**
Cathédrale de
    Notre-Dame **8**
Centre Pompidou **11**
Tour Eiffel **2**
Hôtel des Invalides
    (Napoléon's Tomb) **3**

Les Halles
    (Forum des Halles) **10**
Musée d'Orsay **5**
Musée du Louvre **6**
Musée Picasso **12**
Musée Rodin **4**
Panthéon **9**
Place de la Bastille **13**
Sainte-Chapelle **7**

Attractions in the 1st Arrondissement

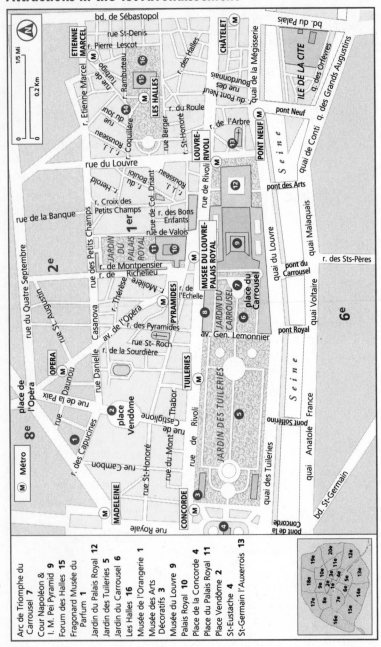

Arc de Triomphe du
Carrousel **7**
Cour Napoléon &
I. M. Pei Pyramid **9**
Forum des Halles **15**
Fragonard Musée du
Parfum **1**
Jardin du Palais Royal **12**
Jardin des Tuileries **5**
Jardin du Carrousel **6**
Les Halles **16**
Musée de l'Orangerie **1**
Musée des Arts
Décoratifs **3**
Musée du Louvre **9**
Palais Royal **10**
Place de la Concorde **4**
Place du Palais Royal **11**
Place Vendôme **2**
St-Eustache **4**
St-Germain l'Auxerrois **13**

Attractions in the 3rd–4th Arrondissements

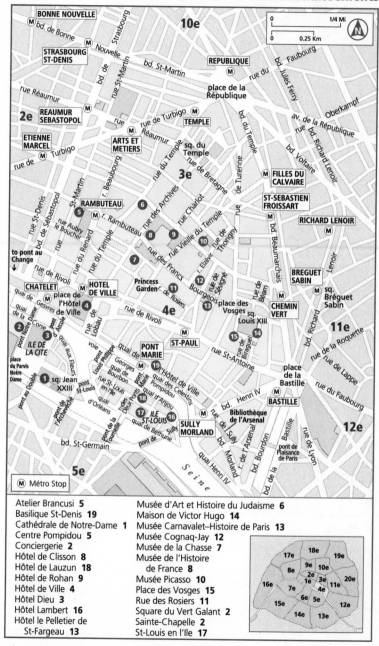

Métro Stop Ⓜ

Atelier Brancusi **5**
Basilique St-Denis **19**
Cathédrale de Notre-Dame **1**
Centre Pompidou **5**
Conciergerie **2**
Hôtel de Clisson **8**
Hôtel de Lauzun **18**
Hôtel de Rohan **9**
Hôtel de Ville **4**
Hôtel Dieu **3**
Hôtel Lambert **16**
Hôtel le Pelletier de
St-Fargeau **13**

Musée d'Art et Histoire du Judaisme **6**
Maison de Victor Hugo **14**
Musée Carnavalet–Histoire de Paris **13**
Musée Cognaq-Jay **12**
Musée de la Chasse **7**
Musée de l'Histoire
de France **8**
Musée Picasso **10**
Place des Vosges **15**
Rue des Rosiers **11**
Square du Vert Galant **2**
Sainte-Chapelle **2**
St-Louis en l'Ile **17**

Attractions in the 5th–6th Arrondissements

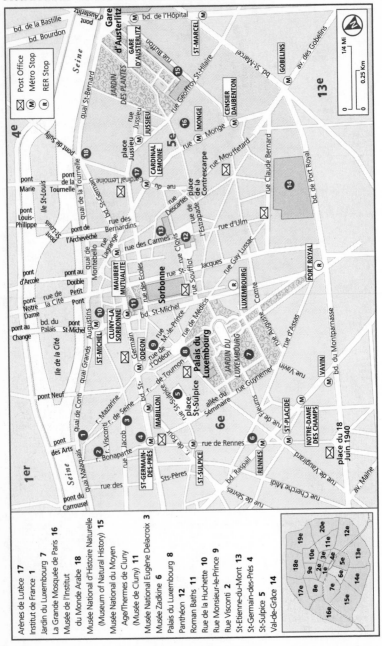

Arènes de Lutèce 17
Institut de France 1
Jardin du Luxembourg 7
La Grande Mosquée de Paris 16
Musée de l'Institut
  du Monde Arabe 18
Musée National d'Histoire Naturelle
  (Museum of Natural History) 15
Musée National du Moyen
  Age/Thermes de Cluny
  (Musée de Cluny) 11
Musée National Eugène Delacroix 3
Musée Zadkine 6
Palais du Luxembourg 8
Panthéon 12
Roman Baths 11
Rue de la Huchette 10
Rue Monsieur-le-Prince 9
Rue Visconti 2
St-Etienne-du-Mont 13
St-Germain-des-Prés 4
St-Sulpice 5
Val-de-Grâce 14

Attractions in the 7th Arrondissement

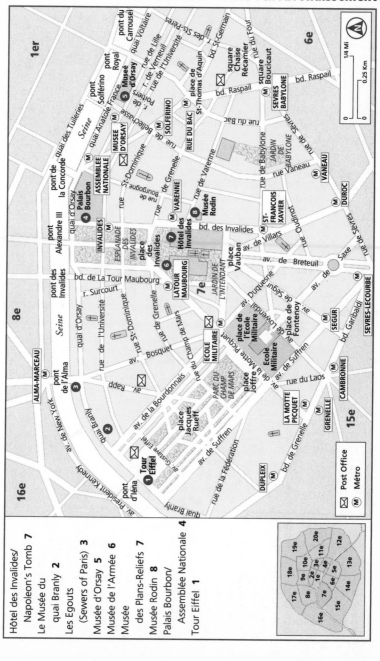

Hôtel des Invalides/
Napoleon's Tomb **7**

Le Musée du
quai Branly **2**

Les Egouts
(Sewers of Paris) **3**

Musée d'Orsay **5**

Musée de l'Armée **6**

Musée
des Plans-Reliefs **7**

Musée Rodin **8**

Palais Bourbon/
Assemblée Nationale **4**

Tour Eiffel **1**

⊠ Post Office
Ⓜ Métro

Attractions in the 8th Arrondissement

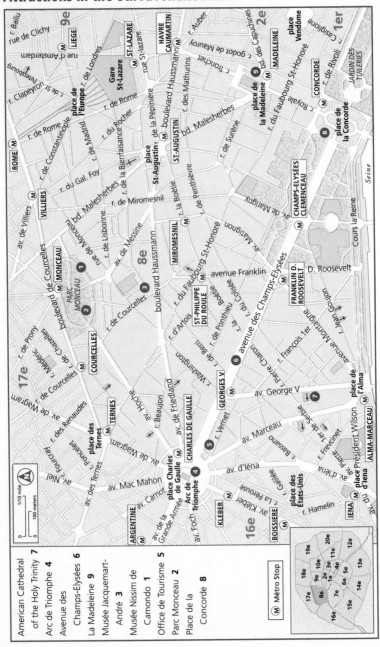

American Cathedral of the Holy Trinity **7**
Arc de Triomphe **4**
Avenue des Champs-Élysées **6**
La Madeleine **9**
Musée Jacquemart-André **3**
Musée Nissim de Camondo **1**
Office de Tourisme **5**
Parc Monceau **2**
Place de la Concorde **8**

Ⓜ Métro Stop

Attractions in the 16th Arrondissement

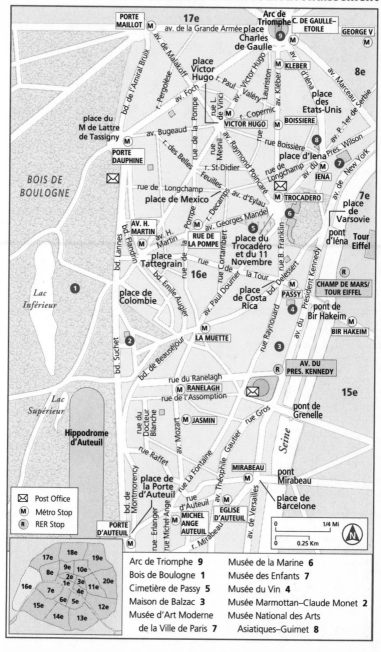

Post Office ⊠
Métro Stop Ⓜ
RER Stop Ⓡ

Arc de Triomphe **9**
Bois de Boulogne **1**
Cimetière de Passy **5**
Maison de Balzac **3**
Musée d'Art Moderne
   de la Ville de Paris **7**

Musée de la Marine **6**
Musée des Enfants **7**
Musée du Vin **4**
Musée Marmottan–Claude Monet **2**
Musée National des Arts
   Asiatiques–Guimet **8**

Attractions in the 18th Arrondissement

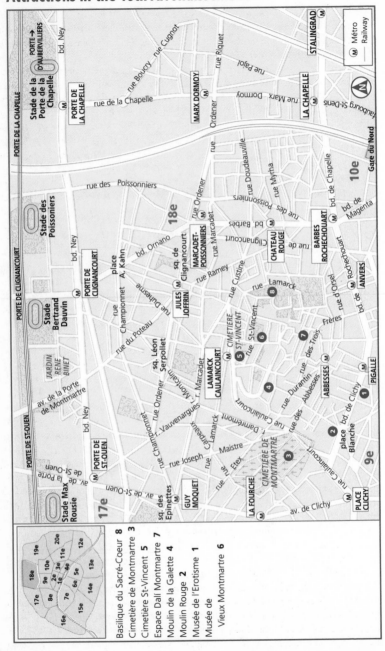

Basilique du Sacré-Coeur 8
Cimetière de Montmartre 3
Cimetière St-Vincent 5
Espace Dalí Montmartre 7
Moulin de la Galette 4
Moulin Rouge 2
Musée de l'Erotisme 1
Musée de
    Vieux Montmartre 6

Cathédrale de Notre-Dame *✹✹✹*   Notre-Dame is the heart of Paris and even of the country itself: Distances from the city to all parts of France are calculated from a spot at the far end of place du Parvis, in front of the cathedral, where a circular bronze plaque marks **Kilomètre Zéro.**

The cathedral's setting on the banks of the Seine has always been memorable. Founded in the 12th century by Maurice de Sully, bishop of Paris, Notre-Dame has grown over the years, changing as Paris has changed, often falling victim to whims of taste. Its flying buttresses (the external side supports, giving the massive interior a sense of weightlessness) were rebuilt in 1330. Though many disagree, we feel Notre-Dame is more interesting outside than in, and you'll want to walk all around it to fully appreciate this "vast symphony of stone." Better yet, cross over the pont au Double to the Left Bank and view it from the quay.

The histories of Paris and Notre-Dame are inseparable. Many prayed here before going off to fight in the Crusades. The revolutionaries who destroyed the Galerie des Rois and converted the building into a secular temple didn't spare "Our Lady of Paris." Later, Napoleon crowned himself emperor here, yanking the crown out of Pius VII's hands and placing it on his own head before crowning his Joséphine empress (see David's *Coronation of Napoléon* in the Louvre). But carelessness, vandalism, embellishments, and wars of religion had already demolished much of the previously existing structure.

The cathedral was once scheduled for demolition, but because of the popularity of Victor Hugo's *Hunchback of Notre-Dame* and the revival of interest in the Gothic period, a movement mushroomed to restore the cathedral to its original glory. The task was completed under Viollet-le-Duc, an architectural genius. The houses of old Paris used to crowd in on Notre-Dame, but during his redesign of the city, Baron Haussmann ordered them torn down to show the cathedral to its best advantage from the parvis. This is the best vantage for seeing the three sculpted 13th-century portals (the Virgin, the Last Judgment, and St. Anne).

On the left, the **Portal of the Virgin** depicts the signs of the zodiac and the coronation of the Virgin, an association found in dozens of medieval churches. The restored central **Portal of the Last Judgment** depicts three levels: the first shows Vices and Virtues; the second, Christ and his Apostles; and above that, Christ in triumph after the Resurrection. The portal is a close illustration of the Gospel according to Matthew. Over it is the remarkable **west rose window** *✹✹*, 9.5m (31 ft.) wide, forming a showcase for a statue of the Virgin and Child. On the far right is the **Portal of St. Anne,** depicting scenes such as the Virgin enthroned with Child; it's Notre-Dame's best-preserved and most perfect piece of sculpture. Equally interesting (though often missed) is the **Portal of the Cloisters** (around on the left), with its dour-faced 13th-century Virgin, a survivor among the figures that originally adorned the facade. (Alas, the Child she's holding has been decapitated.) Finally, on the Seine side of Notre-Dame, the **Portal of St. Stephen** traces that saint's martyrdom.

If possible, come to see Notre-Dame at sunset. Inside, of the three giant medallions warming the austere cathedral, the **north rose window** *✹✹* in the transept, from the mid–13th century, is best. The main body of the church is typically Gothic, with slender, graceful columns. In the **choir,** a stone-carved screen from the early–14th century depicts such biblical scenes as the Last Supper. Near the altar stands the 14th-century *Virgin and Child* *✹*, highly venerated among Paris's faithful. In the **treasury** are displayed vestments and gold objects, including crowns. Exhibited is a cross presented to

Notre-Dame de Paris

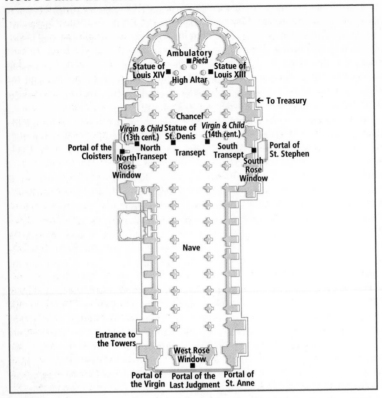

Haile Selassie, former emperor of Ethiopia, and a reliquary given by Napoleon. Notre-Dame is especially proud of its relic of the True Cross and the Crown of Thorns.

To visit the **gargoyles** ★★ immortalized by Hugo, you have to scale steps leading to the twin **towers,** rising to a height of 68m (223 ft.). Once there, you can inspect devils (some giving you the raspberry), hobgoblins, and birds of prey. Look carefully, and you may see hunchback Quasimodo with Esmeralda.

Approached through a garden behind Notre-Dame is the **Mémorial des Martyrs Français de la Déportation de 1945 (Deportation Memorial),** out on the tip of Ile de la Cité. Here, birds chirp and the Seine flows gently by, but the memories are far from pleasant. The memorial commemorates the French citizens who were deported to concentration camps during World War II. Carved into stone are these blood-red words (in French): "Forgive, but don't forget." The memorial is open Monday to Friday from 8:30am to 9:45pm, and Saturday and Sunday from 9am to 9:45pm. Admission is free.

6 place du Parvis Notre-Dame, 4e. ✆ 01-42-34-56-10. www.monum.fr. Admission free to cathedral. Towers 5.50€ ($7.15) adults, 4.50€ ($5.85) seniors and ages 18–25, free for children under 18. Treasury 5.50€ ($7.15) adults, 4.50€ ($5.85) seniors and ages 5–25, free for children under 5. Cathedral year-round daily 8am–6:45pm. Towers and crypt Apr–Sept daily 9:30am–6:30pm (until 11pm Sat–Sun June–Aug); Oct–Mar daily 10am–5:30pm. Museum Wed and Sat–Sun 2–5pm. Treasury Mon–Sat 2:30–6:30pm; Sun 1:30–5:30pm. Métro: Cité or St-Michel. RER: St-Michel.

Hôtel des Invalides/Napoleon's Tomb ✱✱✱   In 1670, the Sun King decided to build this "hotel" to house soldiers with disabilities. It wasn't an entirely benevolent gesture, considering that the men had been injured, crippled, or blinded while fighting his battles. When the building was finally completed (Louis XIV had long been dead), a gilded dome by Jules Hardouin-Mansart crowned it, and its corridors stretched for miles. The best way to approach the Invalides is by crossing over the Right Bank via the early-1900s pont Alexander-III and entering the cobblestone forecourt, where a display of massive cannons makes a formidable welcome.

Before rushing on to Napoleon's Tomb, you may want to visit the world's greatest military museum, the **Musée de l'Armée.** In 1794, a French inspector started collecting weapons, uniforms, and equipment, and with the accumulation of war material over time, the museum has become a documentary of man's self-destruction. Viking swords, Burgundian battle axes, 14th-century blunderbusses, Balkan *khandjars,* American Browning machine guns, war pitchforks, salamander-engraved Renaissance serpentines, a 1528 Griffon, musketoons, grenadiers . . . if it can kill, it's enshrined here. As a sardonic touch, there's even the wooden leg of General Daumesnil, the governor of Vincennes who lost his leg in the battle of Wagram. Oblivious to the irony of committing a crime against a place that documents man's evil nature, the Nazis looted the museum in 1940.

Among the outstanding acquisitions are suits of armor worn by the kings and dignitaries of France, including Louis XIV. The best are in the new Arsenal. The most famous one, the "armor suit of the lion," was made for François I. Henri II ordered his suit engraved with the monogram of his mistress, Diane de Poitiers, and (perhaps reluctantly) that of his wife, Catherine de Médicis. Particularly fine are the showcases of swords and the World War I mementos, including those of American and Canadian soldiers—seek out the Armistice Bugle, which sounded the cease-fire on November 7, 1918, before the general cease-fire on November 11. The west wing's Salle Orientale has arms of the Eastern world, including Asia and the Mideast Muslim countries, from the 16th century to the 19th century. Turkish armor (look for Bajazet's helmet) and weaponry, and Chinese and Japanese armor and swords are on display.

Then there's that little Corsican who became France's greatest soldier. Here you can see the death mask Antommarchi made of him, as well as an oil by Delaroche painted at the time of Napoleon's first banishment (Apr 1814) and depicting him as he probably looked, paunch and all. The First Empire exhibit displays Napoleon's field bed with his tent; in the room devoted to the Restoration, the 100 Days, and Waterloo, you can see his bedroom as it was at the time of his death on St. Helena. The Turenne Salon contains other souvenirs, such as the hat Napoleon wore at Eylau; the sword from his Austerlitz victory; and his "Flag of Farewell," which he kissed before departing for Elba.

You can gain access to the **Musée des Plans-Reliefs** through the west wing. This collection shows French towns and monuments done in scale models (the model of Strasbourg fills an entire room), as well as models of military fortifications since the days of the great Vauban.

A walk across the Cour d'Honneur (Court of Honor) delivers you to the **Eglise du Dôme,** designed by Hardouin-Mansart for Louis XIV. The architect began work on the church in 1677, though he died before its completion. The dome is the second-tallest monument in Paris (the Tour Eiffel is the tallest, of course). The hearse used at the emperor's funeral on May 9, 1821, is in the Napoleon Chapel.

To accommodate **Napoleon's Tomb** ⟨★★★⟩, the architect Visconti had to redesign the church's high altar in 1842. First buried on St. Helena, Napoleon's remains were exhumed and brought to Paris in 1840 on the orders of Louis-Philippe, who demanded that the English return the emperor to French soil. The remains were locked inside six coffins in this tomb made of red Finnish porphyry, with a green granite base. Surrounding it are a dozen Amazon-like figures representing Napoleon's victories. Almost lampooning the smallness of the man, everything is done on a gargantuan scale. In his coronation robes, the statue of Napoleon stands 2.5m (8¼ ft.) high. The grave of the "King of Rome," his son by second wife Marie-Louise, lies at his feet. Surrounding Napoleon's Tomb are those of his brother, Joseph Bonaparte; the great Vauban, who built many of France's fortifications; World War I Allied commander Foch; and the vicomte de Turenne, the republic's first grenadier (actually, only his heart is entombed here).

Place des Invalides, 7e. ⟨© 01-44-42-37-72. www.invalides.org. Admission to Musée de l'Armée, Napoléon's Tomb, and Musée des Plans-Reliefs 7.50€ ($9.75) adults, 5.50€ ($7.15) students, free for children under 18. Oct–Mar daily 10am–5pm; Apr–Sept daily 10am–6pm; June–Aug daily 10am–7pm. Closed Jan 1, May 1, Nov 1, and Dec 25. Métro: Latour-Maubourg, Varenne, Invalides, or St-Francois-Xavier.

Musée d'Orsay ⟨★★★⟩   Architects created one of the world's great museums from an old rail station, the neoclassical Gare d'Orsay, across the Seine from the Louvre and the Tuileries. Don't skip the Louvre, of course, but come here even if you have to miss all the other art museums in town. The Orsay boasts an astounding collection devoted to the watershed years 1848 to 1914, with a treasure trove by the big names plus all the lesser-known groups (the symbolists, pointillists, nabis, realists, and late romantics). The 80 galleries also include Belle Epoque furniture, photographs, objets d'art, and architectural models. A cinema shows classic films.

A monument to the Industrial Revolution, the Orsay is covered by an arching glass roof allowing in floods of light. It displays works ranging from the creations of academic and historic painters like Ingres to romanticists such as Delacroix, to neorealists like Courbet and Daumier. The Impressionists and post-Impressionists, including Manet, Monet, Cézanne, van Gogh, and Renoir, share space with the fauves, Matisse, the cubists, and the expressionists in a setting once used by Orson Welles to film a nightmarish scene in *The Trial,* based on Kafka's unfinished novel. You'll find Millet's sunny wheat fields, Barbizon landscapes, Corot's mists, and Tahitian Gauguins all in the same hall.

But it's the Impressionists who draw the crowds. When the nose-in-the-air Louvre chose not to display their works, a great rival was born. Led by Manet, Renoir, and Monet, the Impressionists shunned ecclesiastical and mythological set pieces for a light-bathed Seine, faint figures strolling in the Tuileries, pale-faced women in hazy bars, and even vulgar rail stations such as the Gare St-Lazare. And the Impressionists were the first to paint that most characteristic feature of Parisian life: the sidewalk cafe, especially in the artists' quarter of Montmartre.

The most famous painting from this era is Manet's 1863 ***Déjeuner sur l'herbe (Picnic on the Grass),*** whose forest setting with a nude woman and two fully clothed men sent shock waves through respectable society when it was first exhibited. Two years later, Manet's ***Olympia*** created another scandal by depicting a woman lounging on her bed and wearing nothing but a flower in her hair and high-heeled shoes; she's attended by an African maid in the background. Zola called Manet "a man among eunuchs."

One of Renoir's most joyous paintings is here: the *Moulin de la Galette* (1876). Degas is represented by his paintings of racehorses and dancers; his 1876 cafe scene, *Absinthe,* remains one of his most reproduced works. Paris-born Monet was fascinated by the effect of changing light on Rouen Cathédrale and brought its stone bubbles to life in a series of five paintings; our favorite is *Rouen Cathédrale: Full Sunlight.* Another celebrated work is by an American, Whistler's *Arrangement in Grey and Black: Portrait of the Painter's Mother,* better known as *Whistler's Mother.* It's said that this painting heralded modern art, though many critics denounced it at the time because of its funereal overtones. Whistler was content to claim he'd made "Mummy just as nice as possible."

1 rue de Bellechasse or 62 rue de Lille, 7e. ⓒ 01-40-49-48-14. www.musee-orsay.fr. Admission 9€ ($12) adults, 7€ ($9.10) ages 18-24, free ages 17 and under. Tues–Wed and Fri–Sun 9:30am–6pm; Thurs 9:30am–9:45pm. Closed Dec 25, Jan 1 and May 1. Métro: Solférino. RER: Musée d'Orsay.

Musée du Louvre 🌟🌟🌟   The Louvre is the world's largest palace and museum. As a palace, it leaves us cold except for the **Cour Carrée.** As a museum, it's one of the greatest art collections ever. To enter, pass through I. M. Pei's controversial 21m (69-ft.) **glass pyramid** 🌟—a startling though effective contrast of the ultramodern against the palace's classical lines. Commissioned by the late president François Mitterrand and completed in 1989, it allows sunlight to shine on an underground reception area with a complex of shops and restaurants. Ticket machines relieve the long lines of yesteryear.

People on one of those "Paris-in-a-day" tours try to break track records to get a glimpse of the Louvre's two most famous ladies: the beguiling *Mona Lisa* and the armless *Venus de Milo* 🌟🌟🌟. The herd then dashes on a 5-minute stampede in pursuit of *Winged Victory* 🌟🌟🌟, the headless statue discovered at Samothrace and dating from about 200 B.C. In defiance of the assembly-line theory of art, we head instead for David's *Coronation of Napoleon,* showing Napoleon poised with the crown aloft as Joséphine kneels before him, just across from his *Portrait of Madame Récamier* 🌟, depicting Napoleon's opponent at age 23; she reclines on her sofa agelessly in the style of classical antiquity.

Then a big question looms: Which of the rest of the 30,000 works on display would you like to see?

Between the Seine and rue de Rivoli, the Palais du Louvre suffers from an embarrassment of riches, stretching for almost a kilometer (half a mile). In the days of Charles V, it was a fortress, but François I, a patron of Leonardo da Vinci, had it torn down and rebuilt as a royal residence. Less than a month after Marie Antoinette's head and body parted company, the Revolutionary Committee decided the king's collection of paintings and sculpture should be opened to the public. At the lowest point in its history, in the 18th century, the Louvre was home for anybody who wanted to set up

---

⟮*Tips* Leaping over the Louvre Line

If you don't want to wait in line at the entrance to the Louvre pyramid, or use the automatic ticket machines, you can order tickets over the phone (ⓒ **08-92-68-46-94**) with a credit card. You can also order advance tickets and take a virtual tour at www.louvre.fr. Tickets can be mailed to you in the U.S., or you can pick them up at any Paris branch of the FNAC electronics chain.

The Louvre

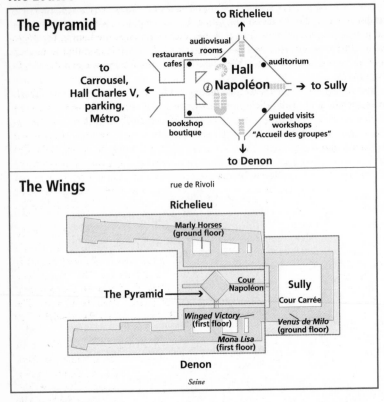

The Pyramid

to Richelieu

audiovisual rooms

restaurants
cafes

Hall Napoléon

auditorium

to Carrousel, Hall Charles V, parking, Métro

→ to Sully

bookshop boutique

guided visits workshops "Accueil des groupes"

to Denon

The Wings

rue de Rivoli

Richelieu

Marly Horses (ground floor)

The Pyramid →

Cour Napoléon

Sully

Cour Carrée

Winged Victory (first floor)

Venus de Milo (ground floor)

Mona Lisa (first floor)

Denon

Seine

housekeeping. Laundry hung in the windows, corners were pigpens, and families built fires to cook their meals in winter. Napoleon ended all that, chasing out the squatters and restoring the palace. In fact, he chose the Louvre as the site of his wedding to Marie-Louise.

So where did all these paintings come from? The kings of France, notably François I and Louis XIV, acquired many of them, and others were willed to or purchased by the state. Many contributed by Napoleon were taken from reluctant donors: The church was one especially heavy and unwilling giver. Much of Napoleon's plunder had to be returned, though France hasn't yet seen its way clear to giving back all the booty.

The collections are divided into seven departments: Egyptian Antiquities; Oriental Antiquities; Greek, Etruscan, and Roman Antiquities; Sculpture; Painting; Decorative Arts; and Graphic Arts. A number of galleries, devoted to Italian paintings, Roman glass and bronzes, Oriental antiquities, and Egyptian antiquities, were opened in 1997 and 1998. If you don't have to do Paris in a day, you might want to visit several times, concentrating on different collections or schools of painting. Those with little time should take a guided tour.

Acquired by François I to hang above his bathtub, Leonardo's ***La Gioconda (Mona Lisa)*** ✯✯✯ has been the source of legend for centuries. Note the guard and bulletproof glass: The world's most famous painting was stolen in 1911 and found in Florence in

1913. At first, both the poet Guillaume Apollinaire and Picasso were suspected, but it was discovered in the possession of a former Louvre employee, who'd apparently carried it out under his overcoat. Two centuries after its arrival at the Louvre, the *Mona Lisa* in 2003 was assigned a new gallery of her own. Less well known (but to us even more enchanting) are Leonardo's *Virgin and Child with St. Anne* and the *Virgin of the Rocks.*

After paying your respects to the "smiling one," allow time to see some French works stretching from the Richelieu wing through the entire **Sully wing** and even overflowing into the **Denon wing.** It's all here: Watteau's *Gilles* with the mysterious boy in a clown suit staring at you; Fragonard's and Boucher's rococo renderings of the aristocracy; and the greatest masterpieces of David, including his stellar 1785 *The Oath of the Horatii* and the vast and vivid *Coronation of Napoleon.* Only Florence's Uffizi rivals the Denon wing for its Italian Renaissance collection—everything from Raphael's *Portrait of Balthazar Castiglione* to Titian's *Man with a Glove.* Veronese's gigantic *Wedding Feast at Cana*, a romp of Venetian high society in the 1500s, occupies an entire wall (that's Paolo himself playing the cello).

Of the Greek and Roman antiquities, the most notable collections, aside from the *Venus de Milo* and *Winged Victory,* are fragments of a **Parthenon frieze** (in the Denon wing). In Renaissance sculpture, you'll see Michelangelo's *Esclaves (Slaves),* originally intended for the tomb of Julius II but sold into other bondage. The Denon wing houses masterpieces such as Ingres's *The Turkish Bath,* the **Botticelli frescoes** from the Villa Lemmi, Raphael's *La Belle Jardinière,* and Titian's *Open Air Concert.* The Sully wing is also filled with old masters, such as Boucher's *Diana Resting After Her Bath* and Fragonard's *Bathers.*

The **Richelieu wing** reopened in 1993 after lying empty for years. Now, with an additional 69,000 sq. m (743,000 sq. ft.) of exhibition space, it houses northern European and French paintings, along with decorative arts, sculpture, Oriental antiquities (a rich collection of Islamic art), and the Napoleon III salons. One of its galleries displays 21 works that Rubens painted in a space of only 2 years for Marie de Médicis's Palais de Luxembourg. The masterpieces here include Dürer's *Self-Portrait,* Van Dyck's *Portrait of Charles I of England,* and Holbein the Younger's *Portrait of Erasmus of Rotterdam.*

When you tire of strolling the galleries, you may like a pick-me-up at the Richelieu Wing's **Café Richelieu** (© **01-49-27-99-01**) or at **Café Marly,** 93 rue de Rivoli, 1er (© **01-49-26-06-60**). Boasting Napoleon III opulence, the Marly is a perfect oasis. Try a cafe crème, a club sandwich, a pastry, or something from the bistro menu.

34–36 quai du Louvre, 1er. Main entrance in the glass pyramid, Cour Napoléon. © **01-40-20-53-17**, 01-40-20-50-50 for operator, or 08-92-68-46-94 for advance credit card sales. www.louvre.fr. Admission 8.50€ ($11); children younger than 18 free; free to all 1st Sun of every month. Sat–Mon and Thurs 9am–5:30pm; Wed and Fri 9am–9:30pm. 1½-hr. English-language tours (Mon and Wed–Sun) 6€ ($7.80), free for children younger than 13 with museum ticket. Métro: Palais-Royal–Musée du Louvre.

Sainte-Chapelle Countless writers have called this tiny chapel a jewel box, yet that hardly suffices, nor can it be called "a light show." Go when the sun is shining, and you'll need no one else's words to describe the remarkable effects of natural light on Sainte-Chapelle. You approach the church through the Cour de la Sainte-Chapelle of the Palais de Justice. If it weren't for the chapel's 74m (243-ft.) spire, the law courts here would almost swallow it up.

Begun in 1246, the bi-level chapel was built to house relics of the True Cross, including the Crown of Thorns acquired by St. Louis (the Crusader king, Louis IX) from the emperor of Constantinople. (In those days, cathedrals throughout Europe were busy acquiring relics for their treasuries, regardless of their authenticity. It was a seller's, perhaps a sucker's, market.) Louis IX is said to have paid heavily for his relics, raising the money through unscrupulous means. He died of the plague on a crusade and was canonized in 1297.

You enter through the *chapelle basse* **(lower chapel),** used by the palace servants; it's supported by flying buttresses and ornamented with fleur-de-lis designs. The king and his courtiers used the *chapelle haute* **(upper chapel),** one of the greatest achievements of Gothic art; you reach it by ascending a narrow spiral staircase. On a bright day, the 15 stained-glass windows seem to glow with Chartres blue and with reds that have inspired the saying "wine the color of Sainte-Chapelle's windows." The walls consist almost entirely of the glass, 612 sq. m (6,588 sq. ft.) of it, which had to be removed for safekeeping during the Revolution and again during both world wars. In the windows' Old and New Testament designs are embodied the hopes and dreams (and the pretensions) of the kings who ordered their construction. The 1,134 scenes depict the Christian story from the Garden of Eden through the Apocalypse; you read them from bottom to top and from left to right. The great rose window depicts the Apocalypse.

Ste-Chapelle stages **concerts** in March to November; tickets cost 19€ to 25€ ($25–$33). Call ✆ **01-44-07-12-38** from 11am to 6pm daily for details.

Palais de Justice, 4 bd. du Palais, 4e. ✆ **01-53-40-60-80.** www.monum.fr. 6.50€ ($8.45) adults, 4.50€ ($5.85) ages 18–25, free 17 and younger. Daily 9am–5pm. Métro: Cité, St-Michel, or Châtelet–Les Halles. RER: St-Michel.

Tour Eiffel 🟊🟊🟊   This is without doubt one of the most recognizable structures in the world. Weighing 7,000 tons, but exerting about the same pressure on the ground as an average-size person sitting in a chair, the wrought-iron tower wasn't meant to be permanent. Gustave-Alexandre Eiffel, the French engineer whose fame rested mainly on his iron bridges, built it for the 1889 Universal Exhibition. (Eiffel also designed the framework for the Statue of Liberty.) Praised by some and denounced by others (some called it a "giraffe," the "world's greatest lamppost," or the "iron monster"), the tower created as much controversy in the 1880s as I. M. Pei's glass pyramid at the Louvre did in the 1980s. What saved it from demolition was the advent of radio—as the tallest structure in Europe, it made a perfect spot to place a radio antenna (now a TV antenna).

The tower, including its TV antenna, is 317m (1,040 ft.) high. On a clear day you can see it from 65km (40 miles) away. An open-framework construction, the tower unlocked the almost unlimited possibilities of steel construction, paving the way for

---

⟨*Value*⟩ Tour Eiffel Bargain

The least expensive way to see the Tour Eiffel (www.tour-eiffel.fr) is to walk up the first two floors at a cost of 7.80€ ($10; 4.50€/$5.85 first floor). That way, you also avoid the long lines waiting for the elevator—although the views are less spectacular from this platform. If you dine at the tower's own **Altitude 95** (✆ **01-45-55-20-04**), an Eiffel restaurant on the first floor, management allows patrons to cut to the head of the line.

> **Tips   Time Out at the Tower**
>
> To see the Eiffel Tower best, don't sprint—approach it gradually. We suggest taking the Métro to the Trocadéro stop and walking from the Palais de Chaillot to the Seine to get the full effect of the tower and its surroundings; then cross the pont d'Iéna and head for the base, where you'll find elevators in two of the pillars—expect long lines. (When the tower is open, you can see the 1889 lift machinery in the east and west pillars.) You visit the tower in three stages: The first landing provides a view over the rooftops, as well as a cinema museum showing films, restaurants, and a bar. The second landing offers a panoramic look at the city. The third landing gives the most spectacular view; Eiffel's office has been re-created on this level, with wax figures depicting the engineer receiving Thomas Edison.

skyscrapers. Skeptics said it couldn't be built, and Eiffel actually wanted to make it soar higher. For years it remained the tallest man-made structure on earth, until skyscrapers such as the Empire State Building surpassed it.

We could fill an entire page with tower statistics. (Its plans spanned 5,400 sq. m/18,000 sq. ft. of paper, and it contains 2.5 million rivets.) But forget the numbers. Just stand beneath the tower, and look straight up. It's like a rocket of steel lacework shooting into the sky.

In 2004 it became possible to ice-skate inside the Eiffel Tower, doing figure eights while taking in views of the rooftops of Paris. Skating takes place on an observation deck 57m (188 ft.) above ground. The rectangular rink is a bit larger than an average tennis court, holding 80 skaters at once—half the capacity of New York City's Rockefeller Center rink. Rink admission and skate rental are free, once you pay the initial entry fee below.

To get to **Le Jules Verne** (© **01-45-55-61-44**), the second-platform restaurant, take the private south foundation elevator. You can enjoy an aperitif in the piano bar and then take a seat at one of the dining room's tables, all of which provide an inspiring view. The menu changes seasonally, offering fish and meat dishes that range from filet of turbot with seaweed and buttered sea urchins to veal chops with truffled vegetables. Reservations are recommended.

Champ de Mars, 7e. © 01-44-11-23-23. www.tour-eiffel.fr. Admission to 1st landing 4.20€ ($5.45), 2nd landing 7.70€ ($10), 3rd landing 11€ ($14.30). Stairs to 2nd floor 3.80€ ($4.95). Sept–May daily 9:30am–11:45pm; June–Aug daily 9am–12:45am. Fall and winter, stairs open only to 6pm. Métro: Trocadéro, Ecole Militaire, or Bir Hakeim. RER: Champ de Mars–Tour Eiffel.

3 The Major Museums

Turn to "The Top Attractions," earlier, for a comprehensive look at the **Musée du Louvre** and the **Musée d'Orsay**.

Centre Pompidou ✹✹✹   Reopened in January 2000 in what was called in the 1970s "the most avant-garde building in the world," the restored Centre Pompidou is packing in the art-loving crowds again. The dream of former president Georges Pompidou, this center for 20th- and 21st-century art, designed by Richard Rogers and

---

Value **The Museum Discount Card**

If you're a culture buff, consider buying a **Paris Museum Pass,** which admits you to some 70 museums in Paris and its environs. You do the math—if you plan to visit three or four museums, the card is usually worth the investment. A pass good for 2 days costs 30€ ($39); for 4 consecutive days, 45€ ($59); and for 6 consecutive days, 60€ ($78). Cards are available at all major museums and Métro stations. For more information, contact **Association InterMusees,** 4 rue Brantôme, 3e (℃ **01-44-61-96-60;** www.parismuseumpass.fr; Métro: Rambuteau).

Renzo Piano, opened in 1977 and quickly became the focus of controversy. Its bold exoskeletal architecture and the brightly painted pipes and ducts crisscrossing its transparent facade (green for water, red for heat, blue for air, and yellow for electricity) were jarring in the old Beaubourg neighborhood. Perhaps the detractors were right all along—within 20 years, the building began to deteriorate so badly that a major restoration was necessary. The renovation added 450 sq. m (4,844 sq. ft.) of exhibit space and a rooftop restaurant, a cafe, and a boutique; in addition, a series of auditoriums were created for film screenings and dance, theater, and musical performances. Access for visitors with disabilities has also been improved.

The Centre Pompidou encompasses five attractions:

Musée National d'Art Moderne (National Museum of Modern Art) ⋆⋆⋆ has a large collection of 20th- and 21st-century art. With some 40,000 works, this is the big attraction, though only about 850 works can be displayed at one time. If you want to view some real charmers, seek out Calder's 1926 *Josephine Baker,* one of his earlier versions of the mobile, an art form he invented. You'll also find two examples of Duchamp's series of dada-style sculptures he invented in 1936: *Boîte en Valise* (1941) and *Boîte en Valise* (1968). And every time we visit, we have to see Dalí's *Hallucination partielle: Six images de Lénine sur un piano* (1931), with Lenin dancing on a piano.

In the **Bibliothèque Information Publique (Public Information Library),** people have free access to a million French and foreign books, periodicals, films, records, slides, and microfilms in nearly every area of knowledge. The **Centre de Création Industriel (Center for Industrial Design)** emphasizes the contributions made in the fields of architecture, visual communications, publishing, and community planning; and the **Institut de Recherche et de Coordination Acoustique-Musique (Institute for Research and Coordination of Acoustics/Music)** brings together musicians and composers interested in furthering the cause of contemporary and traditional music. Finally, you can visit a re-creation of the Jazz Age studio of Romanian sculptor Brancusi, the **Atelier Brancusi** ⋆, a minimuseum slightly separated from the rest of the action.

The museum's **forecourt** is a free "entertainment center" featuring mimes, fire-eaters, circus performers, and sometimes musicians. Don't miss the nearby **Stravinsky fountain,** containing mobile sculptures by Tinguely and Saint Phalle.

Place Georges-Pompidou, 4e. ℃ 01-44-78-12-33. www.centrepompidou.fr. Admission 10€ ($13) adults, 8€ ($10) students, free for children younger than 18. Wed–Mon 11am–9pm. Métro: Rambuteau, Hôtel de Ville, or Châtelet–Les Halles.

Jeu de Paume   After knowing many roles, this museum has become a center for photography and video, exploring "the world of images, their uses, and the issues they raise." Its exhibitions not only display photography but mechanical images. It is one of the finest museums of its type in the world, and it changing exhibitions, many of them daringly avant-garde.

For years the National Gallery in the Jeu de Paume, in the northeast corner of the Tuileries gardens, was one of the treasures of Paris, displaying some of the finest words of the impressionists. In 1986 that collection was hauled off to the Musée d'Orsay, much to the regret of many. Following a 9.7€- ($12.6-) million face-lift, this Second Empire building has been transformed into state-of-the-art galleries.

Originally, in this part of the gardens, Napoleon III built a ball court on which *jeu de paume,* an antecedent of tennis, was played—hence the museum's name. The most infamous period in the National Gallery's history came during the Nazi occupation, when it served as an "evaluation center" for works of modern art. Paintings from all over France were shipped to the Jeu de Paume; art condemned by the Nazis as "degenerate" was burned.

1 Place de la Concorde, 8e. ⓒ 01-47-03-12-50. Admission 6€ ($7.80) adults, 3€ ($3.90) students and children. Tues noon–9pm; Wed–Fri noon–7pm; Sat–Sun 10am–7pm. Métro: Concorde.

Le Musée du quai Branly ★★★   The architect, Jean Nouvel, said he wanted to create something "unique, poetic, and disturbing." And so he did with the opening of this $265-million museum, which took a decade to launch. There was even scandal: the terra-cotta figures from Nigeria turned out to be smuggled. At long last under one roof nearly 300,000 tribal artifacts from Africa, Asia, Oceania, and the Americas have been assembled. Galleries stand on sculpted pillars that evoke totem poles. Set in a lush, rambling garden on the Left Bank in the shadow of the Eiffel Tower, this is the greatest museum to open in Paris since Pompidou.

Housed in four spectacular buildings with a garden walled off from the quai Branly, are the art, sculpture, and cultural materials of a vast range of non-Western civilizations, separated into different sections that represent the traditional cultures of Africa, East and Southeast Asia, Oceania, Australia, the Americas, and New Zealand. The pieces here come from the now-defunct Musée des Arts Africains et Oceaniens, from the Louvre, and from the Musée de l'Homme. Temporary exhibits are shown off in boxes all along the 183m-long (600 ft.) exhibition hall.

Incredible masterpieces are on display made by some very advanced traditional civilizations; some of the most impressive exhibits present tribal masks of different cultures, some of which are so lifelike and emotional in their creation that you can feel the fear and elation involved in their use, which is well documented by descriptions in English. Allow 2 hours for a full visit; also take a stroll in their carefully manicured garden, or have a café au lait in their small cafeteria across from the main building. There are numerous entrances to the museum grounds from the area near the Eiffel Tower; the main entrance is on quai Branly.

27–37 quai Branly and 206–208 rue de Université, 7e. ⓒ 01-56-61-70-00. www.quaibranly.fr. Admission 8.50€ ($11) adults, 6€ ($7.80) students 18–26 and seniors. Children 17 and younger free. Tues–Sun 10am–6:30pm (until 9:30pm Thurs). Métro: Alma-Marceau. RER: Pont d'Alma.

Musée Carnavalet-Histoire de Paris ★★ *Kids*   If you enjoy history, but history tomes bore you, spend some time here for insight into Paris's past, which comes alive in such details as the chessmen Louis XVI used to distract himself while waiting to go to the guillotine. The comprehensive and lifelike exhibits are great for kids. The building, a Renaissance palace, was built in 1544 by Pierre Lescot and Jean Goujon, and

ιater acquired by Mme de Carnavalet. The great François Mansart transformed it between 1655 and 1661.

The palace is best known for one of history's most famous letter writers, Mme de Sévigné, who moved here in 1677. Fanatically devoted to her daughter (she moved in with her because she couldn't bear to be apart), she poured out nearly every detail of her life in her letters, virtually ignoring her son. A native of the Marais district, she died at her daughter's château in 1696. In 1866, the city of Paris acquired the mansion and turned it into a museum. Several salons cover the Revolution, with a bust of Marat, a portrait of Danton, and a model of the Bastille (one painting shows its demolition). Another salon tells the story of the captivity of the royal family at the Conciergerie, including the bed in which Mme Elisabeth (the sister of Louis XVI) slept and the dauphin's exercise book.

Exhibits continue at the **Hôtel le Pelletier de St-Fargeau,** across the courtyard. On display is furniture from the Louis XIV period to the early 20th century, including a replica of Marcel Proust's cork-lined bedroom with his actual furniture, including his brass bed. This section also exhibits artifacts from the museum's archaeological collection, including some Neolithic pirogues, shallow oak boats used for fishing and transport from about 4400 to 2200 B.C.

23 rue de Sévigné, 3e. ⟨🕐⟩ **01-44-59-58-58.** www.carnavalet.paris.fr. Free admission. Special exhibits from 5€ ($6.50). Tues–Sun 10am–6pm. Métro: St-Paul or Chemin Vert.

Musée de l'Orangerie ⟨⟩   In the Tuileries stands this gem among galleries. It has an outstanding collection of art and one celebrated painting on display: Claude Monet's exquisite *Nymphéas* (1915–27), in which water lilies float amorphously on the canvas. The water lilies are displayed as the artist intended them to be—lit by sunlight in large oval galleries that evoke the shape of the garden ponds at his former Giverny estate.

Creating his effects with hundreds and hundreds of minute strokes of his brush (one irate 19th-century critic called them "tongue lickings"), Monet achieved unity and harmony, as he did in his Rouen Cathedral series and his haystacks. Artists with lesser talent might have stirred up "soup." But Monet, of course, was a genius. See his lilies and evoke for yourself the mood and melancholy as he experienced them so many years ago. Monet continued to paint his water landscapes right up until his death in 1926, although he was greatly hampered by failing eyesight.

The renovated building also houses the art collections of two men, John Walter and Paul Guillaume, who are not connected to each other, except that they were both married at different times to the same woman. Their collection includes more than 24 Renoirs, including *Young Girl at a Piano.* Cézanne is represented by 14 works, notably *The Red Rock,* and Matisse by 11 paintings. The highlight of Rousseau's nine works displayed here is *The Wedding,* and the dozen paintings by Picasso reach the pinnacle of their brilliance in *The Female Bathers.* Other outstanding paintings are by Utrillo (10 works in all), Soutine (22), and Derain (28).

Jardin des Tuileries, 1er. ⟨🕐⟩ **01-44-77-80-07.** Admission 6.50€ ($8.45) adults, 4.50€ ($5.85) students younger than 26 years of age. Free first Sun of every month. Wed–Mon 12:30–7pm (until 9pm Fri). Métro: Concorde.

Musée des Arts Décoratifs   In the northwest wing of the Louvre's Pavillon de Marsan, this museum holds a treasury of furnishings, fabrics, wallpaper, objets d'art, and items displaying living styles from the Middle Ages to the present. Notable are the 1920s Art Deco boudoir, bath, and bedroom done for couturier Jeanne Lanvin by the designer Rateau, plus a collection of the works donated by Jean Dubuffet. Decorative art from the Middle Ages to the Renaissance is on the second floor; collections from the 17th, 18th, and 19th centuries occupy the third and fourth floors. The fifth floor has specialized centers, such as wallpaper and drawings, and exhibits detailing fashion, textiles, toys, crafts, and glass trends.

Palais du Louvre, 107 rue de Rivoli, 1er. ℂ 01-44-55-57-50. www.lesartsdecoratifs.fr. Admission 8€ ($10) adults, 6.50€ ($8.45) ages 18–25, free for children younger than 18. Tues–Fri 11am–6pm and Sat–Sun 10am–6pm. Métro: Palais-Royal or Tuileries.

Musée Jacquemart-André 𝒜𝒜   This is the finest museum of its type in Paris, the treasure trove of a couple devoted to 18th-century French paintings and furnishings, 17th-century Dutch and Flemish paintings, and Italian Renaissance works. Edouard André, the last scion of a family that made a fortune in banking and industry in the 19th century, spent most of his life as an army officer stationed abroad; he eventually returned to marry a well-known portraitist of government figures and the aristocracy, Nélie Jacquemart, and they went on to compile a collection of rare decorative art and paintings in this 1850s town house.

In 1912, Mme Jacquemart willed the house and its contents to the Institut de France, which paid for an extensive renovation and enlargement. The salons drip with gilt and are the ultimate in *fin-de-siècle* style. Works by Bellini, Carpaccio, Uccelo, Van Dyck, Rembrandt *(The Pilgrim of Emmaus),* Tiepolo, Rubens, Watteau, Boucher, Fragonard, and Mantegna are complemented by Houdon busts, Savonnerie carpets, Gobelin tapestries, Della Robbia terra cottas, and an awesome collection of antiques. The 18th-century Tiepolo frescoes of spectators on balconies viewing Henri III's 1574 arrival in Venice are outstanding.

Take a break with a cup of tea in Mme Jacquemart's high-ceilinged dining room, adorned with 18th-century tapestries. Salads, tarts, *tourtes* (pastries filled with meat or fruit), and Viennese pastries are served during museum hours.

158 bd. Haussmann, 8e. ℂ 01-45-62-11-59. www.musee-jacquemart-andre.com. Admission 9.50€ ($12) adults, 7€ ($9.10) children 7–17, free for children younger than 7. Daily 10am–6pm. Métro: Miromesnil or St-Philippe-du-Roule.

Musée Marmottan–Claude Monet 𝒜𝒜   In the past, an art historian or two would sometimes venture here to the edge of the Bois de Boulogne to see what Paul Marmottan had donated to the Académie des Beaux-Arts. Hardly anyone else did until 1966, when Claude Monet's son Michel died in a car crash, leaving a then–$10 million bequest of his father's art to the little museum. The Académie suddenly found itself with 130-plus paintings, watercolors, pastels, and drawings. Monet lovers could now trace the evolution of the great man's work in a single museum. The collection includes more than 30 paintings of Monet's house at Giverny and many of water lilies, his everlasting fancy, plus **Willow** (1918), **House of Parliament** (1905), and a **Renoir portrait** of the 32-year-old Monet. The museum had always owned Monet's **Impression: Sunrise** (1872), from which the Impressionist movement got its name. Paul Marmottan's original collection includes fig-leafed nudes, First Empire antiques, assorted objets d'art, Renaissance tapestries, bucolic paintings, and crystal chandeliers. You can also see countless miniatures donated by Daniel Waldenstein. The works of other Impressionists are also included, among them Degas, Manet, Pissarro, Renoir, Auguste Rodin, and Alfred Sisley.

2 rue Louis-Boilly, 16e. ℂ 01-44-96-50-33. www.marmottan.com. Admission 7€ ($9.10) adults, 4.50€ ($5.85) ages 8–24, free for children 7 and younger. Tues–Sun 10am–6pm. Métro: La Muette. RER: Bouilainvilliers, line C.

Musée National du Moyen Age/Thermes de Cluny (Musée de Cluny) ✿✿

Along with the Hôtel de Sens in the Marais, the Hôtel de Cluny is all that remains of domestic medieval architecture in Paris. Enter through the cobblestoned **Cour d'Honneur (Court of Honor),** where you can admire the flamboyant Gothic building with its vines, turreted walls, gargoyles, and dormers with seashell motifs. First, the Cluny was the mansion of a rich 15th-century abbot, built on top of/next to the ruins of a Roman bath (see below). By 1515, it was the residence of Mary Tudor, widow of Louis XII and daughter of Henry VII and Elizabeth of York. Seized during the Revolution, the Cluny was rented in 1833 to Alexandre du Sommerard, who adorned it with medieval artworks. After his death in 1842, the government bought the building and the collection.

This collection of medieval arts and crafts is superb. Most people come to see *The Lady and the Unicorn Tapestries* ✿✿✿, the most acclaimed tapestries of their kind. All the romance of the age of chivalry—a beautiful princess and her handmaiden, beasts of prey, and house pets—lives on in these remarkable yet mysterious tapestries discovered only a century ago in Limousin's Château de Boussac. Five seem to deal with the senses (one, for example, depicts a unicorn looking into a mirror held by a dour-faced maiden). The sixth shows a woman under an elaborate tent with jewels, her pet dog resting on an embroidered cushion beside her, with the lovable unicorn and his friendly companion, a lion, holding back the flaps. The background forms a rich carpet of spring flowers, fruit-laden trees, birds, rabbits, donkeys, dogs, goats, lambs, and monkeys.

The other exhibits range widely: Flemish retables; a 14th-century Sienese John the Baptist and other sculptures; statues from Sainte-Chapelle (1243–48); 12th- and 13th-century crosses, chalices, manuscripts, carvings, vestments, leatherwork, jewelry, and coins; a 13th-century Adam; and recently discovered heads and fragments of statues from Notre-Dame de Paris. In the fan-vaulted medieval chapel hang tapestries depicting scenes from the life of St. Stephen.

Downstairs are the ruins of the **Roman baths,** from around A.D. 200. The best-preserved section is seen in room X, the frigidarium (where one bathed in cold water). Once it measured 21×11m (69×36 ft.), rising to a height of 15m (49 ft.), with stone walls nearly 1.5m (5 ft.) thick. The ribbed vaulting here rests on consoles evoking ships' prows. Credit for this unusual motif goes to the builders of the baths, Paris's boatmen. During Tiberius's reign, a column to Jupiter was found beneath Notre-Dame's chancel and is now on view in the court; called the "Column of the Boatmen," it's believed to be the oldest sculpture created in Paris.

158 bd. Haussmann, 8e. ⓒ 01-45-62-11-59. www.musee-moyenage.fr. Admission 9.50€ ($12) adults, 7€ ($9.10) children 7–17, free for children younger than 7. Daily 10am–6pm. Métro: Miromesnil or St-Philippe-du-Roule.

Musée National Eugène Delacroix

This museum is for Delacroix groupies, among whom we include ourselves. If you want to see where he lived, worked, and died, this is worth at least an hour. Delacroix (1798–1863) is something of an enigma to art historians. Even his parentage is a mystery. Many believe Talleyrand was his father. One biographer saw him "as an isolated and atypical individualist—one who respected traditional values, yet emerged as the embodiment of Romantic revolt." Baudelaire called him "a volcanic crater artistically concealed beneath bouquets of flowers." The museum is on one of the Left Bank's most charming squares, with a romantic garden. A large arch on a courtyard leads to Delacroix's studio—no poor artist's studio, but the creation of a solidly established man. Sketches, lithographs, watercolors, and oils are hung throughout. If you want to see more of Delacroix's work, head to the Chapelle des Anges in St-Sulpice (p. 214).

6 place de Furstenberg, 6e. © 01-44-41-86-50. www.musee-delacroix.fr. Admission 5€ ($6.50) adults, free for children 17 and younger. Wed–Mon 9:30am–5pm. Métro: St-Germain-des-Prés, Mabillon.

Musée Picasso 𝄞𝄞 When it opened at the beautifully restored Hôtel Salé (Salt Mansion, built by a man who made his fortune by controlling the salt distribution in 17th-c. France) in the Marais, the press hailed it as a "museum for Picasso's Picassos," and that's what it is. The state acquired the world's greatest Picasso collection in lieu of his family's paying $50 million in inheritance taxes: 203 paintings, 158 sculptures, 16 collages, 19 bas-reliefs, 88 ceramics, and more than 1,500 sketches and 1,600 engravings, along with 30 notebooks. These works span some 75 years of the artist's life and ever-changing style.

The range of paintings includes a remarkable 1901 self-portrait; *The Crucifixion* and *Nude in a Red Armchair;* and *Le Baiser (The Kiss), Reclining Nude,* and *Man with a Guitar,* all painted at Mougins on the Riviera in 1969 and 1970. Stroll through the handsome museum and find your own favorite—perhaps the wicked *Jeune Garçon à la Langouste (Young Man with a Lobster),* painted in Paris in 1941. Several intriguing studies for *Les Demoiselles d'Avignon,* which shocked the establishment and launched cubism in 1907, are also on display. Because the collection is so vast, temporary exhibits featuring items such as his *Studies of the Minotaur* are held twice per year. Also here is Picasso's own treasure trove of art, with works by Cézanne, Rousseau, Braque, Derain, and Miró. Picasso was fascinated with African masks, many of which are on view.

In the Hôtel Salé, 5 rue de Thorigny, 3e. © 01-42-71-25-21. www.musee-picasso.fr. Admission 9.50€ ($12) adults, 7.50€ ($9.75) seniors and ages 18–25, free for children younger than 18. Apr–Sept Wed–Mon 9:30am–6pm; Oct–Mar Wed–Mon 9:30am–5:30pm. Closed Dec 25 and Jan 1. Métro: St-Paul, Filles du Calvaire, or Chemin Vert.

Musée Rodin 𝄞𝄞 Today Rodin is acclaimed as the father of modern sculpture, but in a different era, his work was labeled obscene. The world's artistic taste changed, and in due course, in 1911, the French government purchased Rodin's studio in this graystone 18th-century mansion in the Faubourg St-Germain. The government restored the rose gardens to their 18th-century splendor, making them a perfect setting for Rodin's most memorable works.

In the courtyard are three world-famous creations. Rodin's first major public commission, *The Burghers of Calais,* commemorated the heroism of six citizens of Calais who in 1347 offered themselves as a ransom to Edward III in return for ending his siege of their port. Perhaps the single best-known work, *The Thinker,* in Rodin's own words, "thinks with every muscle of his arms, back, and legs, with his clenched fist and gripping toes." Not completed when Rodin died, *The Gate of Hell,* as he put it, is "where I lived for a whole year in Dante's *Inferno.*"

Finds **Looking for a Quick Escape?**

The little alley behind the Musée Rodin winds its way down to a pond with fountains, flower beds, and even sand pits for children. It's one of the most idyllic hidden spots in Paris.

Inside, the sculpture, plaster casts, reproductions, originals, and sketches reveal the freshness and vitality of a remarkable artist. You can almost see his works emerging from marble into life. Everybody is attracted to *Le Baiser (The Kiss),* of which one critic wrote, "The passion is timeless." Upstairs are two versions of the celebrated and condemned *Nude of Balzac,* his bulky torso rising from a tree trunk (Albert E. Elsen commented on the "glorious bulging" stomach). Included are many versions of his *Monument to Balzac* (a large one stands in the garden), Rodin's last major work. Other significant sculptures are the soaring *Prodigal Son; The Crouching Woman* (the "embodiment of despair"); and *The Age of Bronze,* an 1876 study of a nude man modeled after a Belgian soldier. (Rodin was falsely accused of making a cast from a living model.) Generally overlooked is a room devoted to Rodin's mistress, Camille Claudel, a towering artist in her own right. She was his pupil, model, and lover, and created such works as *Maturity, Clotho,* and the recently donated *The Waltz* and *The Gossips.*

In the Hôtel Biron, 77 rue de Varenne, 7e. ℂ 01-44-18-61-10. www.musee-rodin.fr. Admission 6€ ($7.80) adults, 4€ ($5.20) ages 18–25, free for children younger than 18. Apr–Sept Tues–Sun 9:30am–5:45pm; Oct–Mar Tues–Sun 9:30am–4:45pm. Métro: Varenne, Invalides, or Saint-Francois-Xavier.

4 Specialty Museums

Be sure to turn to "The Top Attractions" and "The Major Museums," both earlier in this chapter, for the cream of the crop. "Especially for Kids," later in this chapter, includes museums that parents and kids alike will love. The museums below represent the curious, fascinating, and sometimes arcane balance of Paris's offerings.

ART & MUSIC MUSEUMS

Musée Bourdelle *(★ (Finds* Here you can see works by Rodin's star pupil, Antoine Bourdelle (1861–1929), who became a celebrated artist in his own right. Along with changing exhibitions, the museum permanently displays the artist's drawings, paintings, and sculptures, and lets you wander through his studio, garden, and house. The original plaster casts of some of his greatest works are on display, but what's most notable here are the 21 studies of Beethoven. Though some of the exhibits are poorly captioned, you'll still feel the impact of Bourdelle's genius.

16–18 rue Antoine-Bourdelle, 15e. ℂ 01-49-54-73-74. www.paris.fr/musees/bourdelle. Admission to the permanent collection 4.50€ ($5.85) adults, 3€ ($3.90) seniors, 2.20€ ($2.85) ages 14–25, free for children 13 and younger. Tues–Sun 10am–6pm. Métro: Montparnasse-Bienvenüe.

Musée Cognacq-Jay *(★* The founders of La Samaritaine department store, Ernest Cognacq and his wife, Louise Jay, were fabled for their exquisite taste. To see what they accumulated from around the world, head for this museum in the 16th-century Hôtel Denon, with its Louis XV and Louis XVI paneled rooms. Some of the 18th century's most valuable decorative works are exhibited, ranging from ceramics and porcelain to delicate cabinets and paintings by Canaletto, Fragonard, Greuze, Chardin, Boucher, Watteau, and Tiepolo.

In the Hôtel Donon, 8 rue Elzévir, 3e. ℂ 01-40-27-07-21. Free admission. Tues–Sun 10am–5:30pm. Métro: St-Paul.

Musée d'Art Moderne de la Ville de Paris & Musée des Enfants This museum bordering the Seine has a permanent collection of paintings and sculpture owned by the city, but come here only if visits to the d'Orsay and Louvre haven't satiated you. It presents ever-changing exhibits on individual artists from all over the world or on trends in international art. You'll find works by Chagall, Matisse, Léger, Rothko, Braque, Dufy, Picasso, Utrillo, and Modigliani. Seek out Pierre Tal Coat's *Portrait of Gertrude Stein,* and keep Picasso's version of this difficult subject in mind. The Musée des Enfants has exhibits and shows for children.

11 av. du Président-Wilson, 16e. ⓒ 01-53-67-40-00. www.mam.paris.fr. Free admission to general collections; temporary exhibition admission 5€–7€ ($6.50–$9.10). Tues–Sun 10am–6pm. Métro: Iéna or Alma-Marceau.

Musée de la Musique   In the $120-million stone-and-glass Cité de la Musique, this museum serves as a tribute and testament to music. You can view 4,500 instruments from the 16th century to the present, as well as paintings, engravings, and sculptures that relate to musical history. It's all here: cornets disguised as snakes, mandolins, lutes, zithers, music boxes, even an early electric guitar. Models of the world's great concert halls and interactive display areas give you a chance to hear and better understand musical art and technology.

In the Cité de la Musique, 221 av. Jean-Jaurès, 19e. ⓒ 01-44-84-44-84. www.cite-musique.fr. Admission 7€ ($9.10) adults, 5.60€ ($7.30) students 19–25, 3.50€ ($4.55) children younger than 19. Tues–Sat noon–6pm; Sun 10am–6pm. Métro: Porte de Pantin.

Musée Edith Piaf *Finds*   This privately run museum is filled with Piaf memorabilia such as photos, costumes, and personal possessions. The daughter of an acrobat, Giovanna Gassion grew up in this neighborhood and assumed the name of Piaf ("little sparrow"); her songs, like "La Vie en Rose" and "Non, Je Ne Regrette Rien," eventually were heard around the world. You must phone in advance for the security code you need to buzz your way in. Nearby is the **Villa Calte,** a beautiful example of the architecture many locals are trying to save (ask for directions at the Piaf museum). Fronted by an intricate wrought-iron fence, the house has a pleasant garden where parts of Truffaut's *Jules et Jim* were filmed.

5 rue Crespin-du-Gast, 11e. ⓒ 01-43-55-52-72. Free admission but donations appreciated. Mon–Wed 1–6pm and Thurs 9am–noon, through advance appointment only. Métro: Ménilmontant.

Musée National des Arts Asiatiques-Guimet 🌟🌟   This is one of the most beautiful Asian museums in the world, and it houses one of the world's finest collections of Asian art. Some 3,000 pieces of the museum's 45,000 works are on display. The Guimet, opened in Lyon but transferred to Paris in 1889, received the Musée Indochinois du Trocadéro's collections in 1931 and the Louvre's Asian collections after World War II. The most interesting exhibits are Buddhas, serpentine monster heads, funereal figurines, and antiquities from the temple of Angkor Wat. Some galleries are devoted to Tibetan art, including fascinating scenes of the Grand Lamas entwined with serpents and demons.

6 place d'Iéna, 16e. ⓒ 01-56-52-53-00. www.museeguimet.fr. Admission 6€–8€ ($7.80–$10). Free for ages 17 and younger. Wed–Mon 10am–6pm. Métro: Iéna.

Musée Nissim de Camondo 🌟   Visit this museum for a keen insight into the decorative arts of the 18th century. The pre–World War I town house was donated to the Musée des Arts Décoratifs by Comte Moïse de Camondo in memory of his son, Nissim, a French aviator killed in combat during World War I. The museum is like the home of an aristocrat—rich with needlepoint chairs, tapestries (many from Beauvais or Aubusson), antiques, paintings, bas-reliefs, silver, Chinese vases, crystal chandeliers, Sèvres porcelain, Savonnerie carpets, and even an Houdon bust. The Blue Salon, overlooking Parc Monceau, is most impressive. The kitchen of the original mansion has been reopened in its original form, capable of serving hundreds of dinner guests at one time, with few alterations from its original Belle Epoque origins. Fittings and many of the cooking vessels are in brass or copper, and the walls are tiled.

63 rue de Monceau, 8e. ⓒ **01-53-89-06-40.** www.lesartsdecoratifs.fr. Admission 6€ ($7.80) adults, 4.50€ ($5.85) ages 18–25, free for children 17 and younger. Wed–Sun 10am–5:30pm. Closed Jan 1, May 1, Bastille Day (July 14), and Dec 25. Métro: Villiers.

Musée Zadkine   This museum near the Jardin du Luxembourg was once the home of sculptor Ossip Zadkine (1890–1967), and his collection has been turned over to the city for public viewing. Included are some 300 pieces of sculpture, displayed in the museum and the garden. Some drawings and tapestries are also exhibited. At these headquarters, where he worked from 1928 until his death, you can see how he moved from "left wing" cubist extremism to a renewed appreciation of the classic era. You can visit his garden for free even if you don't want to go into the museum—in fact, it's one of the finest places to relax in Paris on a sunny day, sitting on a bench taking in the two-faced *Woman with the Bird.*

100 bis rue d'Assas, 6e. ⓒ **01-55-42-77-20.** www.zadkine.paris.fr. Free admission to permanent collections. Exhibition admission 4.50€ ($5.85) adults, 2€ ($2.60) for ages 26 and younger. Tues–Sun 10am–6pm. Métro: Notre-Dame des Champs or Vavin.

CRAFT & INDUSTRY MUSEUMS

Manufacture Nationale des Gobelins ⚑★   Did you know a single tapestry can take 4 years to complete, employing as many as three to five full-time weavers? The founder of this dynasty, Jehan Gobelin, came from a family of dyers and clothmakers; in the 15th century, he discovered a scarlet dye that made him famous. By 1601, Henri IV imported 200 weavers from Flanders to make tapestries full time. Until this endeavor, the Gobelin family hadn't made any tapestries. Colbert, Louis XIV's minister, bought the works, and under royal patronage the craftsmen set about executing designs by Le Brun. After the Revolution, the industry was reactivated by Napoleon. Today, Les Gobelins is a viable business entity, weaving tapestries for museums and historical restorations around the world. Throughout most of the week, the factories are closed to casual visitors, who are never allowed to wander at will. But if you'd like an insight into this medieval craft, you can participate, 3 days a week, in one of two guided tours, each lasting 90 minutes and each conducted in French. The tour guide will showcase the history of the enterprise and expose you to views of weavers and needlepoint artisans as they painstakingly ply their craft, patiently inserting stitch after laborious stitch, often while standing or seated behind huge screens of thread. If you don't speak French, pamphlets in English are distributed, each outlining the context of the lecture.

42 av. des Gobelins, 13e. ⓒ **01-44-54-19-33.** Tours in French (with English pamphlets) 8€ ($10) adults, 6€ ($7.80) ages 7–24, free for children younger than 7. Tues–Thurs 2 and 2:45pm. Métro: Gobelins.

Musée d'Art et Histoire du Judaisme ⚑★★   Security is tight, but it's worth the effort. In the Hôtel de St-Aignan, dating from the 1600s, this museum of Jewish history has been handsomely and impressively installed. The development of Jewish culture is traced not only in Paris, but also in France itself, as well as in Europe. Many of the exhibitions are devoted to religious subjects, including menorahs, Torah ornaments, and ark curtains, in both the Ashkenazi and Sephardic traditions. For us, the most interesting documents relate to the notorious Dreyfus case. Also on parade is a collection of illuminated manuscripts, Renaissance Torah arks, and paintings from the

18th and 19th centuries, along with Jewish gravestones from the Middle Ages. The best display is of the artwork by leading Jewish painters and artists ranging from Soutine to Zadkine, from Chagall to Modigliani.

Hôtel de St-Aignan, 71 rue du Temple, 3e. ℂ 01-53-01-86-60. www.mahj.org. Admission 9.50€ ($12) adults, 7€ ($9.10) ages 18–26, free for children younger than 18. Mon–Fri 11am–6pm; Sun 10am–6pm. Métro: Rambuteau.

Musée National de Céramique de Sèvres 𝒜𝒜   This museum boasts one of the world's finest collections of faience and porcelain, some of which belonged to Mme du Barry, Mme de Pompadour's successor as Louis XV's mistress (Mme de Pompadour *loved* Sèvres porcelain). On view is porcelain patterned with the Pompadour rose (which the English called the *rose du* Barry), a style much in vogue in the 1750s and 1760s. The painter Boucher made some of the designs used by the factory, as did the sculptor Pajou (he created the bas-reliefs for the Opéra at Versailles). The factory pioneered what became known as the *Louis Seize* (Louis XVI) style—it's all here, plus lots more, including works from Sèvres's archrival, Meissen. Technically, this attraction is not in Paris, but in an adjacent suburb (Sèvres) that's just across the bridge from the extreme western tip of the 15th Arrondissement. To get here, take the Métro to Pont de Sèvres; then walk westward across the bridge that spans the Seine.

Place de la Manufacture, 92310, Sèvres. ℂ 01-41-14-04-20. www.musee-ceramique-sevres.fr. Admission 4.50€ ($5.85) adults, 3€ ($4.20) ages 18–25, free for children 18 and younger. Druing special exhibitions both adults and ages 18–25 (who are also adults, of course) pay a supplement of 1.20 euros ($1.60) in addition to the regular admission cited above. Wed–Mon 10am–5pm. Métro: Pont de Sèvres.

HISTORY MUSEUMS

Musée de l'Histoire de France (Musée des Archives Nationales) 𝒜   The official home of the archives that reflect the convoluted history of France, this small but noteworthy palace was first built in 1371 as the **Hôtel de Clisson** and later acquired by the ducs de Guise, who figured prominently in France's bloody wars of religion. In 1705, most of it was demolished by the prince and princess de Soubise, through their architect, the much-underrated Delamair, and rebuilt with a baroque facade. The princesse de Soubise was once the mistress of Louis XIV, and apparently, the Sun King was very generous, giving her the funds to remodel and redesign the palace into one of the most beautiful buildings in the Marais. *Tip:* Before entering through the building's main entrance, the gracefully colonnaded Cour d'Honneur (Court of Honor), walk around the corner to 58 rue des Archives, where you'll see the few remaining vestiges—a turreted medieval gateway—of the original Hôtel de Clisson.

In the early 1800s, the site was designated by Napoleon as the repository for his archives, and it has served that function ever since. The archives contain documents that predate Charlemagne. But depending on the policies of the curator, only some of them are on display at any given moment, and usually as part of an ongoing series of temporary exhibitions that sometimes spill out into the **Hôtel de Rohan,** just around the corner on the rue Vieille du Temple.

Within these exhibitions, you're likely to see the facsimiles of the penmanship of Marie Antoinette in a farewell letter she composed just before her execution; Louis XVI's last will and testament; and documents from Danton, Robespierre, Napoleon I, and Joan of Arc. The archives have the only known sketch of the Maid of Orléans that was completed during her lifetime. Even the jailers' keys from the long-since-demolished Bastille are here. Despite the undeniable appeal of the documents it shelters, one of the most intriguing aspects of this museum involves the layout and decor of rooms that have changed very little since the 18th century. One of the finest is the **Salon de la Princesse** (aka the *Salon Ovale*), an oval room with sweeping expanses of gilt and crystal and a series of artfully executed ceiling frescoes by Van Loo, Boucher, and Natoire.

In the Hôtel de Soubise, 60 rue des Francs-Bourgeois, 3e. © **01-40-27-60-96**. Admission 3€ ($3.90) adults, 2.30€ ($3) ages 18–25, free for children younger than 18. Mon and Wed–Fri 10am–12:30pm and 2–5:30pm; Sat–Sun 2–5:30pm. Métro: Hôtel-de-Ville or Rambuteau.

Paris-Story *(Kids* This very touristy, 45-minute multimedia show retraces the city's history in a state-of-the-art theater. The 2,000 years since Paris's birth unroll to the music of such musicians as Wagner and Piaf. Maps, portraits, and scenes from dramatic times are projected on the large screen as a running commentary (heard through headphones in one of 13 languages) gives details about art, architecture, and events. Many visitors come here for a preview of what they want to see; others stop for an in-depth look at what they've already visited.

11 bis rue Scribe, 9e. © **01-42-66-62-06**. www.paris-story.com. Admission 10€ ($13) adults, 6€ ($7.80) students/younger than age 18. Children younger than 6 free. Daily 10am–6pm. Shows begin every hour on the hour. Métro: Opéra. RER: Auber.

THE OFFBEAT

Fragonard Musée du Parfum *(Finds* This perfume museum is in a 19th-century theater on one of Paris's busiest thoroughfares. As you enter the lobby through a courtyard, the scented air will remind you of why you're there—to appreciate perfume enough to buy a bottle in the ground-floor shop. But first, a short visit upstairs introduces you to the rudiments of perfume history. The copper containers with spouts and tubes were used in the distillation of perfume oils, and the exquisite collection of perfume bottles from the 17th century to the 20th century is impressive.

39 bd. des Capucines, 9e. © **01-42-60-37-14**. www.fragonard.com. Free admission. Mon–Sat 9am–6pm. Métro: Opéra.

Musée de l'Erotisme A tribute to the primal appeal of human sexuality, this art gallery/museum is in a 19th-century town house that had been a raunchy cabaret. It presents a tasteful but risqué collection of art and artifacts, with six floors boasting an array of exhibits like erotic sculptures and drawings. The oldest object is a palm-size Roman *tintinabulum* (bell), a phallus-shaped animal with the likeness of a nude woman riding astride it. Modern objects include resin, wood, and plaster sculptures by French artist Alain Rose and works by American, Dutch, German, and French artists. New for 2005 is a collection of erotic and satirical cartoons by well-known Dutch artist Willem. Also look for everyday items with erotic themes from South America (terra-cotta pipes shaped like phalluses) and the United States (a 1920s belt buckle that resembles a praying nun when it's fastened and a nude woman when it's open). The gift shop sells Asian amulets, African bronzes, and terra-cotta figurines from South America. There's also a gallery where serious works of art are sold.

72 bd. de Clichy, 18e. © **01-42-58-28-73**. www.musee-erotisme.com. Admission 8€ ($10) adults, children under 18 not permitted. Daily 10am–2am. Métro: Blanche.

Musée de l'Institut du Monde Arabe Many factors have contributed to France's preoccupation with the Arab world, but three of the most important include trade links that developed during the Crusades, a large Arab population living today in France, and the memories of France's lost colonies in North Africa. For insights into the way France has handled its relations with the Arab world, consider making a trek to this bastion of Arab intellect and aesthetics. Designed in 1987 by architect Jean Nouvel and funded by 22 different, mostly Arab countries, it includes expositions on calligraphy, decorative arts, architecture, and photography produced by the Arab/Islamic world, and insights into its religion, philosophy, and politics. There's a bookshop on-site, a replica of a Medina selling high-quality gift and art objects, and archival resources that are usually open only to bona-fide scholars. Views from the windows of the on-site Moroccan restaurant encompass Notre-Dame, l'Ile de la Cité, and Sacré-Coeur. Guided tours start at 3pm Tuesday to Friday or at 4:30pm on Saturday and Sunday.

1 rue des Fossés St-Bernard, 5e. ☏ 01-40-51-38-38. www.imarabe.org. Entrance to permanent exhibitions 5€ ($6.50) adults, 4€ ($5.20) students, free for children under 12. Entrance to temporary exhibits 8€–15€ ($10–$20) adults, 6€–11€ ($7.80–$14) students, free for children under 12. Tues–Sun 10am–6pm. Métro: Jussieu, Cardinal Lemoine, Sully-Morland.

Musée du Vin   This museum is in an ancient stone-and-clay quarry used by 15th-century monks as a wine cellar. It provides an introduction to the art of wine making, displaying various tools, beakers, cauldrons, and bottles in a series of exhibits. The quarry is right below Balzac's house (p. 219), and the ceiling contains a trap door he used to escape from his creditors.

5 rue des Eaux, 16e. ☏ 01-45-25-63-26. www.museeduvinparis.com. Admission 8.50€ ($11) adults, 7.50€ ($9.75) seniors, 7€ ($9.10) students and children. Tues–Sun 10am–6pm. Métro: Passy.

5 The Major Churches

Turn to "The Top Attractions," earlier in this chapter, for a full look at the **Cathédrale de Notre-Dame, Basilique du Sacré-Coeur,** and **Sainte-Chapelle.**

American Cathedral of the Holy Trinity   This cathedral is one of Europe's finest examples of Gothic Revival architecture and a center for the presentation of music and art. It was consecrated in 1886, and George Edmund Street, best known for the London Law Courts, created it. Aside from the architecture, you'll find remarkable pre-Raphaelite stained-glass windows illustrating the *Te Deum,* an early-15th-century triptych by an anonymous painter (probably a monk) known as the Roussillon Master; a needlepoint collection including kneelers depicting the 50 state flowers; and the 50 state flags in the nave. A **Memorial Cloister** commemorates Americans who died in Europe in World War I and all the victims of World War II. Documentation in several languages explains the highlights. The cathedral is also a center of worship, with a schedule of Sunday and weekday services in English. Les Arts George V, a cultural organization, presents reasonably priced choral concerts, lectures, and art shows.

23 av. George V, 8e. ☏ 01-53-23-84-00. Free admission. Mon–Fri 9am–5pm. Métro: Alma-Marceau or George V.

Basilique St-Denis 🕮🕮   In the 12th century, Abbot Suger placed an inscription on the bronze doors here: "Marvel not at the gold and expense, but at the craftsmanship of the work." France's first Gothic building that can be precisely dated, St-Denis was constructed between 1137 and 1281 and was the "spiritual defender of the State" during the reign of Louis VI ("The Fat"). The facade has a rose window and a crenellated parapet on the top similar to the fortifications of a castle. The stained-glass windows—in stunning mauve, purple, blue, and rose—were restored in the 19th century.

The first bishop of Paris, St. Denis became the patron saint of the monarchy, and royal burials began in the 6th century and continued until the Revolution. The sculpture designed for the **tombs**—some two stories high—spans French artistic

The Royal Heart of the Boy Who Would Be King

In a bizarre twist, following a mass in 2004, the heart of the 10-year-old heir to the French throne, Louis XVII, was laid to rest at **Saint-Denis Basilica**, 2 rue de Strasbourg, St.-Denis (✆ **01-48-09-83-54**), near the graves of his parents, Marie Antoinette and Louis XVI. The heart was pickled, stolen, returned, and, 2 centuries later, DNA tested. In ceremonies recognizing the royal heart, more than 2 centuries of rumor and legend surrounding the child's death were put to rest. Genetic testing has persuaded even the most cynical historians that the person who might have been the future Louis XVII never escaped prison. The boy died of tuberculosis in 1795, his body ravaged by tumors. The child's corpse was dumped into a common grave, but not before a doctor secretly carved out his heart and smuggled it out of prison in a handkerchief. The heart of the dead boy was compared with DNA of hair trimmed from Marie-Antoinette during her childhood in Austria. It was a perfect match.

development from the Middle Ages to the Renaissance. (There are guided tours in French of the Carolingian-era crypt.) François I was entombed at St-Denis, and his funeral statue is nude, though he demurely covers himself with his hand. Other kings and queens here include Louis XII and Anne de Bretagne, as well as Henri II and Catherine de Médicis. Revolutionaries stormed through the basilica during the Terror, smashing many marble faces and dumping royal remains in a lime-filled ditch in the garden. (These remains were reburied under the main altar during the 19th c.) Free organ concerts are given on Sundays at 11:15am.

Place de l'Hôtel-de-Ville, 2 rue de Strasbourg, St-Denis. ✆ **01-48-09-83-54**. Admission 6.50€ ($8.45) adults and 4.50€ ($5.85) seniors and students 18–25, free for children under 18. Apr–Sept Mon–Sat 10am–6:15pm, Sun noon–6:15pm; Oct–Mar Mon–Sat 10am–5:15pm, Sun noon–5:15pm. Closed Jan 1, May 1, Dec 25. Métro: St-Denis.

La Grande Mosquée de Paris ✦   This beautiful pink marble mosque was built in 1922 to honor the North African countries that had given aid to France during World War I. Today, North Africans living in Paris gather on Friday, the Muslim holy day, and during Ramadan to pray to Allah. Short tours are given of the building, its central courtyard, and its Moorish garden; guides present a brief history of the Islamic faith. However, you may want to just wander around on your own and then join the students from nearby universities for couscous and sweet mint tea at the Muslim **Restaurant de la Mosquée de Paris** (✆ **01-43-31-18-14**), adjoining the grounds, open daily from noon to 3pm and 7 to 10:30pm.

2 place du Puits-de-l'Ermite, 5e. ✆ **01-45-35-97-33**. www.mosquee-de-paris.net. Admission 2€ ($2.60), free for children under 8. Sat–Thurs 9am–noon and 2–6pm. Métro: Place Monge.

La Madeleine ✦✦   La Madeleine is one of Paris's minor landmarks, dominating rue Royale, which culminates in place de la Concorde. Though construction began in 1806, it wasn't consecrated until 1842. Resembling a Roman temple, the building was intended as a monument to the glory of the Grande Armée (Napoleon's idea, of course). Later, several alternative uses were considered: the National Assembly, the Bourse, and the National Library. Climb the 28 steps to the facade, and look back: You'll be able to see rue Royale, place de la Concorde and its obelisk, and (across the Seine) the dome of the Hôtel des Invalides. Don't miss Rude's *Le Baptême du Christ,* to the left as you enter.

Place de la Madeleine, 8e. ℂ 01-42-65-52-17. www.eglise-lamadeleine.com. Free admission. Mon–Sat 9am–7pm, Sun 8am–1:30pm and 3:30–7pm. Métro: Madeleine.

St-Etienne-du-Mont 𝓻𝓻 Once there was an abbey here, founded by Clovis and later dedicated to St. Geneviève, the patroness of Paris. Such was the fame of this popular saint that the abbey proved too small to accommodate the pilgrimage crowds. Now part of the Lycée Henri IV, the Tour de Clovis (Tower of Clovis) is all that remains of the ancient abbey—you can see the tower from rue Clovis. Today, the task of keeping St. Geneviève's cult alive has fallen on this church, practically adjoining the Panthéon. The interior is Gothic, an unusual style for a 16th-century church. Building began in 1492 and was plagued by delays until the church was finally finished in 1626.

Besides the patroness of Paris, such men as Pascal and Racine were entombed here. Because of the destruction of church records during the French Revolution, church officials aren't sure of the exact locations in which they're buried. St. Geneviève's tomb was destroyed during the Revolution, but the stone on which her coffin rested was discovered later, and her relics were gathered for a place of honor at St-Etienne. The church possesses a remarkable early-16th-century **rood screen:** Crossing the nave, it's unique in Paris—called spurious by some and a masterpiece by others. Another treasure is a wood **pulpit,** held up by Samson, clutching a bone in one hand, with a slain lion at his feet. The fourth chapel on the right when you enter contains impressive 16th-century stained glass.

1 place St-Geneviève, 5e. ℂ 01-43-54-11-79. Free admission. With the exception of some of France's school holidays, when hours may vary slightly, the church is open year-round as follows: Mon noon–7:30pm; Tues–Fri 8:45am–7:30pm; Sat 8:45am–noon and 2–7:45pm; and Sun 8:45am–12:15pm and 2:30–7:45pm. Métro: Cardinal Lemoine or Luxembourg.

St-Eustache 𝓻𝓻 This Gothic and Renaissance church completed in 1637 is rivaled only by Notre-Dame. Mme de Pompadour and Richelieu were baptized here, and Molière's funeral was held here in 1673. The church has been known for organ recitals ever since Liszt played in 1866. Inside rests the **black-marble tomb** of Jean-Baptiste Colbert, the minister of state under Louis XIV; atop the tomb is his marble effigy flanked by statues of *Abundance* by Coysevox and *Fidelity* by Tuby. The church's most famous painting is Rembrandt's *The Pilgrimage to Emmaus.* There's a side entrance on rue Rambuteau.

2 rue du Jour, 1er. ℂ 01-42-36-31-05. www.st-eustache.org. Free admission. Daily 9:30am–7pm. Sun Mass 9:30am, 11am, and 6pm; Sun organ recitals 5:30pm. Métro: Les Halles.

St-Germain-des-Prés It's one of Paris's oldest churches, from the 6th century, when a Benedictine abbey was founded here by Childebert, son of Clovis. Alas, the marble columns in the triforium are all that remain from that period. The Normans nearly destroyed the abbey at least four times. The present building has a Romanesque

---

Moments **Gregorians Unplugged**

St-Germain-des-Prés stages wonderful concerts on the Left Bank; it boasts fantastic acoustics and a marvelous medieval atmosphere. The church was built to accommodate an age without microphones, and the sound effects will thrill you. For more information, call ℂ 01-55-42-81-33. Arrive about 45 minutes before the performance if you'd like a front-row seat. Tickets are 15€ to 50€ ($20–$65).

nave and a Gothic choir with fine capitals. At one time, the abbey was a pantheon for Merovingian kings. Restoration of the site of their tombs, **Chapelle de St-Symphorien,** began in 1981, and unknown Romanesque paintings were discovered on the triumphal arch. Among the others interred here are Descartes (his heart, at least) and Jean-Casimir, the king of Poland who abdicated his throne. The Romanesque tower, topped by a 19th-century spire, is the most enduring landmark in St-Germain-des-Prés. Its church bells, however, are hardly noticed by the patrons of Les Deux Magots across the way.

When you leave the church, turn right on rue de l'Abbaye and have a look at the 17th-century pink **Palais Abbatial.**

3 place St-Germain-des-Prés, 6e. ℂ 01-55-42-81-33. www.eglise-sgp.org. Free admission. Mon–Sat 8am–7:45pm; Sun 9am–8pm. Métro: St-Germain-des-Prés.

St-Germain l'Auxerrois   Once it was the church for the Palais du Louvre, drawing an assortment of royalty, courtesans, men of art and law, and local artisans. Sharing place du Louvre with Perrault's colonnade, the church contains only the foundation stones of its original 11th-century belfry. The chapel that had stood here was greatly enlarged in the 14th century by the addition of side aisles and became a beautiful church, with 77 sq. m (829 sq. ft.) of stained glass, including some rose windows from the Renaissance. The intricately carved **church-wardens' pews** are outstanding, based on 17th-century Le Brun designs. Behind them is a **15th-century triptych** and **Flemish retable,** so poorly lit you can hardly appreciate it. The organ was ordered by Louis XVI for Sainte-Chapelle. Many famous men were entombed here, including the sculptor Coysevox and the architect Le Vau. Around the chancel is an intricate **18th-century grille.**

The saddest moment in the church's history was on August 24, 1572, the evening of the St. Bartholomew Massacre. The tower bells rang, signaling the supporters of Catherine de Médicis, Marguerite de Guise, Charles IX, and the future Henri III to launch a slaughter of thousands of Huguenots, who'd been invited to celebrate the marriage of Henri de Navarre to Marguerite de Valois.

2 place du Louvre, 1er. ℂ 01-42-60-13-96. Free admission. Daily 8am–7pm. Métro: Louvre-Rivoli.

St-Sulpice   Pause first outside St-Sulpice. The 1844 fountain by Visconti displays the sculpted likenesses of four bishops of the Louis XIV era: Fenelon, Massillon, Bossuet, and Flechier. Work on the church, at one time Paris's largest, began in 1646. Though laborers built the body by 1745, work on the bell towers continued until 1780, when one was finished and the other left incomplete. One of the priceless treasures inside is Servandoni's rococo **Chapelle de la Madone (Chapel of the Madonna),** with a Pigalle statue of the Virgin. The church has one of the world's largest organs, comprising 6,700 pipes; it has been played by musicians like Marcel Dupré and Charles-Mari Widor.

The real reason to come here is to see the Delacroix frescoes in the **Chapelle des Anges (Chapel of the Angels),** the first on your right as you enter. Look for his muscular Jacob wrestling (or dancing?) with an effete angel. On the ceiling, St. Michael is having some troubles with the Devil, and yet another mural depicts Heliodorus being driven from the temple. Painted in Delacroix's final years, the frescoes were a high point in his baffling career. If these impress you, pay the painter tribute by visiting the Musée Delacroix (see "The Major Museums," earlier).

Rue St-Sulpice, 6e. ℂ 01-46-33-21-78. Free admission. Daily 7:30am–7:30pm. Métro: St-Sulpice.

Val-de-Grâce 🏛🏛   According to an old proverb, to understand the French you must like Camembert cheese, the pont Neuf, and the dome of Val-de-Grâce. Its origins go back to 1050, when a Benedictine monastery was built here. In 1619, Louis XIII appointed as abbess Marguerite Veni d'Arbouze, who asked Louis's wife, Anne of Austria, for a new monastery. After 23 years of a childless marriage, Anne gave birth to a boy who went on to be known as the Sun King. To express his gratitude, Louis XIII approved the rebuilding of the church, and at the age of 7, on April 1, 1645, the future Louis XIV laid Val-de-Grâce's first stone. Mansart was the main architect, and to him we owe the facade in the Jesuit style. Le Duc, however, designed the dome, and Mignard added the frescoes. Le Mercier and Le Muet also had a hand in the church's fashioning. The church was turned into a military hospital in 1793 and an army school in 1850.

1 place Alphonse-Laveran, 5e. ℂ 01-40-51-47-28. Admission 5€ ($6.50) adults, 2.50€ ($3.25) children and students, free for children under 6. Tues–Wed noon–6pm; Sat–Sun 1:30–5pm. Métro: Port Royal.

6 Architectural & Historic Highlights

Arènes de Lutèce   Discovered and partially destroyed in 1869, this amphitheater is Paris's most important Roman ruin after the baths in the Musée de Cluny (p. 204). Today, the site is home to a small arena, not as grand as the original, and gardens. You may feel as if you've discovered a private spot in the heart of the city, but don't be fooled. Your solitude is sure to be interrupted, if not by groups of students playing soccer, then by parents pushing strollers down the paths. This is an ideal spot for a picnic; bring a bottle of wine and baguettes to enjoy in this vestige of the ancient city of Lutétia.

At rues Monge and Navarre, 5e. No phone. Free admission. Mon–Fri 8am–9pm; Sat–Sun 9am–9pm. Métro: Jussieu.

Bibliothèque Nationale de France, Site Tolbiac/François Mitterrand   The French National Library opened in 1996 with a futuristic design by Dominique Perrault (a quartet of 24-story towers evoking the look of open books); this is the last of the *grand projets* of the late François Mitterrand. It boasts the same grandiose scale as the Cité de la Musique and houses the nation's literary and historic archives; it's regarded as a repository of the French soul, replacing outmoded facilities on rue des Archives. The library incorporates space for 1,600 readers at a time, many of whom enjoy views over two levels of a garden-style courtyard that seems far removed from Paris's urban congestion.

This is one of Europe's most user-friendly academic facilities, emphasizing computerized documentation and microfiche—a role model that will set academic and literary priorities well into the future. The public has access to as many as 180,000 books, plus thousands of periodicals, with an additional 10 million historic (including medieval) documents available to qualified experts. Though the appeal of this place extends mainly to serious scholars, a handful of special exhibits might interest you, as well as concerts and lectures. Concert tickets rarely exceed 15€ ($20) for adults and 10€ ($13) for students, seniors, and children; a schedule is available at the library.

Quai François-Mauriac, 13e. ℂ 01-53-79-59-59. www.bnf.fr. Admission 3.30€ ($4.30). No one under 16 admitted. Mon 2–8pm; Tues–Sat 10am–8pm; Sun 1–7pm. Closed Sept 6–19. Métro: Bibliothèque François-Mitterrand.

Conciergerie 🏛🏛   London has its Bloody Tower, and Paris has its Conciergerie. Even though the Conciergerie had a long regal history before the Revolution, it was forever stained by the Reign of Terror and lives as an infamous symbol of the time when carts pulled up constantly to haul off fresh supplies of victims for Dr. Guillotin's wonderful little invention.

Much of the Conciergerie was built in the 14th century as an extension of the Capetian royal Palais de la Cité. You approach through its landmark twin towers, the **Tour d'Argent** (where the crown jewels were stored at one time) and **Tour de César,** but the **Salle des Gardes (Guard Room)** is the actual entrance. Even more interesting is the dark and foreboding Gothic **Salle des Gens d'Armes (Room of People at Arms),** utterly changed from the days when the king used it as a banquet hall. However, architecture plays a secondary role to the list of prisoners who spent their last days here. Few in its history endured tortures as severe as those imposed on Ravaillac, who assassinated Henri IV in 1610. In the Tour de César, he received pincers in the flesh and had hot lead and boiling oil poured on him like bath water before being executed (see the Hôtel de Ville entry below). During the Revolution, the Conciergerie became a symbol of terror to the nobility and enemies of the State. A short walk away, the Revolutionary Tribunal dispensed a skewed, hurried justice—if it's any consolation, the jurists didn't believe in torturing their victims, only in decapitating them.

After being seized by a crowd of peasants who stormed Versailles, Louis XVI and Marie Antoinette were brought here to await their trials. In failing health and shocked beyond grief, *l'Autrichienne* ("the Austrian," as she was called with malice) had only a small screen (sometimes not even that) to protect her modesty from the gaze of guards stationed in her cell. By accounts of the day, she was shy and stupid, though the evidence is that on her death, she displayed the nobility of a true queen. (What's more, the famous "Let them eat cake," which she supposedly uttered when told the peasants had no bread, is probably apocryphal—besides, at the time, cake flour was less expensive than bread flour, so even if she said this, it wasn't meant coldheartedly.) It was shortly before noon on the morning of October 16, 1793, when the executioners arrived, grabbing her and cutting her hair, as was the custom for victims marked for the guillotine.

Later, the Conciergerie housed other prisoners, including Mme Elisabeth; Mme du Barry, mistress of Louis XV; Mme Roland ("O Liberty! Liberty! What crimes are committed in thy name!"); and Charlotte Corday, who killed Marat while he was taking a sulfur bath. In time, the Revolution consumed its own leaders, such as Danton and Robespierre. Finally, one of Paris's most hated men, public prosecutor Fouquier-Tinville, faced the guillotine to which he'd sent so many others. Among the few interned here who lived to tell the tale was American Thomas Paine, who reminisced about his chats in English with Danton.

1 quai de l'Horloge, 4e. ☏ **01-53-40-60-93.** www.monum.fr. Admission 6.50€ ($8.45) adults, 4.50€ ($5.85) ages 18–25, free for children under 18. Daily 9:30am–6pm. Métro: Cité, Châtelet, or St-Michel. RER: St-Michel.

Hôtel de Ville ☼ On a large square with fountains and early-1900s lampposts, the 19th-century Hôtel de Ville isn't a hotel, but Paris's grandiose City Hall. The medieval structure it replaced had witnessed countless municipally ordered executions. Henri IV's assassin, Ravaillac, was quartered alive on the square in 1610, his body tied to four horses that bolted in opposite directions. On May 24, 1871, the Communards doused the City Hall with petrol, creating a blaze that lasted for 8 days. The Third Republic ordered the structure rebuilt, with many changes, even creating a Hall of Mirrors evocative of that at Versailles. For security reasons, the major splendor of this building is closed to the public. However, the information center sponsors exhibits on Paris in the main lobby.

29 rue de Rivoli, 4e. (✆) **01-42-76-43-43**. Free admission. Information center Mon–Sat 10am–6pm. Métro: Hôtel de Ville.

Institut de France ⟨✦⟩ Designed by Louis Le Vau, this dramatic baroque building with an enormous cupola is the seat of all five academies that dominate France's intellectual life—Française, Sciences, Inscriptions et Belles Lettres, Beaux Arts, and Sciences Morales et Politiques. The members of the Académie Française (limited to 40), guardians of the French language referred to as "the immortals," gather here. Many are unfamiliar figures (though Jacques Cousteau and Marshall Pétain were members), and the academy is remarkable for the great writers and philosophers who have *not* been invited to join—Balzac, Baudelaire, Diderot, Flaubert, Descartes, Proust, Molière, Pascal, Rousseau, and Zola, to name only a few. The cenotaph was designed by Coysevox for Mazarin.

23 quai de Conti, 6e. (✆) **01-44-41-44-41**. www.institut-de-france.fr. Free admission (guests can walk into courtyard only). Guided tours Sat–Sun. Métro: Louvre-Rivoli.

La Grande Arche de La Défense ⟨✦⟩ Designed as the architectural centerpiece of the sprawling satellite suburb of La Défense, outside the 16th Arrondissement, this massive steel-and-masonry arch rises 35 stories. It was built with the blessing of the late François Mitterrand and extends the magnificently engineered straight line linking the Louvre, Arc de Triomphe du Carrousel, Champs-Elysées, Arc de Triomphe, avenue de la Grande Armée, and place du Porte Maillot. The arch is ringed with a circular avenue patterned after the one around the Arc de Triomphe. The monument is tall enough to shelter Notre-Dame beneath its heavily trussed canopy. An elevator carries you up to an observation platform, where you get a view of the carefully planned geometry of the surrounding streets.

You'll notice nets rigged along the Grande Arche. When pieces of Mitterrand's *grand projet* started falling to the ground, they were erected to catch the falling fragments. If only such protection existed for all politicians' follies!

1 place du parvis de La Défense, Puteaux. (✆) **01-49-07-27-57**. Admission 7.50€ ($9.75) for adults, 6€ ($7.80) ages 6–25, free 5 and younger. Daily 10am–7pm (until 8pm Apr–Sept). Métro: Grande Arche de la Défense.

Palais Bourbon/Assemblée Nationale ⟨✦⟩ The French parliament's lower house, the Chamber of Deputies, meets at this 1722 mansion built by the duchesse de Bourbon, a daughter of Louis XIV. You can make reservations for one of two types of visits as early as 6 months in advance. Tours on art, architecture, and basic French government processes are given Monday, Friday, and Saturday. They're in French (in English with advance booking). You may also observe sessions of the National Assembly, held Tuesday afternoon and all day Wednesday and Thursday beginning at 9:30am. Remember, this is a working government building, and all visitors are subject to rigorous security checks.

33 quai d'Orsay, 7e. (✆) **01-40-63-64-08**. www.assemblee-nationale.fr. Free admission. Hours vary, so call ahead. Métro: Assemblée Nationale.

Palais Royal ⟨✦✦⟩ The Palais Royal was originally known as the Palais Cardinal, for it was the residence of Cardinal Richelieu, Louis XIII's prime minister. Richelieu had it built, and after his death it was inherited by the king, who died soon after. Louis

XIV spent part of his childhood here with his mother, Anne of Austria, but later resided at the Louvre and Versailles. The palace was later owned by the duc de Chartres et Orléans (see the entry for Parc Monceau under "Parks & Gardens"), who encouraged the opening of cafes, gambling dens, and other public entertainment. Though government offices occupy the Palais Royal and are not open to the public, do visit the **Jardin du Palais Royal,** an enclosure bordered by arcades. Don't miss the main courtyard, with the controversial 1986 Buren sculpture—280 prison-striped columns, oddly placed.

Rue St-Honoré, 1er. No phone. Free admission. Métro: Palais Royal–Musée du Louvre.

Panthéon 𝕽𝕽   Some of the most famous men in French history (Victor Hugo, for one) are buried here on the crest of the mount of St. Geneviève. In 1744, Louis XV vowed that if he recovered from a mysterious illness, he'd build a church to replace the Abbaye de St. Geneviève. He recovered but took his time fulfilling his promise. It wasn't until 1764 that Mme de Pompadour's brother hired Soufflot to design a church in the form of a Greek cross with a dome reminiscent of St. Paul's in London. When Soufflot died, his pupil Rondelet carried out the work, completing the structure 9 years after his master's death.

After the Revolution, the church was converted to a "Temple of Fame" and became a pantheon for the great men of France. Mirabeau was buried here, though his remains were later removed. Likewise, Marat was only a temporary tenant. Voltaire's body was exhumed and placed here—and allowed to remain. In the 19th century, the building changed roles so many times—a church, a pantheon, a church again—that it was hard to keep its function straight. After Hugo was buried here, it became a pantheon once again. Other notable men entombed within are Rousseau, Soufflot, Zola, and Braille. Only one woman has so far been deemed worthy of placement here: Marie Curie, who joined her husband, Pierre. Most recently, the ashes of André Malraux were transferred to the Panthéon because, according to President Jacques Chirac, he "lived [his] dreams and made them live in us." As Charles de Gaulle's culture minister, Malraux decreed the arts should be part of the lives of all French people, not just Paris's elite.

Before entering the crypt, note the striking frescoes: On the right wall are scenes from Geneviève's life, and on the left is the saint with a white-draped head looking out over medieval Paris, the city whose patron she became, as well as Geneviève relieving victims of famine with supplies.

Place du Panthéon, 5e. ℂ 01-44-32-18-00. www.monum.fr. Admission 7.50€ ($9.75) adults, 4.80€ ($6.25) ages 18–25, free for children under 18. Apr–Sept daily 10am–6:30pm; Oct–Mar daily 10am–6pm (last entrance 45 min. before closing). Métro: Cardinal Lemoine or Maubert-Mutualité.

7 Literary Landmarks

If there's a literary bone in your body, you'll feel a vicarious thrill on discovering the haunts of the writers and artists who've lived, worked, and played in Paris.

Take the Métro to place St-Michel to begin your tour. As you wander away from the Seine, you'll encounter **rue de la Huchette,** one of the Left Bank's most famous streets. Its inhabitants were immortalized in Eliot Paul's *The Last Time I Saw Paris.* Continuing on, you'll enter the territory of the Beat Generation, home to the **Café Gentilhomme** (no longer there) described by Jack Kerouac in *Satori in Paris.* Allen Ginsberg's favorite, the **Hôtel du Vieux-Paris,** 9 rue Gît-le-Coeur, 6e, still attracts those in search of the Beats.

Stroll down **rue Monsieur-le-Prince,** the "Yankee alleyway," where Richard Wright, James McNeill Whistler, Henry Wadsworth Longfellow, and Oliver Wendell Holmes lived at one time or another. During a visit in 1959, Martin Luther King, Jr., came to call on Richard Wright, the Mississippi-born African-American novelist famous for *Native Son.* King climbed to the third-floor apartment at **no. 14** to find that Wright's opinions on the civil rights movement conflicted with his own. Whistler rented a studio at **no. 22,** and in 1826, Longfellow lived at **no. 49.** Oliver Wendell Holmes, Sr., lived at **no. 55.** After strolling along this street, you can dine at the haunts of Kerouac and Hemingway. (See our recommendation of **Crémerie-Restaurant Polidor,** 41 rue Monsieur-le-Prince, 6e, on p. 165.) Or cross back over to the Right Bank for a drink at the famed **Hôtel de Crillon,** 10 place de la Concorde, 8e (p. 219), where heroine Brett Ashley broke her promise to rendezvous with Jake Barnes in Hemingway's *The Sun Also Rises.* Zelda and F. Scott Fitzgerald lifted their glasses here as well.

For details on **Harry's New York Bar,** 5 rue Daunou, 2e, see section 5, "Literary Haunts" in chapter 11. For a description of **Les Deux Magots, Le Procope,** and **La Rotonde,** see section 6, "The Top Cafes" in chapter 7. For coverage of the bookstore **Shakespeare and Company,** see section 2, "Shopping A to Z," in chapter 10.

Here are two great museums for hard-core literary fans:

Maison de Balzac   In the residential district of Passy, near the Bois de Boulogne, sits this modest house with a courtyard and garden. Honoré de Balzac fled to this house in 1840, after his possessions and furnishings were seized, and lived here for 7 years (to see him, you had to know a password). If a creditor knocked on the rue Raynouard door, Balzac was able to escape through the rue Berton exit. The museum's most notable memento is Balzac's "screech-owl" (his nickname for his tea kettle), which he kept hot throughout the night as he wrote *La Comédie Humaine.* Also enshrined are Balzac's writing desk and chair, and a library of special interest to scholars. The little house is filled with caricatures of Balzac. A biographer once wrote: "With his bulky baboon silhouette, his blue suit with gold buttons, his famous cane like a golden crowbar, and his abundant, disheveled hair, Balzac was a sight for caricature."

47 rue Raynouard, 16e. ① **01-55-74-41-80.** www.paris.fr/musees/balzac. Admission free for permanent collection. Exhibition admission 4€ ($5.20) adults, 3€ ($3.90) seniors, 2€ ($2.60) 14–26, free for children 13 and under. Tues–Sun 10am–6pm. Métro: Passy or La Muette.

Maison de Victor Hugo ⓐ   Today, theatergoers who've seen *Les Misérables,* even those who haven't read anything by Paris's 19th-century novelist, come to place des Vosges to see where Hugo lived and wrote. Some thought him a genius, but Cocteau called him a madman, and an American composer discovered that in his old age, he was carving furniture with his teeth! From 1832 to 1848, the novelist/poet lived on the second floor of the Hôtel Rohan Guéménée. The museum owns some of Hugo's furniture, as well as pieces that once belonged to Juliette Drouet, the mistress with whom he lived in exile on Guernsey, one of the Channel Islands.

Worth the visit are Hugo's drawings, more than 450, illustrating scenes from his own works. Mementos of the great writer abound, including samples of his handwriting, his inkwell, and first editions of his works. A painting of Hugo's 1885 funeral procession at the Arc de Triomphe is on display, as are many portraits and souvenirs of his family. Of the furnishings, a chinoiserie salon stands out. The collection even contains Daumier caricatures and a bust of Hugo by David d'Angers, which, compared with Rodin's, looks saccharine.

6 place des Vosges, 4e. ℂ **01-42-72-10-16.** www.musee-hugo.paris.fr. Free admission. Tues–Sun 10am–6pm. Métro: St-Paul, Bastille, or Chemin-Vert.

8 Parks & Gardens

JARDIN DES TUILERIES

The spectacular statue-studded **Jardin des Tuileries** ✴✴, bordering place de la Concorde, 1er (ℂ **01-40-20-90-43;** Métro: Tuileries or Concorde), is as much a part of Paris as the Seine. Le Nôtre, Louis XIV's gardener and planner of the Versailles grounds, designed the gardens. Some of the gardens' most distinctive statues are the 18 enormous bronzes by Maillol, installed within the **Jardin du Carrousel,** a subdivision of the Jardin des Tuileries, between 1964 and 1965, under the direction of Culture Minister André Malraux.

About 100 years before that, Catherine de Médicis ordered a palace built here, the **Palais des Tuileries;** other occupants have included Louis XVI (after he left Versailles) and Napoleon. Twice attacked by Parisians, it was burned to the ground in 1871 and never rebuilt. The gardens, however, remain. In orderly French manner, the trees are arranged according to designs, and even the paths are arrow-straight. Bubbling fountains break the sense of order and formality.

JARDIN DU LUXEMBOURG

Hemingway once told a friend that the **Jardin du Luxembourg** ✴✴, in the 6th Arrondissement (Métro: Odéon; RER: Luxembourg), "kept us from starvation." He related that in his poverty-stricken days in Paris, he wheeled a baby carriage (the vehicle was considered luxurious) through the garden because it was known "for the classiness of its pigeons." When the gendarme went across the street for a glass of wine, the writer would eye his victim, preferably a plump one; lure him with corn; "snatch him, wring his neck"; and hide him under the blanket. "We got a little tired of pigeons that year," he confessed, "but they filled many a void."

The Luxembourg has always been associated with artists, though children, students, and tourists predominate nowadays. Watteau came this way, as did Verlaine. Balzac didn't like the gardens at all. In 1905, Gertrude Stein would cross them to catch the Batignolles/Clichy/Odéon omnibus, pulled by three gray mares, to meet Picasso in his studio at Montmartre, where he painted her portrait.

Marie de Médicis, the wife of Henri IV, ordered the **Palais du Luxembourg** built on this site in 1612, shortly after she was widowed. A Florentine by birth, the regent wanted to create another Pitti Palace, where she could live with her "witch" friend, Leonora Galigal. Architect Salomon de Brossee wasn't entirely successful, though the overall effect is Italianate. Alas, the queen didn't get to enjoy the palace, as her son, Louis XIII, forced her into exile when he discovered she was plotting to overthrow him. She died in poverty in Cologne. For her palace, she'd commissioned 21 paintings from Rubens, which glorified her life, but they're now in the Louvre. You can visit the palace Monday, Friday and Saturday from 10:30am to 2:30pm, but you must call ℂ **01-44-54-19-49** to make a reservation. The cost is 10€ ($13) per person.

You don't really come to the Luxembourg to visit the palace; the gardens are the attraction. For the most part, they're in the classic French tradition: well groomed and formally laid out, the trees planted in patterns. Urns and statuary on pedestals—one honoring Paris's patroness, St. Geneviève, with pigtails reaching to her thighs—encircle a central water basin. Kids can sail a toy boat, ride a pony, or attend an occasional

Grand Guignol puppet show. And you can play *boules* (lawn bowling) with a group of elderly men who wear black berets and have Gauloises dangling from their mouths.

One of the most spectacular parks in Europe is the **Bois de Boulogne** ✲✲, Porte Dauphine, 16e (𝄞 **01-40-67-90-82;** Métro: Les Sablons, Porte Maillot, or Porte Dauphine), often called the "main lung" of Paris. Horse-drawn carriages traverse it, but you can also drive through. You can discover its hidden pathways, however, only by walking. You could spend days in the Bois de Boulogne and still not see everything.

Porte Dauphine is the main entrance, though you can take the Métro to Porte Maillot as well. West of Paris, the park was once a forest kept for royal hunts. It was in vogue in the late 19th century: Along avenue Foch, carriages with elegantly attired and coiffured Parisian damsels would rumble along with their foppish escorts. Nowadays, it's more likely to attract run-of-the-mill picnickers. (Be careful at night, when hookers and muggers proliferate.)

When Napoleon III gave the grounds to the city in 1852, they were developed by Baron Haussmann. Separating Lac Inférieur from Lac Supérieur is the **Carrefour des Cascades** ✲ (you can stroll under its waterfall). The Lower Lake contains two islands connected by a footbridge. From the east bank, you can take a boat to these idyllically situated grounds, perhaps stopping off at the cafe/restaurant on one of them.

Restaurants in the bois are numerous, elegant, and expensive. The **Pré Catelan** ✲ contains a deluxe restaurant of the same name (𝄞 **01-44-14-41-14**), occupying a gem of a Napoleon III–style château, and also a Shakespearean theater in a garden planted with trees mentioned in the bard's plays. Nearby is **La Grande Cascade** (𝄞 **01-45-27-33-51**), once a hunting lodge for Napoleon III.

Jardin d'Acclimatation (𝄞 **01-40-67-90-82;** www.jardindacclimatation.fr), at the northern edge of the park, is for children, with a zoo, an amusement park, and a narrow-gauge railway (see "Especially for Kids," later in this chapter, for more details). Two racetracks, the **Hippodrome de Longchamp** ✲✲✲ and the **Hippodrome d'Auteuil,** are in the park (see "A Day at the Races," below). The Grand Prix is run in June at Longchamp (the site of a medieval abbey). Fashionable Parisians always turn out for this, the women in their finest haute couture. To the north of Longchamp is the **Grand Cascade,** an artificial waterfall.

In the western section of the bois, the 24-hectare (59-acre) **Parc de Bagatelle** ✲ (𝄞 **01-43-28-47-63**) owes its existence to a bet between the comte d'Artois (later Charles X) and Marie Antoinette, his sister-in-law. The comte wagered he could erect a small palace in less than 3 months, so he hired nearly 1,000 craftsmen (cabinetmakers, painters, Scottish landscape architect Thomas Blaikie, and others) and irritated the locals by requisitioning all shipments of stone and plaster arriving through Paris's west gates. He won his bet. If you're here in late April, it's worth visiting the Bagatelle just for the tulips. In late May, one of the finest rose collections in Europe is in full bloom. For some reason, as the head gardener confides to us, "This is the major rendezvous point in Paris for illicit couples."

Parc de Bagatelle is open daily from 9am to dusk, charging adults 2€ ($2.60) and those ages 7 to 26 .50€ (65¢); it's free for children 6 and under.

PARC MONCEAU

Much of **Parc Monceau** ✲, 8e (𝄞 **01-42-27-39-56;** Métro: Monceau or Villiers), is ringed with 18th- and 19th-century mansions, some evoking Proust's *Remembrance of Things Past.* Carmontelle designed it in 1778 as a private hideaway for the duc d'Orléans (who came to be known as Philippe-Egalité), at the time the richest man in France. The duke was noted for his debauchery and pursuit of pleasure, so no ordinary park would do. It was opened to the public in the days of Napoleon III's Second Empire.

Monceau was laid out with an Egyptian-style obelisk, a medieval dungeon, a thatched farmhouse, a Chinese pagoda, a Roman temple, an enchanted grotto, various chinoiseries, and a waterfall. These fairy-tale touches have largely disappeared except for a pyramid and an oval naumachia fringed by a colonnade. Now the park is filled with solid statuary and monuments, one honors Chopin. In spring, the red tulips and magnolias are worth the airfare to Paris.

9 Cemeteries

Sightseers often view Paris's cemeteries as being somewhat like parks—suitable places for strolling. The graves of celebrities are also major lures. Père-Lachaise, for example, is a major attraction; the other cemeteries are of lesser interest.

Cimetière de Montmartre ✶ This cemetery, established in 1795, lies west of Montmartre and north of boulevard de Clichy. Russian dancer **Vaslav Nijinsky**, novelist **Alexandre Dumas *fils*,** impressionist **Edgar Degas,** and composers **Hector Berlioz** and **Jacques Offenbach** are interred here, along with **Stendhal** and lesser literary lights like **Edmond** and **Jules de Goncourt** and **Heinrich Heine.** A more recent tombstone honors **François Truffaut,** film director of the *nouvelle vague* (new wave). We like to pay our respects at the tomb of **Alphonsine Plessis,** heroine of *La Dame aux Camélias,* and **Mme Récamier,** who taught the world how to lounge. **Emile Zola** was buried here, but his corpse was exhumed and promoted to the Panthéon in 1908. In 1871, the cemetery was used for mass burials of victims of the Siege and the Commune.

20 av. Rachel (west of the Butte Montmartre and north of bd. de Clichy), 18e. ✆ 01-53-42-36-30. Sun–Fri 8am–6pm; Sat 8:30am–6pm (closes at 5:30pm in winter). Métro: La Fourche.

Cimetière de Passy This cemetery runs along Paris's old northern walls, south and southwest of Trocadéro. It's a small graveyard sheltered by chestnut trees, but it contains many gravesites of the famous—a concierge at the gate can guide you. Painters **Edouard Manet** and **Romaine Brooks** and composer **Claude Debussy** are tenants. Many great literary figures since 1850 were interred here, including **Tristan Bernard, Jean Giraudoux,** and **François de Croisset.** Also present are composer **Gabriel Fauré;** aviator **Henry Farman;** actor **Fernandel;** and high priestess of the city's most famous literary salon, **Natalie Barney,** along with **Renée Vivien,** one of her many lovers.

2 rue du Comandant-Schloesing, 16e. ✆ 01-43-28-47-63. Free admission. Mar–Nov daily 8am–6pm; Dec–Feb daily 8:30am–5:30pm. Métro: Trocadéro.

Cimetière du Montparnasse ✶ In the shadow of the Tour Montparnasse, this debris-littered cemetery is a burial ground of yesterday's celebrities. A map to the left of the main gateway will direct you to the gravesite of its most famous couple, **Simone de Beauvoir** and **Jean-Paul Sartre.** Others resting here include **Samuel Beckett; Guy de Maupassant; Pierre Larousse** (famous for his dictionary); **Capt. Alfred Dreyfus;** auto tycoon **André Citroën;** sculptors **Ossip Zadkine** and **Constantin Brancusi;** actress **Jean Seberg;** composer **Camille Saint-Saëns;** photographer **Man Ray;** and poet **Charles Baudelaire,** who'd already written about "plunging into the abyss, Heaven or Hell." In 2005, the cemetery interred the remains of American intellectual and activist **Susan Sontag,** who wanted to be buried in the same cemetery as some of her favorite writers.

Père-Lachaise Cemetery

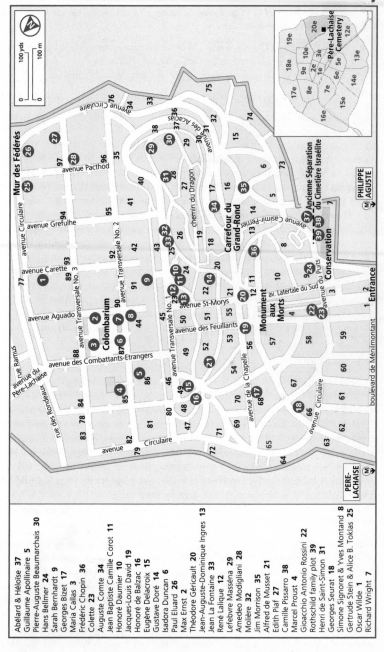

Abélard & Héloïse **37**
Guillaume Apollinaire **5**
Pierre-Auguste Beaumarchais **30**
Hans Bellmer **24**
Sarah Bernhardt **9**
Georges Bizet **17**
Maria Callas **3**
Frédéric Chopin **36**
Colette **23**
Auguste Comte **34**
Jean Baptiste Camille Corot **11**
Honoré Daumier **10**
Jacques-Louis David **19**
Honoré de Balzac **16**
Eugène Delacroix **15**
Gustave Doré **14**
Isadora Duncan **6**
Paul Eluard **26**
Max Ernst **2**
Théodore Géricault **20**
Jean-Auguste-Dominique Ingres **13**
Jean La Fontaine **33**
René Lalique **12**
Lefebvre Masséna **29**
Amedeo Modigliani **28**
Molière **32**
Jim Morrison **35**
Alfred de Musset **21**
Edith Piaf **27**
Camille Pissarro **38**
Marcel Proust **4**
Gioacchino Antonio Rossini **22**
Rothschild family plot **39**
Henri de Saint-Simon **31**
Georges Seurat **18**
Simone Signoret & Yves Montand **8**
Gertrude Stein & Alice B. Toklas **25**
Oscar Wilde **1**
Richard Wright **7**

223

3 bd. Edgar-Quinet, 14e. (©) 01-44-10-86-50. Mon–Fri 8am–6pm; Sat 8:30am–6pm; Sun 9am–6pm (closes at 5:30pm Nov–Mar). Métro: Edgar-Quinet.

Cimetière du Père-Lachaise ★★★   When it comes to name-dropping, this cemetery knows no peer; it has been called the "grandest address in Paris." A free map of Père-Lachaise is available at the newsstand across from the main entrance (additional map on p. 223).

Everybody from **Sarah Bernhardt** to **Oscar Wilde** to **Richard Wright** is resting here, along with **Honoré de Balzac, Jacques-Louis David, Eugène Delacroix, Maria Callas, Max Ernst,** and **Georges Bizet. Colette** was taken here in 1954; her black granite slab always sports flowers, and legend has it that cats replenish the roses. In time, the "little sparrow," **Edith Piaf,** followed. The lover of George Sand, poet **Alfred de Musset,** was buried under a weeping willow. Napoleon's marshals, **Ney** and **Masséna,** lie here, as do **Frédéric Chopin** and **Molière. Marcel Proust's** black tombstone rarely lacks a tiny bunch of violets (he wanted to be buried beside his friend/lover, composer **Maurice Ravel,** but their families wouldn't allow it).

Some tombs are sentimental favorites: Love-torn graffiti radiates 1km (half a mile) from the grave of Doors singer **Jim Morrison.** The great dancer **Isadora Duncan** came to rest in the Columbarium, where bodies have been cremated and "filed" away. If you search hard enough, you can find the tombs of that star-crossed pair **Abélard** and **Héloïse,** the ill-fated lovers of the 12th century—at Père-Lachaise, they've found peace at last. Other famous lovers also rest here: A stone is marked **"Alice B. Toklas"** on one side and **"Gertrude Stein"** on the other; and eventually, France's First Couple of film were reunited when **Yves Montand** joined his wife, **Simone Signoret.** (Montand's gravesite attracted much attention in 1998: His corpse was exhumed in the middle of the night for DNA testing in a paternity lawsuit. He wasn't the father.)

Covering more than 44 hectares (109 acres), Père-Lachaise was acquired by the city in 1804. Nineteenth-century sculpture abounds, as each family tried to outdo the others in ostentation. Monuments also honor Frenchmen who died in the Resistance or in Nazi concentration camps. Some French Socialists still pay tribute at the **Mur des Fédérés,** the anonymous gravesite of the Communards who were executed in the cemetery on May 28, 1871. When these last-ditch fighters of the Commune, the world's first anarchist republic, made their final desperate stand against the troops of the French government, they were overwhelmed, lined up against the wall, and shot in groups. A handful survived and lived hidden in the cemetery for years like wild animals, venturing into Paris at night to forage for food.

16 rue de Repos, 20e. (©) 01-55-25-82-10. www.pere-lachaise.com. Mon–Fri 8am–6pm; Sat 8:30am–6pm; Sun 9am–6pm (closes at 5:30pm Nov–to early Mar). Métro: Père-Lachaise or Philippe Auguste.

Cimetière St-Vincent   Because of the artists and writers who have their resting places in the modest burial ground of St-Vincent, with a view of Sacré-Coeur on the hill, it's sometimes called "the most intellectual cemetery in Paris"—but that epithet seems more apt for other graveyards. Artists **Maurice Utrillo** and **Théopile-Alexandre Steinien** were buried here, as were musician **Arthur Honegger** and writer **Marcel Aymé.** More recently, burials have included the remains of French actor **Gabriello,** film director **Marcel Carné,** and painter **Eugène Boudin.**

6 rue Lucien-Gaulard, 18e. (©) 01-46-06-29-78. Mar 6–Nov 5 Mon–Sat 8:30am–6pm, Sun 9am–6pm; Nov 6–Mar 5 Mon–Fri 8am–5:15pm, Sat 8:30am–5:15pm, Sun 9am–5:15pm. Métro: Lamarck-Caulaincourt.

10 Paris Underground

Les Catacombes ⊛   Every year, an estimated 50,000 visitors explore some 910m (2,986 ft.) of tunnel in these dank catacombs to look at 6 million ghoulishly arranged, skull-and-crossbones skeletons. First opened to the public in 1810, this "empire of the dead" is now illuminated with electric lights over its entire length. In the Middle Ages, the catacombs were quarries, but by the end of the 18th century, overcrowded cemeteries were becoming a menace to public health. City officials decided to use the catacombs as a burial ground, and the bones of several million persons were transferred here. In 1830, the prefect of Paris closed the catacombs, considering them obscene and indecent. During World War II, the catacombs were the headquarters of the French Resistance.

1 place Denfert-Rochereau, 14e. © **01-43-22-47-63**. Admission 5€ ($6.50) adults, 3.10€ ($4.05) seniors, 2.50€ ($3.25) ages 14–25, free for children under 14. Tues–Sun 10am–5pm (ticket office 10am–4pm). Métro: Denfert-Rochereau.

Les Egouts ⊛   Some sociologists assert that the sophistication of a society can be judged by the way it disposes of waste. If so, Paris receives good marks for its mostly invisible sewer network. Victor Hugo is credited with making them famous in *Les Misérables:* Jean Valjean takes flight through them, "all dripping with slime, his soul filled with a strange light." Hugo also wrote, "Paris has beneath it another Paris, a Paris of sewers, which has its own streets, squares, lanes, arteries, and circulation."

In the early Middle Ages, drinking water was taken directly from the Seine, and wastewater poured onto fields or thrown onto the unpaved streets transformed the urban landscape into a sea of rather smelly mud. Around 1200, the streets were paved with cobblestones, and open sewers ran down the center of each. These open sewers helped spread the Black Death, which devastated the city. In 1370, a vaulted sewer was built on rue Montmartre, draining effluents into a Seine tributary. During Louis XIV's reign, improvements were made, but the state of waste disposal in Paris remained deplorable.

During Napoleon's reign, 31km (19 miles) of sewer were constructed beneath Paris. By 1850, as the Industrial Revolution made the manufacture of iron pipe and steam-digging equipment more practical, Baron Haussmann developed a system that used separate channels for drinking water and sewage. By 1878, it was 580km (360 miles) long. Beginning in 1894, the network was enlarged, and laws required that discharge of all waste and storm-water runoff be funneled into the sewers. Between 1914 and 1977, an additional 966km (600 miles) were added. Today, the network of sewers is 2,093km (1,300 miles) long.

The city's sewers are constructed around four principal tunnels, one 5.5m (18 ft.) wide and 4.5m (15 ft.) high. It's like an underground city, with the street names clearly labeled. Sewer tours begin at pont de l'Alma on the Left Bank, where a stairway leads into the city's bowels. Visiting times might change during bad weather, as a storm can make the sewers dangerous. The tour consists of a film, a small museum visit, and then a short trip through the maze. *Warning:* The smell is pretty bad, especially in summer.

Pont de l'Alma, 7e. © **01-53-68-27-82**. Admission 4€ ($5.20) adults; 3.20€ ($4.15) seniors, students, and children 5–16; free for children under 5. May–Sept Sat–Wed 11am–5pm; Oct–Apr Sat–Wed 11am–4pm. Métro: Alma-Marceau. RER: Pont de l'Alma.

11 A Day at the Races

Paris boasts an army of avid horse-racing fans who get to the city's eight racetracks whenever possible. Information on current races is available in newspapers and magazines such as *Tierce, Paris-Turf, France-Soir,* and *L'Equipe,* all sold at kiosks throughout the city.

The epicenter of Paris horse racing is the **Hippodrome de Longchamp** 𝕮𝕮𝕮, in the Bois de Boulogne, 16e (© **01-44-30-75-00**; RER or Métro: Porte Maillot and then a free shuttle bus on race days only). Established in 1855, during the autocratic but pleasure-loving reign of Napoleon III, it's the most prestigious, boasts the greatest number of promising thoroughbreds, and awards the largest purse in France. The most important events at Longchamp are the **Grand Prix de Paris** in late June and the **Prix de l'Arc de Triomphe** in early October.

Another racing venue is the **Hippodrome d'Auteuil,** also in the Bois de Boulogne (© **01-40-71-47-47**; Métro: Porte Auteuil; then walk). Known for its steeplechases and obstacle courses, it sometimes attracts more than 50,000 Parisians at a time. Spectators appreciate the park's promenades as much as they do the equestrian events. Races are conducted from early March to late November.

12 Neighborhood Highlights

Some of Paris's neighborhoods are attractions unto themselves. The 1st Arrondissement probably has a higher concentration of attractions per block than anywhere else. Though all Paris's neighborhoods are worth wandering, some are more interesting than others. This is especially true of Montmartre, the Latin Quarter, and the Marais, so we've featured them as walking tours in chapter 9.

ISLANDS IN THE STREAM: ILE DE LA CITE & ILE ST-LOUIS

For a map of Ile de la Cite and Ile St-Louis, please refer to the map of the same name in the color insert at the beginning of this book.

ILE DE LA CITE 𝕮𝕮𝕮 **WHERE PARIS WAS BORN**   Medieval Paris, that blend of grotesquerie and Gothic beauty, bloomed on this island in the Seine (Métro: Cité). Ile de la Cité, which the Seine protects like a surrounding moat, has been known as "the cradle" of Paris ever since. As Sauval once observed, "The Island of the City is shaped like a great ship, sunk in the mud, lengthwise in the stream, in about the middle of the Seine."

Few have written more movingly about its heyday than Victor Hugo, who invited the reader "to observe the fantastic display of lights against the darkness of that gloomy labyrinth of buildings; cast upon it a ray of moonlight, showing the city in glimmering vagueness, with its towers lifting their great heads from that foggy sea." Medieval Paris was a city not only of legends and lovers, but also of blood-curdling tortures and brutalities. No story illustrates this better than the affair of Abélard and his charge Héloïse, whose jealous uncle hired ruffians to castrate her lover. (The attack predictably quelled their ardor; he became a monk, and she, an abbess.) You can see their graves at Père-Lachaise (see "Cemeteries," above).

Because you'll want to see all the attractions on Ile de la Cité, begin at the cathedral of Notre-Dame. Proceed next to the Sainte-Chapelle, moving west. After a visit there, you can head northeast to the Conciergerie. To cap off your visit, and for the best scenic view, walk to the northwestern end of the island for a view of the bridge, pont Neuf, seen from square du Vert Galant.

The island's stars, as mentioned, are **Notre-Dame, Sainte-Chapelle,** and the **Conciergerie**—all described earlier. Across from Notre-Dame is the **Hôtel Dieu,** built from 1866 to 1878 in neo-Florentine style. This is central Paris's main hospital, replacing the 12th-century hospital that ran the island's entire width. Go in the main entrance, and take a break in the spacious neoclassical courtyard whose small garden and fountain make a quiet oasis.

Don't miss the ironically named **pont Neuf** (New Bridge) at the tip of the island opposite from Notre-Dame. The span isn't new—it's Paris's oldest bridge, begun in 1578 and finished in 1604. In its day, it had two unique features: It was paved, and it wasn't flanked with houses and shops. Actually, with 12 arches, it's not one bridge but two (they don't quite line up)—one from the Right Bank to the island and the other from the Left Bank to the island. At the **Musée Carnavalet** (p. 201), a painting called *The Spectacle of Buffoons* shows what the bridge was like between 1665 and 1669. Duels were fought on it, the nobility's great coaches crossed it, peddlers sold their wares, and entertainers such as Tabarin went there to seek a few coins from the gawkers. As public facilities were lacking, the bridge also served as a *de facto* outhouse.

Just past pont Neuf is the "prow" of the island, the **square du Vert Galant.** Pause to look at the equestrian statue of beloved Henri IV, who was assassinated by Ravaillac (see the entry for the Conciergerie). A true king of his people, Henri was also (to judge from accounts) regal in the boudoir—hence the nickname "Vert Galant" (Old Spark). Gabrielle d'Estrées and Henriette d'Entragues were his best-known mistresses, but they had to share him with countless others, some of whom would casually catch his eye as he was riding along the streets. In fond memory of the king, the little triangular park continues to attract lovers. It appears to be a sunken garden because it remains at its natural level; the rest of the Cité has been built up during the centuries.

ILE ST-LOUIS ★★

Cross the pont St-Louis, the footbridge behind Notre-Dame, to Ile St-Louis, and you'll find a world of tree-shaded quays, town houses with courtyards, restaurants, and antiques shops. (You can also take the Métro to Sully-Morland or Pont Marie and cross the bridge.) The fraternal twin of Ile de la Cité, Ile St-Louis is primarily residential; nearly all the houses were built from 1618 to 1660, lending the island a remarkable architectural unity. Plaques on the facades identify the former residences of the famous. **Marie Curie** lived at 36 quai de Béthune, near pont de la Tournelle, and sculptor **Camille Claudel** (Rodin's mistress) lived and worked in the Hôtel de Jassaud, 19 quai de Bourbon.

The most exciting mansion—though perhaps with the saddest history—is the 1656–57 **Hôtel de Lauzun,** 17 quai d'Anjou, built for Charles Gruyn des Bordes. He married Geneviève de Mouy and had her initials engraved on much of the interior decor; their happiness was short-lived, because he was convicted of embezzlement and sent to prison in 1662. The next occupant was the duc de Lauzun, who resided there for only 3 years. He had been a favorite of Louis XIV until he asked for the hand of the king's cousin, the duchesse de Montpensier. Louis refused and had Lauzun tossed into the Bastille. Eventually, the duchesse pestered Louis into releasing him, and they married secretly and moved here in 1682, but domestic bliss eluded them—they fought often and separated in 1684. Lauzun sold the house to the grandnephew of Cardinal Richelieu and his wife, who had such a grand time throwing parties, they went bankrupt. Baron Pichon bought it in 1842 and rented it out to a hashish club.

Tenants Baudelaire and Gaultier regularly held hashish soirees in which Baudelaire did research for his *Les Paradis Artificiels* and Gaultier for his *Le Club des Hachichins*. Now the mansion belongs to the city and is used to house official guests. The interior is sometimes open for temporary exhibits, so call the tourist office.

Hôtel Lambert, 2 quai d'Anjou, was built in 1645 for Nicholas Lambert de Thorigny. The portal on rue St-Louis-en-l'Ile gives some idea of the splendor within, but the house's most startling element is the oval gallery extending into the garden. Designed to feature a library or art collection, it's best viewed from the beginning of quai d'Anjou. Voltaire and his mistress, Emilie de Breteuil, lived here; their quarrels were legendary. The mansion also housed the Polish royal family for over a century before becoming the residence of actress Michèle Morgan. It now belongs to the Rothschild family and isn't open to the public.

Nos. 9, 11, 13, and 15 quai d'Anjou also belonged to the Lamberts. At **no. 9** is the house where painter/sculptor/lithographer Honoré Daumier lived from 1846 to 1863, producing hundreds of caricatures satirizing the bourgeoisie and attacking government corruption. He was imprisoned because of his 1832 cartoon of Louis-Philippe swallowing bags of gold extracted from the people.

Near the Hôtel de Lauzun is the church of **St-Louis-en-l'Ile,** no. 19 bis rue St-Louis-en-l'Ile. Despite a dour exterior, the ornate interior is one of the finest examples of Jesuit baroque. Built between 1664 and 1726, this church is still the site of many weddings—with all the white stone and gilt, you'll feel as if you're inside a wedding cake. Look for the 1926 plaque reading "In grateful memory of St. Louis in whose honor the city of St. Louis, Missouri, USA, is named."

RIGHT BANK HIGHLIGHTS

LES HALLES *𝒢* For 8 centuries, **Les Halles** (Métro: Les Halles; RER: Châtelet–Les Halles) was the city's major wholesale fruit, meat, and vegetable market. In the 19th century, Zola called it "the underbelly of Paris." The smock-clad vendors, beef carcasses, and baskets of vegetables all belong to the past, for the original market, with zinc-roofed Second Empire "iron umbrellas," has been torn down. Today the action has moved to a steel-and-glass edifice at Rungis, a suburb near Orly. In 1979 the **Forum des Halles,** 1–7 rue Pierre-Lescot, 1er, opened. This large complex, much of it underground, contains shops, restaurants, and movie theaters. Many of the shops are unattractive, but others contain a wide display of merchandise that has made the mall popular with residents and visitors.

For many visitors, a night on the town still ends in the wee hours with a bowl of onion soup at Les Halles, usually at **Au Pied de Cochon (The Pig's Foot),** 6 rue Coquillière, 1er (𝒞 **01-40-13-77-00;** p. 132), or at **Au Chien Qui Fume (The Smoking Dog),** 33 rue du Pont-Neuf, 1er (𝒞 **01-42-36-07-42**). One of the classic scenes of old Paris was elegantly dressed Parisians (many fresh from Maxim's) standing at a bar drinking cognac with blood-smeared butchers. Some writers have suggested that 19th-century poet Gérard de Nerval introduced the custom of frequenting Les Halles at such an unearthly hour.

A newspaper correspondent described today's scene: "Les Halles is trying to stay alive as one of the few places where one can eat at any hour of the night."

LEFT BANK HIGHLIGHTS

ST-GERMAIN-DES-PRES *𝒢𝒢* This neighborhood in the 6th Arrondissement (Métro: St-Germain-des-Prés) was the postwar home of existentialism, associated with

Sartre, De Beauvoir, Camus, and an intellectual bohemian crowd that gathered at **Café de Flore, Brasserie Lipp,** and **Les Deux Magots** (see chapter 7). Among them, black-clad poet and singer Juliette Greco was known as *la muse de St-Germain-des-Prés,* and to Sartre, she was the woman who had "millions of poems in her throat." Her long hair, black slacks, black sweater, and black sandals launched a fashion trend adopted by young women everywhere. In the 1950s, new names appeared, such as Françoise Sagan, Gore Vidal, and James Baldwin, but by the 1960s, tourists were firmly entrenched.

St-Germain-des-Prés still retains an intellectually stimulating bohemian street life, full of many interesting bookshops, art galleries, *cave* (basement) clubs, bistros, and coffeehouses. But the stars of the area are two churches, **St-Germain-des-Prés,** 3 place St-Germain-des-Prés, and **St-Sulpice,** rue St-Sulpice (for both, see "The Major Churches," earlier in this chapter), and the **Musée National Eugène Delacroix,** 6 place de Furstenberg (p. 204). Nearby, **rue Visconti** was designed for pushcarts and is worth visiting today. At **nos. 20–24** is the residence where dramatist Jean-Baptiste Racine died in 1699. And at **no. 17** is the house where Balzac established his printing press in 1825. (The venture ended in bankruptcy, forcing the author back to his writing desk.) Such celebrated actresses as Champmeslé and Clairon also lived here.

MONTPARNASSE ☆☆   For the "Lost Generation," life centered around the cafes of Montparnasse, at the border of the 6th and 14th arrondissements (Métro: Montparnasse-Bienvenüe). Hangouts like the **Dôme, Coupole, Rotonde,** and **Sélect** became legendary, as artists—especially American expats—turned their backs on touristy Montmartre. Picasso, Modigliani, and Man Ray came this way, and Hemingway was also a popular figure. So was Fitzgerald when he was poor (when he wasn't, you'd find him at the Ritz). Faulkner, MacLeish, Duncan, Miró, Joyce, Ford Maddox Ford, and even Trotsky spent time here.

The most notable exception was Gertrude Stein, who never frequented the cafes. To see her, you had to wait for an invitation to her salon at **27 rue de Fleurus.** She bestowed this favor on Sherwood Anderson, Elliot Paul, Ezra Pound, and, for a time, Hemingway. When Pound launched himself into a beloved chair and broke it, he incurred Stein's wrath, and Hemingway decided there wasn't "much future in men being friends with great women."

American expatriate writer Natalie Barney, who moved to Paris as a student in 1909 and stayed for more than 60 years, held her grand salons at **20 rue Jacob** (actually in St-Germain-des-Prés). Every Friday, her salon attracted the literati of her day, such as Gertrude Stein, Djuna Barnes, Colette, Sherwood Anderson, T. S. Eliot, Janet Flanner, James Joyce, Sylvia Beach, Marcel Proust, and William Carlos Williams. The group met on and off for half a century, interrupted only by two world wars. Near place de Furstenberg, Barney's former residence is landmarked but not open to the public. In the garden you can see a small Doric temple bearing the inscription *A l'Amitié,* "to friendship."

Aside from the literary legends, one of the most notable characters was **Kiki de Montparnasse** (actually named Alice Prin). She was raised by her grandmother in Burgundy until her mother called her to Paris to work. When a sculptor discovered her, she became an artist's model and adopted her new name; soon she became a prostitute and would bare her breasts for anyone who'd pay three francs. She sang at **Le Jockey,** 127 bd. du Montparnasse, which no longer exists. In her black hose and

Moments **Memorial to a Princess**

Place de l'Alma (Métro: Alma-Marceau) has been turned into a tribute to the late Diana, princess of Wales, killed in an auto accident August 31, 1997, in a nearby underpass. The bronze flame in the center is a replica of the one in the Statue of Liberty and was a gift from the *International Herald Tribune* to honor Franco-American friendship. Many bouquets and messages (and even graffiti) are still placed around the flame.

Paris has also opened the **Center for Nature Discovery, Garden in Memory of Diana, Princess of Wales,** at 21 rue des Blancs-Manteaux in the Marais. The small park, which you can visit daily during daylight hours, is devoted to teaching children about nature and gardening and contains flowers, vegetables, and decorative plants.

garters, she captivated dozens of men, among them Frederick Kohner, who went so far as to title his memoirs *Kiki of Montparnasse*. Kiki later wrote her own memoirs, with an introduction by Hemingway. Papa called her "a Queen," noting that it was "very different from being a lady."

Completed in 1973 and rising 206m (676 ft.) above the skyline, the **Tour Montparnasse** (℗ **01-45-38-52-56;** www.tour-montparnasse.com; Métro: Montparnasse-Bienvenüe) was denounced by some as "bringing Manhattan to Paris." The city soon passed an ordinance outlawing any further structures of this size in the heart of Paris. Today, the modern tower houses an underground shopping mall, as well as much of the infrastructure for the Gare de Montparnasse rail station. You can ride an elevator up to the 56th floor (where you'll find a bar and restaurant) and then climb three flights to the roof terrace. The view encompasses virtually every important Paris monument, including Sacré-Coeur, Notre-Dame, and La Défense. Admission is 9€ ($12) for adults, 6.50€ ($8.45) for students, and 4€ ($5.20) for kids 7 to 15. Free for children 6 and under. It's open April to September daily 9:30am to 11:30pm, October to March daily 9:30am to 10:30pm (Métro: Montparnasse-Bienvenue).

The life of Montparnasse still centers around its cafes and exotic nightclubs, many only a shadow of what they used to be. Its heart is at the crossroads of **boulevard Raspail** and **boulevard du Montparnasse,** one of the settings of *The Sun Also Rises*. Hemingway wrote that "boulevard Raspail always made dull riding." Rodin's controversial statue of Balzac swathed in a large cape stands guard over the prostitutes who cluster around the pedestal. Balzac seems to be the only one in Montparnasse who doesn't feel the weight of time.

13 Especially for Kids

If you're staying on the Right Bank, take the children for a stroll through the **Jardin des Tuileries** (p. 220), where there are donkey rides, ice-cream stands, and a marionette show; at the circular pond, you can rent a toy boat. On the Left Bank, similar treats exist in the **Jardin du Luxembourg** (p. 220). After a visit to the Eiffel Tower, you can take the kids for a donkey ride in the **Champ de Mars.**

A Paris tradition, **puppet shows** are worth seeing for their colorful productions; they're a genuine French child's experience. At the Jardin du Luxembourg, puppets reenact plots set in Gothic castles and Oriental palaces; many critics say the best puppet shows are held in the Champ de Mars.

On Sunday afternoon, French families head to the **Butte Montmartre** to bask in the fiesta atmosphere. You can join in: Take the Métro to Anvers, and walk to the *funiculaire* (the cable car that carries you up to Sacré-Coeur). Once up top, follow the crowds to place du Tertre, where a Sergeant Pepper–style band will usually be blasting off-key and you can have the kids' pictures sketched by local artists. You can take in the views of Paris from the various vantage points and treat your children to ice cream. For a walking tour of Montmartre, see chapter 9.

Your kids may want to check out the Gallic versions of Mickey Mouse and his pals, so see chapter 12, "Side Trips from Paris," for **Disneyland Paris.**

MUSEUMS

Cité des Sciences et de l'Industrie *Kids*   A city of science and industry has risen here from unlikely ashes. When a slaughterhouse was built on the site in the 1960s, it was touted as the most modern of its kind. It was abandoned in 1974, and the location on the city's northern edge presented the government with a problem. What could be built in such an unlikely place? In 1986, the converted premises opened as the world's most expensive ($642-million) science complex, designed to "modernize mentalities" in the service of modernizing society.

The place is so vast, with so many exhibits, that a single visit gives only an idea of the scope of the Cité. Busts of Plato, Hippocrates, and a double-faced Janus gaze silently at a tube-filled riot of high-tech girders, glass, and lights. The sheer dimensions pose a challenge to the curators of its constantly changing exhibits. Some exhibits are couched in Gallic humor—imagine using the comic-strip adventures of a jungle explorer to explain seismographic activity. **Explora,** a permanent exhibit, occupies the three upper levels of the building and examines four themes: the universe, life, matter, and communication. The Cité also has a **multimedia library,** a **planetarium,** and an **"inventorium"** for kids. The silver-skinned geodesic dome called **La Géode**—a 34m-high (112-ft.) sphere with a 370-seat theater—projects the closest thing to a 3-D cinema in Europe and has several surprising additions, including a real submarine.

The Cité is in the **Parc de La Villette,** an ultramodern science park surrounding some of Paris's newest housing developments. This is Paris's largest park—twice the size of the Tuileries. The playgrounds, fountains, and sculptures are all innovative. Here you'll find a belvedere, a video workshop for children, and information about exhibits and events, along with a cafe and restaurant.

Finds The "Beach" of Paris

Relaxing under a palm tree on a chaise lounge sounds more Caribbean than Parisian, but a nearly 4.8km (3-mile) stretch of sandy shore has opened along the Seine. With the Eiffel Tower looming in the background, visitors and locals can splash in fountains, swing in hammocks, play volleyball, or enjoy a picnic. Just don't go into the polluted water of the murky Seine. The Paris beach opened in the late summer of 2003, after tons of sand were poured into concrete bases along the river.

In the Parc de La Villette, 30 av. Corentine-Cariou, La Villette, 19e. ✆ **01-40-05-70-00**. www.cite-sciences.fr. Cité Pass (entrance to all exhibits) 7.50€ ($9.75) adults, 5.50€ ($7.15) ages 7–24, free 6 and under. Tues–Sat 10am–6pm; Sun 10am–7pm. Métro: Porte de La Villette.

Musée Grévin ✸ *(Kids)*   The Grévin is Paris's number-one waxworks. Comparisons with Madame Tussaud's are almost irresistible, but it isn't all blood and gore and doesn't shock as much as Tussaud's. It presents French history in a series of tableaux. Depicted is the 1429 consecration of Charles VII in the Cathédrale de Reims (armored Joan of Arc, carrying her standard, stands behind the king); Marguerite de Valois, first wife of Henri IV, meeting on a secret stairway with La Molle, who was soon to be decapitated; Catherine de Médicis with Florentine alchemist David Ruggieri; Louis XV and Mozart at the home of the marquise de Pompadour; and Napoleon on a rock at St. Helena, reviewing his victories and defeats. Visitors will also find displays of contemporary sports and political figures, as well as 50 of the world's best-loved film stars.

Two shows are staged frequently throughout the day. The first, called the **"Palais des Mirages,"** starts off as a sort of Temple of Brahma and, through magically distorting mirrors, changes first into an enchanted forest and then into a fête at the Alhambra in Granada. A magician is the star of the second show, **"Le Cabinet Fantastique";** he entertains children of all ages.

10 bd. Montmartre, 9e. ✆ **01-47-70-85-05**. www.grevin.com. Admission 18€ ($23) adults, 16€ ($21) students, 11€ ($14) children 6 to 14, 9€ ($11) children 5 and under. Mon–Fri 10am–6:30pm, Sat–Sun 10am–7pm. Ticket office closes at 5:30pm. Métro: Grands Boulevards.

Musée National d'Histoire Naturelle (Museum of Natural History) ✸ *(Kids)*
This museum in the Jardin des Plantes, founded in 1635 as a research center by Guy de la Brosse, physician to Louis XIII, has a range of science and nature exhibits. At the entrance of the **Grande Gallery of Evolution**, two 26m (85-ft.) skeletons of whales greet you. One display containing the skeletons of dinosaurs and mastodons is dedicated to endangered and vanished species. Galleries specialize in paleontology, anatomy, mineralogy, and botany. Within the museum's grounds are **tropical hothouses** containing thousands of species of unusual plant life and a **menagerie** with small animals in simulated natural habitats.

57 rue Cuvier, 5e. ✆ **01-40-79-54-79**. www.mnhn.fr. Admission 8€ ($10) adults, 6€ ($7.80) students, seniors over 60, and children 4–13. Wed–Mon 10am–6pm. Métro: Jussieu or Gare d'Austerlitz.

AN AMUSEMENT PARK
Jardin d'Acclimatation ✸ *(Kids)*   Paris's definitive children's park is the 20-hectare (49-acre) Jardin d'Acclimatation in the northern part of the Bois de Boulogne. This is the kind of place that amuses tykes and adults but not teenagers. The visit starts with a ride on a green-and-yellow or green-and-red narrow-gauge train from Porte Maillot to the Jardin entrance, through a stretch of wooded park. The train operates at 10-minute intervals daily from 10:30am until the park closes; one-way fare costs 1.25€ ($1.65). En route you'll find a **house of mirrors,** an **archery range,** a **miniature-golf course, zoo animals,** a **puppet theater** (performances Wed, Sat, Sun, and holidays), a **playground,** a **hurdle-racing course, junior-scale rides, shooting galleries,** and **waffle stalls.** You can trot the kids off on a **pony** (Sat and Sun only) or join them in a **boat** on a mill-stirred lagoon. **La Prévention Routière** is a miniature roadway operated by the Paris police: Youngsters drive through in small cars equipped to start and

stop, and are required by two genuine gendarmes to obey str' changes. Inside the gate is an easy-to-follow map.

In the Bois de Boulogne, 16e. ☎ **01-40-67-90-82**. www.jardindacclimatation.fr. Admis' dren 3 and under. June–Sept daily 10am–7pm; Oct–May daily 10am–6pm. Métro: Sablons.

A ZOO

Parc Zoologique de Paris *(Kids*

There's a modest zoo in the Jardin des Plantes, but without a doubt, the best zoo is here on the southeastern outskirts of Paris, quickly reachable by Métro. Many of this modern zoo's animals, which seem happy and are playful, live in settings similar to their natural habitats, hemmed in by rock barriers, not bars or cages. You'll never see an animal in a cage too small for it. The lion has an entire veldt to himself, and you can lock eyes comfortably across a deep moat. On a cement mountain like Disneyland's Matterhorn, exotic breeds of mountain goats and sheep leap from ledge to ledge or pose gracefully for hours while watching the penguins in their pools at the mountain's foot. Keep well back from the bear pools, or you might get wet.

In the Bois de Vincennes, 53 av. de St-Maurice, 12e. ☎ **01-44-75-20-14**. Admission 5€ ($6.50; all ages). Daily 9am–5:30pm. Métro: Porte Dorée.

14 Organized Tours

BY BUS

Before plunging into sightseeing on your own, you may like to take the most popular get-acquainted tour in Paris: **Cityrama**, 2 rue des Pyramides, 1er (☎ **01-44-55-61-00;** Métro: Palais-Royal–Musée du Louvre). On a double-decker bus with enough windows for Versailles, you take a 2-hour ride through the city. You don't go inside any attractions, but you get a look at the outside of Notre-Dame and the Eiffel Tower, among other sites, and it helps you get a feel for the city. There's commentary in eight languages on earphones. Tours depart daily at 10am, 11am, and 2:30pm. A 1½-hour orientation tour is 18€ ($23) adults, 8.50€ ($11) children. A morning tour with interior visits to the Louvre costs 39€ ($51). Half-day tours to Versailles (59€/$77) and Chartres (55€/$72) are a good value and relieve some of the hassle associated with visiting those monuments. A joint ticket that includes Versailles and Chartres costs 95€ ($124). A tour of the nighttime illuminations leaves daily at 10pm in summer, 7pm in winter, and costs 22€ ($29); it tends to be tame and touristy.

The **RATP** (☎ **08-92-68-77-14;** www.ratp.fr), which runs regular public transportation, also operates the **Balabus,** a fleet of orange-and-white big-windowed motor coaches. The only drawback is their limited operating times: Sunday and national holidays from 12:30 to 8:30pm, from April to the end of September. Itineraries run in both directions between Gare de Lyon and the Grand Arche de La Défense. Three Métro tickets will carry you along the entire route. You'll recognize the bus, and the route it follows, by the *Bb* symbol on its side and on signs posted along its route.

CRUISES ON THE SEINE

A boat tour on the Seine provides vistas of the riverbanks and some of the best views of Notre-Dame. Many boats have sun decks, bars, and restaurants. **Bateaux-Mouche** (☎ **01-40-76-99-99;** www.bateaux-mouches.fr; Métro: Alma-Marceau) cruises depart from the Right Bank of the Seine, adjacent to pont de l'Alma, and last about

---

Moments Friday Night "Rando" Fever

The Paris Roller Rando takes over the city on Friday nights, "rando" being short for _randonnée,_ meaning tour or excursion. The starting time is around 10pm at the place d'Italie (also the name of the Métro stop). Roller folk from Paris and throughout Ile de France amass here to begin their 3-hour weekly journey through the city on rollerblades. Every Friday three motorcycle policemen lead the way with dome lights flashing, signaling moving cars to get out of the way. First-aid wagons follow the "rollers." On an average night in Paris, some 20,000 rollers show up. Many visitors like to stay up late that night to watch these "mad, mad Parisians" in all their crazed "rollermania."

---

75 minutes. Tours leave daily at 20- to 30-minute intervals from 10am to 11pm between April and September. Between October and March, there are at least five departures daily between 11am and 9pm, with a schedule that changes according to demand and the weather. Fares are 8€ ($10) for adults and 4€ ($5.20) for children 4 to 13. Dinner cruises depart daily at 8:30pm, last 2 hours, and cost 95€ to 125€ ($124–$163). On dinner cruises, jackets and ties are required for men.

Some people enjoy excursions on the Seine and its canals. The 3-hour **Seine et le Canal St-Martin** tour, offered by **Paris Canal** (© 01-42-40-96-97), requires reservations. The tour begins at 9:30am on the quays in front of the Musée d'Orsay (Métro: Solférino) and at 2:30pm in front of the Cité des Sciences et de l'Industrie at Parc de la Villette (Métro: Porte de la Villette). Excursions negotiate the waterways of Paris, including the Seine, an underground tunnel below place de la Bastille, and the Canal St-Martin. Tours are offered twice daily from mid-March to mid-November; the rest of the year, on Sunday only. As you glide along the waterways, recorded commentary in French and English relates how building supplies and food staples were hauled, with relative efficiency, into central Paris during the capital's building boom in the Napoleonic age of the 19th century. The cost is 17€ ($22) for adults, 14€ ($18) for seniors over 60 and students ages 12 to 25, 10€ ($13) ages 4 to 11, and free for children under 4.

BIKE TOURS

Some of the best-orchestrated bike tours in Paris are conducted in English and offered by **Fat Tire Bike Tours** (© 01-56-58-10-54; www.fattirebiketoursparis.com); they depart from a spot that's immediately adjacent to the south leg _(pilier sud)_ of the Eiffel Tower. (Look for a large yellow sign advertising the tours.) Between mid-February and mid-December, bike tours depart daily at 11am, and between May and September, an additional tour is offered at 3:30pm. Between April and October, an additional tour is offered at night, departing at 7pm from the same spot. The cost of any tour includes use of a bike and a protective helmet. _**Hint:**_ If you're interested in participating in one of these bike tours, we recommend that you schedule your ascent to the upper levels of the Eiffel Tower for either immediately before or after your bike tour and that you arrive in clothing appropriate for a two-wheeled, self-propelled jaunt through the monumental avenues of central Paris. The cost is 24€ ($31) per person for the day tour and 28€ ($36) for the night tour. The night tour is more festive than the day tour and includes a complimentary ride aboard the bateaux mouches, the big-windowed panoramic boats that chug along the Seine beneath some of the most famous bridges in Europe.

OTHER TOURS

The first audio-guided tours of Paris have been launched by **Audio Visit,** which takes you through such famous neighborhoods as the Champs-Elysées district, Louvre/Opéra, and Montmartre. English commentaries are available, costing 8€ ($10) per half-day or 15€ ($20) for both audioguide and bike during the same time frame. Rentals of the audioguide are available at the Syndicat d'Initiative de Montmartre, 21 place du Tertre, 18e; Paris Story, 11 bis, rue Scribe, 9e; and Maison Roue Libre, Forum de Halles, 1 Passage Montdétour, 1er. For more information, call © **04-78-29-60-72,** or visit www.audiovisit.com.

Context:Paris (© **888/467-1986** in the U.S., or 06-13-09-67-11; www.context paris.com) is an organization of graduate students and art-history professors who lead thematic walking tours of the city. Tours range from 1-hour orientation "chats" to 4-hour in-depth visits of the Louvre. Being academics, the guides try to create a college seminar feeling without being too obtuse and scholarly. Context:Paris also rents cell-phones, arranges transportation, and organizes culinary excursions. Prices vary widely depending on what itinerary you select, but many tours cost 50€ to 60€ ($65–$78) per person.

CRACKING THE "DA VINCI CODE"

When thousands of visitors carrying dog-eared copies of Dan Brown's *The Da Vinci Code* started pouring into the Louvre asking questions raised by the best-selling novel, tour guides caught on quickly. Today, Paris bustles with organized tours of fans wanting to explore the book's locations, such as the **Louvre** (p. 195) and **St-Sulpice** (p. 214). With the film version, starring Tom Hanks, seen around the world in theaters and on DVD, interest in *The Da Vinci Code* shows no sign of waning.

The plot kicks off with the murder of the fictional Louvre curator, Jacques Saunière, in the museum's Grand Gallery. The church of St-Sulpice was home to the brass meridian marker and stone obelisk that play a key role in the novel's search for the Holy Grail.

Be warned that the *Mona Lisa* at the Louvre does not hang in the place as described by Brown in his blockbuster. And at St-Sulpice, Father Paul Roumanet has put up a sign for the thousands of fans streaming into the church in search of clues. "Contrary to fanciful allegations in a recent best-selling novel, this is not a vestige of a pagan temple," the sign reads. It also specifies that the initials "P" and "S" featured on circular windows refer to Saint Peter and Saint Sulpice—not to the imaginary Priory of Sion, the secret society that is charged with protecting the Holy Grail in the novel. Roumanet fears that readers of Dan Brown's novel don't take it for fiction but "take it as established truth—and that is not at all the case."

Lovers of the novel are booking the following tours to visit actual locations for the mega-hit that has sold millions of copies.

Paris Muse offers you both a private museum tour of the Louvre, exploring the themes of the book, or else a group walking tour of the book-related locales in Paris

(© **06-73-77-33-52** in France; www.parismuse.com). The 2-hour private tour costs 110€ ($143) for individuals or 90€ ($117) per person for parties of two or more. A less expensive walking tour takes place on Friday at 10:30am and 1pm, lasting 2 hours and costing 30€ ($39) per person. The meeting point for this tour is 23 Place Vendôme, 1er. More detailed information about meeting your guide will be sent when you reserve by e-mail.

Another walking tour lasts 2 hours and costs 25€ ($33) per person, and it's operated by **Viator Tours** (contact the outfit by searching www.viator.com). Participants meet in front of the Ritz Hotel at Place Vendôme. For both tours above, take the Métro to Tuileries.

Strolling Around Paris

The best way to discover Paris is on foot. Our favorite walks are along the Seine and down the Champs-Elysées from the Arc de Triomphe to the Louvre. In this chapter we highlight the attractions of Montmartre, the Latin Quarter, and the Marais.

For more walking tours in the City of Light, see *Frommer's Memorable Walks in Paris*.

WALKING TOUR 1	MONTMARTRE

Start:	Place Pigalle (Métro: Pigalle).
Finish:	Place Pigalle.
Time:	5 hours, more if you break for lunch. It's a 4km (2½-mile) trek.
Best Time:	Any day it isn't raining. Set out by 10am at the latest.
Worst Time:	After dark.

Soft-white three-story houses and slender barren trees stick up from the ground like giant toothpicks—that's how Utrillo, befogged by absinthe, saw Montmartre. Toulouse-Lautrec painted it as a district of cabarets, circus freaks, and prostitutes. Today, Montmartre remains truer to the dwarfish Toulouse-Lautrec's conception than it does to Utrillo's.

Before all this, Montmartre was a sleepy farm community with windmills dotting the landscape. The name has always been the subject of disagreement, some arguing it originated from the "mount of Mars," a Roman temple at the top of the hill, others asserting it's "mount of martyrs," a reference to the martyrdom of St. Denis, who was beheaded here with fellow saints Rusticus and Eleutherius.

Turn right after leaving the Métro station and go down boulevard de Clichy; turn left at the Cirque Medrano, and begin the climb up rue des Martyrs. On reaching rue des Abbesses, turn left and walk along this street, crossing place des Abbesses. Go uphill along rue Ravignan, which leads to tree-studded place Emile-Goudeau, in the middle of rue Ravignan. At no. 13, across from the Timhôtel, is the:

❶ Bateau-Lavoir (Boat Washhouse)
Though gutted by fire in 1970, this building, known as the cradle of cubism, has been reconstructed by the city. While Picasso lived here (1904–12), he painted

one of the world's most famous portraits, *The Third Rose* (of Gertrude Stein), as well as *Les Demoiselles d'Avignon*. Other residents were van Dongen, Jacob, and Gris; Modigliani, Rousseau, and Braque had studios nearby.

Rue Ravignan ends at place Jean-Baptiste-Clément. Go to the end of the street and cross onto rue Norvins (on your right). Here rues Norvins, St-Rustique, and des Saules collide a few steps from rue Poulbot, a scene captured in a famous Utrillo painting. Turn right and go down rue Poulbot. At no. 11 you come to:

❷ Espace Dalí Montmartre

The phantasmagoric world of Espace Dalí Montmartre (📞 **01-42-64-40-10**) features 300 original Dalí works, including his famous 1956 lithograph of Don Quixote.

Rue Poulbot crosses tiny:

❸ Place du Calvaire

Here you have a panoramic view of Paris. On this square once lived artist/painter/lithographer Maurice Neumont (a plaque marks the house).

From place du Calvaire, head east along rue Gabrielle, taking the first left north along the tiny rue du Calvaire, which leads to:

❹ Place du Tertre

This old town square is tourist central. All around the square are terrace restaurants with dance floors and colored lights, while Sacré-Coeur gleams through the trees. The cafes overflow with people, as do the indoor and outdoor art galleries. Some of the "artists" still wear berets (you'll be asked countless times if you want your portrait sketched). The square is so loaded with local color that it can seem gaudy and inauthentic.

TAKE A BREAK
Many restaurants in Montmartre, especially those around place du Tertre, are unabashed tourist traps. An exception is **La Crémaillère 1900**, 15 place du Tertre, 18e (📞 **01-46-06-58-59**). As its name suggests, this is a Belle Epoque dining room, retaining much of its original look, including many paintings. You can sit on the terrace opening onto the square or retreat to the courtyard garden. A full menu is served throughout the day, including a standard array of French classics. Go any time daily from 9am to 12:30am.

Right off the square fronting rue du Mont-Cenis is:

❺ St-Pierre

Originally a Benedictine abbey, this church has played many roles: a Temple of Reason during the Revolution, a food depot, a clothing store, and even a munitions factory. These days, one of Paris's oldest churches is back to being a church.

Facing St-Pierre, turn right and follow rue Azaïs to:

❻ Sacré-Coeur

The basilica's Byzantine domes and bell tower loom above Paris and present a wide vista (see "The Top Attractions: From the Arc de Triomphe to the Tour Eiffel" in chapter 8). Behind the church, clinging to the hillside, are steep, crooked little streets that have survived the march of progress.

Facing the basilica, take the street on the left (rue du Cardinal-Guibert); then go left onto rue du Chevalier-de-la-Barre and right onto rue du Mont-Cenis. Continue on this street to rue Cortot; then turn left. At no. 12 is the:

❼ Musée de Vieux Montmartre

Musée de Vieux Montmartre (📞 **01-46-06-61-11**) presents a collection of mementos of the neighborhood. Luminaries such as Dufy, van Gogh, Renoir, and Suzanne Valadon and her son, Utrillo, occupied this 17th-century house, and it was here that Renoir put the final touches on his *Moulin de la Galette* (see below).

From the museum, turn right, heading up rue des Saules past a winery, a reminder of the days when Montmartre was a farming village on the outskirts of Paris. A grape-harvesting festival is held here every October. The intersection of rue des Saules and rue St-Vincent is one of the most visited and photographed corners of the butte. Here, on one corner, sits what was the famous old:

❽ Cabaret des Assassins

This was long ago renamed **Au Lapin Agile** (see "Chansonniers" in chapter 11). Picasso and Utrillo frequented this little cottage, which numerous artists have patronized and painted. On any given afternoon, French folk tunes, love ballads, army songs, sea chanteys, and music-hall ditties stream out of the cafe and onto the street.

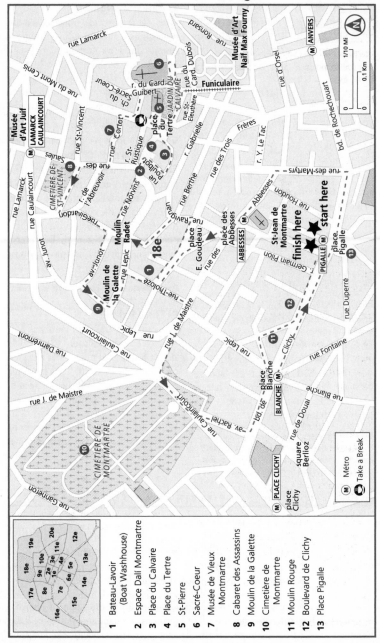

1/10 Mi

0   0.1 Km

Ⓜ ANVERS

Ⓜ LAMARCK CAULAINCOURT

Musée d'Art Juif

Musée d'Art Naïf Max Fourny

Funiculaire

CIMETIÈRE DE ST-VINCENT

18e

ABBESSES

St-Jean de Montmartre

finish here ★
start here ★

Ⓜ PIGALLE

place Pigalle

Moulin de la Galette

Moulin Radet

CIMETIÈRE DE MONTMARTRE

Ⓜ BLANCHE

place Blanche

square Berlioz

Ⓜ PLACE CLICHY

place Clichy

Ⓜ Métro

☉ Take a Break

1 Bateau-Lavoir (Boat Washhouse)
2 Espace Dalí Montmartre
3 Place du Calvaire
4 Place du Tertre
5 St-Pierre
6 Sacré-Coeur
7 Musée de Vieux Montmartre
8 Cabaret des Assassins
9 Moulin de la Galette
10 Cimetière de Montmartre
11 Moulin Rouge
12 Boulevard de Clichy
13 Place Pigalle

Turn left on rue St-Vincent, passing the Cimetière St-Vincent on your right (see "Cemeteries" in chapter 8). Take a left onto rue Girardon and climb the stairs. In a minute or two, you'll spot on your right two of the *moulins* (windmills) that used to dot the butte. One of these, at no. 75, is the:

❾ Moulin de la Galette

This windmill (entrance at 1 av. Junot) was built in 1622 and was immortalized in oil by Renoir (the painting is in the Musée d'Orsay). When it was turned into a dance hall in the 1860s, it was named for the *galettes* (cakes made with flour ground inside the mills) that were sold here. Later, Toulouse-Lautrec, van Gogh, and Utrillo visited the dance hall. A few steps away, at the angle of rue Lepic and rue Girardon, is the Moulin Radet, now part of a restaurant.

Turn right onto rue Lepic and walk past no. 54. In 1886, van Gogh lived here with his brother, Guillaumin. Take a right turn onto rue Joseph-de-Maistre and then left again on rue Caulaincourt until you reach the:

❿ Cimetière de Montmartre

This final resting place is second in fame only to Père-Lachaise and is the haunt of Nijinsky, Dumas fils, Stendhal, Degas, and Truffaut, among others (see "Cemeteries" in chapter 8).

From the cemetery, take avenue Rachel; turn left onto boulevard de Clichy; and go to place Blanche, where stands a windmill even better known than the one in Renoir's painting, the:

⓫ Moulin Rouge

One of the world's most-talked-about nightclubs, the Moulin Rouge was immortalized by Toulouse-Lautrec. The windmill is still here, and so is the can-can, but the rest has become an expensive, slick variety show with an emphasis on undraped women (see "Nightclubs & Cabarets" in chapter 11).

From place Blanche, you can begin a descent on:

⓬ Boulevard de Clichy

En route, you'll have to fight off the pornographers and hustlers trying to lure you into sex joints. With some rare exceptions, notably the citadels of the *chansonniers* (songwriters), boulevard de Clichy is one gigantic tourist trap. But everyone who comes to Paris invariably winds up here.

The boulevard strips and peels its way down to where you started:

⓭ Place Pigalle

The center of nudity in Paris was named after a French sculptor, Pigalle, whose closest brush with nudity was a depiction of Voltaire in the buff. Toulouse-Lautrec had his studio right off the square at 5 av. Frochot. Of course, place Pigalle was the notorious "Pig Alley" of World War II. When Edith Piaf was lonely and hungry, she sang in the alleyways, hoping to earn a few francs for the night.

WALKING TOUR 2   THE LATIN QUARTER

Start:	Place St-Michel (Métro: St-Michel).
Finish:	The Panthéon.
Time:	3 hours, not counting stops. The distance is about 2.5km (1½ miles).
Best Time:	Any weekday from 9am to 4pm.
Worst Time:	Sunday morning, when everybody is asleep.

This is the precinct of the Université de Paris (known for its most famous branch, the Sorbonne), where students meet and fall in love over café crème and croissants. Rabelais named it the Quartier Latin after the students and professors who spoke Latin in the classroom and on the streets. The sector teems with restaurants, cafes, bookstalls, *caveaux* (basement nightclubs), *étudiants* (students), *clochards* (bums), and *gamins* (kids).

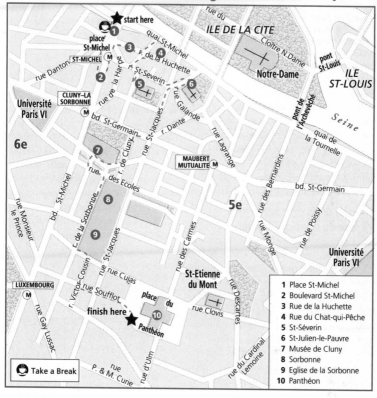

1 Place St-Michel
2 Boulevard St-Michel
3 Rue de la Huchette
4 Rue du Chat-qui-Pêche
5 St-Séverin
6 St-Julien-le-Pauvre
7 Musée de Cluny
8 Sorbonne
9 Eglise de la Sorbonne
10 Panthéon

A good starting point for your tour is:

❶ Place St-Michel

Balzac used to draw water from the fountain (Davioud's 1860 sculpture of St-Michel slaying the dragon) when he was a youth. This was the scene of frequent skirmishes between the Germans and the Resistance in the summer of 1944, and the names of those who died here are engraved on plaques around the square.

>
> **TAKE A BREAK**
> Open 24 hours, **Café le Départ St-Michel**, 1 place St-Michel (☎ **01-43-54-24-55**), lies on the banks of the Seine. The decor is warmly modern, with etched mirrors reflecting the faces of a diversified crowd. If you want to fortify yourself for your walk, opt for one of the warm or cold snacks, including sandwiches.

To the south, you find:

❷ Boulevard St-Michel

Also called by locals Boul' Mich, this is the main street of the Latin Quarter as it heads south. It's a major tourist artery and won't give you great insight into local life. For that, you can branch off to any streets that feed into the boulevard and find cafes, bars, gyro counters, ice-cream stands, crepe stands, and bistros such as those seen in movies set in Paris in the 1950s. The Paris Commune began here in 1871, as did the student uprisings of 1968.

From place St-Michel, with your back to the Seine, turn left down:

❸ Rue de la Huchette

This typical street was the setting of Elliot Paul's *The Last Time I Saw Paris* (1942). Paul first wandered here "on a soft summer evening, and entirely by chance," in 1923 and then moved into no. 28, the Hôtel Mont-Blanc. Though much has changed, some of the buildings are so old that they have to be propped up by timbers. Paul captured the spirit of the street more evocatively than anyone, writing of "the delivery wagons, makeshift vehicles propelled by pedaling boys, pushcarts of itinerant vendors, knife-grinders, umbrella menders, a herd of milk goats, and the neighborhood pedestrians." (The local bordello has closed, however.) Today, you see lots of Greek restaurants.

Branching off this street to your left is:

❹ Rue du Chat-qui-Pêche

This is said to be the shortest, narrowest street in the world, with not one door and only a handful of windows. It's usually filled with garbage or lovers or both. Before the quay was built, the Seine sometimes flooded the cellars of the houses, and legend has it that an enterprising cat took advantage of its good fortune and went fishing in the confines of the cellars—hence the street's name, which means "Street of the Cat Who Fishes."

Now retrace your steps toward place St-Michel and turn left at the intersection with rue de la Harpe, which leads to rue St-Séverin. At the intersection, take a left to see:

❺ St-Séverin

A flamboyant Gothic church named for a 6th-century recluse, St-Séverin was built from 1210 to 1230 and was reconstructed in 1458, over the years adopting many of the features of Notre-Dame, across the river. The tower was completed in 1487 and the chapels from 1498 to 1520; Hardouin-Mansart designed the Chapelle de la Communion in 1673 when he was 27, and it contains some beautiful Roualt etchings from the 1920s. Before entering, walk around the church to examine the gargoyles, birds of prey, and reptilian monsters projecting from its roof. To the right, facing the church, is the 15th-century "garden of ossuaries."

The stained glass inside St-Séverin, behind the altar, is a stunning adornment using great swaths of color to depict the seven sacraments.

After visiting the church, go back to rue St-Séverin and follow it to rue Galande; then continue on until you reach:

❻ St-Julien-le-Pauvre

This church is on the south side of square René-Viviani. First, stand at the gateway and look at the beginning of rue Galande, especially the old houses with the steeples of St-Séverin rising across the way; it's one of the most frequently painted scenes on the Left Bank. Enter the courtyard, and you'll be in medieval Paris. The garden to the left has the best view of Notre-Dame. Everyone from Rabelais to Thomas Aquinas has passed through the doors of this church. Before the 6th century, a chapel stood on this spot. The present church goes back to the Longpont monks, who began work on it in 1170 (making it the oldest church in Paris). In 1655, it was given to the Hôtel Dieu and in time became a small warehouse for salt. In 1889, it was presented to the followers of the Melchite Greek rite, a branch of the Byzantine church.

Return to rue Galande and turn left at the intersection with rue St-Séverin. Continue until you reach rue St-Jacques, turn left, and turn right when you reach boulevard St-Germain. Follow this boulevard to rue de Cluny, turn left, and head toward the entrance to the:

❼ Musée de Cluny

Even if you're rushed, see *The Lady and the Unicorn* tapestries and the remains of the Roman baths. (See "The Major Museums" in chapter 8.)

After your visit to the Cluny, exit onto boulevard St-Michel, but instead of heading back to place St-Michel, turn left and walk to place de la Sorbonne and the:

❽ Sorbonne

One of the most famous academic institutions in the world, the Sorbonne was founded in the 13th century by Robert de Sorbon, St. Louis's confessor, for poor students who wished to pursue theological studies. By the next century it had become the most prestigious university in the West, attracting such professors as Thomas Aquinas and Roger Bacon and such students as Dante, Calvin, and Longfellow. Napoleon reorganized it in 1806. The courtyard and galleries are open to the public when the university is in session. In the Cour d'Honneur are statues of Hugo and Pasteur. At first glance from place de la Sorbonne, the Sorbonne seems architecturally undistinguished. In truth, it was rather indiscriminately reconstructed in the early 1900s. A better fate lay in store for the:

❾ Eglise de la Sorbonne

Built in 1635 by Le Mercier, this church contains the marble tomb of Cardinal Richelieu, a work by Girardon based on a design by Le Brun. At his feet is the remarkable statue *Learning in Tears*.

From the church, go south on rue Victor-Cousin and turn left at rue Soufflot. At the street's end is place du Panthéon and the:

❿ Panthéon

Sitting atop Mont St-Geneviève, this nonreligious temple is the final resting place of such distinguished figures as Hugo, Zola, Rousseau, Voltaire, and Curie. (See "Architectural & Historic Highlights" in chapter 8.)

WALKING TOUR 3   THE MARAIS

Start:	Place de la Bastille (Métro: Bastille).
Finish:	Place de la Bastille.
Time:	4½ hours, with only brief stops en route. The distance is about 4.5km (2¾ miles).
Best Time:	Monday to Saturday, when more buildings and shops are open. If interiors are open, often you can walk into courtyards.
Worst Time:	Toward dusk, when shops and museums are closed and it's too dark to admire the architectural details.

When Paris began to overflow the confines of Ile de la Cité in the 13th century, the citizenry started to settle in Le Marais, a marsh that was once flooded by the Seine. By the 17th century, the Marais had become the center of aristocratic Paris, and some of its great *hôtels particuliers* (mansions), many now restored or still being spruced up, were built by the finest craftsmen in France. In the 18th and 19th centuries, fashion deserted the Marais for the expanding Faubourg St-Germain and Faubourg St-Honoré. Industry took over and once-elegant hotels deteriorated into tenements. There was talk of demolishing the neighborhood, but in 1962 the community banded together and saved the historic district.

Today, the 17th-century mansions are fashionable once again. The *International Herald Tribune* called this area the latest refuge for the Paris artisan fleeing the tourist-trampled St-Germain-des-Prés. (However, that doesn't mean the area doesn't get its share of tourist traffic—quite the contrary.) The "marsh" sprawls across the 3rd and 4th arrondissements, bounded by the Grands Boulevards, rue du Temple, place des Vosges, and the Seine. It has become Paris's center of gay/lesbian life, particularly on rues St-Croix-de-la-Bretonnerie, des Archives, and Vieille-du-Temple, and is a great area for window-shopping at trendy boutiques, up-and-coming galleries, and eclectic stores.

Begin your tour at the site that spawned one of the most celebrated and abhorred revolutions in human history:

❶ Place de la Bastille

On July 14, 1789, a mob attacked the Bastille prison here, igniting the French Revolution. Now, nothing of this symbol of despotism remains. Built in 1369, it loomed over Paris with eight huge towers. Within them, many prisoners, some sentenced by Louis XIV for "witchcraft," were kept, the best known being the "Man in the Iron Mask." Yet when the revolutionary mob stormed the fortress, only seven prisoners were discovered. (The Marquis de Sade had been shipped to the madhouse 10 days earlier.) The authorities had discussed razing it, so the attack meant little. But what it symbolized and what it unleashed can never be undone, and each July 14 the country celebrates Bastille Day with great festivity. Since the late 1980s, what had been scorned as a grimy-looking traffic circle has become an artistic focal point, thanks to the construction of the Opéra Bastille on its eastern edge.

It was probably easier to storm the Bastille in 1789 than it is now to cross over to the center of the square for a close-up view of the:

❷ Colonne de Juillet

The July Column doesn't commemorate the Revolution, but honors the victims of the July Revolution of 1830, which put Louis-Philippe on the throne after the heady but wrenching victories and defeats of Napoleon Bonaparte. The winged God of Liberty, whose forehead bears an emerging star, crowns the tower.

From place de la Bastille, walk west along rue St-Antoine for about a block. Turn right and walk north along rue des Tournelles, noting the:

❸ Statue of Beaumarchais

Erected in 1895, it honors the 18th-century author of *The Barber of Seville* and *The Marriage of Figaro*, set to music by Rossini and Mozart, respectively.

Continue north for a long block along rue des Tournelles; then turn left at medieval-looking rue Pas-de-la-Mule (Footsteps of the Mule), which will open suddenly onto the northeastern corner of enchanting:

❹ Place des Vosges

This is Paris's oldest square and once its most fashionable, boasting 36 brick-and-stone pavilions rising from covered arcades that allowed people to shop no matter what the weather. The buildings were constructed according to a strict plan: The height of the facades is equal to their width, and the height of the triangular roofs is half the height of the facades. In 1559, Henri II was killed while jousting on a spot near the Hôtel des Tournelles; his widow, Catherine de Médicis, had the place torn down. The current square was begun in 1605 on Henri IV's orders and called place Royal; the king intended the square to be the scene of businesses and social festivities and even planned to live there, but Ravaillac had other plans and assassinated Henri 2 years before its completion in 1612. By the 17th century, the square was the home of many aristocrats. During the Revolution, it was renamed place de l'Invisibilité, and its statue of Louis XIII was stolen (and probably melted down). A replacement now stands in its place.

In 1800, the square was renamed place des Vosges because the Vosges département (an administrative unit) was the first in France to pay its taxes to Napoleon. The addition of chestnut trees sparked a controversy; critics say they spoil the perspective. Even though its fortunes waned when the Marais went out of fashion, place des Vosges is back big-time. Over the years, the famous often took up residence: Descartes, Pascal, Cardinal Richelieu, courtesan Marion Delorme, Gautier, Daudet, and Mme de Sévigné all lived here. But its best-known occupant was Victor Hugo (his home, now a museum, is the only house open to the public).

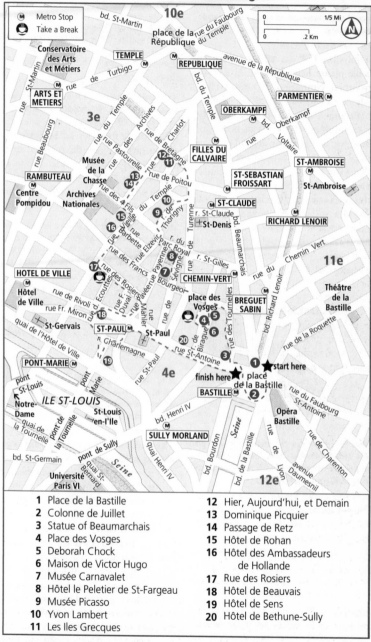

- (M) Metro Stop
- (☺) Take a Break

0 — 1/5 Mi
0 — .2 Km

10e

bd. St-Martin
rue du Faubourg du Temple
place de la République
avenue de la République

Conservatoire des Arts et Métiers
TEMPLE (M)
REPUBLIQUE (M)
PARMENTIER (M)
rue de Turbigo

ARTS ET METIERS
bd. du Temple
OBERKAMPF (M)
bd. Oberkampf
rue Voltaire

rue St-Martin
rue Beaubourg
3e
rue du Temple
rue des Archives
rue de Charlot
rue de Bretagne
FILLES DU CALVAIRE (M)
ST-AMBROISE (M)

Musée de la Chasse
rue Pastourelle
rue de Poitou
ST-SEBASTIEN FROISSART (M)
St-Ambroise

RAMBUTEAU (M)
rue des 4 Fils
rue du Temple
ST-CLAUDE (M)
r. St-Claude
RICHARD LENOIR (M)

Centre Pompidou
Archives Nationales
rue Vieille du Temple
r. de Thorigny
St-Denis
bd. Beaumarchais

rue Barbette
Parc Royal
r. du Parc Royal
r. St-Gilles
Chemin Vert
11e

HOTEL DE VILLE
rue des Francs Bourgeois
rue de Sévigné
CHEMIN-VERT (M)
rue du Chemin Vert
Théâtre de la Bastille

Hôtel de Ville
rue de Rivoli
rue Elzévir
place des Vosges
BREGUET SABIN (M)
rue de la Roquette

rue Fr. Miron
rue des Rosiers
rue Vieille du Temple
rue des Tournelles
rue de Birague

quai de l'Hôtel de Ville
St-Gervais
ST-PAUL (M)
St-Paul
r. Charlemagne
rue St-Paul
4e
r. St-Antoine

PONT-MARIE (M)
pont Marie
finish here ★
place de la Bastille
BASTILLE (M)
rue du Faubourg St-Antoine

pont St-Louis
ILE ST-LOUIS
St-Louis en-l'Ile
bd. Henri IV
Opéra Bastille
rue de Charenton

Notre-Dame
quai de la Tournelle
pont de la Tournelle
SULLY MORLAND (M)
Seine
avenue Daumesnil

pont de Sully
bd. St-Germain
Université Paris VI
quai St-Bernard
Seine
quai Henri IV
bd. Bourdon
bd. de la Bastille
12e
rue de Lyon

start here ★ place de la Bastille

1 Place de la Bastille	12 Hier, Aujourd'hui, et Demain
2 Colonne de Juillet	13 Dominique Picquier
3 Statue of Beaumarchais	14 Passage de Retz
4 Place des Vosges	15 Hôtel de Rohan
5 Deborah Chock	16 Hôtel des Ambassadeurs de Hollande
6 Maison de Victor Hugo	17 Rue des Rosiers
7 Musée Carnavalet	18 Hôtel de Beauvais
8 Hôtel le Peletier de St-Fargeau	19 Hôtel de Sens
9 Musée Picasso	20 Hôtel de Bethune-Sully
10 Yvon Lambert	
11 Les Iles Grecques	

Place des Vosges is the centerpiece of many unusual, charming, and/or funky shops. At 20 place des Vosges is one of the best of these:

❺ Deborah Chock

This shop (✆ **01-48-04-86-86**) sells reproductions of the colorful and contemporary paintings of Deborah Chock, who is noted for the pithy phrases on the background of her paintings that reflect insights from the worlds of poetry, philosophy, and psychoanalysis. The address is at 20 place des Vosges, and hours are 10am to 1pm and 2 to 7pm, but call ahead because times can vary. It is sometimes closed on Monday and Tuesday. Use it as a debut before you explore the many other art galleries in the neighborhood. The staff is English-speaking and well versed in the currents of the Paris art scene.

TAKE A BREAK
Two cafes hold court from opposite sides of place des Vosges, both serving café au lait, wine, *eaux de vie* (brandies), sandwiches, pastries, and tea: **Ma Bourgogne** at no. 19 (✆ **01-42-78-44-64**), on the western edge, and **La Chope des Vosges**, at no. 22 (✆ **01-42-72-64-04**).

Near the square's southeastern corner at 6 place des Vosges, commemorating the life and times of a writer whose works were read with passion in the 19th century, is the:

❻ Maison de Victor Hugo

Hugo's former home is now a museum (✆ **01-42-72-10-16**) and literary shrine (see "Literary Landmarks" in chapter 8). Hugo lived there from 1832 to 1848, when he went into voluntary exile on the Channel Islands after the rise of the despotic Napoleon III.

Exit place des Vosges from its northwestern corner (opposite the Maison de Victor Hugo) and walk west along rue des Francs-Bourgeois until you reach the intersection with rue de Sévigné; then make a right. At no. 23 is the:

❼ Musée Carnavalet

This 16th-century mansion is now a museum (✆ **01-44-59-58-32**) devoted to the history of Paris and the French Revolution (see "The Major Museums" in chapter 8).

Continue to a point near the northern terminus of rue de Sévigné, noting no. 29 (now part of the Carnavalet). This is the:

❽ Hôtel le Peletier de St-Fargeau

The structure bears the name of its former occupant, who was considered responsible for the death sentence of Louis XVI. It's used for offices and can't be visited.

At the end of the street, make a left onto lovely rue du Parc-Royal, lined with 17th-century mansions. It leads to place de Thorigny, where at no. 5 you'll find the:

❾ Musée Picasso

The museum occupies the **Hôtel Salé,** built by a salt-tax collector (see "The Major Museums" in chapter 8). You can visit the museum now or come back at the end of the tour.

Walk northeast along rue Thorigny and turn left onto rue Debelleyme. After a block, near the corner of rue Vieille-du-Temple, at 108 rue Vieille-du-Temple, is a particularly worthwhile art gallery (among dozens in this neighborhood):

❿ Yvon Lambert

This gallery (✆ **01-42-71-09-33**) specializes in contemporary and sometimes radically avant-garde art by international artists. The art is displayed in a cavernous main showroom, spilling over into an annex room. An excellent primer for the local arts scene, it provides an agreeable contrast to the 17th-century trappings all around you.

Continue north for 2 short blocks along rue Debelleyme until you reach rue de Bretagne. Anyone who appreciates a really good deli will want to stop at 14 rue de Bretagne:

⓫ Les Iles Grecques

This deli (✆ **01-42-71-00-56**) is the most popular of the area's ethnic take-out restaurants, a perfect place to buy picnic supplies before heading to square du Temple (up rue de Bretagne) or place des Vosges. You'll find moussaka, stuffed eggplant, stuffed grape leaves, olives, *tarama* (a savory paste made from fish roe), and both meatballs and vegetarian balls. It's open Monday from 4 to 8pm and Tuesday to Sunday from 10am to 2pm and 3:30 to 8pm.

After you fill up on great food, note that at the same address is:

⑫ Hier, Aujourd'hui, et Demain

At this shop (✆ **01-42-77-69-02**) you can appreciate France's love affair with 1930s Art Deco. Michel, the owner, provides an array of bibelots and art objects, with one of the widest selections of colored glass in town. Works by late-19th-century glassmakers such as Daum, Gallé, and Legras are shown. Some items require special packing and great care in transport; others can be carted home as souvenirs.

Now walk southeast along rue Charlot to no. 10 at the corner of rue Pastourelle, where you'll be tempted by the fabrics of:

⑬ Dominique Picquier

Looking to redo your settee? This stylish shop (✆ **01-42-72-39-14**) sells a wide roster of fabric (50% cotton, 50% linen) that stands up to rugged use. Most patterns are based on some botanical inspiration, such as ginkgo leaves, vanilla pods and vines, and magnolia branches. Most cost 95€ ($124) per meter (3¼ ft.), although some, particularly plush velvets, can go as high as 118€ ($153) per meter.

Nearby, at 9 rue Charlot, adjacent to the corner of rue Charlot and rue du Perche, is the Marais's large experimental art gallery, the:

⑭ Passage de Retz

Opened in 1994, this avant-garde gallery (✆ **01-48-04-37-99**) has about 630 sq. m (6,781 sq. ft.) of space to show off its highly amusing exhibits. It has shown Japanese textiles, American abstract expressionist paintings, modern Venetian glass, contemporary Haitian paintings, and selections from affiliated art galleries in Québec.

Walk 1 block farther along rue Charlot, turn left for a block onto rue des 4 Fils; then go right on rue Vieille-du-Temple to no. 87, where you'll come across Delamair's:

⑮ Hôtel de Rohan

The fourth Cardinal Rohan, the larcenous cardinal of the "diamond necklace scandal" that led to a flood of destructive publicity for Marie Antoinette, once lived here. The first occupant of the hotel was reputed to be the son of Louis XVI. The interior is usually closed to the public except during an occasional exhibit. If it's open, check out the amusing **Salon des Singes (Monkey Room).** Sometimes you can visit the courtyard, which boasts one of the finest sculptures of 18th-century France, *The Watering of the Horses of the Sun,* with a nude Apollo and four horses against a background of exploding sunbursts. (If you want to see another Delamair work, detour to 60 rue des Francs-Bourgeois to see the extraordinary Hôtel de Soubise, now housing the **Musée de l'Histoire de France** [p. 209].)

Along the same street, at no. 47, is the:

⑯ Hôtel des Ambassadeurs de Hollande

Here, Beaumarchais wrote *The Marriage of Figaro.* It's one of the most splendid mansions in the Marais and, despite its name, was never occupied by the Dutch embassy.

Continue walking south along rue Vieille-du-Temple until you reach:

⑰ Rue des Rosiers

Rue des Rosiers (Street of the Rosebushes) is one of the most colorful and typical streets remaining from Paris's old Jewish quarter, and you'll find an intriguing blend of living memorials to Ashkenazi and Sephardic traditions. The Star of David shines from some of the shop windows; Hebrew letters appear, sometimes in neon; couscous is sold from shops run by Moroccan, Tunisian, or Algerian Jews; restaurants serve kosher food; and signs appeal for Jewish liberation. You'll come across many delicacies you might have read about but never seen, such as sausage stuffed in a gooseneck, roots of black horseradish, and pickled lemons.

TAKE A BREAK
The street offers a cornucopia of ethnic restaurants that remain steadfast to their national origins. The most frequented is **L'As du Falafel**, 34 rue des Rosiers (℃ **01-48-87-63-60**). This is both a kosher falafel kiosk and a small restaurant. Some clients have claimed that it serves the "best falafel on the planet." Since we haven't tasted all versions, we're not sure. But the falafel is superb, costing 6€ ($7.80) sitdown, but only 4€ ($5.20) to go. It's open Monday to Thursday and Sunday noon to midnight; Friday noon to 6pm.

Take a left onto rue des Rosiers and head down to rue Pavée, which gets its name because it was the first street in Paris, sometime during the 1300s, to have cobblestones placed over its open sewer. At this "Paved Street," turn right and walk south until you reach the St-Paul Métro stop. Make a right along rue François-Miron and check out no. 68, the 17th-century:

⑱ Hôtel de Beauvais

Though the facade was damaged in the Revolution, it remains one of Paris's most charming hotels. A plaque announces that Mozart lived here in 1763 and played at the court of Versailles. (He was 7 at the time.) Louis XIV presented the mansion to Catherine Bellier, wife of Pierre de Beauvais and lady-in-waiting to Anne of Austria; she reportedly had the honor of introducing Louis, then 16, to the facts of life. To visit the interior, apply to the **Association du Paris Historique** on the ground floor.

Continue your walk along rue François-Miron until you come to a crossroads, where you take

a sharp left along rue de Jouy, cross rue Fourcy, and turn onto rue du Figuier, where at no. 1 you'll see the:

⑲ Hôtel de Sens

The structure was built between the 1470s and 1519 for the archbishops of Sens. Along with the Cluny on the Left Bank, it's the only domestic architecture remaining from the 15th century. Long after the archbishops had departed in 1605, the wife of Henri IV, Queen Margot, lived here. Her new lover, "younger and more virile," slew her old lover as she looked on in amusement. Today, the hotel houses the Bibliothèque Forney (℃ **01-42-78-14-60**). Leaded windows and turrets characterize the facade; you can go into the courtyard to see more ornate stone decoration—the gate is open Tuesday to Friday from 1:30 to 8:15pm and Saturday from 10am to 8:15pm.

Retrace your steps to rue de Fourcy, turn right, and walk up the street until you reach the St-Paul Métro stop again. Turn right onto rue St-Antoine and continue to no. 62:

⑳ Hôtel de Bethune-Sully

Work began on this mansion in 1625, on the order of Jean Androuet de Cerceau. In 1634, it was acquired by the duc de Sully, once Henri IV's minister of finance. After a straitlaced life as the "accountant of France," Sully broke loose in his declining years, adorning himself with diamonds and garish rings and a young bride who had a thing for very young men. The hotel was acquired by the government just after World War II and is now the seat of the National Office of Historical Monuments and Sites, with an information center and a bookshop inside. Recently restored, the relief-studded facade is especially appealing. You can visit the interior with a guide on Saturday or Sunday at 3pm and can visit the courtyard and the garden any day; chamber-music concerts are frequently staged here.

10

Shopping in Paris

You don't have to buy anything to appreciate shopping in Paris—just soak up the art form the French have made of rampant consumerism. Peer in the *vitrines* (display windows), absorb cutting-edge ideas, witness new trends, and take home with you a whole new education in style.

1 The Shopping Scene

BEST BUYS

FOODSTUFFS   Nothing makes a better souvenir than a product of France brought home to savor later. Supermarkets are located in tourist neighborhoods; stock up on coffee, designer chocolates, mustards (try Maille or Meaux brands), and perhaps American products in French packages for the kids. However, to be sure you don't try to bring home a prohibited foodstuff, see section 2, "Entry Requirements," in chapter 3, "Planning Your Trip to Paris."

FUN FASHION   Sure, you can buy couture or *prêt-à-porter* (ready-to-wear), but French teens and trendsetters have their own stores where the latest looks are affordable. Even the dime stores in Paris sell designer copies. In the stalls in front of the department stores on boulevard Haussmann, you'll find some of the latest accessories, guaranteed for a week's worth of small talk once you get home.

PERFUMES, MAKEUP & BEAUTY TREATMENTS   A discount of 20% to 30% makes these items a great buy; qualify for a VAT refund (see below), and you'll save 40% to 45% off the Paris retail price, allowing you to bring home goods at half the U.S. price. Duty-free shops abound in Paris and are always less expensive than the ones at the airports.

For bargain cosmetics, try out French dime-store and drugstore brands such as **Bourjois** (made in the Chanel factories), **Lierac**, and **Galenic**. **Vichy**, famous for its water, has a skin-care and makeup line. The newest retail trend in Paris is the *parapharmacie*, a type of discount drugstore loaded with inexpensive brands, health cures, beauty regimes, and diet plans. These usually offer a 20% discount.

GETTING A VAT REFUND

The French **value-added tax** (**VAT—TVA** in French) is 19.6%, but you can get most of that back if you spend 182€ ($237) or more in any store that participates in the VAT refund program. Most stores participate.

Once you meet your required minimum purchase amount, you qualify for a tax refund. The amount of the refund varies with the way the refund is handled and the fee some stores charge you for processing it. So the refund at a department store may be 13%, whereas at a small shop it may be 15% or even 18%.

Tips **Shopping Etiquette**

When you walk into a French store, it's traditional to greet the owner or sales clerk with a direct address, not a fey smile or even a weak *"Bonjour."* Only a clear and pleasant *"Bonjour, madame/monsieur"* will do.

And if you plan to enter the rarefied atmospheres of the top designer boutiques (to check out the pricey merchandise, if not to buy anything), be sure to dress the part. You don't need to wear couture, but do leave the sneakers and sweat suit back at your hotel. The sales staff will be much more accommodating if you look as if you belong there.

You'll receive **VAT refund papers** in the shop; some stores, like Hermès, have their own, while others provide a government form. Fill in the forms before you arrive at the airport and expect to stand in line at the Customs desk for as long as half an hour. You must show the goods at the airport, so have them on you or visit the Customs office before you check your luggage. Once the papers are mailed, a credit will appear, often months later, on your credit card bill. All refunds are processed at the point of departure from the **European Union (EU),** so if you're going to another EU country, don't apply for the refund in France.

Be sure to mark the paperwork to request that your refund be applied to your credit card so you aren't stuck with a check in euros, which may be hard to cash. This also ensures the best rate of exchange. In some airports, you're offered the opportunity to get your refund back in cash, which is tempting. But if you accept cash in any currency other than euros, you'll lose money on the conversion rate.

To avoid refund hassles, ask for a Global Refund form ("Shopping Checque") at a store where you make a purchase. When leaving an EU country, have it stamped by Customs, after which you take it to a Global Refund counter at one of more than 700 airports and border crossings in France. Your money is refunded on the spot. For information, contact **Global Refund Canada,** Box 2020 Station, Main Brampton, Ontario L6T 353 (© **800/993-4313** or 905/791-9078; www.globalrefund.com).

DUTY-FREE BOUTIQUES

The advantage of duty-free shops is that you don't have to pay the VAT, so you avoid the red tape of getting a refund. Both Charles de Gaulle and Orly airports have shopping galore (de Gaulle has a virtual mall with crystal, cutlery, chocolates, luggage, wine, pipes and lighters, lingerie, silk scarves, perfume, knitwear, jewelry, cameras, cheeses, and even antiques). You'll also find duty-free shops on the avenues branching out from the Opéra Garnier, in the 1st Arrondissement. Sometimes bargains can be found, but most often not.

BUSINESS HOURS

Usual shop hours are Monday to Saturday from 10am to 7pm, but hours vary, and Monday mornings don't run at full throttle. Small shops sometimes close for a 2-hour lunch break and some do not open at all until after lunch on Monday. Thursday is the best day for late-night shopping, with stores open to 9 or 10pm.

Sunday shopping is limited to tourist areas and flea markets, though there's growing demand for full-scale Sunday hours. The department stores are now open on the five Sundays before Christmas. The **Carrousel du Louvre,** a mall adjacent to the Louvre, is hopping on Sunday but closed on Monday. The tourist shops lining rue de Rivoli across from the Louvre are open on Sunday, as are the antiques villages, flea markets, and specialty events. Several food markets enliven the streets on Sunday. For our favorites, see the box "Food Markets" (p. 263). The **Virgin Megastore** on the Champs-Elysées, a big teen hangout, pays a fine to stay open on Sunday.

GREAT SHOPPING NEIGHBORHOODS

Here are the best of the shopping arrondissements:

1ST & 8TH ARRONDISSEMENTS These two arrondissements adjoin each other and form the heart of Paris's best Right Bank shopping strip—they're one big hunting ground. This area includes the **rue du Faubourg St-Honoré,** where the big designer houses are, and the **Champs-Elysées,** with hot mass-market and teen scenes. At one end of the 1st is the **Palais Royal,** one of the best shopping secrets in Paris, where an arcade of boutiques flanks each side of the garden of the former palace.

Also here is **avenue Montaigne,** Paris's most glamorous shopping street, boasting 2 blocks of ultrafancy shops, where you float from big name to big name and in a few hours can see everything from Dior to Caron. Avenue Montaigne is also the address of **Joseph,** a British design firm, and **Porthault,** maker of the poshest sheets in the world.

2ND ARRONDISSEMENT Right behind the Palais Royal is the **Garment District (Sentier),** as well as a few sophisticated shopping secrets, such as **place des Victoires.**

In the 19th century, this area became known for its *passages,* glass-enclosed shopping streets—in fact, the world's first shopping malls. They were also the city's first buildings to be illuminated by gaslight. Many have been torn down, but a dozen or so have survived. Of them all, we prefer **Passage de Grand Cerf,** between 145 rue St-Denis and 10 rue Dussoubs (Métro: Bourse), lying a few blocks from the Beaubourg. It's a place of wonder, filled with everything from retro-chic boutiques to (increasingly) Asian-themed shops. What's exciting is to come upon a discovery, perhaps a postage-stamp-size shop with a special jeweler who creates unique products such as jewel-toned safety pins.

3RD & 4TH ARRONDISSEMENTS The border between these two arrondissements gets fuzzy, especially around **place des Vosges,** center stage of the Marais. The districts provide several dramatically different shopping experiences.

On the surface, the shopping includes the "real people stretch" (where all the non-millionaires shop) of **rue de Rivoli** and **rue St-Antoine,** featuring everything from Gap and a branch of Marks & Spencer to local discount stores and mass merchants. Many shoppers will also be looking for **La Samaritaine,** 19 rue de la Monnaie, once the most famous department store in France. It occupied four noteworthy buildings erected between 1870 and 1927. These buildings have been sold and are undergoing renovation to be completed in 2012. The new owner has not made his intentions clear about the future of this Parisian landmark.

Hidden in the Marais is a medieval warren of twisting streets chockablock with cutting-edge designers and up-to-the-minute fashions and trends. Start by walking around place des Vosges for galleries, designer shops, and special finds; then dive in and lose yourself in the area leading to the Musée Picasso.

Finally, the 4th is the home of the **Bastille,** an up-and-coming area for artists and galleries, where you'll find the newest entry on the retail scene, the **Viaduc des Arts** (which actually stretches into the 12th). It's a collection of about 30 stores occupying a series of narrow vaulted niches under what used to be railroad tracks. They run parallel to avenue Daumesnil, centered on boulevard Diderot.

6TH & 7TH ARRONDISSEMENTS   Though the 6th is one of the most famous shopping districts in Paris—it's the soul of the Left Bank—a lot of the good stuff is hidden in the zone that turns into the residential district of the 7th. **Rue du Bac,** stretching from the 6th to the 7th in a few blocks, stands for all that wealth and glamour can buy.

9TH ARRONDISSEMENT   To add to the fun of shopping the Right Bank, the 9th sneaks in behind the 1st, so if you choose not to walk toward the Champs-Elysées and the 8th, you can head to the city's big department stores, all built in a row along **boulevard Haussmann** in the 9th. Department stores include not only the two big French icons, **Au Printemps** and **Galeries Lafayette,** but also a large branch of Britain's **Marks & Spencer.**

2 Shopping A to Z

ANTIQUES

Argenterie de Turenne ★ *Finds*   Inside, you'll find old-fashioned gentility and masses of silver, both secondhand sterling and plated, much of it made in France during the 19th and early 20th centuries. The array of trays, water pitchers, cutlery, napkin rings, tumblers, and punchbowls is staggering, but what many visitors find amazing is that congenially battered, silver-plated forks and spoons are sold by weight, at the rate of 60€ ($78) per kilo (about 2 lbs.), although most clients prefer to buy forks, knives, and spoons piecemeal, from 5€ ($6.50) each. The store lies within the Marais, a short walk from place des Vosges, on a block that's lined with purveyors of other old-fashioned grace notes that include antique glassware and porcelain. Open Tuesday to Saturday 10:30am to 7pm. 19 rue de Turenne, 4e. ✆ **01-42-72-04-00.** Métro: St-Paul.

Le Louvre des Antiquaires ★★   Across from the Louvre, this store offers three levels of fancy knickknacks and 250 vendors. It's just the place if you're looking for 30 matching Baccarat-crystal champagne flutes from the 1930s, a Sèvres tea service from 1773, or a signed Jean Fouquet gold-and-diamond pin. Too stuffy? No problem. There's always the 1940 Rolex with the aubergine crocodile strap. Prices can be high, but a few reasonable items are hidden here. What's more, the Sunday scene is fabulous, and there's a cafe with a variety of lunch menus. Pick up a free map and brochure of the premises from the information desk. Open Tuesday to Sunday 9am to 7pm. Closed Sunday July to Aug. 2 place du Palais Royal, 1er. ✆ **01-42-97-27-27.** Métro: Palais-Royal.

Village St-Paul   This isn't an antiques center, but a cluster of dealers in their own hole-in-the-wall hideout. It really hops on Sunday. Bring your camera, because inside the courtyards and alleys is a dream vision of hidden Paris: dealers in a courtyard selling furniture and other decorative items in French-country and formal styles. The rest of the street, stretching from the river to the Marais, is also lined with dealers. Open Thursday to Monday 11am to 7pm. 23–27 rue St-Paul, 4e. No phone. Métro: St-Paul.

ART

Artcurial ★★   Set within minimalist showrooms in one of the most spectacular 19th-century mansions in Paris, this is one of the best outlets in Europe for contemporary art. Since it was established in 1975, it has represented megastars such as Man

Ray and the "enfant terrible" of France's postwar intelligentsia, Jean Cocteau. Today, the names of showcased artists read like a *Who's Who* of contemporary art: Arman, Sonia de Launay, and Niki de Saint Phalle for painting and sculpture; Claude Lalanne for jewelry design; and Matta for contemporary carpets. Director Pierre-Alain Challier's bilingual staff is well versed in the merits of each individual artist on display. Despite an address that might be among the most expensive in the world (the intersection of avenue Montaigne and Champs-Elysées), the place is more welcoming than, and not as forbidding as, its location implies. Open Monday to Saturday 9am to 7pm. 61 av. Montaigne, 8e. ℭ 01-42-99-16-16. www.artcurial.com. Métro: Franklin-D-Roosevelt.

Galerie Adrien Maeght 𝕽𝕽𝕽   This art house is among the most famous names, selling contemporary art on a fancy Left Bank street that's far more fashionable than the bohemian Left Bank that Picasso knew. Open Monday 10am to 6pm; Tuesday to Saturday 9:30am to 7pm. 42 rue du Bac, 7e. ℭ 01-45-48-45-15. www.maeght.com. Métro: Rue du Bac.

Galerie 27   This tiny closet sells lithographs by famous artists of the early 20th century, including Picasso, Miró, Braque, and Léger. Contemporary artists are also represented. Open Tuesday to Saturday 10am to 1pm and 2:30 to 7pm. 27 rue de Seine, 6e. ℭ 01-43-54-78-54. Métro: St-Germain-des-Prés or Odéon.

J. C. Martinez 𝕽   In its way, this is one of the most charming and old-fashioned art galleries in Paris. Established in the mid-1970s within a single room that's loaded with at least 400 separate boxes, it specializes in antique prints and engravings, most of them crafted between the late 1700s and around 1910, and some even earlier. You can rummage randomly through the inventories here, depending on how rare they are. But if your parameters are more specialized, the staff will guide you toward whatever subject interests you the most. If you're interested in engravings of birds, botany, fashion, sailing ships, floral arrangements, architectural renderings, or horse races, there's at least one box devoted to that particular subject. And if you're interested in the way the borders of France and its internal regions have been organized and reorganized since the days of the *ancien régime,* there's a wondrous collection of maps crafted at different times of the nation's complicated history. Open Monday 10am to 12:30pm and 2:30 to 7pm; Tuesday to Friday 10am to 7pm; Saturday 10:30am to 7pm. 21 rue St-Sulpice, 6e. ℭ 01-43-26-34-53. Métro: Odéon or Mabillon.

La Maison Rouge 𝕽   The so-called "red house," created by Antoine de Galbert, has an ever-changing decor, as well as a constantly rotating display of the latest work of the "hot" artists of Paris. A large, well-laid-out, avant-garde space awaits you. Open Wednesday to Sunday 11am to 7pm (9pm on Thursday). Since this place is a virtual museum of art, an admission is charged: 6.50€ ($8.45) adults, 4.50€ ($5.85) ages 3 to 18 and senior citizens. 10 bd. de la Bastille, 12e. ℭ 01-40-01-08-81. www.lamaisonrouge.org. Métro: Quai de la Rapée.

Viaduc des Arts   This complex of boutiques and crafts workshops occupies the vaulted spaces beneath one of the 19th-century railway access routes into the Gare de Lyon. Around 1990, crafts artists, including furniture makers, potters, glassblowers, and weavers, began renting the niches beneath the viaduct, selling their wares to homeowners and members of Paris's decorating trades. Several trendsetting home-furnishing outfits have rented additional spaces. Stretching for more than 2 blocks

Finds **An Open-Air Canvas Gallery**

The **Paris Art Market** (*©* **01-53-57-42-60**) is "the place to go" on a Sunday. At the foot of Montparnasse Tower, this market is like an open-air gallery and has done much to restore the reputation of Montparnasse (14e) as a *quartier* for artists. Some 100 artists participate, including painters, sculptors, and photographers, even jewelers and hat makers. Head for the mall along the boulevard Edgar Quinet for the best work. Go anytime on Sunday between 10am and 7:30pm (Métro: Montparnasse).

between the Opéra Bastille and the Gare de Lyon, it allows one to see what Parisians consider chic in terms of home decorating. Open Monday to Saturday 11am to 7pm. 119 av. Daumesnil, 12e. *©* **01-44-75-80-66**. www.viaduc-des-arts.com. Métro: Bastille, Ledru-Rollin, Reuilly-Diderot, or Gare-de-Lyon.

BOOKS

If you like rare and unusual books, patronize one of the *bouquinistes,* the owners of those army-green stalls that line the Seine. This is where tourists in the 1920s and 1930s went to buy "dirty" French postcards. You might get lucky and come across some treasured book, such as an original edition of Henry Miller's *Tropic of Cancer,* which was banned for decades in the United States.

Brentano's   A block from the Opéra Garnier, Brentano's is a large English-language bookstore selling guides, maps, novels, and nonfiction as well as greeting cards, postcards, holiday items, and gifts. Open Monday to Saturday 10am to 7:30pm. 37 av. de l'Opéra, 2e. *©* **01-42-61-52-50**. www.brentanos.fr. Métro: Opéra or Pyramides.

Galignani   Sprawling over a large street level and supplemented by a mezzanine, this venerable wood-paneled bookstore has thrived since 1810. Enormous numbers of books are available in French and English, with a special emphasis on French classics, modern fiction, sociology, and fine arts. Looking for English-language translations of works by Balzac, Flaubert, Zola, or Colette? Most of them are here; if not, they can be ordered. Open Monday to Saturday 10am to 7pm. 224 rue de Rivoli, 1er. *©* **01-42-60-76-07**. Métro: Tuileries.

Les Mots à la Bouche   This is Paris's largest, best-stocked gay bookstore. You can find French- and English-language books as well as gay-info magazines such as *Illico, Blue, e.m@le, Carol's Girlfriends,* and *Lesbia.* You'll also find lots of free pamphlets advertising gay/lesbian venues and events. Open Monday to Saturday 11am to 11pm; Sunday 1 to 9pm. 6 rue Ste-Croix-la-Bretonnerie, 4e. *©* **01-42-78-88-30**. www.motsbouche.com. Métro: Hôtel-de-Ville.

Librairie le Bail-Weissert   Paris is filled with rare book shops, but this one has the best collection of atlases, rare maps, and engravings from the 15th century to the 19th century. The shop sells original topographical maps of European and world cities, along with various regions of Europe. There's also a superb collection of architectural engravings. Open Monday to Friday 10am to 12:30pm and 2 to 7pm; Saturday 2 to 7pm. 5 rue Lagrange, 5e. *©* **01-43-29-72-59**. www.lebail-weissert.com. Métro: Maubert-Mutualité or St-Michel.

Shakespeare and Company *✩* The most famous bookstore on the Left Bank is Shakespeare and Company, on rue de l'Odéon, home to Sylvia Beach, "mother confessor to the Lost Generation." Hemingway, Fitzgerald, and Stein were frequent patrons, as was Anaïs Nin, the diarist noted for her description of struggling American artists in 1930s Paris. Nin helped her companion, Henry Miller, publish *Tropic of Cancer,* a book so notorious in its day that returning Americans who tried to slip copies through Customs often had them confiscated as pornography. (When times were hard, Nin herself wrote pornography for a dollar a page.) Long ago, the shop moved to rue de la Bûcherie, a musty old place where expatriates still swap books and literary gossip and foreign students work in exchange for modest lodgings. Check out the lending library upstairs. Open daily 11am to midnight. 37 rue de la Bûcherie, 5e. © 01-43-25-40-93. www.shakespeareco.org. Métro: St-Michel.

Taschen   This store is a Germany-based publishing house that's known for coffee-table books. Erudite, high-profile, and glossy, most of them focus on architecture, art, photography, or eroticism. If you're in the market for a sweeping overview of the organization's past projects, this is the store for you. It is one of only two retail outlets in the world solely devoted to Taschen products (the other is in Cologne). Prices range from 7€ ($9.10) for a simple but provocative paperback to 5,000€ ($6,500) for a blockbuster collection of fashion photographs focusing on the best works of Helmut Newton. Open Tuesday to Saturday 11am to 7pm. 2 rue de Buci, 6e. © 01-40-51-79-22. Métro: Odeon.

Tea and Tattered Pages   At this largely English-language paperback bookshop, you can take a break from browsing to have tea. Though it's out of the way, an extra dose of charm makes it worth the trip. Open Monday to Saturday 11am to 7pm; Sunday noon to 6pm. 24 rue Mayet, 6e. © 01-40-65-94-35. www.teaandtatteredpages.com. Métro: Duroc.

Village Voice Bookshop   This favorite of expatriate Yankees is on a side street in the heart of the best Left Bank shopping district, near some of the gathering places described in Gertrude Stein's *The Autobiography of Alice B. Toklas.* Opened in 1981, the shop is a hangout for literati. Its name has nothing to do with the New York weekly. Open Monday 2 to 8pm; Tuesday to Saturday 10am to 8pm; Sunday 2 to 7pm. 6 rue Princesse, 6e. © 01-46-33-36-47. www.villagevoicebookshop.com. Métro: Mabillon.

W. H. Smith France   This store provides books, magazines, and newspapers published in English (most titles are from Britain). You can get the *Times* of London, of course, and the Sunday *New York Times* is available every Monday. There's a fine selection of maps and travel guides, plus a special children's section that includes comics. Open Monday to Saturday 9am to 7:30pm; Sunday 1 to 7:30pm. 248 rue de Rivoli, 1er. © 01-44-77-88-99. Métro: Concorde.

CERAMICS, CHINA & PORCELAIN

La Maison Ivre   This charming shop is perfect for country-style ceramics that add authenticity to French-country decor. It carries an excellent selection of handmade pottery from all over France, with an emphasis on Provençal and southern French ceramics, including ovenware, bowls, platters, plates, pitchers, mugs, and vases. Open Monday to Saturday 10:30am to 7pm. 38 rue Jacob, 6e. © 01-42-60-01-85. www.maison-ivre.com. Métro: St-Germain-des-Prés.

Limoges-Unic/Madronet   Housed in two shops on the same street, this store is crammed with crystal of Daum, Baccarat, Lalique, Haviland, and Bernardaud. You'll also find other table items: glass and crystal, silver, whatever your heart desires. They'll ship your purchases, and English is widely spoken. Open Monday to Saturday 11am to 6pm. 34 and 58 rue de Paradis, 10e. ℂ **01-47-70-34-59.** Métro: Gare de l'Est.

Manufacture Nationale de Sèvres ⓖ★★   Once endorsed and promoted by the mistresses of Louis XV, Sèvres today manufactures only 4,000 to 5,000 pieces of porcelain every year. Of these, many are reserved as replacements for government and historical entities. Open Tuesday to Friday 11am to 7pm. 4 place André-Malraux, 1er. ℂ **01-47-03-40-20.** Métro: Palais-Royal.

CHILDREN: FASHION & TOYS

Au Nain Bleu ⓖ   This is the largest, oldest, and most centrally located toy store in Paris. More important, it's probably the fanciest toy store in the world. But don't panic—in addition to the expensive stuff, you'll find rows of cheaper items on the first floor. Open Monday 2 to 7pm, Tuesday to Saturday 10am to 7pm. 408 rue St-Honoré, 8e. ℂ **01-42-65-20-00.** www.aunainbleu.com. Métro: Concorde or Madeleine.

Bonpoint   This outlet is part of a chain that helps parents transform their darlings into models of well-tailored conspicuous consumption. Though you'll find some garments for real life, the primary allure of the place lies in its tailored, traditional—and expensive—garments by the "Coco Chanel of the children's garment industry," Marie-France Cohen. The shop sells clothes for boys and girls from newborn to age 16. Open Monday to Saturday 10am to 6pm. 15 rue Royale, 8e. ℂ **01-47-42-52-63.** Métro: Concorde.

Orchestra Kazibao ⓕ*inds*   If you prefer clothes that have hip, hot style and color, but are wearable, washable, and affordable, forget Bonpoint, and try this small shop— it's a representative of a truly sensational French line of clothes for toddlers, and it's only a block from place de la Madeleine. Open Monday to Saturday 11am to 7pm. 18 rue Vignon, 9e. ℂ **01-42-66-24-74.** Métro: Madeleine.

CRYSTAL

Baccarat ⓖ★★   Opened in 1764, Baccarat is one of Europe's leading purveyors of full-lead crystal. You won't be able to comparison-shop Baccarat crystal at its four branches—a central organization sets rigid prices. The most prestigious outlet is on place de la Madeleine, but the outlet at 11 place des Etats-Unis, 16e, is larger and contains the **Musée Baccarat.** A third branch at rue de la Paix sells only women's jewelry, in which real gemstones (usually colored stones like rubies and sapphires) are sometimes interspersed with cut crystal for that flashy "is it real or is it fake?" look. A fourth branch is in the Hotel Concorde La Fayette at the Palais des Congrès–Côté Ternes, at place du Général Koenig. Branches are open Tuesday to Friday 10am to 7pm; Monday and Saturday 10am to 7:30pm. 11 place de la Madeleine, 8e ℂ **01-42-65-36-26.** Métro: Madeleine. Also: 11 place des Etats-Unis, 16e. ℂ **01-40-22-11-22.** Métro: Boissière.

Lalique ⓖ★   Lalique is known for its smoky frosted-glass sculpture, Art Deco crystal, and unique perfume bottles. The shop sells a wide range of merchandise, including leather belts with Lalique buckles and silk scarves at about 213€ ($277), designed to compete directly with those sold by Hermès. Open Monday to Wednesday 10am to 6:30pm; Thursday to Friday 9:30am to 6:30pm; Saturday 9:30am to 7pm. 11 rue Royale, 8e. ℂ **01-53-05-12-12.** www.cristallalique.fr. Métro: Concorde.

DEPARTMENT STORES

Au Bon Marché   Don't be fooled by the name ("low-budget" or "cheap") of this two-part Left Bank department store—for about 20 years, it has worked hard to position itself in the luxury market, selling fashion for men, women, and children; furniture; upscale gifts; and housewares. Some visitors compare it with Bloomingdale's. This is the oldest department store in Paris, dating from 1852. Of course, it can't compete with the *grand magasins* (department stores) like Galeries Lafayette (see below), except in one category: Au Bon Marché has a superior rug department, which it has fine-tuned as its specialty since 1871. It also has one of the largest food halls in Paris. Open Monday to Wednesday and Friday 9:30am to 7pm; Thursday 10am to 9pm; Saturday 9:30am to 8pm. 22–24 rue de Sèvres, 7e. ℭ 01-44-39-80-00. www.lebonmarche.fr. Métro: Sèvres-Babylone.

Au Printemps ℛℛ Take a look at the facade of this store for a reminder of the Gilded Age. Inside, the merchandise is divided into housewares (**Printemps Maison**), women's fashion (**Printemps de la Mode**), and men's clothes (**Le Printemps de l'Homme**). This is better for women's and children's fashions than is Galeries Lafayette. As for the top names in perfume, it's in a dead heat with Galeries Lafayette. Although visitors feel more pampered in Galeries Lafayette, Au Printemps's customer service is dazzling, putting all major department stores in Paris to shame. Check out the magnificent stained-glass dome, through which turquoise light cascades into the sixth-floor **Café Flo,** where you can have a coffee or a full meal. Interpreters at the Welcome Service in Printemps de la Mode will help you find what you're looking for, claim your VAT refund, and so on. Au Printemps also has a tourist discount card, offering a flat 10% discount. Open Monday to Wednesday and Friday to Saturday 9:35am to 7pm; Thursday 9:35am to 9pm. 64 bd. Haussmann, 9e. ℭ 01-42-82-50-00. www.printemps.com. Métro: Havre-Caumartin. RER: Auber or Haussmann–St-Lazare.

Colette Named after the great French writer, Colette is a swank citadel for à la mode fashion. It buzzes with excitement, displaying fashions by some of the city's most promising young talent, including Marni and Lucien Pellat-Finet. This is for the sophisticated shopper who'd never be caught dead shopping at Galeries Lafayette and the like. Not to be overlooked are home furnishings by such designers as Tom Dixon and even zany Japanese accessories. Even if you don't plan to buy anything, patronize the tea salon, with its fresh quiches, salads, and cakes, plus three-dozen brands of bottled water. Open Monday to Saturday 11am to 7:30pm. 213 rue St-Honoré, 1er. ℭ 01-55-35-33-90. www.colette.fr. Métro: Tuileries or Pyramides.

Galeries Lafayette ℛℛℛ Opened in 1896, with a lobby capped by an early-1900s stained-glass cupola classified as a historic monument, Galeries Lafayette is Europe's largest department store. If you have time for only one department store, make it this one. This store could provision a small city with everything from perfume to fashion. It is even more user-friendly than Au Printemps, and in fashion it places more emphasis on upcoming designers. It also concentrates on an upscale roster of everything you need to furnish and maintain a home; thousands of racks of clothing for men, women, and children; and a staggering array of cosmetics, makeup products, and perfumes. Menswear is concentrated in a section called **Galfa;** also in the complex is **Lafayette Gourmet,** one of the fanciest grocery stores in Paris, selling culinary exotica at prices usually lower than those at Fauchon (see "Food: Chocolate, Honey, Patés & More," later), **Lafayette Sports, Galeries Lafayette Mariage** (for wedding accessories), and two other general-merchandise stores, both known simply as **"GL."** The floor above street level has a concentration of high-end, semi-independent boutiques, including Cartier, Vuitton, and Prada Sport. A fashion show is held at least once daily, usually in the **Salon Opéra.** At the street-level **Welcome Desk,** a multilingual staff will tell you

Finds A Touch of Africa in the Marais

A stroll down rue Elzévir in the Marais is like a trip to Senegal. Valeria Schlumberger, a Frenchwoman who lives for part of the year on Ile de Gorée, off the coast of Dakar, has opened up several storefronts on this street in the Marais, all under the umbrella organization of La Compagnie du Sénégal et de l'Afrique de l'Ouest (www.csao.fr). You can find beautiful hand-woven and hand-dyed bolts of cloth that make fabulous curtains, cushion covers, or quilts. Many decorative items are made of recycled material, such as metallic bits and pieces from tin cans, or even aerosol sprays. Multicolored carpets are sold, along with basketwork and paintings. The leading outlets, all in the 3rd Arrondissement, include **The Boutique,** 1–3 rue Elzévir (© **01-42-71-33-17**); and **La Gallery,** 9 rue Elzévir (© **01-44-54-90-50**). **La Jokko,** 5 rue Elzévir (© **01-42-74-35-96**), is a languid bar, ideal for drinking between rounds of shopping. At the association's restaurant, **Le Petit Dakar,** 6 rue Elzévir (© **01-44-59-34-74**), you can order such native specialties as grouper with cassava and rice, topped off by litchi ice cream.

where to find various items in the store, where to get a taxi back to your hotel, and so on. Open Monday to Wednesday and Friday to Saturday 9:30am to 6:45pm; Thursday 9:30am to 9pm. 40 bd. Haussmann, 9e. © **01-42-82-34-56**. Métro: Chaussée d'Antin. RER: Auber.

Talmaris (★ (Finds   This is called the world's smallest department store. Actually, it's a boutique showcase for Alain-Paul Ruzé, who spends 6 months a year traveling the world picking up treasures, which he brings back to Paris and sells at this outlet. He's likely to turn up with just about anything, perhaps an American flag from the 1700s, discovered in a Greenwich Village flea market in Manhattan. Both costly and less expensive items are sold. Open Monday to Saturday 10am to 7pm. 61 av. Mozart, 16e. © **01-42-88-20-20**. www.talmaris.com. Métro: Ranelagh.

FABRICS

Souleiado (★   This is the only Paris branch of one of Provence's most successful purveyors of the bright fabrics and thick pottery of France's southern tier. Fabrics are measured out by scissors-wielding saleswomen and then sold by the meter for seamstresses to whip into curtains, tablecloths, or whatever. In a separate shop just around the corner, at 78 rue de Seine (same phone), there are displays of table settings, housewares, and gift items, each reflecting the bright sunshine and colors (usually ocher, cerulean blue, and a strong medium green) of the Midi. Open Monday 10:30am to 6:30pm,; Tuesday to Saturday 10:30am to 7pm. 3 rue Lobineau, 6e. © **01-43-54-62-25**. www.souleiado.fr. Métro: Odéon or Mabillon.

FASHION
CUTTING-EDGE CHIC

Azzedine Alaïa   Alaïa, who became the darling of French fashion in the 1970s, is the man who put body consciousness back into Paris chic. If you can't afford the current collection, try the **stock shop** around the corner at 18 rue de la Verrerie, 4e (© **01-42-72-19-19**; Métro: Hotel-de-Ville), where last year's leftovers are sold at serious discounts. Both outlets sell leather trench coats, knit dresses, pleated skirts, cigarette pants, belts, purses, and fashion accessories. Open Monday to Saturday 10am to 7pm. 7 rue de Moussy, 4e. © 01-42-72-19-19. Métro: Hôtel-de-Ville.

BCBG/Max Azria   You'll quickly get the sense that someone spent hours meticulously selecting the women's clothing and accessories featured on three floors of this stylish boutique where everything is "BCBG" (*bon chic, bon genre*—a designation for things chic, restrained, and tasteful). Things here are, indeed "BCBG," but in brighter colors than you might expect, judging from the samba-inspired and highly theatrical front windows. Come here for women's sportswear, evening wear (at least some of it in silk mousseline), costume jewelry, and accessories. The staff seems thoughtful and sensitive to its clientele. The place stocks European sizes 34 to 44, which translate roughly to U.S.-derived sizes 0 to 12. It's open Monday to Saturday 10am to 7:30pm. 412 rue St-Honoré, 8e. © 01-40-20-16-50. www.bcbg.com. Métro: Concorde or Madeleine.

Courrèges   The house of Courrèges, founded in 1961, now maintains only one retail outlet in all of France: a sprawling, futuristic-looking showcase where the combined fashion statements of more than 40 years of fashion design are assembled into one blockbuster venue. The designs, once associated with moonwalks and the expanding space-age programs, are back and hot again. Even those white vinyl go-go boots and disco purses in silver metallic cloth are back in style, with special emphasis on neon tones of red and white, plastic, and a sense of whimsy and fun. André Courrèges, the founder, is in semiretirement: Coqueline, his wife, boldly forges ahead with ideas and venues for the 21st century. Open Monday to Saturday 10am to 7pm. 40 rue François Premier, 8e. © 01-53-67-30-00. www.courreges.com. Métro: Alma-Marceau.

Jean-Paul Gaultier   Supporters of this high-camp, high-fashion mogul describe him as an avant-garde classicist without allegiance to any of the aesthetic restrictions of the bourgeoisie. Detractors call him a glorified punk rocker with a gimmicky allegiance to futurist models as interpreted by *Star Trek*. Whatever your opinion, it's always refreshing and insightful, especially for fashion buffs, to check out France's most iconoclastic designer. Gaultier's line of purses, priced from around 800€ ($1,040) each, are available in luxurious textures of leather, silk, or satin and are directly inspired by street fashion as it evolved in the urban environments of Los Angeles and New York. There's a franchise branch of his store at 6 rue Vivienne, 2e (© **01-42-86-05-05;** Métro: Bourse), but the company's main branch, and the site of its biggest inventories, is at avenue George V. Open Monday and Saturday 10:30am to 7pm; Tuesday to Friday 10am to 7pm. 44 av. George V, 8e. © 01-44-43-00-44. Métro: George V.

DESIGNER BOUTIQUES & FASHION FLAGSHIPS

There are two primary fields of dreams in Paris when it comes to showcasing the international big names: rue du Faubourg St-Honoré and avenue Montaigne. Though the Left Bank is gaining in status, with such recent additions as Dior, Armani, and Vuitton, the heart of the international designer parade is on the Right Bank.

  Rue du Faubourg St-Honoré is so famous and fancy, it's simply known as "the Faubourg." It was the traditional miracle mile until recent years, when the really exclusive shops shunned it for the wider and even more deluxe avenue Montaigne at the other end of the arrondissement. (It's a long but pleasant walk from one fashion strip to the other.) **Avenue Montaigne** is filled with almost unspeakably fancy shops, but a few of them have affordable cafes (try Joseph at no. 14), and all have sales help who are usually cordial to well-dressed customers.

The mix is quite international—from British (**Joseph**) to German (**Jil Sander**) to Italian (**Krizia**). **Chanel, Lacroix, Porthault, Ricci, Dior,** and **Ungaro** are a few of the big French names. Also check out some of the lesser-known creative powers, and don't miss a visit to **Caron.** Most of the designer shops sell men's and women's clothing. The Faubourg hosts other traditional favorites: **Hermès, Lanvin, Jaeger, Rykiel,** and the upstart **Façonnable,** which sells preppy men's clothing in the United States through a business deal with Nordstrom. Lanvin has its own men's shop (**Lanvin Homme**), with a cafe perfect for a light (and affordable) lunch.

Alain Figaret   Alain Figaret is one of France's foremost designers of men's shirts and women's blouses. Though this store has a broad range of fabrics, 100% cotton is its specialty. Also, check out the silk neckties in distinctively designed prints and the silk scarves for women. In recent years, inventories have been expanded to include pajamas, polo shirts, undergarments, and vests for both men and women. If you're comparison-shopping, Figaret and Charvet (see below) are half a block apart. Open Monday to Saturday 10am to 7:30pm. 21 rue de la Paix, 2e. ✆ **01-42-65-04-99.** www.alain-figaret.fr. Métro: Opéra.

Chanel ✪   If you can't have the sun, the moon, and the stars, at least buy something with Coco Chanel's initials on it—either a serious fashion statement (drop-dead chic) or something fun and playful (tongue-in-chic). Karl Lagerfeld's designs come in all flavors and have added a subtle twist to Chanel's classicism. This store is adjacent to the Chanel couture house and behind the Ritz, where Mlle Chanel once lived. Check out the beautiful staircase of the *maison* before you shop the two-floor boutique—it's well worth a peek. Open Monday to Saturday 10am to 7pm. 29 rue Cambon, 1er. ✆ **01-42-86-28-00.** Métro: Concorde or Tuileries.

Charvet   The duke of Windsor made Charvet famous, but Frenchmen of distinction have been buying their shirts here for years. The store sells ties, pocket squares, underwear, and pajamas as well, plus women's shirts, all custom-tailored or straight off the peg. Open Monday to Saturday 10am to 7pm. 28 place Vendôme, 1er. ✆ **01-42-60-30-70.** Métro: Opéra.

Christian Dior   This fashion house is set up like a small department store, selling men's, women's, and children's clothing, as well as affordable gift items, makeup, and perfume on the street level. For several years, cutting-edge Brit designer John Galliano has been in charge of the collections. Unlike some of the other big-name fashion houses, Dior is very approachable. Open Monday to Saturday 10am to 7pm. 30 av. Montaigne, 8e. ✆ **01-40-73-73-73.** Métro: Franklin-D-Roosevelt.

Givenchy ✪   Hubert de Givenchy made fashion news around the world with his establishment, in 1962, of the company that continues its lonely role as a *couturier* (custom-made clothier) for elegant women. Today, from chic premises set one floor above street level, the art form of custom-made women's clothing continues, a tradition that has died out except for just a handful of other practitioners. Be forewarned that if you're interested in custom-made clothing, advance appointments are necessary, and prices are stratospheric. But on the street level of the same premises, you'll find the flagship of the Givenchy empire, specializing in women's ready-to-wear. Just across the street, you'll find the official outlet for Givenchy's women's accessories, including purses and bags, scarves, shoes, and whatever it takes to keep a stylish woman-of-a-certain-age looking fabulous. A short walk away is **Givenchy Hommes,** where upscale, ready-to-wear clothing is inventoried for men. Both outlets maintain the same hours: Monday to Saturday 10am to 7pm. 8 av. George V, 8e. ℰ **01-44-31-49-91.** www.givenchy.fr. Métro: George V. Givenchy Hommes: 56 rue François Premier, 8e. ℰ **01-40-76-07-27.** Métro: Alma-Marceau

Hermès ℱℱ   France's single most important status item is a scarf or tie from Hermès. Patterns on these illustrious scarves, retailing for about 240€ ($312), have recently included the galaxies, Africa, the sea, the sun, and horse racing and breeding. But the choices don't stop there—this large flagship store has beach towels and accessories, dinner plates, clothing for men and women, a large collection of Hermès fragrances, and even a saddle shop; a package of postcards is the least expensive item sold. Ask to see the private museum upstairs. Outside, note the horseman on the roof with his scarf-flag flying. Open Monday to Saturday 10:30am to 6:30pm. 24 rue du Faubourg St-Honoré, 8e. ℰ **01-40-17-46-00.** Métro: Concorde.

Louis Vuitton ℱ   Its luggage is among the most famous and prestigious in the world, a standard accessory aboard the first-class cabins of aircraft flying transatlantic and transpacific. Not content to cover the world's luggage with his initials, Vuitton has branched into leather goods, writing instruments, travel products, and publishing. Look for the traditional collection of leather, including Vuitton's monogrammed brown-on-brown bags in printed canvas, on the street level. The mezzanine showcases upscale pens, writing supplies, and stationery. The top floor carries the company's newest line: women's shoes and bags. Open Monday to Saturday 10am to 7pm. 6 place St-Germain-des-Prés, 6e. ℰ **01-45-49-62-32.** Métro: St-Germain-des-Prés.

Yves Saint Laurent   Long gone are the 1970s, when anything Yves St-Laurent did was touted by the international press as a sign of his genius and the fashionable French dressed up in his luxurious versions of Cossack costumes, replete with boleros, riding boots, and copies of antique jewelry from the Russian steppes. Hours of all branches are Monday 11am to 7pm; Tuesday to Saturday from 10:30am to 7pm. With the shutdown in 2003 of his couture department and the worldwide availability of off-the-rack Saint-Laurent franchises selling mass-market clothing around the world, there are now only four outlets in Paris that sell his clothing. 6 and 12 place St-Sulpice, 6e. ℰ **01-43-29-43-00** and ℰ **01-43-26-84-40.** www.ysl.com. Métro: St-Sulpice. Other locations at 32 (men) and 38 (women) rue du Faubourg St-Honoré, 8e. ℰ **01-53-05-80-80** and ℰ **01-42-65-74-59.** Métro: Madeleine or Concorde.

DISCOUNT & RESALE

Anna Lowe ℱ *Value*   Adjacent to the Bristol Hotel, one of the most expensive addresses in Paris, is one of the city's premier boutiques for women who want to purchase heavily discounted clothing (new, with labels intact) from some of the world's best-known fashion designers. Expect discounts of up to 50% on last year's collections from such artists as Valentino, Thierry Mugler, John Galliano, Chanel, Versace, and many more. Your find might be what a model wore down the runway at last year's fashion show, excess inventories from factories that—for whatever reason—never got paid, or overstock from boutiques looking to make room for new inventories. Prices are reasonable, and the labels, in many cases, still retain their old magic and sense of chic. Open Monday to Saturday 10am to 7pm. 104 rue du Faubourg St-Honoré, 8e. ℰ **01-42-66-11-32.** www.annalowe.com. Métro: Miromesnil.

Annexe des Créateurs ℱℱ *Value*   Few stores in Paris receive as much publicity as this high-end, ultraglamorous discount outlet, where the collections of top-drawer designers are discounted by 30% to 70%. Charming owner and founder Edwige Meister inventories the only slightly worn but out-of-date women's wear of Stella McCartney, Versace, Moschino, Gaultier, Vivienne Westwood, and others. The staff insists that garments are in "perfect or near-perfect condition" and usually derive from terribly wealthy, obsessively stylish women who refuse to wear any garment more than once. It "isn't inconceivable," according to Mlle Meister, for a client to sell (on consignment) a garment in one of these two boutiques and then immediately pass through the interconnecting door to buy a secondhand but mint-condition garment in the boutique's counterpart a few steps away. Open Tuesday to Saturday 11am to 7pm. 19 rue Godot de Mauroy, 9e. (✆ 01-42-65-46-40. www.annexedescreateurs.com. Métro: Madeleine.

Au Gré du Vent This is where the wives of diplomats and millionaires and self-made women from all arenas of Parisian life arrive, discreetly, with plastic shopping bags loaded with occasionally worn couture, which Au Gré du Vent sells on consignment. Hanging enticingly in this cheerful store—depending on that day's inventory—might be garments from Chanel, Hermès, Prada, Gucci, Dolce & Gabbana, Kenzo, Louis Vuitton, Pierre Balmain, or Gaultier. You won't always find the size or style you're looking for, but a woman with a sense of adventure can have a lot of fun here. Open Tuesday to Saturday 10:30am to 7pm. 10 rue des Quatre Vents, 6e. (✆ 01-44-07-28-73. Métro: Odéon.

Défilé des Marques French TV stars often shop here, picking up St. Laurent, Dior, Lacroix, Prada, Chanel, Versace, Hermès, and others at a fraction of the price. Yes, it sells discounted Hermès scarves as well. Low prices here derive from the owners' skill at picking up used clothing from last year's collections in good condition and, in some cases, retro-chic clothing from collections of many years ago, sometimes from estate sales. Open Tuesday to Saturday 11am to 8pm. 171 rue de Grenelles, 7e. (✆ 01-45-55-63-47. Métro: Latour-Maubourg.

Limoges-Unic & Madronet In two shops a 3-minute walk from each other, you'll find Limoges china and anything else you might need for the table—glass, crystal, and silver. It pays to drop into both stores, whose inventories vary according to the season and the whims of the buyers. Open Monday to Saturday 10am to 7pm. 34 and 58 rue de Paradis, 10e. (✆ 01-47-70-34-59. Metro: Gare-de-l'est.

Réciproque Forget about serious bargains, but celebrate what could be your only opportunity to own designer clothing of this caliber. Within a series of six storefronts side by side along the same avenue, you'll find used clothing from every major name in fashion, along with shoes, accessories, menswear, and wedding gifts. Everything has been worn, but some items were worn only on fashion runways or during photo shoots. Open Tuesday to Friday 11am to 7pm; Saturday 10:30am to 7pm. 88–101 rue de la Pompe, 16e. (✆ 01-47-04-30-28. Métro: Pompe.

SR Store This is where great designer Sonia Rykiel dumps all that good stuff she didn't sell in main-line boutiques. Everything in both outlets, which lie within about 2 blocks of each other, is half of the retail price charged when the garment was originally released. Both branches are open Tuesday to Friday 10:45am to 6:45pm; Saturday 10:45am to 7pm. 64 rue d'Alésia, 14e. (✆ 01-43-95-06-13. www.soniarykiel.com. Métro: Alésia. Also: 110–112 rue d'Alésia, 14e. (✆ 01-45-43-80-86. Métro: Alésia.

VINTAGE COUTURE
Didier Ludot Fashion historians salivate when they're confronted with an inventory of vintage haute couture. In this frenetically stylish shop, albeit at prices that rival

Food Markets

Outdoor markets are plentiful in Paris. Some of the better known are the **Marché Buci** (see "Markets," below); the **rue Mouffetard market,** open Tuesday to Sunday from 9:30am to 1pm and Tuesday to Saturday from 4 to 7pm (6e; Métro: Monge or Censier-Daubenton); and the **rue Montorgueil market,** behind the St-Eustache church, open Monday to Saturday from 9am to 7pm (1er; Métro: Les Halles). The trendiest market is **Marché Biologique,** along boulevard Raspail, a tree-lined stretch lying between rue de Rennes and rue du Cherche-Midi, 6e. It's open Sunday from 8:30am to 6:30pm (Métro: Montparnasse).

what you'd expect to pay for a serious antique, you'll find a selection of gowns and dresses created between 1900 and 1980 for designing women who looked *faaabulous* at Maxim's, at chic cocktail parties on the avenue Foch, in Deauville, or wherever. Open Monday to Saturday 11am to 7pm. 24 Galerie de Montpensier, in the arcades surrounding the courtyard of the Palais Royal, 1er. (C) **01-42-96-06-56.** Métro: Palais-Royal.

FOOD: CHOCOLATE, HONEY, PATES & MORE

Christian Constant 𝒦𝒦   Opened in 1970, Christian Constant sells some of Paris's most delectable chocolates by the kilo. Each is a blend of ingredients from Ecuador, Colombia, or Venezuela, usually mingled with scents of spices and flowers such as orange blossoms, jasmine, the Asian blossom ylang-ylang, and vetiver and *verveine* (herbs usually used to brew tea). Open Monday to Friday 8:30am to 9pm; Saturday to Sunday 8am to 8:30pm. 37 rue d'Assas, 6e. (C) **01-53-63-15-15.** Métro: St-Placide.

Fauchon 𝒦𝒦𝒦   At place de la Madeleine stands one of the city's most popular sights—not the church, but Fauchon, a hyper-upscale mega-delicatessen that thrives within a city famous for its finicky eaters. It's divided into three divisions that include an *épicerie* (for jams, crackers, pastas, and exotic canned goods); a *pâtissier* (for breads, pastries, and chocolates); and a *traiteur* (for cheeses, terrines, pâtés, caviar, and fruits). Prices are steep, but the inventories—at least to serious foodies—are fascinating. At some of the counters, you'll indicate to attendants what you want from behind glass display cases and get an electronic ticket, which you'll carry to a *caisse* (cash register). Surrender your tickets, pay the tally, and then return to the counter to pick up your groceries. In other cases, you simply load up a shopping basket with whatever you want and pay for your purchases at a cash register, just as you would at any grocery store.

On the same premises, Fauchon has a restaurant, **Brasserie Fauchon,** and a tea salon, which showcases the pastry-making talents of its chefs. Among the many offerings is a *Paris-Brest,* a ring in the shape of a bicycle wheel that's loaded with pastry cream, almond praline, butter cream, and hazelnut paste capped with almonds. Open Monday to Saturday 9:30am to 7pm. 26 place de la Madeleine, 8e. (C) **01-70-39-38-00.** www.fauchon.fr. Métro: Madeleine.

Hédiard   This 1850 temple of *haute gastronomie* has been renovated, perhaps to woo visitors away from Fauchon. The decor is a series of salons filled with almost Disneyesque displays meant to give the store the look of an early-1900s spice emporium.

Hédiard is rich in coffees, teas, jams, and spices. The decor changes with whatever holiday (Halloween, Easter, Bastille Day) or special promotion (the coffees of Brazil, the teas of Ceylon) is in effect at the time. Upstairs, you can eat at the Restaurant de l'Epicerie. Open Monday to Saturday 9am to 11pm. 21 place de la Madeleine, 8e. ✆ **01-43-12-88-88**. Métro: Madeleine.

Jadis et Gourmande   This chain of chocolatiers has a less lofty reputation than Christian Constant and more reasonable prices. It's best known for its alphabetical chocolate blocks, which allow you to spell out any message (well . . . almost), in any language. *"Merci"* comes prepackaged. Specialties that are even more delectable are *pralines fondants*, a mixture of praline, nuts, and chocolate that begins to melt the moment it hits your taste buds. Open Monday 1 to 7pm; Tuesday to Friday 10am to 7pm, and Saturday 11am to 7pm. 27 rue Boissy d'Anglais, 8e. ✆ **01-42-65-23-23**. www.jadiset gourmande.fr. Métro: Madeleine. An even larger premises, with greater quantities of the same inventories, is at 88 bd. du Port-Royal, 5e. ✆ **01-43-26-17-75**. RER: Port-Royal.

Jean-Paul Hévin   One of the great chocolatiers of Paris, its owner has mastered the fusion of *chocolat* with *fromage* (cheese, of course). Sweet luscious chocolates with tart cheeses such as Camembert or Roquefort are infused to satisfy both the cheese fan and the chocolate lover's sweet tooth. Savory chocolates are also served without cheese. New offerings—unique in Paris—have caused this place to become one of the most acclaimed in Europe for chocolate devotees. Open Monday to Saturday 10am to 7:30pm. 231 rue St-Honoré, 6e. ✆ **01-45-51-99-64**. www.jphevin.com. Métro: Tuileries or Concorde.

Le Maison du Miel   Running "The House of Honey" has been a family tradition since before World War I. The entire store is devoted to products made from honey: honey oil, honey soap, and various honeys to eat, including one made from heather. This store owes a tremendous debt to the busy bee. Monday to Saturday 9:15am to 7pm. 24 rue Vignon, 9e. ✆ **01-47-42-26-70**. www.lamaisondumiel.com. Métro: Madeleine, Havre-Caumartin, or Opéra.

Maison de la Truffe ⭐ *Finds*   Cramped and convivial, with a charming staff, the layout of this shop was modeled after a Parisian's fantasy of an affable, cluttered, old-fashioned butcher shop in Lyon. It's an excellent source for foie gras, caviar, black and white truffles, and other high-end foodstuffs. Artfully assembled gift baskets are a house specialty. One corner is devoted to a restaurant where many (but not all) of the dishes contain the costly items (especially truffles) sold in the shop. Examples include noodles or risottos with truffles and caviar with all the fixings. A prix-fixe menu costs 20€ ($26) without truffles and 65€ ($85) with truffles. Most main courses cost 30€ to 98€ ($39–$128), except for caviar, which begins at 175€ ($228) and can go up to 5,000€ ($6,500) per person. The restaurant is open during the open hours of the shop, although the last food order is accepted 45 minutes prior to closing. Open Monday to Saturday 9:30am to 9pm. 19 place de la Madeleine, 8e. ✆ **01-42-65-53-22**. www.maison-de-la-truffe.fr. Métro: Madeleine or Auber.

Poilâne ⭐⭐   One of Paris's best-loved bakeries, Poilâne hasn't changed much since it opened in 1932. Come here to taste and admire the beautiful loaves of bread decorated with simple designs of leaves and flowers that'll make you yearn for an all-but-vanished Paris. Specialties include apple tarts, butter cookies, and a chewy sourdough loaf cooked in a wood-burning oven. Breads can be specially wrapped to stay fresh during your journey home. *Note:* Cherche-Midi location open Monday to Saturday 7:15am to 8:15pm; Grenelle location Tuesday to Sunday 7:15am to 8:15pm. 8 rue du

Cherche-Midi, 6e. ℂ **01-45-48-42-59**. www.poilane.fr. Métro: St-Sulpice. Also: 49 bd. de Grenelle, 15e. ℂ **01-45-79-11-49**. Métro: Dupleix.

JEWELRY

Bijoux Burma   If you can't afford any of the spectacular and expensive bijoux at the city's world-famous jewelers, come here to console yourself with some of the best fakes anywhere. This quality costume jewelry is the secret weapon of many a Parisian woman. Open Monday to Saturday 10:30am to 6:45pm. 50 rue François-Premier, 8e. ℂ **01-42-66-21-51**. Métro: Franklin-D-Roosevelt.

Cartier 👁👁   One of the most famous jewelers in the world, Cartier has prohibitive prices to match its glamorous image. Go to gawk, and if your pockets are deep enough, pick up an expensive trinket. Open Monday to Saturday 10:30am to 7pm. 23 place Vendôme, 1er. ℂ **01-44-55-32-20**. www.cartier.com. Métro: Opéra or Tuileries.

Van Cleef & Arpels 👁👁   Years ago, Van Cleef's designers came up with an intricate technique that remains a vital part of its allure—the invisible setting, wherein a band of sparkling gemstones, each cut to interlock with its neighbor, creates an uninterrupted flash of brilliance. Come browse with the rich and famous. Open Monday to Friday 10:30am to 7pm, Saturday 11am to 7pm. 22 place Vendôme, 1er. ℂ **01-53-45-35-50**. www.vancleef-arpels.com. Métro: Opéra or Tuileries.

KITCHENWARE

A. Simon   Established in 1884, this large kitchenware shop supplies restaurants and professional kitchens. But it will also cover your table with everything from menu cards and wine tags to knives, copper pots, and pans—not to mention white paper doilies and those funny little paper things they put on top of the tablecloth at bistros. Open Monday 1:30 to 6:30pm; Tuesday to Saturday 9am to 6:30pm. 48 and 52 rue Montmartre, 2e. ℂ **01-42-33-71-65**. Métro: Les Halles.

Dehillerin   Established in 1820, Dehillerin is Paris's most famous cookware shop, in the "kitchen corridor" alongside A. Simon (see above) and several other kitchenware stores. The shop has more of a professional feel to it than beginner-friendly A. Simon, but don't be intimidated. Equipped with the right tools from Dehillerin, you, too, can learn to cook like a master chef. Open Monday 9am to 12:30pm and 2 to 6pm; Tuesday to Saturday 9am to 6pm. 18 rue Coquillière, 1er. ℂ **01-42-36-53-13**. www.e-dehillerin.fr. Métro: Les Halles.

LEATHER GOODS

Morabito   This glamorous leather purveyor was originally established by an Italian entrepreneur on the place Vendôme in 1905. In the 1990s, it was partially acquired by an organization in Tokyo. Today, from a site on the glamorous rue François-Premier, it sells chicer-than-thou handbags that begin at a bare minimum of 480€ ($624). Morabito also has suitcases—some of the best in Paris—for men and women. Open Monday to Saturday 10am to 7pm. 55 rue François-Premier, 1er. ℂ **01-53-23-90-40**. www.morabitoparis.com. Métro: George V.

LINGERIE

Cadolle   Herminie Cadolle invented the brassiere in 1889. Today, her family manages the store she founded, and they still make specialty brassieres for the Crazy Horse Saloon. This is the place to go if you want made-to-order items or are hard to fit.

Open Monday to Saturday 9:30am to 1pm and 2 to 6:30pm. 14 rue Cambon, 1er. ✆ **01-42-60-94-22**. www.cadolle.fr. Métro: Concorde.

Nikita This is the discount sales outlet for all the big names in women's lingerie, including Bolero, Lise Charmel, Lejaby, Simone Pérèle, and Aubade. Most of the lingerie sold here is 20% to 30% less than its counterparts in Right Bank boutiques. Open Monday to Saturday 9:30am to 7:30pm; Sunday 9:30am to 1:30pm. 22 rue Levis, 17e. ✆ **01-42-12-01-30**. Métro: Villiers.

Sabbia Rosa Everything here is filmy, silky, and sexy. Look for undergarments (slips, brassieres, and panties) and the kind of negligees that might have been favored by Brigitte Bardot in *And God Created Woman*. Even Madonna has been spotted shopping for panties here. Open Monday to Saturday 10am to 7pm. 73 rue des Sts-Pères, 6e. ✆ **01-45-48-88-37**. Métro: Sèvres-Babylone or St-Germain.

MALLS

Carrousel du Louvre If you want to combine an accessible location, a fun food court, boutiques, and plenty of museum gift shops with a touch of culture, don't miss the Carrousel. Always mobbed, this is one of the few venues allowed to open on Sunday. There's a Virgin Megastore, a branch of The Body Shop, and several other emporiums for conspicuous consumption. Check out Diane Claire for the fanciest souvenirs you've ever seen. Open Tuesday to Sunday 10am to 8pm. 99 rue de Rivoli, 1er. ✆ **01-43-16-47-10**. Métro: Palais-Royal or Musée du Louvre.

Les Trois Quartiers Named after the junction of the three neighborhoods (Madeleine, Opéra, and Concorde) where it sits, this is a mall of at least 13 upscale boutiques specializing in clothing, perfume, cosmetics for men and women, and household accessories. The largest is Madelios, a menswear store that stocks more than 50 brand names, including Ralph Lauren, Hugo Boss, and Burberry. Open Monday to Saturday 10am to 7pm. 21 bd. de la Madeleine, 1er. ✆ **01-42-97-80-06**. Métro: Madeleine.

Marché St-Germain Throughout the 19th and most of the 20th century, this site functioned as an open-air market where Parisian consumers acquired daily portions of fresh fruits, vegetables, cheeses, meats, and fish. Since its transformation into a modern (and enclosed) shopping mall, there remain only about 20 different food merchants, each showcasing ultrafresh foodstuffs. The remaining space is now occupied by about a dozen middle-bracket purveyors of men's and women's clothing, shoes, housewares, and gift items. Also on the premises are about a half-dozen bars, pubs, and restaurants, many of them themed as Irish, Latino, or Scandinavian venues. Most of the shops within the compound are open Monday to Saturday 10am to 8pm. The restaurants and bars each maintain individualized hours of their own. The market's executive headquarters are at 14 rue Lobineau, 6e. ✆ **01-43-26-01-44**. Métro: Mabillon. The market itself lies within the area enclosed by the rues Lobineau, Mabillon, and Clément.

Montparnasse Shopping Centre This shopping center is sort of a quick-fix mini mall in a business center and hotel (Le Méridien) complex, with a small branch of Galeries Lafayette and some inexpensive boutiques. Visiting it is really worthwhile only if you also take a trip across the street to Inno, with its deluxe supermarket in the basement. Open Monday to Saturday 8:30am to 10pm. Between rue de l'Arrivée and 22 rue du Départ, 14e. No phone. Métro: Montparnasse-Bienvenüe.

MARKETS

Marché aux Fleurs   Artists and photographers love to capture the Flower Market on canvas or film. The stalls are ablaze with color, and each is a showcase of flowers, most of which escaped the perfume factories of Grasse on the French Riviera. The Flower Market is along the Seine, behind the Tribunal de Commerce. On Sunday, it becomes the **Marché aux Oiseaux (Bird Market).** Open daily 8:30am to 4pm. Place Louis-Lépine, Ile de la Cité, 4e. No phone. Métro: Cité.

Marché aux Puces de la Porte de Vanves   This weekend event sprawls along two streets and is the best flea market in Paris—dealers swear by it. There's little in terms of formal antiques and furniture. It's better for old linens, used Hermès scarves, toys, ephemera, costume jewelry, perfume bottles, and bad art. Asking prices tend to be high, as dealers prefer to sell to nontourists. On Sunday, there's a food market one street over. Open Saturday to Monday 6:30am to 4:30pm. Av. Georges-Lafenestre, 14e. No phone. Métro: Porte de Vanves.

Marché aux Puces St-Ouen de Clignancourt ⟨★⟩   Paris's most famous flea market is a grouping of more than a dozen flea markets—a complex of 2,500 to 3,000 open stalls and shops on the northern fringe of the city, selling everything from antiques to junk, from new to vintage clothing. The market begins with stalls of cheap clothing along avenue de la Porte de Clignancourt. As you proceed, various streets will tempt you. Hold on until you get to rue des Rosiers; then turn left. Vendors start bringing out their offerings around 9am Saturday to Monday and take them in around 6pm. Hours are a tad flexible, depending on weather and crowds. Monday is traditionally the best day for bargain seekers—attendance is smaller and merchants demonstrate a greater desire to sell.

First-timers always want to know two things: "Will I get any real bargains?" and "Will I get fleeced?" It's all relative. Obviously, dealers (who often have a prearrangement to have items held for them) have already skimmed the best buys. And it's true that the same merchandise displayed here will sell for less in the provinces. But for the visitor who has only a few days to spend in Paris—and only half a day for shopping—the flea market is worth the experience.

Dress casually and show your knowledge if you're a collector. Most dealers are serious and get into the spirit of things only if you speak French or make it clear you know what you're doing. The longer you stay, the more you chat and show your respect for the goods, the more room you'll have for negotiating. Most of the markets have restroom facilities; some have central offices to arrange shipping.

Cafes, pizza joints, and even a few restaurants are scattered around. Almost without exception, they are bad. The exception is **Le Soleil,** 109 av. Michelet, St-Ouen (⟨℡⟩ **01-40-10-08-08**), which was converted from a cafe into a family-run restaurant by Louis-Jacques Vannucci. Catering to flea-market shoppers, the restaurant looks as if it were flea market–decorated as well. The French food is excellent, especially the sautéed chicken in a light cream sauce, the green-bean salad tossed with tomato cubes, and the fresh Norman cod and the tiny mussels cooked in a rich broth. Open daily for lunch and Thursday to Saturday for dinner. *Note:* Beware of pickpockets and teenage troublemakers while shopping the market. Open Saturday to Monday 9am to 7pm. Av. de la Porte de Clignancourt, 18e. No phone. www.marchesauxpuces.fr. Métro: Porte de Clignancourt (turn left, cross bd. Ney, and then walk north on av. de la Porte Montmartre). Bus: 56, 85, 155, or 166.

The Scent of a Parisian

If there's one reason international shoppers come to Paris, it's cosmetics—after all, the City of Light is the world capital of fragrances and beauty supplies. These are a few of our favorite perfume and makeup shops:

Although you can buy **Parfums Caron** scents in any duty-free or discount *parfumerie*, it's worth visiting the source of some of the world's most famous perfumes. The tiny shop is at 34 av. Montaigne, 8e (© **01-47-23-40-82**; Métro: Franklin-D-Roosevelt), boasting old-fashioned glass beakers filled with fragrances and a hint of yesteryear. Fleur de Rocaille, a Caron scent, was the featured perfume in the movie *Scent of a Woman*. Store hours are Monday to Saturday from 10am to 6:30pm.

While there are other branches, and you can test Goutal bathroom amenities at many upscale hotels, the sidewalk mosaic tile and the unique scents make the **Annick Goutal,** at 14 rue Castiglione, 1er (© **01-42-60-52-82**; Métro: Concorde), worth stopping by. Try Eau d'Hadrien for a unisex splash of citrus and summer. Store hours are Monday to Saturday from 10am to 7pm.

Shiseido, the world's fourth-largest maker of cosmetics and skin-care goods, has become more prominent thanks to the efforts of the **Salons du Palais Royal Shiseido,** 142 Galerie de Valois, Palais Royal, 1er (© **01-49-27-09-09**; Métro: Palais-Royal). In addition to an awesome array of skin-care products and makeup, it stocks 21 exclusive unisex fragrances created by the company's artistic director, Serge Lutens. Don't be afraid to wander in and ask for some scent strips. Open Monday to Saturday from 10am to 7pm.

Marché aux Timbres This is where Audrey Hepburn figured it out in *Charade*, remember? At this stamp collector's paradise, nearly two dozen stalls are set up on a permanent basis under shady trees on the eastern edge of the Rond-Point. The variety of stamps is almost limitless—some common, some quite rare. Generally open Thursday to Sunday 10am to 6pm. Av. Matignon, off the Champs-Elysées at Rond-Point, 8e. No phone. Métro: Franklin-D-Roosevelt or Champs-Elysées–Clemenceau.

Marché Buci This traditional French food market is set up at the intersection of two streets and is only a block long, but what a block it is! Seasonal fruits and vegetables cover tabletops, and chickens spin on the rotisserie. One stall is entirely devoted to big bouquets of fresh flowers. Monday mornings are light. Open daily 9am to 7pm. Rue de Buci, 6e. No phone. Métro: St-Germain-des-Prés.

MUSIC
FNAC This is a large chain of music and book stores known for their wide selection and discounted prices. Eight branches are in Paris, with the largest being at 136 rue de Rennes, Montparnasse. Other locations include rue St-Lazare, avenue des Champs-Elysées, Forum des Halles, avenue des Ternes, and avenue d'Italie. All are open Monday

SHOPPING A TO Z

to Saturday 10am to 7:30pm except Champs-Elysées, which is open daily noon to midnight. 136 rue de Rennes, 6e. ✆ **01-49-54-30-00.** Métro: St-Placide.

Virgin Megastore Paris has three branches of Europe's biggest, most widely publicized CD and record store. The Champs-Elysées branch is the city's largest music store; a bookstore and cafe are downstairs. The store's opening in a landmark building helped to rejuvenate the avenue. You'll find a Virgin Megastore at each airport. Open Monday to Saturday 10am to midnight; Sunday noon to midnight (other locations: Carrousel du Louvre, Sunday to Tuesday 10am to 8pm, Wednesday to Saturday 10am to 10pm; Gare Montparnasse, Monday to Thursday 7am to 8pm, Friday 7am to 9pm, Saturday 7am to 8pm). 52–60 av. des Champs-Elysées, 8e. ✆ **01-49-53-50-00.** Métro: Franklin-D-Roosevelt.

PERFUME & MAKEUP (DISCOUNT)
Catherine *(Finds)* This family-owned shop sells an impressive stock of all the big-name perfumes and cosmetics at discounts of 20% to 25%. In addition, its paperwork is usually extremely well organized, allowing refunds of the value-added tax (VAT) to be cleared quickly through Customs. Many on the staff speak English. Open Tuesday to Saturday 9am to 7pm; Monday 10:30am to 7pm. 7 rue Castiglione, 1er. ✆ **01-42-61-02-89.** Métro: Concorde.

Editions de Parfums Fréderic Malle *(★ (Finds)* If the big brand-name perfumes that are sold at every duty-free airport in Europe bore you, consider a visit to this boutique where brands are more personalized. This is the only outlet of an organization founded in 2000 by master perfumer Fréderic Malle, whose nose is as sensitive as that of any wine expert. Each of the scents sold here comes in a standardized bottle in either a 50ml size priced at 65€ to 120€ ($85–$156), depending on the scent, or a 100ml size priced at 85€ to 180€ ($111–$234). Scents are designed for either men or women; come in varying intensities of floral, spice, or "Oriental" motifs; and carry names that include Iris Poudre, Noir Epices, En Passant, and one of the best-sellers, Musc Ravageur. There's a lot of elegant chichi about this place (the paneled decor was designed by superdecorators Andrée Putnam and Olivier Lempereur), but the scents inside are often lovely. One of the things we like best about the place is the framed photographic portraits of each of the men and women who created the original scents sold within the boutique. Open Monday 1pm to 7pm and Tuesday to Saturday 11am to 7pm. 37 rue de Grenelle, 7e. ✆ **01-42-22-77-22.** www.editionsdeparfums.com. Métro: Rue du Bac.

Freddy Parfums (IFRAH) The discounts here are fabulous: up to 40% on perfumes, handbags, cosmetics, silk scarves, and neckties. Freddy of Paris is near American Express and the Opéra. Open Monday to Friday 10am to 7pm, Saturday 10am to 6pm. 3 rue Scribe, 9e. ✆ **01-47-42-63-41.** Métro: Opéra.

Maki You get some of the best deals in cosmetics and makeup here. In fact, it's the place where French actors and many models come for quality makeup products at discounted prices. The shop lies in the middle of a theater area. The staff often advises you about makeup. Open Tuesday to Saturday 11am to 1pm and 2:30 to 6:30pm. 9 rue Mansart, 9e. ✆ **01-42-81-33-76.** Métro: Blanche.

SHOES
Rodolphe Menudier This boutique elevates shoe buying to an artistic experience akin to a visit to a high-tech, postmodern museum. The black-lacquer and brushed-stainless-steel decor includes one wall sheathed in silver-painted leather and another

---

Finds   Sign of the Times

A shop such as **La Plaque Emaillées et Gravée Jacquin** stands in sharp contrast to the mass merchandise in most department stores. Established in 1908, when the Art Nouveau craze swept Paris, the outfit has done a respectable business promoting turn-of-the-20th-century Parisian charm ever since. Its specialty is the custom manufacture of cast-iron plaques, enameled and baked, commemorating virtually any event, person (including yourself), or piece of real estate that appeals to you. Phillippe Jacquin, the owner, offers a variety of shapes, sizes, and colors for the finished product. Expect to pay around 65€ to 150€ ($85–$195) for a street sign–size plaque and much more for plaques that can measure up to about 2m (6½ ft.) wide, suitable perhaps for a storefront. It will take 3 to 4 weeks for your plaque to be manufactured, after which it can be shipped. Shipping can be expensive and, in our opinion (because of the cast-iron nature of what's in the package), complicated. Much smaller plaques, some ready-made, are also available. Open Monday to Friday 9am to 1pm and 2 to 6pm. It's located at 18 bd. des Filles-du-Calvaire, 11e (© **01-47-00-50-95**; www.jacquinpub.com; Métro: St-Sébastien).

---

entirely faced in slate. These high-glam grace notes provide a backdrop for a small collection of stylish, but relatively conservative, men's shoes and a large collection of both standard and fetishistic shoes for ladies. Expect an inventory with footwear designed either for the office or, say, a prolonged schlep through the streets and museums of Paris. But if you're in the market for frighteningly high spike heels, in colors that include gold, silver, or outrageously patterned fabric, or the kind of high-altitude platform shoes that are definitely not for anyone with vertigo, this shop might be for you. Open Monday 11am to 7pm; Tuesday to Saturday 10am to 7pm. 14 rue Castiglione, 1er. © **01-42-60-86-27**. Métro: Tuileries.

SOUVENIRS & GIFTS

Au Nom de la Rose   Tasteful and frilly, this flower shop and gift boutique sells many of the floral arrangements that decorate local hotels and restaurants, as well as gift objects that are scented, emblazoned, or permeated with "the spirit or scent of the rose." Expect an overwhelming mass of flowers, many of them temporarily resting in glassed-in coolers, as well as rose-hip jams and marmalades, scented soaps and candles, rosewater-based perfumes, and decorative items for the home and kitchen. A "refinement" (their words) that you might consider either hopelessly decadent or whimsical and charming, depending on your point of view, is a perfume that's specifically designed to enhance the allure of your bedsheets. Open Monday to Saturday from 9am to 9pm, and Sunday from 9am to 2pm. 46 rue du Bac, 7e. © **01-42-22-22-12**. www.aunomdelarose.fr. Métro: Rue du Bac.

La Tuile à Loup   This emporium has been selling authentic examples of all-French handcrafts since around 1975, making a name through its concentration of hand-produced woven baskets, cutlery, and woodcarvings. Especially appealing are the hand-painted crockery and charming stoneware from such traditional manufacturers as Quimper and Malicorne and from small-scale producers in the Savoie Alps and

Alsace. Open Monday 1 to 7pm; Tuesday to Saturday 10:30am to 7pm. 35 rue Daubenton, 5e. ℰ **01-47-07-28-90**. www.latuilealoup.com. Métro: Censier-Daubenton.

STATIONERY

Cassegrain ℛ Nothing says elegance more than thick French stationery and note-
cards. Cassegrain, originally an engraver in 1919, offers beautifully engraved stationery, most often in traditional patterns, and business cards engraved to order.
Several other items for the desk, many suitable for gifts, are for sale as well; there
are even affordable pencils and pens, leather wallets, and small desktop accessories.
Open Monday to Saturday 10am to 7pm. 422 rue St-Honoré, 8e. ℰ **01-42-60-20-08**. www.
cassegrain.fr. Métro: Concorde.

SWEATERS

Georgina Brandolini ℛ The namesake owner was the former spokesperson for the
Valentino interests. Branching out on her own, she has set her sights on the sweater.
"No one makes them anymore," she laments. Therefore, she has set out to design her
own. Arguably, her sweaters are the best in Paris, or at least the most original. Prices
aren't cheap, but the quality is high and she caters to both sexes. Open Tuesday to Saturday 10:30am to 1pm and 2 to 7pm. 16 bd. Raspail, 8e. ℰ **01-45-44-27-96**. www.georgina
brandolini.com. Métro: Rue du Bac or Sèvres-Babylone.

TABLEWARE

Conran Shop This shop might remind you of an outpost of the British Empire,
valiantly imposing Brit aesthetics and standards on the French-speaking world. Inside,
you'll find articles for the kitchen and dining room; glass and crystal vases; fountain
pens and stationery; reading material and postcards; and even a selection of chocolates, teas, and coffees to help warm up a foggy English day. Open Monday to Friday
10am to 7pm; Saturday 10am to 7:30pm. 117 rue du Bac, 7e. ℰ **01-42-84-10-01**. www.
conranshop.fr. Métro: Sèvres-Babylone.

Geneviève Lethu This Provençal designer has shops all over France, with 19 others in and around Paris, all selling her clever and colorful Pottery Barn–meets–French
Mediterranean tableware. The newer designs stress influences from India, South
America, and Africa as well. Energy, style, and verve are rampant, and the prices are
moderate. Open Monday to Saturday 10:15am to 7pm. 95 rue de Rennes, 6e. ℰ **01-45-44-
40-35**. www.genevievelethu.com. Métro: St-Sulpice.

WINES

Lavinia ℛ This is the largest wine-and-spirits store in Europe, opening in 2002 to
great acclaim in Paris. Spread over three floors near place de la Madeleine, it stocks
more than 3,000 brands of French wine and spirits, along with more than 2,000
brands from other parts of the world. A simple lunch-only restaurant is on-site, as well
as a tasting bar. Wine sales here are big business and reflective of France's marketing
ideas as regards its favorite beverage. This is the only place in Paris where you can buy
a good bottle of South Dakota wine. But who would want to? Open Monday to Friday 10am to 8pm; Saturday 9am to 8pm. 3–5 bd. de la Madeleine, 1er. ℰ **01-42-97-20-20**.
www.lavinia. fr. Métro: Madeleine.

Les Caves Taillevent This is a temple to the art of making fine French wine. Associated with one of Paris's grandest restaurants, Taillevent, it occupies the street level

and cellar of an antique building. Stored here are more than 25,000 bottles of wine, with easy access in nearby warehouses to almost a million more. Open Monday 2 to 7:30pm; Tuesday to Saturday 9am to 7:30pm. 199 rue du Faubourg St-Honoré, 8e. ℂ 01-45-61-14-09. Métro: Charles de Gaulle–Etoile.

Nicolas *Finds* This is the flagship store of this chain of wine boutiques, and as such, its vintages are likely to be more esoteric and rare than what you'd find in any of the other 400-or-so members of its chain. Scattered over three floors of a large space near La Madeleine are fairly priced bottles of mainstream wines such as Alsatian Gewürztraminers and Collioures from Languedoc-Roussillon. Nicholas also stocks some exceptionally rare vintages, such as a Romanée-Conti from Burgundy, whose 1961 vintage sells for around 7,900€ ($10,270) per bottle. Open Monday to Friday 9:30am to 8:30pm, Saturday 9:30am to 8pm. 31 place de la Madeleine, 8e. ℂ 01-42-68-00-16. www.nicolas.com. Métro: Madeleine.

11

Paris After Dark

When darkness falls, the City of Light lives up to its name—the monuments and bridges are illuminated, and the glow of old-fashioned and modern street lamps, the blaze of sidewalk-cafe windows, and the glare of neon signs flood the avenues and boulevards. Parisians start the serious part of their evenings as Anglos stretch, yawn, and announce it's time for bed. Once the workday is over, most people go to a cafe to meet with friends over a drink and perhaps a meal (see section 6, "The Top Cafes," in chapter 7); then, they may head home or proceed to a restaurant or the theater; and much later, they may show up at a bar or a dance club.

In this chapter, we describe Paris's after-dark diversions—from attending a Molière play at the Comédie-Française to catching a cancan show at the Moulin Rouge to sipping a Sidecar at Harry's New York Bar to partying at Le Queen with all the boys.

1 The Performing Arts

LISTINGS Announcements of shows, concerts, and operas are plastered on kiosks all over town. You'll find listings in the weekly *Pariscope,* an entertainment guide with a section in English, or the English-language bimonthly *Boulevard.* Performances start later in Paris than in London or New York—from 8 to 9pm—and Parisians tend to dine after the theater. You may not want to do the same, because many of the less expensive restaurants close as early as 9pm.

TICKETS Paris has many ticket agencies, most near the Right Bank hotels. *Avoid them if possible.* You can buy the cheapest tickets at the box office of the theater or at discount agencies that sell tickets at discounts of up to 50%. One is the **Kiosque Théâtre,** 15 place de la Madeleine, 8e (no phone; www.kiosquetheatre.com; Métro: Madeleine), offering leftover tickets for about half-price on the day of performance. Tickets for evening performances are sold Tuesday to Saturday from 12:30 to 8pm. For matinees, tickets are sold Saturday from 12:30 to 2pm and Sunday from 12:30 to 4pm. Other branches are in the basement of the Châtelet–Les Halles Métro station and in front of Gare Montparnasse.

Students with ID can often get last-minute tickets by applying at the box office an hour before curtain time.

The easiest (and most expensive) way to get tickets, especially if you're staying in a first-class or deluxe hotel, is to ask your concierge to arrange for them. A service fee is added, but it's a lot easier if you don't want to waste precious hours in Paris trying to secure often-hard-to-get tickets.

Tickets for festivals, concerts, and the theater are easy to obtain through one of these locations of the **FNAC** record store chain: 136 rue de Rennes, 6e (© **01-49-54-30-00;** Métro: St. Placide); or 1–7 rue Pierre-Lescot, in the Forum des Halles, 1er. (© **01-40-41-40-00;** Métro: Châtelet–Les Halles).

For information and tickets to just about any show in Paris (also Dijon, Lyon, and Nice), **Keith Prowse** has a New York office if you'd like to make arrangements before you go. It's at 234 W. 44th St., Suite 1000, New York, NY 10036 (© **800/669-8687;** www.keithprowse.com). The Paris office is at 7 rue de Clichy, 9e (© **01-42-81-88-98;** Métro: Place de Clichy). They will mail tickets to your home, fax confirmation, or leave tickets at the box office in Paris. There's a markup of 20% (excluding opera and ballet) over box-office price, plus a U.S. handling charge of $8. Hotel and theater packages are also available.

THEATER

Comédie-Française 𝒜𝒜   Those with even a modest understanding of French can delight in a sparkling production of Molière at this national theater, established to keep the classics alive and promote important contemporary authors. Nowhere else will you see the works of Molière and Racine so beautifully staged. The box office is open daily from 11am to 6pm, but the hall is dark from mid-July to early September. In 1993 a Left Bank annex was launched, the **Comédie Française-Théâtre du Vieux-Colombier,** 21 rue du Vieux-Colombier, 4e (© **01-44-39-87-00**). Though its repertoire varies, it's known for presenting serious French dramas. Discounts are available if you reserve in advance. 2 rue de Richelieu, 1er. © 08-25-10-16-80. www.comedie-francaise.fr. Tickets 28€ ($36) adults, 15€ ($20) 26 and under. Métro: Palais-Royal or Musée du Louvre.

OPERA, DANCE & CLASSICAL CONCERTS

Cité de la Musique 𝒜𝒜𝒜   This testimony to the power of music has been the most widely applauded, the least criticized, and the most innovative of the late François Mitterrand's *grands projets*. At the city's northeastern edge in what used to be a run-down and depressing neighborhood, this $120-million stone-and-glass structure incorporates a network of concert halls, a library and research center for the study of all kinds of music, and a museum (see section 4, "Specialty Museums," in chapter 8). The complex hosts a rich variety of concerts, ranging from Renaissance music through 19th- and 20th-century works, including jazz and traditional music from nations around the world. 221 av. Jean-Jaurès, 19e. © 01-44-84-45-00, or 01-44-84-44-84 for tickets. www.cite-musique.fr. Tickets 18€–40€ ($23–$52) for 4:30 and 8pm concerts. Métro: Porte de Pantin.

Opéra Bastille 𝒜𝒜𝒜   This controversial building—it has been called a "beached whale"—was designed by Canadian architect Carlos Ott, with curtains by Japanese designer Issey Miyake. Since the house's grand opening in July 1989, the Opéra National de Paris has presented works such as Mozart's *Marriage of Figaro* and Tchaikovsky's *Queen of Spades*. The main hall is the largest of any French opera house, with 2,700 seats, but music critics have lambasted the acoustics. The building contains two other concert halls, including an intimate 250-seat room that usually hosts chamber music. Both traditional opera performances and symphony concerts are presented here, as well as both classical and modern dance. Several concerts are given for free in honor of certain French holidays. Write ahead for tickets. 2 place de la Bastille, 4e. © 08-92-89-90-90 or 01-40-01-17-89. Tickets 8€–175€ ($10–$228) opera, 12€–80€ ($16–$104) dance. Métro: Bastille.

Opéra Comique This is a charming venue for light opera, on a smaller scale than Paris's major opera houses. Built in the late 1890s in an ornate style that might remind you of the Opéra Garnier, it's the site of small productions of operas such as *Carmen, Don Giovanni, Tosca,* and *Palleas & Melisande.* There are no performances from mid-July to late August. The box office, however, is open year-round Monday 9am to 2pm and 3:15 to 6pm; Tuesday to Saturday 9am to 9pm; Sunday 11am to 3pm and 4:15 to 7pm. 5 rue Favart, 2e. ℭ **08-25-00-00-58.** www.opera-comique.com. Tickets 7€–100€ ($9.10–$130). Métro: Richelieu-Drouot.

Opéra Garnier 🎭🎭🎭 Once the haunt of the Phantom, this is the premier venue for dance and once again for opera. Charles Garnier designed this 1875 rococo wonder during the heyday of the French Empire; the facade is adorned with marble and sculpture, including *The Dance* by Carpeaux. Following a year-long renovation, during which the Chagall ceiling was cleaned and air-conditioning was added, the facade gleams as it did for Napoleon III. You can see the original gilded busts and statues, the rainbow-hued marble pillars, and the mosaics. The Opéra Garnier combines ballet and opera, and provides one of the most elegant evenings you can spend in the City of Light. Because of the competition from the Opéra Bastille, the Garnier has made great efforts to present more up-to-date dance works such as choreography by Twyla Tharp, Agnes de Mille, and George Balanchine. The box office is open Monday to Saturday from 11am to 6:30pm. Place de l'Opéra, 9e. ℭ **08-92-89-90-90** or 01-40-01-18-50. Tickets 5€–160€ ($6.50–$208) opera, 12€–80€ ($16–$104) dance. Métro: Opéra.

Salle Pleyel 🎭🎭🎭 New York has its Carnegie Hall, but for years Paris lacked a permanent home for its orchestra. That is, until 2006 when the restored Salle Pleyel opened once again. Built in 1927 by the piano-making firm of the same name, Pleyel was the world's first concert hall designed exclusively for a symphony orchestra. Ravel, Debussy, and Stravinsky performed their masterpieces here, only to see the hall devastated by fire less than 9 months after its opening. The original sound quality was never recovered because of an economic downturn. In 1998, real estate developer Hubert Martigny purchased the concert hall and pumped $38 million into it, restoring the art deco spirit of the original and also refining the acoustics it once knew. Nearly 500 seats were removed to make those that remained more comfortable. The Orchestre Philarmonique de Radio France and the Orchestre de Paris now have a home worthy of their reputations, and the London Symphony Orchestra makes Pleyel its venue in Paris. The box office is open Monday to Friday 10am to 6pm. 252 rue du Faubourg-St-Honoré, 8e. ℭ **01-42-52-13-13.** www.sallepleyel.fr. Tickets 10€–130€ ($13–$169). Métro: Miromesnil.

Théâtre des Champs-Elysées This Art Deco theater, attracting the haute couture crowd, hosts both national and international orchestras (such as the Vienna Philharmonic) as well as opera and ballet. The box office is open Monday to Saturday from 10am to 6pm. There are no performances in August. 15 av. Montaigne, 8e. ℭ **01-49-52-50-50** for box office. www.theatrechampselysees.fr. Tickets 6€–160€ ($7.80–$208). Métro: Alma-Marceau.

Théâtre National de Chaillot Part of the architectural complex facing the Eiffel Tower, this is one of the city's largest concert halls, hosting cultural events that are announced on billboards in front. Sometimes (rarely) dance is staged here, or you might see a brilliantly performed play by Marguerite Duras. The box office is

---

Moments The Music of Angels

Some of the most moving music in Paris echoes through its churches, with sounds that can take you back to the Middle Ages. At **Eglise de St-Eustache,** rue Rambuteau, 1er (*(C)* **01-42-36-31-05;** Métro: Les Halles), High Mass with the organ playing and the choir singing is at 11am on Sunday. In summer, concerts are played on the organ, marking the church's role in holding the premiere of Berlioz's *Te Deum* and Liszt's *Messiah.* Tickets to these special concerts sell for 12€–40€ ($16–$52). It's open daily 9:30am to 7pm.

The **American Church in Paris,** 65 quai d'Orsay, 7e (*(C)* **01-40-62-05-00;** www. acparis.org; Métro: Invalides or Alma-Marceau), sponsors free concerts from September to June on Sundays at 5pm. You can also attend free concerts at **Eglise St-Merry,** 76 rue Verrerie, 4e (*(C)* **01-42-71-48-15;** Métro: Hôtel-de-Ville). These performances are staged with variable musicians based on their availability, from September to July on Saturdays at 8:30pm, and again on Sundays at 4pm.

---

open Monday to Saturday from 11am to 7pm, Sunday 1 to 5pm. 1 place du Trocadéro, 16e. *(C)* **01-53-65-30-00.** www.theatre-chaillot.fr. Tickets 27€–32€ ($35–$42) adults, 21€–27€ ($27–$35) seniors over 60, 12€–17€ ($16–$22) under age 25. Métro: Trocadéro.

2 The Club & Music Scene

Paris is still a late-night mecca, and both the quantity and variety of nightlife exceed that of other cities. Nowhere else will you find such a huge, mixed array of nightclubs, bars, dance clubs, cabarets, jazz dives, music halls, and honky-tonks.

A MUSIC HALL

Olympia   Charles Aznavour and other big names appear in this cavernous hall. The late Yves Montand performed once, and the show was sold out 4 months in advance. Today, you're more likely to catch Gloria Estefan. A typical lineup might include an English rock group, Italian acrobats, a French singer, a dance troupe, juggling American comedians (doing much of their work in English), and the featured star. A witty master of ceremonies and an onstage band provide a smooth transition. Performances usually begin at 8:30pm Tuesday to Saturday, with Sunday matinees at 5pm. 28 bd. des Capucines, 9e. *(C)* **01-55-27-10-00** or 08-92-68-33-68. www.olympiahall.com. Tickets 22€–75€ ($29–$98). Métro: Opéra or Madeleine.

CHANSONNIERS

Chansonniers (literally, songwriters) provide a bombastic musical satire of the day's events. This combination of parody and burlesque is a time-honored Gallic amusement and a Parisian institution. Songs are often created on the spot, inspired by the "disaster of the day."

Au Lapin Agile *✦*   Picasso and Utrillo patronized this little cottage near the top of Montmartre, then known as the Cabaret des Assassins, and it has been painted by many artists, including Utrillo. You'll sit at carved wooden tables in a dimly lit room with walls covered by bohemian memorabilia and listen to French folk tunes, love ballads, army songs, sea chanteys, and music-hall ditties. You're encouraged to sing along, even if it's only the *"oui, oui, oui—non, non, non,"* the refrain of "Les Chevaliers de la Table Ronde." Open Tuesday to Sunday 9pm to 2am. 22 rue des Saules, 18e. ℭ **01-46-06-85-87.** www.au-lapin-agile.com. Cover (includes 1 drink) 24€ ($31), 17€ ($22) students. Métro: Lamarck Caulaincourt.

Théâtre des Deux Anes   Since 1920, this theater has staged satires of the foibles, excesses, and stupidities of French governments. Favorite targets are President Jacques Chirac and other mandarins of the *hexagone française.* Cultural icons, French and foreign, receive a grilling that's very funny and sometimes caustic. The place considers itself more of a theater than a cabaret and doesn't serve drinks or refreshments. The 2½-hour show is conducted in rapid-fire French slang, so if your syntax isn't up to par, you won't appreciate its charms. Performances are given Tuesday through Saturday at 8:30pm, with matinees on Sunday at 3pm; closed July to September. 100 bd. de Clichy, 18e. ℭ **01-46-06-10-26.** www.2anes.com. Tickets 37€–41€ ($48–$53). Métro: Place Clichy.

NIGHTCLUBS & CABARETS

Decidedly expensive, these places give you your money's worth by providing lavishly spectacular floor shows. They generally attract an older crowd and are definitely not youth-oriented.

Chez Michou   The setting is blue, the master of ceremonies wears blue, and the spotlights bathe performers in yet another shade of blue. Cross-dressing belles bear names such as Hortensia and DuDuche; they lip-sync in costumes from haute couture to haute concierge, paying tribute to such Americans as Whitney Houston and Tina Turner and to French stars such as Mireille Mathieu, Sylvie Vartan, and Brigitte Bardot. If you don't want dinner, you'll have to stand at the bar, paying a compulsory 35€ ($46) for the first drink. Dinner is served nightly at 8:30pm (reservations required); shows begin nightly at 11pm. 80 rue des Martyrs, 18e. ℭ **01-46-06-16-04.** www.michou.fr. Cover (including dinner, aperitif, wine, coffee, and show) 99€ ($129). Métro: Pigalle.

Crazy Horse Saloon   Since 1951, this sophisticated strip joint has thrived, thanks to good choreography and a sly, coquettish celebration of the female form. The theme binding each of the 5-minute numbers (featuring gorgeous dancers in erotic costumes) is La Femme in her various states: temperamental, sad, dancing/bouncy, or joyful. Dance numbers that endure season after season include "Le Laser" and "The Erotic Lesson." Dinner is served at Chez Francis, a restaurant under separate management a few steps away. Shows last just under 2 hours. You'll find a small number of women among the audience of mainly businessmen. Shows Sunday to Friday 8:30 and 11pm; Saturday at 7:30, 9:45, and 11:50pm. 12 av. George V, 8e. ℭ **01-47-23-32-32.** www.lecrazyhorseparis.com. Reservations recommended. Cover (includes 2 drinks) 90€ ($117); dinner spectacle 135€–170€ ($176–$221). Métro: George V or Alma Marceau.

Folies-Bergère   The Folies-Bergère has been an institution since 1869. Josephine Baker, the African-American singer who danced in a banana skirt and threw bananas into the audience, became "the toast of Paris" here. According to legend, the first GI to reach Paris at the 1944 Liberation asked for directions to the club. Don't expect the naughty and slyly permissive, skin-and-glitter revue that used to be the trademark of this place. In 1993, that all ended with a radical restoration of the theater and a reopening under new management. Today, it's a conventional 1,600-seat theater devoted to a frequently changing roster of big-stage performances in French, many of which are adaptations of Broadway blockbusters. Recent examples have included restagings of *Fame* and *Saturday Night Fever,* and a revue of male strippers inspired by

America's Chippendales. There's even been a relatively highbrow reenactment of one of the classics of the French-language repertory, *L'Arlésienne,* by 19th-century playwright Alphonse Daudet. True, there's always an acknowledgment of the nostalgia value of the old-time, much naughtier Folies-Bergère, and endless nods to the stars of yesterday (especially Josephine Baker and her topless act with bananas), but if you're looking for artful nudity presented with unabashed Parisian permissiveness, head for the Crazy Horse Saloon or the Lido. An on-site restaurant serves dinners in one of the theater's salons, but most spectators opt just for the show, and not the meal. Shows are usually given Tuesday to Saturday at 9pm and Sunday at 3pm. 34 rue Richer, 9e. ℂ 01-44-79-98-60 or 08-92-68-16-50. www.foliesbergere.com. Tickets 25€–84€ ($33–$109). Métro: Grands Boulevards or Cadet.

L'Ane Rouge This red-and-black minitheater has been a showcase for French satire and humor since it opened shortly after World War II. You'll enjoy a well-flavored dinner of French specialties, followed by a 2-hour medley of French-language standup comedy, ribald stories, and politicized jokes. If your knowledge of French is zero, you won't enjoy this place; ditto if you hate being singled out by a comedian in front of a crowd. Dinner served nightly at 8pm; shows nightly 10pm to midnight. 3 rue Laugier, 17e. ℂ 01-43-80-79-97. www.diners-spectacles.com. Tickets 45€ ($59); fixed-price dinner (includes access to show) 50€–100€ ($65–$130), which includes 1 drink. Reservations recommended. Métro: Ternes.

Le Canotier du Pied de la Butte The worst thing you can say about this place is that it's touristy, but visitors share a genuine appreciation of the nuances, lyricism, and poetry of popular French songs. Each performance includes appearances by two men and two women, who interact with their own versions of the hits made famous by Piaf, Montand, Brel, and Chevalier. Nostalgia is unleashed by the bucketful in a cozy red, black, and white theater with room for no more than 70. Performances Monday to Saturday 9 to 10:30pm. 62 bd. Rochechouart, 18e. ℂ 01-46-06-02-86. Reservations required. Cover 20€–38€ ($26–$49) including first drink. Métro: Anvers.

Le Paradis Latin Built in 1889 by Alexandre-Gustave Eiffel, with the same metallic skeleton as the famous tower, Le Paradis Latin represents the architect's only venture into theater design. The place is credited with introducing vaudeville and musical theater to Paris. In 1903 the building was a warehouse, but in the 1970s it was transformed into a successful cabaret whose singers, dancers, and special effects extol the fun, frivolity, and permissiveness of the City of Light. The show includes tasteful nudity (they contrast their more dignified nudity—breasts only—with the more blatant and unabashed nudity at Crazy Horse), a ventriloquist, and a trapeze artist. The master of ceremonies speaks in French and English. Dinner Wednesday to Monday 8pm; reviews at 9:30pm. 28 rue Cardinal-Lemoine, 5e. ℂ 01-43-25-28-28. Cover 82€ ($107) including a glass of champagne; dinner and show 117€–170€ ($152–$221). Métro: Jussieu or Cardinal Lemoine.

Lido de Paris The Lido competes with the best Las Vegas has to offer. Its $15-million-production, *C'est Magique,* reflects a dramatic reworking of the classic Parisian cabaret show, with eye-popping special effects, water technology using more than 60,000 gallons per minute, and even aerial and aquatic ballet. The show, the most expensive ever produced in Europe, uses 70 performers, $4 million in costumes, and a $2-million lighting design with lasers. There's even an ice rink and swimming pool that appears and disappears. The 45 topless Bluebell Girls, those legendary showgirls, are still here. Chef Paul Bocuse is the consultant for the culinary offerings. 116 bis av. des Champs-Elysées, 8e. ℂ 800/227-4884 in the U.S., or 01-40-76-56-10. www.lido.fr. Dinner dance (7:30pm) and show (11:30pm) 140€–210€ ($182–$273); show only (9:30 and 11:30pm) 100€ ($130). Price includes half-bottle of champagne per person. Métro: George V.

Moulin Rouge This is a camp classic. The establishment that Toulouse-Lautrec immortalized is still here, but the artist would probably have a hard time recognizing it. Colette created a scandal here by offering an on-stage kiss to Mme de Morny, but shows today have a harder time shocking audiences. Try to get a table—the view is much better on the main floor than from the bar. What's the theme? It's strip routines and the saucy sexiness of *la Belle Epoque,* and of permissive Paris between the wars. Handsome men and girls, girls, girls, virtually all topless, keep the place going. Dance finales usually include two dozen of the belles doing a topless cancan. Revues begin nightly at 9 and 11pm. 82 bd. Clichy, place Blanche, 18e. ℂ 01-53-09-82-82. www.moulinrouge. fr. Cover including champagne 87€–97€ ($113–$126); 7pm dinner and show 140€–170€ ($182–$221). Métro: Blanche.

Nouveau Casino Some Paris-watchers consider this the epitome of the hyperhip countercultural scene that blossoms along the rue Oberkampf every night. In a former movie theater adjacent to the Café Charbon, it's a large, drafty space centered on a dance floor and an enormous bar crafted to resemble an iceberg. Live concerts take place nightly between 8pm and 1am; on Friday and Saturday, the party continues from 1am till dawn, with a DJ who spins some of the most avant-garde dance music in Paris. Celebrity spotters have picked out Prince Albert of Monaco and such French-language film stars as Vincent Cassel and Mathieu Kassovitz. 109 rue Oberkampf, 9e. ℂ 01-43-57-57-40. www.nouveaucasino.net. Admission to concerts 12€–13€ ($16–$17); to disco 5€–20€ ($6.50–$26). Métro: St-Maur, Parmentier, or Ménilmontant.

JAZZ, SALSA, ROCK & MORE

The great jazz revival that long ago swept America is still going strong here, with Dixieland, Chicago, bop, and free-jazz rhythms being pounded out in dozens of jazz cellars, mostly called *caveaux.* Most clubs are between rue Bonaparte and rue St-Jacques on the Left Bank. The crowds that attend clubs to hear rock, salsa, and the like are definitely young, often in their late teens, 20s, or early 30s. The exception to that is in the clubs offering jazz nights, where jazz-lovers span all ages.

Baiser Salé In a cellar lined with jazz-related paintings, a large bar, and videos that show jazz greats of the past (Charlie Parker, Miles Davis), this is an appealing club. Everything is mellow and laid-back, with an emphasis on the music. Genres include Afro-Caribbean, Afro-Latino, salsa, merengue, rhythm and blues, and sometimes fusion. 58 rue des Lombards, 1er. ℂ 01-42-33-37-71. www.lebaisersale.com. Cover Tues–Sun 8€ ($10) or 16€ ($21) after 10pm. Free Mon. Métro: Châtelet.

Bus Palladium A single room with a very long bar, this rock-'n'-roll temple has varnished hardwoods and fabric-covered walls that barely absorb the reverberations of nonstop recorded music. You won't find techno, punk, jazz, blues, or soul here. It appeals to hard-core, mostly heterosexual, rock wannabes ages 25 to 35. Alcoholic drinks cost 5€ to 15€ ($6.50–$20); on Tuesdays, women drink free. It's open Tuesday to Saturday 11pm to 5am. 6 rue Fontaine, 9e. ℂ **01-53-21-07-33.** Cover 12€–20€ ($16–$26) for men, and Fri–Sat for women. Métro: Blanche or Pigalle.

Caveau de la Huchette ✿ This celebrated jazz *caveau,* reached by a winding staircase, draws a young crowd, mostly students, who dance to the music of well-known jazz combos. In pre-jazz days, Robespierre and Marat frequented the place. Sunday to Thursday 9:30pm to 2:30am; Friday to Saturday and holidays 9:30pm to 4am. 5 rue de la Huchette, 5e. ℂ **01-43-26-65-05.** www.caveaudelahuchette.fr. Cover 11€ ($14) Sun–Thurs, 13€ ($17) Fri–Sat; students under 25 9€ ($12). Métro/RER: St-Michel.

Caveau des Oubliettes ✿ It's hard to say which is more intriguing—the entertainment and drinking or the setting. An *oubliette* is a dungeon with a trap door at the top at its only opening, and the name is accurate. Located in the Latin Quarter, just across the river from Notre-Dame, this night spot is housed in a genuine 12th-century prison, complete with dungeons, spine-tingling passages, and scattered skulls, where prisoners were tortured and sometimes pushed through portholes to drown in the Seine. The *caveau* is beneath the subterranean vaults that many centuries ago linked it with the fortress prison of Petit Châtelet. Today patrons laugh, drink, talk, and flirt in the narrow *caveau* or else retreat to the smoke-filled jazz lounge. There's a free jam session every night, perhaps Latin jazz or rock. At some point on Friday and Saturday nights concerts are staged (a cover is assessed at this time). 52 rue Galande, 5e. ℂ **01-46-34-23-09.** Cover 12€ ($16) Fri–Sat. Open daily 5pm–2am. Métro: St-Michel.

La Chapelle des Lombards *finds* The club's proximity to the Opéra Bastille seems incongruous, considering the African/Caribbean jazz and Brazilian samba that's the norm. It's a magnet for South American and African expatriates, and the rhythms and fire of the music propel everyone onto the dance floor. Open Tuesday to Sunday 11pm to 6am. 19 rue de Lappe, 11e. ℂ **01-43-57-24-24.** Cover 15€–19€ ($20–$25) including first drink. Women free Thurs before midnight. Métro: Bastille.

Le Bilboquet This restaurant/jazz club/piano bar, where the film *Paris Blues* was shot, offers some of the best music in the city. Jazz is featured daily, 9:30pm to 1:30am, on the upper level in the restaurant, a wood-paneled room with a copper ceiling, brass-trimmed bar, and Victorian candelabra. The menu is limited but classic French; dinner will run you 55€ ($72) and is served Monday to Saturday 8pm to 2am. 13 rue St-Benoît, 6e. ℂ **01-45-48-81-84.** Cover 18€ ($23). Métro: St-Germain-des-Prés.

Le Duc des Lombards Comfortable and appealing, this low-key jazz club replaced an older club 10 years ago. Performances begin nightly at 9pm and continue (with breaks) for 5 hours, touching on everything from free jazz to more traditional such forms as hard bop. Concerts begin at 9:30pm. 42 rue des Lombards, 1er. ℂ **01-42-33-22-88.** Cover 19€–25€ ($25–$33). Métro: Châtelet.

Le Gibus Attracting a pulsating under-30 crowd, this is one of the best-known rock clubs in Paris, patronized by both gays and straights. It opens every night late as a dance club, entertaining its diverse medley of counterculture Parisians and visitors. Depending on that week's schedule, you'll be confronted with a rotating series of themes, ranging from "Club Trance" to "Party Up." There might be a live rock band or even a drag show presented as part of the evening's rhythms. Friday and Saturday attract the most gays. Friday and Saturday 10:30pm to either 3 or 6am. 18 rue du Faubourg du Temple, 11e. ℂ **01-47-00-78-88.** Cover 10€–20€ ($13–$26). Métro: République.

Les Etoiles   Since 1856, this old-fashioned music hall has shaken with the sound of performers at work and patrons at play. Its newest incarnation is as a restaurant discothèque where the music is exclusively salsa and the food is Cuban. Expect simple but hearty portions of fried fish, shredded pork or beef, rice, beans, and flan, as bands from Venezuela play to a crowd that already knows or quickly learns how to dance to Latin American rhythms. 61 rue du Château d'Eau, 10e. © 01-47-70-60-56. Cover 22€ ($29; includes meal); for nondiners 12€ ($16; includes drink). Tues–Sat 9pm–3am. Métro: Château d'Eau.

Le Sunset/Le Sunside   A staple on the Parisian jazz circuit since 1976, Le Sunset/ Le Sunside maintains two separate bar areas, one on street level and one in the cellar, where separate jazz shows—each 3 hours in duration—begin at 8:30pm and 10pm, respectively. Expect a decor that (in the cellar) emulates a Métro station, thanks to a sheath of gloss-white tiles, and a roster of French, Italian, and U.S.-derived artists including Roy Haynes, Aldo Romano, Richard Galliano, and more recently Steve Grossman, Mark Turner, and Simon Goubert. Whereas Le Sunset is dedicated to electric jazz and world music, Le Sunside is a temple of more conservative and classic jazz. Doors open nightly at 8:30pm. 60 rue des Lombards, 1er. © 01-40-26-46-60. www.sunset-sunside.com. Cover 20€–22€ ($26–$29). Métro: Châtelet.

New Morning   Jazz maniacs come to drink, talk, and dance at this enduring club. It's sometimes a scene, attracting such guests as Spike Lee and Prince. The place is especially popular with jazz groups from central and southern Africa. It opens nightly at 8pm, with concerts beginning at 9pm. 7 rue des Petites-Ecuries, 10e. © 01-45-23-51-41. www.newmorning.com. Cover 17€–21€ ($22–$27). Métro: Château-d'Eau.

Slow Club ☆☆   One of the most famous jazz cellars in Europe, with medieval ceiling vaults that make the music reverberate in an evocative way, this venue hosts a revolving set of artists who tend to focus on New Orleans–style jazz. Most of the hip folks who flock here are in their 30s and early 40s. The club schedules live music Thursday through Saturday; on Wednesday, it features recorded music, everything from swing to rock 'n' roll. Open 10pm to 3:30am. 130 rue de Rivoli, 1er. © 01-42-33-84-30. Cover 13€ ($17). Métro: Châtelet, Louvres-Rivoli.

DANCE CLUBS

The nightspots below are among hundreds of places where people in their 20s or early 30s go to dance—distinct from others where the main attraction is the music. The area around the church of **St-Germain-des-Prés** is full of dance clubs, but they come and go so quickly that you could arrive to find a hardware store in the place of last year's white-hot club—but like all things in nature, the new springs up to replace the old. Check *Time Out: Paris* or *Pariscope* to get a sense of current trends. Most of these clubs don't really get going until well after 10pm.

Batofar ☆   Self-consciously proud of its status as a club that virtually everybody views as hip, Batofar sits on a converted barge that floats on the Seine, sometimes attracting hundreds of gyrating dancers, most of whom are in their 20s and 30s. House, garage, techno, and live jazz by groups that hail from (among other places) Morocco, Senegal, and Germany sometimes add to the mix. Come here for an insight into late-night Paris at its most raffish and countercultural, and don't even try to categorize the patrons. Beer will cost around 8.50€ ($11) a bottle. Open Tuesday to Saturday from 6pm to 3 or 4am, depending on business. Closed November to March. Facing 11 quai François Mauriac, 13e. © 01-53-60-17-30. Cover 12€–16€ ($16–$21). Métro: Quai de la Gare.

After-Dark Diversions: Dives, Drag, & More

On a Paris night, the cheapest entertainment, especially if you're young, is "the show" at the tip of Ile de la Cité, behind Notre-Dame. A sort of Gallic version of the Sundowner Festival in Key West, Florida, it attracts just about everyone who ever wanted to try his or her hand at performance. The spontaneous entertainment usually includes magicians, fire-eaters, jugglers, mimes, and music makers from all over, performing against the backdrop of the illuminated cathedral. This is one of the greatest places in Paris to meet young people in a sometimes-euphoric setting.

Also popular is a stroll along the Seine after 10pm. Take a graveled pathway down to the river from the Left Bank side of pont de Sully, close to the Institut du Monde Arabe, and walk to the right, away from Notre-Dame. This walk, which ends near place Valhubert, is the best place to see spontaneous Paris in action at night. Joggers and saxophone players come here, and many Parisians arrive for impromptu dance parties.

To quench your thirst, wander onto Ile St-Louis and head for the **Café-Brasserie St-Regis**, 6 rue Jean-du-Bellay, 4e, across from pont St-Louis (© 01-43-54-59-41; Métro: Pont Marie). If you want to linger, you can order a *plat du jour* or a coffee at the bar. But try doing as the Parisians do: Get a 3€ ($3.90) beer to go *(une bière à emporter)* in a cup and take it with you on a stroll around the island. The cafe is open daily until midnight.

Cab ★★ If you've ever wanted to dance in a basement under the Louvre, it doesn't get much classier than this joint patronized by French models, Arab businessmen, women with a past, and children of the rich. Dim lighting illuminates black leather furniture, and there are two bars with shiny black or glass surfaces. There is also a trio of different seating areas. Music is house and electro, with various hip-hop songs and other American hits mixed in. We even heard Michael Jackson one night (remember him?). Open Wednesday and Friday to Sunday 11:30pm to 4:30am. Place du Palais royal, 1er. © 01-58-62-56-25. Cover 20€ ($26), including 1 drink. Métro: Palais Royal-Musée du Louvre.

Club Zed *(Finds)* Hip, breezy, and very French, this popular nightspot in a former bakery with a vaulted masonry ceiling may surprise you with its mix of musical offerings, including samba, rock 'n' roll, 1960s pop, and jazz. Specific theme parties, such as the one at Halloween, where virtually everyone comes in costume, are a delight. Open Thursday 10:30pm to 3am; Friday and Saturday 11pm to 5:30am. 2 rue des Anglais, 5e. © 01-43-54-93-78. Cover 10€ ($13) Thurs, 18€ ($23) Fri–Sat, including first drink. Métro: Maubert-Mutualité.

Favela Chic No other nightclub in Paris succeeds at satirizing and respecting Brazilian-ness as effectively as this one. Set in the grungy-trendy Oberkampf nightclub district, it attracts good-looking, trendy men and women who come to dance, flirt, and chat in any of a dozen languages. There's definitely a fashionable slant to this place, but as regards the specific style, that's anybody's guess. Live music alternates with recorded music. Open Tuesday to Thursday 7:30pm to 2am, Friday

If you're caught waiting for the Métro to start running again at 5am, try the **Sous-Bock Tavern**, 49 rue St-Honoré, 1er (© **01-40-26-46-61**; Métro: Les Halles or Louvres-Rivoli), open daily from 11am to 5am. Young drinkers gather here to sample from 250 varieties of beer or 20 varieties of whisky. The dish to order is a platter of mussels—curried, with white wine, or with cream sauce; they go well with the brasserie-style fries.

If drag shows aren't your cup of tea, how about *Last Tango in Paris?* At **Le Tango**, 11 rue au Maire, 3e (© **01-42-72-17-78**; Métro: Arts et Métiers), memories of Evita and Argentina live on. On site is a ballroom called *La Boîte à Frissons*. The evening starts at 10:30pm, with couples dancing until 12:30am, featuring the waltz, the tango, *pasadoble,* the polka, rock 'n' roll and cha cha. After that, the dance floor turns into a disco. The cover is 7€ ($9.10). It's open Friday and Saturday from midnight to 5am.

If you're looking for a sophisticated, laid-back venue, consider the **Sanz-Sans**, 49 rue du Faubourg St-Antoine, 4e (© **01-44-75-78-78**; Métro: Bastille or Ledru Rollin), a multi-ethnic playground where the children of prominent Parisians mingle, testifying to the unifying power of jazz. In this red-velvet duplex, the most important conversations seem to occur over margaritas on the stairway or the back-room couches. The later it gets, the sexier the scene becomes. No cover is charged.

and Saturday until 4am. 18 rue du Faubourg du Temple, 11e. © 01-40-03-02-66. www.favelachic. com. Cover Fri–Sat 10€ ($13), including one drink. Métro: République.

La Balajo   Established in 1936, this dance club is where Edith Piaf won the hearts of Parisian music lovers. Today, it's easy to compare La Balajo with New York City's Roseland—an old-fashioned venue steeped in Big Band nostalgia, which sometimes manages to shake the dust out for special parties and events. Afternoon sessions focus on tangos, *paso dobles,* and waltzes, and are more staid than their late-night counterparts. Evenings attract a younger crowd (age 20–35-ish), who groove to a mixture, depending on the DJ, of house, garage, techno, and old-fashioned disco. Open Thursday 10pm to 4:30am; Friday and Saturday 10pm to 5:30am; and Sunday 3 to 7pm. 9 rue de Lappe, 11e. © 01-47-00-07-87. www.balajo.fr. Cover (includes 1 drink) 8€ ($10) for afternoon sessions, 16€–20€ ($21–$26) for night sessions. Métro: Bastille.

La Java   This bal-musette dance hall was once one of the most important in Paris; Piaf and Maurice Chevalier made their names here. Today, you can still waltz on what one critic called "retro fetish night," or even tango on Sunday afternoon. Brazilian and Latin themes predominate on some nights. Overall, it's one of the best places in Paris for the old-fashioned pleasures of couples arm-in-arm on a dance floor. 105 rue du Faubourg du Temple, 11e. © 01-42-02-20-52. Cover 5€–22€ ($6.50–$29). Métro: Belleville, Goncourt.

La Loco   Next to the Moulin Rouge, this club is popular with American students and is especially busy on Sunday. People dance to rock and techno, though occasionally metal concerts are staged. La Loco is one of the largest clubs in Paris. In the *sous-sol* (the basement, the coolest of the three levels), you can even see the remnants of an old railway line (hence the name). The Bar Americain looks more Roman with fake statuary and columns crowned by lions. Daily 11pm to 5am. 90 bd. De Clichy, 18e. © 01-53-41-88-88. Cover 5€–20€ ($6.50–$26). Métro: Blanche.

Le New Riverside This Left Bank cellar from the 18th century attracts droves of jaded clubgoers who appreciate the indestructible premises and classic rock from the '70s. Expect patrons ages 20 to 40; women, especially when unaccompanied, are almost always admitted free. Open daily 11am to dawn. 7 rue Grégoire-de-Tours, 6e. © 01-43-54-46-33. Cover (includes 1 drink) 12€–15€ ($16–$20) for men, and after midnight Fri–Sat for women. Métro: Odéon, Mabillon, or Odéon.

Le Saint Occupying three medieval cellars in the university area, this place attracts a crowd of people in their 20s and 30s who dance (to music from the U.S. and Europe), drink, and soak up the Left Bank student-dive scene. Vacationers will enjoy this fun spot, and its "young love beside the Seine" vibe can be a hoot. Wednesday to Sunday 11pm to 6am. 7 rue St-Séverin, 5e. © 01-40-20-43-23. Cover (includes 1 drink) 10€–15€ ($13–$20). Métro: St-Michel or Cluny-La Sorbonne.

Les Bains Douches The name, "The Baths," comes from this hot spot's former function as a Turkish bath that attracted gay clients, none more notable than Marcel Proust. It may be hard to get in if the doorman doesn't think you're trendy and *très chic*. Yes, that was Jennifer Lopez we saw whirling around the floor. Dancing begins at midnight, and a supper club–like restaurant is upstairs. Meals cost 40€ to 50€ ($52–$65). On certain nights this is the hottest party atmosphere in Paris, and Mondays are increasingly gay, although sexual preference is hardly an issue at this club. "We all walk the waterfront," one DJ enigmatically told us. Open Tuesday to Saturday 11pm to 6am. 7 rue du Bourg-l'Abbé, 3e. © 01-48-87-01-80. www.lesbainsdouches. net. Cover 10€–20€ ($13–$26). Métro: Etienne Marcel.

Les Coulisses Montmartre has more tourist traps than anywhere in Paris, but this fairly new club has some legitimacy; it's a good spot for drinking and dancing. It consists of a basement-level dance club, a first-floor bar, and a restaurant on the second floor. The decor changes all the time, but management usually sticks to baroque and medieval themes. The restaurant is open Tuesday to Saturday 9pm to midnight. The club is open from 11pm to 5am. 1 rue St. Rustique, 18e. © 01-42-62-89-99. Cover 20€–30€ ($26–$39) Fri–Sat; no cover for restaurant patrons. Métro: Abbesses or Funiculaire de Montmartre.

Rex Club This echoing blue-and-orange space emulates the techno-grunge clubs of London, complete with an international mood-altered crowd enjoying the kind of music that only those ages 18 to 28 could love. A host of DJs, including techno-circuit celeb Laurent Garnier, is on hand. Open Wednesday to Saturday 11:30pm to 7am. 5 bd. Poissonnière, 2e. © 01-42-36-10-96. www.rexclub.com. Cover 10€–15€ ($13–$20). Métro: Bonne Nouvelle.

3 Bars, Pubs & Clubs

WINE BARS

Many Parisians now prefer wine bars to traditional cafes or bistros. The food is often better, and the ambience more inviting. For cafes, see section 6, "The Top Cafes," in chapter 7.

Au Sauvignon   This tiny spot has tables overflowing onto a covered terrace and a decor that features old ceramic tiles and frescoes done by Left Bank artists. Wines range from the cheapest Beaujolais to the most expensive Puligny-Montrachet. A glass of wine costs 4.50€ to 6€ ($5.85–$7.80). To go with your wine, choose an Auvergne specialty, such as goat cheese or a terrine. Fresh Poilâne bread is ideal with ham, pâté, or goat cheese. Open daily 8am to 10pm. Closed in August. 80 rue des Sts-Pères, 7e. (℃) **01-45-48-49-02.** Métro: Sèvres-Babylone or Saint Sulpice.

Aux Négociants   Ten minutes downhill from the north facade of Sacré-Coeur, this *bistro à vins* has flourished since 1980 as an outlet for wines produced in the Loire Valley. Artists, vendors, and office workers come here, linked by an appreciation of wine, costing 3.60€ to 4.50€ ($4.70–$5.85) per glass, and the *plats du jour,* costing 13€ ($17). Open Monday noon to 2:30pm; Tuesday to Friday noon to 2:30pm and 7 to 10:30pm. 27 rue Lambert, 18e. (℃) **01-46-06-15-11.** Métro: Lamarck Caulaincourt or Château Rouge.

Juveniles   This wine bar prides itself on experimenting with a wide roster of wines from "everywhere." High-quality but lesser-known wines from Spain, France, California, and Australia decant for 3€ to 9€ ($3.90–$12) per glass. Anything you like, including the "wine of the week," can be hauled away uncorked from the wine boutique here. An assortment of tapas-inspired platters is also available for 5.50€ to 18€ ($7.15–$23). Bar open Monday 6pm to midnight and Tuesday to Saturday noon to midnight. 47 rue de Richelieu, 1er. (℃) **01-42-97-46-49.** Métro: Palais-Royal.

La Tartine   Mirrors, brass details, and frosted-globe chandeliers make La Tartine look like a movie set of old Paris. At least 60 wines are offered at reasonable prices, including seven kinds of Beaujolais and a large selection of Bordeaux by the glass. Glasses of wine cost 3.50€ to 6€ ($4.55–$7.80), and the *charcuterie* platter costs 16€ ($21). We recommend the light Sancerre wine and goat cheese from the Loire Valley. Open daily 8am to 2am. 24 rue de Rivoli, 4e. (℃) **01-42-72-76-85.** Métro: St-Paul.

Le Sancerre   Engagingly old-fashioned, with an agreeable staff and food prepared fresh every day, this wine bar specializes in vintages from the Loire Valley and Sancerre. The latter, produced in red, rosé, and white, is known for its not-too-dry fruity aroma and legions of fans who believe it should be more celebrated. Other wine choices include chinon and saumur wine (both from the Loire Valley), as well as pinot de Bourgogne (from Burgundy), gamay (from the Ardèche Valley in France's southwest), and chenas (from the Beaujolais). Food items usually include *andouillettes* (chitterling sausages), omelets with flap mushrooms, fresh oysters, and quiche. Glasses of wine cost 3.10€ to 5.20€ ($4.05–$6.75); simple platters of food cost 8.50€ to 14€ ($11–$18) each. Open Monday to Friday 8am to 4pm and 6:30 to 11pm; Saturday 8:30am to 4pm. 22 av. Rapp, 7e. (℃) **01-45-51-75-91.** Métro: Alma-Marceau.

Les Bacchantes   This place prides itself on offering more wines by the glass— at least 90—than any other wine bar in Paris; prices range from 2€ to 6€ ($2.60– $7.80). It also does a hefty restaurant trade in well-prepared *cuisine bourgeoise.* Its cozy, rustic setting—with paneling, and chalkboards announcing vintages and platters— attracts theatergoers before and after performances at the Théâtre Olympia, as well as anyone interested in carefully chosen vintages from esoteric or small-scale winemakers. Wines are mainly from France, but you'll also find examples from neighboring countries. 21 rue Caumartin, 9e. (℃) **01-42-65-25-35.** Métro: Havre-Caumartin.

Willi's Wine Bar 🌟🌟   Journalists and stockbrokers head for this popular wine bar in the financial district. It offers about 300 kinds of wine, including a dozen specials you can taste by the glass for 3€ to 18€ ($3.90–$23). Lunch is the busiest time; on quiet evenings, you can better enjoy the warm ambience. Daily specials are likely to include lamb brochette with cumin or Lyonnais sausage in truffled vinaigrette, plus a spectacular dessert such as chocolate terrine. A fixed-price menu costs 19€ to 25€ ($25–$33) at lunch, 34€ ($44) at dinner. The restaurant is open Monday to Saturday noon to 2:30pm and 7 to 11pm; the bar, Monday to Saturday noon to midnight. 13 rue des Petits-Champs, 1er. ℂ **01-42-61-05-09.** www.williswinebar.com. Métro: Bourse, Pyramides, or Palais-Royal.

BARS, PUBS & CLUBS

These "imported" places trying to imitate American cocktail bars or British pubs mostly strike an alien chord. But that doesn't prevent fashionable Parisians from barhopping (not to be confused with cafe-sitting). Many bars in Paris are youth-oriented. But if you're an older traveler who prefers to take your expensive drink in one of the grand-luxe bars of the world, Paris has those as well. The bars at the **Plaza Athénée** or **Ritz,** for example, are among the grandest in the world and provide a uniquely Parisian experience for those who want to don their finest apparel and take along a gold-plated credit card. In general, bars and pubs are open daily from 11am to 1:30am.

Académie de la Bière 🅥🅐🅛🅤🅔   The decor is paneled and rustic, an appropriate foil for an "academy" whose curriculum includes more than 153 kinds of beer from micro-breweries. More than half of the dozen beers on tap are from small-scale breweries in Belgium that deserve to be better known than that country's bestseller, Stella Artois. Snack-style food is available, including platters of mussels, assorted cheeses, and sausages with mustard. Open Sunday to Thursday noon to 2am and Friday and Saturday noon to 3am. 88 bis bd. du Port-Royal, 5e. ℂ **01-43-54-66-65.** RER: Port Royal.

Bar du Crillon 🌟🌟   Though some visitors consider the Bar du Crillon too self-consciously elegant, its social and literary history is remarkable. Hemingway set a climactic scene of *The Sun Also Rises* here, and through the years it has attracted diplomats from the U.S. Embassy as well as visiting heiresses, stars, starlets, and wannabes. Sonia Rykiel decorated the bar. Another option down the hall is the Edwardian-style **Jardin d'Hiver,** where you can order tea, cocktails, or coffee. In the Hôtel de Crillon, 10 place de la Concorde, 8e. ℂ **01-44-71-15-39.** Métro: Concorde.

Bar Hemingway/Bar Vendôme   In 1944, during the liberation of Paris, Ernest Hemingway made history by ordering a drink at the Ritz Bar while gunfire from retreating Nazi soldiers was still audible in the streets. Today the Ritz commemorates the event with bookish memorabilia, rows of newspapers, and stiff drinks. Look for the bar's entrance, and homages to other writers such as Proust, near the hotel's rue Cambon entrance. If you develop a thirst in the daytime, when the Bar Hemingway isn't open, head for the Bar Vendôme, near the hotel's place Vendôme entrance. The setting is just as cozy and woodsy, albeit a bit more grand. In the Hôtel Ritz, 15 place Vendôme, 1er. ℂ **01-43-16-33-65.** Tues–Sat 5pm–1am.Métro: Opéra or Concorde.

Barrio Latino   This multilevel emporium of good times, Gallic flair, and Latin charm occupies a space designed by Gustav Eiffel in the 19th century. Tapas bars and dance floors are on the street level *(rez-de-chaussée)* and third floor *(3eme étage);* a Latin restaurant is on the second floor *(2eme étage).* Staff members roll carts loaded with tapas around the floors, selling them like hot dogs at an American baseball game. The restaurant specializes in food that French palates find refreshing: Argentine steaks, Brazilian *feijoada* (a bean-based dish that's similar to cassoulet), and Mexican chili, all of which taste wonderful with beer, caipirinhas, cuba libres, or rum punches. The clientele is mixed, mostly straight, partly gay, and 100% blasé about matters such as an individual's sexuality. 46 rue du Faubourg St-Antoine, 12e. ℂ 01-55-78-84-75. Cover 20€ ($26) for nondiners Thurs–Sat after 9pm. Métro: Bastille.

Bob Cool   A hot Parisian Left Bank bar, this rendezvous point attracts a hip and rather laid-back coterie of friends to its precincts not far from the famous street, rue St-André-des-Arts. Tables and chairs are found in the front room, with banquettes in the back. Writers and artists, ranging in age from 18 to 60, are drawn here, especially during the happy hour from 5 to 9pm, when you buy one drink and get the second free. The bartender selects the music, be it rock, Latino, house or soca. On our last visit, Dominican Republic merengue was the rage. Open Tuesday to Saturday 5pm to 2am. 15 rue des Grands Augustins, 6e. ℂ 01-46-33-33-77. Métro: Odéon or St-Michel.

Bound   Catering to a cool, fashionable, international crowd, this is an artfully decorated, busy bar and supper club that is hip, stylish, and a lot of fun. Set in the heart of one of Paris's most expensive residential and commercial neighborhoods (real-estate brokers refer to it as "the Golden Triangle"), it's laid out in one enormous street-floor area that boasts a rose stone bar said to be the longest in Paris. Cutting-edge music plays; deep armchairs are scattered artfully throughout; and a restaurant, specializing in international and Asian/French/Pacific Rim cuisine, including sushi, serves late suppers for around 70€ ($91) per person. Open Sunday to Friday noon to 2am; Saturday 7pm to 2am. 49–51 av. George V, 8e. ℂ 01-53-67-84-60. Métro: George V.

Buddha Bar   The food is mediocre, but that doesn't seem to matter to the fashion-istas on the see-and-be-seen circuit. A giant Buddha presides over the vast dining room, where a combination of Japanese sashimi, Vietnamese spring rolls, Chinese lac-quered duck, and various Asian fusion dishes are served. Many patrons come here to drink at the lacquered bar, found upstairs from the street-level dining room. From the upper perch you can observe the action of the swanky international patrons below. The music is spacey, the atmosphere electric, and some of the prettiest women and handsomest hunks in Paris are in attendance nightly. The location is near the Champs Elysées and place de la Concorde. 8 rue Boissy d'Anglais, 8e. ℂ 01-53-05-90-00. Daily 4pm–2am. Métro: Concorde.

Chez Richard   This is our favorite bar in the 4th Arrondissement and a great place for people-watching, lying inside a courtyard off rue Vieille-du-Temple. The interior is lined with stone, and the ceiling fans and palm leaves evoke old Algiers (once a French colony). The action is on three levels, and hip music is played in the back-ground. Happy hour daily from 5 to 8pm is very popular with Left Bank young people. The bartenders are among the hippest in town. Open Monday to Saturday 6pm to 2am (closed 2 weeks in August). 37 rue Vieille-du-Temple, 4e. ℂ 01-42-74-31-65. Métro: Hôtel-de-Ville.

China Club   Designed to recall France's 19th-century colonies in Asia or a bordello in 1930s Shanghai (on the ground floor) and England's empire-building zeal in India (upstairs), the China Club lets you chitchat or flirt with the singles who crowd into the street-level bar, and then escape to calmer, more contemplative surroundings upstairs. You'll see regulars from the worlds of fashion and the arts, along with postshow celebrants from the nearby Opéra Bastille. A street-level Chinese restaurant serves dinner daily from 7pm to 2am; in the more animated cellar bar, live music prevails Thursday and Saturday from 10pm to 1am. 50 rue de Charenton, 12e. ℂ **01-43-43-82-02.** Métro: Bastille or Ledru Rollin.

La Belle Hortense   There are dozens of other bars and cafes near this one, but none maintains a bookstore in back, and few seem so self-consciously aware of their roles as ersatz literary salons. Come for a glass of wine and participation in a discussion within what's defined as "a literary bar." It's named after a pulpy 19th-century romance *(La Belle Hortense)* set within the neighborhood. Glasses of wine cost 3€ to 7€ ($3.90–$9.10). Open daily 5pm to 2am. 31 rue Vieille-du-Temple, 4e. ℂ **01-48-04-71-60.** Métro: Hôtel de Ville.

Le Bar   Because of the crush of wannabes who scheme, maneuver, and manipulate their way into the bar of this ultraprestigious hotel, there's absolutely no guarantee that you'll get in, so make sure you have an alternative plan. Should you get inside, you'll find a street-level location of rich-looking paneling, high tables, barrel-shaped armchairs, glossy bar tops, and the kind of lighting that makes almost anyone look fabulous. Chat here can get bitchy, and it's anyone's guess how rich the pampered crowd really is. Be prepared for theme cocktails that in many cases are too pink, too cloying, and certainly too expensive at 24€ ($31). Open daily 6pm to 2am. In the Hotel Plaza-Athénée, 25 av. Montaigne, 8e. ℂ **01-53-67-66-00.** Métro: Alma-Marceau.

Le Bar de L'Hôtel   A Left Bank hotel is home to the city's most romantic bar. Oscar Wilde checked out long ago, but the odd celebrity still shows up: We were once 15 minutes into a conversation before realizing we were speaking to Jeanne Moreau. Drinks are expertly mixed, the place sleek and chic, and conversations are held at a discreet murmur. It would be hard to find a better place for a romantic rendezvous. In L'Hôtel, 13 rue des Beaux-Arts, 6e. ℂ **01-44-41-99-00.** Métro: St-Germain-des-Prés.

Le Forum   Patrons, who include frequent business travelers, compare this place with a private club in London. The comparison is due partly to the polished oak paneling and ornate stucco, and partly to the selection of single-malt whiskeys. You can also try 180 cocktails, including many that haven't been popular since the Jazz Age. Champagne by the glass is common, as is that social lubricant, the martini. Open Monday to Friday noon to 2am; Saturday 5:30pm to 2am. 4 bd. Malesherbes, 8e. ℂ **01-42-65-37-86.** www.bar-le-forum.com. Métro: Madeleine.

Le Fumoir   At Le Fumoir, the well-traveled crowd that lives or works in the district provides a kind of classy raucousness. The decor is a lot like that of an English library, with about 6,000 books providing a backdrop to the schmoozing. A Swedish chef prepares an international menu featuring meal-size salads (the one with scallops and lobster is great), roasted codfish with zucchini, and roasted beef in red-wine sauce. More popular are the stiff mixed drinks, the wines and beers, and the dozen or so types of cigars. Open daily 11am to 2am. 6 rue de l'Amiral-de-Coligny, 1er. ℂ **01-42-92-00-24.** www.lefumoir.com. Métro: Louvre-Rivoli.

Man Ray   This chic rendezvous off the Champs-Elysées is dedicated to the photographer and American Dadaist Man Ray, who felt more comfortable roaming Montparnasse than the 8th. Many of his photos decorate the club. This spot is a media favorite, because its owners include Johnny Depp, Sean Penn, and John Malkovich. The discreet entry is through wrought-iron doors with virtually no sign. In the basement is a restaurant presided over by two winged Indonesian goddesses. The bar upstairs is big and bustling, and the club often schedules jazz. 32 rue Marbeuf, 8e. ℭ 01-56-88-36-36. www.manray.fr. Métro: Franklin-D-Roosevelt.

Mojito Habana Amid a decor that evokes colonial Havana under Batista, with lots of green upholsteries, wood panels, and deep sofas, you'll find a three-tiered place with a restaurant (it charges around 50€/$65 for a full meal); a piano bar (music begins at 11pm every night the place is open, and at 10pm on Tues); and a cigar lounge. Jazz concerts are featured Tuesday night. Cocktails, including cuba libres, cost 13€ ($17) each. Entrance is always free. And the music that's in the background is international rock and pop, not solely salsa and merengue. It's open Monday to Saturday from noon to 5am. And it attracts a lot of nattily dressed business travelers. 19 rue de Presbourg, 16e. ℭ 01-45-00-84-84. Métro: Etoile.

Moosehead Throughout this very Left Bank place, you'll be surrounded by the restaurant's primary decorative theme: anything and everything to do with ice hockey. As such, the walls are lined with framed photographs of hockey players in action, as well as jerseys and memorabilia that reflect the favorite sport, and some of the favorite teams of the owners and many of the staff. Expect a rough-and-ready, sports-loving crowd that includes many Canadian, British, Irish, French, and American sports fans. Depending on the weather and the mood of the organizers, theme nights here include beach parties (at which some of the less inhibited clients strip to their underpants within sight lines of whimsically useless beach parasols) and country-western bashes. Open Monday to Friday 4pm to 2am; Saturday to Sunday 11am to 3am. 16 rue des Quatre Vents, 6e. ℭ 01-46-33-77-00. www.mooseheadparis.com. Métro: Odéon.

4 Gay & Lesbian Bars & Clubs

Gay life is centered on **Les Halles** and **Le Marais,** with the greatest concentration of gay and lesbian clubs, restaurants, bars, and shops between the Hôtel de Ville and Rambuteau Métro stops. Gay dance clubs come and go so fast that even the magazines devoted to them, such as *Illico*—distributed free in the gay bars and bookstores—have a hard time keeping up. For lesbians, there is *Lesbian Magazine*. Also look for Gai Pied's *Guide Gai* and *Pariscope*'s regularly featured English-language section, "A Week of Gay Outings." Also important for both men and women is *Têtu Magazine,* sold at most newsstands.

Café Cox, 15 rue des Archives, 4e (ℭ 01-42-72-08-00), gets so busy in the early evening that the crowd stands on the sidewalk. This is where you'll find the most mixed gay crowd in Paris—from hunky American tourists to sexy Parisian men. Another hot place in Les Halles is Le Tropic Café, 66 rue des Lombards, 1er (ℭ 01-40-13-92-62; Métro: Châtelet–Les Halles), where the trendy, good-looking crowd parties until dawn. A restaurant with a bar popular with women is Okawa, 40 rue Vieille-du-Temple, 4e (ℭ 01-48-04-30-69; Métro: Hôtel de Ville), where trendy lesbians (and some gay men) enjoy happy hour. Le 3w, 6 rue des Ecouffes, 3e (ℭ 01-48-87-39-26; Métro: St-Paul), is a bar for gay women where an unattached female can usually find a drinking buddy.

Amnesia Café The Amnesia's function and crowd may change during the day, but you'll always find a cadre of local gays. This cafe/tearoom/bistro/bar includes two bar areas, a mezzanine, and a cellar bar, Amni-Club, open in the evening. The drinks of choice are beer, cocktails, and *café amnesia,* a specialty coffee with whisky and Chantilly cream. Deep armchairs, soft pillows, and 1930s accents create an ambience conducive to talk and laughter. Open daily 11am to 2am, Friday and Saturday until 3am. 42 rue Vieille-du-Temple, 4e. (✆ **01-42-72-16-94**. Métro: Hôtel de Ville or St. Paul.

Banana Café   This popular bar is a stop for gays visiting or doing business in Paris. Occupying two floors of a 19th-century building, it has walls the color of an overripe banana, dim lighting, and a policy of raising the drink prices after 10pm, when things become really interesting. There's a street-level bar and a cellar dance floor that features a live pianist and recorded music—sometimes with dancing. On many nights, go-go dancers perform from spotlit platforms in the cellar. Open daily from 5:30pm to 4 or 5am. 13 rue de la Ferronnerie, 1er. (✆ **01-42-33-35-31**. www.bananacafeparis.com. Métro: Châtelet–Les Halles.

La Champmeslé   With dim lighting, background music, and comfortable banquettes, La Champmeslé offers a cozy meeting place for women and a few (about 5%) "well-behaved" men. Paris's leading women's bar is in a 300-year-old building with exposed stone, ceiling beams, and 1950s-style furnishings. Thursday night, one of the premier lesbian events in Paris, a cabaret, begins at 10pm. 4 rue Chabanais, 2e. (✆ **01-42-96-85-20**. Mon–Sat 3pm–dawn. Métro: Pyramides or Bourse.

Le Central   Established in 1980 in a 300-year-old town house, Le Central is a staple of gay men's life in the Marais. Outfitted with decor of battered paneling and windows that wrap around on two sides, it attracts local residents who make the place their hangout, along with goodly numbers of attractive male tourists and the Parisians who appreciate them. Don't be surprised if the friendships you forge here are with other Yanks, Aussies, or Brits. A small gay hotel is upstairs. Open Monday to Friday from 4pm to 2am; Saturday to Sunday from 2pm to 2am. 33 rue Vieille-du-Temple, 4e. (✆ **01-48-87-99-33**. www.hotelcentralmarais.com. Métro: Hôtel de Ville.

Le Depot   This gay pleasure palace stages everything from Queer Mother Nights to Putanas at Work. Patrons wander the rooms downstairs searching for their companion of the night. The pickup area and best cruising grounds are in the section where porno flicks are being shown on television sets mounted on the walls. The many back rooms allow you to get better acquainted with your catch of the evening. After 11pm, lesbians patronize the upstairs dance floor. The age range here is from 18 to 50. The post-Sunday-brunch gay tea dance, starting at 5pm, is one of the happening events of Paris. Open daily from 2pm to 8am. 10 rue aux Ours, 3e. (✆ **01-44-54-96-96**. Cover 7.50€–12€ ($9.75–$16). Métro: Etienne-Marcel.

Le Pulp   This is one of the most popular lesbian dance clubs, looking like a burgundy-colored, 19th-century French music hall. It's best to show up before midnight. The venue, as the French like to say, is *très cool*, with cutting-edge music played in a setting that just happens to discourage the presence of men. Open Wednesday to Saturday from 11:30pm until dawn. 25 bd. Poissonnière, 2e. (✆ **01-40-26-01-93**. www.pulp-paris.com. Cover 10€ ($13) Fri–Sat (includes 1 drink). Métro: Grands Boulevards.

Le Queen   Should you miss gay life à la New York, seek out the flashing purple sign near the corner of avenue George V. This place is often mobbed, primarily by gay men and, to a lesser degree, chic women who work in fashion and film. Look for drag shows, muscle shows, striptease by danseurs atop the bars, and everything from '70s-style disco nights to foam parties (only in summer), when cascades of suds descend onto the dance floor. Go very, very late: The place opens at midnight and stays open until 6 or 7am. 102 av. des Champs-Elysées, 8e. (✆ **01-53-89-08-90**. www.queen.fr. Cover 10€–20€ ($13–$26). Fri–Sat. Métro: Franklin-D-Roosevelt or George V.

Open Café/Café Cox   Although this side-by-side pair of gay men's bars are independent, their clienteles are so interconnected, and there's such traffic between them, that we—like many other residents of this neighborhood—usually jumble them together. Both define themselves as bars rather than dance clubs, but on particularly busy nights, one or another couple might actually begin to dance. Simple cafe-style food is served from noon to around 5pm. Don't come here with preconceptions about what type of guy you're likely to find—patrons can include just about every type of man that roams the streets of gay Europe today. Open Sunday to Thursday from 11am to 2am, Friday to Saturday to 4am. 17 rue des Archives, 4e. ℂ **01-42-72-26-18** or 01-42-72-08-00. Métro: Hôtel de Ville.

Sundays at La Scala   In gay Paris, Sunday nights used to be dull until a group of entrepreneurs gained access to the sleek basement-level interior of an otherwise mostly straight nightclub in the shadow of City Hall. The flamboyantly extroverted venue attracts a clientele of mostly gay men who flirt, dance, and cavort on a glossy dance floor till around 2am, theoretically in time to allow for a productive workweek. Open Wednesday to Sunday 11pm to dawn. 188 rue de Rivoli, 1er. ℂ **01-42-61-64-00.** Cover 12€–15€ ($16–$20; includes 1 drink). Women admitted free except on Sat night. Métro: Hôtel de Ville, Tuileries, or Palais-Royal.

5 Literary Haunts

Harry's New York Bar ℛ   At *sank roo doe noo,* as the ads tell you to instruct your cabdriver, is the most famous bar in Europe—possibly in the world. Opened on Thanksgiving Day 1911 by an expatriate named MacElhone, it's where members of the World War I ambulance corps drank themselves silly. In addition to being Hemingway's favorite, Harry's is where the white lady and sidecar cocktails were invented; it's also the reputed birthplace of the Bloody Mary and the headquarters of a loosely organized fraternity of drinkers known as the International Bar Flies.

The historic core is the street-level bar, where CEOs and office workers loosen their ties on more or less equal footing. Daytime crowds are from the neighborhood's insurance, banking, and travel industries; evening crowds include pre- and post-theater groupies and night owls who aren't bothered by the gritty setting and unflattering lighting. A softer, somewhat less macho ambience reigns in the cellar, where a pianist provides music Tuesday to Saturday from 10pm to 2am. 5 rue Daunou, 2e. ℂ **01-42-61-71-14.** Métro: Opéra.

Rosebud   The popularity of this place known for a bemused and indulgent attitude toward anyone looking for a drink and some talk hasn't diminished since the 1950s. The name refers to the beloved sled of Orson Welles's *Citizen Kane.* Around the corner from Montparnasse's famous cafes and thick in associations with Sartre and de Beauvoir, Ionesco, and Duras, Rosebud draws a crowd ages 35 to 65, though the staff has recently noticed the appearance of students. Drop in at night for a glass of wine, a shot of whisky, or a hamburger or chili con carne. Open daily 7pm to 2am. 11 bis rue Delambre, 14e. ℂ **01-43-35-38-54** or 01-43-20-44-13. Métro: Vavin.

12

Side Trips from Paris

Paris is the center of a curious landlocked island known as the **Ile de France.** Shaped roughly like a saucer, it's encircled by a thin ribbon of rivers: the **Epte, Aisne, Marne,** and **Yonne.** Fringing these rivers are forests with famous names—**Rambouillet, St-Germain, Compiègne,** and **Fontainebleau.** These forests are said to be responsible for Paris's clear, gentle air and the unusual length of its spring and fall. This may be debatable, but there's no argument that they provide the capital with a fine series of day trips, all within easy reach.

The forests surrounding Paris were once the domain of royalty and the aristocracy, and they're still sprinkled with the magnificent châteaux of their former masters. Together with ancient villages, glorious cathedrals, and cozy country inns, they make the Ile de France irresistible. In this chapter, we offer only a handful of the possibilities for day jaunts. For a more extensive list, see *Frommer's France 2008.*

1 Versailles ⟨★⟩

21km (13 miles) SW of Paris, 71km (44 miles) NE of Chartres

For centuries, the name of the Parisian suburb of Versailles resounded through the consciousness of every aristocratic family in Europe. The palace here outdazzled every other kingly residence in Europe—it was a horrendously expensive scandal and a symbol to later generations of a regime obsessed with prestige above all else.

Back in the *grand siècle* (the 17th century), all you needed was a sword, a hat, and a bribe for the guard at the gate. Provided you didn't look as if you had smallpox, you'd be admitted to the **Château de Versailles,** where you could stroll through salon after glittering salon—watching the Sun King rise—and dress and dine and do even more intimate things while you gossiped, danced, plotted, flirted, and trysted.

You get to see only half of the palace's treasures; the rest are closed to the public. Some 3.2 million visitors arrive annually; on average, they spend 2 hours.

ESSENTIALS

GETTING THERE   To get to Versailles, catch the **RER** line C5 to Versailles-Rive Gauche at the Gare d'Austerlitz, St-Michel, Musée d'Orsay, Invalides, Ponte de l'Alma, Champ de Mars, or Javel stop, and take it to the Versailles Rive Gauche station. The trip takes 35 to 40 minutes. The round-trip fare is 5.50€ ($7.15); Eurailpass holders travel free on the RER but need to show the pass at the ticket kiosk to receive an RER ticket. **SNCF trains** make frequent runs from Gare St-Lazare and Gare Montparnasse in Paris to Versailles: Trains departing from Gare St-Lazare arrive at the Versailles Rive Droite railway station; trains departing from Gare Montparnasse arrive at Versailles Chantiers station.

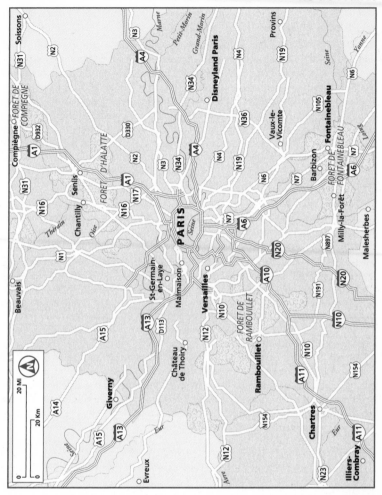

Both Versailles stations are within a 10-minute walk of the château, and we recommend the walk as a means of orienting yourself to the town, its geography, its scale, and its architecture. If you can't or don't want to walk, you can take bus B, or (in midsummer) a shuttle bus marked CHATEAU from either station to the château for either a cash payment of around 2€ ($2.60; drop the coins directly into the coin box near the driver) or the insertion of a valid ticket for the Paris Métro. Because of the vagaries of the bus schedules, we highly recommend the walk. Directions to the château are clearly signposted from each railway station.

If you're **driving,** exit the *périphérique* (the ring road around Paris) on N10 (av. du Général-Leclerc), which will take you to Versailles; park on place d'Armes in front of the château.

VISITOR INFORMATION The **Office de Tourisme** is at 2 bis av. de Paris (*℃* **01-39-24-88-88;** fax 01-39-24-88-89).

EVENING SPECTACLES Recognizing the value of the palace as a national symbol, the French government offers a program of fireworks and illuminated fountains, "Les Fêtes de Nuit de Versailles," on about 7 to 10 widely publicized dates between late August and early September, usually beginning at 9:30pm. Observers, who sit in bleachers near the palace's boulevard de la Reine entrance, close to the Fountain *(Bassin)* of Neptune, are treated to a display of fireworks, prerecorded classical music, and up to 200 players (none of whom utters a line) in period costume, portraying the glories of France as symbolized by Louis XIV and the courtiers of the *ancien régime.* Shows are big on pomp and strong on visuals, and last about 90 minutes. Tickets range from 30€ to 85€ ($39–$111). Gates open around 90 minutes prior to showtime. For information, call *℃* **01-30-83-78-98.**

DAYTIME SPECTACLES Saturdays and Sundays from April to early October, between 11:30am and noon and 3:30 and 5pm, the French government broadcasts classical music throughout the park and opens the valves on as many fountains as are currently in operation as part of a program known as *Les Grands Eaux Musicals de Versailles.* The spectacles showcase the landscaping vision of the palace's designers and encourage participants to walk, promenade, or meander the vast park, enjoying the juxtaposition of supremely grand architecture with lavish waterworks. Afternoon events include water coming out of more jets than during the somewhat less lavish morning events. Admission to any part of the park during these spectacles costs 7€ ($9.10) adults or 5.50€ ($7.15) ages 10 to 18, free for children under 10. For information, call *℃* **01-30-83-78-88.**

You can purchase tickets to all spectacles at Versailles up until about a half-hour prior to the day or night of any performance from the ticket office in the *Accueil-Billeterie* on Place d'Armes, immediately across from the main facade of the palace, or from any French branch of the FNAC department store (FNAC's central phone number is *℃* **01-55-21-57-93**).

TOURING VERSAILLES

Château de Versailles ★★★ Within 50 years, the Château de Versailles was transformed from Louis XIII's hunting lodge into an extravagant palace. Begun in 1661, its construction involved 32,000 to 45,000 workmen, some of whom had to drain marshes and move forests. Louis XIV set out to build a palace that would be the envy of Europe and created a symbol of opulence copied, yet never duplicated, the world over.

Wishing (with good reason) to keep an eye on the nobles of France, Louis XIV summoned them to live at his court. Here he amused them with constant entertainment and lavish banquets. To some he awarded such tasks as holding the hem of his robe. While the aristocrats played at often-silly intrigues and games, the peasants on the estates sowed the seeds of the Revolution.

When Louis XIV died in 1715, his great-grandson Louis XV succeeded him and continued the outrageous pomp, though he is said to have predicted the outcome: *"Après moi, le déluge"* ("After me, the deluge"). His wife, Marie Leszczynska, was shocked by the blatant immorality at Versailles.

Versailles

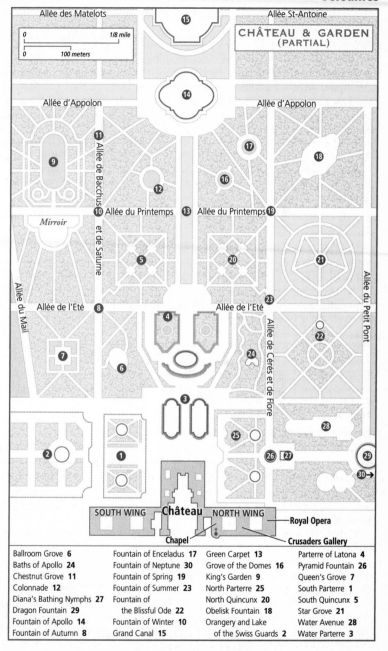

CHÂTEAU & GARDEN
(PARTIAL)

Allée des Matelots

Allée d'Appolon

Allée d'Appolon

Allée de Bacchus et de Saturne

Mirroir

Allée du Printemps

Allée du Printemps

Allée du Mail

Allée de l'Eté

Allée de l'Eté

Allée de Cérès et de Flore

Allée du Petit Pont

SOUTH WING   Château   NORTH WING

Chapel   Royal Opera

Crusaders Gallery

Ballroom Grove **6**	Fountain of Enceladus **17**	Green Carpet **13**	Parterre of Latona **4**
Baths of Apollo **24**	Fountain of Neptune **30**	Grove of the Domes **16**	Pyramid Fountain **26**
Chestnut Grove **11**	Fountain of Spring **19**	King's Garden **9**	Queen's Grove **7**
Colonnade **12**	Fountain of Summer **23**	North Parterre **25**	South Parterre **1**
Diana's Bathing Nymphs **27**	Fountain of Winter **10**	North Quincunx **20**	South Quincunx **5**
Dragon Fountain **29**	Fountain of	Obelisk Fountain **18**	Star Grove **21**
Fountain of Apollo **14**	the Blissful Ode **22**	Orangery and Lake	Water Avenue **28**
Fountain of Autumn **8**	Grand Canal **15**	of the Swiss Guards **2**	Water Parterre **3**

A Return to Faded Glory

The French government is going to pour out $455 million into a grand restoration of Versailles and its splendid gardens. The project, it is estimated, will take 17 years, but the attraction—one of the most visited in Europe—will remain open during the work in progress. The grand design of the architects is to make the palace, dating from the 17th century, look much as it did when it was home to Louis XIV, XV, and the ill-fated XVI. Some features will be removed, such as a wide staircase ordered built by King Louis-Philippe in the château's last major rebuilding in the 1830s. Other features will be added, including a replica of the *grille royale* that was torn out after the 1789 Revolution. Facilities for those with disabilities will also improve.

The next monarch, Louis XVI, found his grandfather's behavior scandalous—in fact, on gaining the throne, he ordered that the "stairway of indiscretion" (secret stairs leading to the king's bedchamber) be removed. The well-intentioned but weak king and his queen, Marie Antoinette, were well liked at first, but the queen's frivolity and spending led to her downfall. Louis and Marie Antoinette were at Versailles on October 6, 1789, when they were notified that mobs were marching on the palace. As predicted, *le déluge* had arrived.

Napoleon stayed at Versailles but never seemed fond of it. Louis-Philippe (who reigned 1830–48) prevented the destruction of the palace by converting it into a museum dedicated to the glory of France. To do that, he had to surrender some of his own riches. Decades later, John D. Rockefeller contributed toward the restoration of Versailles, and work continues today.

The magnificent **Grands Appartements** ✺✺✺ are in the Louis XIV style; each bears the name of the allegorical painting on the ceiling. The best-known and largest is the **Hercules Salon** ✺✺, with a ceiling painted by François Lemoine depicting the Apotheosis of Hercules. In the **Mercury Salon** (with a ceiling by Jean-Baptiste Champaigne), the body of Louis XIV was put on display in 1715; his 72-year reign was one of the longest in history.

The most famous room at Versailles is the 71m-long (233-ft.) **Hall of Mirrors** ✺✺✺. Begun by Mansart in 1678 in the Louis XIV style, it was decorated by Le Brun with 17 arched windows faced by beveled mirrors in simulated arcades. On June 28, 1919, the treaty ending World War I was signed in this corridor. The German Empire was proclaimed here in 1871.

The royal apartments were for show, but Louis XV and Louis XVI retired to the **Petits Appartements** ✺✺ to escape the demands of court etiquette. Louis XV died in his bedchamber in 1774, a victim of smallpox. In a second-floor apartment, which you can visit only with a guide, he stashed away first Mme de Pompadour and then Mme du Barry. Attempts have been made to return the Queen's Apartments to their appearance in the days of Marie Antoinette, when she played her harpsichord in front of special guests.

Louis XVI had a sumptuous **Library,** designed by Jacques-Ange Gabriel. Its panels are delicately carved, and the room has been restored and refurnished. The **Clock**

Room contains Passement's astronomical clock, encased in gilded bronze. Twenty years in the making, it was completed in 1753. The clock is supposed to keep time until the year 9999. At age 7, Mozart played for the court in this room.

Gabriel designed the **Opéra** ✸✸ for Louis XV in 1748, though it wasn't completed until 1770. In its heyday, it took 3,000 candles to light the place. Hardouin-Mansart built the harmoniously gold-and-white **Royal Chapel** in 1699, dying before its completion. Louis XVI married Marie Antoinette here in 1770, while he was the dauphin.

Spread across 100 hectares (250 acres), the **Gardens of Versailles** ✸✸✸ were laid out by landscape artist André Le Nôtre. At the peak of their glory, 1,400 fountains spewed forth. *The Buffet* is an exceptional fountain, designed by Mansart. One fountain depicts Apollo in his chariot pulled by four horses, surrounded by tritons rising from the water. Le Nôtre created a Garden of Eden using ornamental lakes and canals, geometrically designed flower beds, and avenues bordered with statuary. On the mile-long **Grand Canal,** Louis XV used to take gondola rides with his favorite of the moment.

Inaugurated late in 2004, developments within the sprawling infrastructure created by the monarchs of France include the opening of *Les Grandes Ecuries* (the Stables), avenue Rockefeller, immediately opposite the château's main front facade, where the horses and carriages of the kings were housed. Visitors can watch a team of up to a dozen students, with their mounts, strut their stuff during hour-long riding demonstrations within the covered, 17th-century amphitheater of the historic stables. Horse lovers will appreciate the equestrian maneuvers that this riding school shows off during these presentations, but they shouldn't go with any expectations that the horsemanship will re-create exclusively 17th- and 18th-century styles. With a painted backdrop that reflects a circus theme, and with costumes that are colorful and artful but not exclusive to Versailles during its heyday, the focus is on showmanship and equestrian razzmatazz rather than exact replication of period costumes or riding styles. Each demonstration lasts about an hour. Demonstrations are conducted Tuesday to Thursday, and Saturday and Sunday, at 10am and 11am, when entrance costs 8€ ($10). There's an additional presentation every Saturday and Sunday at 2pm, when admission costs 16€ ($21). There are no discounts for students or seniors, and persons under 10, accompanied by an adult, enter free. For additional information, contact the château directly at ✆ **01-30-83-78-00.**

Incidentally, participation in this event provides the only official way a visitor to Versailles can easily gain entrance to the stables, which contain a warren of narrow stalls for horses, as well as a large space with a plastered ceiling that's used as the amphitheater for displays of horsemanship.

On Christmas 1999, one of the worst storms in France's history destroyed some 10,000 historic trees on the grounds. Blowing at 161kmph (100 mph), gusts uprooted 80% of the trees planted during the 18th and 19th centuries. They included pines from Corsica planted during Napoleon's reign, tulip trees from Virginia, and a pair of junipers planted in honor of Marie Antoinette. Still, much remains to enchant you, and the restored gardens get better every month.

Place d'Armes. ✆ 01-30-83-78-00. www.chateauversailles.fr. Palace 14€ ($18) adults; 10€ ($13) adults after 4pm, seniors over 59, and ages 18–25. Both Trianons and Le Hameau 16€ ($21) adults; 10€ ($13) adults after 3:30pm, seniors over 59, and ages 18–25. Everything free for children under 18. Palace Apr–Oct Tues–Sun 9am–6:30pm; Nov–Mar Tues–Sun 9am–5:30pm. Trianons and Le Hameau Tues–Sun noon–6pm. Grounds daily dawn–dusk.

Impressions

When Louis XIV finished the Grand Trianon (Grand Pavilion), he told [Mme de] Maintenon he had created a paradise for her, and asked if she could think of anything now to wish for. . . . She said she could think of but one thing—it was summer, and it was balmy France—yet she would like well to sleigh ride in the leafy avenues of Versailles! The next morning found miles and miles of grassy avenues spread thick with snowy salt and sugar, and a procession of those quaint sleighs waiting to receive the chief concubine of the gaiest and most unprincipled court that France has ever seen!

—Mark Twain, *The Innocents Abroad* (1869)

Musée Lambinet ✮ (Finds) Often overlooked by visitors to Versailles, the Musée Lambinet is filled with treasures seized from the French court during the Revolution. Here are all the antiques, the carved wood paneling, even religious art and other objets d'art so beloved by Marie Antoinette and the mistresses of Louis XV such as Madame de Pompadour and Madame du Barry. The sumptuous mansion from 1751 is also filled with paintings (no great masterpieces, however), along with weaponry, and rare porcelain (look for the Du Barry rose). Also on view are rare displays illustrating the lives of Jean-Paul Marat, the radical journalist, and his murderer, Charlotte Corday, as depicted in stage plays and films.

54 bd. De la Reine. ✆ 01-39-50-30-32. Admission 5.30€ ($6.90). Tues–Sun 2–5:45pm.

The Trianons & The Hamlet A long walk across the park will take you to the **Grand Trianon (Grand Pavilion)** ✮✮, in pink-and-white marble. Le Vau built a Porcelain Trianon here in 1670, covered with blue-and-white china tiles, but it was fragile and soon fell into ruin. So, in 1687, Louis XIV commissioned Hardouin-Mansart to build the Grand Trianon. Traditionally, it has been a place where France has lodged important guests, though de Gaulle wanted to turn it into a weekend retreat. Nixon once slept here in the room where Mme de Pompadour died. Mme de Maintenon also slept here, as did Napoleon. The original furnishings are gone, of course, with mostly Empire pieces there today.

Gabriel, the designer of place de la Concorde in Paris, built the **Petit Trianon** ✮✮ in 1768 for Louis XV. Louis used it for his trysts with Mme du Barry. When he died, Louis XVI presented it to his wife, and Marie Antoinette adopted it as her favorite residence, a place to escape the rigid life and oppressive scrutiny at the main palace. Many of the current furnishings, including a few in her rather modest bedchamber, belonged to the ill-fated queen.

Rousseau's theories about recapturing the natural beauty and noble simplicity of life were much in favor in the late 18th century, and they prompted Marie Antoinette to have Mique build her the 12-house **Le Hameau (Hamlet)** on the banks of the Grand Trianon Lake in 1783. She wanted a chance to experience the simplicity of peasant life—or at least peasant life as seen through the eyes of a frivolous queen. Dressed as a shepherdess, she would come here to watch sheep being tended and cows being milked, men fishing, washerwomen beating their laundry in the lake, and donkey carts bringing corn to be ground at the mill. The interiors of the hamlets cannot be visited, but the surrounding informal landscaping—in obvious contrast to the formality of the other gardens at Versailles—and bizarre origins make views of their exteriors one of the most popular attractions here.

Follow the signs from the place d'Armes (to the immediate right after entering the Palace of Versailles). See above for admission times and hours to visit.

WHERE TO DINE

Le Potager du Roy ☆ MODERN FRENCH   Philippe Letourneur spent years perfecting a distinctive cuisine and now adds novelty to the dining scene in Versailles. Letourneur rotates his skillfully prepared menu with the seasons. Examples are foie gras with vegetable-flavored vinaigrette, *pot-au-feu* of vegetables with foie gras, cream of lentil soup with scallops, roasted duck with *navarin* of vegetables, and roasted codfish with roasted peppers in the style of Provence. Looking for something unusual and earthier? Try fondant of pork jowls with fresh vegetables.

1 rue du Maréchal-Joffre. ✆ **01-39-50-35-34.** Reservations required. Main courses 26€–33€ ($34–$43). Fixed-price menu 40€ ($52). AE, MC, V. Tues–Sat noon–1:30pm and 7:30–9:30pm.

Les Trois Marches ☆☆☆ MODERN FRENCH   The food here is of the highest order—and so are the prices. Chef Gérard Vié, known for the inventiveness of his *cuisine bourgeoise,* serves the finest food in Versailles. His greenhouse-inspired dining room is remarkable for its expanses of glass and its intimate size (55 seats). In summer, you can dine under the canopy on the front terrace. Begin with lobster salad flavored with fresh herbs and served with an onion soufflé; foie gras of duckling; galette of potatoes with bacon, chardonnay, and Sevruga caviar; or citrus-flavored scallop bisque. The chef is a great innovator, especially when it comes to main courses: pigeon roasted and flavored with rosé and accompanied with celeriac and truffles; North Atlantic lobster served with carrot juice and creamy lobster bisque; filets of John Dory served with braised eggplant, squid, and squid ink; or filet of sea bass with a "cake" of eggplant. If you can't choose a single dessert, opt for the assortment. Some patrons find the staff a bit too stiff and patronizing.

In the Hôtel Trianon Palace, 1 bd. de la Reine. ✆ **01-39-50-13-21.** Reservations required. Main courses 75€–100€ ($98–$130); fixed-price lunch 58€ ($75) Tues–Fri only; fixed-price dinner 160€–180€ ($208–$234). AE, DC, MC, V. Tues–Sat 1–2pm and 7:30–9:30pm. Closed Aug.

L'Resto du Rio ☆ FRENCH   This informal bistro lies in an 18th-century building overlooking the western facade of the palace at Versailles. Orange and apricot tones prevailing in the main dining room evoke an autumnal theme. The chef prepares an appetizing array of dishes, including specialties such as duck foie gras with caramelized apples or salmon smoked with birch branches. For a main course, we'd recommend such dishes as fresh sole or else sautéed scallops in a parsley sauce. A seasonal specialty is wild doe with chestnuts. For dessert, there are such grand choices as a soufflé flambé with mandarin oranges or omelet Norwegian (called baked Alaska in the U.S.).

1 av. de St-Cloud. ✆ **01-39-50-42-26.** Reservations required. Main courses 15€–16€ ($20–$21); fixed-price lunch 16€–27€ ($21–$35); fixed-price dinner 20€–27€ ($26–$35). AE, MC, V. Tues–Sun noon–2pm and Tues–Sat 7–11pm.

2 The Cathedral at Chartres ☆☆☆

97km (60 miles) SW of Paris, 76km (47 miles) NW of Orléans

Many observers feel the architectural aspirations of the Middle Ages reached their highest expression in the glorious Cathédrale de Chartres. Come to see its soaring architecture; highly wrought sculpture; and above all, its stained glass, which gave the world a new color: Chartres blue. It takes a full day to see Chartres.

GETTING THERE   From Paris's Gare Montparnasse, **trains** run directly to Chartres, taking less than an hour. Tickets cost 25€ ($33) round-trip. Call © **08-92-35-35-35.** If **driving,** take A10/A11 southwest from the *périphérique* and follow signs to Le Mans and Chartres. (The Chartres exit is clearly marked.)

VISITOR INFORMATION   The **Office de Tourisme** is on place de la Cathédrale (© **02-37-18-26-26;** fax 02-37-21-51-91).

SEEING THE CATHEDRAL

Cathédrale Notre-Dame de Chartres 🟊🟊🟊   Reportedly, Rodin once sat for hours on the sidewalk, admiring this cathedral's Romanesque sculpture. His opinion: Chartres is the French Acropolis. When it began to rain, a kind soul offered him an umbrella, which he declined, so transfixed was he by this place.

The cathedral's origins are uncertain; some have suggested it grew up over an ancient Druid site that later became a Roman temple. As early as the 4th century, there was a Christian basilica here. An 1194 fire destroyed most of what had by then become a Romanesque cathedral but spared the western facade and crypt. The cathedral you see today dates principally from the 13th century, when it was rebuilt with the efforts and contributions of kings, princes, churchmen, and pilgrims from all over Europe. One of the world's greatest high Gothic cathedrals, it was the first to use flying buttresses to support the soaring dimensions within.

French sculpture in the 12th century broke into full bloom when the **Royal Portal** 🟊🟊🟊 was added. A landmark in Romanesque art, the sculptured bodies are elongated, often stylized, in their long, flowing robes. But the faces are amazingly (for the time) lifelike, occasionally winking or smiling. In the central tympanum, Christ is shown at the Second Coming, with his descent depicted on the right and his ascent on the left. Before entering, walk around to both the **North Portal** and the **South Portal,** each from the 13th century. They depict such biblical scenes as the expulsion of Adam and Eve from the Garden of Eden.

Inside is a celebrated **choir screen;** work on it began in the 16th century and lasted until 1714. The niches, 40 in all, contain statues illustrating scenes from the life of the Madonna and Christ—everything from the *Massacre of the Innocents* to the *Coronation of the Virgin.*

However, few rushed visitors ever notice the screen because they're too transfixed by the light from the **stained glass** 🟊🟊🟊. Covering an expanse of more than 2,500 sq. m. (27,000 sq. ft.), the glass is unlike anything else in the world. The stained glass, most of which dates from the 12th and 13th centuries, was spared in both world wars by being painstakingly removed, piece by piece, and stored away. See the windows in the morning, at noon, in the afternoon, at sunset—as often as you can. Like the petals of a kaleidoscope, they constantly change. It's difficult to single out one panel or window above the others, but an exceptional one is the 12th-century *Vierge de la Belle Verrière* **(Our Lady of the Beautiful Window)** on the south side. Of course, there are three fiery rose windows, but you couldn't miss those if you tried.

The **nave,** the widest in France, still contains its ancient floor labyrinth, which formed a mobile channel of contemplation for monks. The wooden *Notre-Dame du Piller* **(Virgin of the Pillar),** to the left of the choir, dates from the 14th century. The

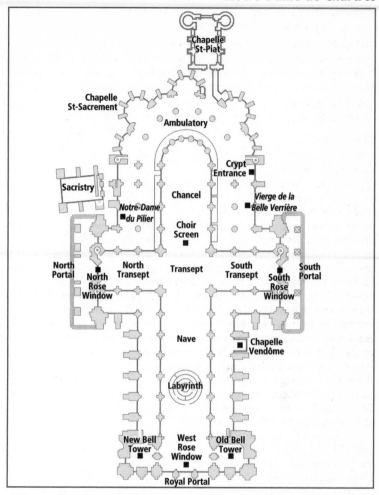

crypt was built over 2 centuries, beginning in the 9th. Enshrined within is **Our Lady of the Crypt,** a 1976 Madonna that replaced one destroyed during the Revolution.

Try to take a tour conducted by Malcolm Miller (© **02-37-28-15-58;** fax 02-37-28-33-03; millercharters@aol.com), an Englishman who has spent 3 decades studying the cathedral and giving tours in English. His rare blend of scholarship, enthusiasm, and humor will help you understand and appreciate the cathedral. He usually conducts 75-minute tours at noon and 2:45pm Monday to Saturday for 10€ ($13) per person. Tours are canceled during pilgrimages, religious celebrations, and large funerals. French-language tours (6.20€/$8.05) start at 10:30am and 3pm from Easter to October and at 2:30pm the rest of the year.

If you're fit enough, don't miss the opportunity, especially in summer, to climb to the top of the tower. Open daily from 8:30am to noon and 2 to 7:30pm, it costs

Moments **Music of the Spheres**

If you're visiting Chartres on a Sunday afternoon, the cathedral has a free 1-hour organ concert at 4:45pm, when the filtered light of the Ile de France sunset makes the western windows come thrillingly alive.

4.60€ ($6) for adults and 3.10€ ($4.05) for students. You can visit the crypt, gloomy and somber but rich with medieval history, only as part of a French-language tour. The cost is 3.10€ ($4.05) per person.

After your visit, stroll through the **Episcopal Gardens** and enjoy yet another view of this remarkable cathedral.

16 Cloître Notre-Dame. ℂ 02-37-21-75-02. www.monum.fr. Free admission to cathedral. Daily 8:30am–7:30pm.

EXPLORING THE OLD TOWN

If time remains, you may want to explore the medieval cobbled streets of the **Vieux Quartier (Old Town)** ✦. At the foot of the cathedral are lanes containing gabled houses and humped bridges spanning the Eure River. From the pont de Bouju, you can see the lofty spires in the background. Try to find **rue Chantault,** which boasts houses with colorful facades, one of which is 8 centuries old.

A highlight of your visit will be **Musée des Beaux-Arts de Chartres** ✦, 29 Cloître Notre-Dame (ℂ **02-37-36-41-39**), next to the cathedral. A former Episcopal palace, the building at times competes with its exhibitions—one part dates from the 15th century and encompasses a courtyard. This museum of fine arts boasts a collection covering the 16th to the 20th centuries, including the work of masters such as Zurbarán, Watteau, and Brósamer. Of particular interest is David Ténier's *Le Concert.* Open from May 3 to October 30 Wednesday to Monday from 10am to noon and 2 to 6pm (closed Sunday morning), the rest of the year, until 5pm. Admission is 3€ ($3.90) for adults, free for children.

WHERE TO STAY

Grand Monarque Best Western The most appealing and desirable hotel in Chartres occupies an imposing civic monument whose 600-year-old foundations and infrastructures were "gentrified" sometime in the 19th century with white stucco, neoclassical detailing, and touches of the baroque. Functioning as an inn since its original construction in the 15th century, and expanded and improved many times since then, it's a grand hotel that remains under the direction of the hardworking members of the Jallerat family. It attracts guests who enjoy its old-world charm—such as Art Nouveau stained glass and Louis XV chairs in the dining room. The guest rooms are decorated with reproductions of antiques; most have sitting areas. Suites have air-conditioning. Bathrooms are motel standard with a tub/shower combination. The hotel provides solid and reliable comfort but not great style. It also has an old-fashioned, unremarkable restaurant.

22 place des Epars, 28005 Chartres. ℂ 800/528-1234 in the U.S., or 02-37-18-15-15. Fax 02-37-36-34-18. www.bw-grand-monarque.com. 55 units. 118€–170€ ($153–$221) double; 200€ ($260) suite. AE, DC, MC, V. Parking 8€ ($10). **Amenities:** 2 restaurants; brasserie; bar; room service; laundry service; dry cleaning; nonsmoking rooms. *In room:* TV, minibar, hair dryer.

Hôtel Châtelet   This modern hotel has many traditional touches. The rustic guest rooms are inviting, with reproductions of Louis XV and Louis XVI furniture. The larger, more expensive units face a garden and avoid street noise. But many windows along the front (street) side of the hotel open onto a view of the cathedral. Each room comes with a tidy, tiled bathroom with tub and shower. In chilly weather, there's a log-burning fire in one of the salons. Breakfast is the only meal served, but numerous restaurants are close by.

6–8 av. Jehan-de-Beauce, 28000 Chartres. ℂ **02-37-21-78-00.** Fax 02-37-36-23-01. www.hotelchatelet.com. **48** units. 65€–81€ ($85–$105) double. Extra person 9.15€ ($12). AE, DC, MC, V. Parking 6€ ($7.80). **Amenities:** Bar; room service; rooms for those w/limited mobility. *In room:* TV, minibar, hair dryer.

WHERE TO DINE

La Vieille Maison 🌟🌟 MODERN FRENCH   Even if the food here weren't superb, the 14th-century building still could be visited for its historic value. The dining room, outfitted in the Louis XIII style, is centered on a narrow ceiling vault, less than 2m (6 ft.) across, crafted of chiseled white stone blocks during the 9th century. Bruno Letartre, the only *maître cuisinier de France* in Chartres, supervises the cuisine. The menu changes four or five times a year, reflecting the seasonality of the Ile de France and its produce. Recent examples have included foie gras of duckling, roasted crayfish with Indian spices, foie gras served on sliced rye bread, brochettes of lobster and scallops with spaghetti, suprême of turbot with baby vegetables and saffron, and noisettes of venison fried with Jamaican and Szechuan pepper and wild mushrooms. Dessert raves go to a thin apple-and-fig tart served with walnut-flavored ice cream.

5 rue au Lait. ℂ **02-37-34-10-67.** www.lavieillemaison.fr. Reservations recommended. Main courses 22€–28€ ($29–$36); fixed-price menu 33€–49€ ($43–$64). MC, V. Wed–Sun noon–2:15pm; Tues–Sat 7–10pm. Closed 1 week in Aug.

Le Geôrges 🌟🌟 FRENCH   The best food and the most upscale dining ambience in Chartres is now found at the town's best hotel, an also-recommended establishment with roots that go back to the 15th century, when the site served food and drink (not as elegant as what you'll find today) to weary travelers and postal workers. Menu items change with the seasons but usually include savory portions of *pâté de Chartres,* made with a combination of minced meats that include wild duck and baked in a giant puff pastry; a steamed combination of crayfish with scallops in wine sauce; and a superb version of roasted veal "Grand Monarque," served with a casserole of mushrooms and cheese. Also interesting is lobster "prepared in the style of perch," with a reduction of apple-flavored Calvados and Newburg (i.e., lobster) sauce. Desserts are sumptuous, and the cheese trolley will warm the heart of any Francophile.

In the Grand Monarque Best Western, 22 place des Epars. ℂ **02-37-18-15-15.** Reservations recommended. Fixed-price menus 39€–55€ ($51–$72). AE, DC, MC, V. Tues–Sun noon–2:45pm; Tues–Sat 7:30–10pm.

3 Giverny 🌟

80km (50 miles) NW of Paris

On the border between Normandy and the Ile de France, Giverny—now the home of the Claude Monet Foundation—is where the great painter lived for 43 years. The restored house and its gardens are open to the public. Budget 2 hours to spend at Giverny.

GETTING THERE   It takes a morning to get to Giverny and to see its sights. Take the Paris-Rouen **train** from Paris's Gare St-Lazare to the Vernon station, where a taxi can take you the 5km (3 miles) to Giverny. Vernon itself lies 40km (25 miles) south-east of Rouen. Perhaps the easiest way to get there is on a full-day **bus tour,** for 65€ ($85) per person, that focuses on Monet's house and garden. Tours depart at 1:45pm Tuesday to Saturday between April and October. You can arrange tours in the summer through **Cityrama,** 149 rue St-Honoré, 1er (℡ **01-44-55-61-00;** Métro: Palais-Royal–Musée du Louvre), or year-round through **American Express,** 11 rue Scribe, 9e (℡ **01-47-14-50-00;** Métro: Opéra).

If you're **driving,** take the Autoroute de l'Ouest (Port de St-Cloud) toward Rouen. Leave the autoroute at Bonnières, and then cross the Seine on the Bonnières Bridge. From here, a direct road with signs leads to Giverny. Expect it to take about an hour; try to avoid weekends. Another approach is to leave the highway at the Bonnières exit and go toward Vernon. Once there, cross the bridge over the Seine and follow signs to Giverny or Gasny (Giverny is before Gasny). This is easier than going through Bonnières, where there aren't many signs.

SHOW ME THE MONET

Claude Monet Foundation ★★★   Born in 1840, the French Impressionist was a brilliant innovator, who excelled at presenting the effects of light at different times of the day. Some critics claim that he "invented light." His paintings of the Rouen cathedral and of water lilies, which one critic called "vertical interpretations of horizontal lines," are just a few of his masterpieces.

Monet first came to Giverny in 1883. Many of his friends used to visit him here at Le Pressoir, including Clemenceau, Cézanne, Rodin, Renoir, Degas, and Sisley. When Monet died in 1926, his son, Michel, inherited the house, but left it abandoned until it decayed. The gardens became almost a jungle, inhabited by river rats. In 1966, Michel died and left it to the Académie des Beaux Arts. It wasn't until 1977 that Gerald van der Kemp, who restored Versailles, decided to work on Giverny. A large part of it was restored with gifts from U.S. benefactors, especially the late Lila Acheson Wallace, former head of *Reader's Digest.*

You can stroll the garden and view the thousands of flowers, including the *nymphéas.* The Japanese bridge, hung with wisteria, leads to a setting of weeping willows and rhododendrons. Monet's studio barge was installed on the pond.

84 rue Claude-Monet Parc Gasny. ℡ 02-32-51-28-21. www.fondation-monet.com. Admission 5.50€ ($7.15) adults, 4€ ($5.20) students, and 3€ ($3.90) children 7–18, free for children under 7. Apr–Oct Tues–Sun 9:30am–6pm. Closed Nov–Mar.

Musée d'Art Americain Giverny ★ *Finds*   Lying about 90m (295 ft.) from Monet's former house and gardens, this museum showcases the U.S.-born artists, mainly Impressionists, who were influenced by Monet and lived at Giverny. Among the more famous painters were John Singer Sargent and William Metcalf, who often summered at Giverny, writing about its glories to other artists. The American painters came from 1887 onward, drawn more by the charm of the village than by the presence of Monet himself. It is estimated that some 100 artists came to live in Giverny, although they did not have much contact, if any, with Monet. He considered these American painters "a nuisance."

99 rue Claude-Monet. ℡ 02-32-51-94-65. www.maag.org. Admission 5.50€ ($7.15) adults, 4€ ($5.20) seniors and students, 3€ ($3.90) children 12–18, free for children under 12. Free to all 1st Sun of each month. Apr–Oct Tues–Sun 10am–6pm. Closed Nov–Mar.

WHERE TO STAY

La Musardiere Giverny has become so popular with visitors that many local homes are opening as B&Bs to accommodate the overnight flow. We find this small inn to be the best of the lot. Just a short walk from Monet's museum and gardens, it is a former manor house opening onto a scenic park filled with ancient trees. The building with its mansard roof dates from 1880 and was around in Monet's time. Many of the antique features and architectural adornments are still in place. Bedrooms are medium in size, attractively and comfortably furnished, each with a small bathroom with tub or shower. The hotel also operates its own restaurant and crêperie.

123 Rue Claude-Monet, 27620 Giverny. ✆ **02-32-21-03-18.** Fax 02-32-21-60-00. 11 units. 59€–77€ ($77–$100) double; 92€–106€ ($120–$138) suite. AE, DC, MC, V. Free parking. **Amenities:** Restaurant; bar. *In room:* TV, hair dryer.

WHERE TO DINE

Auberge du Vieux Moulin TRADITIONAL FRENCH This is a convenient lunch stop near the Monet house. The restaurant is in a stone building with a pair of flowering terraces. The Boudeau family maintains a series of dining rooms filled with original Impressionist paintings. Specialties range from escalope of salmon with sorrel sauce to aiguillettes of duckling with peaches. The kitchen doesn't pretend that the food is anything more than good country fare with a dash of panache. The charm of the staff helps a lot, too. You can walk here from the museum in about 5 minutes; leave your car in the museum lot.

21 rue de la Falaise. ✆ **02-32-51-46-15.** Reservations recommended. Main courses 16€–19€ ($21–$25); fixed-price menu 15€–35€ ($20–$46). AE, MC, V. Dec–Oct daily noon–3pm and 7–10pm.

Baudy FRENCH We hesitate to recommend this place because of the never-ending buses arriving from Paris, but it's a local legend and deserves a look. During the town's 19th-century heyday, the American painters used the pink villa as their lodging. In Monet's time, this place was an *epicerie-buvette* (casual hangout) run by the painter's friends Angelina and Gaston Baudy. Metcalf was the first artist to arrive on Mme Baudy's doorstep, and in time a string of other painters followed. Artists such as Cézanne could be found wandering around the rose garden here. The place no longer has its "legendary two tables," at which Mme Baudy fed the artists, but it now plays host to virtually all visitors to Giverny, feeding them simply prepared, traditional French cuisine, including big, freshly made salads and a changing array of hot food.

81 rue Claude-Monet. ✆ **02-32-21-10-03.** Reservations recommended. Main courses 11€–16€ ($14–$21). Fixed-price menu 19€ ($25). MC, V. Tues–Sat 10am–7pm; Sun 10am–3pm. Closed Nov–Mar.

Restaurant Les Fleurs ✪ FRENCH Capably managed by Michel and Annie Graux, this pleasant, popular restaurant does a large percentage of its business with art lovers. The Claude Monet Foundation is just across the river in Giverny. On the main street of Vernon, 4.8km (3 miles) southwest of the museum, the restaurant focuses on flavorful, familiar *cuisine bourgeoise* that many diners remember fondly from their childhoods. Chef Michel served an apprenticeship with culinary megastar Alain Ducasse. Menu items include fresh fish such as sea bass served with saffron sauce and a flavorful risotto of the day, and sweetbreads braised with parmesan. Other dishes include an array of homemade terrines and pâtés; fresh scallops with lobster-flavored cream sauce; a platter devoted to different preparations of duckling; and a variety of meats grilled, simply and flavorfully, *à la plancha.*

71 rue Sadi-Carnot, Vernon. From the Claude Monet Foundation in Giverny, drive 5km (3 miles) southwest, crossing the Seine, and follow signs to Vernon. (℃ **02-32-51-16-80.** Reservations recommended. Main courses 14€–20€ ($18–$26); fixed-price menu 24€–47€ ($31–$61). AE, MC, V. Tues–Sun noon–2:30pm; Tues–Sat 7:30–10pm. Closed May 1 and Aug 31.

4 Disneyland Paris

32km (20 miles) E of Paris

After provoking some of the most enthusiastic and controversial reactions in recent French history, the multimillion-dollar Disneyland Paris opened in 1992. It's one of the world's most lavish theme parks, conceived on a scale rivaling that of Versailles. European journalists initially accused it of everything from cultural imperialism to the death knell of French culture.

But after goodly amounts of public relations and financial juggling, "Disneyland Paris" has become France's number-one tourist attraction, with 50 million visitors annually. It surpasses the Eiffel Tower and the Louvre in the number of visitors and accounts for 4% of the French tourism industry's foreign currency sales. About 40% of the visitors are French, half from Paris. Disneyland Paris looks, tastes, and feels like the ones in California and Florida—except for the expensive cheeseburgers *"avec pommes frites."*

Situated on a 2,000-hectare (5,000-acre) site (about one-fifth the size of Paris) in the suburb of Marne-la-Vallée, the park incorporates the most successful elements of its Disney predecessors and European flair.

In terms of the other Disney parks (excluding Tokyo), Disneyland Paris definitely lies in the middle, with top honors going to Florida. The California Disneyland emerges as a distant third. The park in Florida is larger than the Paris property, with a greater number of attractions and rides. But Disneyland Paris does a decent job of re-creating the Magic Kingdom. In 2002, the Paris park added **Walt Disney Studios,** focusing on the role of movies in popular culture.

Take 1 day for the highlights, 2 days for more depth.

GETTING THERE   The RER commuter express **rail** network (Line A) stops within walking distance of the park. Board the RER in Paris at Charles-de-Gaulle–Etoile, Châtelet–Les Halles, or Nation. Get off at Line A's last stop, Marne-la-Vallée Chessy, 45 minutes from central Paris. The round-trip fare is 12€ ($16). Trains run daily, every 10 to 20 minutes from 5:30am to midnight.

Shuttle buses connect Orly and Charles de Gaulle airports with each hotel in the resort. Buses depart the airports every 30 to 45 minutes. One-way transport to the park from either airport is 14€ ($18) for adults, 12€ ($16) for children 3 to 11.

If you're **driving,** take A4 east from Paris and get off at Exit 14, DISNEYLAND PARIS. Parking begins at 8€ ($10) per day, but is free if you stay at one of the park hotels. A series of moving sidewalks speeds up pedestrian transit from parking areas to the park entrance.

VISITOR INFORMATION   All the hotels we recommend offer general information on the theme park. For details and reservations at any of its hotels, contact the **Disneyland Paris Guest Relations Office,** located in City Hall on Main Street, U.S.A. (℃ **01-60-30-60-53** in English, or 08-25-30-60-30 in French; www. disneylandparis.com). For information on Disneyland Paris and specific details on the many other attractions and monuments in the Ile de France and the rest of the

> **⌐Tips⌐ Fast Pass Those Long Lines**
>
> Disneyland Paris has instituted a program that's done well at the other parks. With the **Fast Pass** system, visitors to the various rides reserve a 1-hour time block. Within that block, the waiting is usually no more than 8 minutes.

country, contact the **Maison du Tourisme,** Disney Village (B.P. 77705), Marne-la-Vallée (© **01-60-43-33-33**).

ADMISSION Admission varies depending on the season. In peak season, a 1-day park ticket costs 44€ ($57) for adults, 36€ ($47) for children 3 to 12, free for children under 3; a 2-day park-hopper ticket is 95€ ($124) for adults, 78€ ($101) for kids; and a 3-day park-hopper ticket is 119€ ($155) for adults, 98€ ($127) for kids. Peak season is from mid-June to mid-September as well as Christmas and Easter weeks. Entrance to Disney Village is free, though there's usually a cover charge at the dance clubs.

HOURS Hours vary throughout the year, but most frequently are 10am to 8pm. Be warned that autumn and winter hours vary the most; it depends on the weather. It's a good idea to phone ahead if you're contemplating a visit at this time.

SPENDING THE DAY AT DISNEY

Disneyland Paris 🏰🏰🏰 The resort was designed as a total vacation destination: In one enormous unit, the park includes five "lands" of entertainment, a dozen hotels, a campground, an entertainment center (**Disney Village,** with six restaurants of its own), a 27-hole golf course, and dozens of restaurants, shows, and shops. The Disney Village entertainment center is illuminated inside by a spectacular gridwork of lights suspended 18m (60 ft.) above the ground. The complex contains dance clubs, shops, restaurants (one of which offers a dinner spectacle based on the original *Buffalo Bill's Wild West Show*), bars for adults trying to escape their children, a French Government Tourist Office, a post office, and a marina.

Visitors stroll among flower beds, trees, reflecting ponds, fountains, and a large artificial lake flanked with hotels. An army of smiling employees and Disney characters—many of whom are multilingual, including Buffalo Bill; Mickey and Minnie Mouse; and, of course, the French-born Caribbean pirate Jean Laffite—are on hand to greet the thousands of *enfants*.

Main Street, U.S.A., abounds with horse-drawn carriages and barbershop quartets. Steam-powered railway cars embark from the Main Street Station for a trip through a Grand Canyon diorama to **Frontierland,** with its paddlewheel steamers reminiscent of Mark Twain's Mississippi River. Other attractions include a petting zoo—the Critter Corral—at the Cottonwood Creek Ranch, and the Lucky Nugget Saloon, inspired by the Gold Rush era. The steps and costumes of the saloon's cancan show originated in the cabarets of turn-of-the-20th-century Paris.

The park's steam trains chug past **Adventureland**—with its swashbuckling pirates, Swiss Family Robinson treehouse, and reenacted Arabian Nights legends—to **Fantasyland.** Here you'll find the **Sleeping Beauty Castle** *(Le Château de la Belle au Bois Dormant),* whose pinnacles and turrets are an idealized (and spectacular) interpretation of French châteaux. In its shadow are Europeanized versions of *Blanche Neige et*

For Those with Another Day: Walt Disney Studios

Next to Disneyland Paris, **Walt Disney Studios** (© 01-60-30-60-30) takes guests on a behind-the-scenes interactive discovery of film, animation, and television.

The main entrance to the studios, called the **Front Lot,** consists of "Sunset Boulevard," an elaborate sound stage complete with hundreds of film props. The **Animation Courtyard** allows visitors to learn the trade secrets of Disney animators, and the **Production Courtyard** lets guests take a look behind the scenes of film and TV production. At **Catastrophe Canyon,** guests are plunged into the heart of a film shoot. Finally, the **Back Lot** is home to special effects and stunt workshops. A live stunt show features cars, motorbikes, and jet skis.

This ode to Hollywood and the films it produced since the end of its "golden age" has a roller coaster, the Rock 'n' Roller Coaster, featuring the music of Aerosmith, that combines rock memorabilia with high-speed scary twists and turns (completely in the dark); and a reconstruction of one of the explosion scenes in the Hollywood action film *Armaggeddon.*

Admission is 42€ ($55) for adults, 34€ ($44) for children. Hours are daily from 9am to 6pm (opens at 10am during certain seasons of the year).

Les Sept Nains (Snow White and the Seven Dwarfs), Peter Pan, Dumbo, Alice (from Wonderland), the Mad Hatter's Teacups, and Sir Lancelot's Magic Carousel.

Visions of the future are in **Discoveryland,** where tributes to invention and imagination draw from the works of Leonardo da Vinci, Jules Verne, H. G. Wells, the modern masters of science fiction, and the *Star Wars* series.

You'll see characters from *Aladdin, The Lion King, Pocahontas,* and *Toy Story.* As Disney continues to churn out animated blockbusters, look for the newest stars to appear in the theme park.

WHERE TO STAY

You can easily make Disneyland a day trip from Paris—the transportation links are excellent—or spend the night.

The resort's six theme hotels share a reservation service. In North America, call © **407/W-DISNEY.** In France, contact the **Central Reservations Office,** Euro Disney Resort, S.C.A., B.P. 105, F-77777 Marne-la-Vallée Cedex 4 (© **01-60-30-60-30;** www.disneylandparis.com).

VERY EXPENSIVE

Disneyland Hotel 🏰🏰   Mouseketeers who have rich daddies and mommies frequent Disney's poshest resort. At the park entrance, this flagship four-story hotel is Victorian, with red-tile turrets and jutting balconies. The spacious guest rooms are plushly furnished but evoke the image of Disney, with cartoon depictions and candy-stripe decor. The beds are king-size, double, or twin; in some rooms armchairs convert to beds. Accommodations in the rear overlook Sleeping Beauty's Castle and Big Thunder Mountain. Some less desirable units open onto a parking lot. The luxurious bathrooms have marble vanities, showers and tubs, and twin basins. On the Castle Club floor, you get free newspapers, all-day beverages, and access to a well-equipped private lounge.

Disneyland Paris, B.P. 111, F-77777 Marne-la-Vallée Cedex 4. © **01-60-45-65-89.** Fax 01-60-45-65-33. www. disneylandparis.com. 496 units. 323€–501€ ($420–$651) double; from 850€ ($1,105) suite. Rates include breakfast. AE, DC, MC, V. **Amenities:** 2 restaurants; bar; health club with indoor pool; Jacuzzi; sauna; room service; babysitting; laundry service; dry cleaning; nonsmoking rooms; rooms for those w/limited mobility. *In room:* A/C, TV, minibar, hair dryer, safe.

EXPENSIVE

Hotel New York ☆ Picture an Art Deco New York of the 1930s. Inspired by the Big Apple, this hotel centers on a nine-story "skyscraper" flanked by the Gramercy Park Wing and the Brownstones Wing. (Their exteriors resemble row houses.) This convention hotel is less family-friendly than others at the resort. Guest rooms are comfortable, with Art Deco accessories, New York–inspired memorabilia, and roomy combination bathrooms with twin basins and tub/shower combos. Try for one of the units fronting Lake Buena Vista.

Disneyland Paris, B.P. 100, F-77777 Marne-la-Vallée Cedex 4. © **01-60-45-75-92.** Fax 01-60-45-73-33. www. disneylandparis.com. 565 units. 214€–333€ ($278–$433) double; from 565€ ($735) suite. Rates include breakfast. AE, DC, MC, V. **Amenities:** 2 restaurants; bar; indoor and outdoor pools; exercise room; sauna; room service; babysitting; nonsmoking rooms; rooms for those w/limited mobility. *In room:* A/C, TV, minibar, hair dryer, safe.

Newport Bay Club ☆☆ You expect to see the reincarnation of Joe Kennedy walking along the veranda with its slated roofs, awnings, and pergolas. It's very Hyannisport here. It's also the biggest hotel in France. With a central cupola, balconies, and a blue-and-cream color scheme, it recalls a harborfront New England hotel (ca. 1900). The layout features nautically decorated rooms in various shapes and sizes. The most spacious are the corner units. The combination bathrooms are roomy, with deluxe toiletries and tub and shower.

Disneyland Paris, B.P. 105, F-77777 Marne-la-Vallée Cedex 4. © **01-60-45-56-55.** Fax 01-60-45-55-33. www. disneylandparis.com. 1,093 units. 172€–272€ ($224–$354) double; from 395€ ($514) suite. Rates include breakfast. AE, DC, MC, V. **Amenities:** 2 restaurants; bar; indoor and outdoor pools; health club; sauna; room service; nonsmoking rooms; rooms for those w/limited mobility. *In room:* A/C, TV, minibar, safe.

Sequoia Lodge Built of gray stone and roughly textured planking, and capped by a gently sloping green copper roof, this hotel resembles a lodge in a remote section of the Rockies. The hotel consists of a large central building with six 100-unit chalets nearby. The guest rooms are comfortably rustic; each tiled bathroom has a tub and shower.

Disneyland Paris, B.P. 100, F-77777 Marne-la-Vallée Cedex 4. © **01-60-45-52-48.** Fax 01-60-45-51-33. www. disneylandparis.com. 1,011 units. 140€–264€ ($182–$343) double; from 420€ ($546) suite. Rates include breakfast. AE, DC, MC, V. **Amenities:** 2 restaurants; bar (only one); indoor/outdoor pool; health club; sauna; laundry service; dry cleaning; nonsmoking rooms; rooms for those w/limited mobility. *In room:* A/C, TV, minibar, hair dryer.

MODERATE

Hotel Cheyenne/Hotel Santa Fe *Kids* Next door to each other near a re-creation of Texas's Rio Grande, these Old West–style lodgings are the resort's least expensive hotels. The Cheyenne consists of 14 two-story buildings along Desperado Street; the desert-themed Santa Fe encompasses four "nature trails" winding among 42 adobe-style pueblos. The Cheyenne is a favorite among families, offering a double bed and bunk beds. Children have an array of activities, including a play area in a log cabin with a lookout tower and a section where you can explore the "ruins" of an ancient Anasazi village. The only disadvantage, according to some parents, is the absence of a pool.

More recently constructed, but charging the same prices, is the nearby **Kyriad Hotel,** a government-rated two-star hotel designed for families, that evokes the aesthetics and layout of a French country inn. Whenever the Cheyenne and the Santa Fe are full, Disney usually directs the overflow to the Kyriad.

Disneyland Paris, B.P. 115, F-77777 Marne-la-Vallée Cedex 4. ℂ **01-60-45-63-12** (Cheyenne) or 01-60-45-79-22 (Santa Fe). Fax 01-60-45-62-33 (Cheyenne) or 01-60-45-78-33 (Santa Fe). www.disneylandparis.com. 2,000 units. Hotel Cheyenne 82€–177€ ($107–$230) double; Hotel Santa Fe 67€–150€ ($87–$195) double. Rates include breakfast. AE, DC, MC, V. **Amenities:** Restaurant; bar; babysitting; nonsmoking rooms; rooms for those w/limited mobility. *In room:* A/C, TV.

WHERE TO DINE

Disneyland Paris offers a gamut of cuisine in more than 45 restaurants and snack bars. You can live on burgers and fries, or you can experiment at the following upscale restaurants.

Auberge de Cendrillon TRADITIONAL FRENCH   This is a fairy-tale version of Cinderella's country inn, with a glass couch in the center. A master of ceremonies wearing a plumed tricorn hat, embroidered tunic, and lace ruffles welcomes you. There are corny elements, but the chefs go out of their way to make a big deal of French cuisine. For the most part, they succeed admirably. The appetizers set the tone. Our favorites are warm goat-cheese salad with lardons and the smoked salmon platter. Either will put you in the mood for a French classic such as loin of lamb roasted under a zesty mustard coating or flavorful sautéed veal medallions. Because the restaurant follows the park's seasonal schedule, lunch is usually easier to arrange than dinner. There's a lunchtime buffet, served daily between 11:30am and around 2:20pm at a price of 22€ ($29) for adults, and 10€ ($13) for children ages 3 to 11.

Fantasyland. ℂ **01-64-74-24-02.** Reservations recommended. Main courses 20€–27€ ($26–$35); fixed-price menu 29€ ($38) adults, 10€ ($13) children. AE, DC, MC, V. Mid-July to Aug daily 11:30am–9:30pm; rest of year daily 11:30am–4pm, Sat–Sun 11:30am–4pm.

California Grill 🎃🎃 *Kids* CALIFORNIAN/FRENCH   The resort's showcase restaurant serves cuisine that's the equivalent of the fare at a one-Michelin-star restaurant. Focusing on the lighter specialties for which the Golden State is famous, with many concessions to French palates, the elegant restaurant accommodates both adults and children gracefully. Even French food critics are impressed with the oysters prepared with leeks and salmon. We also embrace the appetizer of foie gras with roasted red peppers, and rate as simply fabulous the roasted pigeon with braised Chinese cabbage and black-rice vinegar. Another winning selection is fresh salmon roasted over beechwood and served with a sprinkling of walnut oil, sage sauce, asparagus, and fricassee of forest mushrooms. Many items are specifically for children. If you want a quiet, mostly adult venue, go here as late as your hunger pangs will allow.

In the Disneyland Hotel. ℂ **01-60-45-65-76.** Reservations required. Fixed-price menu 44€–71€ ($57–$92); children's menu 15€ ($20). AE, DC, MC, V. Daily 6:30–10:30pm.

Inventions *Value* INTERNATIONAL   This may be the only buffet restaurant in Europe where animated characters from the Disney films (including Mickey and Minnie) go table-hopping. With views over a park, the restaurant contains four enormous buffet tables devoted to starters, shellfish, main courses, and desserts. Selections are wide, portions can be copious, and no one leaves hungry. Don't expect *grande cuisine*—that's the domain of the more upscale California Grill (see the previous listing), in the same hotel. What you'll get is a sense of American bounty and culinary generosity, with ample doses of cartoon fantasy.

In the Disneyland Hotel. ⌀ **01-60-45-65-83.** Lunch buffet 35€ ($46) adults, 18€ ($23) children 7–11, 16€ ($21) children 3–6; dinner buffet 46€ ($60) adults, 24€ ($31) children 7–11, 18€ ($23) children under 7. AE, DC, MC, V. Daily 12:30–3pm and 6–10:30pm.

DISNEYLAND AFTER DARK

The premier theatrical venue is **Le Legende de Buffalo Bill** in Disney Village (⌀ **01-60-45-71-00**). The twice-per-night stampede of entertainment recalls the show that once traveled the West with Buffalo Bill and Annie Oakley. You'll dine at tables arranged amphitheater-style around a rink where sharpshooters, runaway stagecoaches, and dozens of horses and Indians ride fast and perform alarmingly realistic acrobatics. A Texas-style barbecue, served in an assembly line by waiters in 10-gallon hats, is part of the experience. Despite its corny elements, it's not without its charm. Wild Bill is dignified and the Indians are suitably brave. Shows start at 6:30 and 9:30pm; the cost (dinner included) is 59€ ($77) for adults, 39€ ($51) for children 3 to 11.

5 Fontainebleau ✶

60km (37 miles) S of Paris, 74km (46 miles) NE of Orléans

Within the vestiges of a forest that bears its name (Forêt de Fontainebleau), this suburb of Paris has offered refuge to French monarchs throughout the country's history. Kings from the Renaissance valued it because of its nearness to rich hunting grounds and its distance from the slums and smells of the city. Napoleon referred to the Palais de Fontainebleau, which he embellished with his distinctive monogram and decorative style, as "the house of the centuries." Many pivotal and decisive events have occurred inside, perhaps none more memorable than when Napoleon stood on the horseshoe-shaped exterior stairway and bade farewell to his shattered army before departing for Elba.

After the glories of Versailles, a visit to Fontainebleau can be a bit of a letdown, especially if you visit on the day after you saw Versailles. Fontainebleau, although a grand château, actually looks like a place where a king could live, whereas Versailles is more of a production. If you stay for lunch, a trip to Fontainebleau should last a half-day.

GETTING THERE **Trains** to Fontainebleau depart from the Gare de Lyon in Paris. The trip takes 45 minutes each way and costs 7.50€ ($9.75) one-way. Fontainebleau's railway station lies 3km (1¾ miles) north of the château, in the suburb of Avon. A local bus (marked simply CHATEAU and part of line A) makes the trip to the château at 15-minute intervals Monday through Saturday and at 30-minute intervals on Sunday; the fare is 1.40€ ($1.80) each way. If you're **driving,** take A6 south from Paris, exit onto N191, and follow signs.

VISITOR INFORMATION The **Office de Tourisme** is at 4 rue Royale, Fontainebleau (⌀ **01-60-74-99-99**), opposite the main entrance to the château.

SEEING THE PALACE

Musée National du Château de Fontainebleau ✦✦✦ Napoleon's affection for this palace was understandable. He followed the pattern of a succession of French kings in the pre-Versailles days who used Fontainebleau as a resort and hunted in its forests. François I tried to turn the hunting lodge into a royal palace in the Italian Renaissance style, bringing artists, including Benvenuto Cellini, there to work for him. Under this patronage, the School of Fontainebleau gained prestige, led by painters Rosso Fiorentino and Primaticcio. The artists adorned the 63m-long (206-ft.) **Gallery of François I** ✦✦✦, where stucco-framed panels depict such scenes as *The Rape of Europa* and the monarch holding a pomegranate, a symbol of unity. The salamander, the symbol of the Chevalier king, is everywhere.

Sometimes called the Gallery of Henri II, the **Ballroom** ✦✦✦ displays the interlaced initials "H&D," referring to Henri and his mistress, Diane de Poitiers. Competing with this illicit tandem are the initials "H&C," symbolizing Henri and his ho-hum wife, Catherine de Médicis. At one end of the room is a monumental fireplace supported by two bronze satyrs, made in 1966 (the originals were melted down during the Revolution). At the other side is the balcony of the musicians, with sculptured garlands. The ceiling displays octagonal coffering adorned with rosettes. Above the wainscoting is a series of frescoes, painted between 1550 and 1558, that depict mythological subjects such as *The Feast of Bacchus*. An architectural curiosity is the richly adorned **Louis XV Staircase** ✦✦. The room above it was originally decorated by Primaticcio for the bedroom of the duchesse d'Etampes, but when an architect was designing the stairway, he simply ripped out her floor. Of the Italian frescoes that were preserved, one depicts the queen of the Amazons climbing into Alexander the Great's bed.

When Louis XIV ascended to the throne, he neglected Fontainebleau because of his preoccupation with Versailles. However, he wasn't opposed to using the palace for houseguests, specifically such unwanted ones as Queen Christina, who had abdicated the throne of Sweden in a fit of religious fervor. Under the assumption that she still had "divine right," she ordered the brutal murder of her companion Monaldeschi, who had ceased to please her. Though Louis XV and then Marie Antoinette took an interest in Fontainebleau, the château found its renewed glory under Napoleon. You can wander around much of the palace on your own, visiting sites evoking the Corsican's 19th-century imperial heyday. They include the **throne room** where he abdicated rule of France, his **offices,** his monumental **bedroom,** and his **bathroom.** Some of the smaller Napoleonic Rooms contain his personal mementos and artifacts.

After your trek through the palace, visit the **gardens** and especially the **carp pond;** the gardens, however, are only a prelude to the Forest of Fontainebleau.

Place du Général-de-Gaulle. ✆ 01-60-71-50-70. www.musee-chateau-fontainebleau.fr. Combination ticket including private *appartements* 6.50€ ($8.45) adults, 4.50€ ($5.85) students 18–25; ticket to *petits appartements* and Napoleonic rooms 3€ ($3.90) adults, 2.30€ ($3) students 18–25, free for children under 14. June–Sept Wed–Mon 9:30am–6pm; Oct–May Wed–Mon 9:30am–5pm.

WHERE TO STAY

Grand Hôtel de l'Aigle-Noir (The Black Eagle) ✦ This mansion, once the home of Cardinal de Retz, sits opposite the château. The formal courtyard entrance has a high iron/board grille and pillars crowned by black eagles. It became a hotel in 1720 and is the finest lodging in Fontainebleau, far superior in amenities and style to the Hôtel Napoleon. The rooms are decorated with Louis XVI, Empire-, or

Fontainebleau

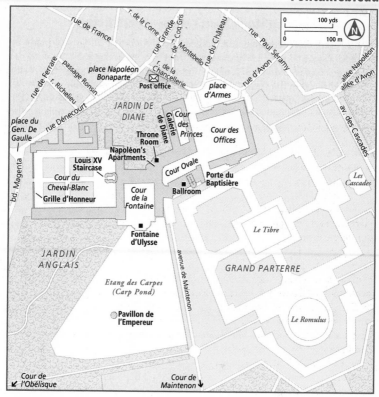

Regency-era antiques or reproductions, with plush beds and elegant bathroom amenities. All but four units have a tub/shower combination. Enjoy a drink in the Napoleon III–style piano bar before dinner.

27 place Napoleon-Bonaparte, 77300 Fontainebleau. © **01-60-74-60-00.** Fax 01-60-74-60-01. www.hotel aiglenoir.fr. 18 units. 160€–170€ ($208–$221) double; 260€–380€ ($338–$494) suite. AE, DC, MC, V. Parking 9€ ($12). **Amenities:** Restaurant; bar; indoor pool; fitness center; sauna; room service; laundry service; dry cleaning; nonsmoking rooms; 2 rooms for those w/limited mobility. *In room:* A/C, minibar, hair dryer.

WHERE TO DINE

Le Caveau des Ducs TRADITIONAL FRENCH   This reasonably priced restaurant occupies a former storage cellar. It sits underground, beneath a series of 17th-century stone vaults built by the same masons who laid the cobblestones of rue de Ferrare. Although the food is simple, the setting—with lots of wood and flickering candles—is dramatic. Menu items include staples such as snails in garlic butter, roast leg of lamb with garlic-and-rosemary sauce, and virtually everything that can be concocted from the body of a duck (terrines, magret, and confits). Filet of rump steak with brie sauce is tasty, as are platters of sole, crayfish tails, and salmon on a bed of pasta. Especially flavorful are strips of veal in morel-studded cream sauce on a bed of pasta.

24 rue de Ferrare. © **01-64-22-05-05.** Reservations recommended. Main courses 16€–25€ ($21–$33); fixed-price menu 24€–39€ ($31–$51). AE, MC, V. Daily noon–2pm and 7–10pm.

Moments **Hiking along Trails Left by French Kings**

The Forest of Fontainebleau is riddled with *sentiers* (hiking trails) made by French kings and their entourages who went hunting in the forest. A *Guide des Sentiers* is available at the tourist information center (see above). Bike paths also cut through the forest. You can rent bikes at the Fontainebleau-Avon rail depot. At the station, go to the kiosk, **A La Petite Reine** (*©* **01-60-74-57-57**). The cost of a regular bike is 13€ ($17) per half-day, 20€ ($26) for a full day. The kiosk is open Monday to Friday from 9:30am to 6pm, Saturday and Sunday from 10am to 7pm.

Le François-1er (Chez Bernard) *©* TRADITIONAL FRENCH   The premier dining choice in Fontainebleau has Louis XIII decor, winemaking memorabilia, and walls that the owners think are about 200 years old. If weather permits, sit on the terrace overlooking the château and the cour des Adieux. In game season, the menu features hare, duck liver, and partridge. Other choices include a cassoulet of snails with flap mushrooms and garlic-flavored cream sauce, magret of duckling with cassis sauce, *rognon de veau* (veal kidneys) with mustard sauce, and a salad of baby scallops with crayfish. Chef Bernard Crogiez's cuisine is meticulous, with an undeniable flair.

3 rue Royale. *©* **01-64-22-24-68**. Reservations required. Main courses 17€–28€ ($22–$36); fixed-price lunch Mon–Fri only 15€ ($20); fixed-price dinner 29€ ($38). AE, MC, V. Tues–Sat noon–2:30pm; Mon–Sat 7:30–9:45pm.

Appendix A: Paris History 101

1 A Concise History of the City of Light

IN THE BEGINNING

Paris emerged at the crossroads of three major traffic arteries on the muddy island in the Seine that today is known as Ile de la Cité.

By around 2000 B.C., the island served as the fortified headquarters of the Parisii tribe, who called it Lutétia. The two wooden bridges connecting the island to the river's left and right banks were among the region's most strategically important, and the settlement attracted the attention of the Roman Empire. In his *Commentaries,* Julius Caesar described his conquest of Lutétia, recounting how its bridges were burned during the Gallic War of 52 B.C. and how the town on the island was pillaged, sacked, and transformed into a Roman-controlled stronghold.

Within a century, Lutétia became a full-fledged Roman town, and some of the inhabitants abandoned the frequently flooded island in favor of higher ground on what is today the Left Bank. By A.D. 200, barbarian invasions threatened the stability of Roman Gaul, and the populace from the surrounding hills flocked to the island's fortified safety. Over the next 50 years, a Christian community gained a foothold there. According to legend, St. Denis served as the city's first bishop (around 250). By this time the Roman Empire's political power had begun to wane in the region, and the cultural and religious attachment of the community to the Christian bishops of Rome grew even stronger.

During the 400s, with the decline of the Roman armies, Germanic tribes from the east (the Salian Franks) were able to invade the island, founding a Frankish dynasty and prompting a Frankish-Latin fusion in the burgeoning town. The first of these Frankish kings, Clovis (466–511), founder of the Merovingian dynasty, embraced Christianity as his tribe's religion and spearheaded an explicit rejection of Roman cultural imperialism by encouraging the adoption of Parisii place names like "Paris," which came into common usage during this time.

The Merovingians were replaced by the Carolingians, whose heyday began with Charlemagne's coronation in 800. The Carolingian Empire sprawled over western Germany and eastern France, but Paris was never its capital. The city remained a commercial and religious center, sacred to the memory of St. Geneviève, who reputedly protected Paris when the Huns attacked it in the final days of the Roman Empire. The Carolingians came to an end in 987, when the empire fragmented because of the growing regional, political, and linguistic divisions between what would become modern France and modern Germany. Paris became the seat of a new dynasty, the Capetians, whose kings ruled France throughout the Middle Ages. Hugh Capet (938–96), the first of this line, ruled as comte de Paris and duc de France from 987 to 996.

THE MIDDLE AGES

Around 1100, Paris began to emerge as a great city, boasting on its Left Bank a university that attracted scholars from all over Europe. Meanwhile, kings and bishops began building the towering Gothic cathedrals of France, one of the greatest of which became Paris's Notre-Dame, a monument rising from the beating heart of the city. Paris's population increased greatly, as did the city's mercantile activity. During the 1200s, a frenzy of building transformed the skyline with convents and churches (including the jewel-like Sainte-Chapelle, completed in 1248, after just 2 years). During the next century, the increasingly powerful French kings added dozens of monuments of their own.

As time passed, Paris's fortunes became closely linked to the power struggles between the French monarchs in Paris and the various highly competitive feudal lords of the provinces. Because of this tug of war, Paris was dogged by civil unrest, takeovers by one warring faction after another, and a dangerous alliance between the English and the powerful rulers of Burgundy during the Hundred Years' War. Around the same time, the city suffered a series of plagues, including the Black Death. To the humiliation of the French monarchs, the English army invaded the city in 1422. Joan of Arc (ca. 1412–31) tried unsuccessfully to reconquer Paris in 1429, and 2 years later the English, supported by a tribunal of French ecclesiastics, burned her at the stake in Rouen. Paris was reduced to poverty and economic stagnation, and its embittered and greatly reduced population turned to banditry and street crime to survive.

Despite Joan's tragic end, the revolution she inspired continued until Paris was finally taken from the English in 1436. During the following several decades, the English retreated to the port of Calais, abandoning their once-mighty French territories. France, under the leadership of Louis XI (1423–83), witnessed an accelerating rate of change that included the transformation of a feudal and medieval social system into the nascent structure of a modern state.

THE RENAISSANCE & THE REFORMATION

The first of the Renaissance monarchs, François I (1494–1547), began an enlargement of Paris's Louvre (which had begun as a warehouse storing the archives of Philippe Auguste before being transformed into a Gothic fortress by Louis IX in the 1100s) to make it suitable as a royal residence. Despite the building's embellishment and the designation of Paris as the French capital, he spent much of his time at other châteaux amid the hunting grounds of the Loire Valley. Many later monarchs came to share his opinion that Paris's narrow streets and teeming commercialism were unhealthy and chose to reside elsewhere.

In 1549, however, Henri II (1519–59) triumphantly established his court in Paris and successfully ruled France from

Dateline

- 2000 B.C. Lutétia thrives along a strategic crossing of the Seine, the headquarters of the Parisii tribe.
- 52 B.C. Julius Caesar conquers Lutétia during the Gallic Wars.
- A.D. 150 Lutétia flourishes as a Roman colony, expanding to the Left Bank.
- 200 Barbarian Gauls force the Romans to retreat to the fortifications on Ile de la Cité.

- 300 Lutétia is renamed Paris; Roman power weakens in northern France.
- 350 Paris's Christianization begins.
- 400s The Franks invade Paris, with social transformation from the Roman to the Gallo-Roman culture.
- 466 Clovis, founder of the Merovingian dynasty and first non-Roman ruler of Paris since the Parisii, is born.

- 800 Charlemagne, founder of the Carolingian dynasty, is crowned Holy Roman Emperor and rules from Aachen in modern Germany.
- 987 Hugh Capet, founder of France's foremost early medieval dynasty, rises to power; his family rules from Paris.
- 1100 The Université de Paris attracts scholars from throughout Europe.

within its borders, solidifying the city's role as the nation's undisputed capital. Following their ruler's lead, fashionable aristocrats quickly began to build *hôtels particuliers* (private residences) on the Right Bank, in a marshy low-lying area known as Le Marais (the swamp).

It was during this period that the Paris we know today came into existence. The expansion of the Louvre continued, and Catherine de Médicis (1518–89) began building her Palais des Tuileries in 1564. From the shelter of dozens of elegant urban residences, France's aristocracy imbued Paris with its sense of architectural and social style, as well as the Renaissance's mores and manners. Stone quays were added to the Seine's banks, defining their limits and preventing future flood damage, and royal decrees established a series of building codes. To an increasing degree, Paris adopted the planned perspectives and visual grace worthy of the residence of a monarch.

During the late 1500s and 1600s, the French kings persecuted Protestants. The bloodletting reached a high point under Henri III (1551–89) during the St. Bartholomew's Day massacre of 1572. Henri III's tragic and eccentric successor, Henri IV (1553–1610), ended the Wars of Religion in 1598 by endorsing the Edict of Nantes, offering religious freedom to the Protestants of France. Henri IV also laid out the lines for one of Paris's memorable squares: place des Vosges. A deranged monk infuriated by the king's support of religious tolerance stabbed him to death in 1610.

After Henri IV's death, his second wife, Marie de Médicis (1573–1642), acting as regent, planned the Palais du Luxembourg (1615), whose gardens have functioned ever since as a rendezvous point for Parisians. In 1636, Cardinal Richelieu (1585–1642), who virtually ruled France during the minority of Louis XIII, built the sprawling premises of the Palais Royal. Under Louis XIII (1601–43), two uninhabited islands in the Seine were joined with landfill, connected to Ile de la Cité and to the mainland with bridges, and renamed Ile St-Louis. Also laid out was the Jardin des Plantes, whose flowers and medicinal herbs were arranged according to their scientific and medical categories.

THE SUN KING & THE FRENCH REVOLUTION

Louis XIV (1638–1715) was crowned king of France when he was only 9 years old. Cardinal Mazarin (1602–61), Louis's Sicilian-born chief minister, dominated the government in Paris during the Sun

---

- **1200s** Paris's population and power grow, though it is often unsettled by plagues and feudal battles.
- **1422** England invades Paris during the Hundred Years' War.
- **1429** Joan of Arc tries to regain Paris for the French; the Burgundians later capture and sell her to the English, who burn her at the stake in Rouen.

- **1500s** François I, first of the French Renaissance kings, embellishes Paris but chooses to maintain his court in the Loire Valley.
- **1549** Henri II rules from Paris; construction of public and private residences begins, many in the Marais.
- **1564** Construction begins on Catherine de Médicis' Palais des Tuileries; building facades in Paris move from half-

timbered to more durable chiseled stonework.
- **1572** The Wars of Religion reach their climax with the St. Bartholomew's Day massacre of Protestants.
- **1598** Henri IV, the most eccentric and enlightened monarch of his era, endorses the Edict of Nantes, granting tolerance to Protestants; a crazed monk fatally stabs him 12 years later.

continues

King's minority. This era marked the emergence of the French kings as absolute monarchs. As if to concretize their power, they embellished Paris with many of the monuments that still serve as symbols of the city. These included new alterations to the Louvre and the construction of the pont Royal, quai Peletier, place des Victoires, place Vendôme, Champs-Elysées, and Hôtel des Invalides. Meanwhile, Louis XIV absented himself from the city, constructing, at a staggering expense, the Château de Versailles, 21km (13 miles) to the southwest. Today, the palace stands as the single most visible monument to the most flamboyant era of French history.

Meanwhile, the rising power of England, particularly its navy, represented a serious threat to France, otherwise the world's most powerful nation. One of the many theaters of the Anglo-French conflict was the American Revolution, during which the French kings supported the Americans in their struggle against the Crown. Ironically, within 15 years, the revolutionary fervor the monarchs had nurtured crossed the Atlantic and destroyed them. The spark that kindled the fire came from Paris itself. For years before the outbreak of hostilities between the Americans and the British, the Enlightenment and its philosophers had fostered a new generation of thinkers who opposed absolutism, religious fanaticism, and superstition. Revolution had been brewing for almost 50 years, and after the French Revolution's explosive events, Europe was completely changed.

Though it began with moderate aims, the Revolution had soon turned the radical Jacobins into overlords, led by Robespierre (1758–94). On August 10, 1792, troops from Marseilles, aided by a Parisian mob, threw Louis XVI (1754–93) and his Austrian-born queen, Marie Antoinette (1755–93), into prison. Several months later, after countless humiliations and a bogus trial, they were guillotined at place de la Révolution (later renamed place de la Concorde) on January 21, 1793. The Reign of Terror continued for another 18 months, with Parisians of all political persuasions fearing for their lives.

THE RISE OF NAPOLEON

It required the militaristic fervor of Napoleon Bonaparte (1769–1821) to unite France once again. Considered then and today a strategic genius with almost limitless ambition, he restored to Paris and France a national pride that had diminished during the Revolution's horror. After many impressive political and military victories, he entered Paris in 1799, at the age of 30, and crowned

- **1615** Construction begins on the Palais du Luxembourg for Henri IV's widow, Marie de Médicis.
- **1636** The Palais Royal is launched by Cardinal Richelieu; soon, two marshy islands in the Seine are interconnected and filled in to create Ile St-Louis.
- **1643** Louis XIV, the "Sun King," one of the most powerful rulers since the Caesars,

rises to power; he moves his court to the newly built Versailles.
- **1776** The American Declaration of Independence strikes a revolutionary chord in France.
- **1789** The French Revolution begins.
- **1793** Louis XVI and his Austrian-born queen, Marie Antoinette, are publicly guillotined.

- **1799** Napoleon Bonaparte crowns himself Master of France and embellishes Paris further with neoclassical splendor.
- **1803** Napoleon abandons French overseas expansion and sells Louisiana to America.
- **1812** Napoleon is defeated in the Russian winter campaign.

himself "First Consul and Master of France." In 1804, he named himself emperor of France.

A brilliant politician, Napoleon moderated the atheistic rigidity of the early adherents of the Revolution by establishing peace with the Vatican. Soon thereafter, the legendary love of Parisians for their amusements began to revive; boulevard des Italiens became the rendezvous point of the fashionable, while boulevard du Temple, which housed many of the capital's theaters, became the favorite watering hole of the working class. In his self-appointed role as a French Caesar, Napoleon continued to alter Paris's face with the construction of the neoclassical arcades of rue de Rivoli (1801), the Arc du Carrousel, and Arc de Triomphe, and the neoclassical grandeur of La Madeleine. On a less grandiose scale, the city's slaughterhouses and cemeteries were sanitized and moved away from the center of town, and new industries began to crowd workers from the countryside into the cramped slums of a newly industrialized Paris.

Napoleon's victories had made him the envy of Europe, but his infamous retreat from Moscow during the winter of 1812 reduced his formerly invincible army to tatters as 400,000 Frenchmen lost their lives. After a complicated series of events that included his return from exile,

Napoleon was defeated at Waterloo by the armies of the English, the Dutch, and the Prussians. Exiled to the British-held island of St. Helena in the remote South Atlantic, he died in 1821, possibly the victim of an unknown poisoner. Sometime later, his body was returned to Paris and interred in a massive porphyry sarcophagus in the Hôtel des Invalides, Louis XIV's monument to the ailing and fallen warriors of France.

In the power vacuum that followed Napoleon's expulsion and death, Paris became the scene of intense lobbying over France's future. The Bourbon monarchy was soon reestablished, but with reduced powers. In 1830, the regime was overthrown. Louis-Philippe (1773–1850), duc d'Orléans and the son of a duke who had voted in 1793 for the death of Louis XVI, was elected king under a liberalized constitution. His prosperous reign lasted for 18 years, during which England and France more or less collaborated on matters of foreign policy.

Paris reveled in its prosperity, grateful for the money and glamour that had elevated it to one of the world's top cultural and commercial centers. Paris opened its first railway line in 1837 and erected its first gas-fed streetlights shortly after. It was a time of wealth, grace, culture, and expansion, though the industrialization

---

- **1814** Aided by a coalition of France's enemies, especially England, the Bourbon monarchy under Louis XVIII is restored.
- **1821** Napoleon Bonaparte dies.
- **1824** Louis XVIII dies, and Charles X succeeds him.
- **1830** Charles X is deposed, and the more liberal Louis-Philippe is elected king; Paris prospers as it industrializes.

- **1848** A violent working-class revolution deposes Louis-Philippe, who's replaced by autocratic Napoleon III.
- **1853–70** On Napoleon III's orders, Baron Haussmann redesigns Paris's landscapes and creates the Grands Boulevards.
- **1860s** The Impressionist style of painting emerges.
- **1870** The Franco-Prussian War ends in the defeat of France; Paris is threatened by Prussian

cannons placed on the outskirts of the city; a revolution in the aftermath of this defeat destroys the Palais des Tuileries and overthrows the government; the Third Republic rises with its elected president, Marshal MacMahon.
- **1878–1937** Several international expositions add monuments to the Paris skyline, including the Tour Eiffel and Sacré-Coeur.

continues

of certain working-class districts produced great poverty. The era also witnessed the development of French cuisine to the high form that still prevails, while a newly empowered bourgeoisie reveled in its attempts to create the good life.

THE SECOND EMPIRE

In 1848, a series of revolutions spread from one European capital to the next. The violent upheaval in Paris revealed the dissatisfaction of members of the working class. Fueled by a financial crash and scandals in the government, the revolt forced Louis-Philippe out. That year, Emperor Napoleon's nephew, Napoleon III (1808–73), was elected president by moderate and conservative elements. Appealing to the property-owning instinct of a nation that hadn't forgotten the violent Revolution of less than a century before, he established a right-wing government and assumed complete power as emperor in 1851.

In 1853, Napoleon III undertook Europe's largest urban redevelopment project by commissioning Baron Eugène-Georges Haussmann (1809–91) to redesign Paris. Haussmann created a vast network of boulevards interconnected with a series of squares that cut across old neighborhoods. While this reorganization gave the capital the look for which it's now famous, screams of outrage sounded throughout the neighborhoods split apart by construction. By 1866, the entrepreneurs of an increasingly industrialized Paris began to regard the Second Empire as a hindrance. In 1870, during the Franco-Prussian War, the Prussians defeated Napoleon III at Sedan and held him prisoner, along with 100,000 of his soldiers. Paris was threatened with bombardments from German cannons, by far the most advanced of their age, set up on the city's eastern periphery.

Although agitated diplomacy gained a Prussian withdrawal, international humiliation and perceived military incompetence sparked a revolt in Paris. One of the immediate effects was the burning of one of Paris's historic landmarks, the Palais des Tuileries. Today, only the gardens of this once-great palace remain. The events of 1870 ushered in the Third Republic and its elected president, Marshal Marie Edme Patrice Maurice de MacMahon (1808–93), in 1873.

Under the Third Republic, peace and prosperity gradually returned, and Paris regained its glamour. Universal expositions held in 1878, 1889, 1900, and 1937 were catalysts for the construction of such enduring monuments as the Trocadéro, the Palais de Chaillot, the Tour Eiffel, the

- **1895** Capt. Alfred Dreyfus, a Jew, is wrongfully charged with treason and sentenced to life on Devil's Island. The incident will lead to one of the major French political scandals of the 19th century.
- **1898** Emile Zola publishes *J'Accuse* in defense of Dreyfus and flees into exile in England.

- **1906** Dreyfus is finally exonerated, and his rank is restored.
- **1914–18** World War I rips apart Europe.
- **1940** German troops invade Paris; the French government, under Marshal Pétain, evacuates to Vichy, while the French Resistance under Gen. Charles de Gaulle maintains symbolic headquarters in London.

- **1944** U.S. troops liberate Paris; de Gaulle returns in triumph.
- **1948** The revolt in the French colony of Madagascar costs 80,000 French lives; France's empire continues to collapse in Southeast Asia and equatorial Africa.
- **1954–62** War begins in Algeria and is eventually lost; refugees flood Paris, and the nation becomes divided over its North African policies.

Grand Palais and the Petit Palais, and the neo-Byzantine Sacré-Coeur. The *réseau métropolitain* (the Métro) was constructed, providing a model for subway systems throughout Europe.

WORLD WAR I

International rivalries and conflicting alliances led to World War I, which, after decisive German victories for 2 years, degenerated into the mud-slogged horror of trench warfare. Industrialization during and after the war transformed Paris and its environs into one of the largest metropolitan areas in Europe, undisputed ever since as the center of France's intellectual and commercial life.

Immediately after the Allied victory, grave economic problems, coupled with a populace demoralized from years of fighting, encouraged the rise of Socialism and the formation of a Communist party, both movements centered in Paris. Also from Paris, the French government, led by the vindictive Georges Clemenceau (1841–1929), occupied Germany's Ruhr Valley—then and now one of that country's most profitable and industrialized regions—and demanded every centime of reparations it could wring from its humiliated neighbor, a policy that contributed to the outbreak of World War II.

THE 1920s—AMERICANS IN PARIS

The so-called Lost Generation, led by American expatriates Gertrude Stein and Alice B. Toklas, topped the list of celebrities who "occupied" Paris after World War I, ushering in one of its most glamorous eras. The living was cheap in Paris. Two people could manage for about a year on a $1,000 scholarship, provided they could scrape up another $500 or so in extra earnings. Paris attracted the *littérateur, bon viveur,* and drifter. Such writers as Henry Miller, Ernest Hemingway, and F. Scott Fitzgerald all lived here. Even Cole Porter came, living first at the Ritz and then at 13 rue de Monsieur. James Joyce, half blind and led around by Ezra Pound, arrived in Paris and went to the salon of Natalie Barney. She became famous for pulling off such stunts as inviting Mata Hari to perform a Javanese dance completely nude at one of her parties, labeled "for women only, a lesbian orgy." Novelist Colette was barred, though she begged her husband to let her go.

With the collapse of Wall Street, many Americans returned home, except hardcore artists such as Henry Miller, who wandered around smoking Gauloises and writing *Tropic of Cancer,* which was banned in America. "I have no money, no

- **1958** France's Fourth Republic collapses; General de Gaulle is called out of retirement to head the Fifth Republic.
- **1968** Paris's students and factory workers engage in a general revolt; the French government is overhauled in the aftermath.
- **1981** François Mitterrand is elected France's first Socialist president since the 1940s; he's reelected in 1988.
- **1989** Paris celebrates the bicentennial of the French Revolution.
- **1992** Euro Disney opens on the outskirts of Paris.
- **1994** François Mitterrand and Queen Elizabeth II ride under the English Channel in the new Chunnel.
- **1995** Jacques Chirac is elected over Mitterrand, who dies the following year; Paris is crippled by a general
strike; terrorists bomb the subway.
- **1997** Authorities enforce strict immigration laws, causing strife for African and Arab immigrants and dividing the country; French voters elect Socialist Lionel Jospin as Chirac's new prime minister.
- **1998** Socialists triumph in local elections across France.

continues

resources, no hopes. I am the happiest man alive," Miller said. Eventually, he met diarist Anaïs Nin, and they began to live a life that gave both of them material for their prose. But even such die-hards as Miller and Nin eventually realized that 1930s Paris was collapsing as war clouds loomed. Gertrude and Alice remained in France as other American expats fled to safer shores.

THE WINDS OF WAR

Thanks to an array of alliances, when Germany invaded Poland in 1939, France had no choice but to declare war. Within a few months, on June 14, 1940, Nazi armies marched down the Champs-Elysées and passed beneath the Arc de Triomphe. Newsreel cameras recorded the French openly weeping at the sight. The city suffered little from the war materially, but for 4 years it survived in a kind of half-life—cold, dull, and drab—fostering scattered pockets of fighters who resisted sometimes passively and sometimes with active sabotage.

During the Nazi occupation of Paris, the French government, under Marshal Henri Pétain (1856–1951), moved to the isolated resort of Vichy and cooperated (or collaborated, depending on your point of view) with the Nazis. Tremendous internal dissension, the memory of which still simmers today, pitted many factions against one another. The Free French Resistance fled for its own safety to London, where it was headed by Charles de Gaulle (1880–1970). On September 9, 1945, a government of national unity was formed under de Gaulle's presidency. A constituent National Assembly was then elected. De Gaulle's disagreement with the National Assembly led in January 1946 to the tendering of his resignation.

POSTWAR PARIS

Despite gains in prestige and prosperity after the end of World War II, Paris was rocked many times by internal dissent as domestic and international events embroiled the government in controversy. In 1951, Paris celebrated the 2,000th anniversary of the city's founding and poured much energy into rebuilding its image as a center of fashion, lifestyle, and glamour. Paris became internationally recognized as both a staple in the travel diets of many North Americans and a beacon for art and artists.

The War of Algerian Independence (1954–58), in which Algeria sought to change from being a French *département* (an integral extension of the French nation) to being an independent country, was an anguishing event, more devastating than the earlier loss of France's colonies. The population of France (Paris in particular) ballooned as French citizens

- 1999 The euro is introduced; on Christmas Day a violent storm assaults Paris and the Ile de France, damaging buildings and toppling thousands of trees.
- 2002 France replaces its national currency, the franc, and switches to the euro, the new European currency.
- 2003 Attacks on French Jews mark the rise of anti-Semitism, the worst since WWII.
- 2005 Mostly French Arab rioters attack Paris suburbs, as violence spreads to French cities.
- 2006 Massive demonstrations against a new labor law are held in Paris and other cites. Jacques Chirac revokes the law.

fled Algeria and returned with few possessions and much bitterness. In 1958, as a result of the enormous loss of lives, money, and prestige in the Algerian affair, France's Fourth Republic collapsed, and de Gaulle was called out of retirement to form a new government, the Fifth Republic. In 1962, the Algerian war ended with victory for Algeria, as France's colonies in central and equatorial Africa became independent one by one. The sun had finally set on the French Empire.

In 1968, a general revolt by Parisian students, whose activism mirrored that of their counterparts in the United States, turned the capital into an armed camp, causing a near collapse of the national government and the very real possibility of total civil war. Though the crisis was averted, for several weeks it seemed as if French society were on the brink of anarchy.

CONTEMPORARY PARIS

In 1981, François Mitterrand (1916–96) was elected the first Socialist president of France since before World War II by a very close vote. Massive amounts of capital were taken out of the country, and though the drain slowed after initial jitters, many wealthy Parisians still prefer to invest their money elsewhere.

Paris today still struggles with social unrest in Corsica and with Muslim fundamentalists both inside and outside France. In the mid-1990s, racial tensions continued to nag at France as the debate over immigration raged. Many right-wing political parties have created a racial backlash against North Africans and against "corruptive foreign influences" in general.

On his third try, Jacques Chirac (b. 1932), a longtime mayor of Paris, won the presidency of France in 1995 with 52% of the vote. Mitterrand turned over the reins on May 17 and died shortly thereafter. France embarked on a new era, but Chirac's popularity faded in the wake

of unrest caused by an 11.5% unemployment rate. In the spring of 1998, France ousted its Conservative parties in an endorsement of Prime Minister Lionel Jospin (b. 1937) and his Socialist-led government. The triumph of Jospin and his Communist and Green Party allies represented a disavowal of the center-right Conservatives. This was a stunning blow to Chirac's neo-Gaullists and the center-right parties led by François Leotard, and to Jean-Marie Le Pen's often-fanatical National Front.

By putting the Left back in charge, the French had voted against all the new ideas proposed for pushing their country into competitiveness and out of its economic doldrums. But Jospin's popularity gradually diminished, and in the elections of 2002, he was voted out of office and announced his retirement from politics. Jacques Chirac came back into power and became one of the most powerful leaders opposing the United States' war in Iraq.

In 1999, France joined 11 other European Union countries in adopting the euro as its standard of currency, though the French franc remained in circulation until March 2002. The new currency, it is hoped, will accelerate the creation of a single economy, comprising nearly 300 million Europeans, with a combined gross national product approaching, by some estimates, $9 trillion, larger than that of the United States.

In February 2005, President George W. Bush flew to Europe to mend fences with some of his worst critics, notably French President Chirac. The two political foes, who will never be great friends, found common ground on such issues as Syria and Lebanon. Iraq remained a thorny problem. Chirac, a self-styled expert on cows after serving as a former agriculture minister, was not invited to Bush's Texas ranch. When asked why not, Bush enigmatically said, "I'm looking for a good cowboy."

Late in 2005, decades of pent-up resentment felt by the children of African immigrants exploded into an orgy of violence and vandalism. Riots began in the suburbs of Paris and spread around the country. Throughout France, gangs of youths battled the French police, torched schools, cars, and businesses, and even attacked commuter trains. Rioting followed in such cities as Dijon, Marseilles, and Rouen. Most of the rioters were the sons of Arab and black African immigrants, Muslims living in a mostly Catholic country. The reason for the protests? Leaders of the riots claimed they live "like second-class citizens," even though they are French citizens. Unemployment is 30% higher in the ethnic ghettos of France.

In the spring of 2006, Jacques Chirac signed a law that made it easier for employers to fire workers, which set off massive demonstrations across France. Some one million protesters staged marches and strikes against the law, which was rescinded on April 10, 2006.

Against a backdrop of discontent regarding issues of unemployment, immigration, and healthcare, the charismatic Nicolas Sarkozy swept into the presidential office in May 2007. It remains to be seen whether his campaign promises to break from "politics as usual" translate into real change, especially for many of France's disenchanted youths.

Appendix B:
Glossary of Useful Terms

It is often amazing how a word or two of halting French will change your hosts' disposition in their home country. At the very least, try to learn a few numbers, basic greetings, and—above all—the life-raft phrase, *Parlez-vous anglais?* ("Do you speak English?") As it turns out, many people do speak passable English and will use it liberally, if you demonstrate the basic courtesy of greeting them in their language. Go out, try our glossary, and don't be bashful. *Bonne chance!*

1 Useful French Words & Phrases

English	French	Pronunciation
Yes/No	**Oui/Non**	Wee/Noh
Okay	**D'accord**	*Dah*-core
Please	**S'il vous plaît**	Seel voo *play*
Thank you	**Merci**	*Mair*-see
You're welcome	**De rien**	Duh ree-*ehn*
Hello (during daylight)	**Bonjour**	Bohn-*jhoor*
Good evening	**Bonsoir**	Bohn-*swahr*
Goodbye	**Au revoir**	O ruh-*vwahr*
What's your name?	**Comment vous appellez-vous?**	Kuh-*mahn* voo za-pell-ay-voo?
My name is	**Je m'appelle**	*Jhuh* ma-pell
How are you?	**Comment allez-vous?**	Kuh-*mahn* tahl-ay-voo?
So-so	**Comme ci, comme ça**	Kum-*see*, kum-*sah*
I'm sorry/excuse me	**Pardon**	Pahr-*dohn*

GETTING AROUND & STREET SMARTS

English	French	Pronunciation
Do you speak English?	**Parlez-vous anglais?**	Par-lay-voo zahn-*glay*?
I don't speak French	**Je ne parle pas français**	Jhuh ne parl pah frahn-*say*
I don't understand	**Je ne comprends pas**	Jhuh ne kohm-*prahn* pas
Could you speak more loudly/more slowly?	**Pouvez-vous parler plus fort/plus lentement?**	Poo-*vay* voo par-lay ploo for/ploo lan-te-*ment*?
What is it?	**Qu'est-ce que c'est?**	Kess kuh *say*?
What time is it?	**Qu'elle heure est-il?**	Kel uhr eh-*teel*?
What?	**Quoi?**	Kwah?
How? or What did you say?	**Comment?**	Ko-*mahn*?

English	French	Pronunciation
When?	Quand?	Kahn?
Where is?	Où est?	Ooh eh?
Who?	Qui?	Kee?
Why?	Pourquoi?	Poor-*kwah*?
here/there	ici/là	ee-*see*/lah
left/right	à gauche/à droite	a goash/a drwaht
straight ahead	tout droit	too drwah
Fill the tank (of a car), please	Le plein, s'il vous plaît	Luh plan, seel-voo-*play*
I want to get off at	Je voudrais descendre à	Jhe voo-*dray* day-son drah-ah
airport	l'aéroport	lair-o-*por*
bank	la banque	lah bahnk
bridge	le pont	luh pohn
bus station	la gare routière	lah gar roo-tee-*air*
bus stop	l'arrêt de bus	lah-*ray* duh boohss
by means of a car	en voiture	ahn vwa-*toor*
cashier	la caisse	lah *kess*
cathedral	la cathedral	lah ka-tay-*dral*
church	l'église	lay-*gleez*
driver's license	permis de conduire	per-*mee* duh con-*dweer*
elevator	l'ascenseur	lah sahn *seuhr*
entrance (to a building or a city)	une porte	ewn port
exit (from a building or a freeway)	une sortie	ewn sor-*tee*
gasoline	du pétrol/de l'essence	duh pay-*troll*/de lay-*sahns*
hospital	l'hôpital	low-pee-*tahl*
luggage storage	la consigne	lah kohn-*seen*-yuh
museum	le musée	luh mew-*zay*
no smoking	défense de fumer	day-*fahns* de *fu*-may
one-day pass	ticket journalier	tee-*kay* jhoor-nall-ee-*ay*
one-way ticket	aller simple	ah-*lay* sam-pluh
police	la police	lah po-*lees*
round-trip ticket	aller-retour	ah-*lay* re-*toor*
second floor	premier étage	prem-ee-*ehr* ay-*taj*
slow down	ralentir	rah-lahn-*teer*
store	le magasin	luh ma-ga-*zehn*
street	rue	roo
subway	le métro	le *may*-tro

English	French	Pronunciation
telephone	**le téléphone**	luh tay-lay-*phone*
ticket	**un billet**	uh *bee*-yay
toilets	**les toilettes/les WC**	lay twa-*lets*/les vay-*say*

NECESSITIES

English	French	Pronunciation
I'd like	**Je voudrais**	Jhe voo-*dray*
a room	**une chambre**	ewn *shahm*-bruh
the key	**la clé (la clef)**	la clay
How much does it cost?	**C'est combien?/**	Say comb-bee-*ehn?*/Sah coot
	Ça coûte combien?	comb-bee-*ehn?*
That's expensive	**C'est cher/chère**	Say share
Do you take credit cards?	**Est-ce que vous acceptez**	Es-kuh voo zaksep-*tay* lay
	les cartes de credit?	kart duh creh-*dee?*
I'd like to buy	**Je voudrais acheter**	Jhe voo-*dray* ahsh-*tay*
aspirin	**des aspirines/des aspros**	deyz ahs-peer-*eenl*/
		deyz ahs-*proh*
condoms	**des préservatifs**	day pray-ser-va-*teef*
dress	**une robe**	ewn robe
envelopes	**des envelopes**	days ahn-veh-*lope*
gift	**un cadeau**	uh kah-*doe*
handbag	**un sac**	uh sahk
hat	**un chapeau**	uh shah-*poh*
map of the city	**un plan de ville**	uh plahn de *veel*
newspaper	**un journal**	uh zhoor-*nahl*
phone card	**une carte téléphonique**	ewn cart tay-lay-fone-*eek*
postcard	**une carte postale**	ewn carte pos-*tahl*
road map	**une carte routière**	ewn cart roo-tee-*air*
shoes	**des chaussures**	day show-*suhr*
soap	**du savon**	dew sah-*vohn*
stamp	**un timbre**	uh *tam*-bruh
writing paper	**du papier á lettres**	dew pap-pee-*ay* a *let*-ruh

IN YOUR HOTEL

English	French	Pronunciation
Are taxes included?	**Est-ce que les taxes**	Ess-keh lay taks son
	sont comprises?	com-*preez?*
balcony	**un balcon**	uh bahl-cohn
bathtub	**une baignoire**	ewn bayn-*nwar*
hot and cold water	**l'eau chaude et froide**	low showed ay fwad

English	French	Pronunciation
Is breakfast included?	**Petit déjeuner inclus?**	Peh-*tee* day-jheun-*ay* ehn-*klu?*
room	**une chambre**	ewn *shawm*-bruh
shower	**une douche**	ewn dooch
sink	**un lavabo**	uh la-va-*bow*
suite	**une suite**	ewn sweet
We're staying for . . . days	**On reste pour . . . jours**	Ohn rest poor . . . jhoor

NUMBERS & ORDINALS

English	French	Pronunciation
zero	**zéro**	*zare*-oh
one	**un**	oon
two	**deux**	duh
three	**trois**	twah
four	**quatre**	*kaht*-ruh
five	**cinq**	sank
six	**six**	seess
seven	**sept**	set
eight	**huit**	wheat
nine	**neuf**	noof
ten	**dix**	deess
eleven	**onze**	ohnz
twelve	**douze**	dooz
thirteen	**treize**	trehz
fourteen	**quatorze**	kah-*torz*
fifteen	**quinze**	kanz
sixteen	**seize**	sez
seventeen	**dix-sept**	deez-*set*
eighteen	**dix-huit**	deez-*wheat*
nineteen	**dix-neuf**	deez-*noof*
twenty	**vingt**	vehn
thirty	**trente**	trahnt
forty	**quarante**	ka-*rahnt*
fifty	**cinquante**	sang-*kahnt*
one hundred	**cent**	sahn
one thousand	**mille**	meel
first	**premier**	*preh*-mee-ay
second	**deuxième**	*duhz*-zee-em
third	**troisième**	*twa*-zee-em
fourth	**quatrième**	*kaht*-ree-em

English	French	Pronunciation
fifth	cinquième	*sank*-ee-em
sixth	sixième	*sees*-ee-em
seventh	septième	*set*-ee-em
eighth	huitième	*wheat*-ee-em
ninth	neuvième	*neuv*-ee-em
tenth	dixième	*dees*-ee-em

THE CALENDAR

English	French	Pronunciation
Sunday	dimanche	dee-*mahnsh*
Monday	lundi	luhn-*dee*
Tuesday	mardi	mahr-*dee*
Wednesday	mercredi	mair-kruh-*dee*
Thursday	jeudi	jheu-*dee*
Friday	vendredi	vawn-druh-*dee*
Saturday	samedi	sahm-*dee*
yesterday	hier	ee-*air*
today	aujourd'hui	o-jhord-*dwee*
this morning/this afternoon	ce matin/cet après-midi	suh ma-*tan*/set ah-preh mee-*dee*
tonight	ce soir	suh *swahr*
tomorrow	demain	de-*man*

2 Food, Menu & Cooking Terms

English	French	Pronunciation
I would like to eat	Je voudrais manger	Jhe voo-*dray* mahn-*jhay*
Please give me	Donnez-moi, s'il vous plaît	Doe-nay-*mwah*, seel voo play
a bottle of	une bouteille de	ewn boo-*tay* duh
a cup of	une tasse de	ewn tass duh
a glass of	un verre de	uh vair duh
a plate of breakfast	une assiette de le petit-déjeuner	ewn ass-ee-*et* duh luh puh-*tee* day-zhuh-*nay*
a cocktail	un apéritif	uh ah-pay-ree-*teef*
the check/bill	l'addition/la note	la-dee-see-*ohn*/la noat
dinner	le dîner	luh dee-*nay*
a knife	un couteau	uh koo-*toe*
a napkin	une serviette	ewn sair-vee-*et*
a spoon	une cuillère	ewn kwee-*air*
Cheers!	A votre santé!	Ah vo-truh sahn-*tay*!

English	French	Pronunciation
fixed-price menu	**un menu**	uh may-*new*
fork	**une fourchette**	ewn four-*shet*
Is the tip/service included?	**Est-ce que le service est compris?**	Ess-ke luh ser-*vees* eh com-*pree?*
Waiter!/Waitress!	**Monsieur!/ Mademoiselle!**	Mun-*syuh*/Mad-mwa-*zel*
wine list	**une carte des vins**	ewn cart day *van*
appetizer	**une entrée**	ewn en-*tray*
main course	**un plat principal**	uh plah pran-see-*pahl*
tip included	**service compris**	sehr-*vees* cohm-*pree*
wide-ranging sampling of the chef's best efforts	**menu dégustation**	may-*new* day-gus-ta-see-*on*

MEATS

English	French	Pronunciation
beef stew	**du pot-au-feu**	dew poht o *fhe*
marinated beef braised with red wine and served with vegetables	**du boeuf à la mode**	dew bewf ah lah *mhowd*
chicken	**du poulet**	*dew poo*-lay
rolls of pounded and baked chicken, veal, or fish, often pike, usually served warm	**des quenelles**	day ke-*nelle*
chicken, stewed with mushrooms and wine	**du coq au vin**	dew cock o *vhin*
frogs' legs	**des cuisses de grenouilles**	day cweess duh gre-*noo*-yuh
ham	**du jambon**	dew jahm-*bohn*
lamb	**de l'agneau**	duh lahn-*nyo*
rabbit	**du lapin**	dew lah-pan
sirloin	**de l'aloyau**	duh lahl-why-*yo*
steak	**du bifteck**	dew beef-*tek*
filet steak, embedded with fresh green or black peppercorns, flambéed and served with a cognac sauce	**un steak au poivre**	uh stake o *pwah*-vruh
double tenderloin, a long muscle from which filet steaks are cut	**du Chateaubriand**	dew *sha*-tow-bree-ahn

English	French	Pronunciation
stewed meat with white sauce, enriched with cream and eggs	**de la blanquette**	duh lah blon-*kette*
veal	**du veau**	dew *voh*

FISH

English	French	Pronunciation
fish (freshwater)	**du poisson de rivière/ du poisson d'eau douce**	dew *pwah*-sson duh ree-vee-*aire/*dew pwah-sson d'o *dooss*
fish (saltwater)	**du poisson de mer**	dew *pwah*-sson duh *mehr*
Mediterranean fish soup or stew made with tomatoes, garlic, saffron, and olive oil	**de la bouillabaisse**	duh lah booh-ya-*besse*
herring	**du hareng**	dew ahr-*rahn*
lobster	**du homard**	dew oh-*mahr*
mussels	**des moules**	day *moohl*
mussels in herb-flavored white wine with shallots	**des moules marinières**	day moohl mar-ee-nee-*air*
oysters	**des huîtres**	dayz hoo-*ee*-truhs
shrimp	**des crevettes**	day kreh-*vette*
smoked salmon	**du saumon fumé**	dew sow-mohn fu-*may*
tuna	**du thon**	dew tohn
trout	**de la truite**	duh lah tru-*eet*

SIDES & APPETIZERS

English	French	Pronunciation
butter	**du beurre**	dew bhuhr
bread	**du pain**	dew pan
goose liver	**du foie gras**	dew fwah grah
potted and minced pork and pork byproducts, prepared as a roughly chopped pâté	**des rillettes**	day ree-*yett*
rice	**du riz**	dew ree
snails	**des escargots**	dayz ess-car-*goh*

FRUITS & VEGETABLES

English	French	Pronunciation
cabbage	**du choux**	dew *shoe*
eggplant	**de l'aubergine**	duh loh-ber-*jheen*
grapes	**du raisin**	dew ray-*zhan*
green beans	**des haricots verts**	day ahr-ee-coh *vaire*
lemon/lime	**du citron/du citron vert**	dew cee-*tron*/dew cee-*tron vaire*
pineapple	**de l'ananas**	duh lah-na-*nas*
potatoes	**des pommes de terre**	day puhm duh *tehr*
potatoes au gratin	**des pommes de terre dauphinois**	day puhm duh tehr doh-feen-wah
french-fried potatoes	**des pommes frites**	day puhm *freet*
spinach	**des épinards**	dayz ay-pin-*ards*
strawberries	**des fraises**	day *frez*

SOUPS & SALADS

English	French	Pronunciation
fruit salad	**une salade de fruit/une macédoine de fruits**	ewn sah-lahd duh *fweel* / ewn mah-say-doine duh fwee
green salad	**une salade verte**	ewn sah-lahd *vairt*
lettuce salad	**une salade de laitue**	ewn sah-lahd duh lay-tew
onion soup	**de la soupe à l'oignon**	duh lah soop ah low-*nyon*
salad, native to Nice, composed of lettuce, tuna, anchovies, capers, tomatoes, olives, olive oil, wine vinegar, and herbs	**une salade Niçoise**	ewn sah-lahd nee-*swaz*
sauerkraut	**de la choucroute**	duh lah chew-*kroot*
vegetable soup with basil	**de la soupe au pistou**	duh lah soop oh pees-tou

BEVERAGES

English	French	Pronunciation
beer	**de la bière**	duh lah bee-*aire*
milk	**du lait**	dew *lay*
orange juice	**du jus d'orange**	dew joo d'or-*ahn*-jhe
water	**de l'eau**	duh lo
red wine	**du vin rouge**	dew vhin *rooj*
white wine	**du vin blanc**	dew vhin *blahn*
coffee (black)	**un café noir**	uh ka-fay *nwahr*

English	French	Pronunciation
coffee (with cream)	**un café crème**	uh ka-fay *krem*
coffee (with milk)	**un café au lait**	uh ka-fay o *lay*
coffee (decaf)	**un café décaféiné** (slang: **un déca**)	un ka-fay day-kah-fay-*nay* (uh *day*-kah)
coffee (espresso)	**un café espresso** (**un express**)	uh ka-fay e-*sprehss-o* (un ek-*sprehss*)
tea	**du thé**	dew *tay*
herbal tea	**une tisane**	ewn tee-*zahn*

DESSERTS

English	French	Pronunciation
cake	**du gâteau**	dew gha-tow
cheese	**du fromage**	dew fro-*mahj*
thick custard dessert with a caramelized topping	**de la crème brulée**	duh lah krem bruh-*lay*
caramelized upside-down apple pie	**une tarte tatin**	ewn tart tah-*tihn*
tart	**une tarte**	ewn tart
vanilla ice cream	**de la glace à la vanille**	duh lah glass a lah vah-*nee*-yuh
fruit, especially cherries, cooked in batter	**du clafoutis**	dew kla-foo-*tee*

Index

See also Accommodations and Restaurant & Cafe indexes, below.

ACCOMMODATIONS

RESTAURANTS & CAFES

THE NEW TRAVELOCITY GUARANTEE

EVERYTHING YOU BOOK WILL BE RIGHT, OR WE'LL WORK WITH OUR TRAVEL PARTNERS TO MAKE IT RIGHT, RIGHT AWAY.

*To drive home the point,
we're going to use the word "right" in every single sentence.*

Let's get right to it. Right to the meat! Only Travelocity guarantees everything about your booking will be right, or we'll work with our travel partners to make it right, right away. Right on!

Here's a picture taken smack dab right in the middle of Antigua, where the guarantee also covers you.

The guarantee covers all but one of the items pictured to the right.

Now, you may be thinking, "Yeah, right, I'm so sure." That's OK; you have the right to remain skeptical. That is until we mention help is always right around the corner. Call us right off the bat, knowing that our customer service reps are there for you 24/7. Righting wrongs. Left and right.

For example, what if the ocean view you booked actually looks out at a downright ugly parking lot? You'd be right to call – we're there for you. And no one in their right mind would be pleased to learn the rental car place has closed and left them stranded. Call Travelocity and we'll help get you back on the right track.

Now if you're guessing there are some things we can't control, like the weather, well you're right. But we can help you with most things – to get all the details in righting,* visit **travelocity.com/guarantee**.

*Sorry, spelling things right is one of the few things not covered under the guarantee.

I'd give my right arm for a guarantee like this, although I'm glad I don't have to.

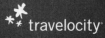